ORIENTATION TO THE COUNSELING PROFESSION

ADVOCACY, ETHICS, AND ESSENTIAL PROFESSIONAL FOUNDATIONS

Bradley T. Erford

Loyola University Maryland

Pearson

Boston   Columbus   Indianapolis   New York   San Francisco   Upper Saddle River
Amsterdam   Cape Town   Dubai   London   Madrid   Milan   Munich   Paris   Montreal   Toronto
Delhi   Mexico City   Sao Paulo   Sydney   Hong Kong   Seoul   Singapore   Taipei   Tokyo

Vice President and Executive Publisher: Jeffery W. Johnston
Acquisitions Editor: Meredith D. Fossel
Editorial Assistant: Nancy Holstein
Vice President, Director of Marketing: Quinn Perkson
Marketing Manager: Amanda L. Stedke
Senior Marketing Coordinator: Brian Mounts
Senior Managing Editor: Pamela D. Bennett
Senior Project Manager: Mary M. Irvin
Senior Operations Supervisor: Matt Ottenweller
Senior Art Director: Diane Lorenzo
Cover Designer: Candace Rowley
Cover Art: SuperStock
Full-Service Project Management: Suganya Karuppasamy, GGS Higher Education Resources, PMG
Composition: GGS Higher Education Resources, PMG
Printer/Binder: R. R. Donnelley & Sons Company
Cover Printer: R. R. Donnelley & Sons Company
Text Font: Garamond

Every effort has been made to provide accurate and current Internet information in this book. However, the Internet and information posted on it are constantly changing, so it is inevitable that some of the Internet addresses listed in this textbook will change.

Library of Congress Cataloging-in-Publication Data

Erford, Bradley T.
   Orientation to the counseling profession : advocacy, ethics, and essential professional foundations / Bradley T. Erford.
      p. cm.
   Includes bibliographical references and index.
   ISBN-13: 978-0-13-228351-9 (alk. paper)
   ISBN-10: 0-13-228351-4 (alk. paper)
1. Counseling—United States.   2. Educational counseling—United States.   I. Title.
BF636.6.E75 2009
361'.06—dc22

2009004382

10 9 8 7 6 5 4 3 2 1

www.pearsonhighered.com

ISBN 13: 978-0-13-228351-9
ISBN 10:   0-13-228351-4

This effort is dedicated to
The One: the Giver of energy, passion, and understanding;
who makes life worth living and endeavors worth pursuing and accomplishing;
the Teacher of love and forgiveness.

BRIEF CONTENTS

CONTENTS

**Chapter 3   Ethical and Legal Issues in Counseling
■ Lynn E. Linde, Bradley T. Erford, and
Amy Cheung   55**

PREFACE

Orientation to the Counseling Profession: Advocacy, Ethics, and Essential Professional Foundations provides a comprehensive overview of the major tenets of the counseling profession, including advocacy and multicultural counseling; licensure; professional associations; ethical/legal issues; consultation; supervision; outcomes research; and the counseling process with diverse applications across the lifespan, settings, and specialties. By contrast, nearly all introductory counseling orientation texts on the market approach the field from a dated and more global "helping professions" perspective. New counselor preparation initiatives expose counselors in training to essential current and future practices that help students orient to the future of counseling practice.

The content of *Orientation to the Counseling Profession* is precisely aligned with the 2009 CACREP standards because CACREP defines the standard of quality in the counselor preparation field. This text helps CACREP-accredited programs meet the CACREP standards, and non-CACREP programs provide counselors in training with the most current professional training standards. The text is structured into four sections: Foundations of Professional Counselor Identity, Counseling Processes and Approaches, Client Issues and Advocacy, and The Effectiveness of Counseling.

Section One, Foundations of Professional Counselor Identity, provides an in-depth look at the foundational issues in counseling, covering historical and future issues, professional identity, associations, credentialing, and legal and ethical dimensions of practice. Chapter 1, Becoming a Professional Counselor: Philosophical, Historical, and Future Considerations, by Susan H. Eaves, Bradley T. Erford, and Mardi K. Fallon, explores the definition and philosophical underpinnings of the terms *counseling* and *professional counselor*. Key to this understanding is the development of a firm foundation in the knowledge of the numerous historical events and key people that gave rise to the counseling profession. Finally, important issues facing counselors as the profession moves into the future are identified and discussed, including outcome-based research, managed care, multiculturalism, technology, and gatekeeping.

In Chapter 2, Professional Counseling Organizations, Licensure, Certification, and Accreditation, by Joshua C. Watson, Bradley T. Erford, Katie Tasch, David M. Kaplan, and Grafton T. Eliason, students are introduced to the American Counseling Association (ACA) and its divisions, branches, and organizational affiliates so that students can become familiar with the wide array of professional associations advocating for counselors and clients. This chapter offers a glimpse of the many credentials that professional counselors can earn. An overview of state licensure, national certification, and counselor education program accreditation processes is provided to answer student questions early on, and to make students aware of the choices that exist for future professional credentialing. Various accountability mechanisms found at the state level for educational systems and mental health agencies are also reviewed.

Section One ends with Chapter 3, Ethical and Legal Issues in Counseling, by Lynn E. Linde, Bradley T. Erford, and Amy Cheung. The chapter is a comprehensive introduction to ethical and legal issues in counseling practice, covering the ACA and ASCA ethical codes, confidentiality/privilege, subpoenas, malpractice, records and personal notes, child abuse, suicide, HIPAA, FERPA, minor consent, and ethical decision making. A professional counselor must always remember that how one conducts oneself personally and professionally reflects not only on oneself, but also on one's colleagues.

Section Two, Counseling Processes and Approaches, provides an in-depth review of counseling theories, process, skills, multicultural competence, consultation, supervision, and counseling career choices. Chapter 4, Theories of Counseling, by Dana Heller Levitt and Alissa Bray, portrays the nature and quality of the counseling relationship as more significant than any other factor in counseling. Regardless of the setting, whether one is working with individuals, families, or groups, counselors have a professional responsibility to develop a foundation and clear rationale for their theoretical orientation to serve clients best. Professional counselors operate out of theories that best fit their personal philosophies of human change and the counseling process. Chapter 4 highlights the significance of theory to counseling practice and provides a brief overview of the major theoretical paradigms. Students will also explore their own beginning preferences for theoretical orientation with the intent of continuing their personal and professional exploration to discover their personal style.

Chapter 5, The Counseling Process, by Donna Starkey Sheperis and Cyrus Marcellus Ellis, orients students to counseling processes and approaches, providing a brief overview of the stages of the counseling process and approaches to helping clients. The counseling process embodies the art and science of helping. Professional counselors bring their training, experience, and personalities into the process. Once initiated, counseling occurs over a series of stages that includes information gathering, application of theory to generate relevant goals, treatment, assessment, and termination. In Chapter 5, students beginning the path to becoming counselors are encouraged to consider their fit with the process and profession of counseling.

Chapter 6, Counseling Microskills, by Joseph B. Cooper, provides an overview of the fundamental skills that constitute the key elements of effective helping relationships. The skills in this chapter focus on Ivey and Ivey's (2007) microskills hierarchy. At the heart of this hierarchy is the basic listening sequence, an interrelated set of skills that not only fosters the development of rapport with clients, but also aids in the identification of interventions to help achieve a successful resolution to the clients' presenting concerns. Examples of the skills in use, along with practice exercises to foster individual skill development, are provided.

In Chapter 7, Multicultural Counseling, by Danica G. Hays and Geneva M. Gray, multicultural counseling applications are reviewed to help students integrate principles of cultural diversity into the counseling process from early on in their training. This chapter features multicultural applications of identity development and counselor competency. Just as important, multicultural implications are highlighted throughout the other sections of the book. Cultural identity developmental processes and culturally specific information and intervention strategies are presented across the cultural dimensions of socioeconomic status, race, ethnicity, gender, sexual orientation, spirituality, ability level, and age.

In Chapter 8, Consultation and Supervision, by Mark A. Young and Alan Basham, introductions to consultation and supervision are provided to help students understand the theory and practical applications of these two essential counselor roles. In particular, the supervision chapter helps counselors in training to understand how to get the most out of their relationships with supervisors and helps them to understand what will be expected of them as future supervisors to the next generation of counselors in training. Models, techniques, types of activities, and important skills used to fulfill the role of consultant or supervisor are presented.

Finally, Section Two concludes with Chapter 9, Settings and Counseling Career Choices, by Nadine E. Garner, James P. Valle, and Nichole Hinkle. This chapter reviews the various major counseling specialties and practice settings, helping all counselors in training to understand what counselors from different specialties do. Often, students embark on their journeys to become counselors without knowing precisely the "kind" of counselor they eventually want to become. This chapter helps students explore these possibilities early in their program to inform their future decisions. This chapter also describes the unique characteristics of working as a professional counselor in the increasingly multicultural settings of elementary and secondary schools; college and university campuses; the mental health settings of community/agency, hospitals, corrections, and private practice; and the various settings for rehabilitation counselors. Also included in the chapter are boxes, titled "A Counselor's Reflection," that invite the student, through suggested activities and first-person accounts, to consider the various counseling career choices in a personal, hands-on way.

Section Three, Client Issues and Advocacy, explores the knowledge, skills, and attitudes required of the counselor when working with clients across the lifespan and with common presenting problems (e.g., substance use, eating disorders, behavioral difficulties). Chapter 10, Human Development through the Lifespan, by Ann Vernon, briefly describes developmental characteristics of infancy and toddlerhood (birth to age 3 years), early childhood (ages 4 to 6 years), middle childhood (ages 6 to 11 years), early adolescence, midadolescence, and later adolescence (ages 11 to 24 years), young adulthood (ages 24 to 40 years), middle adulthood (ages 40 to 60 years), and later adulthood (ages 60 years and older). The information in these approximate age categories serves as a basis for examples of interventions that helping professionals can use to facilitate development at several of these stages.

Chapter 11, Assessment, Case Conceptualization, Diagnosis, and Treatment Planning, by Gail Mears, reviews each of these major counseling tenets. Assessment is the systematic gathering of information to address a client's presenting concerns effectively. A case conceptualization reflects how the professional counselor understands the nature of the presenting problems and includes a diagnostic formulation. Treatment plans outline counseling outcome expectations and interventions to meet these expectations.

Chapter 12, Client Issues, by Catherine Y. Chang and Amy L. McLeod, provides a broad overview of the general categories of client issues (i.e., drug and alcohol counseling, mental health counseling, career counseling, and rehabilitation counseling). The field of counseling is becoming increasingly specialized, with certifications and licensures available for addictions counselors (National Certified Addictions Counselor [NCAC]; Master Addiction Counselor [MAC]), mental health counselors (Licensed Professional Counselor [LPC]—term may vary depending on the state), career counselors, and rehabilitation counselors (Certified Rehabilitation Counselor [CRC]). Although these areas are not distinct, and clients may enter counseling with a mental health and a substance abuse issue, a career and a rehabilitation issue, or any combination of the four, it is important for professional counselors to have a basic understanding of each area.

An innovative facet of this text is the integration of advocacy counseling and the introduction of professional advocacy strategies. Chapter 13, Advocating for the Counseling Profession, by Amy Milsom, answers important questions about advocacy counseling, including: What does it mean to advocate for the counseling profession? Why is professional advocacy important? In what ways can professional counselors advocate for the profession? Counselors best serve their clients by advocating for a strong professional presence in the public and legislative venues. A positive view of the counseling profession by citizens and legislators helps remove barriers for clients and promote the worth and dignity of diverse individuals.

In addition, obtaining social justice for clients demands that professional counselors understand and practice advocacy counseling according to the standards developed by the ACA. Chapter 14, Advocacy Counseling: Being an Effective Agent of Change for Clients, by Donna M. Gibson, proposes that the core purpose of advocacy counseling is to address external barriers that interfere with human development. Although this purpose can be met by advocating for the profession of counseling, it is often met by advocating at the individual client level. Through an examination of the advocacy competency domains (American Counseling Association, 2006), specific guidelines are provided on how to increase clients' empowerment and how to be a successful advocacy counselor.

Section Four, The Effectiveness of Counseling, addresses the crucial issues of accountability in counseling. The future of the counseling profession lies in our ability to show that counseling practices are effective in helping clients reach their stated goals. Counselors in training need to learn to conduct needs assessments, outcome studies, and program evaluation to determine what services are needed, and the effects of those services. Chapter 15, Accountability in Counseling, by Bradley T. Erford, proposes that accountability is a central responsibility of all professional counselors. At its core, accountability shows the effect that a professional counselor has in producing changes in clients and program stakeholders. The conduct of outcome studies is approached from traditional research methods perspectives and more contemporary perspectives, including action research and single-subject research designs.

Counselors also need to realize that a great wealth of extant literature exists to inform their daily counseling practice with clients. This literature is reviewed in Chapter 16, Outcome Research in Counseling, by Susan H. Eaves and Bradley T. Erford, to bolster the student's knowledge of what does and does not work in counseling, so counselors can use effective counseling interventions. Professional counselors have an ethical responsibility to use counseling methods grounded in theory and empirically validated through research. It is now known that counseling is effective in many forms and for many client conditions. This chapter reviews research on the effectiveness of counseling in several areas: client-counselor characteristics, individual approaches, group approaches, career intervention, and school-based student interventions. This body of information should be used by professional counselors to inform their practice and increase treatment efficacy.

Orientation to the Counseling Profession: Advocacy, Ethics, and Essential Professional Foundations provides a wealth of information on the most foundational and emerging issues of the counseling profession. It was specifically designed to orient counselors in training, regardless of specialty area, to the profession of counseling that we have all dedicated our careers and lives to improving. Enjoy!

SUPPLEMENTAL INSTRUCTIONAL FEATURES

Supplemental to this book are pedagogical tools helpful to counselor educators choosing to use this book as a course textbook. The companion *Instructor's Manual* contains at least 25 multiple-choice questions and 10 essay questions per chapter. Numerous case studies and activities included in the text can stimulate lively classroom discussions. Links to MyHelpingLab were inserted into the text at relevant junctures to help students find video links to demonstrate visually the principles in practice.

ACKNOWLEDGMENTS

I thank Lacey Wallace and Katie Tasch, graduate assistants extraordinaire, for their tireless assistance in the preparation of the original manuscript and ancillaries. All of the contributing authors are to be commended for lending their expertise in the various topical areas. As always, Meredith Fossel, Nancy Holstein, Mary Irvin, and Kevin Davis of Pearson have been wonderfully responsive and supportive. At GGS Higher Education Resources PMG, thanks go to Suganya Karuppasamy and her production team. Finally, special thanks go to the outside reviewers whose comments helped to provide substantive improvement to the original manuscript: Yvonne L. Callaway, Eastern Michigan University; Wade Leuwerke, Drake University; and Peter M. del Rosario, Marist College.

ABOUT THE EDITOR

Bradley T. Erford, Ph.D., NCC, LCPC, LPC, LP, is a professor in the School Counseling Program of the Educational Specialties Department in the School of Education at Loyola University Maryland. He is the recipient of the American Counseling Association (ACA) Research Award, ACA Hitchcock Distinguished Professional Service Award, ACA Professional Development Award, and ACA Carl D. Perkins Government Relations Award. He has also been inducted as an ACA Fellow. In addition, he has received the Association for Assessment in Counseling and Education (AACE)/Measurement and Evaluation in Counseling and Development Research Award, the AACE Exemplary Practices Award, the AACE President's Special Merit Award, the Association for Counselor Education and Supervision's Robert O. Stripling Award for Excellence in Standards, Maryland Association for Counseling and Development (MACD) Maryland Counselor of the Year, the MACD Counselor Advocacy Award, the MACD Professional Development Award, the MACD Professional Service Award, the MACD Outstanding Programming Award, and the MACD Counselor Visibility Award. He has co-authored and edited a number of texts, including *The American Counseling Association Encyclopedia of Counseling* (ACA, 2009); *Transforming the School Counseling Profession* (Pearson, 2002, 2006, 2010); *Professional School Counseling: A Handbook of Principles, Programs and Practices* (Pro-Ed, 2004, 2009); *Orientation to the Counseling Profession* (Pearson, 2010); *Developing Multicultural Competence: A Systems Approach* (Pearson, 2010); *35 Techniques Every Counselor Should Know* (Pearson, 2010); *Group Counseling in the Schools* (Pearson, 2010); *Group Work: Processes and Applications* (Pearson, 2010); *Crisis Prevention and Intervention* (Pearson, 2010) *Group Activities: Firing Up for Performance* (Pearson, 2007); *Assessment for Counselors* (Houghton Mifflin/Lahaska Press, 2007); *Research and Evaluation in Counseling* (Houghton Mifflin/Lahaska Press, 2008); *Educational Applications of the WISC-IV* (Western Psychological Services, 2006); and *The Counselor's Guide to Clinical, Personality and Behavioral Assessment* (Houghton Mifflin/Lahaska Press, 2005). His research specialization falls primarily in development and technical analysis of psychoeducational tests and has resulted in the publication of numerous refereed journal articles, book chapters, and published tests. He is an ACA Governing Council Representative; Past President of the AACE; Past Chair and Parliamentarian of the ACA—Southern Region; Past President of the MACD; Past Chair of the ACA's Task Force on High Stakes Testing, Standards for Test Users Task Force, Interprofessional Committee, and Public Awareness and Support Committee; Chair of the Convention Committee and Past Chair of the Screening Assessment Instruments Committee for the AACE; Past President of Maryland Association for Counselor Education and Supervision; Past President of Maryland Association for Measurement and Evaluation; and Past President of the Maryland Association for Mental Health Counselors. He is also an editorial board member of the *Journal of Counseling and Development*, and an ad hoc reviewer for *Counselor Education and Supervision, Measurement and Evaluation in Counseling and Development, Educational and Psychological Measurement*, and *Psychological Reports*. Dr. Erford has been a faculty member at Loyola since 1993 and is a Licensed Clinical Professional Counselor, Licensed Professional Counselor, Nationally Certified Counselor, Licensed Psychologist, and Licensed School Psychologist. Prior to arriving at Loyola, Dr. Erford was a school psychologist/counselor in the Chesterfield County (VA) Public Schools. He maintains a private practice specializing in assessment and treatment of children and adolescents. He holds a Ph.D. in counselor education from The University of Virginia, an M.A. in school psychology from Bucknell University, and a B.S. in biology/psychology from Grove City College (PA). He teaches courses in testing and measurement, psychoeducational assessment, lifespan development, research and evaluation in counseling, school counseling, counseling techniques, and stress management (not that he needs it).

ABOUT THE AUTHORS

Alan Basham, Ph.D., is a counselor educator at Eastern Washington University, where he teaches in CACREP School Counseling and Mental Health Counseling programs. He is past president of the Washington Counseling Association and the Association for Spiritual, Ethical and Religious Values in Counseling (ASERVIC), a division of the ACA. Alan has written invited chapters in several texts, coauthored a volume on leadership ethics and teamwork, drafted the ACA's *Code of Leadership*, and contributed to the ACA's position papers on *High Stakes Testing* and *Test User Qualifications*. He is especially interested in integrating spirituality into the counseling process and in applying Native American perspectives.

Alissa Bray is currently completing her doctorate in counselor education at Ohio University. Her areas of interest include theory development and multicultural issues in counseling. She has co-taught several master's-level counseling courses, including theories and techniques. Research and professional presentations have explored the connection between graduate training and practice, specifically how theories are employed in community counseling. Following the completion of her dissertation, Alissa will pursue her career in community counseling and counselor education.

Catherine Y. Chang, Ph.D., is an associate professor and Program Coordinator of the Counselor Education and Practice Doctoral Program in the Department of Counseling and Psychological Services at Georgia State University. She received her doctorate in counselor education from the University of North Carolina at Greensboro. Her areas of research interest include multicultural counseling and supervision, Asian and Korean concerns, and multicultural issues in assessment.

Amy Cheung, M.Ed., is a graduate of the school counseling program at Loyola University and a professional school counselor in the Howard County Public School System (MD).

Joseph B. Cooper, PhD., LPC, NCC is an assistant professor in the department of counseling at Marymount University in Arlington, VA. He received his doctorate in counselor education at the University of North Carolina at Charlotte. Prior to completing his doctorate, Dr. Cooper worked for 10 years providing individual, family, and group substance abuse and mental health counseling in the agency and school settings. His current research interests include motivational interviewing, attachment theory, intensive short-term dynamic psychotherapy, and neurophysiology.

Susan H. Eaves, Ph.D., NCC, LPC, received her doctorate in counselor education from Mississippi State University. She has worked with children, adolescents, and adults, with experience conducting group therapy and commitment screenings. Dr. Eaves's research interests include marital infidelity, sexually risky behaviors, assessment, and borderline personality disorder.

Grafton T. Eliason, Ed.D., LPC, NCC, is an assistant professor in the Department of Counselor Education and Services at California University of Pennsylvania. He has published on the topics of death, dying, and spirituality, and has a special interest in existential philosophy and religion. He received his doctorate in counselor education and supervision from Duquesne University, and he is an ordained Presbyterian minister.

Cyrus Marcellus Ellis, Ph.D., completed his doctoral study at The University of Virginia and is an associate professor in the counseling program at Governors State University with primary teaching responsibilities in the community counseling sequence. His research interests include self-concept development, addiction and recovery, race- based information, social justice, and social and cultural foundations.

Mardi K. Fallon, M.Ed., LSW, PCC, is a doctoral candidate at the University of Cincinnati. She works as a mental health therapist in a Community Mental Health Center in Cincinnati. She is currently specializing in work with reactive attachment disorder and helping preschool children become socially and emotionally ready for kindergarten.

Nadine E. Garner, Ed.D., LPC, is an associate professor in the Psychology Department and the graduate program coordinator of School Counseling at Millersville University of Pennsylvania. She is the co-author of the ASCA book, *A School with Solutions: Implementing a Solution-focused/Adlerian-based Comprehensive School Counseling Program.* Dr. Garner created the workshop *A Multiple Intelligences Approach to Conflict Resolution,* which she presents internationally. As a former K-12 professional school counselor at Scotland School for Veterans' Children, Dr. Garner developed a comprehensive conflict resolution/peer mediation program.

Donna M. Gibson, Ph.D., LPC/I, NCC, completed her doctorate in counseling and counselor education at the University of North Carolina at Greensboro and is an assistant professor in the counselor education programs at the University of South Carolina. She has served as Member-at-Large for Membership and President of AACE. Her research interests include pedagogical issues in teaching assessment, K-12 career assessment, leadership in school counseling and counselor education, and relational/cultural theory.

Geneva M. Gray, Ph.D., LPC, is an assistant professor at Argosy University–Atlanta Campus. She received her doctoral degree in Counselor Education and Practice from Georgia State University in 2007. She is a licensed professional counselor in Georgia and provides clinical services for children, adolescents, and families. She has completed research in the areas of addictions, LGBT issues in counseling, and multiculturalism.

Danica G. Hays, Ph.D., LPC, NCC, is an assistant professor in the Department of Educational Leadership and Counseling at Old Dominion University. She has conducted individual and group counseling in community mental health, university, and hospital settings. Her research interests include qualitative methodology, assessment and diagnosis, domestic violence intervention, and multicultural and social justice issues in counselor preparation and community mental health.

Nichole Hinkle, M.Ed., is a middle school counselor and a graduate of the school counseling program at Millersville University of Pennsylvania.

David M. Kaplan, Ph.D., NCC, is a past president of the American Counseling Association and its current Chief Professional Officer. Dr. Kaplan's publications include one book, eight book chapters, and 33 journal articles. He has conducted about 200 professional presentations on such topics as professional issues in counseling, counseling ethics, family counseling, and counseling association management. He has been recognized with honors from the American Counseling Association (Fellow), the International Association of Marriage and Family Counselors (Distinguished Service Award), the Association for Adult Development and Aging (Presidential Award for Mentorship), and the New York Counseling Association (Distinguished Legislative Service Award).

Dana Heller Levitt, Ph.D., is an associate professor of Counselor Education at Montclair State University. She received her master's and doctoral degrees from the University of Virginia. In addition to eating disorders and body image, Dr. Levitt also focuses on religiosity, ethics, and training and supervision for counselors across settings.

Lynn E. Linde, Ed.D., is Coordinator of Clinical Experiences in the School Counseling program at Loyola University Maryland. She received her doctorate in counseling from

George Washington University. She is a former Branch Chief for Pupil Services at the Maryland State Department of Education and representative to the American Counseling Association (ACA) Governing Council. She is an ACA Fellow, Past Chair of the ACA— Southern Region, and Past President of the Maryland Association for Counseling and Development. George Washington University. She is a former Branch Chief for Pupil Services at the Maryland State Department of Education and representative to the ACA Governing Council. She is an ACA Fellow, past chair of ACA–Southern Region and past president of the Maryland Association for Counseling and Development.

Amy L. McLeod, Ed.S., LPC, NCC, is a doctoral student in the counselor education and practice program at Georgia State University. Her research interests include multicultural issues in counselor education and supervision, assessment and diagnosis, women's issues, and crisis and trauma counseling.

Gail Mears, Psy.D., is a counselor educator at Plymouth State University, Plymouth, NH. She is a licensed Clinical Mental Health Counselor, teaches mental health counseling courses, and supervises internships. She has 27 years' experience as a psychotherapist with a broad range of clients. In addition to her work as an Associate Professor of Counselor Education, she provides counseling services to college students through the Plymouth State College Counseling and Human Relations Center and the Plymouth State University Community Clinic, where she serves as the clinic director. She is the current President of the American Mental Health Counselors Association.

Amy Milsom, Ph.D., NCC, LPC, is an associate professor at Clemson University. She earned her doctorate from Penn State University and is a former middle and high school counselor. Her primary research interests are in the areas of students with disabilities, school counselor preparation and professionalism, and group work.

Donna Starkey Sheperis, Ph.D., LPC, NCC, is an assistant professor of Counselor Education at Delta State University in Cleveland, where she teaches community counseling courses, including ethics. She is a long-time, active member of the counseling profession and a regular presenter at the state and national level in the field of counseling ethics and the client-counselor relationship.

Katie Tasch, M.Ed., is a graduate of the school counseling program at Loyola University Maryland. She is a professional school counselor at the elementary level in Baltimore County Public Schools (MD) and a former classroom teacher with 9 years' experience. Her undergraduate degree is in elementary education from York College of Pennsylvania, where she graduated with honors. She is a proud member of the ACA and ASCA, and, in her spare time, she enjoys running a drama club for elementary age students.

James P. Valle, Ph.D., is an assistant professor in the Elementary and Early Childhood Education Department at Millersville University of Pennsylvania. Dr. Valle's specialty areas include designing interdisciplinary curricula with an emphasis in language and literacy. Dr. Valle developed a literacy curriculum for correctional facilities that use comprehensive treatment programs and has served as a consultant for schools and families in the area of home schooling evaluation. His interests include integrating song writing and production with literacy.

Ann Vernon, Ph.D., NCC, LMHC, is professor emeritus and former Coordinator of Counseling at the University of Northern Iowa and a therapist in private practice where she works extensively with children, adolescents, and their parents. Dr. Vernon is the former Director of the Midwest Center for REBT and Vice-President of the Albert Ellis Board of Trustees. She is the author of numerous books, chapters, and articles, including *Thinking, Feeling, Behaving* and *What Works When with Children and Adolescents*.

Joshua C. Watson, Ph.D., LPC, NCC, ACS, completed his doctoral study at the University of North Carolina at Greensboro and is an associate professor in the counselor education program at Mississippi State University–Meridian with primary teaching responsibilities in assessment and educational statistics courses. His research interests include counseling student-athletes, wellness, and counselor training issues.

Mark A. Young, Ph.D., LPC, NCC, completed his doctorate at Idaho State University and currently is an assistant professor in the mental health counseling program at Eastern Washington University. His teaching and research interests are in couples and family counseling, supervision, and professional development.

Foundations of Professional Counselor Identity

1

Becoming a Professional Counselor

Philosophical, Historical, and Future Considerations

SUSAN H. EAVES, BRADLEY T. ERFORD,
AND MARDI K. FALLON

PREVIEW

This initial chapter explores the definition and philosophical underpinnings of the terms "counseling" and "professional counselor." Key to this understanding is the development of a firm foundation in the numerous historical events and key individuals that gave rise to the counseling profession. Also, important issues facing professional counselors as the profession moves into the future are identified and discussed, including outcome-based research, managed care, multiculturalism, technology, and gatekeeping.

COUNSELING AND PROFESSIONAL COUNSELORS: WHERE WE ARE

A thorough understanding of the counseling profession's origin and historical progression provides a framework within which the counseling student can increase his or her identification with the profession, gain a sense of pride in the profession, develop an identity as a professional counselor, understand where that identity fits within the larger scheme, and be armed with knowledge necessary to advocate for the profession. Perhaps even more importantly, this understanding ensures the next generation of professional counselors will continue to move forward, not mistake innovation for history, anticipate how events will impact the profession, and be more likely to make important contributions.

In the 1990s, authors (e.g., Gladding, 1996; Heppner et al., 1995) warned that the field of counseling could cease as a specialty or become obsolete if specialization and preparedness did not continue. Understanding the history of counseling along with its current status seems an appropriate and necessary place to begin. In the words of Samuel Gladding (1996, p. 99), "we must be aware of who we are." What better way to gain such awareness than first to understand where we came from and how we arrived at this current place. A profession without a history lacks direction and trajectory, and for this reason counseling students and new professionals must gain a complete understanding of the profession they have chosen. This chapter discusses what counseling is today, the philosophy underlying counseling, the history of the profession, and the current trends within the field.

Before delving into the past, a look at the current status, meaning, and philosophy of the counseling profession is warranted. While the practice of offering counsel has probably always occurred in some fashion, counseling as a distinct profession is relatively new compared with other helping fields. In addition, the general public, as well as professional counselors themselves, are often perplexed by and have difficulty ascertaining the true meaning, purpose, and intention of what counseling is, what it is not, and how it differs from other closely related helping professions.

The meaning of counseling can be ambiguous for several reasons. First, the word "counseling" has been used broadly to refer to everything from a financial consultant to a lawyer. Second, the word has carried different connotations over the years even within the counseling profession. Finally, the word "counseling" describes many different activities a counselor actually does (e.g., educate, coordinate, advocate, assess). For the sake of clarity, counseling is in fact specific, specialized, and distinguishable from other mental health disciplines by its philosophy, its evolution, and its focus.

Nearly 40 years ago, the purpose of a counselor was said "to facilitate wise choices and decisions" or "to promote adjustment or mental health" (Tyler, 1969, p. 10). Clearly there are two agendas being represented here. This is due to the fact that counseling largely evolved from the guidance movement, yet actively differentiated itself from psychotherapy (Gladding, 1996). Historically, **guidance** referred to guiding, or helping others make choices about vocation, lifestyle, or education. **Psychotherapy** assumed a medical model, meaning the person receiving help was sick. The goal of psychotherapy was to alleviate the sickness, with the therapist as expert using information about the client's past to provide insight into thoughts previously kept out of awareness. Table 1.1 provides some distinctions between historical conceptions of counseling and psychotherapy.

Today, counseling and psychotherapy are no longer defined along two seemingly divergent roles or definitions, such as outlined in Table 1.1. Rather, counseling encompasses and embraces the various roles that have become synonymous with the word. More recently, **counseling** has been defined as follows:

> . . . a proactive, holistically oriented process for helping persons learn to cope with problems of living and for promoting healthy development. It is an interpersonal

TABLE 1.1 Historical Distinctions Between "Counseling" and "Psychotherapy"

Psychotherapy	Counseling
Long-term (up to 2 years)	Short-term (less than 6 months)
Medical model	Wellness model
Alleviate symptoms	Improve quality of life
Past is most important	Focus on the here and now
Goal of insight	Goal of change
Therapist as expert	Counselor as collaborator

process involving a professional with the requisite graduate education and experience in counseling (the counselor), using scientifically validated methods, working with an individual, family, group, organization, or segment of a community that is seeking assistance (the client). This process involves empowering the client to decide on feasible goals and to identify, develop, and use personal and environmental resources to attain these goals. Depending on the nature of the client's situation, the process may be: (a) **facilitative** (that is, assisting healthy growth to occur in an unimpeded manner), (b) **preventive** (that is, preventing a difficulty from arising), (c) **remedial** (that is, redirecting maladaptive pattern of development to a healthy course), (d) **rehabilitative** (that is, assisting the client to compensate for existing limitations in ability to cope by promoting the use of other strengths that the client possesses), and/or (e) **enhancing** (that is, improving the client's quality of life above its present level). (Hershenson, Power, & Waldo, 1996, p. 6)

While the definition by Hershenson et al. certainly seems encompassing of the various intricacies of counseling, it is important to examine briefly the agreed upon commonalities between the definitions offered by the American Counseling Association (ACA) and Division 17 (Counseling Psychology) of the American Psychological Association (APA). According to these two professional organizations, the definition of counseling encompasses the following:

1. Counseling is a profession that requires graduate education; necessitates adherence to ethical standards; and encourages licensure, certification, and organizational membership and involvement.
2. Counseling is holistic and concerns itself with treating the entire person, although without stepping outside of one's area of competence.
3. Counseling focuses on relatively healthy functioning individuals who are experiencing difficulty.
4. Counseling is empirically driven and based on theoretically sound underpinnings and interventions.
5. Counseling involves the facilitation of change, behaviorally, cognitively, and emotionally.

The ACA and APA go further to address one additional commonality in definitions: Counseling includes various areas of specialty that include a refined and advanced accrual of knowledge after the general requirements of a professional counselor's education are met. Under the counseling umbrella, specialties include school and college counseling, career counseling, mental health or community counseling, marriage and family counseling, rehabilitation counseling, addictions and offender counseling, and gerontological counseling (American Counseling Association, 2006a). It is important to caution against divisiveness, however. "*Counselor* is a noun and other words like *mental health* and *school* are modifiers" (Gladding, 1996, p. 102).

According to the 2006–2007 edition of the U.S. Department of Labor, *Occupational Outlook Handbook,* there were 601,000 counselors in the United States when this data was collected just 3 years earlier. Within the field of counseling, subspecialty areas were dispersed as follows: 248,600 educational, career, and school counselors; 131,000 rehabilitation counselors; 96,000 mental health counselors; 76,000 substance abuse and behavioral disorder counselors; 24,000 marriage and family therapists; and 25,000 other counselors (www.bls.gov/oco/pdf/ocos067.pdf).

How Do Counselors Differ From Psychologists and Social Workers?

As will become clear in the historical overview later in the chapter, counseling shares a common history with psychology. Many of the theories and techniques professional counselors use to help clients and students meet personal, social, career, and academic counseling goals are the same as those used by psychologists. Indeed, the emergence of counseling psychology within the field of psychology led to the subsequent emergence of mental health counseling.

The primary difference lies in education and training; ordinarily, the practice of psychology requires a doctoral degree, whereas the practice of counseling ordinarily requires a master's degree. That said, much of the basic course work at the master's level is very similar, if not identical, in psychology and counseling programs. However, to become a licensed psychologist in most states, a doctoral degree in psychology is required. Also, some of the clinical training for psychologists is usually conducted in an inpatient setting to help psychology trainees gain experience in the treatment of the more severe psychiatric disorders. While some of the training counselors receive is equivalent to that received by many psychologists, the focus of the training is usually approached from a developmental or wellness approach—hence the term "mental health counselor." Both counselors and psychologists are licensed by state regulatory agencies.

Social work and counseling also share many commonalities. In fact, social workers in many ways blazed the trail for counselors. Licensed clinical social workers were able to pass state laws and regulations recognizing their title and practice at the master's level. In addition, the more recent focus among professional counselors on social justice and client advocacy has traditionally been a prominent role of social workers, although for counselors such an emphasis also was apparent in the counseling profession as far back as Frank Parsons in the early 1900s. While the clinical skills of social workers are in many ways equivalent to professional counselors and psychologists, the training of social workers focuses more heavily on identifying systemic barriers to client success and identification and access to resources that will help clients overcome those barriers. Social workers, psychologists, and professional counselors all provide individual and group interventions to clients in private practice, community agencies, and, in many states, schools.

Each profession has its own professional associations and licensing boards that advocate for professional issues and strive to protect the public. For professional counselors, the unified national association that advocates for all counselors regardless of specialty is the ACA. For psychologists, it is the APA. For social workers, it is the National Association for Social Work (NASW).

THE PHILOSOPHICAL UNDERPINNINGS OF COUNSELING

The values and beliefs of the counseling profession are a distinct aspect that separates it from other helping professions. In some ways, the philosophy of counseling has changed less than any other facet throughout its history. First articulated by Remley (1992) and later documented and expanded upon by Hershenson et al. (1996) and Remley and Herlihy (2007), several underlying philosophical assumptions characterize and unite the counseling profession.

Within a **wellness perspective**, the goal of counseling is not to relieve the client of problematic symptoms (i.e., the illness model, which focuses on the absence of symptoms), but rather to strive for optimal functioning and health in life. Maslow (1968) refers to this as the process of **self-actualizing**, whereas Rogers (1961) describes it as a process of becoming **fully functioning**. Regardless of the phrasing used, both are intended to focus on striving for a state of satisfaction and reaching one's full potential, rather than a focus on meeting immediate needs and alleviating symptoms. Myers, Sweeney, and Witmer (2000) discuss the use of a wellness model in counseling and offer the following as areas of concentration within a wellness perspective: **spirituality** (e.g., belief in a higher power, optimism, purpose, worship or meditation, values, and transcendence); self-direction (e.g., worthiness, mastery, rational beliefs, coping, problem solving, creativity, humor, health, self-care, and identity); work and leisure; friendship; and love. Through these venues, professional counselors assist clients in striving for their own wellness.

A **developmental perspective** is the second characteristic of the philosophy of counseling. Professional counselors understand the issues clients bring to the counseling relationship within a developmental framework. What this means is that many of the problems viewed as pathological by other helping professionals are instead viewed by professional counselors as normal responses to abnormal events, or simply as transitory issues in response to change (Remley & Herlihy, 2001).

Within developmental course work provided to counselors in training, the timing-of-events model states that reactions to events and change depend heavily on whether or not the change was expected during that developmental phase of life. Events that occur as expected are considered **on time**, whereas events that occur earlier or later than expected, or perhaps not at all, are considered **off time**. Crises may result from the unexpected timing of events (Papalia, Olds, & Feldman, 2004). For instance, a pregnancy for many individuals may be a happy and planned event, whereas for a high school student, it may spur a crisis. Similarly, the death of a parent is an event that most people will experience in their life. However, for an 8-year-old boy, this event will have additional repercussions because it occurred much earlier than typically expected.

A third focus unique to the counseling philosophy is that of **empowerment**. Because counselors work within a developmental model, realizing that many issues presented in counseling are normal and temporary, and because wellness is emphasized, professional counselors encourage and foster independence of the client from the helping relationship. In this way, clients can gain the confidence to navigate their future lives and problems, without becoming dependent on the counselor each time a new issue arises. Empowerment is defined as:

> . . . the process by which people, organizations, or groups who are powerless (a) become aware of the power dynamics at work in their life context, (b) develop the skills and capacity for gaining some reasonable control over their lives, (c) exercise this control without infringing upon the rights of others, and (d) support the empowerment of others in their community. (McWhirter, 1991, p. 224)

Empowerment begins within the therapeutic relationship as the professional counselor alters the power differential between counselor and client in such a way that the client becomes an equal partner in the helping process. What occurs within the counseling setting becomes transferable and generalizable to the world outside of the counseling setting, helping clients to gain a sense of control over their own lives. At a minimum, professional counselors have a basic understanding that clients are the experts of their own lives and are capable and responsible enough to develop the necessary skills to live independently (McWhirter, 1991; Remley & Herlihy, 2001). In some ways related to empowerment, professional counselors also focus on social and client advocacy, multicultural sensitivity, and multicultural counseling competence in our global society. These topics will be addressed in great detail in subsequent chapters.

It is generally agreed that individuals do not operate independently from their environment. Because of this, there is a belief that not only does the individual influence the environment, but also the environment influences the individual. Problems presented for counseling must be viewed within the larger scope and context of the client's worldview. Professional counselors make every effort to understand and conceptualize the client's issues with respect to that client's political, social, familial, and economic context, as these variables surely influence the client's current state. However, the professional counselor does not place blame or responsibility for the client's presenting concerns on these environmental factors, but rather encourages the client to take responsibility for change within that system (Hershenson et al., 1996; McWhirter, 1991).

One final note regarding the philosophy of counseling is warranted. Counseling is to be proactive and preventive, often through education and resources provided to the community. When intervention is necessary, however, it is preferable that it occur during the early stages of the problem. Because professional counselors believe that everyone can benefit from counseling, it is preferred that individuals experiencing even mild distress seek help rather than waiting until the distress evolves into a true crisis (Kleist & White, 1997; Remley & Herlihy, 2001). In essence, the professional counselor understands the client from a developmental model and in relation to his or her environment, works toward wellness, prefers prevention or early intervention, and attempts to empower the client.

THINK ABOUT IT 1.1

If you could change one thing about the philosophy of counseling, what would it be? How might this one change affect the course of history and the profession as we know it today?

HOW WE GOT HERE: PEOPLE, ISSUES, AND SOCIETAL FORCES THAT HAVE SHAPED THE COUNSELING PROFESSION

Throughout history, every society has found methods beyond the family to provide direction and support as they have struggled with questions of who they were and who they might become. In some instances, the individuals who delivered such guidance were philosophers, physicians, priests, medicine men, or teachers (Herr & Erford, 2007). Before the 1900s, most guidance took the form of giving advice or imparting knowledge. However, along with social reform, population changes, educational concerns, and the rise of industrialization, came the birth of a profession known as counseling. While the historical events influencing the counseling profession are numerous, only some of the most important events are discussed in detail here and in subsequent chapters. Figure 1.1 provides a timeline and brief notice of other historical events important to our understanding of the counseling profession's genesis and development.

1907	Jesse B. Davis introduced the first guidance course as part of the school curriculum
1908	Frank Parsons founded the Vocational Bureau of the Civic Services
1908	Clifford Beers authored *A Mind That Found Itself,* changing societal attitudes of the mentally ill
1909	Parson's *Choosing a Vocation* was published following his death 1 year earlier
1909	*Binet-Simon Scale* was translated into English
1909	Freud was invited to the United States to present his ideas on neurosis
1913	National Vocational Guidance Association was founded as the first counseling association
1914	World War I began, and psychological instruments were used for screening purposes
1917	*Smith-Hughes Act* provided funding for vocational education in schools
1917	*Army Alpha* and *Army Beta* tests were designed for the military
1921	Rorschach published his projective inkblot test
1921	Child guidance clinics were created
1922	Alfred Adler began using collective counseling, or group therapy
1927	*The Strong Vocational Interest Blank* was developed by Edward K. Strong, Jr.
1929	Great Depression began after the stock market crashed
1929	The first family and marriage counseling center was opened in New York
1930s	E. G. Williamson developed the first theory of counseling from the work of Parsons
1935	Murray and Morgan developed the *Thematic Apperception Test* (TAT)
1935	Alcoholics Anonymous was founded
1937	Recovery Incorporated was founded, a mental health self-help group
1938	Buros published Volume 1 of *Mental Measurements Yearbook*
1939	First edition of the *Dictionary of Occupational Titles* (DOT) was published
1939	*Wechsler-Bellevue Intelligence Scale* was introduced
1939	World War II began, and counselors were widely used for classification, screening, and treatment
1940s	Certification of school counselors was established
1940	Otto Rank, Alfred Adler, Karen Horney, Erich Fromm, Erik Erikson, and Victor Frankl came to the United States to escape Nazi persecution
1940	The *Minnesota Multiphasic Personality Inventory* (MMPI) was published
1942	Carl Rogers published *Counseling and Psychotherapy,* introducing client-centered therapy
1946	*National Mental Health Act* was introduced
1948	*The Occupational Outlook Handbook* was published
1949	The *Graduate Record Exam* (GRE) was published
1949	The *Wechsler Intelligence Scale for Children* (WISC) was published
1950	Theory development began to flourish, including systematic desensitization, rational-emotive therapy, transactional analysis, and career development
1952	American Personnel and Guidance Association (APGA) (later to become ACA) was formed by a merging of four entities, which became the founding divisions: The National Vocational Guidance Association (NVGA; now known as the National Career Development Association [NCDA]); the National Association of Guidance and Counselor Trainers (NAGCT; now known as the Association for Counselor Education and Supervision [ACES]); the Student Personnel Association for Teacher Education (SPATE; now known as the Counseling Association for Humanistic Education and Development [C-AHEAD]); and the American College Personnel Association (ACPA)

(Continued)

FIGURE 1.1 Counseling time line.

1953	American School Counselor Association (ASCA) joined APGA as a division
1957	The Russians launched *Sputnik,* spurring the creation of NDEA the following year
1958	American Rehabilitation Counselor Association (ARCA) was chartered
1958	*National Defense Education Act* (NDEA) was passed, expanding the training of school counselors
1960s	Existentialism, family systems, and cognitive theories became popular
1962	Wrenn, in *The Counselor in a Changing World,* first introduced the concept of the culturally encapsulated counselor
1963	The *Community Mental Health Centers Act* made it possible to build and staff many mental health centers across the United States
1964	APGA recommended a branch be formed in every state
1964	*Civil Rights Act* was passed
1965	The Association for Assessment in Counseling (AAC) was chartered
1966	The National Employment Counselors Association (NECA) was chartered
1966	ERIC Clearinghouse was established
1967	APA legislation committee proposed a restriction on who can provide counseling
1972	Association for Multicultural Counseling and Development (AMCD) was chartered
1972	International Association for Addictions and Offender Counselors (IAAOC) was chartered
1973	Association for Specialists in Group Work (ASGW) was chartered
1973	Southern Association for Counselor Education and Supervision (SACES) established the first counselor licensure committee
1974	Association for Spiritual Ethical and Religious Values in Counseling (ASERVIC) was chartered
1974	Congress passed the *Family Educational Rights and Privacy Act* (FERPA)
1974	APGA adopted position paper "Counselor Licensure: Position Statement" calling for licensure legislation efforts in all 50 states
1974	American Rehabilitation Counselors Association (ARCA) certified rehabilitation counselors
1975	Congress passed the *Education for All Handicapped Children Act* (Public Law 94-142)
1975	Virginia passed the first regulatory act for professional counselors
1976	*Career Education Incentive Act* was provided for career education within schools
1978	The American Mental Health Counselors Association (AMHCA) was chartered
1979	AMHCA certified mental health counselors
1979	Following Virginia's example, Arkansas passed the second licensure law, and Alabama became the third state to achieve licensure
1983	American Personnel and Guidance Association (APGA) changed its name to the American Association for Counseling and Development (AACD)
1983	National Board for Certified Counselors (NBCC) was established
1984	Association for Counselors and Educators in Government (ACEG) was chartered
1986	Association for Adult Development and Aging (AADA) was chartered
1989	International Association for Marriage and Family Counselors (IAMFC) was chartered
1990	*Americans with Disabilities Act* was passed
1991	American College Counselors Association (ACCA) was chartered
1992	American Association for Counseling and Development (AACD) changed its name to the American Counseling Association (ACA)
1994	State licensure, certification, or registry adopted in 41 states
1994	NBCC certified more than 19,000 counselors

FIGURE 1.1   Counseling time line (*Continued*).

1996	Association for Gay, Lesbian, and Bisexual Issues in Counseling (AGLBIC) was chartered
1997	ACA Governing Council developed a cohesive definition of counseling
2001	More than 31,000 counselors held the NCC certification
2002	Counselors for Social Justice (CSJ) was chartered
2003	ASCA created *The ASCA National Model: A Framework for School Counseling Programs*
2004	Association for Creativity in Counseling (ACC) was chartered
2007	Nevada became the 49th state to license professional counselors; only California had not

FIGURE 1.1 Counseling time line (*Continued*).

1900–1920

In the late 1800s and early 1900s, the United States was in the midst of making the transition from a national economy that was, in general, agriculturally based to an economy that was increasingly based in manufacturing and industrial processes. As this transition ensued, urbanization and occupational diversity increased, as did national concerns about strengthening industrial education as a way to prepare young people to enter the growing opportunities in the workforce. Such goals effectively required information about how people could identify and get access to emerging jobs. By the turn of the 20th century, particularly in urban areas, such information was so differentiated and comprehensive that families or local neighborhoods could no longer be the primary sources of occupational information or of the allocation of jobs; other, more formal mechanisms, including vocational guidance in schools, became necessary (Herr & Erford, 2007).

Societal changes also were occurring in reference to views of mental illness. Before the early 20th century, there was a widespread belief that heredity irrevocably determined the fate of each individual. Because of this assumption, containment of individuals considered mentally ill, rather than futile attempts at treatment, was the acceptable goal of the healthy members of society. However, this established way of thinking gradually began to shift, and mentally ill individuals came to be viewed with consideration of their environment and social context (Hershenson et al., 1996).

Three events within 3 years led three separate individuals to emerge as leaders and innovators in the development of counseling. In 1907, a school superintendent named **Jesse B. Davis** made a progressive suggestion for that time. He felt strongly that his teachers should provide a lesson each week focusing on character, problem solving, and prevention in an effort to restore the moral fiber of American society, and in doing so, designated 117 English teachers as vocational counselors (Gladding, 2004).

One year later, a Yale graduate named **Clifford Whittingham Beers** recounted his time as a patient in a mental health facility and wrote:

> I soon observed that the only patients who were not likely to be subjected to abuse were the very ones least in need of care and treatment. The violent, noisy, and troublesome patient was abused because he was violent, noisy, and troublesome.

The patient too weak, physically or mentally, to attend to his own wants was frequently abused because of that very helplessness.... (1908, p. 116)

Containing this and other similarly horrendous and compelling statements, *A Mind That Found Itself* (Beers, 1908) unequivocally provided the incentive for the **mental hygiene movement**. Beers purposefully set out to use his written accounts to bring about such a change in societal attitudes. Through affiliations with wealthy and influential individuals, he also created reform through organization and legislation, leading to the establishment of the National Mental Health Association in 1909 and later the National Alliance for the Mentally Ill.

THINK ABOUT IT 1.2

If Clifford Beers was committed to an inpatient psychiatric hospital today, would his experience be different than it was in 1903? If so, how would it be different?

Around the same time, a lawyer, a teacher, a social worker, and an engineer amalgamated into one man who became best known as a social reformer. **Frank Parsons**, considered the Father of the American guidance movement, was many things before becoming the founder of the Vocational Bureau of Boston in 1908, serving as a vocational counselor and the director. He believed that growth and prevention were necessary for social reform, and in May 1908, he presented, through lecture, his idea for systematic guidance. Just a few months later, he died, leaving his most important work, *Choosing a Vocation,* to be published the following year (Tang & Erford, 2004; Zunker, 2002). This book, combined with his ideas and work while living, set forth the framework that later became the basis for personality psychology's **trait theory**.

According to Parsons, ideal choices of vocation result from an understanding of one's capabilities and interests, matched with knowledge and facts about different vocation options, to produce a good fit between the two. In other words, Parsons was the first to propose that to be happy and successful in your career, you must consider what you are interested in and good at, taking into account the qualifications and compensation for that line of work, to make an informed and rational decision (Zunker, 2002).

Together, these three men, Jesse B. Davis, Clifford W. Beers, and Frank Parsons, changed the meaning and making of mental health and guidance. Their changes ultimately resulted in the development of the counseling profession.

While great strides were taking place in guidance and mental health, psychologists were progressing in their understanding of human behavior. **Sigmund Freud**, an Austrian originally trained as a neurologist, began publishing his observations from a single case study before the turn of the century. In 1909, he was invited to the United States to present his ideas on neurosis at various universities, although strong resistance to these ideas prevented the inclusion of his work in textbooks for years to come (Burger, 2004). Meanwhile, in Germany, Wilhelm Wundt was being credited with developing the first experimental psychology laboratory, and **William James** modified this design and incorporated it into practice in the United States. James was interested in the whole person, cognitively, affectively, and behaviorally, and used a laboratory-type setting to gain insight into the reasons for human behavior. Other psychologists, such as G. Stanley Hall, Burrhus Frederick (B. F.) Skinner, and Max Wertheimer, were also developing their own approaches to understanding how individuals developed and behaved around this same time, stressing the importance of gaining knowledge and developing theory through observation and scientific inquiry (Glosoff, 2005).

Not only did Wundt inspire James, but he was perhaps most influential to the field because of his work in measurement. Evaluating the reaction times of children to various stimuli and standardizing experimental procedures contributed greatly to the measurement movement. **James Cattell** became interested in measurable differences between individuals while studying under Wundt. Upon returning to the United States, similar to William James, Cattell incorporated and expanded upon what he had learned in Germany. The term "mental test" was first used by Cattell, and he was the first to focus on measuring mental abilities and intelligence. Although Cattell did much to give impetus to the measurement movement, especially as it applied to measuring mental abilities, the first true intelligence test was not published until 1905—hence the term "the 1905 scale," also known as the *Binet-Simon Scale,* which was later translated, revised, and published in the United States as the *Stanford-Binet* (Glosoff, 2005; Zunker, 2002).

While the *Stanford-Binet* certainly contributed to the testing movement, the need for measuring the emotional and intellectual abilities and deficiencies of large groups of people became most obvious as World War I began. Nearly 1.5 million people needed classification to enter and serve in the armed services. This need gave rise to the use of large-scale psychological instruments, a process known as **psychometrics**. Specifically, the *Army Alpha* and *Army Beta* tests were developed. The *Army Alpha* was used with English-speaking recruits who could read, and the *Army Beta* tested illiterate and non–English-speaking recruits. The use of such large-scale testing services created a need for more counselors equipped to administer and interpret the tests; these individuals later became known as **psychometrists** (Glosoff, 2005; Zunker, 2002).

The time leading up to 1920 included several additional events that have a unique place in the history of counseling. First, in 1913, the **National Vocational Guidance Association (NVGA)** was founded and within 2 years began publishing a bulletin that would later become the flagship journal for the entire profession of counseling. This bulletin, after several changes in title and focus, became what is now known as the *Journal of Counseling and Development* (since 1984), serving as a "living history of the issues confronting the profession" (Williams & Buboltz, 1999, p. 345).

The role of the federal government has at times been instrumental to the counseling profession, as related to guidance and mental health. In addition to the government's commissioning of psychological testing for would-be members of the armed services, the *Smith-Hughes Act* of 1917 established grants to support vocational education in public schools and counselor-training departments at major universities (Zunker, 2002).

Finally, group counseling formats had already proven their usefulness before 1920. Groups were being used in hospitals with similarly diagnosed medical patients, in schools to assist in vocational decision making, and with immigrants to assist with adjustment to American culture (Hershenson et al., 1996).

1920–1940

As the United States came into crisis, the guidance movement continued to gain acceptance and become more widely used, while simultaneously coming under scrutiny as it became obvious that its focus was too narrow to meet the needs of society. During the Great Depression, a time of massive unemployment and economic hardship, desperation surrounded the search for employment. As millions sought entry back into the workforce, society became convinced of betterment if only those who were re-employed did so in a way that increased satisfaction and efficacy. Because of this, the focus became the ability to place "square pegs in square holes" (Glosoff, 2005, p. 12).

Now the very aspect of guidance that helped to promote and legitimatize it also became a point of controversy. Primarily, guidance was criticized for largely ignoring aspects of human development and experience, and instead, for relying too heavily on testing instruments for the constricted purpose of career placement (Gladding, 2004). With the economy in seeming disrepair, career placement was but one small piece of the puzzle, with mental health issues arising for even the most stable of individuals. Still, instrumentation maintained center stage in guidance, and instruments such as *The Strong Vocational Interest Blank,* developed by Edward K. Strong, Jr., in 1927, provided much needed standardized support materials for the guidance movement, setting a course that would continue for the next several decades (Zunker, 2002).

As society changed, so too did the field of counseling. Inspired by John Dewey's philosophy of education and his own belief in the testing movement, **E. G. Williamson** developed a theory of counseling known as clinical counseling, based on the assumption that personality consists of measurable traits related to occupational choices. This scientific empirical method was tailored to each client with the goal of problem solving and decision making, as relevant to choosing a vocation. Herein lay the problem, as counseling was still heavily focused on occupational concerns.

In 1921, there was an increased interest in the mental health of children, and **child guidance demonstration clinics** were created in many U.S. cities. This movement also took a scientific approach as it emphasized the early detection of emotional disorders through testing and diagnosis. Intervention and treatment involved psychoanalysis or modifying the child's environment (Hershenson et al., 1996).

There were some exceptions to the standard interventions and treatments offered by these child guidance clinics, however. Relationship therapy, play therapy, and neo-Freudian techniques were all beginning to take shape. In one such child guidance clinic in Rochester, New York, **Carl Rogers**, a clinical psychologist initially trained in psychometrics, began to develop an interest in these new relationship therapies. Rogers was in the beginning stages of developing his own nondirective and client-centered therapy, heavily influenced by the relationship therapies that so interested him.

In 1922, **Alfred Adler** began using a form of group therapy he termed **collective counseling**, which he applied to his work with children and prison populations. He also began using family councils in his treatment of children, allowing him to gain input from and insight into the families, while helping them to understand that many problems with children relate to existing problems within the family. While Adler was developing these approaches to group counseling, so too was J. L. Moreno in his formulation of the Theater of Spontaneity, a foundation for the creation of **psychodrama**, Gestalt techniques, and encounter therapies (Gladding, 2002).

In 1929, the first marriage and family counseling center was established by Abraham and Hannah Stone in New York City. This marked the beginning of marriage and family counseling as a specialization within the field of counseling. Also during this period, self-help groups continued to increase in popularity, and in 1935, **Alcoholics Anonymous** was established as a self-help approach to alcohol addiction. Two years later, Recovery, Inc., a self-help group for mental illness, was founded. Finally, the individual focused theory of psychoanalysis began to be incorporated into group formats, acknowledging the influence of social forces and biology on the individual's behavior (Gladding, 2002; Hershenson et al., 1996).

During the Great Depression, there was a need for counselors to work with unemployed individuals in nontraditional ways. Guidance centers housed within school settings were no longer adequate in scope to meet the needs of society. As a response to the Great Depression, society began to understand the importance of the economy, and that the chances for improvement were greater if people were successfully matched to careers and were satisfied with their work (Glosoff, 2005). Nonschool guidance workers within social agencies came to the forefront of counseling because they were now in the position to create the greatest amount of change within society. Counseling became available to adults and children, and settings expanded to include public schools, colleges, and community settings (Brown & Srebalus, 2003).

Although the public had become far more aware and interested in mental health and vocational counseling by this time, the necessary funding from the federal government was not available. Before the Great Depression, funding had been provided almost solely by the individual states and various private foundations. However, the financial role assumed by the government began to change as the Great Depression made it obvious that there was a need for social welfare programs, access to health services, and research on mental health (Hershenson et al., 1996).

In direct response to the Great Depression, legislation by the federal government increased as well. The *Wagner-Peyser Act* of 1933 established the U.S. Employment Service. The Civilian Conservation Corps was created in 1933, and the Works Progress Administration was established in 1935. All of these legislative initiatives were designed to provide employment for the masses who could not find jobs during this period. In 1939, the first edition of the *Dictionary of Occupational Titles* was published by the U.S. Employment Service, becoming a much-needed source of information for vocational counselors (Zunker, 2002).

THINK ABOUT IT 1.3

If you could ask one person in the history of counseling a question, who would it be, what would you ask them, and why? How might they respond?

1940–1960

World War II created a reality that few could deny. More than a million men were rejected for military service for psychiatric reasons, alerting the United States to the extensiveness of mental health problems within society. Psychiatric evaluations and mental hygiene clinics became commonplace at recruitment, training, and separation centers in an effort to sort the various servicemen correctly. Of those who were able to serve, many suffered from what was then called **battle fatigue**, shell shock, or war neurosis, a condition today known as post-traumatic stress disorder. Mental health professionals were able to treat many of these men and return them to active duty. Because of these experiences, the federal government and the general public began to take notice of the need for mental health prevention and treatment. As a result, the *National Mental Health Act* of 1946 was enacted, authorizing funds for research and training in the areas of prevention, diagnosis, and treatment of mental health disorders (Hershenson et al., 1996).

As the need for mental health counseling increased, so too did the need for guidance and vocational counseling. Not only were women now entering the workforce at record numbers, but also returning veterans needed assistance with re-entrance. In addition, the need for rehabilitation counselors became obvious because many veterans were now disabled in some capacity and needed assistance with the transition back to a productive and meaningful civilian life (Glosoff, 2005).

With the 1940s came a new direction in counseling and guidance that differed in theory and approach from the widely used model of E. G. Williamson. Williamson's pervasive approach to counseling consisted of information gathering, evaluation, diagnosis, and treatment. In 1942, Carl Rogers, who a decade earlier was beginning to shape his nondirective approach, published *Counseling and Psychotherapy* in an effort to propose his now completed theory of **client-centered counseling**. In contrast to Williamson, Rogers focused on the client, who was viewed as the expert on his or her own life and was considered responsible for the direction of change and growth within counseling. Rogers believed that with the right therapeutic environment and conditions, clients would move in a positive direction. Rogers placed new emphasis on counseling techniques, training and education of counselors, research, understanding the counseling process, necessary conditions for effectiveness, and the goals of counseling (Glosoff, 2005). Activity 1.1 will further stimulate your thinking about the approaches of Williamson and Rogers.

ACTIVITY 1.1

A common debate during the 1940s to 1960s was whether the ideas of Williamson (e.g., test them and train them) or Rogers (e.g., accept them and listen to them) were more advanced and helpful. First, research further the ideas of E. G. Williamson and Carl Rogers. Next, divide the group in half, with one half espousing the ideas of Williamson, and the other half espousing the ideas of Rogers. Have each side debate the importance of their views.

During this same time, there was an influx of European existentialists and neo-Freudians who escaped from Nazi persecution and the Holocaust. Otto Rank, Alfred Adler, Karen Horney, Erich Fromm, Erik Erikson, and Victor Frankl immigrated to the United States for safe harbor. Similar to the work of Rogers, their approaches differed compared with the prevalent assessment and diagnostic perspective common to the United States, as well as with the behavioral, trait personality, and Freudian psychoanalytic perspectives. It is believed that the influence of their views helped to shape the growth and acceptance of humanism within the United States, and contributed to the work and vision of men such as Rollo May, Abraham Maslow, and Carl Rogers (Glosoff, 2005).

Developments in the field of counseling after World War II were of extraordinary importance. Beginning in the early 1950s, increased funds were made available for training counseling professionals, building facilities, and staffing them. Within this decade alone, the field of counseling began to grow as a distinct entity. First, the American Personnel and Guidance Association (APGA) was established to organize groups interested in counseling and guidance. Next, Division 17 (Counseling Psychology) was developed within the APA because some APA members voiced an interest in working with less pathological clients.

Finally, the government passed the *National Defense Education Act* in response to the panic created by the Russians' launch of the first satellite to achieve Earth's orbit. The launching of ***Sputnik*** created a fear within Americans that the Soviet Union would become stronger politically because they had proven their superiority with space technology. All over the world, news stories repeated the idea that Americans had failed to produce adequately trained students in math and the sciences, resulting in inferior capabilities compared with the Russians. In an effort to direct large numbers of students quickly into math and science courses, Congress created programs to increase the number of school counselors who could provide such direction to students (Herr & Erford, 2007; Remley & Herlihy, 2001).

THINK ABOUT IT 1.4

If you could create a dialogue, a conversation, between two influential individuals in the history of counseling, who would they be, and what might they say to one another?

1960–1980

The 1960s and 1970s were a time of rapid societal changes. The unequal rights of women and racial minorities were recognized, and federal and state legislatures passed numerous laws to address these inequities. These efforts continue today. This increased emphasis on addressing social injustices coincided with a concomitant increase in counselors.

During the 1960s and 1970s, such a high demand arose for school counselors that colleges and universities could not keep pace. Rushed training and increased responsibilities led to confusion about the exact role of the school counselor. Leaders within the APGA collaborated to define roles and functions of the school counselor, increasing cohesion and clarity. With the development of a clearer professional identity came the need for guidelines to protect and guide the development of the profession of counseling. This need led to **accreditation** of programs through the Council for the Accreditation of Counseling and Related Educational Programs (CACREP) and the creation of certification and licensing boards (Glosoff, 2005).

Toward the end of the 1950s, theory development began to flourish with Joseph Wolpe's systematic desensitization, Albert Ellis's rational-emotive therapy, Eric Berne's transactional analysis, and Donald Super's career development theories. Later in the 1960s, existentialism, family systems, and cognitive theories evolved. Group therapy modalities also became common during this time, with the most popular groups being basic encounter groups (i.e., personal growth groups emphasizing awareness through emotions) and marathon groups (i.e., extended groups lasting for an extended and consecutive period of time) (Gladding, 2002). Developmental psychology became popular at this time and was considered a primary focus of the counseling profession as the 1960s began. However, with the Vietnam War, the women's movement, and the civil rights movement, other issues and concerns began to take precedence.

In 1963, the *Community Mental Health Centers Act* promoted the growth of counseling as a field that addressed issues within the community in direct response to increased problems with alcoholism, drug use, marital discord, and family crisis. This important piece of legislation provided funds for community-based mental health programs in an effort to increase prevention and decrease hospitalization. For the first time in the history of counseling, the school was no longer the primary counseling setting. A necessary response to the upcoming plans to close large state mental hospitals, this Act led to the development of crisis centers, drop-in clinics, battered women shelters, rape counseling centers, and runaway centers. Similar to the school counseling profession, the mental health arena was now overwhelmed with community needs and understaffed and undertrained. As the number of mental health professionals grew, these professional counselors actively pursued increased recognition and training (Hershenson et al., 1996).

1980 to the Present

A growing awareness of **pluralism** began to take place with an interest in how ethnicity, society, culture, gender, and personal biases affected behavior and treatment. Counseling services in all settings became more specialized, with more stringent educational requirements, more advanced degrees, and licensure and certification.

Toward the end of the 1970s, the APGA began to question its vision and purpose, and it was decided that its previous professional identification of guidance and personnel seemed to have passed. During the 1981 APGA Annual Convention, the Editorial Board of *The Personnel and Guidance Journal* held a discussion, later contributing resulting statements to be published within the journal. Samuel Gladding was quoted to say,

> APGA's present dilemma stems from a lack of identity. We simply do not know collectively if we are a part of what has traditionally been thought of as guidance...or what has emerged vigorously in the last 20 years, counseling psychology.... As a profession, it has been difficult for us not to identify ourselves as one or the other. With this difficulty has come confusion, stumbling, and seemingly a lack of direction. (Barclay et al., 1981, p. 132)

Shortly after this, the APGA changed its name to the American Association for Counseling and Development (AACD) to reflect the changes occurring in the profession and to renew a commitment to the field of counseling. Just 9 years later, in 1992, the name changed again to what is known today as the **American Counseling Association (ACA)**.

THINK ABOUT IT 1.5

Before discussing current trends, consider for a moment what you believe to be the most important issue or trend in the counseling profession today. What changes do you think need to occur, or what aspects do you think need to be attended to more closely?

WHERE WE ARE GOING

It is clear from this historical overview that counseling is a young field, still in its adolescence, continuing to develop its identity, and striving for recognition and respect from the public, legislators, and other mental health professions. An examination of the past helps us to understand the rich history of the counseling profession, but also helps us to identify pressing issues on the horizon that will continue to challenge professional counselors in the future. Some of these future challenges include outcome-based research, managed care, multiculturalism, technology, and gatekeeping.

Outcome-Based Research and Future Needs

There is a growing effort to narrow the gap between research and practice in an effort to train and educate scientist-practitioners. A **scientist-practitioner** is one who is adept at and able to integrate scientific research and counseling practice to form a more exact science. The scientist-practitioner model actually emanated from the APA's Boulder Conference in 1949, and the counseling profession shares much of its history with the psychology profession.

In the 1980s, a review of the existing body of literature revealed a lack of relevant information for counseling practitioners. It was suggested that research take a more qualitative focus in an effort to produce new information with greater applicability for the everyday counselor. Twenty years later, Norcross and Hill (2003) noted an increased emphasis on empirically supported treatments, but still encouraged a continued focus on objective understanding, while incorporating therapeutic factors specific to the professional counselor. Still, a struggle remains in place to do just that. (See Chapter 16 for an in-depth discussion of the counseling outcome literature.)

While it is agreed that counseling interventions must continue to gain empirical support, it is also recognized that many human factors, which are not easily measured, account for successful counseling outcomes. Counseling is a complex activity not easily researched. Difficulty in designing research suitable for such complexity is not the only factor hindering the integration of outcome-based research. While the burden of proof seems to rest most heavily on those doing the research and disseminating the knowledge, a strong commitment by researchers to produce such information is not enough. Ideally, master's level counselors themselves also would take part in producing research, and at a minimum would be trained thoroughly enough in research methodology to understand the applicability of the findings (Wampold, 2002).

According to Williams and Buboltz (1999, p. 345),

The content of a professional journal can also, to an extent, reflect the types of research and practical topics that are popular during a given historical period. . . .

By examining the articles published in a journal, one is able to determine the issues and trends that likely have an impact on counseling practice.

Because attention to a profession's journals can provide an inside perspective of professional concerns and issues current to that profession, a look at several content analyses and editorial notes is warranted. In 2005, Laura Hensley Choate, the Editor of the *Journal of College Counseling,* encouraged research and submission of manuscripts with strong, applicable, and clear relevance to the practicing counselor. In 2006, Kaye W. Nelson and Stephen Southern, Editor and Assistant Editor, respectively, of *The Family Journal: Counseling and Therapy for Couples and Families,* discussed the findings of a content analysis. They stated that the journal would continue to support research on wellness, prevention, and healthy relationships, but urged a stronger focus on training and supervision, multicultural issues, addictions, divorce, gender issues, and spirituality in relationships, all issues relevant to practice. Similar urges can be seen in other journals shaping the field of counseling.

Managed Care

Beginning in the late 1980s, the issue of **managed care** became a double-edged sword. While it insists on accountability and forces the professional counselor to deliver effective services, it also tends simultaneously to stifle the entire health care profession with its bureaucratic philosophies. In the 1990s, Gladding (1996, p. 102) presciently stated, "[t]he road ahead in counseling is fraught with managed care and groups who would deny us our traditions and competencies."

Originally developed as a means of protecting clients from unnecessary services and fees, managed care has evolved into a system designed to cut costs with reduced professional regard for the client's best interest. Decisions regarding the client's treatment often are made by staff with little or no counseling background. Often, only clients with serious mental illness diagnoses are allowed payment for services. Clearly, ethical considerations are a concern, especially as they pertain to confidentiality and privacy, freedom of choice with regard to a counselor, and rights to collaborative decisions regarding the course of treatment (Nystul, 2006).

Professional counselors often find themselves in a situation to reduce the quality of services offered in an attempt to stay within the number of allotted sessions, "upcode" a diagnosis to qualify for counseling services, or abandon the client because of financial necessity, as a reduced number of sessions necessitates increasing the number of other clients. More recent changes within the managed care system include consideration of coverage for diagnoses outside the DSM-IV-TR as well as the inclusion of mental health professionals on staff and boards involved in decision-making processes. In addition, counselors are being educated in brief, solution-focused counseling skills to maintain quality services within a reduced time frame (Glosoff, 2005).

Multiculturalism and Diversity

Often referred to as the "fourth force" in counseling (with psychoanalysis, behavior, and humanism being the first three), **multiculturalism** has gained much attention over the past several decades. It remains a current issue for the field of counseling, however, because there is still much change and innovation needed. Wrenn (1962) first introduced the concept of the **culturally encapsulated counselor**—meaning professional counselors perceive others through their own narrow cultural lens, without regard for the cultural values and experiences of the client. Since that time, social forces, demographic changes, and legislation have provided the impetus for change, while research and scholarship have proliferated, expanding our understanding and practice in the field.

There is still much to be done, however. In essence, the multicultural movement seeks to reconceptualize existing theories, therapies, and techniques to be encompassing of more diverse populations. It does not seek to do away with the theories currently in use, but rather calls for a modification in such a way as to espouse a more diversified perspective. Simply put, existing treatments have been empirically validated with a predominantly White, male, educated, middle-class population. However, individuals who seek counseling are not always White, male, educated, or middle-class (Glosoff, 2005; Remley & Herlihy, 2001).

Cultural differences not only take into consideration issues related to race and ethnicity, but also issues related to gender, social class, sexual orientation, age, disability, and religion, among others. Because of this contradiction, counseling processes ranging from the beginning stage, establishing a relationship, to the final stage, termination, are lacking in comprehensiveness, exactness, and client goal attainment (Glosoff, 2005; Remley & Herlihy, 2001). However, there are steps professional counselors can take to help ensure ethical multicultural practice.

First, awareness and self-evaluation are crucial. Counselors must constantly and consistently examine themselves for preconceived notions and biases, and acknowledge the value-based assumptions they make. Second, professional counselors must make every effort to increase their knowledge of the populations and clients they are working with. Finally, professional counselors should seek to translate and adapt appropriately the skills and techniques currently in use to culturally diverse clients (Glosoff, 2005).

Technology

Beginning in the 1990s, technology and Internet use in counseling began to grow at a tremendous rate. Since that time, the use of **technology** can be observed in counseling in numerous beneficial ways. Internet searches provide a fast and efficient way for professional counselors, counseling students, counselor educators, and clients to access information on various counseling-related topics, although the soundness of this information could sometimes be questionable. Databases, assessment tools, diagnosis screening, consultation, supervision, education, and referrals are only a few of the many appropriate uses of computers in counseling-related ways.

More recently, computers are being used for actual counseling (i.e., Internet counseling), leading some to question the ethical implications. There are some tasks inherent to the counseling process that can best be served by computers, allowing professional counselors greater efficiency in their work. Few would argue that computers are a valuable resource for responsibilities considered more clerical in nature, such as data entry, scheduling and appointments, referrals, and community resource contact. However, relationship building and clinical judgment are limited at best within the confines of the computer as the counseling setting. In other words, there is a recent trend to conduct counseling through computers (e.g., e-mail counseling, bulletin board counseling, chat room counseling, e-coaching), rather than in more traditional face-to-face formats. This trend is wrought with well-founded concerns.

Advocates of the use of computers for counseling purposes voice admirable positions. They claim that this modality is beneficial because it allows previously underserved subpopulations (e.g., individuals in remote areas, individuals with physical impairments or disabilities) easier access to counseling services. It can also be viewed as less anxiety provoking for clients who perceive a relationship through a computer to be less threatening and more anonymous.

Having noted the benefits that may have originally spurred the use of computers in counseling, the potential problems should be noted as well. The credentials of many on-line counselors are questionable, as are their ethical practices and quality of services. Additionally, counseling sites accessible today may not exist in 6 months' time, confidentiality cannot be ensured, and cultural factors and nonverbal behaviors are completely impossible to gauge and appreciate fully.

Gatekeeping

The issue of **gatekeeping** is gaining momentum in the counseling profession; gatekeeping refers to the screening, remediation, and dismissal of students poorly fit for the counseling profession. A student who shows emotional impairment, inappropriate relationship skills, and unethical behavior should be evaluated more closely to determine if these issues are problematic or constitute true impairment. Vacha-Haase, Davenport, and Kerewsky (2004) provide working definitions of "problematic" and "impairment" and delineate between the two. A student who is problematic displays behavior that is unacceptable and inappropriate, whereas an impaired student shows signs of mental illness or emotional distress that would impact and hinder effective functioning as a professional counselor. Gatekeepers should make every effort to differentiate between truly unacceptable and acceptable behavior, as well as distress that is developmentally normal versus that which is not.

Gaubatz and Vera (2002) estimate that more than 10% of master's level counseling students are poorly or marginally suited for the field. Of this 10%, faculty members intervened in just over half of all cases, meaning that approximately 5% of all counseling students granted admission into counseling programs are either remediated or dismissed each school year. This also indicates that another 5% become **gateslippers**, who receive no intervention and are instead graduated.

When examining key determining factors to the gatekeeping issue, Gaubatz and Vera found that (a) CACREP-accredited programs have 10% fewer overlooked gateslippers; (b) programs with a larger adjunct-to-faculty ratio have higher numbers of gateslippers; (c) programs with fewer tenured faculty have higher numbers of gateslippers; and (d) programs whose faculty are concerned about being sued by students receiving poor teaching evaluations or feel pressure from the institution not to screen have higher numbers of gateslippers. Having formalized gatekeeping procedures in place was found to be the most important predictor of graduating fewer problematic and impaired counseling students; Gaubatz and Vera (2002) stated "any program that institutes formalized procedures will reduce the number of deficient students it graduates" (p. 304).

It is beyond the scope of this chapter to review all of the current trends and issues facing the field of counseling. A specific discussion of advocacy, pharmacotherapy, creativity, spirituality, and assessment would be warranted, but for now complete Activity 1.2 to identify trends and issues in society that will affect future generations of counselors.

ACTIVITY 1.2

With your classmates, make a time line for the next 10 years of counseling. Give some thought to where the field has been so as to predict more accurately where you believe the field is going. Include important events, legislation, or key people in regard to the five trends discussed above.

Summary

The importance of understanding the origination of a profession cannot be overstated. It is crucial to have a clear sense of what the counseling profession is and is not, what influenced it on the way to its existing status, and what issues require current and future attention. It is necessary to understand that counseling is defined in many ways, but for the purpose of our profession, counseling incorporates a holistic, proactive, preventive, and rehabilitative viewpoint, focusing on facilitating healthy growth, redirecting unhealthy development, and improving the current quality of life.

The philosophy of counseling was discussed as it relates to a wellness, developmental, and empowering perspective. Within the wellness perspective, professional counselors focus not only on symptom reduction, but also on improving the client's optimal being. Within a developmental perspective, professional counselors understand and view client concerns within a lifespan development framework, understanding that many reactions are appropriate given the surrounding conditions or are temporary. Also, from an empowerment perspective, clients are encouraged and assisted to gain the confidence and independence to use life skills and exercise control over their life.

Accounts of the history of counseling most frequently begin with the landmark contributions of Jesse B. Davis, Frank Parsons, and Clifford W. Beers. Davis designated teachers as guidance counselors and incorporated character building into class time; Beers exposed the inhumane treatment of mentally ill individuals and worked with influential people to bring about a change in societal attitudes; and Parsons was the first to state that to be happy in a career, a person must first consider what he or she is good at.

Beginning with these accounts, the influence of guidance and psychotherapy on the developing counseling profession could easily be seen. The measurement movement, the use of group formats, the development of counseling theory, World War I and World War II, the rise of humanism, changes in legislation and funding, and movement toward accreditation all were influential in shaping the field. The current trends and issues in the counseling profession were also discussed. Included among these were outcome-based research, managed care, multiculturalism, technology in counseling, and gatekeeping.

This chapter provides the profession's historical progression, enabling the counseling student to begin developing a framework within which to increase identification with the profession, gain a sense of pride in that profession, develop an identity as a professional counselor, advocate for the profession, and make important and innovative contributions to the profession.

2

Professional Counseling Organizations, Licensure, Certification, and Accreditation

JOSHUA C. WATSON, BRADLEY T. ERFORD,
KATIE TASCH, DAVID M. KAPLAN, AND GRAFTON T. ELIASON

PREVIEW

This chapter highlights the positive role professional organizations have played in the identity development of the counseling profession and in providing various services to counselors and clients. An in-depth examination of the American Counseling Association (ACA) provides the reader with an overview of the various divisions, branches, policies, and professional partners, as well as professional development and other numerous benefits for both counselors and students. This chapter offers a glimpse at the many credentials that can be earned by professional counselors (i.e., state licensure, state certification, national certification) and counselor education programs (i.e., accreditation). Various accountability procedures found at the state level for educational systems and mental health agencies are also reviewed.

PROFESSIONAL COUNSELING ORGANIZATIONS

Professional counselors, working through professional counselor organizations, have achieved a great deal over the past 50 years. The lives of professional counselors and the clients we serve would be quite different if these organizations had never existed. Ponder for a moment how the counseling world might look without the influence and hard work of professional counseling organizations.

Professional counselors would not be licensed in any state. Expectations for ethical professional practice would not exist, and the public would not be protected, as professional counselors would not be held accountable to various codes of ethics. Third-party reimbursement from health insurance companies would not be possible for professional counselors. The U.S. Department of Veterans Affairs would still exclude rehabilitation and mental health counselors from providing mental health services to armed service veterans. Professional school counselors would continue to find the title "guidance counselor" on the office door, while being inundated and preoccupied with administrative tasks, leaving the office primarily to take care of lunch and bus duties. Graduate counseling programs, if they existed at all, would consist of less than 30 credits, have 100 hours (or less) of field experience, and be viewed by other mental health professions as providing far less than a professional level of training.

However, thanks to the hard work and efforts within professional counseling associations, much-needed change and advancement have been brought to the field of counseling, which has benefited professional counselors, counselors in training, and individuals seeking counseling services. It is incumbent that all professional counselors, counselor educators, and counseling students join and be active members of counseling associations to advance the profession, demonstrate professionalism, maintain counseling skills, and partake in the many benefits that counseling organizations offer.

Navigating through the acronym-rich world of these organizations can be daunting, even for experienced professional counselors. Here is just one dizzying example: *NYAADA is a division of NYCA, which is a branch of ACA. It is also a state division of AADA, which is itself an ACA division.* This sentence translates to: "The New York Association for Adult Development and Aging (NYAADA) is a division of the New York Counseling Association (NYCA). NYCA is the New York branch of the American Counseling Association (ACA). The NYAADA is also a state division of the Association for Adult Development and Aging (AADA), which is the ACA division that focuses on adult development across the lifespan" (Figure 2.1). Whew! Got that? To help you sort out the professional associations, this chapter provides a synopsis of major counseling associations and partners, as well as the benefits and services provided to counseling students and professional counselors.

American Counseling Association (ACA)

The **American Counseling Association (ACA)** speaks to and for professional counselors across all settings and specialties, making it the world's largest association for counselors with more than 40,000 members in the United States and 50 additional countries. The ACA gives members the opportunity to stay in touch with issues across the entire counseling spectrum. It also allows members to benefit from ideas and approaches from areas outside

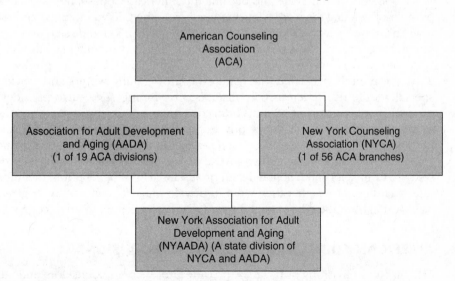

FIGURE 2.1 The relationship between ACA, divisions, state branches, and state divisions.

their specialty. As an example, the annual ACA Conference has more than 500 sessions that cover greater than two dozen specialties.

Professional school counselors can attend programs that focus on school counseling, but they can also attend workshops on establishing a private practice, a topic that may not appear in a conference devoted exclusively to school counseling. Career counselors can go to sessions that speak to career development, but they also have the opportunity to attend family counseling workshops, an area sparsely covered at most career development conferences. A rehabilitation counselor can find programs on assisting clients with disabilities, but also can attend sessions on normal human development and abilities. The same type of interactive dialogue and participation is provided in ACA publications, the ACA website (www.counseling.org), on-line continuing education (CE), and many other services and products.

It is interesting to view the evolution of the counseling profession through the specific titles that ACA has held over the years. ACA was founded in 1952 as the American Personnel and Guidance Association (APGA). This title reflected the four organizations that came together to form ACA: the National Vocational Guidance Association, the National Association of Guidance and Counselor Trainers, the Student Personnel Association for Teacher Education, and the American College Personnel Association. It seems pretty clear from reviewing the names of the founding ACA divisions that the roots of the profession are in education and career development.

In 1983, the organization changed its name from the APGA to the American Association for Counseling and Development (AACD). This name change signified the emergence of a professional identity that could be distinguished from other mental health professions such as psychology and social work. For the first time, counseling was in the title of the professional organization for the entire world to see. The initial focus on career development had blossomed into a niche held by no other helping profession: human development across the lifespan that focuses on positive human growth, rather than focusing on human pathology. The word "development" was also added to the Association's title.

The most recent name change occurred in 1992, when AACD dropped the word "development" from the title and became the American Counseling Association (ACA). The purpose of deleting the word "development" from the title was to unite and reflect the common link between association members. Additionally, this change signified a growing recognition that counseling was becoming established as a core mental health profession.

The ACA issues two publications to all members. The ACA publishes *Counseling Today,* a monthly magazine that features award-winning writers and articles on topics of special and general interest to counselors. *Counseling Today* also provides employment advertisements and advertisements from companies offering products for counselors, as well as monthly columns for students, private practitioners, and others. The ACA also publishes the *Journal of Counseling and Development,* ACA's flagship journal that includes articles of interest to the entire membership of ACA, as the topics reach across all specialties and work settings. Counselors and mental health professionals can benefit from the informative literature regardless of whether they work in private practice, community or government agencies, hospitals, or the educational setting (elementary school through college).

AMERICAN COUNSELING ASSOCIATION DIVISIONS

The nineteen divisions of the ACA provide professional counselors and students with a unique opportunity to focus on specific areas of interest. The ACA divisions also provide information, resources, and leadership opportunities for their members. Each division elects its own division officers who preside over independent activities and represent an active voice in national ACA governance (i.e., the ACA Governing Council). By joining one or more divisions of the ACA, opportunities are also given to members within a division to enhance professional identity and practice.

Divisions are sometimes categorized as belonging to either the "passion" divisions or the "work setting" divisions (Figure 2.2). **Passion divisions** focus on areas of expertise and topics of interest. For example, if one is passionate about multicultural and ethnic minority counseling, in addition to belonging to the ACA, one might also belong to the Association for Multicultural Counseling and Development (AMCD). By being an active member of the AMCD, not only can one keep abreast and knowledgeable of all the latest research, theories, and counseling implications for multicultural and ethnic minority counseling, but one can also help advance this area of counseling by taking on leadership roles within the organization, promoting the goals and mission of the organization to other colleagues and aspiring colleagues, and conducting and sharing one's own research on this topic with others in the field.

Of the 19 divisions within the ACA, 9 are considered passion divisions. The remaining 10 ACA divisions can be classified as **work setting divisions**, which focus on the various specialties and specific work settings within professional counseling. For example, in addition to belonging to the ACA, a professional school counselor might also belong to the American School Counselor Association (ASCA) to keep abreast of the latest research, topics, trends, and theories helping professional school counselors in the work setting. However, one should not judge a book by its cover, or in this case, judge an association by its title. Titles alone do not tell the history, mission, goals, and values of an ACA division. Therefore, all 19 divisions are explored in more detail.

American College Counseling Association

Chartered in 1991, the **American College Counseling Association (ACCA)** is one of the newest divisions of the American Counseling Association (ACA) (American Counseling Association, 2007). The ACCA focuses on professional counselors who provide service at institutions of higher education and fosters student development in colleges, universities, and technical and community college settings. Additionally, the ACCA strives to improve college counseling and ethical practice, while promoting communication and cooperation within and among other collegiate institutions and professional organizations to enhance college student development and the profession of counseling in the higher education setting. The ACCA publishes the *Journal of College Counseling* and a newsletter, *Visions*. For more information on this work setting division, visit www.collegecounseling.org.

American Mental Health Counselors Association

Chartered in 1978, the **American Mental Health Counselors Association (AMHCA)** represents clinical mental health counselors. The AMHCA mission is to use education, advocacy, licensing, and professional development to improve the profession of mental health counseling. The AMHCA not only rallies behind the professional mental health counselor, but also "advocates for client-access to quality services within the health care industry" (www.counseling.org/AboutUs/DivisionsBranchesAndRegions/TP/Divisions/CT2.aspx). The AMHCA publishes the *Journal of Mental Health Counseling* and a newsletter, *The Advocate*. For more information on this work setting division, visit www.amhca.org.

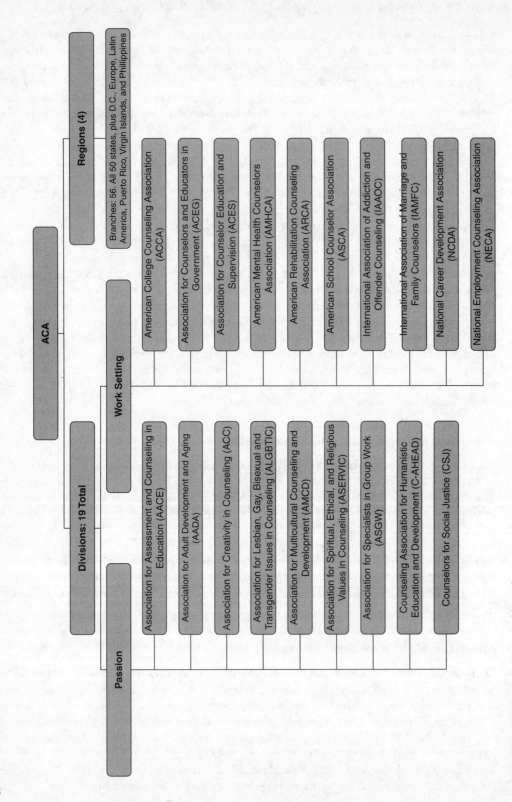

FIGURE 2.2 ACA divisions and branches.

American Rehabilitation Counseling Association

The **American Rehabilitation Counseling Association (ARCA)**, chartered in 1958, advocates for the counseling needs of individuals with disabilities. The ARCA mission is focused on promoting excellence in professional rehabilitation counseling, research, consultation, and professional development to enhance the development of individuals with disabilities throughout their lifespan. The ARCA stresses its equal commitment to eliminating environmental and attitudinal barriers in an effort to create more opportunities for individuals with disabilities, such as in education, employment, and community activities. The ARCA publishes a newsletter and scholarly journal, the *Rehabilitation Counseling Bulletin*. For more information on this work setting division, visit www.arcaweb.org.

American School Counselor Association

Chartered in 1953, the **American School Counselor Association (ASCA)** advocates and expands the image and influence of professional school counselors. In addition to advocacy, the ASCA promotes leadership, collaboration, and systemic change in the field of school counseling. The ASCA empowers professional school counselors with the knowledge and skills to help improve student success at school, home, and in the community. Additionally, the ASCA focuses on helping professional school counselors enhance the personal, social, and career development areas of student life. ASCA members work with students, educators, parents, and community members to provide a positive learning environment. The ASCA mission is to represent professional school counselors from elementary school settings through higher education institutions and to promote professionalism and ethical practices. The ASCA publishes a journal, *Professional School Counseling*, and the *ASCA School Counselor* magazine. For more information about the ASCA, visit www.schoolcounselor.org.

Association for Adult Development and Aging

"Chartered in 1986, AADA serves as a focal point for information sharing, professional development, and advocacy related to adult development and aging issues; [and] addresses counseling concerns across the lifespan" (www.counseling.org/AboutUs/DivisionsBranchesAndRegions/TP/Divisions/CT2.aspx). The **Association for Adult Development and Aging (AADA)** finds ways to improve the standards and services professionals give to adults of all ages by "improving the skills and competence of American Counseling Association members, expanding professional work opportunities in adult development and aging, promoting the lifelong development and well-being of adults, promoting standards for professional preparation for counselors of adults across the lifespan." The AADA sees creating partnerships with other organizations as a key initiative to improving the standards of care that is given to adults of all ages. The AADA publishes a journal, *Adultspan,* and newsletter, *Adultspan Newsletter.* For more information about this passion division, visit www.aadaweb.org.

Association for Assessment in Counseling and Education

The **Association for Assessment in Counseling and Education (AACE)** was originally chartered in 1965 as the Association for Measurement and Evaluation in Guidance. Later, it became known as the Association for Assessment in Counseling. In 2003, the organization became known as the AACE. As evident in the AACE vision and mission statements, this organization is an advocate for the counseling profession's effective use of assessment and research. The AACE's vision proclaims it is an "organization of counselors, educators, and other professionals that advances the counseling profession by providing leadership, training, and research in the creation, development, production, and use of assessment and diagnostic techniques" (www.theaaceonline.com/about.htm). Its mission is to promote and recognize scholarship, professionalism, leadership, and excellence in the development and use of assessment and diagnostic techniques in counseling. The AACE publishes a highly rated journal, *Measurement and Evaluation in Counseling and Development,* and a newsletter, *AACE Newsnotes.* For more information on this ACA passion division, visit www.theaaceonline.com.

Association for Counselor Education and Supervision

Originally called the National Association of Guidance and Counselor Trainers, the **Association for Counselor Education and Supervision (ACES)** was a founding association of the ACA in 1952 (American Counseling Association, 2007). The ACES is the home for counselor educators and professional counselors who provide supervision. The ACES advocates for quality graduate education and supervision of counselors in all work settings. The ACES is a strong supporter of the accreditation process and professional development, through which the ACES strives to improve education, credentialing, and supervision of counselors. The ACES publishes a journal, *Counselor Education and Supervision*, and a newsletter, *The Spectrum.* For more information on this work setting division, visit www.acesonline.net.

Association for Counselors and Educators in Government

The **Association for Counselors and Educators in Government (ACEG)** was originally chartered in 1984 as the Military Educators and Counselors Association to support all members of the armed services and their families by providing them with meaningful guidance, counseling, and educational programs. This included individuals and family members in the following categories: active duty, retired, civilian employees of the Department of Defense, or employees of other government agencies. Members voted in 1994 to change the name of the organization to the ACEG. Today, the ACEG continues to counsel clients and their families in local, state, and federal government or in military-related agencies. The ACEG publishes the *ACEG Newsletter.* For more information on this work setting division, visit www.dantes.doded.mil/dantes_web/organizations/aceg/index.htm.

Association for Creativity in Counseling

The ACA's newest division, formed in 2004 as the **Association for Creativity in Counseling (ACC)**, is a "forum for counselors, counselor educators, creative arts therapists and counselors in training to explore unique and diverse approaches to counseling" (www.aca-acc.org/Public.htm). From art and dance therapy to creativity in psychotherapy, the ACC's goal is to promote greater awareness, advocacy, and understanding of diverse and creative approaches to counseling. The ACC publishes the *Journal of Creativity in Mental Health* and the *ACC Newsletter.* For more information on this passion division, visit www.aca-acc.org.

Association for Lesbian, Gay, Bisexual, and Transgender Issues in Counseling

The **Association for Lesbian, Gay, Bisexual, and Transgender Issues in Counseling (ALGBTIC)** was originally chartered in 1975 as the Association for Gay, Lesbian and Bisexual Issues in Counseling. Throughout its existence as a division of the ACA, the ALGBTIC has fought hard to be recognized by the ACA and other divisions as an organization to promote awareness, rather than an association based on member sexual orientation. The mission of the ALGBTIC is to provide education to promote awareness, understanding, and equality to clients and counselors of minority sexual orientations. In addition, the ALGBTIC strives to improve standards and identify barriers related to gay, lesbian, bisexual, and transgendered counseling. The ALGBTIC identifies issues related to lesbian, gay, bisexual, and transgendered clients and advocates for the reduction of stereotypical thinking and homosexual prejudice. The ALGBTIC publishes *The Journal of LGBT Issues in Counseling* and a newsletter, the *ALGBTIC News*. For more information on this passion division, visit, www.algbtic.org.

Association for Multicultural Counseling and Development

Chartered in 1972 as the Association of Non-White Concerns in Personnel and Guidance, the **Association for Multicultural Counseling and Development (AMCD)** works to improve cultural, ethnic, and racial understanding in counseling. The AMCD's mission is to advance multicultural issues throughout the counseling profession by enhancing awareness about racial and ethnic diversity in human growth and development, addressing racial and ethnic differences, examining theory development and research, and providing leadership and training (www.amcdaca.org). While the AMCD is dedicated to improving ethnic and racial understanding, it also extends to planning personal growth activities and creating educational opportunities for culturally diverse populations. An additional claimed responsibility of this organization is defending human and civil rights, while ensuring that those rights remain a major focus for the ACA and its divisions. The AMCD publishes the *Journal of Multicultural Counseling and Development* and the *AMCD Newsletter*. For more information on this passion division, visit www.amcdaca.org.

Association for Specialists in Group Work

The **Association for Specialists in Group Work (ASGW)** was chartered in 1973. The mission of the ASGW is to provide professional leadership in the field of group work, establish group work standards for professional training, and support research and the dissemination of knowledge in the various aspects of group counseling. In addition, the ASGW strives to foster diversity and dignity in groups, use group process to extend counseling, use a forum for professional counselors to obtain innovative and developing concepts in group work, and provide modeling of effective group practice. The ASGW publishes the *Journal for Specialists in Group Work* and the newsletter *The Groupworker*. For more information on this passion division, visit www.asgw.org/index.asp.

Association for Spiritual, Ethical, and Religious Values in Counseling

The creation of this professional association was a twofold process dating back to 1951, when the Catholic Guidance Council was formed as part of New York's Archdiocese to promote counseling and guidance in the parochial schools. The need for this organization spread nationally, which led to the development of the National Conference of Guidance Councils in 1958. During this same time period, a small group of counselors, many of whom were influential in forming the New York diocesan council, attended the 1955 American Personnel and Guidance Association (APGA) in Chicago and formed the Catholic Counselors in the APGA. In 1961, these two groups merged and created the National Catholic Guidance Conference; however, divisional charter status was not awarded until 1974. Three years later, the charter changed its name to the Association for Religious Values in Counseling. The division was again renamed in 1993 as the **Association for Spiritual, Ethical, and Religious Values in Counseling (ASERVIC)**.

Although this organization has a strong background in Catholic heritage, today ASERVIC is no longer dominated by one specific religious affiliation. Rather, "ASERVIC is devoted to professionals who believe that spiritual, ethical, religious, and other human values are essential to the full development of the person and to the discipline of counseling" (www.counseling.org/AboutUs/DivisionsBranchesAndRegions/TP/Divisions/CT2.aspx). As a result, ASERVIC believes in and promotes the infusion of spirituality, ethics, and religious values in counselor training and application. ASERVIC publishes a journal, *Counseling and Values,* and its newsletter, *INTERACTION,* is an on-line publication. For more information on this passion division, visit www.aservic.org/index.html.

Counseling Association for Humanistic Education and Development

Nicknamed, "the heart and conscience of the counseling profession," the **Counseling Association for Humanistic Education and Development (C-AHEAD)** has a rich history dating back to 1931 beginning as the Teachers College Personnel Association, which was dedicated to personnel workers who trained teachers. The name changed in 1946 to the Personnel Section of the American Association of Teacher Colleges and changed again in 1951 to the Student Personnel Association for Teacher Education. In 1952, the Student Personnel Association for Teacher Education joined three other organizations to form the APGA, which later became the ACA. C-AHEAD is one of the four founding associations of ACA.

C-AHEAD is based on the philosophical principles of the humanistic approach to counseling, and its mission is to focus on ways to empower and advocate for the client to make a difference. As a result, another important philosophy of this organization is to know the client rather than the diagnosis. C-AHEAD provides its members with a forum to exchange information about humanistically oriented counseling practices. Additionally, this organization "promotes changes that reflect the growing body of knowledge about humanistic principles applied to human development and potential" (www.counseling.org/AboutUs/DivisionsBranchesAndRegions/TP/Divisions/CT2.aspx). C-AHEAD publishes the *Journal of Humanistic Counseling Education and Development* and a newsletter, *Infochange.* For more information on this passion division, visit www.c-ahead.com.

Counselors for Social Justice

The **Counselors for Social Justice (CSJ)**, chartered in 2002, "is a community of counselors, counselor educators, graduate students, and school and community leaders who seek equity and an end to oppression and injustice affecting clients, students, counselors, families, communities, schools, workplaces, governments, and other social and institutional systems" (http://counselorsforsocialjustice.com/mission.html). To accomplish this mission, the CSJ maintains an active support network, implements social action strategies, challenges oppressive systems of privilege and power, uses on-line resources to maintain social justice advocacy, and disseminates inequalities that face counselors, clients, students, and communities. The CSJ publishes the *Journal for Social Action in Counseling and Psychology* and a newsletter, the *Activist*. For more information on this passion division, visit http://counselorsforsocialjustice.com.

International Association of Addiction and Offender Counselors

The **International Association of Addiction and Offender Counselors (IAAOC)** was originally chartered in 1972 as the Public Offender Counselor Association. "Members of IAAOC advocate the development of effective counseling and rehabilitation programs for people with substance abuse problems, other addictions, and adult and/or juvenile public offenders" (www.counseling.org/AboutUs/DivisionsBranchesAndRegions/TP/Divisions/CT2.aspx). The IAAOC's mission is to provide advancement and leadership in the fields of addictions and offender counseling. This organization supports research, training, prevention, treatment, and advocacy of the addicted and forensic/criminal justice populations. The IAAOC publishes the *Journal of Addictions and Offender Counseling* and the *IAAOC Newsletter*. For more information on this work setting division, visit www.iaaoc.org.

International Association of Marriage and Family Counselors

Chartered in 1989, the **International Association of Marriage and Family Counselors (IAMFC)** promotes excellence in the practice of couples and family counseling. "Members help develop healthy family systems through prevention, education, and therapy" (www.counseling.org/AboutUs/DivisionsBranchesAndRegions/TP/Divisions/CT2.aspx). The IAMFC is notable for its publications, media products, and exploration forum for family-related issues, involving diverse professionals, and emphasizing collaboration. The IAMFC encourages counselors to advocate for the value and dignity of all families. The IAMFC publishes *The Family Journal* and a newsletter, *The Family Digest*. For more information on this work setting division, visit www.iamfc.com.

National Career Development Association

Originally founded in 1913 as the National Vocational Guidance Association, the **National Career Development Association (NCDA)** was the first counseling association in existence. The NCDA was one of the four founding associations of the ACA. The mission of the NCDA is to "promote career development for all people across the lifespan through public information, member services, conferences, and publications" (www.counseling.org/AboutUs/DivisionsBranchesAndRegions/TP/Divisions/CT2.aspx). The NCDA publishes the highly rated *Career Development Quarterly* and a newsletter, *Career Developments*. For more information on this work setting division, visit http://ncda.org/.

National Employment Counseling Association

Originally chartered in 1966, the **National Employment Counseling Association (NECA)** began as a division of the ACA under the title of National Employment Counselors Association. The NECA is committed to offering professional leadership to individuals who counsel those in the employment or career development setting. The NECA membership expands to a diverse work setting, which includes individuals from private practice; business and industry; community agencies; colleges and universities; and federal, state, and local government. The NCDA publishes the highly rated *Journal of Employment Counseling* and the *NECA Newsletter*. For more information on this work setting division, visit http://geocities.com/employmentcounseling/neca.html.

Now complete Activity 2.1 to find out more about the ACA, its divisions and other entities, and counseling-related publications and information. Then complete Activity 2.2 to test your memory for the ACA divisions and their expressed missions. Finally, complete Activity 2.3 by picking the three ACA divisions that most interest you.

ACTIVITY 2.1   FINDING CURRENT RESEARCH

It is important for professional counselors to have recent knowledge of issues and findings in counseling. Many professional counseling organizations provide current research and information pertinent to the counseling field. The following are activities that can be done to increase your knowledge base of these up-to-date findings:

1. Journals can be located at a local college or county library for hard copy articles and text. Professional journals often also can be accessed on-line through the journal's specific website or www.psycline.org/journals/psycline.html, Psycline, an on-line guide to psychology and social science journals on the web. Choose a topic of special interest to you as a professional and find five research articles discussing this topic.
2. Go to your university library, choose a topic of special interest from the text holdings, and read the book.
3. Not all information found on the Internet has been evaluated by an expert in the field. However, this does not mean that there is no beneficial information on the World Wide Web.
   a. Psychwatch.com is the on-line resource for professionals in psychology and psychiatry. It has numerous links to other counseling disciplines and resources, including on-line journals, licensure information, and software.
   b. Psychcentral.com is a mental health and psychology website providing peer-reviewed information since 1995. This site has a resource directory of current topics related to counseling and psychology, along with symptom and treatment links to mental health disorders.
   c. Information can also be located at professional organizations' homepages, including the ACA, www.counseling.org, and the ASCA, www.schoolcounselor.org.
4. Take all of the information found during your research of journals, books, and Internet sites. Write a short literature review to illustrate the knowledge you have gained from this activity.

AMERICAN COUNSELING ASSOCIATION REGIONS AND BRANCHES

For the purposes of the ACA, the United States is broken into four **regions**: Midwest, North Atlantic, Southern, and Western. The four region designations allow ACA members who are not members of ACA divisions to have representation through an ACA Governing Council Representative. See Table 2.1 to find which region your state or territory of residence is in. Regions are composed of branches.

TABLE 2.1 ACA Regional Breakdown

Midwest	North Atlantic	Southern	Western
Illinois	Connecticut	Alabama	Alaska
Indiana	Delaware	Arkansas	Arizona
Iowa	European	Florida	California
Kansas	Maine	Georgia	Colorado
Michigan	Massachusetts	Kentucky	Hawaii
Minnesota	New Hampshire	Latin America	Idaho
Missouri	New Jersey	Louisiana	Montana
Nebraska	New York	Maryland	Nevada
North Dakota	Pennsylvania	Mississippi	New Mexico
Ohio	Puerto Rico	North Carolina	Oregon
Oklahoma	Rhode Island	South Carolina	Philippines
South Dakota	Vermont	Tennessee	Utah
Wisconsin	Washington, D.C.	Texas	Washington State
		Virginia	Wyoming
		West Virginia	

ACTIVITY 2.2

Find the division of the ACA that best fits the following descriptions.

___ 1. Counselor educators with a humanistic orientation.

___ 2. Professional counselors who lead groups.

___ 3. Professional counselors who advocate quality services within the health care industry.

___ 4. Professional counselors in employment and career development settings.

___ 5. Professional counselors concerned with lifespan concerns and senior citizens.

___ 6. Professional counselors who are engaged in societal issues, seeking social action.

___ 7. Psychometrists; testing specialists.

___ 8. A founding association; now concerned with career development.

___ 9. Counselors of clients (and their families) in local, state, and federal government, or in military-related agencies.

___10. Emphasizes the need for quality education and supervision of professional counselors.

___11. Works to improve cultural, ethnic, and racial empathy and understanding.

___12. Professional counselors who work for the full development of the individual through values, religious, ethical, and spiritual issues.

(Continued)

___13. Professional counselors promoting healthy family systems.

___14. Professional counselors fostering student development in higher education.

___15. Professional counselors who work with substance abuse.

___16. Professional counselors who work in the school system.

___17. Professional counselors who work with disabled clients.

___18. Educates counselors in the area of sexual identity.

___19. Professional counselors interested in using creative arts with clients.

a. Association for Assessment in Counseling and Education (AACE)

b. Association for Adult Development and Aging (AADA)

c. Association for Creativity in Counseling (ACC)

d. American College Counseling Association (ACCA)

e. Association for Counselors and Educators in Government (ACEG)

f. Association for Counselor Education and Supervision (ACES)

g. Association for Gay, Lesbian, Bisexual, and Transgender Issues in Counseling (AGLBTIC)

h. Association for Multicultural Counseling and Development (AMCD)

i. American Mental Health Counselors Association (AMHCA)

j. American Rehabilitation Counseling Association (ARCA)

k. American School Counselor Association (ASCA)

l. Association for Spiritual, Ethical, and Religious Values in Counseling (ASERVIC)

m. Association for Specialists in Group Work (ASGW)

n. Counseling Association for Humanistic Education and Development (C-AHEAD)

o. Counselors for Social Justice (CSJ)

p. International Association of Addiction and Offender Counselors (IAAOC)

q. International Association of Marriage and Family Counselors (IAMFC)

r. National Career Development Association (NCDA)

s. National Employment Counseling Association (NECA)

ACTIVITY 2.3

The three divisions that best fit my career interests are:

1.

2.

3.

Branches represent the grassroots of counseling. The ACA has 56 branches, including one for each state, plus the District of Columbia, Europe, Latin America, Puerto Rico, Virgin Islands, and the Philippines. (*Note:* Some branches are currently "inactive.") Branches provide something that a national organization cannot: a local connection. Branches enable professional counselors to network with other professional counselors in their town, county, state, or territory through local and state conferences and workshops. Branches are in touch with the issues that are pertinent to their particular state and so can target resources, training, and advocacy to a specific need or issue.

For example, the Illinois Counseling Association provides members with specific information on health insurance companies that provide counselor reimbursement in the Chicago area. The Kentucky Counseling Association provides information on how to find a school counseling position in Kentucky. The Texas Counseling Association has a referral bank where state residents can find Association members who are practitioners. The Maine Counseling Association, through its branch division the Maine School Counselor Association, links to a vital resource for school counselors in Maine: The Maine Comprehensive School Counseling Model. Often local or statewide services such as these are of greatest importance to resident counselors and students in training, and beyond the scope of national association missions. Branch associations fill these needs.

Branches also play a vital role in advocating for state legislation that is in the best interest of counselors, clients, and the public. A great example concerns now defeated legislation in Indiana that would have restricted use of more than 200 tests and inventories to only licensed psychologists and prevented counselors from using these instruments in mental health centers, rehabilitation agencies, or independent practice. The bill may have been signed into law by the Governor of Indiana if not for a coalition formed by the National Board for Certified Counselors (NBCC) and the Fair Access Coalition on Testing, consisting of professional counselors, social workers, test publishers, marriage and family therapists, and other professional groups. This coalition was able to convince the Governor not to sign the bill. As a result, counselors in Indiana can continue to provide assessment services within their scope of practice and training to residents of Indiana.

In another example, the ACA, AMHCA, and NBCC helped counselors in Nevada form a coalition to pursue licensure, and in 2007 Nevada became the 49th state to achieve that goal. The California Coalition for Counseling Licensure, with the financial backing of the NBCC and ACA, is attempting to achieve licensure for professional counselors in California, the final remaining state.

OTHER PROFESSIONAL COUNSELING ORGANIZATIONS

The ACA partners with other professional organizations to provide its members with various resources. Such resources include a competitive liability insurance program and a charitable foundation. All professional counselors are committed to academic excellence and high standards within the counseling setting. As a result, additional relationships exist within the counseling world among an honor society for counselors (Chi Sigma Iota [CSI]), university accreditation for counseling programs (Council for Accreditation of Counseling and Related Educational Programs [CACREP] and National Council on Rehabilitation Education [CORE]), and a national counseling certification organization (NBCC), each of which is briefly introduced.

American Counseling Association Insurance Trust, Inc.

In today's world where personal liability lawsuits have become more commonplace, insurance companies serve an essential role. As a result, the ACA has teamed up with an independent corporation, the **American Counseling Association Insurance Trust, Inc. (ACAIT)**, which promotes and administers quality insurance coverage and services. ACA members and groups in the human development professions can benefit from ACAIT's competitive rates. Whether you work with individuals, families, or difficult populations such as sex offenders, the ACAIT offers broad coverage professional liability insurance.

The ACAIT governing board of trustees consists of insurance experts and professional counselors. The ACAIT also uses licensed insurance underwriters and agents to write and provide insurance for professional counselors, students, multidisciplinary groups, business owners, and nonprofit organizations. The ACAIT also offers auto, homeowners, and group life and health plans, which include disability income, business overhead expense, term life, customized major medical, catastrophic major medical, short-term major medical, hospital protection, accidental death and dismemberment, dental, longer-term care, and Medicare supplement insurance.

American Counseling Association Foundation

The **American Counseling Association Foundation (ACAF)** encourages and supports counselor well-being and the well-being of those the counselors serve. This foundation was established in 1979. Since its inception, the ACAF has supported counseling students with essay competitions; honored outstanding educators and practitioners; published a free weekly column, *The Counseling Corner,* in approximately 300 U.S. newspapers; and used the Growing Happy and Confident Kids project to reach out to elementary school students to help them deal with and develop skills to face the problems that plague our schools (e.g., bullying, violence, substance abuse, gangs). Most recently, the ACAF established the Counselors Care Fund, which reaches out to counselors and branches affected by hurricanes Katrina and Rita. The ACAF remains a professional partner of the ACA through tax-deductible gifts from corporations, individuals, foundations, and ACA divisions and branches.

Chi Sigma Iota

Chi Sigma Iota (CSI) is the counseling profession's official honorary society. This independent membership organization distinguishes the outstanding contributions of individuals to the profession and recognizes spectacular achievement in counseling. Numerous universities sponsor local chapters of CSI. For further information, see www.csi-net.org.

Council for Accreditation of Counseling and Related Educational Programs

Created in 1981, the **Council for Accreditation of Counseling and Related Educational Programs (CACREP)** is an independent council that accredits institutions with graduate-level counselor preparation programs. To ensure quality training in the field of counseling, the CACREP promotes high standards, imparts rigorous and objective reviews of established programs, and works with other credentialing organizations. For further information, see www.cacrep.org. Chapter 3 contains much more information on the CACREP.

National Board for Certified Counselors

The **National Board for Certified Counselors (NBCC)** is a voluntary, nonprofit, non-governmental, independent corporation that advances professional counselor credentials. To help counselors advance their credentialing, the NBCC administers the national certification process; identifies counselors who have chosen to become nationally board certified; and manages the certification examination and specialty certificates for addictions counselors, clinical mental health counselors, and school counselors. Much more information regarding the NBCC follows later in this chapter. See also www.nbcc.org.

PROFESSIONAL DEVELOPMENT

Regardless of professional work setting, CE and professional development is a must for professional counselors. Whether to obtain certificate or license renewal, to increase occupational opportunities, or for career development, CE is a reality that stretches well beyond the receipt of a graduate degree, state licensure, or national certification. Obtaining licenses and certifications guarantees that professional counselors will need CE professional development opportunities because the licensing or certifying entities require it.

The purpose of professional development is to help the professional counselor maintain or increase counseling knowledge and skills. Continuing professional development can be costly and time-consuming, so the ACA and its divisions and branches offer quality and affordable CE courses presented by experts in an assortment of subject areas, allowing participants to partake at their own convenience.

The ACA offers CE courses on-line. Participants who have access to the Internet can obtain on-line CE credit at times most convenient to their busy schedules. The ACA offers members three ways to obtain on-line CE credit. First, the ACA offers three-credit and five-credit on-line courses with a corresponding examination. Second, the ACA offers an individual the capability to read articles in the *Journal of Counseling and Development* and take corresponding examinations, whereby each article is worth one CE credit. Finally, the ACA offers an individual the option to read from selected ACA book chapters and take corresponding examinations, whereby each book chapter is worth one CE credit. The ACA warns, however, that before enrolling in the on-line courses, one should confirm that on-line credits are accepted by one's state licensure board or certification body. Although most state licensure boards and certification renewal bodies accept on-line courses for CE credit, not all do at this time.

Another option provided by the ACA is the ACA Home Study Program. Similar to the on-line courses, this program can be completed at one's leisure, whether at home, in the office, or in the car. The home study kit includes a videotape, audiotape, or CD-ROM, reference materials, and the examination. Leading-edge information is presented by nationally renowned instructors, allowing participants the opportunity to earn CE hours.

Members can also subscribe to the *Legal & Regulatory Compliance* newsletter and take the quarterly examinations to earn CE credit. The *Legal & Regulatory Compliance* newsletter helps subscribers learn about the existing and emerging laws and regulations in layperson terms.

Finally, national, state, and regional conferences provide an opportunity for counseling professionals to contribute to the field through presentations and to expand their knowledge base as educators and practitioners. For example, CE contact hours can be earned at the ACA Annual Convention. During this convention, the ACA offers the ACA Learning Institute, where more than 40 skill-building workshops are offered during the 2-day preconvention time period. In addition, the ACA offers the Annual Conference Content Sessions every spring, where more than 400 educational opportunities are available for professional counselors and mental health practitioners. Numerous other professional counseling organizations at the state and national levels offer myriad opportunities for professional development.

BENEFITS OF JOINING PROFESSIONAL COUNSELING ORGANIZATIONS

Professional counseling organizations have developed benefits and services to meet best the needs of their members. Counselors are kept informed of current issues and updates in the profession through publications including books, journals, newsletters, webpages, and listserves. Members of the ACA receive the quarterly *Journal of Counseling and Development* and the professional monthly newsletter *Counseling Today*. Many organizations provide grants, awards, and scholarships through foundations supporting students, research, mentoring, advocacy, service, and humanitarian efforts in the counseling field. In addition, employment listings are often provided for state and national opportunities. Assistance in job searches, resume writing, interviewing skills, and occupational trends may be included.

Additional Benefits for Professional Counselor Members

The ACA considers its professional members, counselors and counselor educators, to be the "linchpin" to helping clients and students meet the daily challenges they face. As a result, the ACA and its divisions and branches are dedicated to providing members with resources, products, information, and services to help them meet success. The ACA also trusts its professional members to make important decisions about the future of counseling and the ACA by encouraging them to run for elected offices and serve on committees. The ACA keeps its professional members abreast of the information, ideas, and experiences created at the annual conventions by publishing the information on *VISTAS Online*. Finally, the ACA offers its professional members multiple opportunities to receive CE credit and teach courses for others to obtain their CE credits.

Additional Benefits for Student Members

The ACA and its divisions and branches recognize that students are the future of the counseling profession and provide students with the resources to begin a career in counseling. Students are offered opportunities through the ACAF Graduate Student Essay Contest. All runners-up and the first-place winners receive a 1-year membership to the ACA. The first-place winner also receives a monetary reward. Another competition offered to students is the Ethics Case Study Competition. Graduate students at both master's and doctoral levels are given the opportunity to think critically about and analyze a probable ethical case, generate an appropriate ethical decision, and make a plan to respond to the decision.

    The ACA in conjunction with the ACAF offers the Ross Trust Graduate Student Scholarship Competition. The competition begins every fall and is for students studying to be a professional school counselor in elementary, middle, or high school. Fifteen scholarships are awarded yearly, of which ten are for master's level students and five are for doctoral students. Another benefit is having listserves available to student members as a means to communicate with other professional counseling students locally, nationally, and internationally.

Divisions and branches of the ACA also offer student and professional member benefits and opportunities. The ASCA offers its members professional liability insurance, the *ASCA School Counselor* Magazine, *Professional School Counseling* journal, Annual Conference discounts, access to the ASCA website and on-line resources, government relationships, and level-specific message boards. An accounting of the membership benefits of the ACA, its 19 divisions, and 56 branches would require an entire book. Joining associations relevant to your location and professional aspirations is a smart decision *and* a great investment in your future and that of your profession.

Ethical Standards

Professional organizations have been instrumental in setting professional and ethical standards for counselors and counselor education programs. Ethical codes work to standardize guidelines for professional practice, continually evolving to meet contemporary needs and issues (see Chapter 3). Ultimately, both counselors and clients benefit. In addition to liability insurance, professional organizations often provide specific services such as ethical or legal consultation for counselors.

Lobbying

National and state organizations work diligently to advocate politically for the counseling profession. In many cases, success has been the result of a unified effort on the part of professional counseling organizations and their members. It is important to continue to represent the interests of the profession and to influence positively public policy and legislation regarding the field of counseling.

Supporting the Mission of the Profession

As you can tell from the information on organizations presented so far, there are many exciting opportunities for professional involvement. Of course, joining a professional association costs money, and joining numerous organizations costs a lot of money. So a question new counselors often ask is, "Which organizations should I belong to, and which credentials should I pursue?" There is no clearly agreed upon answer to this question.

We suggest that all professional counselors, and especially students, join the ACA and their state branch. This gives professionals a contact with the associations that serve all counselor interests at the state and national levels. If you have a work setting division (e.g., school counselor, mental health counselor, career counselor), you would be wise to join that national division and the affiliated state division. We also suggest that professional counselors pursue national certification, such as the National Certified Counselor (NCC), and state licensure or certification, which are often needed to engage in private practice or work for nonprofit agencies or school systems.

Joining professional organizations and pursuing professional credentials shows your commitment to professional standards, places you in contact with like-minded professionals at the national and state levels, and keeps you informed of important work and legislative issues. If you are passionate about certain counseling specialties (e.g., assessment, social justice, multiculturalism), you are encouraged to join the national divisions and state affiliates that serve those causes. There are numerous opportunities to get involved, attend professional development events, and advocate on the part of your clients and profession. Getting involved in professional organizations and pursuing professional credentials is the best way to develop and maintain your professional identity and serve the best interests of your clients and students.

RELATIONSHIP BETWEEN THE AMERICAN COUNSELING ASSOCIATION AND THE AMERICAN PSYCHOLOGICAL ASSOCIATION

The ACA is the national association for all counselors, regardless of specialty area, and serves the interests of all professional counselors. The American Psychological Association is the national association for all psychologists, regardless of specialty area, and serves the interests of all psychologists. On the one hand, the two associations often work in concert to accomplish legislative or professional goals shared in common. On the other hand, turf issues sometimes arise between counselors and psychologists. Because psychological associations at the national and state levels have existed longer than counseling associations, they are often better known by the public and better respected by legislators.

Turf battles continue to occur in some states. In the late 1990s through 2008, psychologists in Maryland and Indiana attempted to restrict the use of psychological tests by professional counselors, whom they deemed as a class of professionals "unqualified" to administer, score, and interpret competently, even though the professional counselors in those states meet the established licensure board and test publisher standards. Such restrictions, claimed the psychologist advocates in those states, protected the public from harm (even though no claim of harm resulting from the use of psychological tests was ever made against a licensee of either state). Despite the claims of protecting the public, such restrictions were clearly aimed at supply and demand economics and restraint of trade, as stated in several opinions by the Maryland Attorney General's office.

These are only a few of the numerous reasons to join and maintain membership in counseling organizations and to pursue professional credentials. Without strong professional organizations, the rights of professional counselors are jeopardized, meaning that the protection of the public is likewise jeopardized.

KEY CHALLENGES THAT REMAIN TO BE ADDRESSED BY COUNSELING PROFESSIONALS

As an emerging profession, counseling still has numerous issues to address. Many of the more conceptual issues were addressed at the end of Chapter 1 and are discussed in subsequent chapters. A lengthy treatise of these issues is beyond the scope of this text—in truth, a new set of issues evolves every 10 or so years, is identified and focused upon by professional organizations and legislators, and, it is hoped, is successfully resolved.

A key issue that has been ongoing and that is likely continue for the next decade or longer is professional identity. Several of the authors in this book are involved in 20/20: A Vision for the Future of Counseling, an initiative undertaken by the ACA and 30 counseling associations and entities to identify and address issues of pressing importance to the future of the counseling profession—issues that need to be resolved by 2020.

Professional identity is a huge issue that will continue to evolve. A side effect of our emerging profession is that the affiliated associations have become a looser consortium of entities, which in some cases has led to a loosening of ties and bonds between the ACA and some of its divisions. All national divisions are autonomous entities, and have historically shared a convergent purpose, mission, and activities. However, not all division leaders see or desire the counseling profession to be a unified one.

For example, in 2003, after repeated warnings of bylaws violations, the ACA Governing Council voted to serve a notice of revocation of the charters of two of its larger divisions, the ASCA and the AMHCA. While the divisions soon re-established compliance, and the charters were actually never revoked, the disintegration caused by the intraprofessional conflict lingers. To this day, some school counselors and mental health counselors believe the ASCA and AMHCA disaffiliated from the ACA, although they did not. Some still do not see the counseling profession as a unified profession, an identity issue that will need to be resolved in the near future.

History has taught us that unity often coalesces during times of threat, and, fortunate or not, there are no serious threats to dismantle the counseling profession at this time. The profession is poised to accomplish two long-held goals in the near future. First, California is the only state without a licensure law that recognizes the title of professional counselor. Within a period of about a quarter century, 49 states and several territories have passed licensure laws. Second, the ACA has long advocated for professional counselors to achieve parity with psychologists and social workers with third-party insurance reimbursement providers, including governmental programs. We are very close to obtaining this goal, but must also fight to maintain it. The current difficulties in the area of parity come from the profession's relatively recent embodiment. Much of the original legislation was written before professional counselors existed, and as the legislation comes up for refunding by governmental agencies and legislatures, some lawmakers, often at the urging of constituents who just happen to represent competing mental health service providers, resist revising provider status and adding professional counselors to the list of qualified providers. Professional counselors must maintain vigilance over all that has been gained, and strive to expand the provision of mental health services to a public who counts on qualified, highly trained professionals for essential care.

The education, training, and recognition of highly qualified counselors is the responsibility of counselor educators, counselor supervisors, and the professionals and organizations that develop and administer accreditation and credentialing processes. The remainder of this chapter introduces the reader to the accreditation and credentialing processes that permeate the profession and raise the quality of counselors to meet high standards of professionalism.

NATIONAL ACCREDITATION

Accreditation is pursued by a university, college, or educational institution to demonstrate compliance with high professional, educational, or training standards developed by an independent professional review board. Accreditation is one way for counselor education programs at institutions of higher education to show that quality education and training is being imparted to students. Many students look at a school's accreditation status when applying to graduate counseling programs. This is not to say that only accredited programs are of high quality, but that programs that have achieved accreditation demonstrate attainment and adherence to high professional standards.

Two major types of accreditation exist in the United States. Institutional accreditation involves a general review of operational and curricular practices at an entire university, college, or school. Specialized accreditation focuses on a particular program or field of study, such as counseling, teacher education, or medicine. Accreditation enhances an institution's reputation. It requires programs to undergo periodic self-examination, continuous assess-ment, and quality improvements to adhere to and exceed standards. Also, institutions often pursue accreditation because it allows access to federal funding and student loans. Two accrediting organizations of primary interest to counselors and counseling programs are the CACREP and CORE.

The CACREP, established in 1981, accredits graduate counselor preparation programs in the United States by setting high educational training standards, influencing and advanc-ing the professional preparation of future professional counselors to serve in a complex and diverse society. The CACREP has had a tremendous impact upon the counseling profession as more than 200 U.S. institutions have achieved CACREP accreditation, and nearly all state licensure boards and the NBCC have modeled their educational requirements upon the CACREP required curriculum. The CACREP (2009) defines accreditation as:

> . . . a system for recognizing educational institutions and professional programs affiliated with those institutions for a level of quality performance and integrity based on review against a specific set of published criteria or standards. In the United States, accreditation represents a unique process of voluntary, nongovern-mental review of educational institutions and professional preparation programs that has been historically described as a self-regulating peer review process. The process includes (1) the submission of a self-study document that demonstrates how standards are being met, (2) an on-site review by a selected group of peers, and (3) a decision by an independent board or commission that either grants or denies accredited status based on how well the standards are being met.

The CACREP reviews programs offering master's degrees in career counseling; college counseling; clinical mental health counseling; marital, couple, and family counseling/therapy; school counseling; and student affairs. The CACREP also reviews doctoral degree programs in counselor education and supervision. The CACREP follows a process of program review and approval that features six steps: (1) self-study and application, (2) initial review, (3) on-site visit, (4) team report, (5) institutional response, and (6) accreditation decision. Accreditation decisions include (a) full 8-year accreditation, (b) 2-year provisional accreditation (minor defi-ciencies to address in a follow-up report), or (c) denial of accreditation.

The CACREP Board undertakes a standard revisions process every 8 years to improve continuously the responsiveness of accredited programs to diverse professional and societal changes. The CACREP Board is composed of 11 professional members and two public mem-bers, but relies on more than 300 trained volunteers who serve as initial reviewers or con-duct on-site reviews. Many university counseling programs are housed in departments of education that may undergo accreditation by external accrediting organizations. For exam-ple, many schools or departments of education undergo accreditation by the National Council for Accreditation of Teacher Education (NCATE). The NCATE insists that counseling programs within NCATE-accredited institutions align with CACREP standards, indicating again the influence and respect the CACREP holds within the United States as the leader in setting high standards for counselor education training programs. Learn more about CACREP by visiting their website at www.cacrep.org.

Another accrediting organization in the field of professional counseling is the **National Council on Rehabilitation Education (CORE)**, which was established to evaluate higher education programs in the field of rehabilitation counseling (Brown & Srebalus, 2003).

CORE was established in 1971 and promotes standards for rehabilitation counseling programs, including mission and objectives, program evaluation, general curriculum requirements, knowledge domains, educational outcomes, clinical experience, administration and faculty, and program support and resources. CORE board members are appointed by the National Rehabilitation Counseling Association) National Council of Rehabilitation Education, ARCA, and Council of State Administrators of Vocational Rehabilitation; two public members are also appointed. Rehabilitation counseling programs are evaluated by the 15–20 member Commission on Standards and Accreditation, and this evaluation is reported to the CORE board for decision. For national certification in the field of rehabilitation counseling, CORE is the accrediting body, not the CACREP.

ACTIVITY 2.4

Investigate the accreditation of your college/university. What is the accrediting body? Many different accreditation entities accredit the university, various departments, and programs. After determining which organizations accredit the university, also research whether there are any other accrediting bodies that recognize your department or program of study. What must your college or university do to be in compliance?

THINK ABOUT IT 2.1

What is the importance of regular reviews of standards for counselor education programs?

STATE ACCREDITATION

Similar to the CACREP, state agencies can approve higher education programs. When a state gives its approval, it is simply stating that the college or university has met the minimum requirements for the statewide standards for all programs at degree granting institutions (Maryland Higher Education Commission, 2007). However, the Maryland Higher Education Commission pointed out that "accreditation goes beyond this to assure that an institution has attained a level of quality recognized by other colleges and universities of the same type."

Many states accredit graduate school counseling programs in conjunction with national accreditation processes. For example, the NCATE, which accepts CACREP accreditation standards and decisions, may coordinate a visit to a college or university with the state department of education. While each entity makes an independent decision, the standards used are often similar. For example, the Maryland State Department of Education has a Division of Certification and Accreditation. Within this division, there are three areas: certification, nonpublic school approval, and program approval for all degree-granting institutions operating in Maryland. "This division certifies teachers and other professional personnel; oversees the preparation and assessment of candidates for principal; and approves the educational programs of nonpublic schools."

STATE PROFESSIONAL CERTIFICATION AND OTHER CREDENTIALS

Credentialing in the counseling world occurs when professionals demonstrate they have met high standards of education, knowledge, and experience. Out of necessity, credentialing laws and regulations for the counseling profession have been left to state legislatures and other regulatory agencies, and as a result, credentialing procedures may differ in different states. There are some commonalities, however, primarily as a result of advocacy efforts by professional counseling organizations.

Gladding (2004) pointed out that there are four levels of credentialing procedures, ranging from least prestigious to most prestigious, which include inspection, registration, certification, and licensure. **Inspection** is an examination by state agencies to determine if professional counselors are practicing in a way that is conducive to public safety, health, and welfare standards. This inspection is often done with professional counselors who are employed by state agencies. During an inspection, personnel are interviewed, and program case notes and agency procedures are scrutinized.

The next type of state credential is **registration**. To qualify for a registry, one's state legislature must have passed a law that allows professional groups to document or list the individuals within the profession who have met specific standards. Generally, those standards include certification. Registries are often published, giving the public a resource. In addition, listing one's name on the registry provides another means for advertisement of services.

Certification for title restrictions is provided for individuals within a given profession who have met higher standards than others within the same profession group. Higher standards often involve the completion of a graduate program, carrying out a specific number of hours or years within the field, and passing an examination to show competency in the given area. Take, for example, the lucrative world of number crunching. Accountants and financial analysts alike can work in the financial industry, but only individuals who have met the higher standards may use the title "certified public accountant" (CPA) or "certified financial analyst" (CFA). However, one who has earned the title of CPA cannot use the title CFA, and one who has earned the title of CFA cannot use the title CPA, as both titles require different procedures and examinations. If one has met the high standards for the CPA and the CFA, one can use both titles.

The same is true for the field of counseling. For example, many within the mental health profession, volunteer or professional, with little or much training, may work with clients with addictions. However, only professionals who have met the high standards of the certification process may use the title "certified addictions counselor." Professionals meeting these specific standards apply for this certification from a professional certification board.

STATE LICENSURE

Licensure is another level of state credentialing procedures and the most prestigious. Licensure is the process by which individual state legislatures regulate the title, practice, or both of an occupational group. As a profession, counseling began pushing for licensure in the 1970s. Beginning with Virginia in 1976, nearly every state has since adopted a counseling licensure law. As of 2007, licensure laws existed in every state (including the District of Columbia) except for California. As more states adopt counseling licensure laws regulating the title and scope of practice, the visibility of professional counselors is increased among the helping professions, managed care organizations, and the general public (Bemak & Espina, 1999).

Licensure laws vary by state. In many of these states, the licensure laws are written as practice acts, while some are written as title acts. **Practice acts** prohibit the practice of professional counseling without first obtaining licensure. These acts are designed to ensure public health, safety, and welfare. In states where practice acts are in place, individuals must successfully complete all specified education, training, and examination requirements before becoming licensed. Nearly every state has adopted some form of practice act for the licensure of professional counselors (American Counseling Association, 2006g).

Title acts restrict the use of a professional title to individuals granted licensure by their appropriate state credentialing agency. In other words, various individuals or groups of practitioners may engage in counseling and counseling-related activities without being licensed (e.g., psychologists, social workers); however, only individuals who have successfully completed all state licensing requirements can call themselves **licensed professional counselors**. Many states have licensure laws that function as title and practice acts.

Also, title acts in different states may result in professional counselors being referred to by different titles or names. For example, in Pennsylvania, the title is "licensed professional counselor," whereas in Pennsylvania's neighbor to the south, Maryland, the title is "licensed clinical professional counselor," and in Pennsylvania's neighbor to the north, New York, the title is "licensed mental health counselor." Different state legislatures draft different bills leading to different laws. This is one of the reasons that the portability of licensure from one state to another is so problematic; not to mention why it is so confusing to make sense out of the "alphabet soup" that follows some professionals' names (e.g., Bradley T. Erford, PhD, NCC, LCPC, LPC, LP, LSP: where PhD = Doctor of Philosophy in counselor education from The University of Virginia; NCC = National Certified Counselor issued by NBCC; LCPC = Licensed Clinical Professional Counselor from Maryland; LPC = Licensed Professional Counselor from Virginia; LP = Licensed Psychologist from Pennsylvania; and LSP = Licensed School Psychologist from Virginia).

To become licensed, individuals must satisfy their respective state's licensing requirements. Although these requirements vary by state, they all include some combination of educational background, supervised counseling experience, and the successful passing of a comprehensive counseling practice examination. Each of these criteria is discussed.

Education

Applicants for licensure are required to complete a master's degree in counseling at an accredited college or university before applying for licensure. The minimum amount of semester hours required is 48, with most states now requiring at least 60 semester hours of graduate study. In addition to the number of hours required, many state licensing boards include specific course work that must be included in one's graduate training, ordinarily aligning with CACREP educational standards.

Supervised Experience

In addition to earning the appropriate academic degree, licensure applicants must document supervised counseling experience. State requirements range from 2,000 to 4,500 hours of supervised experience. In most cases, these hours are to be accumulated in a specific time frame (e.g., 2 years). These hours typically include time spent in individual counseling, group counseling, case staffing, record keeping, and face-to-face supervision. Supervised experience usually means the work experience must be conducted concurrently with individual, triadic, or small group face-to-face supervision with a qualified supervisor licensed by a state board to practice counseling (e.g., a licensed professional counselor), or a related mental health service (e.g., psychology, social work).

Some state counseling boards are considering requirements that applicants for licensure as a professional counselor receive supervision specifically from a licensed professional counselor to facilitate the applicant's professional identity and orientation. This proposed practice makes a lot of sense from the professional identity perspective, but may not always be in the best interest of counselors. On the one hand, no one is better equipped to help orient and supervise a mental health counselor than another experienced mental health counselor supervisor and mentor. On the other hand, experienced, qualified, and willing supervisors may be difficult to locate, and other licensed mental health professionals (e.g., licensed psychologists, licensed clinical social workers, psychiatrists) may be just as experienced and capable as supervisors and mentors.

Examination

All states require licensure applicants to pass a comprehensive examination on the practice of professional counseling. All states that regulate counseling use an examination prepared by the NBCC.

American Association of State Counseling Boards

The American Association of State Counseling Boards (AASCB) maintains responsibility for the licensure and certification of counselors in the United States (American Association of State Counseling Boards, 2007). Currently, the AASCB works with 49 states, the District of Columbia, Guam, and Puerto Rico to establish licensure, create common standards, and develop national portability of licensure. To facilitate license portability, or the ability to transfer one's license automatically from one state licensing board to another, the AASCB has devised two formulas for state licensure in a member state. The first formula consists of 48 semester hours and a master's degree in counseling or a related field; course work consistent with CACREP standards and guidelines; 3,000 hours of post-master's supervision; 1,900 hours of direct client contact; 100 hours of clinical supervision; and passage of the licensure examination as recognized by the member state. The second formula consists of 60 semester hours and a master's degree in counseling or a related field; course work consistent with CACREP standards and guidelines with additional course work in specialty area; 4,000 hours of post-master's supervision; 2,500 hours of direct client contact; 5 years of counseling experience in clinical counseling; and passage of the licensure examination as recognized by the member state.

The AASCB allows for extra years of experience to compensate for deficits in course work, supervision hours, and additional testing requirements. The AASCB continues to work with states possessing licensure laws in an effort to unify the counseling state licensure procedure expectations.

LICENSE PORTABILITY

Although the AASCB is working hard to unify the field of counseling, because of different state standards and procedures for licensure, the counseling profession currently does not have a portability agreement for licensed professional counselors. **Portability** refers to the ability of professionals to move their licensed status from state to state (Gerig, 2007). In the past, a licensed counselor moving from one state to another would have to apply for standard entry licensure in the new state regardless of any license or licenses previously held or level of training and experience. Some states have begun addressing this issue by reaching reciprocity agreements with partner states. In these cases, states with similar licensing requirements agree to accept each other's licenses so long as the appropriate fees are paid in the new state.

Because certification, registry, and licensure requirements and procedures differ from state to state, it is important to research what is required. Misuse of qualifications, title, and status are subject to legal penalties, generally misdemeanor violations, which can be imposed by certification, registry, and licensure boards. To avoid misdemeanor offenses and the potential of losing one's ability to practice, it is important to research what is required, especially when relocating. For more information about individual state requirements, as well as information for the District of Columbia, Guam, and Puerto Rico, see Table 2.2. Then complete Activity 2.5 to explore the licensure requirements in your state.

TABLE 2.2 Certification and Licensure Websites by State

State	Website
Alabama	www.abec.alabama.gov/
Alaska	www.dced.state.ak.us/occ/ppco.htm
Arizona	www.bbhe.state.az.us/
Arkansas	www.arkansas.gov/abec/
California	www.california-registry.org/
Colorado	www.dora.state.co.us/registrations
Connecticut	www.ct-clic.com
Delaware	http://dpr.delaware.gov/
District of Columbia	http://hpla.doh.dc.gov/hpla/cwp/view,a,1195,q,488169,hplaNav,l30661l,.asp
Florida	www.doh.state.fl.us/mqa/491
Georgia	www.sos.state.ga.us/plb/counselors
Hawaii	www.hawaii.gov/dcca/areas/pvl/programs/mental
Idaho	www.ibol.idaho.gov/cou.htm
Illinois	www.dpr.state.il.us
Indiana	www.in.gov/pla/bandc/mhcb/licen_mhc.html
Iowa	www.idph.state.ia.us/licensure/board_home.asp?board=be
Kansas	www.ksbsrb.org
Kentucky	http://finance.ky.gov/ourcabinet/caboff/oas/op/procoun
Louisiana	www.lpcboard.org
Maine	www.state.me.us/pfr/olr/categories/cat13.htm
Maryland	www.dhmh.state.md.us/bopc/
Massachusetts	www.mass.gov/reg/boards/mh
Michigan	www.michigan.gov/mdch/0,1607,7-132-7417_27529_27536—,00.html
Minnesota	www.bbht.state.mn.us/
Mississippi	www.lpc.state.ms.us
Missouri	www.pr.mo.gov
Montana	www.swpc.mt.gov

(Continued)

TABLE 2.2 Certification and Licensure Websites by State (*Continued*)

State	Website
Nebraska	www.hhs.state.ne.us/crl/mhcs/mental/mentalhealth.htm
Nevada	http://marriage.state.nv.us/licensing.htm
New Hampshire	www.state.nh.us/mhpb/
New Jersey	www.state.nj.us/lps/ca/medical/familytherapy.htm
New Mexico	www.rld.state.nm.us/b&c/counseling/index.htm
New York	www.op.nysed.gov/mhp.htm
North Carolina	www.ncblpc.org
North Dakota	www.ndbce.org
Ohio	http://cswmft.ohio.gov/
Oklahoma	www.health.ok.gov/program/lpc or nenaw@health.ok.gov
Oregon	www.oblpct.state.or.us
Pennsylvania	www.dos.state.pa.us/bpoa/cwp/view.asp?a=1104&q=433177
Puerto Rico	www.salud.gov.pr/
Rhode Island	www.healthri.org/hsr/professions/mf_counsel.php
South Carolina	www.llr.state.sc.us/pol/counselors
South Dakota	www.doh.sd.gov/brd/counselor
Tennessee	www.state.tn.us/health/Boards/PC_MFT&CPT/
Texas	www.dshs.state.tx.us/counselor
Utah	www.dopl.utah.gov/licensing/professional_counselor.html
Vermont	http://vtprofessionals.org/opr1/allied/
Virginia	www.dhp.virginia.gov
Washington	www.doh.wa.gov
West Virginia	www.wvbec.org
Wisconsin	http://drl.wi.gov/prof/coun/def.htm
Wyoming	http://plboards.state.wy.us/mentalhealth/index.asp

ACTIVITY 2.5

What are the licensure requirements for professional counselors in your state? How many hours of graduate study and supervised clinical experience must an individual have to apply for licensure? What comprehensive examination must he or she pass? Once you have researched your own state, select another state you might consider working in. How are the licensure laws similar between the two states? How are they different?

Certification/Licensure for Professional School Counselors

State governments are given power by the U.S. Constitution to regulate the educational system within their own jurisdiction, leaving ultimate power and authority to reside with the state boards of education. As a result, states establish and implement certification and licensure standards for teachers, administrators, and other personnel, which also includes professional school counselors. Usually, this is done either by the state department itself, using an approved program approach upon which a recommendation for the program results in licensure, or by a division created within the state department, which oversees the credentialing of prospective educators and educational personnel. This division ultimately determines whether or not individuals are qualified to perform in the public schools.

In many states, professional school counselors are certified (in some states called licensed) by the state Department of Education to provide counseling services in the school, similar to the way teachers and principals are certified. Such procedures assure the public that the professionals working with school students have met minimum criteria and standards of education and training.

Benefits and Drawbacks of Counseling Licensure

The adoption of counseling licensure laws by nearly every state would seem to indicate that licensure is a benefit to the public and the counseling profession. Proponents of licensure often cite the safeguarding of client welfare, professional accountability standards, and increased accessibility of services as a few of the major benefits of licensing counselors (Corey, Corey, & Callanan, 2003). Additionally, the benefits to the counselor consist of third-party reimbursement and advertisement. Licensure also has intangible rewards, such as the internal drive to achieve at the highest level within one's profession. However, some see little benefit in licensing counselors. According to Eriksen (1999b), the drawbacks of licensure include its promotion of "turf war" among the mental health disciplines, the cost required to acquire and maintain the license, the geographical limitations it places on practicing counselors, and the lack of any true research evidence supporting its existence.

THINK ABOUT IT 2.2

Do you believe that the enactment of counseling licensure laws has benefited the public and the counseling profession or limited its growth?

NATIONAL CERTIFICATION

National certification of professional counselors is administered by the **National Board of Certified Counselors (NBCC)** and Affiliates, Inc., which was established in 1982 and has become the world's largest counselor certification system, certifying more than 42,000 professional counselors. Counselors who wish to become nationally certified voluntarily submit their credentials to determine if they have met preset, specific standards required to attain the certification NCC, which is basically a "general practice" certification. Requirements for the NCC include specific educational course work, documented experience, endorsements by qualified professionals, and a passing score on the *National Counselor Examination for Licensure and Certification* (NCE).

The NCE is a 200-item test of the knowledge, skills, and abilities necessary for providing professional counseling services. The NCE is not only administered to individuals pursuing national certification, but also has been adopted by most state licensure boards as a required element of the state licensure process. All states that regulate professional counselors require passing at least one of the NBCC-administered examinations. The content areas represented on the NCE are the curricular areas required by the CACREP (i.e., professional orientation and ethical practice, social and cultural foundations, human growth and development, career and lifestyle development, helping relationships, group work, assessment, and research and program evaluation), but these curricular areas have been cross-referenced with five work behavior domains (i.e., fundamentals of counseling, assessment and career counseling, group counseling, programmatic and clinical intervention, professional practice issues). Of the 200 items on each administration of the NCE, 160 are scored, and 40 are under field test development. The NBCC sets a criterion-referenced passing/cutoff score for each administration.

The NCE is used to assess individual performance of those who voluntarily submit to the examination and cannot be used by counselor education programs as a program evaluation device. For the purpose of program evaluation, an NBCC affiliate (the Center for Credentialing and Education) prepares and administers the Counselor Preparation Comprehensive Examination, which is currently used as a program evaluation tool by more than 100 counselor education programs in U.S. colleges and universities.

When a professional counselor becomes an NCC, the counselor can pursue national certification in a specialty area, such as school counseling **(National Certified School Counselor)**, clinical mental health counseling **(Certified Clinical Mental Health Counselor)**, or addictions counseling **(Master Addictions Counselor)**. Each specialty certification requires additional educational, examination, and experience requirements. The NBCC also offers an **Approved Clinical Supervisor** certificate.

The NBCC also promulgates and enforces the *NBCC Code of Ethics,* which sets standards for the ethical behavior of all NCCs. The NBCC also developed and distributes the *Standards for Ethical Practice of Internet Counseling,* which covers Internet counseling relationships; confidentiality in counseling relationships; and legal considerations, licensure, and certification. Finally, the NBCC is a founding member of the Fair Access Coalition on Testing, a nonprofit organization that advocates for the appropriate access to and use of tests by competent professionals. The NBCC has been instrumental in advocating and achieving numerous victories for professional counselors in the United States on various issues, from testing to licensure to incorporation of counselors as service providers within third-party payer networks. In addition, hundreds of NCCs responded to the call for humanitarian and professional assistance during times of national crisis (e.g., 9-11 terrorist attack, Hurricane Katrina).

ACTIVITY 2.6

Explore the NBCC (www.nbcc.org) website to identify recent developments in the counseling profession.

COMMISSION ON REHABILITATION COUNSELOR CERTIFICATION

The oldest of all the national certifications is the **Commission on Rehabilitation Counselor Certification (CRCC)** (see www.crccertification.com/), which issues the Certified Rehabilitation Counselor (CRC) credential. The CRCC is not affiliated with the

NBCC. The CRCC was established in 1974 with the purpose of assuring the public that professionals in the field of rehabilitation counseling meet the quality standards within the profession and practice (Commission on Rehabilitation Counselor Certification, n.d.). To obtain this national certification, applicants must take the certification examination. Beyond this, however, applicants may choose one of six different paths for the remainder of the certification process.

The first path involves completion of a master's degree program that is fully accredited by CORE. In addition, applicants must have participated in a supervised internship consisting of either a 480-hour quarter system or a 600-hour semester system. The second path is identical to the first path, but makes a provision for students who graduated from a program that was not accredited by CORE. In this case, applicants must have an additional one year of supervised experience under a CRC and present a letter stating they are in good standing. The third path to national certification is for applicants who, similar to applicants choosing the second option, did not graduate from an accredited college, but also did not have an internship experience. In this case, applicants are required to complete a 2-year internship under the supervision of a CRC.

The fourth path is designed for students enrolled in an accredited master's degree program for rehabilitation counseling. In addition to the accredited program, students must have 75% of the course work finished, part of which is the internship under the supervision of a CRC, and provide a letter from the CRC stating they are in good standing. However, certification will not be granted until after the master's degree program is complete. The last two options are for applicants who are not U.S. citizens and for applicants with doctorates in rehabilitation counseling. In these situations, applicants must ensure that they have met the requirements from one of the other four options.

Upon completion of this national certification process, one is granted certification for 5 years. For recertification, applicants must complete 150 contact hours of approved CE credit. Otherwise, one must go through the examination process again.

Summary

We hope that you are now aware of the importance of membership in professional organizations. But which should you join? We would like to suggest that you become a member of, at minimum, three associations: ACA, at least one ACA division, and your state ACA branch. We also recommend that you become a NCC and obtain licensure in your state. This will cover all your professional bases.

These organizations keep you informed and educated about trends and new practices across the entire counseling profession, keep you updated in your specialty area, and provide you local networking and advocates for counseling issues in your state or territory. Does joining these counseling organizations run into a bit of money? You bet. Should you do it anyway? Absolutely! It is the price that we all pay for the elevation over the past few decades of counseling into a fully acknowledged and comprehensive profession. Would you expect your physician to be a member of the American Medical Association and your lawyer to be a member of the American Bar Association? Of course. So, too, do our clients expect to be able to reap the benefits of having a counselor who has membership in professional counseling organizations.

Accreditation of institutions of higher education involves a commitment to high curricular and organizational standards. CACREP and CORE are the primary accreditation organizations for counselor education programs. CORE accredits rehabilitation counseling programs and CACREP accredits master's degree programs in career counseling; college counseling; clinical mental health counseling; marital, couple, and family counseling/therapy; school counseling; student affairs; and doctoral degree programs in counselor education and supervision. Credentialing involves the voluntary submission of evidence of a professional counselor's education and experience for comparison with a set of standards and passing an examination of the knowledge and information required for practice as a professional counselor. Verification of counselor credentials can entail inspection, registration, certification, and licensure. National certification is conducted by the NBCC, which also administers the NCE.

The licensing of professional counselors is a state-governed process. Individuals wishing to practice as licensed professional counselors must satisfy all of the licensing board requirements for their respective state. These requirements include graduate course work in counseling and related areas, supervised clinical experience, and a passing score on the designated comprehensive examination for that state. Since counseling licenses are not portable, professional counselors should familiarize themselves with the requirements of any states they might relocate to in the future. Accreditation, national certification, and state licensure serve to construct a strong foundation for the establishment of quality counselor education training programs and continuous professional development so that the public not only is protected from harm by unqualified practitioners, but also is well served by highly qualified professional counselors.

3

Ethical and Legal Issues in Counseling

Lynn E. Linde, Bradley T. Erford,
and Amy Cheung

PREVIEW

This chapter addresses some ethical and legal issues in counseling. As a professional counselor, you must always remember that how you conduct yourself personally and professionally reflects not only upon yourself, but also upon your colleagues. Knowledge and understanding of the issues reviewed in this chapter are only a starting point. Keep up-to-date with the laws, ethics, policies, and procedures that govern professional practice. The implementation of your professional responsibilities will require your undivided attention every day of your professional life.

ETHICAL STANDARDS AND LAWS

The cornerstone of the counseling relationship rests upon the public's trust in the services provided. Each professional counselor has an enormous responsibility to uphold the public trust and must seek high levels of training, education, and supervision in the ethical application of counseling practices. This is particularly essential in a profession such as counseling because counselors usually work with clients and students as lone professionals, often with little oversight and behind closed doors in confidential circumstances. Attention to ethical and legal issues is thus crucial.

One of the greatest challenges facing most professional counselors daily is how to handle appropriately the many different ethical and legal situations they encounter. Because of the nature of counseling, professional counselors must be prepared to help clients who present a variety of challenges. It is often difficult to know all one needs to understand and be able to do. Numerous resources and sources of information can help guide professional counselors as they strive to assist clients in an ethical and legal manner. The professional associations for counselors have created ethical standards for professional behavior and provide a wealth of current information, resources, and training. Federal and state governments continually enact laws and regulations that affect counselors, including the judicial branch, in which courts hand down decisions that directly affect counselors' behavior. In addition, state boards of education and local school systems create policies, guidelines, and procedures that professional school counselors must follow.

Professional counselors are sometimes confused by the difference between ethical standards and laws, and what one should do when these seem to be in conflict with each other. It may be helpful to take a look at the origin of both. **Ethical standards** are usually developed by professional associations to guide the behavior of a specific group of professionals. According to Herlihy and Corey (2006), ethical standards serve three purposes: to educate members about sound ethical conduct, to provide a mechanism for accountability, and to serve as a means for improving professional practice. Ethical standards change and are updated periodically to ensure their relevance and appropriateness.

Ethical standards are based on generally accepted norms, beliefs, customs, and values (Fischer & Sorenson, 1997). The **Code of Ethics** published by the **American Counseling Association (ACA)** (2005a) is based on Kitchener's five moral principles of autonomy, justice, beneficence, nonmaleficence, and fidelity (Forester-Miller & Davis, 1996). **Autonomy** refers to the concept of independence and the ability to make one's own decisions. Professional counselors need to respect the right of clients to make their own decisions based on their personal values and beliefs, and not impose their values on clients. **Justice** means treating each person fairly, but it does not mean treating each person the same way. Rather, counselors should treat clients according to the client needs. **Beneficence** refers to doing good or what is in the best interests of the client. In counseling, it also incorporates the concept of removing conditions that might cause harm. **Nonmaleficence** means doing no harm to others. Finally, **fidelity** involves the concepts of loyalty, faithfulness, and honoring commitments. This means that professional counselors must honor all obligations to the client.

Laws are also based on these same, generally accepted norms, beliefs, customs, and values. However, laws are more prescriptive, have been incorporated into code, and carry greater sanctions or penalties for failure to comply. Laws and ethical standards exist to ensure the appropriate behavior of professionals within a particular context to ensure that the best interests of the client are met. When the two seem to be in conflict with each other, the professional counselor must attempt to resolve the conflict in a responsible manner (Cottone & Tarvydas, 2003). Professional counselors must make their clients aware of the conflict and their ethical standards. Because there are greater penalties associated with laws, the counselor will often follow the legal course of action if there is no harm to the client. Many ethical standards recognize that other mandates must be followed and suggest that professional counselors work to change mandates that are not in the best interests of their clients. Activity 3.1 provides an opportunity to explore the nuances of an ethical/legal conflict.

ACTIVITY 3.1

Consider a situation where the law and ACA ethical standards are in conflict with one another. Role-play with a peer how you might approach your client in explaining the conflict and your ethical standards. What might you do to begin working toward changing legal mandates that are not in the best interest of your client?

Within the ACA, there are multiple codes of ethics. The ACA has its *Code of Ethics* (2005), to which its members must adhere. In addition, several divisions have their own codes of ethics, including the American School Counselor Association (ASCA) and the American Mental Health Counseling Association. Some associations, such as the Association for Specialists in Group Work and the Association for Assessment in Counseling and Education, have developed standards or guidelines for best practices. **Best practice guidelines** are not ethics per se but do recommend practice standards that professional counselors should strive to uphold. These codes of ethics and guidelines parallel the ACA's *Code of Ethics,* but speak more directly to the specialty area. For example, the ASCA's *Code of Ethics* discusses what ethical behavior consists of in a school setting.

Many professional counselors belong to multiple organizations, each of which may have its own code of ethics. They may also hold credentials from organizations or state credentialing boards that have a code of ethics as well. Many counselors are Nationally Certified Counselors, a credential offered by the National Board for Counselor Certification, Inc., which also has a code of ethics. It is often hard to know which code takes precedence. While each professional will have to make that determination individually, there are two general guidelines. First, what is the setting in which one is practicing, and is there a particular code that applies specifically to that setting? Second, in what capacity (e.g., licensed professional counselor, marriage and family therapist, certified school counselor) is the professional operating? Additionally, all codes are similar, and all concern behaving in an appropriate professional manner, operating in the best interests of the client, and practicing within the scope of one's education, training, and experience. If a professional counselor is doing all of this, the existence of multiple codes of ethics should not be a significant issue.

American Counseling Association *Code of Ethics*

The ACA revises its *Code of Ethics* about every 10 years. The sixth and most recent revision took effect in August 2005. There are numerous significant changes from the 1995 *Code of Ethics and Standards of Practice* to the 2005 *Code of Ethics.* The most obvious change is that the Standards of Practice section, which described in behavioral terms the aspirational ethics set forth in the code, has been incorporated into the body of the *Code of Ethics* and is no longer a separate section. Each section now begins with an introduction, which sets the tone for that section and is a beginning point for discussion (American Counseling Association, 2005a). Parts of the *Code of Ethics* have been updated to reflect the current thinking and practice in the field, and several new issues have been added. A glossary of terms has also been added. Now complete Activity 3.2 to consider the current societal issues that may affect the writing of the next ACA *Code of Ethics.*

ACTIVITY 3.2

Society changes over time, affecting the practice of counseling. What are some foreseeable changes spurred by societal issues that might be present in the next revision of the ACA *Code of Ethics*?

The ACA states that the 2005 *Code of Ethics* serves five main purposes, as follows:

The *Code* 1) enables the association to clarify to current and future members, and to those served by members, the nature of the ethical responsibilities held in common by its members; 2) The *Code* helps support the mission of the association; 3) The *Code* establishes the principles that define ethical behavior and best practices of association members; 4) The *Code* serves as an ethical guide designed to assist members in constructing a professional course of action that best serves those utilizing counseling services and best promotes the values of the counseling profession; and 5) The *Code* serves as the basis for processing of ethical complaints and inquiries initiated against members of ACA. (p. 3)

The 2005 ACA *Code of Ethics* (see www.counseling.org/Resources/CodeOfEthics/TP/Home/CT2.aspx) addresses the responsibilities of professional counselors toward their clients, colleagues, workplace, and themselves by delineating the ideal standards for conducting one's behavior. All members are required to abide by the *Code of Ethics,* and action is taken against any member who fails to do so. In effect, as these are the standards of the profession, all professional counselors are held to the *Code of Ethics* by the mental health community, regardless of whether they are members of the ACA.

The *Code of Ethics* is divided into eight areas: (A) The Counseling Relationship; (B) Confidentiality, Privileged Communication, and Privacy; (C) Professional Responsibility; (D) Relationships with Other Professionals; (E) Evaluation, Assessment, and Interpretation; (F) Supervision, Training, and Teaching; (G) Research and Publication; and (H) Resolving Ethical Issues. Each of these areas details specific counselor responsibilities and standards.

In general, the *Code of Ethics* discusses respecting one's client and the background each client brings to the counseling setting; maintaining professional behavior with clients and other professionals; practicing with the best interests of the client in mind; and practicing within the limits of one's training, experience, and education. The last section provides direction for members resolving ethical dilemmas. Highlights from each of these areas are summarized later, but at this point, readers should locate the actual ACA *Code of Ethics* on the ACA website and peruse it in detail.

SECTION A: THE COUNSELING RELATIONSHIP   A key issue addressed in this section is boundaries with clients and dual relationships. The period of time that a professional counselor and former client must wait to engage in romantic or sexual relationships was changed from 2 to 5 years, and the language was expanded to include not just clients, but also romantic partners or family members of former clients. This change highlighted the vulnerable nature of clients in a helping relationship. The previous *Code* emphasized the avoidance of nonprofessional relationships with clients outside of the formal counseling relationship. The current *Code* recognizes that this is not always possible, and recognizes that nonprofessional relationships with clients may even benefit clients (e.g., attending formal ceremonies, hospital visits, membership in community organizations, commerce), albeit when conducted with caution.

Continued emphasis was placed on critical issues, including general client welfare and avoiding harm, appropriate termination of services, fees and bartering, and informed consent. The informed consent provision is particularly important because many state counseling boards now require written consent so that clients can choose a counseling relationship with a qualified provider from an informed consumer position. Section A.2.b specifies that informed consent includes, but is not limited to, purposes, goals, techniques, procedures, limitations, potential risks, and benefits of services; the counselor's qualifications, credentials, and relevant experience; the intended use of tests and reports, fees, and billing arrangements; the right to confidentiality and limitations; the continuation of services should the counselor become incapacitated; obtaining clear information about their records; participating in ongoing treatment planning; and right to refuse treatment at any time and the potential consequences for doing so. In addition, the *Code* addresses the need to balance assent from minors and others incapable of giving consent without the assent of parents and family members who hold the legal rights of consent, protection, and decision making on their behalf. Table 3.1 provides a sample informed consent that addresses these salient points.

Section A also includes new standards for serving the terminally ill and facilitating end-of-life decisions, making the ACA one of the first national associations to address these issues. In doing so, the ACA directs counselors to receive adequate supervision and seek multiple professional collaborations, and help clients exercise self-determination, establish high-quality end-of-life care, and participate maximally in decision making. Finally, the 1999 ACA *Ethical Standards for Internet Online Counseling* was integrated into A.12, broadening the *Code* to address issues of technology in providing counseling services, record keeping, and research applications.

SECTION B: CONFIDENTIALITY, PRIVILEGED COMMUNICATION, AND PRIVACY Several major changes were made to the confidentiality, privileged communication, and privacy section of the *Code of Ethics*. Standard B.1.a was added to remind professional counselors to maintain sensitivity and awareness in regard to cultural meanings of privacy and confidentiality. Counselors should also be respectful of differing views and inform clients with whom, when, and how information will be shared. Another addition was Standard B.3.e, which took into consideration the transmission of confidential information and reflected the growing use of technology throughout the counseling process. This Standard advised counselors to take precautions to ensure confidentiality when using technologies such as computers, electronic mail, or voicemail.

A new and important addition was Standard B.3.f, which asserted that professional counselors should maintain the confidentiality of deceased clients as is consistent with legal requirements and policies. Another significant change involved Standard B.4.b, which was renamed Couples and Family Counseling. The 2005 *Code* stated that professional counselors must clearly recognize who is considered to be "the client," must discuss limitations and expectations of confidentiality during couples and family counseling, and should seek and document an agreement with all involved parties as to their individual rights to confidentiality or obligations to protect the confidentiality of the known information. This differed from the 1995 *Code,* which simply declared that permission was required when disclosing information about one family member to another.

Finally, Section B.5 was expounded upon to address confidentiality and privacy when counseling clients who are minors or adults lacking the capacity to give informed consent. Professional counselors are directed to inform parents and legal guardians of the confidential nature of the counseling relationship as well as establish a working relationship with them to serve clients better. Counselors must also seek permission from the appropriate parties to disclose information. When working with this specific population, counselors are reminded to uphold written policies, federal and state laws, and ethical standards as applicable.

TABLE 3.1 Professional Disclosure Statement*

Bradley T. Erford, PhD
Address
Telephone Numbers & E-mail

I welcome you as a new client and I look forward to working with you. The purpose of this form is to let you know about my approach to counseling, what you can expect from counseling, and my background. This form will also give you an opportunity to give consent for counseling or assessment services.

In my view, the relationship of feelings and thoughts to behavior is crucial to understanding the issues that affect being successful in life. I use a variety of strategies that can help people make sense of their world, strategies that are mostly humanistic and cognitive-behavioral in nature; that is, they are strategies based on the notion people often experience personal difficulties because of relationship issues, and that the way people think about and see themselves and the world influences how they feel and behave. You will be encouraged to engage in strategies to address these issues both during and between our sessions.

Individual counseling offers you a chance to express ideas and concerns to understand your situation better and learn new ways to solve problems. However, there are risks and limitations to counseling. At times, you might experience feelings that are uncomfortable and hard to face. I often compare this process to taking medicine: it may not taste great, but it also might be good for you in the long run. I will do my best to provide an accurate and fair assessment and diagnosis that will help guide our treatment planning and goal setting. We will also discuss this assessment/diagnosis and your resulting treatment plan/goals throughout the counseling process. Counseling is a collaborative process done with your best interests in mind, and the ultimate goal is for you to reach a level of healthy and independent personal functioning.

Of course, you have the right to refuse or terminate treatment at any time, and should you believe either of these options appropriate, I hope you will discuss the potential benefits and risks associated with your decision with me. If at any time I become unavailable to continue providing services to you as a result incapacitation or other cause, I will help transition you to another mental health care provider who can either continue treatment or insure appropriate referral so that your best interests are served.

I specialize in working with children, adolescents, and their families, and provide psycho-educational assessment, as well as individual, group, and family counseling. I am particularly experienced in working with individuals presenting with disruptive, anxious, and depressed behaviors, as well as individuals experiencing learning, divorce, or grief adjustment difficulties, or in need of stress management.

Everything you discuss with me will be kept confidential by me except matters pertaining to (1) suicide or harm to another person; (2) physical/sexual abuse or neglect of minors, persons with disabilities, and the elderly; (3) legal activity resulting in a court order; and (4) anything else as required by law. For those matters, legally and ethically, I would have to break confidentiality and involve others. Except for these conditions, any written information or report that I possess cannot be shared, orally or in writing, with another individual or agency without your express written permission. Tests are administered and reports are produced to facilitate personal diagnosis and treatment. Of course, I would be willing to share information with any other professional or agency that you wish, provided that you sign a written release-of-information form, which I can provide for you. Alternatively, you may share results from written reports or sessions at your discretion because confidentiality applies to my communications, not yours. Ethically guiding my behavior is the ACA Code of Ethics published by the American Counseling Association in Alexandria, VA, the National Board for Certified Counselors (NBCC, Inc.), and the Code of Ethics adopted by the Maryland Board of Professional Counselors and Therapists. Legally, I adhere to U.S. and Maryland statutes.

TABLE 3.1 Professional Disclosure Statement (*Continued*)

As for my background, I have been a licensed professional counselor since 1988. I earned my bachelor's degree (BS) in biology from Grove City College (PA), my master's degree (MA) in school psychology from Bucknell University (PA), and my PhD in counselor education from The University of Virginia. I am a member of the American Counseling Association, and I am a Licensed Clinical Professional Counselor (LCPC), which allows me to practice mental health counseling in Maryland. My LCPC state license was issued by the Board of Professional Counselors and Therapists in Baltimore, MD. I also am a National Certified Counselor (NCC), which is a designation given by the National Board for Certified Counselors (NBCC).

As far as counseling/assessment session fees are concerned, I charge $____ per hour. This same rate applies to time spent on providing special services, such as court appearances. Cost for a standard psychoeducational assessment is $_____ which includes a written report and up to 1 hour for a feedback/interpretation consultation session. I do not participate with third-party payers, such as managed care organizations and insurance companies. By signing this form, you are agreeing to pay this fee on the day the service is provided. Missed appointments without a 24-hour notice will have to be paid for, except for genuine emergencies.

I have attached a business card to this letter. Please feel free to contact me at any time during business hours. If I am unavailable, you can leave a message, and I will get back to you as soon as possible. In the event of an emergency, please call 911 or go to the nearest emergency room.

I hope that you will find this counseling experience to be successful and, in some ways, enjoyable. I thank you very much for taking time to read this. Please sign below to indicate your consent to pursue counseling or assessment services.

Bradley Erford, PhD, LCPC, NCC

LC#

Contact Information:

Board of Professional Counselors and Therapists	American Counseling Association
4201 Patterson Avenue	5999 Stevenson Avenue
Baltimore, MD 21215-2299	Alexandria, VA 22304
410-764-4732	800-347-6647

Note: You do not have to sign this; you have the right to refuse counseling or psychoeducational assessment.

I, _____, fully understand what I have just read and offer my consent for counseling or psychoeducational assessment, free of any pressure to do so. Here is my signature and the date of the signature (that expires one year from now).

_____   _____

Signature   Date

_____   _____

Signature of a custodial parent is required in   Date
cases where the child/adolescent is a minor

*This information is required by the Board of Professional Counselors and Therapists, which regulates all licensed clinical professional counselors in Maryland. You can contact the Board at Board of Professional Counselors and Therapists, 4201 Patterson Avenue, Baltimore, MD 21215-2299, or 410-764-4732.

SECTION C: PROFESSIONAL RESPONSIBILITY This section continued to place emphasis on issues such as professional competence, advertising and soliciting clients, professional qualifications, and public responsibility. One area that was significantly expanded upon involved counselor impairment (Standard C.2.g). Professional counselors must be alert to signs of personal impairment and should refrain from providing or offering services if the impairment could potentially harm a client. If the problem reached the level of professional impairment, the counselor should seek out assistance. Professional counselors are now also required to assist supervisors or colleagues in recognizing impairment and, if necessary, provide assistance, intervention, or consultation.

Standard C.2.h was added to address further the issue of counselor impairment or subsequent termination of practice. This new standard stated that counselors should follow a prepared plan for the transfer of files and clients when they leave a practice. In particular, counselors need to designate a specific colleague or "records custodian," and create a proper plan for file and client transfer in the case of their incapacitation, termination of practice, or death.

Another major change to this section included the addition of Standard C.6.e, which acknowledged that professional counselors must use techniques, modalities, or procedures that have a scientific or empirical foundation and are grounded in theory. If not, counselors should note their procedures or techniques to be "unproven" or "developing." The potential risks and ethical considerations of the procedures or techniques should be explained to the client, and counselors should take all necessary steps to protect the client from any potential harm. Counselors are still required to monitor their effectiveness and take any necessary actions to improve as professionals.

SECTION D: RELATIONSHIPS WITH OTHER PROFESSIONALS This section stressed the importance of interaction and relationships between counselors and other professionals. Professional counselors should become knowledgeable about their colleagues and develop positive working relationships and communication systems. Generally, the 2005 ACA *Code of Ethics* reorganized and renamed most of the standards in this section. It was also recognized that counselors may often be a part of an interdisciplinary team. Several new standards were created to reflect this development.

Professional counselors are reminded to be respectful of differing approaches to counseling services and the traditions and practices of other professional groups (Standard D.1.a). Inclusion of Standards D.1.b and D.1.c specifically addressed interdisciplinary relationships and teamwork, respectively. Professional counselors must work to develop and strengthen relationships with interdisciplinary colleagues. Professional counselors must also keep focused on how best to serve their clients when working in a team environment. To do so, counselors can contribute to and partake in any decisions that could potentially affect the well-being of clients by the use of the values, experiences, and perspectives of the counseling profession and other disciplines. Standard D.1.e reminded counselors that when working with an interdisciplinary team, it is their responsibility to clarify the ethical and professional obligations of individual members and the team as a whole. Professional counselors are encouraged to attempt to resolve ethical concerns initially within the team. If a resolution cannot be made within the team, counselors should pursue other means to address the concerns consistent with the well-being of the client.

SECTION E: EVALUATION, ASSESSMENT, AND INTERPRETATION A noticeable change to this section involved the replacement of the word "tests" with "assessment," which has a more integrative and broader connotation. In addition, "career assessment" was added to several standards, and further details were included. For example, Standard E.1.a now includes specific examples of measurements, including, but not limited to, personality, ability, interest, achievement, intelligence, and performance. It is still recognized that assessment is only one part of the overall counseling process, and that professional counselors must take into account the cultural, social, and personal factors.

Historical and Social Prejudices in the Diagnosis of Pathology (Standard E.5.c) was a new addition to the 2005 *Code* and stated that professional counselors should be aware of social and historical prejudices in the pathologizing and misdiagnosis of specific individuals and groups. In addition, counselors should be cognizant of the role of mental health professionals in the continuation of these problems. Not only does the revised ACA *Code of Ethics* take into consideration historical factors, it was also changed to reflect the current trends in counseling.

The inclusion of Section E.13, Forensic Evaluation: Evaluation for Legal Proceedings, denoted the increased presence of professional counselors in legal proceedings and subsequent legal matters. This new section outlined the primary obligations for counselors, the consent for evaluation, and the necessity to avoid potentially harmful relationships in regard to forensic evaluations. The primary obligation of professional counselors conducting forensic evaluations is to generate objective findings that are supported by appropriate techniques and information. Counselors are entitled to form their own professional opinions, but must define any limitations in their testimonies or reports.

SECTION F: SUPERVISION, TRAINING, AND TEACHING   This section was heavily revised and expanded in certain sections, such as supervisory relationships and student welfare and responsibilities. Focus still remained on fostering professional relationships and creating appropriate boundaries between supervisors and their students. The ethical obligations of both parties are clearly set forth, and counselors should be accurate, honest, and fair during the training and assessment of students.

Areas that were focused upon include counselor supervision and client welfare, counselor supervision competence, supervisory relationships, supervisor responsibilities, counseling evaluation and remediation, responsibilities of counselor educators, student welfare and responsibilities, evaluation and remediation of students, roles and relationships between educators and students, and multicultural/diversity competence in counselor education and training programs. As with Section A, Standards F.3.e and F.10.e were included to address the change from dual relationships to potentially beneficial relationships between counselor educators or supervisors and students. Because the revisions to this section are too numerous and beyond the scope of this chapter, individuals are encouraged to go to the ACA website and consult in-depth the 2005 *Code of Ethics.*

SECTION G: RESEARCH AND PUBLICATION   An important change to note was the replacement of the term "human subjects" with "research participants." The revised *Code* also recognized that independent researchers who may lack access to an Institutional Review Board might design and conduct research programs as well. These independent researchers are advised to seek out and consult with researchers who are acquainted with Institutional Review Board procedures to make appropriate safeguards available to research participants.

Further additions or clarifications included the disposal of research documents and records of relationships with research participants when there are intensive or extended interactions. Professional counselors are obligated to take the appropriate steps to destroy any documents or records that contain confidential data or may identify research participants within a reasonable period after the completion of a research study or project. Section G.3

outlined the restrictions on relationships with research participants that included nonprofessional relationships, sexual or romantic interactions, and sexual harassment, as well as potentially beneficial interactions.

Finally, the publication section of the 2005 *Code of Ethics* was expanded. Standard G.5.b was added, which specifically stated that professional counselors should not plagiarize or present another person's work as their own. In addition, the standard concerning professional review of documents presented for publication was expanded to include making valid publication decisions, reviewing materials in a timely manner, avoiding biases, and evaluating only those documents that fall within one's field of competency.

SECTION H: RESOLVING ETHICAL ISSUES   This final section provided information and suggestions pertaining to the resolution of ethical issues. Three main changes were made in regard to legal conflicts, unfair discrimination, and reporting ethical violations. Standard H.1.b stated that if there was a conflict between ethical responsibilities and laws, professional counselors should make known their commitment to the *Code of Ethics* and work to alleviate the conflict. Counselors may follow legal requirements or regulations if the ethical conflict cannot be resolved in this manner.

The second change included an increase in procedural details for professional counselors reporting a suspected ethical violation (Standard H.2.c). When informal resolution is inappropriate for an ethical violation, or the issue is not correctly resolved, professional counselors are directed to seek out further action, such as referring to voluntary national certification bodies, state or national ethics committees, state licensing boards, or any suitable institutional authorities. It is further stated that this standard is not applicable if a professional counselor has been retained to review the work of the counselor who is in question, or if it would violate any confidentiality rights.

The addition of Standard H.2.g was the final major change to Section H. It was stated that professional counselors absolutely should not deny a person's advancement, admission to academic programs, employment, promotion, or tenure based only upon their having made an ethics complaint or their being the subject of an ethics complaint. This standard provided some protection against unfair discrimination for counselors who have made an ethics complaint or been the subject of one.

American School Counselor Association Ethical Standards for School Counselors

In addition to the ACA, other counseling organizations have established codes of ethics. The ASCA (2004) has developed a parallel set of ethical standards that specifically addresses school counseling. The eight sections of the ASCA code are Responsibilities to Students; Responsibilities to Parents; Responsibilities to Colleagues and Professional Associates; Responsibilities to the School and Community; Responsibilities to Self; Responsibilities to the Profession; Maintenance of Standards; and Resources. As in the ACA's standards, these standards discuss putting the counselee's best interests first, treating each student as an individual and with respect, involving parents as appropriate, maintaining one's expertise through ongoing professional development and learning, and behaving professionally and ethically.

Both the ACA and the ASCA have developed guides to ethical decision making that can be used when a professional counselor is concerned about a particular situation and needs to determine if an ethical dilemma exists. The ACA's model involves seven steps: (a) identify the problem, (b) apply the ACA *Code of Ethics,* (c) determine the nature and dimensions of the dilemma, (d) generate potential courses of action, (e) consider the potential consequences of all options and choose a course of action, (f) evaluate the selected course of action, and (g) implement the course of action (Forester-Miller & Davis, 1996).

C. B. Stone (2005) has taken the ACA model and applied it to the school setting. As Stone and others caution, professional counselors using either of these models or any other ethical decision-making model would not necessarily come to the same conclusion. There is seldom one correct way of handling any given situation, and each counselor brings different background, values, and belief systems to each dilemma. However, if one reflects on the moral principles and continues to practice with these in mind, it is likely that the dilemma can be resolved in the client's best interests.

Remley and Herlihy (2007) suggested four self-tests to consider when a decision has been made. First, in thinking about justice, would you treat others this same way if they were in a similar situation? Second, would you suggest to other counselors this same course of action? Third, would you be willing to have others know how you acted? Fourth, do you have any lingering feelings of doubt or uncertainty about what you did? If you cannot answer in the affirmative to the first three tests and in the negative to the fourth test, perhaps the decision was not ethically sound. It is always appropriate and ethically sound to consult with a colleague when working through a dilemma to ensure that all aspects of the issue have been examined, and that all possible problems have been discussed.

ADDITIONAL SOURCES OF INFORMATION AND GUIDANCE: COURTS, LAWS, AND REGULATIONS

While the ethical standards provide an important foundation for guiding counselor behavior, there are many other sources of information with which professional counselors must become familiar if they are to maintain the highest standards of ethical and legal behavior. These other sources include the courts, laws, and regulations.

Court System

Professional counselors are affected by three main types of laws: **statutory law**, which is created by legislatures; **constitutional law**, which results from court decisions concerning constitutional issues; and **common law**, which results from other court decisions. There are 51 U.S. court systems—the court systems for the 50 states and the federal system. Both state and federal courts can enact decisions affecting counselors, and both are usually composed of tiers. The structure of state courts varies, but generally consists of trial courts that include courts of special jurisdiction, such as juvenile court or small claims court, and courts of appeal.

All states have a court that is the final authority to which cases may be appealed. The name of this court varies across states. For example, in Maryland and New York, it is called the court of appeals; in West Virginia, it is called the supreme court of appeals; in other states, it is called superior court. One must be careful in reading state court decisions to note which court rendered the decision because the names are inconsistent across states. Cases from the highest court in each state may be appealed directly to the U.S. Supreme Court. Decisions from state courts are binding only on individuals living within that state, but may serve as precedent for a similar case in another state.

The federal court system is also a three-tiered system. Approximately 100 U.S. district courts form the basis of the federal system. These courts hear cases that involve federal law, disputes between citizens that involve more than $75,000, and cases where the United States is a party (Fischer, Schimmel, & Kelly, 1999). There are 13 courts of appeals. Decisions from the circuit courts of appeals are binding only on the states within the court's jurisdiction. However, decisions from one court may influence the decision rendered by another court when the same issue arises. Cases from the circuit courts of appeals may be appealed to the U.S. Supreme Court, the highest court in the United States.

Statutory Law

Statutory law is the body of mandates created through legislation passed by the U.S. Congress and state legislatures. Much of the structure of health, mental health, and education, and many of the policies that govern their implementation are found within these mandates. The federal government has authority to pass legislation related only to the powers specified in the Constitution, but numerous laws have been enacted that affect professional counselors. Most legislation influencing counselors is passed by state legislatures and concerns two types of legislation: creating state legislation to implement federal legislation, and enacting new, state-specific legislation. State laws may be more restrictive than federal legislation, but may never be less restrictive. To show how laws affect counseling practice, complete Activity 3.3.

ACTIVITY 3.3

Go to your state's legislative website. Peruse the bills and laws relevant to you as a professional counselor that have been passed recently. How will these affect your practice?

State and Local Agencies: Regulations and Policies

Most state departments of mental health, which ordinarily house licensing boards, such as a board of professional counselors, can enact regulations that are binding upon the practice of counseling within the state. Likewise, most state departments of education have the ability to enact regulations that are binding on the school districts within the state. The regulations often encompass areas not addressed through other state legislation, or add detail to state legislation and may include implementation plans and more specific definitions. State agencies also develop policies, which are often detailed explanations of how to implement a specific law. Last, state agencies may also issue guidelines, which are actually suggestions about how to address a specific issue. In contrast to regulations and policies, guidelines are not mandates and do not have to be followed. However, because they do represent the agency's current thinking regarding a particular issue, local policies generally do not deviate too far from them.

Although it is not a regulation, the state attorney general may issue an **opinion** or advice of counsel. This guidance is frequently in response to a new court case or law or upon request of a state agency. The advice or opinion is the attorney general's legal interpretation of what that law or case means for the agency or agencies affected and usually suggests what the agency needs to do to comply. The advice or ruling is often incorporated into policy or guidelines by the agency.

Local school systems and agencies may also develop their own policies, procedures, and guidelines. School systems, in particular, often take state regulations and policies and rewrite them to reflect their specific local situation; these are often adopted by the local board of education. Local mental health departments or agencies may also define state policies and procedures further to reflect their jurisdiction-specific needs. Finally, individual schools or centers may have additional policies or guidelines in place for certain issues that further direct the manner in which a professional school counselor must act.

Importantly, professional counselors functioning in private practice or agencies other than school systems are not bound by the policies or guidelines developed by the schools, just as professional school counselors are not bound by the policies or guidelines developed by state agencies without school oversight or authority. To show how school or agency policies, procedures, and guidelines affect counseling practice, complete Activity 3.4.

ACTIVITY 3.4

Access a local school's or agency's policies, procedures, and guidelines. Become acquainted with unfamiliar policies and procedures that will directly affect your practice as a professional counselor.

MAKING DECISIONS

Failure to understand the law, and by extension policies, procedures, and guidelines, is an unacceptable legal defense. It is incumbent on the professional counselor to become familiar with all the various sources of information and guidance that are available to perform one's responsibilities in an ethical and legal manner. There are many ways of maintaining current information.

In most work settings, with the exception perhaps of private practice, professional counselors have a supervisor or other individual in authority who can help them become familiar with the regulations, policies, and guidelines relevant to that setting. Most schools and many community agencies have administrative manuals that incorporate all these sources of information into continually updated binders. The ACA newsletter, *Counseling Today,* highlights issues and important, timely topics in counseling, as do other professional journals and newsletters. Many commercially available newsletters cover recent court rulings and their impact in different work settings.

The Internet has become a valuable tool for current information and resources, although one must be careful to authenticate this information. Guillot-Miller and Partin (2003) identified more than 40 sites that include information relevant to ethical and legal practices for professional counselors. The professional associations for counselors and other mental health professionals, institutions of higher education, state and federal government agencies, government-funded organizations, and professional and legal publishers all continuously update their websites and are good sources of current information. Activity 3.5 directs you to explore the sources of information helpful in maintaining ethical and legal practice.

ACTIVITY 3.5

Access applicable sources of information that will guide your decision making as a professional counselor. What sources are available to you so that you can continuously update your knowledge of ethical guidelines and information?

Sometimes mandates seem to be in conflict with each other. In such cases, common sense should prevail. There may be a therapeutically logical reason to follow one particular mandate rather than another one. Professional counselors should follow the logical course of action and document what they did and why. For example, if a counselor is working with a suicidal teenage client but believes that telling the parents would perpetuate an abusive situation, the counselor should handle the situation as an abuse case and inform child protective services about the suicidal behavior. In addition, if a particular policy, guideline, or regulation is not in the best interests of the clients in the counselor's work setting, as per the ethical standards, the counselor should work to change the mandate.

Two other issues are sometimes confusing for professional counselors. The first concerns the different ways in which counselors in different settings operate. Some mandates cover all counselors, particularly mandates that are the result of federal or state legislation or court cases. For example, child abuse and neglect laws apply to all counselors regardless of the setting in which they work. However, the implementation of some mandates, particularly as they become policy and guidelines, may look different in different settings.

Schools have perhaps the greatest number of mandates under which staff must operate, yet professional school counselors seldom need permission to see students (Remley & Herlihy, 2007), particularly if there is an approved comprehensive developmental program. A mental health counselor, employed by an outside center or agency but working either in a school or in a school-based health center, needs signed, informed consent to see the same students. In some cases, local school systems have mandated an opt-in program, which is a program that requires signed, informed consent for students to participate in different aspects of the comprehensive guidance program. In such cases, professional school counselors working in nearby systems or schools may operate differently, perhaps using an opt-out program in which all students participate unless a parent or guardian has expressly (in writing) forbidden the student from participating. For additional practice in adhering to agency or school policies and professional ethics, complete Activity 3.6.

ACTIVITY 3.6

Depending on your intended work setting, construct one of the following:
1. Develop an informed consent form relevant to your work setting.
2. Develop an opt-in or opt-out form for use in a school program.
3. Develop an informed consent form for use with parents and children in a community or private agency setting.

The second issue concerns professional counselors who hold multiple credentials. A counselor may work as a professional school counselor, but hold state certification or licensure and work as a mental health counselor outside of school. The counselor may need permission to do something as a professional school counselor, but not need permission as a mental health counselor, or vice versa. Under which set of mandates should the counselor operate?

The answer to both of these questions is the same: Employees must follow the mandates that apply to their work setting. Professional counselors are required to operate under the mandates of the system that employs them or, in the case of volunteers, the mandates of the entity under whose auspices they are working. If a counselor is employed by an agency or a private practice, he or she must follow the mandates of that entity. If a counselor is employed by a school system as a counselor, he or she must follow the mandates of the local school system. Teachers who have degrees in counseling or another related mental health degree, but who continue to be employed as teachers do not have the same protections as counselors because they are not employed in a mental health capacity. They need to check the policies of their school system carefully to see if they are covered by any protections such as confidentiality.

ADDITIONAL LEGAL CONSIDERATIONS

In developing an ethical stance, professional counselors must take all of the aforementioned sources of information into account. There are several other influences that must be considered, however (Herlihy & Corey, 2007; Hopkins & Anderson, 1990; Stone, 2005). Each counselor brings to every counseling relationship a sum of experiences, education, and training. Each counselor brings to the setting that which makes one unique—that is, values, morals, and spiritual influences. Who a professional counselor is strongly influences the stance taken on issues. Professional counselors must continually be aware of how their own beliefs and values impact the way they think about issues, the clients and their needs, and the options that they perceive to be available. Professional counselors must also continually examine their behavior in light of cultural bias and multicultural understanding. When deciding on a course of action for a client, counselors always try to do what is in the best interests of the client.

Professional Competence

In addition to being knowledgeable about mandates, as was previously discussed, there are further steps that professional counselors should take to ensure ethical and legal behavior. Several of these are mentioned in the ACA *Code of Ethics* (2005), but it is important to re-emphasize them. As reported by Hopkins and Anderson (1990) and Cottone and Tarvydas (2003), professional counselors should:

- Maintain professional growth through continuing education. While counselors must attend continuing education opportunities to renew national credentials, state credentials, or both, it is important to stay current with the theories, trends, and information about clients and different populations.
- Maintain accurate knowledge and expertise in areas of responsibility. Information changes so quickly that professional counselors must ensure they are providing quality and effective services to their clients. One way of achieving this goal is through professional development, but counselors may also gain information through reading, consultation with colleagues, supervision, and other means.

- Accurately represent credentials. As stated in the ethical standards, professional counselors should claim only the credentials they have earned and only the highest degree in counseling or a closely related mental health field. Counselors who hold doctorates in non–mental health fields should not use the title "doctor" in their work as a counselor. This is a particular problem in school settings where counselors might earn doctorates in administration and supervision, or related fields, but continue to work as counselors and use the title "doctor" in their job. Counselors should not imply in any way that their credentials allow them to work in areas in which they are not trained.
- Provide services only for which they are qualified and trained. The easiest way for professional counselors to get into trouble professionally is to provide services for which they are not qualified, either by training or by education. This is particularly true when using counseling techniques. Counselors should have training in using a particular technique before using it. Reading about a technique is not equivalent to implementing it under supervision. Also, professional counselors should not try to work with clients whose problems go beyond their expertise. If professional counselors are put in a situation where there are no other counselors to whom to refer the client, the counselor should consult with colleagues and ask for supervision to ensure the effectiveness of the counseling.

"Can I Be Sued?" and "What Is Malpractice?"

The answer to "Can I be sued?" is, of course, yes. Anyone can be sued for almost anything, particularly in our litigious society. The more important question is, "Will I be found guilty?" The answer to this question is much more complex.

If professional counselors fail to exercise "due care" in fulfilling their professional responsibilities, they can be found guilty of **civil liability**—that is, the counselor committed a wrong against an individual. **Negligence** may be found if the wrong committed results in an injury or damage—in other words, if the duty owed to the client was breached in some way. In counseling, it is more common for counselors to be sued for malpractice. **Malpractice** is the area of tort law that concerns professional conduct. "Malpractice is professional misconduct or any unreasonable lack of skill in the performance of professional duties" (Lovett, as cited in Hopkins & Anderson, 1990, p. 48). Generally, for a counselor to be held liable in tort for malpractice, four conditions have to be met (Stone, 2005): (a) a duty was owed to the plaintiff (client) by the defendant (counselor); (b) the counselor breached the duty; (c) there is a causal link between the breach and the client's injury; and (d) the client suffered some damage or injury.

An example of negligence would be a professional counselor who failed to report an abuse case. The counselor had a duty to the client and failed to fulfill that duty. With malpractice, the client suffered because of lack of skill or inappropriate behavior on the part of the counselor. An example of malpractice would be if a counselor treated a client with an eating disorder through hypnosis when the counselor was not trained to use the technique of hypnosis. The situation may be further complicated if this technique is not recognized as effective for treating eating disorders.

The standard of practice will be used in any liability proceeding to determine if the professional counselor's performance was within accepted practice. The standard of practice question is, "In the performance of professional services, did the counselor provide the level of care and treatment that is consistent with the degree of learning, skill, and ethics ordinarily possessed and expected by reputable counselors practicing under similar circumstances?" (American Counseling Association, 1997, p. 9).

The **standard of practice** will be established through the testimony of peers. These peers, who are called expert witnesses, are considered to be experts in the field under question. For professional school counselors, the expert witnesses would be other school counselors (Stone, 2005). For rehabilitation counselors, the expert witnesses would be other rehabilitation counselors. For mental health counselors, the expert witnesses would be other mental health counselors. The standard is an ever-evolving level of expectation and is influenced by two major factors: education and experience. The standard is not an absolute one, but a variable one. It will be much higher for a professional counselor who has practiced for many years and pursued advanced graduate training or professional development than it will be for a counselor in the first year of practice immediately after graduate school. The more training and experience a counselor possesses, the higher the standard to which the counselor will be held accountable. The assumption is that a professional counselor should know more each year he or she practices through experience and training, and should be held to a higher standard with each additional year. Using this standard of practice, a counselor will usually be found guilty of malpractice if one or more of the following situations occurs (Hopkins & Anderson, 1990):

- The practice was not within the realm of acceptable professional practice.
- The counselor was not trained in the technique used.
- The counselor failed to follow a procedure that would have been more helpful.
- The counselor failed to warn or protect others from a violent client.
- The counselor failed to obtain informed consent.
- The counselor failed to explain the possible consequences of the treatment.

Several professional publications have reported that sexual misconduct is the primary reason that liability actions are initiated against professional counselors. School staff, counselors, and other mental health professionals have been accused of committing sexual abuse or misconduct. It may be that other problems, such as failure to use a more appropriate technique, are actually more common, but that most clients lack the ability to recognize therapeutic problems and may just have a general sense that "it isn't working or helping" and choose to terminate.

Although the number of professional counselors who are sued is increasing, the number still remains small. In schools, parents are more likely to request their child not be included in certain school counseling program activities or to complain to the principal or central administration about a program or behavior. In rare cases, parents may sue. Most cases against school counselors have been rejected by the courts (Fischer & Sorensen, 1997). In school or agency settings, violating or failing to follow mandates would get a professional counselor in trouble faster than almost any other behavior. Depending on the counselor's action, the professional counselor may be reprimanded. In extreme cases, the counselor's employment may be terminated. In clinics and agencies, few counselors are sued over professional practice issues; counselors are more often sued because of sexual conduct or illegal activities. Professional counselors must be knowledgeable about their communities. They may have a legal right to implement certain programs or conduct certain activities, but if the community is not supportive of those activities, they are going to face opposition.

When a professional counselor is faced with any legal action, the first thing the counselor should do is call a lawyer, and then let the counselor supervisor, if there is one, know. Most agencies, clinics, practices, and schools are accustomed to dealing with such legal issues and may even have a procedure for what needs to be done. Professional counselors should never attempt to reason with the client or contact the client's lawyer without advice of counsel. It is important to not provide any information to, or discuss the case with, anyone except the counselor's lawyer or the person designated to help the counselor. Just as professional counselors advise clients to get professional mental health help when they have personal problems, counselors must get legal help when they have legal problems.

Subpoenas

Many professional counselors will receive a **subpoena** at some point in their professional career. Probably the most common reason counselors, and particularly professional school counselors, receive subpoenas is in cases involving custody disputes, child abuse or neglect allegations, and special education disputes. In most cases, the client an attorney is representing believes that counselors may have some information that will be helpful to the case. Professional counselors need to pay attention to subpoenas because they are legal documents. At the same time, consider whether the information being requested is confidential because professional school counselors may be limited in what they can share. Under no circumstances should the counselor automatically comply with the subpoena without discussing it first with the client, the client's attorney, or both, or without consulting the agency's or school system's attorney. According to the ACA (1997), professional counselors should take the following steps when receiving a subpoena:

1. Contact the client or the client's attorney and ask for guidance. If you work for a school system, contact the school system's attorney to seek guidance.
2. If the above-mentioned parties advise you to comply with the subpoena, discuss the implications of releasing the requested information.
3. Obtain a signed informed consent form to release the records. That form should specify all conditions of release: what, to whom, and so forth.
4. If the decision is made not to release the records, the attorney should file a motion to quash (or, in some areas, ask for a protective order). This will allow the counselor to not comply with the subpoena.
5. Maintain a record of everything the counselor and attorneys did; keep notes regarding all conversations and copies of any documents pertaining to the subpoena.

An attorney who wants information may ask a judge to issue a court order. A **court order** permits the release of confidential information, but does not mandate its release. If both a subpoena and a court order are received, the counselor must release the information with or without the client's consent. Failure to do so may result in the counselor being held in contempt of court.

The important things to remember about subpoenas are do not panic and do consult an attorney. Subpoenas are legal documents, but the counselor has enough time to consider the implications to the client of releasing the information and to seek legal advice.

CONFIDENTIALITY

For clients to feel free to share sometimes sensitive and personal information during a counseling session, they must feel that they can trust the professional counselor not to share what is disclosed during sessions with anyone else without their permission. This sense of trust and privacy, called confidentiality, is essential for counseling to be successful. **Confidentiality** is the cornerstone of counseling and is what separates the counseling relationship from other relationships in which information is shared. Confidentiality belongs to the client, not to the counselor. The client always has the right to waive confidentiality or to allow information to be shared with a third party.

Counseling minors presents particular challenges to the issue of confidentiality. Every state sets the age of majority; for most states, it is 18 years of age. Most students are minors younger than age 18 years, who are not legally able to make their own decisions. Students have an ethical right to confidentiality, but the legal rights belong to their parents or guardians (Remley & Herlihy, 2007). Most states protect counselor-client confidentiality. Approximately 20 states protect professional school counselor–student confidentiality through statutes (Cottone & Tarvydas, 2003), but many include significant restrictions.

Professional counselors often ask what to do if parents want to know what is discussed during counseling sessions with their minor children. Legally, parents have the right to know what is being discussed. However, the child might not want the information shared with the parent. Section B.5.b, Responsibility to Parents and Legal Guardians, of the ACA *Code of Ethics* states that:

> Counselors inform parents and legal guardians about the role of counselors and the confidential nature of the counseling relationship. Counselors are sensitive to the cultural diversity of families and respect the inherent rights and responsibilities of parents/guardians over the welfare of the children/charges according to law. Counselors work to establish, as appropriate, collaborative relationships with parents/guardians to best serve clients. (ACA, 2005, p. 8)

This statement leaves professional counselors with a dilemma. To resolve this dilemma, Remley and Herlihy (2007) suggested that the counselor first discuss the issue with the child to determine if the child is willing to disclose the information to the parent. If the child does not want to disclose, the counselor should try to help the parent understand that the best interests of the child are not served by disclosure. If this does not work, the counselor should schedule a joint meeting with the parent and child to discuss the issue. If the parent is still not satisfied, the counselor may have to disclose the information without the child's consent.

Some professional counselors would suggest that this type of situation may reflect some deeper family issue. While the parent or guardian has a legal right to the information, there may be an underlying "family secret" that the parent does not want known, and the counselor should be sensitive to any difficulties the child may be exhibiting. Or, this situation may be the result of cultural differences, and the counselor needs to be sensitive to the family's traditions and beliefs.

Many professional counselors suggest that at the beginning of the first session of each new counseling relationship, the professional school counselor should discuss confidentiality with the client, explain what it means, and point out the limits of confidentiality. Some counselors choose to hang a sign on the wall of their office that outlines this information as a reinforcement to what is discussed in the first session. While this issue seems simple on the surface, in reality it is a very complex issue that has generated a significant amount of research and professional discourse. As the use of technology increases in counseling settings, the discussions will continue and expand. There are significant challenges to keeping electronic information confidential.

Limits to Confidentiality

According to section B.1.a of the ACA *Code of Ethics* (2005, p. 2), "Counselors respect client rights to privacy...." Section B.1.c states, "Counselors do not share confidential information without client consent or without sound legal or ethical justification." Section B.1.d states, "At initiation and throughout the counseling process, counselors inform clients of the limitations of confidentiality and seek to identify foreseeable situations in which confidentiality must be breached." There are several instances, however, in which counselors must break confidentiality. These are delineated in Section B.2.a. The most important of these is the **duty to warn**. When a professional counselor becomes aware that a client is in danger of being harmed, such as in instances of abuse or suicide, or when the client is likely to harm someone else, the counselor may break confidentiality and tell an appropriate person.

The basis for the duty-to-warn standard began with the 1974 Tarasoff case in California. In this case, the client, a graduate student, told his psychologist about his intent to kill a girl (named Tarasoff) who had rejected his advances. The psychologist told the campus police and his supervisor, but did not warn the intended victim or her family. The majority of the California Supreme Court ruled that the psychologist had a duty to warn a known, intended victim. This case established the legal duty to warn and protect an identifiable victim from a client's potential or intended violence and has formed the basis of many other court decisions across the United States. The ACA's *Code of Ethics,* Section B.2.a, now reads, "The general requirement that counselors keep information confidential does not apply when disclosure is required to protect clients or identified others from serious and foreseeable harm..." (p. 2).

In the ensuing decades, some cases have extended the duty-to-warn standard to include types of harm other than violence and foreseeable victims in addition to identifiable victims. Several other situations constrain the limits of confidentiality, as delineated in the ACA *Code of Ethics* (2005):

- *Subordinates.* Confidentiality is not absolute when subordinates, including employees, supervisees, students, clerical assistants, and volunteers, handle records or confidential information. Every effort should be made to limit access to this information, and the assistants should be reminded of the confidential nature of the information they are handling.
- *Treatment teams.* The client should be informed of the treatment team and the information being shared.
- *Consultation.* The professional counselor always has the right to consult with a colleague or supervisor on any case. In such instances, the counselor should provide enough information to obtain the needed assistance, but should limit any information that might identify the client.
- *Groups and families.* In group or family counseling settings, confidentiality is not guaranteed. The counselor may state that what goes on in the sessions is confidential, and the members may agree. However, because there is more than one client in the group, it is impossible to guarantee confidentiality.
- *Third-party payers.* Information will sometimes have to be sent to a mental health provider, insurance company, or other agency that has some legitimate need for the information. The counselor must disclose this information only with the client's permission.
- *Minors.* There are special considerations regarding confidentiality and minors; these are discussed in detail in the next section.

- *Contagious, life-threatening diseases.* In contrast to the duty-to-warn standard, the ACA *Code of Ethics* states that the counselor is justified in disclosing information about a client to an identifiable third party if that party's relationship with the client is such that there is a possibility of contracting the disease and the client does not plan on telling the third party. The word used is "justified," not "should" or "must." This wording leaves it up to the counselor to decide if the third party is at risk and must be warned.
- *Court-ordered disclosure.* Subpoenas were previously discussed. Even if ordered to reveal confidential information by a judge, counselors should limit what they reveal to only what is absolutely necessary.

In summary, confidentiality is a very complex issue, but it is essential to the effectiveness of counseling. Clients have an ethical right to confidentiality, and counselors must make every effort to ensure this right. There are specific cases, however, in which it is not only permissible, but also essential to break confidentiality to protect the client, or others from the client.

Confidentiality and Privileged Communication

The term "confidentiality" is used in discussions about counseling, whereas the term **"privileged communication"** is the legal term used to describe the privacy of the counselor-client communication. Privileged communication exists by statute and applies only to testifying in a court of law. The privilege belongs to the client, who always has the right to waive the privilege and allow the counselor to testify.

Clients have an ethical right to confidentiality, and the ethical standards for the mental health professions detail the boundaries of confidentiality. Privileged communication is more limited; federal, state, and local mandates determine its parameters. Whether a counselor-client relationship is covered by privileged communication varies widely across jurisdictions. Even within a jurisdiction, a counselor in private practice may be covered by privileged communication, but the school counselors who work in that same jurisdiction may not be. It is essential that counselors become familiar with their local mandates and policies to determine the extent to which privileged communication applies to their situation. Activity 3.7 provides an opportunity to think ahead and consider how you might handle circumstances when confidentiality may need to be compromised.

ACTIVITY 3.7

What precautions will you take as a professional counselor to forewarn your clients about the possible limits to confidentiality? Consider how you will approach your client if a breach of confidentiality is necessary, and then practice this approach with a peer.

MINOR CONSENT LAWS

All states have a **minor consent law** that allows certain minors to seek treatment for certain conditions, usually involving substance abuse, mental health, and some reproductive health areas. These laws are based on the federal regulation 42 U.S.C. §§290dd-3; 42 C.F.R. Part 2, which references the confidentiality of patient records for drug and alcohol abuse assessment, referral, diagnosis, and treatment. The law further prohibits the release of these records to anyone without the client's informed consent and includes clients younger than age 18 years even if they are in school and living with parents or guardians.

Over the past decade, there has been a movement to increase the number of student assistance teams and student assistance programs in schools. These teams usually consist of an administrator, one or more student services professionals (e.g., professional school counselor, school social worker, pupil personnel worker, school psychologist, school nurse), and teachers, and may include a substance abuse assessor from a local agency or similar professional. School staff refer students who are suspected to have a substance abuse problem to this team. The team is trained to deal with substance abuse issues and, if they believe the student has a substance abuse problem, have the student assessed and referred for appropriate assistance.

The controversy surrounding this program concerns the role of the parents or guardians in this process. Under the federal law, the student may go from referral through completion of treatment without the parents' or guardians' knowledge. Substance abuse professionals are divided regarding whether it is possible to treat successfully teens who abuse substances without the family's involvement. Other professionals have concerns about the ability of young adolescents to seek treatment without any family knowledge or involvement.

As this federal law has been incorporated into state statute, states have taken different approaches to deciding to whom this law applies and for what. Generally, the patient must be old enough to understand the problem, the treatment options available, and the possible consequences of the problem and the treatment options. Some states may have no age limits and maintain that a minor has the same capacity as an adult to consent to certain services. Some states have decided on a specific age at which the minor may consent to mental health treatment, reproductive or substance abuse services, and treatment for sexually transmitted diseases and AIDS/HIV. According to the Guttmacher Institute's *State Policies in Brief* reports (2000, 2005a, 2005b, 2007), various states handle minor consent issues differently (Table 3.2).

There is tremendous variation across the 50 states in what is permissible under the law. There is also some question as to the applicability of this law to school settings. The laws clearly cover medical personnel and certain conditions. A school nurse is covered, but a professional school counselor or school psychologist may not be covered. It is critical that professional counselors become familiar with the minor consent law in the state in which they work to ensure compliance. A state law may allow a professional counselor to address reproductive issues and substance abuse without parental consent or notification, but a local policy may prohibit such counseling. The laws cover minors seeking advice or treatment or both. If a minor is not seeking help, the law may not apply, and the counselor would follow other policies or procedures in dealing with these issues.

The legal issues aside, this is the law that raises a tremendous number of ethical issues for professional counselors. Numerous professionals have difficulty with the ability of young adolescents, in particular, to access these services without the family's involvement. Should a professional counselor help a 13-year-old with a substance abuse problem seek treatment without the family's knowledge? How successful will the adolescent's recovery be? What about a 15-year-old who is abusing drugs and engaging in risky sexual behaviors? What is the counselor's ethical responsibility in such cases?

TABLE 3.2 The Guttmacher Institute Overview of Minors' Consent Law

Minors may consent to:

State	Contraceptive Services	STD Services	Prenatal Care	Place Minor's Child for Adoption	Medical Care for Minor's Child	Abortion Services	Tx for Alcohol&/ or Drug Abuse	Tx for Mental Health Services	Drop Out of School
Alabama	All+	All*	All	All	All	Parental Consent	All	All	16+
Alaska	All	All	All	All	All	▼(Parental Consent)			16+
Arizona	All	All		All		Parental Consent	All		16+
Arkansas	All	All*	All		All	Parental Consent	All		NA
California	All	All	All	All		▼(Parental Consent)	All*	All*	NA
Colorado	All	All	All	All	All	Parental Notice	All	All*Φ	16+
Connecticut	Some	All		Legal counsel	All	All	All	All	Parental Consent
Delaware	All*	All*	All*	All	All	Parental Notice‡	All	All	16+
Dist. of Columbia	All	All	All	All	All	All	All	All	NA
Florida	Some	All	All		All	Parental Notice	All	All=	Parental Consent
Georgia	All	All*	All	All	All	Parental Notice	All*		16+
Hawaii	All*,+	All*,+	All*,+	All	All		All*		MD[26]
Idaho	All	All+	All	All	All	▼(Parental Consent)	All	All	16+
Illinois	Some	All*	All	All	All	▼(Parental Notice)	All*	All*	16+[30]
Indiana	Some	All		All		Parental Consent	All		Parental Consent
Iowa	All	All			All	Parental Notice	All		MD[32]
Kansas	Some	All*	Some	All	All	Parental Notice	All		MD[32]
Kentucky	All*	All*	All*	Legal counsel	All	Parental Consent	All*	All*@	Parental Notice@

(Continued)

TABLE 3.2 The Guttmacher Institute Overview of Minors' Consent Law (*Continued*)

Minors may consent to:

State	Contraceptive Services	STD Services	Prenatal Care	Place Minor's Child for Adoption	Medical Care for Minor's Child	Abortion Services	Tx for Alcohol&/or Drug Abuse	Tx for Mental Health Services	Drop Out of School
Louisiana	Some	All*		Parental consent	All	Parental Consent	All*		17+
Maine	Some	All*		All	All	All	All*		17+
Maryland	All*	All*	All*	All	All	Parental Notice	All*	All*@	16+
Massachusetts	All	All	All		All	Parental Consent	All[37]	All@	MD[26]
Michigan	Some	All*	All*	Parental consent	All	Parental Consent	All*	All†	All
Minnesota	All*	All*	All*	Parental consent	All	Parental Notice	All*	Parental Consent	
Mississippi	Some	All	All	All	All	Parental Consent	All*Φ		17+
Missouri	Some	All*	All*	Legal counsel	All	Parental Consent	All*[11]		Parental Notice[26]
Montana	All*	All*	All*	Legal counsel	All	▼(Parental Notice)	All*[11]	All@	16+
Nebraska	Some	All		All	All	Parental Notice	All		All[26]
Nevada	Some	All	Some	AllΩ	All	▼(Parental Notice)	All		All[40]
New Hampshire	Some	All†	Some	All		▼(Parental Notice)	All		Parental Consent
New Jersey	Some	All*	All*	All	All	▼(Parental Notice)	All		16+
New Mexico	All	All	All	All	All	▼(Parental Consent)	All	All	Parental Consent
New York	All	All	All	All	All		All	All	16+
North Carolina	All	All	All		All	Parental Consent	All	All	16+

North Dakota		All*,†		All		Parental Consent	All†	All†	16+[26]
Ohio	All	All				Parental Consent	All		NA
Oklahoma	Some	All*	All*	All†	All	Parental Consent and Notice	All	All†	Parental Consent
Oregon	All*	All	All*,Φ		All	Parental Consent	All†	All†	MD[46]
Pennsylvania	Some	All	All	Parental notice	All	Parental Consent	All		17+
Rhode Island	All	All		Parental consent	All	Parental Consent	All		16+
South Carolina	All◇	All◇	All◇	All	All	Parental Consent	16[46]	16[46]	MD[49]
South Dakota	Some	All	All		All	Parental Notice	All		16+
Tennessee	All	All	All	All	All	Parental Consent	All	All@	17+
Texas	Some	All*	All*	All	All	Parental Consent	All	All	NA
Utah	Some	All	All	All	All	Parental Consent and Notice			NA
Vermont	Some	All	All	All	All	Parental Consent	All		16+[53]
Virginia	All	All	All	All	All	Parental Consent	All	All	NA
Washington	All	All†	All	Legal counsel	All		All=	All=	16+
West Virginia	Some	All		All	All	Parental Notice	All	NA	16+[30]
Wisconsin	All	All	All			Parental Consent	All	NA	16+[55]
Wyoming	All	All	All	All	All	Parental Consent	All		
TOTAL	**25+DC**	**50+DC**	**32+DC**	**28+DC**	**30+DC**	**2+DC**	**45+DC**	**21+DC**	**34**

(Continued)

TABLE 3.2 The Guttmacher Institute Overview of Minors' Consent Law (Continued)

Notes:

▼Enforcement permanently or temporarily enjoined by a court order; policy not in effect.

"All" applies to minors 12 and older unless otherwise noted.

"Some" applies to specified categories of minors (those who have a health issue, or are married, pregnant, mature, etc.).

The totals include only those states that allow all minors to consent.

*Physicians may, but are not required to, inform the minor's parents.

†Applies to minors 14 and older.

‡Applies to minors younger than 17.

Ω A court may require parental consent.

Φ Applies to minors 15 and older.

◇Applies to mature minors 15 and younger and to minors 16 and older.

=Applies to minors 13 and older.

@Applies to minors 16 and older.

NA = Not Allowed to drop out.

MD = Minor allowed to decide;

In all but four states, the age of majority is 18. In AI and NE, it is 19, and in PA and MS, it is 21; however, in MS, 18 is the age of consent for health care.

[11]Includes surgery.

[26]Minor may drop out if employed and in MA, MO, and NE is 14, in HI is 15, in MA also if has completed the 6th grade; in NE also if has completed the 8th grade. Otherwise, a minor may drop out at 16 in these states.

[30]Minor may drop out of school before reaching age 16 if employed.

[32]A court may allow a minor to drop out.

[37]Minor may consent if found drug-dependent by two doctors; bars consent to methadone maintenance therapy.

[40]After eighth grade, court determines whether the minor or the parents can make the decision.

[46]Minor must prove to the school board that the minor has acquired "equivalent knowledge" of the high school courses, or consent may be granted by the state school board for minors 16 and 17 who are employed.

[49]Minor who has completed 8th grade may seek court authorization to drop out to work.

[53]Minor must be at least 16, have completed 10th grade, or be excused by the superintendent.

[55]Minor must be at least 16 and have completed 10th grade.

Adapted from "Minors and the Right to Consent to Health Care," by H. Boonstra and E. Nash, 2000, *The Guttmacher Report on Public Policy*, 3(4), pp. 4–8.

The problem this law presents for many professional counselors is that it allows them to assist adolescent clients legally, but may conflict with their personal beliefs. Some professionals believe that behaviors such as these can cause harm to oneself, and they have a duty to warn, which supersedes all other responsibilities. Some professional counselors work with the adolescent to help the adolescent involve the family, whereas others believe that telling the family will work against the adolescent's obtaining help.

Another issue is that many parents do not understand that their children can seek treatment in these areas without parental consent. Parents will be understandably angry and distrustful when they discover their child has a sexually transmitted disease or is abusing substances, and that the professional counselor knew but did not tell them about it. Professional counselors need to be prepared to deal with the aftermath of such discoveries. They need to think through their positions on these issues carefully and be honest with clients about their beliefs. Professional counselors should not wait until they are faced with a situation to figure out where they stand on an issue. To consider this likely scenario, complete Activity 3.8.

ACTIVITY 3.8

How might you address parents who are understandably angry over a minor consent issue, and are now distrustful of you as their child's professional counselor? What precautions might you take to avoid this situation?

RECORDS AND PERSONAL NOTES

Educational Records

Educational records include all records of a student's achievement, attendance, behavior, testing and assessment, school activities, and other information that the school collects and maintains. Schools frequently divide student records into cumulative records, health records, special education records, and confidential records, including psychological evaluations. This division of records is done for the convenience of the school; all these records are considered to be a part of the educational record. The only exceptions are personal notes, reports to Child Protective Services for abuse or neglect, and, in some states, reports from law enforcement agencies regarding students' arrests for reportable offenses.

The inspection, dissemination, and access to student educational records must be in accordance with the ***Family Educational Rights and Privacy Act*** (FERPA) of 1974 (20 U.S.C. 1232g). This law, which is often referred to as the Buckley Amendment, applies to all school districts, preK–12 schools, and postsecondary institutions (colleges) that receive federal funding through the U.S. Department of Education. Nonpublic schools that do not accept federal funding are exempt from this law.

The FERPA has several provisions. The first provision requires that schools or systems annually send a notice to parents or guardians regarding their right to review their children's records and to file a complaint if they disagree with anything in the record. The system has 45 days in which to comply with the parents' request to review the records. There are penalties, including loss of federal funding, for any school or system that fails to comply.

Second, the law limits who may access the records and specifies what personally identifiable information can be disclosed without informed consent—that is, what constitutes directory information or public information. Under FERPA, only individuals "with a legitimate educational interest" can access a student's record. This includes the new school when a student transfers. The sending school may send the records without the parents' consent, but should make every attempt to inform the parent that it has done so. The major exception relates to law enforcement; the school must comply with a judicial order or lawfully executed subpoena. The school must also make whatever information is needed available to the school's law enforcement unit. In emergencies, information relevant to the emergency can be shared (see www.ed.gov/print/policy/gen/guid/fpco/ferpa/index.html). All states and jurisdictions have incorporated FERPA into state statutes and local policies, with some variance among aspects such as what constitutes directory information.

The rights of consent transfer to the student at age 18 years, or when the student attends a postsecondary institution. The law does not specifically limit the rights of parents of students older than 18 years of age who are still in secondary school. Noncustodial parents have the same rights as custodial parents, unless their rights have been terminated or limited by the courts. Stepparents and other family members who do not have custody of the child have no rights under FERPA, unless the court has granted authority.

The ***Protection of Pupil Rights Amendment*** **(PPRA)** of 1978, often called the Hatch Amendment, gives parents additional rights. It established certain requirements when surveys are given to students in preK–12 schools; it does not apply to postsecondary schools because students can consent on their own. If the survey is funded with federal money, informed consent must be obtained for all participating students if students in elementary or secondary schools are required to take the survey, and questions about certain personal areas are included. It also requires informed parental consent before the student undergoes any psychological, psychiatric, or medical examination, testing, or treatment, or any school program designed to affect the personal values or behavior of the student. The Hatch Amendment also gives parents the right to review instructional materials in experimental programs.

The *No Child Left Behind* (NCLB) Act of 2001 included several changes to FERPA and PPRA and continued to increase parents' rights. The changes apply to surveys funded either in part or entirely by any program administered by the U.S. Department of Education. NCLB made minor changes to the seven existing categories concerning surveys and added an additional category. PPRA now requires that:

- Schools and contractors make instructional materials available for review by the parents of participating students if those materials will be used in any Department of Education–funded survey, analysis, or evaluation.
- Schools and contractors obtain written, informed parental consent before students' participation in any Department of Education–funded survey, analysis, or evaluation if information in any of the following areas would be revealed:
  - Political affiliations or beliefs of the parent or student
  - Mental and psychological problems of the family or student
  - Sex behavior or attitudes
  - Illegal, antisocial, self-incriminating, or demeaning behavior
  - Critical appraisals of other individuals with whom the student has close family relationships

- Legally recognized privileged or analogous relationships such as those of lawyers, ministers, and physicians
- Religious practices, affiliations, or beliefs of the student or parent/guardian (newly added)
- Income other than such information as required to determine eligibility or participation in a program (20 U.S.C. 1232h)

The new provisions of PPRA also apply to surveys not funded through the U.S Department of Education programs. These provisions give parents the right to inspect, on request, any survey or instructional materials used as part of the curriculum if created by a third party and involving one or more of the eight aforementioned areas. Parents also have the right to inspect any instrument used to collect personal information that will be used in selling or marketing. Parents always have the right to not grant permission or to opt their child out of participating in any activity involving the eight previously delineated areas. PPRA does not apply to any survey that is administered as part of the *Individuals with Disabilities Education Improvement Act* (IDEIA, 2004).

As can be seen from the previous discussion, there are many constraints in schools to assessment, testing, and surveying students. Because individual school systems, districts, or colleges may have defined this legislation further, it is essential that professional counselors become familiar with the requirements of the policies and procedures for their specific school system.

The word "parents" has been used in the preceding discussion about student records. The law does recognize the right of students older than age 18 years to access their own records, and accords them the same rights as parents of students younger than age 18 years. However, the law does not specifically limit the right of parents whose children are 18 years of age or older to access their child's records, particularly in cases where the child is still living at home and is financially dependent on the parents. The law also gives noncustodial parents the same rights as custodial parents. Unless there is a court order in the child's file that limits or terminates the rights of one or both parents, both parents have the same access to the child's records. School personnel also must provide copies of records such as report cards to both parents if requested.

The word "parent" is used to reference the legal guardian of the child, who may not be the biological or adoptive parent of the child, but some other legally recognized caregiver. Stepparents and other family members have no legal right to the student's records without court-appointed authority, such as adoption or guardianship. This is particularly problematic in situations where a relative provides kinship care—that is, the relative has physical custody 24 hours a day, 7 days a week, but no legal custody of the child. Legally, this person has no educational decision-making rights for the child and cannot access the child's record or give consent. The crack epidemic, incarcerations, and AIDS/HIV have created a situation in which millions of children younger than 18 years of age are involved in informal kinship care situations. Kinship care may be the best situation for these children, but these situations present significant legal implications for schools.

Outside agencies may not access the records of any student without the signed consent of the parent or legal guardian. Some states have worked out interagency agreements wherein a parent signs one form that designates what records may be shared with which agencies, making individual forms unnecessary. Local policies dictate whether signed informed consent is needed to share information at school team meetings, such as student assistance programs, IEP, or student services meetings, when the agency personnel are regular members of the team.

Personal Notes

Personal notes are notes written by professional counselors to serve as an extension of their memories; they are an impression of the client or session. These notes must remain "in the sole possession of the maker" and cannot be shared with anyone except "a substitute maker." A substitute maker is someone who takes over for the counselor in the counselor's position, in the same way a substitute teacher takes over for the regular teacher. In the case of school counselors, a substitute maker is not the counselor who becomes responsible for the child the next year or in the next school.

Personal notes must remain separate from the educational record. When any information in the personal notes is shared, it is no longer confidential. If professional counselors keep their personal notes in their offices, they should keep them separate from all other records and secure, such as in a locked file cabinet. Some counselors keep them in their car or house, but this is unnecessary, unless there are problems with security in the counselor's office.

As technology becomes more common in counseling offices, professionals may prefer to keep their personal notes on the computer. This is not a good idea, unless the counselor can absolutely guarantee that no one can access the program or break through network firewalls. Even keeping the notes on disk is questionable. Stories of computer hackers breaking codes and paralyzing websites for hours are frequently reported in the news. It is preferable to keep notes separate and not tell anyone they exist, even if there is nothing of particular interest in them. The information is confidential, and the professional counselor needs to ensure its security. Information from the notes would be shared only in cases in which there is a clear duty to warn, or when a judge requires that confidentiality be broken and the information shared. Activity 3.9 is meant to stimulate your thinking over how you will handle personal notes pertaining to clients.

ACTIVITY 3.9

How might you store your personal notes as a professional counselor? What precautions will you take to keep them secure? If subordinates are involved, what precautions will you take to ensure confidentiality?

THE *HEALTH INSURANCE PORTABILITY AND ACCOUNTABILITY ACT* (HIPAA) OF 1996

The *Health Insurance Portability and Accountability Act* (**HIPAA**) of 1996 required that the U.S. Department of Health and Human Services adopt national standards for the privacy of individually identifiable health information, outlined patients' rights, and established criteria for access to health records. The requirement that the Department of Health and Human Services also adopt national standards for electronic health care transactions was also included in this law. The Privacy Rule was adopted in 2000 and became effective in 2001. The Privacy Rule set national standards for the privacy and security of protected health information. The rule specifically excludes any individually identifiable health information that is covered by FERPA. Health records in schools that are under FERPA are specifically excluded from HIPAA.

However, the situation is not that simple, particularly in the area of special education. Many schools receive mental, physical, and emotional health assessments of students that have been conducted by outside providers whose practices are covered by HIPAA regulations. In previous years, such assessments and reports automatically became part of the educational record. This may no longer be the case, particularly if the provider requests that the report not be re-disclosed. As HIPAA continues to impact health information, agencies and school systems must develop policies and procedures to address any potential conflicts between FERPA and HIPAA. Professional counselors must be aware of these issues and any school policies.

CHILD ABUSE

Another issue professional counselors must deal with that has clear legal mandates is child abuse and neglect. Efforts to recognize and intervene in child abuse cases began in the late 1800s and were modeled on the prevention of cruelty to animals laws. In 1961, the "battered child syndrome" was legally recognized, and by 1968, all 50 states had laws requiring the reporting of child maltreatment. In 1974, the *National Child Abuse Prevention and Treatment Act* (P.L. 93-247) became a federal law. The act was later reauthorized with changes and renamed the ***Keeping Children and Families Safe Act*** of 2003. The law defined **child abuse** as physical or mental injury, sexual abuse or exploitation, negligent treatment, or maltreatment of a child younger than age 18 years or the age specified by the child protection law of the state in question, by a person who is responsible for the child's welfare, under circumstances that indicate that the child's health or welfare is harmed or threatened (42 U.S.C.S. §5101).

The law is clear regarding who must report cases of child abuse and neglect. Every health practitioner, educator, human services worker, and law enforcement officer must report suspected abuse or neglect, generally within 24 to 72 hours of first "having reason to suspect." It is incumbent on the individual who first suspects the abuse or neglect to call Child Protective Services to report. The oral report must be followed up by a written report in most cases. Each state may have slightly different procedures for reporting; some states allow 7 days for submission of the written report and identify different agencies to which the report must be made. What does not change is the legal mandate to report.

There is no liability for reporting child abuse, even if a subsequent investigation determines no evidence that abuse or neglect occurred, unless the report is made with malice. Most states do have serious penalties for failure to report, however. These penalties may include loss of certification or license, disciplinary action, or termination of employment.

Parents or guardians have no rights to information during this process. The agency, school, or other entity making the report should not inform the parents that a report is being made. It is the responsibility of the department of social services and the law enforcement agency to contact the parent and conduct the investigation. It is critical that professional counselors understand the laws regarding cases of child abuse and neglect and follow the procedures exactly. The individual submitting the report does not have to prove that abuse has occurred; it is enough to have reason to suspect.

Professional counselors are sometimes put in an awkward position when they are not the first person to suspect abuse, but the staff member who does is not willing to make the report and asks the counselor to do it. In such cases, if the staff member will not make the report, professional counselors should do it, but should apprise the administrator of the circumstances surrounding the report. Regardless of who submits the report, the client will need support and assistance throughout the process. Activity 3.10 pertains to handling cases of abuse and neglect.

ACTIVITY 3.10   HANDLING ABUSE AND NEGLECT

Become familiar with local or state processes of reporting suspicions of abuse and neglect to Child Protective Services. What might you do if another professional in your building or agency approaches you about their suspicion of child abuse or neglect?

SUICIDE

For many years, the standard that was used in the counseling profession for dealing with potential suicide cases was based on the Tarasoff case, which was previously discussed. As a result of the Tarasoff case ruling, professional counselors had a duty to warn if there was a foreseeable victim. According to Remley and Herlihy (2005), subsequent court decisions interpreted the case differently; some judges ruled that the duty exists even when there is no foreseeable victim, if individuals are unintentionally injured by the client—classes of persons of which the victim is a member, bystanders, and other individuals. Generally, when dealing with a potentially suicidal client, the professional counselor conducts a lethality assessment, determines the seriousness of the threat, and, based on the seriousness of the threat, decides whether the duty to warn was applicable.

The Eisel case in Maryland changed the standard for many professional school counselors. In that case, two middle school students became involved in Satanism and became obsessed with death and self-destruction. Friends of Nicole Eisel went to their school counselor and told her that Nicole was thinking about killing herself. That counselor consulted with Nicole's school counselor. Both professional school counselors spoke with Nicole, who denied thinking about killing herself. Shortly thereafter, on a school holiday, Nicole's friend, who attended another school, shot Nicole and killed herself in the park behind the school. Mr. Eisel sued the school, the school system, and the professional school counselors. The circuit court dismissed the case. Mr. Eisel appealed to the court of appeals. Its decision of October 29, 1991, stated:

> Considering the growth of this tragic social problem in the light of the factors discussed above, we hold that school counselors have a duty to use reasonable means to attempt to prevent a suicide when they are on notice of a child or adolescent student's suicidal intent. (*Eisel v. Board of Education*, 1991)

Based on the facts of this case as developed to date, a trier of fact could conclude that the duty included warning Mr. Eisel of the danger. The case was remanded back to the circuit court to decide the issue of liability for the school system and the professional school counselors. The case finally concluded 8 years after it began and found the school and professional school counselors had acted appropriately given the circumstances, their training, and the policies in place at the time.

The court's decision had a major impact on professional school counselors in the state of Maryland. This decision removed the counselor's ability to determine whether duty to warn is applicable. As a consequence, professional school counselors in Maryland must always tell the parent whenever there is any indication from a child or someone else that the child is thinking about suicide, regardless of the seriousness of the threat. They must also inform the principal or the principal's designee. Many of Maryland's school systems now apply this procedure to all student services personnel employed by the school system, and other states have implemented similar provisions and policies.

While this case is legally binding only on professional school counselors in Maryland, it has become the standard by which subsequent cases have been decided. For example, a Florida court subsequently made a similar ruling in a similar case, and several other courts are following suit. Professional school counselors must be aware of the policies within their system. The courts clearly are ruling in favor of duty to warn, as opposed to counselor discretion. Professional counselors practicing outside of schools should abide by state statute and policy, but deciding to warn when there is any reason to suspect the client is in danger to self or others is probably a good practice in almost all circumstances, particularly when the client is a minor child.

As this chapter comes to a close, Activities 3.11 through will help you integrate the information on ethical and legal issues in counseling, and apply ethical decision-making principles to numerous scenarios.

ACTIVITY 3.11   ETHICAL DECISION MAKING

For each numbered situation , indicate whether the behavior is ethical (E) or unethical (U), and cite the ACA *Code of Ethics* Standard or Standards that apply. The person in question in each scenario is <u>underlined</u>.

Situation #1: Judy, a counselor educator at a university, has a colleague named <u>John</u> who is opening a private practice in addition to his teaching job. John is building his client caseload by offering special rates to recent graduates of the university counseling program in exchange for providing supervision, which is required for licensing.

E   U   Standard(s) _____

Situation #2: A <u>rehabilitation counselor</u> is conducting a research study. Because raw data includes confidential information about individual participants, the counselor deletes all identifying data before giving the material to the secretary for computer entry.

E   U   Standard(s) _____

Situation #3: <u>Larry</u> Adams has a PhD in history and is a university professor. He also has a master's degree in counseling and is an LPC. He wants to open a part-time private practice, and has business cards printed that say, "Dr. Larry Adams, Individual and Group Counseling."

E   U   Standard(s) _____

Situation #4: A woman enters into a counseling relationship with a male <u>counselor</u> at a mental health center after finishing a treatment program for alcohol addiction. The

(Continued)

woman has a history of violent behavior when intoxicated. Although she has maintained her sobriety for several months, one evening, obviously intoxicated, she calls the counselor and threatens to kill her mother. Despite the client's incoherence, the counselor discerns that she has a gun. The counselor calls the client's mother, but is unable to reach her, and then calls the police.

E   U   Standard(s) _____

Situation #5: A <u>residence hall director</u> who is responsible for hall discipline at a university has a master's degree in counseling. He is approached by students living in his hall who say they would like to address some personal concerns and want him to be their counselor. The residence hall director arranges weekly sessions for counseling with the students.

E   U   Standard(s) _____

Situation #6: A male professional <u>counselor</u> in a mental health center works daily with clients who are taking medications. One of the clients, who has been on Prozac, tells the counselor that she continues to be quite depressed. The counselor says, "No problem, you may need your medication changed. I'll arrange that," and refers the woman to the staff psychiatrist.

E   U   Standard(s) _____

Situation #7: A professional <u>counselor</u> has been encouraging a client to get involved in more social activities to get her out of the house more often. One day, the client unexpectedly shows up at an art class that the counselor is enrolled in, saying that she signed up for the same class. The counselor decides to stay enrolled.

E   U   Standard(s) _____

Situation #8: A professional <u>counselor</u> has been seeing a married couple who have decided to divorce. During the week between sessions, the couple has an argument, and the husband moves out of the house. The wife obtains a restraining order because she fears her husband will harm her or the children as he has in the past. The husband calls the counselor and threatens to bomb the house if his wife does not allow him to see the children. The husband sounds rational, but definitely wants to get even with his wife. The counselor believes the husband is just spouting off.

E   U   Standard(s) _____

Situation #9: <u>Sharon</u>, a counselor in private practice, receives a phone call from a former male friend with whom she has had a sexual relationship. He tells her that he is grieving the death of his father and requests counseling from her. Because Sharon specializes in grief counseling and has not dated him in more than a year, she agrees to counsel him.

E   U   Standard(s) _____

Situation #10: A female <u>graduate student</u> in counseling is doing her internship in a community agency. The administrators tell her that they do not want her to inform clients that she is a student intern. They explain that the clients might think they are getting second-class service if they knew their counselor was in training. The administrators contend that clients are paying (on a sliding scale) for services they receive, and that it would not be psychologically good to give them any information that might cause them to believe they were not getting the best help available. The student did as she was told.

E   U   Standard(s) _____

Situation #11: Robert requests counseling from a counselor in private practice. He indicates that he and his wife are involved in marriage counseling as a couple through an agency in town. Robert says he is undecided about continuing the marriage and would like to sort out his feelings and reach a decision. He intends to continue couples counseling in the meantime. The professional <u>counselor</u> agrees to provide counseling for Robert without requesting permission to contact the other marriage counselor.

E   U   Standard(s) _____

Situation #12: A professional <u>counselor</u> has administered a personality inventory for a Mexican American client. The counselor is aware that this inventory contains several race-sensitive items, but has decided to use it anyway because this particular client seems so well acculturated.

E   U   Standard(s) _____

Situation #13: A <u>family counselor</u> in a mental health clinic has been having weekly sessions with two parents and their adolescent child, a juvenile offender who is about to be released from a detention center. In the past, the juvenile was known to be extremely dangerous and violent, and had made generalized statements of hostility, but with no intended or identifiable victim. The counselor took no action to block his release.

E   U   Standard(s) _____

Situation #14: A professional <u>school counselor</u> is working with a student who is distressed about her family situation, which involves the use of crack cocaine. The counselor has no training in drug counseling, but continues working with the student even though a local family service center has an excellent program for teenagers with parents who abuse substances, and this service is available at no charge.

E   U   Standard(s) _____

Situation #15: As a private practitioner, a professional <u>counselor</u> decides not to purchase malpractice insurance and proceeds to practice without it.

E   U   Standard(s) _____

Situation #16: A high school <u>counselor</u> is contacted by a teacher who reports that Diane, a student in her English class, has written a poem about death. When the teacher talked

(Continued)

with Diane, she threatened to kill herself. The counselor calls Diane into her office, and Diane admits to being deeply despondent and wanting to end her life. Diane begs the counselor not to tell her parents or anyone else. The counselor is concerned for Diane's safety, so she calls her parents to tell them of Diane's suicidal ideation.

E   U   Standard(s) _____

Situation #17: A professional <u>counselor</u> is seeing a client who had been sexually abused as a child. The client expresses frustration that she cannot remember the earliest incidents of abuse, and insists that hypnosis would help her break through this barrier. Although the counselor has no specific training in hypnosis, she agrees to purchase a hypnosis audiotape and attempt the procedure with the client.

E   U   Standard(s) _____

Situation #18: Steve, an HIV-infected man, reveals to his professional <u>counselor</u> that he is infected. After the counselor probes the situation a bit, Steve admits to his counselor that he is embarrassed, is confused, and finds it difficult to talk about his condition. Steve admits that he has unprotected sexual relations and does not disclose his condition to his partners. The counselor agrees to continue providing counseling services only if Steve gives a verbal agreement that he will not have sexual relations with others until he is less confused.

E   U   Standard(s) _____

Situation #19: Joe, a 23-year-old college student, was convicted of illegal possession of controlled substances and is now serving a 2-year probation sentence. He is seeing the <u>college counselor</u>. Joe's probation officer contacts the counselor and requests a report. Although Joe has not signed a release of information, the counselor complies, fearing that not to do so might cause the probation officer to file a negative report on Joe to the court.

E   U   Standard(s) _____

Situation #20: Before seeing a family for counseling, a <u>professional counselor</u> gives a written document explaining the process of counseling to the parents. After reading the informed consent document, the parents sign it and bring the family to counseling. The informed consent document is not given to or described to the children.

E   U   Standard(s) _____

ACTIVITY 3.12

As a future professional counselor, write a reflection on (1) your ethical decision-making process (with emphasis on self-awareness and analysis of the various codes of ethics), and (2) the implications of your values for counseling practice, including the role of your cultural values in counseling.

ACTIVITY 3.13

Place a checkmark in the appropriate column. How ethical is it for a professional counselor to?

	Never	Rarely	Sometimes	Usually	Always
1. Barter with a client for services.					
2. Invite a client to a personal party or social event.					
3. Provide counseling to a friend who is in a crisis.					
4. Accept a gift from a client if the gift is worth less than $10.					
5. Accept a gift from a client if the gift is worth more than $50.					
6. Accept a client's invitation to a special event.					
7. Go out for coffee with a client after a counseling session.					
8. Become friends with a client after termination of the counseling relationship.					
9. Give the home phone number to a client.					
10. Share personal experiences as a member of a self-help group when a client is in attendance.					
11. Occasionally hire a client to baby-sit.					

ACTIVITY 3.14

Answer the following questions regarding the ACA *Code of Ethics* (2005).
1. Are the ethical standards sufficiently comprehensive and specific to guide you in working with diverse client populations? Are you aware of any subtle biases you may have against individuals who are different from you? How can you guard against racial and sexual stereotyping in your counseling relationship with clients?
2. How can you recognize when you are meeting your personal needs at the expense of a client? Do you think it is possible to continue your work as a professional counselor if you do not meet your own needs? Can you think of any values you hold that you might impose on certain clients? If you became aware of personal problems that were negatively affecting your work, what would you do?

(Continued)

3. What might you want to tell clients about the exceptions to confidentiality? Do you think that informing clients about the limits to confidentiality increases or decreases trust? What are your thoughts about confidentiality as it pertains to contagious, fatal diseases? What are your thoughts about confidentiality as it pertains to minor clients?

4. Under what circumstances might you consult with another professional regarding your ethical obligations to a client? How can you determine when a client's condition represents a clear and imminent danger to the client or others? How can you assess the degree of danger?

5. When might you make use of tests as a part of the counseling process? What factors do you need to take into account in selecting, administering, scoring, and interpreting tests? What are the ethical considerations in testing diverse client populations?

6. How can appropriate relationship boundaries between counselor educators and students be determined? What ethical, professional, and social relationship boundaries between counselor educators and students do you see as important? What ethical, professional, and social relationship boundaries between supervisors and supervisees do you see as important?

Summary

If one were to survey practicing counselors regarding the "hot issues" in counseling, the list would likely include eating disorders, HIV/AIDS, self-mutilation, autism and Asperger's syndrome, bullying, harassment, changing family structures, mobility, cultural diversity, sexual orientation, depression, loss and grief, students with special needs, emotional disturbance, gangs, and a host of other topics. So how does a counselor help a 21-year-old who believes he is gay? Or a 16-year-old who is starving herself to death? Or an incarcerated parent who wants the professional counselor to read his letters to his children because the mother will not let him have any contact with his children?

Here are some final words of wisdom to help guide you as a professional counselor.

- Always document in writing what you did and why you did it.
- If you did not follow a policy, document why you did not (e.g., not calling the parent in a suicide case because it was handled as an abuse case).
- Know federal, state, and local laws, regulations, policies, and guidelines.
- Consult with a colleague or supervisor when you have questions or doubts.
- Read and use resources.
- Consult with a lawyer when appropriate.

Professional counselors must be prepared to deal with these issues and more every day of their professional lives. Many of these areas do not have clear laws, regulations, court cases, or policies to guide counselors toward legal and ethical behavior. Professional counselors need to try to do what is in the best interests of their clients, and to help the clients see what that is. They must advocate for their clients because frequently the professional counselor is the only support that the client has. Professional counselors must never stop believing that what they do makes a difference in the lives of clients.

SECTION TWO

Counseling Processes and Approaches

4

Theories of Counseling

DANA HELLER LEVITT AND ALISSA BRAY

PREVIEW

The nature and quality of the counseling relationship is more significant than any other factor in counseling. Given this perspective, why do professional counselors study theories? Whether working with individuals, families, or groups, regardless of the setting, professional counselors have a professional responsibility to develop a foundation and clear rationale of their theoretical orientation to serve clients best. Professional counselors operate out of theories that best fit their personal philosophies of human change and the counseling process. Selecting a theoretical orientation is a career-long process that begins during professional training.

In this chapter, the significance of theory to counseling practice is explored, and a brief overview of the major theoretical paradigms is presented. You will also begin to explore your own initial preferences for theoretical orientation with the intent of continuing your personal and professional exploration to discover your personal style.

THE SIGNIFICANCE OF THEORY

Theories ground us as professional counselors. They provide a means to understand what we are doing, how we are serving clients, and how to explain counseling to clients. People entering counseling are generally not interested in hearing a detailed description of their counselor's philosophical beliefs about the nature of the counseling relationship and human change. Rather, they are seeking guidance about the change process and how the professional counselor can help accomplish that goal. Theories represent clients' realities and what we know to be important and effective elements of the counseling relationship (Hansen, 2006a). Professional counselors must have a firm sense of the counseling process alongside their own philosophies about what works in counseling and how individuals change and grow.

A firm understanding of your beliefs about counseling can help you explain the process to clients, helping them understand the nature of counseling and what can be expected

(Gladding, 2005). This road map for counseling can help you generate new ideas with the client to determine the best course of action and the means to reach goals.

Theories provide a framework for conceptualizing client problems and determining a course of action in counseling (Halbur & Halbur, 2006). For example, a professional counselor who operates from a cognitive-behavioral standpoint would identify a client's struggle with bulimia as faulty logic and plan a course of treatment to reshape thoughts and behaviors. A psychodynamically oriented professional counselor would view the issue through the lens of the client's past and spend counseling time uncovering early triggers and sustaining factors for the disorder.

Ethics of Applying Counseling Theory

One theory does not fit for all clients. A successful approach with one client may be a complete disaster with another. Professional counselors have an ethical responsibility to be culturally competent and to address each client's needs as such. There is no cookie-cutter, "one size fits all," approach to counseling. Despite what some clients may be seeking, professional counselors do not have a handbook of problems and solutions. Professional counselors instead must use their understanding of theory to provide the best possible services to clients. Operating from a clear theoretical framework also means being flexible with that approach to know when it will not work. Activity 4.1 provides an opportunity to explore some of the theoretical underpinnings of your counseling approach.

ACTIVITY 4.1

A second-grade girl is referred for counseling. Recently, she has been having difficulty staying on task during class and difficulty making friends. Her parents were never married and no longer live together. Her teacher reports that the girl came to her the previous day and mentioned something about other students making fun of her on the playground because she does not have a "real" family.
- As a professional counselor, how would you establish rapport?
- What types of questions would you ask her during the first session?
- What strategies would you employ to begin solving some of the problems she is having in school?
- Now, if the student was a 17-year-old Asian boy, what types of alterations would you make to your approach and strategies?

From an ethical standpoint, professional counselors must be clear about their professional orientation to serve clients best. As discussed in Chapter 3, the American Counseling Association (ACA) *Code of Ethics* (2005) provides guidelines for professional and ethical counseling practice. All professional counselors and counselors in training are expected to abide by the principles stated in the *Code of Ethics*. Sections of the *Code of Ethics* pertain specifically to learning and practice associated with theories. Professional counselors must be aware of new trends and best practices in the profession. This includes knowledge of theories and continuing education on theoretical underpinnings in counseling. Professional counselors must also be competent to use the theories they choose to employ in counseling, and must have a firm foundation for the work they perform with clients.

Closely related, and perhaps one of the most fundamental aspects of professional and ethical practice, is continual counselor self-reflection. **Self-awareness** is crucial to counselor development (Meier & Davis, 2005). Because theory is akin to one's philosophy of counseling, counselors must regularly assess their beliefs about the process and their effectiveness with clients. By this manner of self-awareness, professional counselors can determine and strengthen their theoretical beliefs and practices.

Finally, clients must make informed choices about entering into counseling (Halbur & Halbur, 2006). The **informed consent** document that clients receive and sign at the start of counseling serves as a contract for what will transpire. This informed consent must include the professional counselor's theoretical orientation, whether explicitly stated or implied in the description of the approaches used in counseling. Providing clients with this information is not only your ethical and professional responsibility, but also the right of clients to know about you and what they can expect (Remley & Herlihy, 2007). Activity 4.2 encourages exploration and refinement of your theoretical approach by exploring the approaches used by practitioners in the field.

ACTIVITY 4.2   THEORY IN PRACTICE

Interview three practicing counselors about their theoretical orientations. Discuss with them the importance of theory in their current work, how they arrived at their personal theories, and the relationship of their theories to personal philosophies. Are there differences when working with individuals, groups, or families?

What Makes a Good Theory?

Hansen, Stevic, and Warner (1986) suggested five components of a good counseling theory, as follows:

1. The theory is clear and easily understood.
2. The theory is comprehensive.
3. The theory is explicit and heuristic, generating further research.
4. The theory is specifically geared to help clients reach their desired outcomes.
5. The theory is useful to practitioners.

Theories must be sound to be plausible to professional counselors. Literally hundreds of theories exist with more emerging (Ivey & Ivey, 2007). All of these theories can be overwhelming to beginning counselors who are trying to do what is in the best interests of their clients. Professional counselors need a means of organizing the information about theories, applying what works, and building on natural helping capabilities.

Intentionality is a necessity in applying the basic helping skills (Halbur & Halbur, 2006). As mentioned in Chapter 5, skill application is an art and a science. Technical expertise, while important, will not make the most effective professional counselor. A firm, philosophical understanding of the counseling profession and practice, and knowledge of the research behind what you do, will help you in your selection of and adherence to a theory that best fits your natural style of helping. Considering theories with respect to their common elements can help professional counselors determine what works best for whom, and most notably for you as the counselor.

THEORETICAL PARADIGMS

Through self-awareness, professional counselors strengthen their approaches and learn new ways to work with clients. Theoretical orientation remains relatively constant through counselors' development given the connection to personal philosophy. Changes that occur tend to be within the general categories of theories, referred to as **paradigms**. These paradigms are a means of grouping theories based on common characteristics. Multiple theories exist within each paradigm. Table 4.1 provides a summary of the five most prominent paradigms and Table 4.2. summarizes the techniques and multicultural considerations of these paradigms as well as of other important theories.

Theories can be described as having specific and common factors. **Specific factors** are the unique characteristics of a given theory. They are elements that distinguish one theory from another and are often the basis of association with a theory. For example, the empty chair technique is a specific factor for gestalt, a humanistic-existential theory. Disputing irrational beliefs is unique to Albert Ellis' rational emotive behavior therapy (REBT) and the behavioral and cognitive behavioral paradigm. **Common factors** are characteristics that appear in all theoretical perspectives. For example, a therapeutic alliance and a healing setting that promotes client trust through professional counselor competence are common factors. A coherent rationale and set of procedures are also common to all theories. These are important principles to keep in mind as you review the major paradigms and begin to formulate your approach to counseling. To illustrate further the application of theoretical principles, consider the case of Terry in Text box 4.1, then answer the questions posed in Activity 4.3. We will return to this case throughout our discussion of the paradigms and theories.

TABLE 4.1 Theoretical Paradigms: Theories and Theorists

Paradigm	Major Theories	Prominent Theorists
Psychodynamic	Psychoanalysis	Sigmund Freud
	Adlerian	Alfred Adler
	Ego Psychology	Carl Jung
Humanistic/Existential	Person-Centered	Carl Rogers
	Existential	Victor Frankl, Irvin Yalom, Rollo May
	Gestalt	Fritz Perls
Behavioral/ Cognitive-Behavioral	Behavioral	John Watson, B.F. Skinner, Hans Eysenck, Albert Bandura, John Krumboltz
	Cognitive	Aaron Beck
	Cognitive Behavioral Therapy	Donald Meichenbaum
	Rational Emotive Behavior Therapy	Albert Ellis
Systems	Family Systems	Murray Bowen, Virginia Satir
Emergent	Narrative	Michael White, David Epston
	Constructivist	George Kelly
	Feminist	
	Interpersonal Therapy (IPT)	

TABLE 4.2 Theoretical Paradigms: Techniques and Multicultural Considerations

Paradigm	Principles	Techniques	Considerations
Psychodynamic	Predetermined	Free association	Ego and past cultural identity development
	Relationship of events and current functioning	Interpretation	Id, ego, superego development
	Bring unconscious into conscious	Dream analysis	Limited views of women
		Analysis of transference	
Humanistic/ existential	Innate goodness of people	Counseling relationship	Attention to individual's unique perspective
	Self-actualization	Empty chair	Lack of structure
	Freedom and responsibility	Genuineness, empathy, unconditional positive regard	Limited attention to external factors
	Finding meaning	Role play	Common values of love, death, anxiety
	Anxiety	Role reversal	
		"I" statements	
Behavioral/cognitive-behavioral	Changing behavior, negative thought patterns, beliefs	Specify automatic thoughts	Understanding beliefs as identity
	ABCDEs of REBT	Homework	Structure
	Disputing irrational beliefs	Thought stopping	Caution when challenging belief systems
		Cognitive restructuring	
		Token economy	
Systems	Family provides framework for understanding individual	Genograms	Identity patterns
	Differentiation of self	Questioning	Caution when attempting to change multigenerational patterns
		Coaching	Resistance to external input on family
		"I" position	
		Detriangulation	
Narrative	Retell story to create favorable outcomes	Deconstruct problems	Many cultures emphasize storytelling
	Person is not the problem	Externalize problems	High-level processing required
		Miracle question	
		Sparkling moments	

(Continued)

TABLE 4.2 Theoretical Paradigms: Techniques and Multicultural Considerations (*Continued*)

Paradigm	Principles	Techniques	Considerations
Constructivism	Personal reality	Card sort	Insight required
	Personal construct	Identify constructs	Challenges test beliefs and principles
		Repertory	
Feminist	Application of feminist principles: equality, empowerment	Gender role analysis	Addresses shared experiences of oppression
	Mutuality	Empowerment	Political action may be against belief
	Androgyny	Egalitarian relationship	Limited application with men
		Sociocultural exploration of gender	
Interpersonal psychotherapy	Improve interpersonal functioning, social network	Therapeutic alliance	Flexible and adaptable to unique individuals
	Attachment, social, and communication theories	Communication analysis	
	Present focus	Interpersonal incidents	
		Content and process affect	
		Role playing	

The following discussion of theories and paradigms is broad in nature. We encourage you to read further about theories in the references provided throughout this chapter, and to research in greater depth the specific theories of interest.

BOX 4.1

The Case of Terry

Terry is a 23-year-old graduate student in microbiology. Terry recently relocated to the area to pursue graduate study after completing her undergraduate degree at a small college near her hometown. Now living two states and hundreds of miles away from her family, Terry feels that she is experiencing her independence for the first time.

Terry first became interested in science when she received a science kit for her seventh birthday. Her parents encouraged her to study science throughout high school and pushed her toward a biology major when she entered college. Terry has heard on more than one occasion that she is the family's "only hope for a doctor." As first-generation immigrants to the United States, Terry's parents feel that their only daughter must be successful to prove their culture's ability to compete in an American environment.

Terry was referred to counseling following the midterm period of her first term in graduate school. Her roommate discovered numerous cuts on her arms and reported that Terry had seemed down over the past few weeks. When she finally agreed to see a professional counselor, Terry reported that she did not perform well on her midterm exams and was questioning whether she could make it in graduate school. She was concerned about disappointing her parents and bringing shame to their family.

ACTIVITY 4.3   PRESENTING ISSUES

Considering the case of Terry, write your initial reactions to her presenting issues for counseling. Specifically:

1. What is the problem?
2. Who is involved in Terry's dilemma?
3. How is the dilemma affecting Terry?
4. What would you hope to see as the goal of counseling for Terry?
5. What might counseling entail?
6. How will you know that counseling is complete?
7. How does your conceptualization attend to Terry's culture?

Keep your responses in a convenient location as you review the remainder of the chapter. These responses may relate to your emerging theoretical orientation.

Psychodynamic Paradigm

At the time of his work, Sigmund Freud was considered revolutionary in his thinking and conceptualizing of the problems experienced by people, primarily women. Today, many theories are based upon Freud's work, either additive to what he developed or created as an alternative explanation to a theory heavily focused on the past and the subconscious mind. For this reason, the psychodynamic paradigm serves as an introduction and foundation to the other paradigms of counseling theories.

Theories that fall under the psychodynamic paradigm are based largely on insight, unconscious motivation, and personality reconstruction. The psychodynamic paradigm holds that most issues clients face are the result of unresolved issues from their early development. The focus in counseling from a psychodynamic framework is on the relationship of past events with current functioning. In the case of Terry, the professional counselor may question how childhood messages of expected success are affecting her current performance in graduate school and the subsequent feelings she experiences. The psychodynamic approach is very analytic in nature and may require a good deal of time to uncover past issues and make headway into current and future functioning.

PSYCHOANALYSIS   Freud's psychoanalytic theory is probably the most widely recognized theory in the psychodynamic paradigm. Many people may have the image of a wise therapist sitting behind a couch, on which a client lays and contemplates the meaning of past events. Many popular media depictions do little to ameliorate this stereotype and may perpetuate the public's beliefs about the nature of counseling in general. Although this image may have been the form of psychoanalysis in early renditions of the theory, much has changed since Freud's groundbreaking approach to counseling to challenge the means by which professional counselors with a psychoanalytic orientation help their clients.

Freud believed that personality is completely formed in childhood, and that challenges later in life are the result of unresolved conflicts. Consistent with the idea that theories emerge from our personal philosophies and experiences, Freud's background demonstrates his emphasis on childhood and the family. The eldest of eight siblings of an authoritarian father, Freud was particularly close to his mother. His upbringing and religious affiliation (a Jew in Vienna, Austria, in the mid to late 1800s) limited his career aspirations to medicine or law. One might see the basis of Freud's intense self-analysis and his subsequent theories of personality dynamics based upon his own life experiences.

In psychoanalysis, the personality is perceived as being composed of three parts: the **id**, or pleasure principle; the **ego**, or reality principle; and the **superego**, or morality principle (conscience). Conflict among these structures creates anxiety in the individual. The subsequent anxiety is often managed by the ego by employing **defense mechanisms**. These mechanisms help the individual to cope with the anxiety and not be overwhelmed. Defense mechanisms can be either adaptive or damaging. For example, Terry may be turning her frustrations with her parents' expectations inward and harming herself, rather than expressing these feelings to her parents. This process of projecting unwanted emotions to oneself in this case is maladaptive in the sense that Terry is being harmed physically and emotionally.

The goal of psychoanalytic counseling is to bring unconscious drives into consciousness and develop insight into intrapsychic conflicts. Techniques such as free association, interpretation, dream analysis, and analysis of resistance and transference may be employed to assist in the development of insight. As might be expected (and often a criticism of this approach), this process can be quite lengthy and time-consuming.

The psychoanalytic counselor is like a blank screen. Listening, analyzing, and attending to **transference** and **countertransference** issues are essential to successful counseling in the psychoanalytic approach. The therapeutic relationship takes the form of the professional counselor as expert, teaching the client about the intrapsychic processes occurring.

Concepts such as defense mechanisms and transference seem to be relevant for individuals from various backgrounds. The culturally sensitive counselor may encourage individuals from ethnic and racial minority groups to develop an overall ego identity as well as a cultural identity. It is also important for psychoanalytic counselors to address their own potential biases and recognize how countertransference could unintentionally play a part in the counseling process. A limitation for multicultural counseling in psychoanalysis is in the area of gender issues. Women are seen as inferior to men because they do not resolve the Electra complex as completely as it is thought that men resolve the Oedipal complex. This concept and other similar concepts, such as penis envy, have been largely discredited and discontinued.

For independent study on psychoanalysis, consult the following foundational resources:

Freud, A. (1936). *The ego and the mechanisms of defense* (J. Strachey, Trans.). New York: International Universities Press.

Freud, S. (1900/1955). *The interpretations of dreams* (J. Strachey, Trans.). London: Hogarth.

Freud, S. (1923/1933). *New introductory lectures on psychoanalysis* (W. J. H. Sprott, Trans.). New York: Norton.

Freud, S. (1923/1947). *The ego and the id* (J. Strachey, Trans.). London: Hogarth.

ADLERIAN COUNSELING   Alfred Adler, a student of Freud, developed his theory as a result of disagreement with many of the principles his mentor proposed. Adler commended Freud's work on dream interpretation, yet the generalizations Freud drew from dreams and his emphasis on sexual trauma and development did not resonate with him. Herein lies another example of the need to formulate a specifically personally relevant theory of counseling. Adler left Freud's tutelage to develop his approach of focusing on the whole person. This holistic viewpoint approached the client as a whole, indivisible being, capable of growth, seeking social interest and connections with others. Similar to Freud, Adler emphasized the role of childhood in personality development and problem (and solution) formation.

Adler's work has been widely used, yet not widely researched or developed. Adler's work is best known for its emphasis and analysis of birth order and sibling relationships. Sweeney (1998) is one of a few modern Adlerian scholars. Traces of Adler's work are evident in the wellness movement in the counseling profession.

The Adlerian concept of **social interest** lends to the theory's cultural sensitivity. Individuals are encouraged to move beyond themselves to learn about and understand different cultural groups and how they may contribute to the greater society. Cultures that emphasize the family find that many Adlerian concepts fit with their value systems. However, limitations exist where emphasis is placed on changing the autonomous self and in the exploration of early childhood experiences. Some clients may find it inappropriate to reveal family information, or may not want to delve into the past because they may not see the connection to current pressing concerns.

For more information regarding Adlerian counseling, consult the following resources:

Adler, A. (1927). *Understanding human nature*. Greenwich, CT: Fawcett.
Adler, A. (1964). *Social interest. A challenge to mankind*. New York: Capricorn.
Adler, A. (1969). *The practice and theory of individual psychology*. Patterson, NJ: Littlefield, Adams.
Dreikurs, R. (1953). *Fundamentals of Adlerian psychology*. Chicago: Alfred Adler Institute.
Sweeney, T. J. (1998). *Adlerian counseling. A practitioner's approach* (4th ed.). Muncie, IN: Accelerated Development.

OTHER PSYCHODYNAMIC THEORIES   Jungian theory, also referred to as ego psychology, and object-relations theory are other approaches that fit within this paradigm. Although many principles of these theories are used today, more modern adaptations of psychoanalysis and Adlerian counseling are seen more readily in practice. To study a foundational work by Carl Jung, refer to the following resource: Jung, C. G. (1961). *Memories, dreams, reflections*. New York: Vintage.

Humanistic-Existential Paradigm

In contrast to the subconscious focus in the psychodynamic paradigm, the humanistic-existential paradigm is relationship-oriented. Rather than focusing on an individual's unresolved conflicts in the past, the focus here is on current and future functioning. Humanism and existentialism are similar in the belief that human nature is fundamentally good, and people have the freedom and responsibility to grow and develop.

Humanists believe that goodness and worth are qualities that people possess. In the journey toward self-actualization, it is believed that people are purposeful, active, and capable of determining their own behavior (Nugent & Jones, 2005). Similarly, existentialists place an emphasis on the importance of anxiety, freedom, values, and responsibilities, and finding meaning in one's actions (Gladding, 2005). Another parallel between humanists and existentialists is that both emphasize the importance of the client-counselor relationship. The professional counselor must enter the client's subjective world to focus on client perceptions of the presenting issue.

PERSON-CENTERED   Person-centered therapy, developed by Carl Rogers (1951, 1957), is a major theoretical approach in the humanistic framework. Over time, this approach has also been identified as nondirective, client-centered, and Rogerian. According to Rogers, the primary motivating force of humans is **self-actualization**, the tendency to move in the direction of growth, adjustment, socialization, independence, and self-realization (McWhirter & Ishikawa, 2005).

Because people have the basic need for a high self-regard, they attempt to organize their internal and external experiences into an integrated self. During this process of self-actualizing, unhealthy psychological or social influences may hinder an individual from realizing his or her potential as an integrated, productive self. In other words, conflicts develop when individuals' basic needs and their needs to obtain approval from others are inconsistent. Terry, for example, is experiencing conflict between her basic needs for self-actualization and her need for approval from her parents. The professional counselor working with Terry will need to be present and congruent to assist her in moving toward the discovery of her true self.

Rogers (1957) identified three essential characteristics a professional counselor must employ for a therapeutic relationship to be established: genuineness (or congruence), unconditional positive regard, and empathy. **Genuineness** is displaying honesty, sincerity, and directness, while avoiding any personal or professional façade. **Unconditional positive regard** is defined as the professional counselor's ability to accept every aspect of the client's personality, while remaining nonjudgmental and nonevaluative toward the client's feelings, thoughts, and behaviors. **Empathy** is the ability to understand the client's world in the way the client understands it. With Terry, the professional counselor must be open to hearing her experiences and acknowledge her challenges with the situation, regardless of personal opinion. Creating a nonthreatening, anxiety-free relationship would allow Terry to resolve conflicts and reach self-understanding.

Person-centered counseling has had a significant impact in the area of human relations with diverse cultural groups. Many countries have adopted person-centered concepts in counseling as well as cross-cultural communication and education. Multicultural limitations include lack of structure, difficulty translating core conditions to practice, and focus on internal evaluation, rather than external evaluation (Corey, 2005).

The following resources provide more information about person-centered counseling:

Rogers, C. (1942). *Counseling and psychotherapy*. Boston: Houghton Mifflin.
Rogers, C. (1951). *Client-centered therapy*. Boston: Houghton Mifflin.
Rogers, C. (1961). *On becoming a person*. Boston: Houghton Mifflin.
Rogers, C. (1980). *A way of being*. Boston: Houghton Mifflin.

EXISTENTIAL   **Existentialism** stems from Soren Kierkegaard, a 19th century philosopher who focused on the pursuit of becoming an individual. There are many contributors to existentialism as a therapeutic approach, including Ludwig Binswanger, Fyodor Dostoyevski, Friedrich Nietzsche, and Abraham Maslow. In more recent years, notable figures in existential psychotherapy include Rollo May, Victor Frankl, and Irvin Yalom.

The essence of existentialism is that humans are believed to have the capacity for self-awareness, and the freedom and responsibility to make choices that would bring about meaning in their lives. However, along with this freedom comes the reality of living with the consequences of those choices, which could lead to **existential anxiety**. May (1977) asserts that normal anxiety can be healthy and motivational.

Frankl (1963) maintained that despite negative conditions, individuals can preserve their own independent thinking, spiritual freedom, and opportunities for choice. In contrast, an individual who sees life as meaningless and without value would be thought to be in what Frankl termed an **existential vacuum**. A well-functioning person is an individual who authentically experiences reality and expresses needs in a way that is not determined by others. Terry may not be in the existential vacuum, but may be questioning the meaning of her current experiences. While having her first taste of freedom, it will be important for Terry to explore her choices and needs as self-determined and not those of her parents.

Other than concentrating on the client-counselor relationship, there is no systematic way that existential counselors help others. Still, Yalom (2002) was able to emphasize three significant qualities within the existential counseling process: (1) helping clients attend to the **here-and-now**, (2) being open and authentic with clients, and (3) cautiously using self-disclosure.

Specific goals in existential counseling include making clients sensitive to their existence, identifying characteristics unique to each client, assisting clients in enhancing interactions with others, helping clients pursue meaning in life, and promoting present and future decision making that will impact the client's direction in life. Few specific techniques are offered in an existential approach. All interventions are undertaken with the intention of assisting clients to find meaning in their actions.

The existential focus on love, suffering, anxiety, and death, all of which are the universal elements of human life, makes this theory applicable cross-culturally. In contrast, a limitation of multicultural existential counseling involves the emphasis on self-determination and the lack of focus on the environment and the social context. Some clients may feel powerless in the face of external realities such as discrimination, racism, and oppression.

Refer to the following resources for more information on existential counseling:

> Frankl, V. (1963). *Man's search for meaning*. Boston: Beacon.
> May, R. (1953). *Man's search for himself*. New York: Dell.
> May, R. (Ed.). (1961). *Existential psychology*. New York: Random House.
> Yalom, I. D. (1980). *Existential psychotherapy*. New York: Basic Books.

GESTALT THERAPY   Gestalt therapy began in response to the reductionist emphasis in the schools of counseling such as psychoanalysis and behaviorism, which attempted to break an individual's personality or behavior into understandable parts. In contrast, **Gestalt therapy** promoted the idea of wholeness. Frederick (Fritz) Perls and his wife Laura Perls were the major theorists associated with this school of thought.

Similar to person-centered counseling, gestaltists believe that people have the tendency to move toward wholeness or self-actualization. Emphasis is placed on the present as indicated by Perls' (1970) statement: "To me, nothing exists except the now. Now = experience = awareness = reality. The past is no more and the future is not yet. Only the *now* exists" (p. 14).

In contrast to psychoanalysis, which focuses on predetermined and unconscious forces, the gestalt view of human nature is antideterministic; people can become responsible, grow, and change from past events. For example, Terry is experiencing difficulties in her life that are a result of her earlier thoughts, feelings, or experiences. This phenomenon is otherwise referred to as **unfinished business**—in Terry's case, asserting her own interests. The role of the gestalt counselor is to provide an atmosphere that allows Terry to identify and pursue what she needs to grow. Being honest as well as deeply and personally involved with Terry would allow the counselor to help her redirect energy in more positive and adaptive ways of functioning.

Gestalt counselors also directly confront clients with their inconsistencies. They focus on the polarities within people and push clients to correct misconceptions, to express emotions genuinely, and to take responsibility for change. Gestalt techniques may include exercises and experiments such as empty chair, role playing, role reversal, dream analysis, and the use of "I" statements. Other characteristics of gestalt counseling that help clients develop and become mature in the now include awareness of nonverbal and verbal expressions and shedding neurotic tendencies. Perls (1970) identified five layers of neurosis that were thought to impede a client's ability to be in touch with himself or herself. Only when individuals reach the final, or explosive, layer can they be truly authentic and in touch with themselves and others.

Gestalt counseling can be viewed as a culturally sensitive theory because the experiments employed by professional counselors may encourage clients to integrate the polarities that exist between the cultures to which they belong. Gestalt techniques can also be tailored to fit with a client's distinct perception and interpretation of his or her own cultural framework. In contrast, gestalt counseling has an individualistic focus, which may be a conflict for people from cultures that emphasize group values.

Consult the following resources for further study of gestalt therapy:

Perls, F. (1969). *Gestalt therapy verbatim*. Moab, UT: Real People Press.
Perls, F. (1972) *In and out of the garbage pail*. New York: Bantam.
Polster, E., & Polster, M. (1973). *Gestalt therapy integrated: Contours of theory and practice*. New York: Brunner/Mazel.
Zinker, J. (1978). *Creative process in Gestalt therapy*. New York: Random House.

Behavioral/Cognitive-Behavioral Paradigm

Clients seek action. Terry wants to act to change her current dilemma. The behavioral or cognitive-behavioral paradigm is the most action-oriented of the theoretical groupings. Clients are guided to pursue specific tangible changes in behavior and thought. From a practical standpoint, many beginning professional counselors are drawn to this paradigm because of the many tools and techniques it employs. Additionally, professional counselors and clients alike can more readily observe progress in counseling from this perspective.

BEHAVIORAL COUNSELING   John B. Watson was one of the first advocates for **behaviorism**, as he was able to establish that human emotions were acquiescent to conditioning. Over time, behaviorism has incorporated various ideas, practices, and theories. Other theorists associated with this approach include Burroughs Frederick (B.F.) Skinner, Joseph Wolpe, Hans Eysenck, Albert Bandura, and John Krumboltz.

Behavioral theory focuses on how to reinforce, extinguish, or modify a wide range of behaviors. Specifically, it emphasizes the association between feelings and environmental stimuli, and the learning or unlearning of behaviors accordingly. Professional counselors are mainly concerned with the science of observing behavior with the resulting consequence of whether to reward positive behavior or extinguish negative behavior. This is accomplished by eliminating the cause or condition that triggered the behavior. Terry might be presented with alternatives to handle the emotional and academic stresses she faces, with the goal of developing a new set of more adaptive behaviors that can be used in everyday situations. A specific behavioral technique is the **token economy**, where clients gain or lose tokens depending on whether or not they have reached a mutually agreed upon target behavior.

Another behavioral approach involves the stimulus-response model. This model applies **classic conditioning**, or learning through the association of two stimuli. The most well-known example of this model is from Pavlov and his laboratory experiments with dogs. He found that when he paired two stimuli, food and the sound of a bell, the dogs would eventually associate the sound of the bell with food and begin salivating in response to the bell before the food was served. Similarly, certain human emotions such as phobias develop because of paired associations. Once these associations are learned, they can be unlearned and replaced in a procedure referred to as **counterconditioning** or **systematic desensitization**.

The nature of the client-counselor relationship in behavioral counseling differs dramatically from the humanistic-existential approaches. Behavioral counselors function as active teachers, reinforcers, and facilitators who help clients learn, unlearn, or relearn specific ways of behaving. It is also common for professional counselors to enter into the client's environment to instruct people who are a part of helping the client's change process. Beyond the use of reinforcers, behavioral counselors may use other techniques, including systematic desensitization, assertiveness training, implosion and flooding, contingency contracts, and aversive techniques. The ideal outcome of most behavior modification programs is to have the client's new behavior continue after the program has terminated (**response maintenance**) and to have the desired behaviors generalized to environments outside of the counseling setting (Cottone, 1992).

Behavioral counseling has advantages for individuals who are from cultures that do not focus on the experience of catharsis. For example, emphasis is placed on specific behaviors that the client wants to change and the development of problem-solving skills. Behavioral counseling takes into account an individual's environmental conditions that could be contributing to psychological problems, such as sociocultural, political, and social influences. A limitation exists when professional counselors fail to recognize conditions beyond the individual, such as Terry's cultural emphasis on family.

Consult the following resources on behavioral counseling:

Bandura, A. (1969). *Principles of behavior modification*. New York: Holt, Rinehart & Winston.

Skinner, B. F. (1953). *Science and human behavior*. New York: Macmillan.

Watson, J. B. (1925). *Behaviorism*. New York: Norton.

COGNITIVE-BEHAVIORAL   In the 1970s, many professional counselors recognized that behavioral approaches were too limited and saw value in combining them with cognitive approaches. Aaron Beck developed cognitive therapy, an approach that focuses on recognizing and changing negative thoughts and maladaptive beliefs into more realistic and constructive thoughts and beliefs. The essence of cognitive therapy is to focus on the cognitive content or automatic thoughts associated with an individual's reaction to an event. Beck asserted that psychological problems were derived from common processes, such as making incorrect inferences on the basis of incorrect information, being unable to distinguish between reality and fantasy, and faulty thinking. In short, he maintained that how people think basically determines how they feel and behave.

Donald Meichenbaum (1995) is one of the founding theorists of the cognitive-behavioral therapy (CBT) approach. Similar to Beck, he thought that helping people change the way they talk to themselves into more constructive cognitions was central to the counseling process. The maladaptive self-statements that affect individuals' behaviors are termed "cognitive distortions." Following are nine ways of mentally assessing a situation: all-or-nothing thinking, catastrophizing, labeling and mislabeling, magnification and minimization, mind reading, negative predictions, overgeneralization, personalization, and selective abstraction (Gladding, 2005).

The CBT counselor collaborates with the client by sharing the responsibility of selecting goals and bringing about change. Specific techniques, such as specifying automatic thoughts, assigning homework, thought stopping, and cognitive restructuring, are useful in identifying and challenging distorted thoughts. With Terry, the professional counselor may address her all-or-nothing perception of success with being a doctor and being accepted by her parents. Homework might include exploration of others' career decision making to challenge cognitive distortions. There are dozens of creative CBT techniques; they are usually active, time-limited, and structured (Meichenbaum, 1986).

Consult the following resources for further study on cognitive and cognitive-behavioral counseling:

Beck, A. T. (1976). *Cognitive therapy and emotional disorders*. New York: New American Library.

Beck, A. T. (1987). *Love is never enough*. New York: Harper & Row.

Meichenbaum, D. (1977). *Cognitive behavior modification: An integrative approach*. New York: Plenum.

RATIONAL EMOTIVE BEHAVIOR THERAPY   Rational emotive behavior therapy (REBT) is similar to counseling theories that emphasize behaviors and cognitions by placing emphasis on thinking, judging, deciding, analyzing, and doing. Albert Ellis, the founder of REBT, assumes that people contribute to their psychological problems by how they interpret life circumstances and events. This assumption is based on the idea that there is a cause-and-effect relationship between behaviors, cognitions, and emotions. It is thought that people have the potential for rational and irrational thinking.

In other words, while people have a tendency to move toward growth, self-preservation, happiness, and self-actualization, they also have a propensity for self-destruction, intolerance, self-blame, and avoidance of actualizing growth potentials. Ellis stresses the point that people generally feel the way they think. Minimizing irrational beliefs and replacing them with practical and effective beliefs is central to REBT.

The REBT counselor encourages clients to identify irrational ideas that contribute to their disturbed behavior, challenges clients to validate their beliefs, uses logical analysis to dispute the irrational beliefs, and teaches clients how to replace their ideas with more

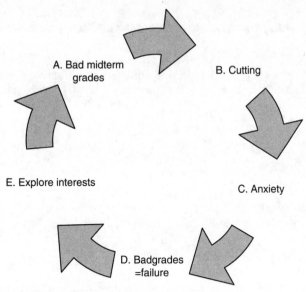

FIGURE 4.1 The ABCDEs of REBT in Terry's case.

rational beliefs. One way to accomplish these goals is to use the ABCDEs of REBT (Figure 4.1).

The letter *A* (Activating Event) represents the activating experience, the letter *B* (Belief) represents what the person believes about the experience, and the letter *C* (Consequence) refers to the subsequent emotional reaction or behavioral response to *B*. The letter *D* (Dispute) represents disputing irrational beliefs, and the letter *E* (Evaluation) refers to the development of a new response. Other specific techniques that may be used in REBT include humor, changing one's language, rational-emotive imagery, role playing, and other behavioral techniques.

The cognitive-behavioral counseling approaches have advantages from a cultural perspective. For example, in the process of identifying and understanding clients' values and beliefs, professional counselors are able to understand fully the clients' conflicting feelings. Also, the emphasis on cognition and behavior and relationship issues, and the structure provided can be beneficial for people from various populations. A limitation of these approaches exists when the professional counselor does not fully understand the cultural background of the client. It is important for professional counselors to proceed with sensitivity and caution when challenging beliefs, values, and ideas. As a brief review of the theoretical approaches described so far, complete Activity 4.4.

For more information on REBT, refer to the following resources:

Ellis, A. (1973). *Humanistic psychotherapy: The rational-emotive approach*. New York: Julian Press.

Ellis, A. (1994). *Reason and emotion in psychotherapy revised*. Secaucus, NJ: Birch Lane.

Ellis, A. (1996). *Better, deeper, and more enduring brief therapy: The rational emotive behavior therapy approach*. New York: Brunner/Mazel.

ACTIVITY 4.4

There are numerous action concepts and approaches in the first three paradigms discussed. Test your knowledge by matching the following theorists with the important concepts.

___ 1. Adler   a. wholeness

___ 2. Freud   b. social interest

___ 3. Meichenbaum   c. self-actualization

___ 4. Ellis   d. spiritual freedom and choice

___ 5. Frankl   e. interpretations of life events

___ 6. Perls   f. defense mechanisms

___ 7. Rogers   g. cognitive distortions

Family Systems Paradigm

In contrast to the counseling approaches discussed so far, the systems approach focuses on the interactive perspective or the communication patterns within the client's family system. In other words, the family provides the framework for understanding how the client behaves and functions in interpersonal relationships. There are many pioneers in family therapy; Murray Bowen developed one of the most comprehensive views of human behavior of any approach to family therapy. The essence of Bowen's model is **differentiation of self**, which is the ability to maintain one's individuality in the face of group influences—the pressures of a person's family (Nichols & Schwartz, 2005).

Bowen asserted that clients have less emotional autonomy than they imagine, and that clients are more dependent and reactive than we realize. Bowenian theory explains how the family, as a multigenerational structure of relationships, shapes the interaction of individuality and togetherness using six concepts: differentiation of self, triangles, emotional cutoff, nuclear family emotional process, multigenerational transmission process, and societal emotional process (Bowen, 1966, 1976).

Normal family development is thought to occur when anxiety is low, family members are well differentiated, and partners are emotionally sound with their families of origin. This becomes difficult as most people leave home during the adolescence-to-adulthood transformation. The result often is that adults react with adolescent sensitivity in their relationships with their parents and with others who interact in a way that is reminiscent of their parents (Nichols & Schwartz, 2005). This is evident in Terry's struggle to communicate her anxiety and pressure to her parents. Bowen states that individuals are likely to repeat problematic behaviors in their own families that have been passed down from past generations unless they explore and resolve these patterns (Kerr & Bowen, 1988).

To help family members identify intergenerational patterns, and to help members differentiate from one another, a professional counselor must remain calm, neutral, and objective, and be differentiated from his or her own family. A Bowenian counselor may work with all members of a family, although it is not necessary because it is believed that changing just one family member may have a direct impact on the entire family system. Specific techniques that may be used include genograms, asking questions, going home again, detri-angulation, person-to-person relationships, differentiation of self, coaching, and the "I-position" (Gladding, 2005; Nichols & Schwartz, 2005).

The **genogram** can be an appropriate tool for professional counselors to identify cul-tural aspects that influence family members' behaviors. Also, evidence suggests that differen-tiation can be applied to individuals from different backgrounds. In contrast, some concepts may be limited in their application to people from diverse backgrounds.

For more information regarding family systems counseling, refer to the following resources:

Bowen, M. (1972). *On the differentiation of self*. In J. Framo (Ed.), *Family interaction: A dialogue between family researchers and family therapists* (pp. 111–173). New York: Springer.

Bowen, M. (1976). *Theory in the practice of psychotherapy*. In P. J. Guerin Jr. (Ed.), *Family therapy: Theory and practice* (pp. 42-90). New York: Gardner Press.

Bowen, M. (1978). *Family therapy in clinical practice*. New York: Aronson.

Emergent Theories

The theories included in the previously discussed paradigms have the distinct quality of being supported and implemented over time. Theories take time to develop and become empirically validated for use in the profession. A fifth paradigm of counseling theory in-cludes the theories that are newer, or emerging, in the profession. Many can fall into this paradigm, including postmodernism (Hansen, 2006a), decisional counseling (Ivey & Ivey, 2007), motivational interviewing, brief and solution-focused counseling, narrative or constructivist approaches, and feminist counseling.

Some emergent theories were developed for specific purposes. For example, motiva-tional interviewing is an approach designed to work with individuals struggling with chem-ical dependency. Brief and solution-focused counseling provides a framework for working in a time-limited, perhaps managed care, counseling environment.

Many emergent theories have been criticized for lacking empirical evidence that the approach works. Some (e.g., feminist) have even been viewed as lacking specific techniques and being more of a philosophy. Hansen (2006b) has posited that it is some philosophical perspective that makes us most effective as professional counselors. Additionally, theories take time to develop. Professional counselors want to avoid the "conference syndrome" approach of applying any new theory they hear or read about in professional development opportunities.

Instead, we propose a more systematic approach to learning about newer theories as they are emerging, seeing what fits with one's personal style of counseling, and applying principles as opportunities arise and the theories become more solidified. For the purposes of this chapter, and to avoid overwhelming the reader, only four emergent theories in counseling are addressed: narrative, constructivist, feminist, and interpersonal counseling.

NARRATIVE THEORY   Terry has a story to tell. She has created a story about her life and present situation, one that she might say needs to be retold. The professional counselor can help Terry to see and create success by helping her to retell her story of wanting to fulfill parental expectations and continual concerns about measuring up to her potential into a story that more accurately fits her desires. Such is the nature of narrative counseling: help clients to retell the stories of their lives to create outcomes that better reflect what they would like to be (Monk, Winslade, Crocket, & Epston, 1997).

One way to conceptualize narrative counseling is to consider a book with many chapters. We can read a book and think we know how it will end in the final chapter. As a metaphor for our lives, we may be comfortable with the opening chapter and a few in between, but we may be dissatisfied with the contents of the book as a whole. Rather than looking to change the problems, a narrative approach suggests rewriting the chapters themselves to create a better perspective on the problems that lie therein. In essence, narrative counseling holds that we are the authors of our own lives (White & Epston, 1990).

Michael White and David Epston are the primary individuals associated with narrative counseling. The concepts of the theory are originally derived from family counseling. White and Epston drew from family therapy expert Gregory Bateson, who suggested that the means for change is to compare one set of events in time with another (White & Epston, 1990). In counseling practice, the goal of narrative counseling is to develop alternative stories for one's life. The counselor would help Terry identify what she would truly like her life to be like, evaluate the possibilities, and determine what must occur in the interim to make this story a reality. The counselor would want Terry to understand that she or her parents are not the problem; rather, the problem itself is the problem. Narrative counseling can assist Terry to shift her perspective of the problem and create a new outlook (story) for her life and circumstances.

The narrative counselor asks many investigative questions to understand what underlies the story and one's self-perception. Techniques used in narrative counseling are encompassed within this idea of questioning and investigating as it relates to retelling one's story. The narrative counselor helps to deconstruct problems, externalizing and separating them from the person and avoiding blame and self-recrimination (Monk et al., 1997). The professional counselor seeks exceptions to the story, times when the outcome of one's actions are inconsistent with what one says or does in the story. These exceptions are referred to as **sparkling moments**, the positive shifts that begin to occur when one can exert control over the problem and begin to create a new story (White & Epston, 1990).

The client and professional counselor work together "against" the problem to identify more favorable stories (Monk et al., 1997). From a cultural standpoint, narrative therapy is consistent with the storytelling nature of some ethnic populations. For example, the Chinese culture is built upon a series of stories handed down from generation to generation and appearing in the form of mythical beliefs. For individuals who come from cultures where storytelling is a part of their practice, narrative therapy can feel familiar and productive. The shift to identifying one's role in changing stories can be challenging, and the narrative counselor must exercise patience and caution to deconstruct problems and not beliefs.

Narrative theory tends to provide an overarching and organizing vision of the problem as separate from the person. This approach can be empowering and eye-opening. Narrative therapy requires a level of insight from the client to be able to tell and then retell the story.

For more information on narrative theory, refer to the following resources:

White, M. & Epston, D. (1989). *Literate means to therapeutic ends.* Adelaide, Australia: Dulwich Centre Publications.

White, M. & Epston, D. (1990). *Narrative means to therapeutic ends.* New York: W.W. Norton & Co.

CONSTRUCTIVIST THEORY   Is one person's perception of a problem another person's reality? How do we derive meaning from our lives, and how do we make sense of this reality? Constructivist theory, based upon the work of George Kelly's (1963) **personal constructs**, suggests that people create their own meaning and realities based upon personal experiences. Constructivism holds that we create our own meaning, and it is the job of the counselor to respect and work with that reality, not to contradict or deny it (Hansen, 2006a).

Terry believes that she must be a successful scientist to please her parents. She is operating under the belief system that success is equal to parental approval. She also believes that people should have personal responsibility for upholding the expectations of a culture. The constructivist counselor would see that Terry is operating under a set of personal constructs, or belief systems, that guide her actions and goals. Personal constructs, as defined by Kelly (1963), are self-beliefs. They guide us in determining the courses of action, the people with whom we associate, and the decisions we make about our own lives. The process of identifying and integrating these personal constructs is at the heart of constructivist counseling.

The constructivist counselor is inquisitive. Constructivism is often paired with narrative techniques such as storytelling and searching for alternative explanations to problems. The goal of constructivism is to create and construe personal reality actively through examination of personal constructs. The professional counselor and client work collaboratively to identify constructs and their origins. Often clients do not emerge with specific strategies to handle situations, but instead focus on personal learning and examination of how they are living authentic lives based on these identified constructs.

One specific technique that stands out from this theory is the use of a **card sort**. The card sort is a means of organizing beliefs into categories to help illustrate the organization of one's system of understanding and operating (Kelly, 1963). The constructivist counselor might help the client to develop a repertory test or grid to illustrate and organize belief systems. For example, Terry might be assisted to determine the major beliefs she has created about family, career, success, and failure. The professional counselor and Terry may identify the basic belief systems to explore further how they are operating in her interactions and decisions regarding her future. In doing so, Terry develops insight and explores the meaning she places on her constructs and the actions she is taking to find meaning in her life.

Similar to the narrative theory, constructivism requires significant insight and a higher level of processing than many traditional approaches. The theory may have limitations in its cross-cultural application in that some cultures expect adherence to their principles. Clients engaged in constructivist counseling are questioning and at times even challenging fundamental belief systems. In Terry's case, the exploration of personal constructs may reveal that culture is not as strong a belief to her as it is to her parents. This may contradict her culture's expectation of respect for parents and elders, and may challenge Terry in creating a new perspective of her situation. Conversely, proponents of constructivist counseling hold that the exploration of beliefs can be the ultimate goal of the theory and can work effectively with most cultures.

Resources for further reading about constructivist counseling include the following:

Kelly, G. A. (1955). *The psychology of personal constructs: A theory of personality*. New York: Norton.

Neimeyer, G. (1992). *Constructivist assessment: A casebook*. Newbury Park, CA: Sage.

FEMINIST COUNSELING   A feminist approach to counseling has been greatly criticized as challenging fundamental cultural beliefs. Feminist counselors operate from the basic philosophy of feminism, and support, respect, and highly value the role of culture in one's life.

The feminist philosophy espouses the equality and rights of women. The feminist movement began during the 1800s and abolition, wherein women were fighting for their voices to be heard (Wood, 2005). This movement continued through voting rights, suffrage, and what is more commonly perceived as the start of feminism, the women's rights movements of the 1960s. The principles of feminism held that women should be perceived as equals with men, have equal rights for employment and opportunities, be given certain inalienable rights to make their own choices, and essentially be treated with a fundamental human respect.

Because of this history, one often perceives feminist counseling as benefiting (or being provided by, for that matter) only women. Much of the literature regarding feminist counseling suggests a woman-centered focus. Chester and Bretherton (2001) identified six themes in feminist counseling from their research with practicing professional counselors: woman-centered, egalitarian, feminism as belief, feminism as action, critique of patriarchy, and a positive vision of the future. Gilbert and Scher (1999) further assert elements of feminist counseling to include empowerment, androgyny, and mutuality within the counseling relationship. The latter citation emphasizes the importance of equality in counseling and in one's life, and carries a more universal position that can benefit women and men. Gender sensitivity in counseling may be a more accurate (and perhaps more palatable) position in applying feminist principles in counseling (Bartholomew, 2003).

How feminist counseling appears to the observer seems to be more questionable. The fact that this approach is an application of feminist principles makes it difficult to identify key feminist counseling theorists. We may look to the work of Carol Gilligan, a preeminent theorist on women's development, Judith Jordan and her colleagues at the Stone Center, and others who all have had an important role in the creation and proliferation of feminist approaches to counseling. The feminist counselor values the female as well the male perspective—ideally the role of gender in our lives (Bartholomew, 2003).

A **gender role analysis** is one of the primary techniques used from this perspective. The gender role analysis is a means of examining with clients messages they received about what it means to be male or female, where these messages are derived, and how they have been employed and are affecting one's functioning (Bartholomew, 2003). Gender role analysis may address another important principle of feminist counseling: **androgyny**.

Based on the pioneering work of Sandra Bem (1981), androgyny challenges the traditional gender roles for men and women. Androgyny suggests that we should value individual characteristics for what they are, regardless of a predefined category. Professional counselors addressing androgyny see that stereotypically masculine and feminine roles are valuable within each individual. A woman who is more aggressive in the workplace and athletic with her peers may also be very sensitive and caring with her partner. Feminist counselors employ gender role analysis to examine these roles and to help the individual put them in an historical and societal context (Hoffman, 2001). The client is helped to see that all of these attributes create her uniqueness. It is often society's views that perpetuate her beliefs that she is somehow aberrant or unacceptable (Chester & Bretherton, 2001). Feminist counseling addresses the societal perceptions and the means by which the individual can take action to implement change. This sociocultural perspective and action as well as a degree of assertiveness are the goals of feminist counseling.

The sociocultural history and viewpoint of feminism contribute to the multicultural sensitivity of this approach in counseling. Feminism has a rich history of working toward equality. Pioneers such as bell hooks and Alice Walker in the 1970s addressed the concern that feminism addressed the concerns of only White, upper-class women (Wood, 2005).

Current feminist movements emphasize and work toward the equal rights of all, including issues of gender, race, ethnicity, and other cultural variables.

Challenges with the feminist theory may be the push for political action. Critics argue that suggesting individuals must see personal issues as political and engage in social change imposes the professional counselor's values, which may be inconsistent with one's cultural beliefs. We instead argue that feminist counselors simply suggest the societal context of issues and explore what, if any, role they would like to have to shape the understanding of one's issues from a broader perspective.

Terry's case is an example of the cultural context and challenges from a feminist perspective. Terry is attempting to fulfill her parents' wishes for her success, a message that may suggest cultural values of parental respect and collectivism. We might also wonder about messages she received about what it means to be female in her culture and in her family. Are there expectations that she will unquestioningly accept her role as a daughter and follow her parents' career aspirations for her? Terry's pursuit of a career in science is nontraditional for women in the United States (even in the 21st century). From a feminist counseling perspective, our gender role analysis might include an exploration of Terry's role in a predominantly male field. This is completed without bias or suggestion that she must stay in or leave the profession. Instead, there is an exploration of what this means to Terry in terms of being female and her identity as a whole. In other words, how does Terry perceive herself and her presenting concern through a gendered lens?

Additional resources regarding feminist counseling include:

> Bem, S. L. (1993). *The lenses of gender.* New Haven, CT: Yale University Press.
> Brown, L. S. (1994). *Subversive dialogues: Theory in feminist therapy.* New York: Basic Books.
> Enns, C. Z. (1997). *Feminist theories and feminist psychotherapies: Origins, themes, and variations.* New York: Haworth.

INTERPERSONAL PSYCHOTHERAPY   Interpersonal psychotherapy (IPT), originally developed for adults with depression, is time-limited and specifically focuses on interpersonal relationships. Goals of IPT include helping clients improve their relationships or their expectations about them, and helping clients improve their social support systems to alleviate their presenting distress. For IPT, the view of human nature is based on the assertion that psychological symptoms are connected to interpersonal distress (Stuart & Robertson, 2003). This approach is derived from three theories: (1) attachment theory, (2) communication theory, and (3) social theory.

Attachment theory is based on the premise that individuals have the intrinsic drive to form interpersonal relationships, a result of the need for reassurance and the desire to be loved. Attachment theory describes the way individuals form, maintain, and end relationships, and hypothesizes that distress occurs as a result of disruptions in an individual's attachment with others. Problem areas specifically addressed by IPT include interpersonal disputes, role transitions, and grief and loss.

While the attachment theory is useful in understanding the more broad, or "macro," social context, the **communication theory** works on a "micro" level, describing the specific ways in which individuals communicate their attachment needs to significant others. In other words, maladaptive attachment styles lead to specific ineffective communications. The result is that the individual's attachment needs are not met.

Social theory contributes to IPT by placing emphasis on interpersonal factors and how those factors contribute to depression or anxiety. One's social support system may be disturbed as a result of an individual's maladaptive response to a particular life event. The level of social support one has directly influences how one handles interpersonal stress. Social theory hypothesizes that poor social support is a fundamental factor in the development of psychological distress (Stuart & Robertson, 2003).

There are three main goals of counseling for IPT: (1) relieving the client's disturbing psychological symptoms; (2) examination of conflict, loss, and transition in the client's relationships; and (3) establishing the client's needs to aid in more effective use of his or her social support system. In contrast to CBT, where the focus is on the client's internal cognitions, IPT focuses on interpersonal communication. Where IPT may focus on cognitions, they are not the primary targets. Likewise, CBT and the other theories of counseling may touch on interpersonal issues, but they are not the focus.

In contrast to analytically oriented theories, which tend to focus on early life experiences in relation to current psychological distress, IPT has a present, here-and-now focus that helps the client improve the current communication and social support systems. In light of its time-limited approach and its here-and-now focus, IPT aims to resolve psychological distress and improve interpersonal communication, rather than to change the underlying cognitions.

The IPT counselor uses the client-counselor relationship to develop insight into the client's interpersonal functioning and to assess the client's attachment style. In the case of Terry, the professional counselor first would need to establish a therapeutic alliance with her to understand her experiences with school and the pressure from her parents. Together, the counselor and Terry would examine Terry's communication patterns and her social support system. What does Terry need to improve her here-and-now interpersonal relationships to build a more effective social support system? What about Terry's attachment style or communication patterns with her parents need to be addressed?

Common techniques of IPT include establishing a therapeutic alliance, communication analysis, describing interpersonal incidents, using content and process affect, and role playing. Because IPT has a solid theoretical foundation and a solid structure, it can be useful for clients from diverse backgrounds. The process and content of IPT counseling is flexible and adaptable, and highlights the unique needs of individuals. IPT takes into account the components of several theoretical paradigms and creates a unique approach to address the individual needs of the client.

Consult the following resources for further reading on IPT:

Bowlby, J. (1969). *Attachment*. New York: Basic Books.

Kiesler, D. J. (1996). *Contemporary interpersonal theory and research: Personality, psychopathology, and psychotherapy*. New York: John Wiley & Sons.

Sullivan, H. S. (1953). *The interpersonal theory of psychiatry*. New York: Norton.

Weissman, M. M., Markowitz, J. C., & Kleman, G. L. (2000). *Comprehensive guide to interpersonal psychotherapy*. New York: Basic Books.

These discussions of the various counseling paradigms offer a sampling of the many theories that exist. The information provided can be very challenging to digest, and even more challenging to determine what fits you as a professional counselor. Now, complete Activities 4.5 through 4.7 to begin considering what you would do as a professional counselor and how that fits within the theoretical perspectives. The next section of this chapter addresses the means by which you can apply theory into your counseling practice.

ACTIVITY 4.5

Match the component with each of the emergent theories identified. Expand upon your understanding by applying concepts from Terry's case.

___ 1. Family systems   a. personal constructs
___ 2. Narrative   b. clients are more dependent and reactive than we realize
___ 3. Feminism   c. develop alternative stories for one's life
___ 4. Constructivism   d. highly value the role of culture in one's life
___ 5. Interpersonal theory   e. relationships are key to development and wellness

When considering Terry's case, what specific issues do each of these theories indicate?

ACTIVITY 4.6   HELPING SKILLS AND THEORETICAL PARADIGMS

Review the basic helping skills of counseling presented in Chapters 5 and 6 (e.g., empathy, active listening, reflection of feeling, paraphrasing, challenging, and confronting). How does each fit within the theoretical paradigms discussed? You will likely find that all helping skills have a place in all theories, with differing emphasis in each. Attend to your personal preference in using each skill. How do they fit with your early leanings toward the theories?

ACTIVITY 4.7

Review your previous perceptions of Terry's case. How do your beliefs about her situation and how *you* might approach counseling align with the counseling theory paradigms discussed in this section?

APPLYING THEORY TO PRACTICE

After reviewing the paradigms and considering culture, counselors must begin to apply theory into their counseling practice. As a beginning counselor, what are the critical components of your approach?

A means of organizing thoughts about theory selection is aligned with your basic beliefs about counseling. The elements of a theory highlight the specific and common factors, personal philosophy, and multicultural considerations discussed in this chapter. Consider each of the following elements in your theory development: view of human nature, goals of counseling, role of the professional counselor, and the techniques or approaches used.

View of Human Nature

How do people change? What motivates people to behave, think, and feel the ways that they do? What do you believe will best help someone grow and develop? These are important questions to ask yourself when considering your own **view of human nature**. The manner in which you believe individuals change will be directly related to the counseling theories to which you subscribe. For example, if you believe that personality is more or less fully constructed in childhood, and change can occur only through regression back to those times, you may be more suited to one of the psychodynamic theories. Conversely, if you believe people are self-determined and control their own destinies, a humanistic-existential approach may be a better match.

Regardless of varying beliefs about how people change, practitioners across settings can agree that change happens only when one is ready to engage in the process. The pioneering work of Prochaska and DiClemente (1982) proposed stages of the change process to explain the manner in which individuals move through changes in thought, behavior, or emotion. Their work originally studied smoking cessation in an adult population and has since been adapted to many issues and populations. Table 4.3 outlines Prochaska and DiClemente's five **stages of change** and how they might appear in counseling practice.

Goals of Counseling

A second important aspect in applying theory to practice is the perceived goals of counseling. Clients may enter counseling wanting immediate answers to difficult problems. We understand that as a profession we are not prone to give direct advice or be problem-solvers. Instead, we give individuals the tools to manage their own problems and to apply them in

TABLE 4.3 Stages of Change

Stage	Description	Application in Practice
Precontemplation	No intent to change	Identify problem as others have presented it to the individual; create ownership
	Unaware that problem exists	
Contemplation	Awareness of problems, but not yet committed to act to change	Weigh pros and cons of problem and solutions
Preparation	Intent and commitment to take action	Address fears, impact of possible change in life
Action	Modify behavior, experiences, or environment to overcome problems	Discuss experience of the change and subsequent feelings
		Consider means to sustain change
Maintenance	Prevent relapse and sustain gains achieved through change	Monitor and discuss new approach to problem

Adapted from "Transtheoretical Therapy: Toward a More Integrative Model of Change," by J. O. Prochaska and C. C. DiClemente, 1982, *Psychotherapy: Theory, Research and Practice, 20*, pp. 161–173.

future situations. An overarching goal of all counseling is to help individuals more effectively manage problems in everyday living.

At first glance, the identification of an overarching goal of counseling may seem to answer all of our questions about this subtopic. However, further examination shows that theories have different beliefs about what counseling should accomplish. Person-centered counselors believe counseling should result in greater self-awareness, behaviorists want to see physical evidence of change in actions, and REBT-oriented counselors assert that changes in thinking and behavior are the ultimate goals of the counseling experience. Your personal beliefs about what individuals should gain from their time in counseling will dictate your determination of approach.

A word of caution: Many new counselors jump to the conclusion that it is their role to determine specific goals for their clients. Specific goals, such as to stop smoking, build a healthy romantic relationship, stay out of prison, or get into college, must be established by the individual seeking counseling. Goal setting is a collaborative venture between professional counselors and clients. The emphasis on elements of goals and the manner in which counseling can assist in reaching them is determined by counselor orientation.

Role of the Professional Counselor

Relative activity or passivity as a professional counselor will help apply theory into practice. As you have read, theories differ in their perceptions of the roles professional counselors play in the therapeutic process. Whether one is collaborator, expert, equal, or indifferent, the role of the professional counselor differs across theories. We have also learnt that many theorists were most successful in being genuine and true to their own preferences for interactions with one another. The professional counselor's role must be consistent with the other elements of theory, and can in great part be determined by your personality and style of interaction. Some professional counselors teeter on the edge of offering advice, whereas others may utter only a few words throughout their time with clients.

Techniques and Approaches

Professional counselors entering the profession may be drawn to approaches that outline specific techniques to be used with clients. For this reason, we have seen many professional counselors begin with a cognitive-behavioral orientation and gradually shift to approaches that offer more flexibility in the process. This phenomenon may be due in part to the level of ambiguity we are willing to endure as we enter into new situations. So much of what we do as professional counselors does not contain a "how-to" manual. We do not have guidelines suggesting, for example, that if a client states his disdain for his mother, we should offer him the opportunity to role-play a preferred interaction with her. We must instead rely on what seems to be consistent with our beliefs about counseling as outlined in the other elements of theory selection.

Some theories are more heavily laden with techniques, whereas others are more amorphous in providing general guidelines about approaches. As you review the theories, what seems to stand out to you as most meaningful and effective? As you enter into the professional counselor role, what do you notice consistently about your approach? Are there certain techniques to which you are more drawn? Do you work more effectively when you can rely on a general approach and employ techniques as needed? Flexibility is a crucial quality of effective counseling. What works well in one counseling interaction may not in another.

Flexibility

Beginning to apply theory to practice requires contemplation of the aforementioned elements. Applying theory also requires flexibility. No two counseling interactions are alike. What works well with one individual may fall flat with another. As we will discuss shortly, few professional counselors operate from truly purist perspectives, and instead combine principles that fit best with their goals, beliefs, and desired roles in counseling. Selecting theory relies on a careful examination of your own personal style. The focus questions presented in Text box 4.2 are intended to assist you in beginning to consider your counseling style and application of theory. Then complete Activity 4.8.

BOX 4.2

Focus Questions on Theory Application

Answer the following questions as honestly as possible as they relate to each element of theoretical orientation. Consider your own beliefs and preferences as you answer the questions.

View of Human Nature
1. How do people change?
2. Are people able to change (self-determined), or is our destiny determined for us?
3. What motivates people to change?

Goals of Counseling
1. What are the common goals for all people in counseling?
2. What is the possibility of change as the result of counseling?
3. What can be reasonably accomplished in the context of counseling?

Role of the Professional Counselor
1. How do you perceive the relationship between professional counselor and client? Equals? Experts?

2. To what extent are you willing to let the client dictate the direction of the session, and to what extent do you believe the professional counselor should determine the focus?
3. To what degree should professional counselors provide guidance through personal disclosure and perspective?

Techniques and Approaches
1. What tools do you believe will be most helpful in communicating with clients?
2. Which basic counseling skills (i.e., reflecting feeling, challenging) are most appealing to you in counseling?
3. What do you believe would be most beneficial to you if a professional counselor was to help you with a present concern?

Review your answers to the above-listed questions, compare them with the information in Tables 4.1 and 4.2 to delineate which theories may be most appealing as you enter into your counseling practice.

ACTIVITY 4.8

Research a specific theory to discover the basic elements of the theory (e.g., the way of looking at human nature, techniques, goals). You may wish to begin your research with the references listed after each theory discussion in the chapter.
- What types of clients and presenting problems would most likely benefit from the use of this theory?
- For what types of clients and presenting problems would it be inappropriate?
- Would you use this theory? Explain.

THEORETICAL INTEGRATION

With so many sound theories from which to choose, it is challenging to select just one. Many professional counselors, as previously stated, rely on more than one theoretical perspective. **Theoretical integration** is the synthesis of the best aspects of several theories with the belief that doing so will produce richer and more meaningful outcomes (Bradley, Parr, & Gould, 1999). Professional counselors operating from an integrative perspective combine the best of what works for them with intentionality. While employing diverse perspectives and techniques, the integrative counselor holds fast to one underlying, foundational theoretical orientation. For example, we might at our core believe and operate from the existential standpoint of finding meaning in life and searching for ultimate existence. Yet working with adolescents in an alcohol treatment facility might require that we employ person-centered techniques to build rapport and behavioral techniques to demonstrate change required for discharge. At our core, however, remains the fundamental belief system of existentialism, which guides the use of supplemental approaches.

Integrative Versus Eclectic Counseling

We are intentional in differentiating integrative and eclectic modes of counseling. **Eclecticism**, in contrast to theoretical integration, is more haphazard in nature. The eclectic counselor is a technical expert, relying on knowledge of approaches and applying what seems to fit at a given time. Eclectic counselors select approaches based on client presenting issues and symptoms. There is a lack of a unified or guiding theory for the professional counselor employing this approach. In many ways, eclecticism feels safe for beginning counselors who feel that they are "flying by the seat of their pants" every time they are faced with a new client and presenting issue. While tempting, always consider more fully what you believe about counseling and use that as your guide.

Why an Integrative Approach?

With the myriad research to demonstrate best practices in counseling, there is ironically a lack of consensus on a single most effective theory. Professional counselors rely instead on the "it depends" mentality of counseling. Not to be confused with eclecticism, theoretical integration offers the professional counselor flexibility in working with various issues and presenting concerns. There exists a level of multicultural responsibility to meet clients where they are when they enter counseling. Also, you must be sure that what you do matches what clients need. Professional counselors can remain authentic in so doing, as the application of elements of theories will differ based upon one's underlying belief systems.

One must also acknowledge the limitations of a purist approach. As discussed earlier, professional counselors work in settings with specific requirements for their clients. For example, community mental health often requires that individuals reach counseling goals and implement change within a shorter time. How is a psychodynamically oriented counselor to work under such managed care dictates? One answer may be simply to maintain the fundamental principles of psychodynamic approaches in selecting cognitive-behavioral strategies to employ in practice. In a school setting, which often offers even more limited time for individual counseling, existentially oriented counselors can help youth explore what is most meaningful in their lives by challenging them to face issues and work in the present-focused framework of reality therapy or gestalt theory.

Being an integrative counselor requires you to be a knowledgeable counselor. Knowledge of the many theories, or at minimum the paradigms, is required to determine consistency in applying varying techniques to support one's foundation. Additionally, exploring one's own beliefs about counseling, as in the previous section, builds a better foundation on which to add supporting approaches. Counseling is a profession valued for flexibility and ability to see multiple dimensions of a problem. Professional counselors must put this in practice by employing what works best to meet a client's needs. Complete Activity 4.9 to explore your personal integrated approach to counseling.

ACTIVITY 4.9   MY INTEGRATED ORIENTATION

Using the figure shown, indicate the various theories you believe will be part of your integrated style of counseling. Consider not only which theories appeal to you for their consistency in beliefs, but also how they will be used. For example, what do you assume to be your core, guiding theory? On what part of the figure do you identify the core? As a humanistically oriented counselor, I (D.H.L.) would identify my core of existentialism at the midsection, or belly, of the figure because I operate from my "gut" in counseling. I tend to "use my hands" as a counselor and supplement my work with approaches in person-centered and CBT. Of course, your integration must be consistent. It would not work well to have a core existential approach and supplement with psychodynamic eyes because of the very different philosophies of these two theories. Place your own core theory at your own identified core on the figure. We have started our own visual depiction of our integrated orientation to help you begin.

Core: Belly; Theory: Existential
Tools: Hands; Person-centered, CBT

My Integrated Theory

As you complete and review your integrated theory, provide a rationale for how these different theories work well together. How do their philosophies complement one another? How is the overall approach depicted here consistent with your own personal beliefs? Your beginning beliefs about the counseling process and change?

Summary

Determining a counseling theory is an involved and lengthy process. The five paradigms discussed here are a starting point to learn more about the counseling theories as you enter into practice. Before foreclosing on a specific theory, we strongly encourage beginning counselors to reflect upon their beliefs about themselves, human nature, and counseling. Aside from the ethical and professional responsibilities for using theory in practice, understanding how counseling works will better prepare you to help clients. A unique perspective on your client's issues that is embedded in your beliefs about how people change and develop will enable you to select appropriate interventions to assist clients to reach their goals. An intentional counselor is a successful counselor, employing a unique integration of personal characteristics and counseling theories.

Answer Key

Activity 4.4   1. b, 2. f, 3. g, 4. e, 5. d, 6. a, 7. c.
Activity 4.5   1. b, 2. c, 3. d, 4. a, 5. e.

To help further your understanding of some of the topics in this chapter, go to MyHelpingLab at the Pearson.com website and view the following video clips:

- Psychodynamic: *Theories of Counseling and Psychotherapy,* Module 3 (Adlerian Therapy, "Using Early Recollections" and "Using Interpretation in Reorientation Stage").
- Humanistic-Existential: *Theories of Counseling and Psychotherapy,* Module 8 (Existential-Humanistic Therapy, "The Power of Listening and Questioning") and Module 1 (Person-Centered Therapy, "An Example of Immediacy").
- Behavioral-Cognitive Behavioral Approaches: *Theories of Counseling and Psychotherapy,* Module 4 (Reality Therapy, "Systemic Planning Through Contracting") and Module 5 (Cognitive Behavioral Therapy, "Connecting Thoughts to Behaviors and Feelings" and "Helping Clients Become More Assertive").
- Family Systems Therapy: *Theories of Counseling and Psychotherapy,* Module 10 (Family Systems Therapy, "Validating a Client's Decisions and Strengths" and "Exploring a Client's Family of Origin"). *Skills/Processes/Techniques,* Module 9 (Systemic and Psycho-Educational Interventions, "Establishing Family Boundaries and Roles" and "Exploring Alliances with Structural Interventions").
- Emergent Theories: *Theories of Counseling and Psychotherapy,* Module 9 (Solution Focused Therapy, "Finding Strength in 'Exceptions'" and "Using a 'Scaling Question'").
- Theoretical Integration: Why an Integrative Approach? *Theories of Counseling and Psychotherapy,* Module 11 (Integrative Therapy, "Delving into Multi-Sensory Experiences" and "Becoming Aware of Behaviors and Emotions").

5

The Counseling Process

DONNA STARKEY SHEPERIS AND CYRUS MARCELLUS ELLIS

PREVIEW

The counseling process embodies the art and science of helping. The client makes the decision to receive services, creating an opportunity for the counseling relationship to begin. Professional counselors bring their training, experience, and personality into the process. Once initiated, counseling occurs over a series of stages that include information gathering, application of theory to generate relevant goals, treatment, assessment, and termination. Students beginning the path to becoming a counselor are encouraged to consider their fit with the process and profession of counseling.

THE PROFESSIONAL COUNSELOR

The profession of counseling provides clients opportunities for healing with a focus on client autonomy and empowerment. Counseling opportunities occur over a range of settings including private practices, schools, and community agencies. As counselors in training, you have probably tried to envision what it will be like to work with clients. Regardless of the setting, the counselor and client develop a powerful relationship to facilitate change. Professional counselors put forth diligent effort to enter this profession, and we recognize that there are some unique dimensions of being a professional counselor that are directly related to effectiveness and the counseling environment. To become an effective professional counselor, we must examine the nature of being a professional counselor as well as some of the important factors of the therapeutic relationship.

Students enter graduate programs in an effort to secure a degree in counseling. Students must do more than reach degree status to practice the profession of counseling; they must truly *become* a counselor. Professional counselors are in a unique position to engage in the powerful process of healing with clients. Professional counselors establish intense relationships with clients willing to become vulnerable in their presence. The prominent dimensions of counseling, established by theory, research, and practice, are the aspects of *becoming* a counselor that are aspired to by students entering graduate programs. All of us have personality characteristics that will influence our counseling. How does one embody the role of the professional counselor?

One of the most significant factors affecting the lives of clients is the makeup of the professional counselor. The professional counselor is central to the counseling process. The professional counselor works with the tools of the profession in the same manner that a surgeon uses medical tools. Counseling theories and techniques are instruments that anyone can read about just as medical tools are instruments that anyone can hold. However, skilled surgeons can use these instruments in ways that individuals without training and discipline cannot; likewise, skilled professional counselors can use their training and discipline in a way that untrained individuals cannot. Activity 5.1 provides an opportunity to consider your fit with the profession of counseling.

ACTIVITY 5.1

Consider what you bring to the role of the professional counselor. You have an initial session with a client. Complete your client's sentence "I just left my new counselor's office. My counselor is _____ and I know I will benefit because _____."

The professional counselor is a special individual who recognizes the need to shape academic training and skills into a fine instrument. The skilled professional counselor is composed of an active placebo and specific counselor characteristics (Kottler, 2003), cross-cultural counseling skills, and a basic counselor paradigm (Hackney, 2001).

Active Placebo and Counselor Characteristics

Kottler (2003) described the notion of there being an **active placebo** at work for professional counselors. The active placebo concept refers to the fact that counselor and client expectations play a major role in the helping process—as large as the actual theories and techniques used in the helping process. Kottler recognized that there are four things that assist professional counselors in their attempt to intervene in the lives of clients. The professional counselor's dress, manner, setting, and style of helping are present in interactions with the public, and if these match the client expectations of what a professional counselor *is,* clients begin to believe that counseling may work for them.

Counselors in training who arrive at this understanding recognize that the active placebo is at work during every moment of their professional lives. In fact, it ought to shape the way in which you conduct your practice, the way in which you are seen by the public, and the manner by which you approach clients and their counseling needs, as well as the way in which you establish your counseling environment.

The active placebo is influenced by more than the explicit expectations of the relationship. Multicultural considerations play essential roles in our personal relationships with others. These considerations are present in the professional counseling relationship as well. Consider your style of relating to others, especially when you meet someone new. Do you tend to be gregarious or reserved? Do you tend to be assertive or deferential? What differences do you notice in your interactions with individuals of the same gender and with individuals of the opposite gender? It is likely that your responses to these questions are influenced, in part, by cultural dynamics.

Much of our personal style of interaction is known to us, that is, we are aware of how we are received by those we meet. However, all of us have blind spots. We are not always aware of our mannerisms and styles of relating that draw others toward us or that may be off-putting to others. Now is the time in your professional development to gather information about your relationship style. Complete Activity 5.2 to explore the active placebo and your relational style.

ACTIVITY 5.2   ACTIVE PLACEBO EXERCISE

Write down how you currently approach personal and professional activities. Do you have a particular manner when interacting with others on a personal level and on a professional level? Explain.

Ask a classmate to comment on your manner in class and other aspects of your behavior.

What do you need to develop an active placebo that would have the public acknowledge that you represent the counseling profession?

Counselor characteristics are also an important part of the therapeutic dynamic. **Counselor characteristics** refer to the personality and the approach of the counselor. Kottler (2003) stated that the professional counselor must to be "vibrant, inspirational, and charismatic" as well as "sincere, loving, and nurturing" and "wise, confident, and self-disciplined" (p. 3). These personal characteristics are essential to motivate and connect with clients struggling with issues ranging from developmental problems to multiple levels of dysfunctional coping mechanisms. Take a minute to consider your own personality and characteristics that will influence your work as a counselor by reading Reflection 5.1 and then completing Activity 5.3.

REFLECTION 5.1

Counseling is heavily influenced by the personal characteristics of the counselor. What traits and skills do you possess that will make you an effective professional counselor?

ACTIVITY 5.3   COUNSELING CHARACTERISTICS EXERCISE

Consider Kottler's list of essential counselor characteristics. Think about your life and describe a time when you have been:

Vibrant
Inspirational
Charismatic
Sincere
Loving
Nurturing
Wise
Confident
Self-disciplined

Cross-Cultural Counseling Competence

Cross-cultural counseling competence is an essential ingredient in counselor preparation. At its very essence, every counseling interaction is cross-cultural in nature. Two (or more) unique individuals enter into the counseling relationship with their own cultural perspectives and experiences. The relationship these individuals create is independent of previous relationships, yet will be influenced by those previous relationships. Some of this impact is discussed later in terms of transference and countertransference. At its most basic level, each counselor-client dynamic is a culture unique unto itself.

Counselors in training prepare for the multicultural practice of professional counseling. Graduate programs may emphasize student understanding of diverse cultures through stand-alone multicultural courses, or programs may infuse multiculturalism throughout the curriculum. Murphy and Dillon (2008) suggest three guidelines for multicultural best practice based on their understanding of the multicultural literature:

1. As clinicians, we need to be aware of our own ethnic, gender, and cultural heritage.
2. We need to acquire knowledge about the cultures and customs of the clients with whom we work.
3. We need to use this self-awareness and knowledge to devise flexible strategies for intervention that are effective and congruent with our client's values (pp. 39–40).

We all have a diverse collection of thoughts and feelings that are not homogeneous to people who may closely match our own racial, class, gender, or ethnic makeup. Each individual brings a lifetime of perceptions and apperceptions that affect each other in the counseling process. This impact, which defines the multicultural dynamic of the relationship, serves to help or hinder the counseling relationship. Your job as counselor is to assess continually the relationship between what is going on in the client's life, in the session, or in your response to the client and the cultural forces at play. Activities 5.4 and 5.5 provide cross-cultural exercises to sensitize you to the power of descriptive labels.

ACTIVITY 5.4   CROSS-CULTURAL EXERCISE

Make a list of words that you have used and that you have heard to describe people who are racially and ethnically similar to you. Then make a list of words you are familiar with that describe people who are different from you, including members of a different gender and socioeconomic class.

Which words do you perceive as coming from feelings of fear, anger, or anxiety? Which words indicate solidarity, understanding, and social justice?

How can you put more words to work in your counselor training that build connections with people who are different from you?

ACTIVITY 5.5   CROSS-CULTURAL EXERCISE: YOUR PERSONAL CULTURAL FRAME OF REFERENCE

You have listed words that generally relate to people similar to and different from you. Now take a moment to consider how you are unique. How do you define your own culture? Consider your demographic factors and the type of family in which you were raised, your current relationships and lifestyle, and characteristics unique to where you live. Write a one-page description of the unique culture that defines you.

Basic Counseling Paradigm

Ultimately, the journey of discovery leads each professional counselor to an end result, the establishment of his or her own **basic counseling paradigm**. A basic counseling paradigm is the manner by which the professional counselor can understand the human condition in all of its various forms. A view of the basic counseling paradigm of the profession has been proposed by Harold Hackney (2001), who recognized that professional counselors work within the role of human growth and development. We serve as the experts on how people may need prevention-based services (e.g., drug prevention, relationship training, premarital counseling) as well as remediation services (e.g., recovery counseling, couples counseling, anger management counseling) across the lifespan.

Hackney's view serves as a foundation for recognition that our theories, techniques, and interventions are guided by the notion that humans have the capacity to live functional lives, but occasionally may need additional coping skills to address particular aspects of their lives. It is important that as a counselor, you formalize your thoughts on the nature of change. What causes client problems, and how are people best helped? Use Activity 5.6 to begin this thought process.

ACTIVITY 5.6   BASIC COUNSELING PARADIGM EXERCISE

Explain how people become healthy, unhealthy, and in need of assistance. How do people get better? Is it because of their thoughts, feelings, relationships, behaviors, or some combination? Explain.

Match your thoughts to how general counseling theories propose people are healthy or unhealthy. What does this say about how your understanding of the human condition is developing?

THE HELPING PROCESS—THE HELPING RELATIONSHIP

What do you think it means to be a helper? Many of us become counselors because of the desire to help others. Perhaps we were helped by someone over the course of our lives, and that has inspired us to become helpers as well. If you have ever received help at a difficult time in your life, or if you have ever given help to someone at a difficult time, you may recognize that the match in relationship between the one giving help and the one receiving help is instrumental. It is this helping relationship that serves as a focal point for counselors in training. It is likely that at some point in your own life you have experienced the benefit of change. For Reflection 5.2, consider change in light of your personal circumstances.

REFLECTION 5.2

Reflect upon a time when you developed awareness or insight that precipitated change in your life. What were the motivating circumstances? What support structures and challenges were in place?

Sharfstein (2005), in a commentary on the power of healing through relationships, recognized that people with serious mental health issues can be assisted through the power of relationships. Sharfstein ended his commentary by recognizing that, "relationships, love, [and] connectedness is what makes life worth living" (p. 213). Sharfstein's commentary is important as we discuss the helping relationship. Professional counselors can get so wrapped up in professional functions such as crisis work, treatment planning, and client stabilization that they forget that many clients are seeking some sort of connection with another human being. In the healing process, clients seek to feel joined with and part of the world around them. What has drawn you to this profession of healing? Take a moment to reflect on your desire to help by engaging in Reflection 5.3.

REFLECTION 5.3

Why do you want to help people? What experiences have you had helping others? What experiences have you had being helped?

Art of Helping

Professional counselors have been trained in the **art of helping** and are able to recognize issues in clients that are detrimental to their overall well-being (Carlson & Ellis, 2004). As you continue your professional growth toward being a full-fledged member of the counseling profession, it is important that you recognize some key dimensions of being a helper to individuals in need of help.

So let's revisit the question, what do you think it means to be a helper? For some, being a helper means that you are a benevolent person who works very hard to provide assistance to people who may need clothing, food, or shelter. For others, it may mean that you take care of people who need help because it comes easy to you. You may extend yourself to others who may need money or someone to talk to when they are expressing difficult personal issues.

For many of us at the beginning of our training, the ability to help others may be the motivating force that supports our decision to become professional counselors. Many of us were helpers all of our lives. We may have helped our parents, our siblings, other family members, and, most especially, we may have been the "counselor" for our friends throughout junior high and high school. When you sit and reflect on why you would open your own emotional well-being to another's struggle, discomfort, and personal pain, is your answer, "I want to help"? Herein lies the doorway into the art of helping—determining why you want to be a helper, and why you want to study how to become a helper.

As a helper intent on practicing the art of counseling, here are some questions for you to reflect on as you approach your training: (a) What does it mean to be a good helper? (b) What would I have to gain from my training to understand the process of helping? (c) What do I bring to my counselor training that will allow me to be a good helper? (d) What parts of my being can get in the way of being a good helper?

These questions mirror comments from Kottler (2003), who recognized that the art of helping others comes from our ability to be in touch with our passion and desire to be in a relationship with another human being. The art of helping others lies within our ability to form a relationship with another human being because we have made a commitment to self, an examination of personal motives for wanting to help others, and a realization that the helping process involves being present and attentive to clients through a variety of clinical approaches and techniques. Kottler stated that professional counselors are people who possess unique characteristics, such as being a vibrant, inspirational, charismatic, loving individual able to be present and available for clients. There is debate within the counseling community on whether we are **scientist-practitioners** or practitioner-scientists (Borders & Bloss, 1994). Does research drive our interventions with clients? Isn't research itself driven by practice? The answer to both of these questions is yes; this is a profession that requires the interplay of art and science. We have explored what it means to be an artist within the counseling profession. What about science?

Helping as a Science

Early on, Haring-Hidore and Vacc (1988) explained the essence of the science of helping for professional counselors. In your introductory course, your professor may cover many of the eight core areas specified by the Council for Accreditation of Counseling and Related Educational Programs (CACREP), one of which is research. When you speak of research, you are speaking of the scientific method, or science. All professional counselors, regardless of specialty area, should use scientific methodology to make practice-based decisions. The American Counseling Association *Code of Ethics* (American Counseling Association, 2005) tells us that we must use evidenced-based practices as professional counselors.

In other words, as counselors, we use scientifically validated methods, tools, and techniques in our work with clients. The science of counseling means that we make treatment decisions that are informed by research and best practices. We learn much of the science of counseling in our graduate programs, but continue to be consumers of research through journals, workshops, and continuing education opportunities to ensure that we stay abreast of the current trends.

The **science of helping** relies upon professional counselors becoming end users of research findings that address assessment and treatment techniques. We recognize that our ability to replicate effective practices comes from our ability to evaluate the effectiveness of treatment protocols because we have learned how to evaluate the methods used by our colleagues in their research. Although most of us will conduct less research and provide more direct services for individuals with addiction, emotional, behavioral, and personal disorders, we are still consumers of research. The outcome data provided by researchers serve as a launching pad for effective interventions and assist us in avoiding methods and techniques that do not facilitate the counseling process.

Haring-Hidore and Vacc (1988) recognized the fact that if we are the end users of research, we must be skilled in the abilities that allow us to digest the results and conclusions of research. Does that mean you have to take a course in statistics? Yes, you do! Does that mean you have to take a course in research? Yes, it does! It is important that you have the skills necessary for working with research findings so that as a practitioner, you can close the divide between research and practice (Crane, Wampler, Sprenkle, Sandberg, & Hovestadt, 2002).

Crane and colleagues recognized that we are not trying to avoid the humanistic qualities of therapy by conducting research. Instead, we must sustain and maintain the emerging clinician's ability to think critically and develop sound procedures for the evaluation of our work, while integrating these findings into our work so that professional practice can be advanced. Advancing the profession means that we understand how the human condition manifests and how to remediate client maladaptive coping mechanisms through sound scientific practices.

A form of research often used in counseling settings is action research. **Action research** is a practical research approach intended to collect information, address a specific problem, and generate solutions. It informs best-practice decisions for counselors and is one method of helping us discover what is working with our clients. By its nature, action research is responsive to a particular need or situation. For example, a counselor in a school may be interested in the perceptions of the teachers she works with on her role as a school counselor. She may survey the teachers to determine if their perceptions match her true job duties. If they do not, she may find herself better able to communicate her role to her colleagues and improve the working relationship. As you read Reflection 5.4, what are the thoughts and feelings you have about research?

REFLECTION 5.4

How do you feel about reading and conducting research? If you could conduct a research study that would answer a burning question you have about counseling, what question would you want answered?

As practitioners, we understand the art and science of counseling. We appreciate the role of theory, and apply current research to our treatment models to serve our clients best. As professional counselors, our goal is to create an environment conducive to client change. What becomes equally important is what actually brings a client in to begin the counseling process.

WHAT BRINGS CLIENTS TO COUNSELING?

As we grow as professional counselors, we think about our practice in various ways. We wonder what our challenges will be. We wonder what opportunities will arise. We wonder where we will work and what our clients will be like. One primary question is: What brings clients to counseling?

Clients enter into counseling to address a host of concerns. A consequence of being a complex human being includes facing the challenges of living, many of which may cause us to have a need for a professional counselor. Not only does life possess the potential for all of us to find our way to a professional counselor, but when we add the additional dimensions of racism, classism, gender inequities, ability differences, ageism, intolerance of differing sexual issues, medical difficulties, lack of individual value, unfulfilling jobs, poor relationships, death, fear, lack of love, and poverty, we may want to ask: Why aren't more people seeking out professional counselors on a daily basis?

Facing the pressures of life and the many conditions that living can uncover in anyone, it becomes clear that the inability to cope with life is the driving force for someone to seek counseling. When clients' temporary fixes fail, and their inability to cope becomes apparent (e.g., too much sex; abusing alcohol; too much smoking; avoidance of issues;

isolation; continuous crying, never crying, too much spending; losing their car, house, job), they make a decision whether or not they will call or ask for a referral for counseling. You will likely help many different types of clients, and some client types will be specialty areas for you. Use Activity 5.7 to consider the client populations you are currently drawn to serve.

ACTIVITY 5.7   HELPER EXERCISE

Write down the types (e.g., populations) of clients you would like to specialize in helping as a professional counselor. What makes you want to help each population? What would you receive from helping such people?

Write down whom (e.g., types, populations) you would not want to help. What makes these groups of people outside of your reach when it comes to providing help? What are the reasons that you give yourself when no one is around for not wanting to help a particular group of people? How does this work with or against your active placebo, counselor characteristics, or view of the human condition?

It can easily be assumed by counselors in training that clients recognize their issues and then sit down with a host of options before them to select a professional counselor. It may also be assumed that clients have the ability to call their HMO or other medical plan and ask for a referral and make their initial appointment and then meet the professional counselor and begin treatment. Certainly there are cases where clients recognize their need for assistance and seek out and select their professional counselor without much delay or hesitation. For the most part, however, potential clients have a hard time requesting help and go through various steps when making the decision to seek counseling.

Although counseling is a necessary service and is generally supported by the community, many potential clients still feel a sense of shame or weakness when thinking of coming to a professional counselor (Sheu & Sedlacek, 2002). Across gender, race, and cultural lines, going to a professional counselor can be viewed as a failure, not manly, reserved for the weak-minded, or a place where only women go to work out their problems.

Potential clients also attempt to answer their own questions about the benefits of going to a professional counselor based on what they have heard (apperceptions), what they believe about professional counselors (connotations), and, for some, their past experiences with professional counselors (perceptions). Additionally, real life makes it hard for potential clients to come into counseling. People may think that a time of distress and maladaptive coping is not a good time to enter into counseling. Clients may believe that, because of life events, "I don't have time for counseling!"

Although we are trained to think that opting for counseling can be a liberating experience, many people see appointments and intake requirements as an additional hardship that they may be better off not incorporating into their hectic lives. All of these dimensions of a person's life provoke potential clients to sift through their fears and doubts about counseling to make a decision to make an appointment and seek help. It is important to address the fact that we *are* our clients. As humans first, and professional counselors second, we are no more immune to these life challenges than are the individuals who seek our services. In fact, most professional counselors would argue that receiving counseling is a prerequisite for providing counseling because it helps us to empathize with the client role. To increase your empathy further, consider the following questions:

1. *Could you give up two and a half hours each week for 15 weeks?* (Counseling is more than the 50-minute session; you must travel there and back, fill out paperwork, and see additional people.)
2. *If you were to see a professional counselor, would you have to miss work?*
3. *Would you have to attempt to move your schedule around?*
4. *Would you have to worry about people knowing where you are going?*
5. *If you are a graduate student going to school at night and have family responsibilities, who would take care of those issues while you were going to your counseling appointments?*

These are just some of the questions going through the minds of potential clients. While there is some variability with the kind of answers that could be given, these are concerns that our potential clients struggle with when trying to decide if they will enter into a counseling relationship. Once committed, they can begin the process of counseling. What would it take for you to enter (or re-enter) counseling? Use Activity 5.8 to consider your relationship with counseling.

ACTIVITY 5.8   THE "WHAT BRINGS YOU TO COUNSELING?" EXERCISE

List three experiences in your life that were or could have been addressed in counseling. What led you to seek counseling or kept you from seeking counseling in those situations?
    If you were going to a counseling session today, what would you want to address?
    Think about a time when you have been frustrated about something. What did you want from the people you talked to about the frustration? How does it feel when others to tell you what you need to think, feel, or do when you are frustrated?

Theorists over the years have considered counseling as a process that occurs in stages. To facilitate an understanding of the counseling process, these stages are discussed in terms of the elements inherent in initiating the relationship, exploring and working together, and integration and termination.

INITIATING COUNSELING

Initiating counseling sets the tone for the working relationship between the client and the professional counselor. During this initial stage, the professional counselor makes a personal connection with the client, defines the process of counseling, and makes a plan for working together. A primary goal at this stage is to create a climate for change. This climate is affected by numerous variables including the setting and structure of counseling. Initiating counseling provides a foundation for establishing the helping relationship necessary to affect change.

Counseling Environment

Counseling occurs in schools, community agencies, organizations, colleges, private practices, and other environments conducive to establishing a helping relationship and providing services. The **counseling environment** refers to the combination of external physical conditions and counselor characteristics that affect the growth and development of clients (Ellis, 2004). The concept of the counseling environment reveals the importance of establishing a safe arena for counseling. Professional counselors are responsible for creating an accepting environment, both physically and interpersonally, that is as free from anxiety and distraction as possible. Counseling generally is most successful in situations that afford the client privacy and offer a setting conducive to intimate conversations. While the physical environment is important, effective counseling requires interpersonal skills. The initial appointment provides the opportunity for work to begin, but ultimately, **relational competence**, or the ability to establish and maintain the helping relationship, is integral to counseling.

Helping Relationship

To understand better the role that the helping relationship plays in the counseling process, it is beneficial to understand the nature of interpersonal relationships in general. Human relationships develop through the exchange of information. You get to know someone by learning bits of information and giving information about yourself. When you meet someone for the first time, you often exchange names, hometowns, majors, and other information that describe you. As you grow closer to someone, you may share hopes, dreams, fears, and insecurities. We make decisions about how much we tell others based on whether or not it is appropriate to the relationship. Some people learn a great deal about us, while others know very little. However, virtually without exception, the exchange of information is reciprocal; that is, we tend to tell others things about us that they are willing to tell us about themselves. Rarely would we tell someone intimate details of our lives if they do not reciprocate and tell us those things about themselves.

Yet that is exactly what clients are asked to do when they enter into a counseling relationship. Clients disclose personal and private information to professional counselors as a necessary part of the process. That disclosure, in a nonreciprocal relationship, violates all of the relationship rules clients have established in their other relationships. What that means for us as professional counselors is that to engage clients successfully in the helping relationship, we have to make it safe for clients to tell us things they normally would not tell another person. Professional counselors have been called "professional inviters of self-disclosure" (Jourard, 1971, p. 15). Creating an environment for successful healing requires professional counselors to relate differently to clients than others in the clients' lives. It is the responsibility of the counselor to greet and interact with the client in such a way as to minimize anxiety and maximize opportunity for healing (Sperry, Carlos, & Kjos, 2003). When have you felt comfortable disclosing to others? Activity 5.9 asks you to consider disclosure from a personal perspective.

ACTIVITY 5.9   DISCLOSURE EXERCISE

Has there ever been a time when you found yourself telling someone more than you expected? What was happening at the time? What caused you to tell this person these things? What was it like? How did you feel afterward? What, if any, consequences were there because of your disclosure?

Egan (2002) proposes a three-stage model for helping that is geared toward helping clients manage the problems of living. He proposes that the client and counselor address three main questions: what is going on, what do I want instead, and how might I get to what I want? Egan's counseling approach focuses on helping clients identify their challenges and devising ways to live more effectively. The clients maintain the power in the relationship as the director of their own lives, and the counselor uses the power of the relationship, along with specific counseling skills, to assist the client.

As the client approaches the presenting problem, the counselor uses empathy and active listening skills to facilitate the story. The counselor helps the client identify any blind spots and focus or prioritize the concerns. This initial stage of the helping relationship is considered exploratory in nature.

Egan conceptualizes the next step, which is related to the question "What do I want instead?" as being aware of possibilities. During this stage of the relationship, the counselor may participate in collaborative brainstorming or serve as a challenger to test the possibilities available to the client. When the client settles on a direction of action, the counselor's role is to help the client develop a plan of action.

During the final action phase, the counselor engages the client in brainstorming again. This additional round of brainstorming has to do with strategies and possible ways of getting to the preferred reality. Action planning results in steps the client can take to reach the goals set in counseling.

Professional Counselor as Healer

Professional counselors work as healers with clients, creating "opportunities for clients to explore issues, take stock of their situations, and make preliminary plans toward self-actualization" (Schmidt, 2002, p. 66). As previously discussed, the personality of the professional counselor is as important to this process as almost any other component of healing (Kottler, 2003). The therapeutic relationship is vital to the healing process. Thirty percent of therapeutic outcome is associated with the interpersonal relationship between the professional counselor and the client (Sperry et al., 2003). In other words, how one interacts with the client is essential to the process of healing.

The professional counselor creates a **climate for change** through the setting and structure of counseling as well as the interpersonal relationship. Counselors create opportunities for reflection and growth by facilitating the client's awareness of possibilities and alternatives. Professional counselors encourage the client's sense of responsibility for acting on one or more of these alternatives (Capuzzi & Gross, 2005). The insight and awareness cultivated in counseling become opportunities. Opportunities become choices and actions. These choices and actions create the changes through which healing occurs.

Role of Theory

To set the stage for successful counseling, a professional counselor must practice from a foundation rooted in theory. It is insufficient only to understand the techniques and interventions of counseling; professional counselors must also be able to conceptualize why the interventions work. **Theory** helps clarify why we do what we do during counseling. In other words, techniques and interventions are how we counsel, but theoretical orientation drives the choices made by the counselor.

Whether practicing from a humanistic, cognitive-behavioral, integrative, or other paradigm, there is an element common across theoretical orientations. Within counseling theory, the concept of empathy is always present. **Empathy** has been defined as a trait and a state (Kunyk & Olson, 2001). People have the ability to experience empathy as a trait—that is, to place ourselves in the shoes of another and take on that person's worldview or perspective. In addition, we have the ability to convey empathy behaviorally through our words and nonverbal behaviors. This state allows others to understand that we are experiencing them, that we see their perspective.

Professional counselors possess and practice the elements of empathy as we provide services to clients. We rely on a cognitive understanding and practical application of the tenets of one or more theories to provide clients with the opportunities for reflection, growth, and change vital for clients to be successful in counseling.

STRUCTURE OF COUNSELING

Let's assume the professional counselor has developed a theoretical grounding; can facilitate helping, healing, empathic relationships; and is operating in a setting conducive to counseling. Now what? The next step in the counseling process is to establish the structure of counseling. **Structure**, explicitly stated and implicitly defined, provides clients and professional counselors a framework within which the practice of counseling can occur. Clients naturally enter counseling with some trepidation, regardless of what extent they want help. Anxiety is normal when confronted with a counseling need, and helping clients understand what to expect from the process helps to address that anxiety (Cochran & Cochran, 2006). Some elements common to providing clients with the structure and expectations of counseling include informed consent, including fee arrangements, frequency and duration of sessions, and what the process will actually look like.

Informed Consent and Confidentiality

Professional counselors are ethically bound to provide clients with **informed consent** (American Counseling Association, 2005). Generally, informed consent occurs in the first session and as frequently as necessary thereafter to ensure that clients are aware of and understand their rights and responsibilities within the counseling relationship. Perhaps the most important issue covered in informed consent is confidentiality and the exceptions to confidentiality. This topic was covered in Chapter 3 in detail.

Another topic to be covered in informed consent is the fee charged by the professional counselor for services, including when payment is expected, and whether or not the counselor files the client's insurance. Professional counselors who are comfortable with discussing privacy, confidentiality, and the benefits and risks of counseling may find themselves uncomfortable discussing fees with clients. Money is a difficult topic for most people to discuss, and counselors are no exception (Trachtman, 1999). The informed consent process, including a written agreement with clients, can actually ease that process by making it clear and explicit from the beginning of the relationship.

A crucial element to the business of counseling is the frequency and duration of sessions. Most individual sessions last 50–60 minutes, but some sessions may last longer; for example, group sessions are frequently 90 minutes in length. Will the client meet weekly? How will appointments be scheduled? What if the client needs to cancel or change an appointment? These issues are best addressed at the beginning of the counseling process. Once clarified, the client and professional counselor can begin to explore fully the reasons for coming in for services. You have probably reviewed copies of informed consent agreements for counseling. Have you considered what you will include in your own practice? Activity 5.10 allows you to begin to put your ideas about informed consent on paper. When your draft is complete, compare it with your classmates, and see if there are other areas you would like to include.

ACTIVITY 5.10   INFORMED CONSENT EXERCISE

Begin to write your own informed consent. What will it look like when you are ready to see clients? How will you describe yourself? What will you expect of clients? What scheduling and fee arrangements would you propose?

Information Gathering

Most professional counselors employ some form of an intake or psychosocial history in the initial session. An **intake** is simply a means of obtaining comprehensive information about a new client. Relevant information to gather in the first session varies from setting to setting (see Appendix A of Erford, 2006, for a sample intake interview). However, typical areas that an intake or psychosocial history cover include the following:

- Client contact information—name, address, referral source, telephone numbers, emergency contact
- Basic demographic information—age, gender, marital status
- A general overview of why the client is seeking services at this time—what brings the client to counseling? Why now?
- A description of the history of the presenting concern—how long has this been occurring? Has it ever been any better or worse?
- Family background, including family of origin and family of creation—what was the client's childhood like? What is the current family structure? Does the client have children?
- Any abuse history—have there ever been times when someone has taken advantage of the client physically or sexually?
- Medical history—does the client have any diagnosed medical disorders? Is the client on any current medications? Has the client ever been hospitalized and if so, for what? At what age were the developmental milestones of walking and talking met? Were there any major childhood accidents or injuries? What about alcohol or drug use?

- Level of education—how far did the client go in school? Did they fail or repeat a grade?
- Present and past occupational status—is the client currently employed? What is the client's occupational history?

Professional counselors generally also include their impressions and recommendations at the conclusion of the intake. These observations set the stage for treatment planning and goal setting. As stated previously, we are our clients. Use Activity 5.11 to conduct an intake on the client you know best—yourself!

ACTIVITY 5.11   INTAKE EXERCISE

Address, for your own situation, the questions standard to a traditional intake or psychosocial history as outlined in this chapter. Write out your responses to these questions. What might a professional counselor see as significant in your responses?

With the counseling structure established, information gathered, and a helping relationship begun, the client and professional counselor begin to explore more deeply the presenting concerns and establish a working relationship conducive to change.

EXPLORING AND WORKING TOGETHER

Throughout this chapter, we have examined the role of the professional counselor and elements of the art and science of counseling. The foundation is set, and the client has entered into counseling. How do we go about the business of counseling? What does the counseling relationship look like?

In the next chapter, you will learn some of the essential nuts and bolts of counseling: counseling skills. The verbal responses of counselors, techniques, nonverbal responses, treatment objectives, and intentionality affect the dynamic of the counseling relationship. As we prepare to address goal setting and client outcome, it is also crucial to explore the relationship levels inherent in the counseling process. Whether in individual, group, or family settings, there exists the real relationship between the client and the counselor and more subtle factors influencing the relationship.

The real relationship is the overt, explicit relationship between the client and the counselor. It includes what is clear, known, and unequivocal about the dynamic between the parties. While such obvious relationship factors are important, they do not capture some of the more implicit subtleties that occur when complex human beings are in relationships. You may already be aware that communication is not only about what you say (e.g., clear, explicit, overt content), but also how you say it (e.g., subtle, implicit, deeper meanings). The same is true in the counseling relationship. The client and the counselor need more than techniques and textbook counseling responses to affect change. The real relationship is influenced by many additional factors, including transference, countertransference, and the working alliance.

"Transference" is a term you have probably heard before. Put simply, transference occurs when a client's emotions from a previous experience are projected, displaced, or *transferred,* onto the counselor and the counseling relationship. This assignment of feelings to the counselor is unconscious and unrelated to the client's actual feelings about the counselor or counseling. Transference includes thoughts or beliefs that are projected into the counseling relationship as well. A classic example of transference is the adolescent client who "parentifies" his adult female counselor because she embodies similar traits, which may be as simple as age and gender, as his mother.

Countertransference occurs when the projection of beliefs, emotions, or experience is from the counselor to the client. We are aware that as counselors we respect our client's values and cultural ways of being, yet we recognize that we cannot operate without our own value set and personal history. You may be of the opinion that as a professional, you will be able to check your personal "stuff" at the door of your counseling office and prevent it from affecting the relationship. Realistically, that is impossible.

As professional counselors who are also human, we acknowledge the certainty of countertransference in the client-counselor relationship. Imagine being a new professional, fresh out of traditional undergraduate and graduate school, approaching work with clients. You are assigned a case in your university counseling center of a woman in her mid-thirties who has returned to school to better her employment opportunities and earning potential. A single mother, she has had a string of failed relationships that have interfered with her job stability. You discover that her current relationship is violent at times, and she has fled to the local domestic violence shelter on two occasions to escape her boyfriend's temper.

Many professional counselors facing such a client would find themselves wondering what keeps the client in the relationship. Treatment goals related to protecting her safety and making healthy relationship choices are indicated. If, as the counselor, you had a history of your mother having been in and out of violent relationships, you may carry feelings of fear, shame, anger, or resentment that affect the feelings you have toward this client. You may find yourself being more directive and perhaps critical of her choices. You may find yourself judging her or comparing her to your mother. While you may believe you have the client's intentions at heart, your personal history would cloud your own objectivity and clarity. Such lack of clarity is an example of the impact of countertransference and an excellent point for counseling supervision. Although largely unconscious, the realities of transference and countertransference are present and affect the real relationship between the client and the counselor.

Another element of the counseling relationship is the working alliance. It is generally accepted that the working or therapeutic alliance is crucial to success in counseling (Anderson, Ogles, & Weis, 1999; Sexton & Whitson, 1994). This alliance is essentially a collaborative environment in which the client and counselor can work and transcends across theoretical orientations. The working alliance relies heavily on the interpersonal skills of the counselor (Anderson et al., 1999) and can be a predictor of a successful counseling experience. Professional counselors who are warm, inviting, and interpersonally sensitive may have a natural ability to form a working alliance with clients.

Graduate training programs often offer classes in facilitative skills to teach these basic interpersonal techniques that are empirically supported as beneficial to the counseling relationship. Assessment tools have been developed to measure the working alliance between the client and the counselor. Such measures include the *Working Alliance Inventory* and the *Barrett-Lennard Relationship Inventory*. The factors of relationship, transference, countertransference, and the working alliance all affect the ability of the client and counselor to explore and work together.

Much of the relationship is established in the early sessions that direct the course of counseling. During initial sessions, crucial information is gathered that leads to the development of a

treatment plan or protocol. Anchored in the relationship between the client and the counselor, this assessment of needs and formulation of goals provides the foundation for the counseling work to be done during this stage.

Goal Setting and Positive Counseling Outcomes

Conducting an initial assessment via the intake process was previously discussed in the context of initiating the counseling relationship. A treatment agenda or plan typically emerges from this intake or psychosocial history. A treatment plan should be a standard practice of professional counselors and include "[d]evelopmental, remedial, and rehabilitative goals and objectives of the counseling process" (Anderson, 1992, p. 23). Treatment planning is not an easy task because it requires a complex assessment of the presenting concerns of the client and the theoretical foundation, experience, and ability of the professional counselor.

Additionally, a periodic assessment of client progress is essential to effective helping. If progress is occurring, do treatment goals need to be altered? Often what seems like the overarching treatment objective for a client changes as more details emerge, and the professional counselor develops a greater understanding of the client's desires and abilities. Ultimately, it is critical to view treatment planning as an ongoing process, rather than a single end product.

How do we know that we are effective as professional counselors? How do we know that our work, reflective powers, and clinical skills have assisted clients in a positive way? How do we know change is occurring? To assess this, we must recognize that change is a process, not a product. Continued assessment is crucial to understanding where the client is in the change process. Treatment goals need to be specific enough to provide a measure of change that the professional counselor and the client can identify, evaluate, and alter as needed. When a goal is reached, and change is noted, it should be celebrated within the client-counselor relationship because a primary responsibility within the counseling relationship is to assess the efficacy of treatment and note any positive counseling outcomes (PCO). When professional counselors speak of treatment efficacy and PCO, we are talking about how well we have intervened in the lives of our clients and how well we have been able to resolve the client's need for counseling (Hackney & Cormier, 2004).

Treatment efficacy is not tied to PCO. It is possible for professional counselors to provide effective treatment practices and at the end of the therapeutic relationship not have achieved PCO in their clients. Instead, treatment efficacy is an issue of truly understanding the maladaptive nature of the human condition and applying theories and techniques to assist clients to re-engage their lives in an adaptive way. Treatment efficacy relates to how well you are able to gain knowledge and skills in approaches emanating from affective, behavioral, cognitive, interpersonal, and somatic theories (Hackney & Cormier, 2004). Treatment efficacy also involves the application of this knowledge and skill set.

It is incumbent upon all professional counselors to understand the integrative nature of issues that confound human beings and lead them to seek treatment. Treatment efficacy is constantly challenged when we reflect upon and review our treatment plans and practices for completeness and consistency or our approach to the client's pathology or issue. We are most effective when we do three things: (a) recognize the best practices available for the issue we are attempting to intervene in, (b) be a true consumer of research concerning the issue we are attempting to intervene in, and (c) recognize the special skills of our approach and the particular limitations of our clinical paradigm.

Positive counseling outcomes (PCO) is related to treatment efficacy, but is not always a result of sound treatment approaches. PCO is a phrase that clinicians use to describe the nature of their intervention and how well their clients have responded to their treatment or developed coping strategies to address the client's issues before entering the counseling relationship. Although a PCO is subjective, many of our colleagues (Hackney, 2001; Oxman & Chambliss, 2003) view PCO as encompassing the following: (a) clients leave the counseling relationship better able to address the issues that brought them into counseling, (b) clients gain increased insight into their life and the ways in which their life provokes adaptive or maladaptive coping abilities, (c) clients develop a plan (written or verbal) that involves their knowledge of their cues for relapse, and (d) treatment goals are achieved.

When clients have a positive counseling outcome, it is evidenced in appreciable ways; for example, clients have stopped smoking, or they are not as depressed as they were before they came into treatment. But the reality is that there will be times when client outcomes are not as positive.

What Happens When Change Does Not Happen?

Change is never guaranteed. The best counseling plans, similar to the best professional counselors, do not always result in a client's goals being accomplished. Numerous factors are related to this possibility. To address these factors, let us consider that successful counseling is grounded in capitalizing on opportunity, the relational competence of the client and the professional counselor, and initiative (i.e., the expectation and desire to change).

Opportunity is compromised when clients fail to attend or are chronically late for regularly scheduled appointments (Cochran & Cochran, 2006). While structure may be established early in the helping relationship, the structure is not valid if it is not followed. Successful professional counselors are skilled at comfortably discussing changes made to the structure by the client. We realize that it may be the professional counselor who has been absent or late, but we are hopeful that the professional counselor would be more attentive to the need of the client than that, and would avoid falling into such a trap.

Relational competence is a two-way street. The most proficiently skilled counselors may not be able to reach clients with whom they cannot seem to relate. Personality being crucial to the process, not all professional counselors can reach all clients. You have likely experienced many qualified, intelligent professors in your college career, and yet it is equally likely that you have learned more from some than others. Why? Those were the instructors you were better able to relate to and with whom you had a more productive learning experience. This same inevitability between teachers and students is true for counselors and clients. What happens when the counselor is approached by a client whose treatment needs are outside of the counselor's boundaries of competence? Reflection 5.5 asks you to consider how you would handle such a situation.

REFLECTION 5.5

A client comes to you for counseling about a specific issue that you have no experience or training in. How do you express this to the client and facilitate a referral?

Finally, there is the concept of initiative, or conversely, **resistance**. Often professional counselors assume resistance is the exception, rather than the norm, but realistically some level of resistance is to be expected in all client-counselor relationships. No matter how desirous the client is of help and change, the risk inherent in the process taps our most human defense mechanisms. Sometimes that resistance may be overt, while at other times, it may be more subtle. As we consider the concept of resistance, reflect on the following questions:

- What concerns would you seek counseling to address?
- What might make you uncomfortable seeking counseling services?
- What counselor characteristics would inhibit your willingness to share intimate concerns?
- What cultural influences are present in this concept of resistance?
- As you reflect on your responses, what do you need to consider about your own style of helping that will maximize client initiative?

In the practice of counseling, voluntary and involuntary participants in the counseling process can present as unwilling or reluctant clients. The involuntary clients who may be court ordered or otherwise placed into counseling against their wishes are less likely to join willingly in the process. Professional counselors in such situations are best served by anticipating anger and defensiveness and viewing the emergence of such as an expected development within the counseling dynamic (Cowan & Presbury, 2000). Openly discussing the circumstances surrounding the counseling relationship is key because professional counselors merely exacerbate the problems that stem from resistance when they pressure clients into participating.

Resistance is to be expected, but may also be culture-bound. For example, prison inmates receiving counseling services are likely to be resistant and not trusting of the counselor or the process. While a measure of resistance is expected in a corrections environment, individuals of chronically oppressed cultures (e.g., African American, Hispanic) show more resistance to counseling than do their White counterparts (Shearer, Myers, & Ogan, 2001). Culturally influenced resistance manifests as the result of differences in language, socio-economic class, and culture-specific value systems (Shearer et al., 2001). Including cultural resistance in the counselor's approach to working with clients would minimize the impact such resistance has on the process of counseling.

More subtle forms of resistance include the initial defensiveness experienced by clients who begin to reveal secretive, difficult, or shameful things to the professional counselor. Frustration and embarrassment may be masked as resistant behaviors as the client becomes less verbal or willing to participate in dialogue about such matters. Clients may be late for, cancel, or miss appointments to avoid the work that constitutes counseling (Cochran & Cochran, 2006). In all situations of resistance, whether subtle or more overt, professional counselors have a variety of options.

In general, it is best to expect and reframe resistance as another way that your client is communicating with you (Schmidt, 2002). Resistance to certain topics tells you that you have entered into risky territory for that client, and those topics should be addressed more sensitively. Resistance does not give you license to avoid a particular topic, however, because often the areas that are most sensitive are the areas that need the most work. Understanding client reactions is key to meeting them at their point of need so as to work best with them within their perspective. Relying on the basic skills of attending to your client, creating an open nonjudgmental climate, and showing patience throughout the process increase the client's trust in the professional counselor and the counseling process, reducing resistance.

Some professional counselor behaviors increase client resistance. Giving advice, solving problems prematurely, and relying on questions as the basis of the relationship may be well intended on the part of the professional counselor, but destructive to the therapeutic relationship (Schmidt, 2002). Professional counselors who have trained long and hard to earn their degrees, license, or certification sometimes approach their work with a certain formality. To minimize resistance, it is suggested that you be flexible with your interaction style and "[l]ower your rank" (Schmidt, 2002, p. 71). Meet the client at his or her level. Formal addresses such as Mrs. Smithers or Dr. Starkey serve only to elevate and distance you from the client. Use of the professional counselor's first name, regardless of age, is encouraged to bridge this gap between the client and the counselor.

INTEGRATION AND TERMINATION

The ultimate goal of counseling is for professional counselors to work themselves out of their jobs with their clients. Does this mean the profession of counseling is on its way out? Absolutely not! The professional counselor is working with each client to facilitate new learning that is applied and integrated into the client's daily functioning. When that occurs, a natural point of **termination** in the client-counselor relationship presents itself. When a client has developed necessary insight to incorporate real change, and there are no other demands present, the counseling work has come to completion.

While it sounds ideal to reach a point of conclusion in counseling as a result of having met previously agreed upon goals, it can in fact be quite challenging. The counseling relationship is, by its very nature, an intimate one. We generally do not walk away from intimate relationships without some measure of anxiety. Likewise in counseling, clients may feel anxious about being "set free from the nest" to manage life without your support. This termination anxiety arises out of a real sense of loss experienced by the client, who has grown to trust and perhaps depend on you as the counselor.

Client termination anxiety may manifest in several ways. Clients may develop new and significant problems as they anticipate the end of the relationship. As a result of feelings of insecurity, they may regress into old patterns of dysfunctional behavior that require continued counseling intervention (Welfel & Patterson, 2005). They may experience real sadness or grief around the loss of their relationship with you as a person. Clients often struggle with termination despite their knowledge that it is healthy and desirable. However, not all clients struggle with termination. In general, the end of the counseling relationship is viewed as a positive event by the client and the professional counselor. To illustrate the challenges of termination, consider Case Study 5.1.

CASE STUDY 5.1

Flo, a 43-year-old woman, entered into a counseling relationship with you 9 months ago to deal with the effects of her recent separation after a 17-year marriage. Flo did not want the separation and was devastated by her husband's departure. Childless, she struggled with why her husband left, how to manage her time and her home without him, and feelings of rejection. She reported sleep and appetite disturbance, poor job performance, and isolating herself from her friends. You worked with her on a weekly basis in individual counseling to address her social fears, her feelings of inadequacy, and her anger at her now ex-husband. During this time, she returned to her previous level of functioning on her job, began sleeping more soundly, showed improved eating habits, joined a weekly professional woman's club, and began socializing again with her friends.

Upon assessing her treatment plan, you both concluded that Flo was making significant progress and was no longer experiencing the symptoms that brought her into counseling in the first place. After determining that you would cut back on the frequency of sessions in an effort to transition her out of services, Flo returned to her next appointment and shared with you her fears about terminating counseling. She stated, "I have come so far and I may not make it on my own! Why can't I continue in weekly counseling just in case I have problems that I can't handle on my own?" Consider your responses to the following questions:

What are the benefits of continuing to work with Flo?

What are the drawbacks?

What areas do you see a need to discuss with her?

What are your feelings about continuing to work with Flo?

While the focus of Case Study 5.1 is on the client response to termination, professional counselors are not immune to their own anxiety related to this stage in the counseling process. If we are lucky as professional counselors, we will find our work with clients to be personally and professionally rewarding. We will like our clients, we will celebrate their successes, and we will miss them when we are no longer working with them. These termination issues will be difficult for us, but may not be as difficult as another form of termination issue—the client who terminates the relationship with us.

Clients will miss appointments, drop out of counseling prematurely, or even declare that the counselor is not a good fit for them. As much as we understand the basis for premature termination on the part of the client, it is still difficult to accept that there is someone who we have been unable to help. In ideal circumstances, both client and counselor will appreciate and acknowledge the need for termination and plan accordingly for its inevitability.

Termination is simply one of the stages of the counseling process. Professional counselors can take several steps to facilitate termination in the most helpful manner possible. Attending to the client's needs and establishing clear follow-up appointments allows the client to participate in the natural ending of the relationship and establish closure. Reviewing the progress in counseling with a focus on the progress made is key (Welfel & Patterson, 2005). Celebrating the successes and changes as a result of counseling acknowledges the client's efforts and growth. Finally, considering what might lead to a return to counseling, and how the client can go about doing so, empowers clients as they leave your care.

Effective professional counselors can establish effective working relationships with clients, identify the core concerns, develop appropriate treatment plans, and work from a core foundation of theory to facilitate change with their clients. Gaining the academic and interpersonal skills necessary to become an effective professional counselor takes diligence and effort on the part of the counseling student. In addition, determining if this career path is appropriate for you is part of what an introduction to the counseling profession course addresses.

BECOMING A PROFESSIONAL COUNSELOR

Many professional counselors enter into the profession for personal reasons. They may have a desire to help others, have had a personally satisfying experience with counseling in the past, be intrigued by how people change, or any combination of reasons. How do you know if the profession is a good fit for your talents, interests, and abilities? Entering into a new field of study as a skilled helper requires students to participate in a discernment process.

Personal Strengths and Challenges

Counselors enter into this profession with a natural style of helping upon which to build. Successful professional counselors develop a skill set that includes their personal strengths and addresses their challenges. You will benefit from examining your own ability to provide opportunity and direction for clients without succumbing to a need to rescue them from their struggles. As a professional counselor, you will grow in your treatment efficacy as you recognize that your own ability to address any of your personal unresolved life events aids in your ability to help others. You will, it is hoped, exude a sense of humor, be flexible, and participate in ongoing supervision and wellness efforts. You will observe your comfort with strong emotion and develop a sense of ease when faced with the distress of others. Another self-check in the discernment process will be your ability to develop, create openness with, and have capacity for intimate relationships.

As a student entering into the counseling field, you will find it necessary to judge wisely the fit between you and the profession. What are your areas of growth? How do you open yourself to the process of not only earning a degree in counseling, but truly becoming a counselor? Your attention to this discernment process will allow you to develop fully throughout your career as a professional counselor. Now complete a final reflection (Activity 5.12) on the counseling process.

ACTIVITY 5.12   A FINAL REFLECTION

Throughout this chapter you have been asked to reflect on your understanding of the profession of counseling, the art and science of counseling, and your role as a counselor. As both gatekeepers and gate openers for this profession, we desire to pave the way for students to become professional counselors and offer you this final reflection opportunity. With this culmination activity, take some time to pull all the bits and pieces together and consider in a discerning way your hopes, strengths, and challenges in becoming a professional counselor. Begin with the following suggestions:

- First, seek your own best counsel by spending time in reflection where you listen to your inner voice, gut feeling, or true self that is your personal source of wisdom.
- Talk with others; claim your talents and strengths; and seek counsel from your instructors, your personal counselor, and your peers about your abilities.

(Continued)

- Listen to your gut—where do you feel pleased and certain? About what do you feel unease or discouragement?
- Above all, trust in who you are, and be mindful that life is unfolding for you in terms of what is best for you. As you attend to the information, cues, and signs around you, the choices about your life path will become clearer.

During this time of mindfulness, consider the following questions:
1. How is my awareness of the dynamics of counseling changing through my exposure to graduate study?
2. How confident am I in my ability to acquire and use the skills involved in the art and science of counseling?
3. How is my understanding, awareness of, and commitment to the fundamental principles of the profession developing?
4. How is my comfort with, and capacity for, intimate relationships changing?

These questions are intended to help you judge wisely the fit between you and the counseling profession and to help you make decisions about opportunities for growth within this discipline. If you encountered answers that you found difficult, exposed areas that you were uncomfortable with, or found matters you were reluctant to consider, these reactions might be an indication that you need to work harder at your choice of counseling as a profession and seek further help in your studies. Reactions that included a sense of peace and determination regarding your professional choice will aid you as you continue in your degree program. Welcome to the profession!

Summary

The professional practice of counseling requires training, experience, and an understanding of the complex nature of interpersonal relationships. The client-counselor relationship is affected by environmental concerns such as the setting and reason for services as well as the personality characteristics of the professional counselor. Expectations that the client and the counselor bring to the counseling opportunity constitute an active placebo and affect the process as much as the training, experience, setting, and personality traits of the professional counselor.

Professional counselors hold a basic competence in cross-cultural work. They have an understanding of the basic counseling paradigm under which they operate and are able to integrate cultural influences within this model of helping. This paradigm is foundational for professional counselors in that it is grounded in

their view of human nature and how people change, their theoretical orientation, techniques, and choice of interventions.

As helpers, professional counselors practice both the art and the science of helping. The art of helping refers to our ability to recognize client concerns and create a climate for change. This intuitive sense is a focus of our graduate training, while being reinforced and expanded through experience with a diverse client population. Additionally, there is a science of helping. As scientist practitioners, we realize the importance of research-driven methods to help our clients best. Whether actual researchers or simply intelligent consumers of our colleagues' research, professional counselors address the art and the science of the counseling profession.

Clients enter counseling for numerous reasons and with many barriers that would keep them from the process. Professional counselors establish an environment and style conducive to creating a therapeutic relationship. Theoretical grounding and an understanding of the interpersonal skills and empathy required to meet clients at their point of need combine to create the greatest opportunity for positive counseling outcomes.

The counseling relationship begins with the necessities of informed consent and the information-gathering or intake process. Using the legal and ethical foundation of informed consent, professional counselors set the structure for the work. Intakes or psychosocial histories provide the initial information needed to develop relevant treatment goals with the client. These goals are regularly assessed with the ultimate goal being to come to a point of termination of services when the work from counseling has become integrated in the client's life. There are challenges within the counseling relationship, however, that may manifest as resistance or even termination anxiety.

As beginning professional counselors, it is critical to understand that one does not simply receive a degree in counseling; rather, one *becomes* a professional counselor. Students who are beginning this process of becoming a counselor are encouraged to consider the concepts presented in this chapter and text in light of how they see themselves fitting within the profession. A thoughtful discernment process is beneficial throughout graduate training and will set the stage for a productive and satisfying career as a professional counselor.

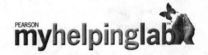

To help further your understanding of some of the topics in this chapter, go to MyHelpingLab at the Pearson.com website and view the following video clips:

- Information Gathering: *Skills, Processes, Techniques*, Module 3 (Diagnostic Assessment, "Assessing Key Components and Presenting Issue") and Module 5 (Focused and Ongoing Assessment, "Helping Clients Assess Bio-Psychological History").
- Goal Setting and Positive Counseling Outcomes: *Theories of Counseling and Psychotherapy,* Module 8 (Existential-Humanistic Therapy, "Goals, Expectations, and the Meaning of Life").

6

Counseling Microskills

JOSEPH B. COOPER

PREVIEW

This chapter provides an overview of the fundamental skills that constitute the key elements of effective helping relationships. The skills in this chapter focus on Ivey and Ivey's (2007) microskills hierarchy. At the heart of this hierarchy is the basic listening sequence, an interrelated set of skills that not only will foster the development of rapport with clients, but also will aid in the identification of interventions to help achieve a successful resolution to the client's presenting concerns. Examples of the skills in use and practice exercises to foster individual skill development are provided.

ESSENTIAL COUNSELING MICROSKILLS

This chapter provides the basic foundational skills involved in effective helping relation-ships. These skills are the foundational tools on which the success of interventions with clients may depend. These skills help to create the necessary conditions from which positive change can take place. These skills provide the client with alliance-building constructs such as empathic understanding, genuineness, and acceptance, and greatly facilitate the develop-ment of a safe therapeutic environment (Rogers, 1951).

In addition, these skills aid in establishing rapport with a client. **Rapport** refers to a harmonious or sympathetic relationship. In helping relationships, the development of rapport starts with the initial contact and continues throughout the counseling process. The professional counselor's primary concern should be on fostering this rapport to develop a cohesive and supportive relationship with the client. The development of rapport is crucial for individuals seeking counseling because this may be the first encounter with a professional counselor, and this interaction may either encourage or discourage the client from seeking counseling in the future or following up for subsequent counseling sessions.

This chapter focuses on Ivey and Ivey's (2007) microskills hierarchy. The microskills represent a set of verbal and behavioral responses that facilitate the process of counseling and alliance formation regardless of the professional counselors' theoretical orientation (Lambert & Ogles, 1997). For some students, discussion of these skills may seem like a redundant review of the basic skills taught in a previous skills course, and for others this may be the first presentation of the skills. Either way, it is important to be aware of and practice effective skills continuously because these skills are the hallmark of effective counseling, and there is always the possibility of implementing ineffective skills over time.

Ivey and Ivey (2007) present these skills as a hierarchy that is organized within a systematic framework. At the bottom of the hierarchy are the basic attending skills, such as patterns of eye contact, body language, and tone of voice. A bit farther up the skills hierarchy is the basic listening sequence, which includes questioning, paraphrasing, summarizing, and reflection of feelings. Each of these basic skills is reviewed with practical examples of the skills in use.

ATTENDING SKILLS

Good communication involves more than just verbal content, for professional counselors communicate with more than just words. Much communication occurs nonverbally. The next time you are engaged in conversation with someone, take a moment to pay attention to all of the nonverbal cues your partner is giving you. What does his or her facial expression say to you? What is conveyed by the look in his or her eyes? Does he or she have a closed or open body stance? Although important in social relationships, these attending skills are even more important in the counseling relationship.

Bedi (2006) surveyed clients who had received counseling and asked them to identify the specific counselor behaviors that most helped to form a working alliance. Following validation and education, clients ranked nonverbal gestures, presentation, and body language as the most important alliance-building factors. These nonverbal attending behaviors communicate a counselor's interest, warmth, and understanding to the client, and include such behaviors as eye contact, body position, and tone of voice.

Eye Contact

Maintaining good **eye contact** is how a professional counselor conveys interest, confidence, and involvement in the client's story (Egan, 2002). Through eye contact, clients know a counselor is focusing on them and is fully committed to the helping process. For clients who have difficulty with closeness, making eye contact can be an important vehicle of change (Vaillant, 1997).

Good eye contact is not the same as staring your client down. There should be natural breaks in eye contact; eye contact should be more of an "ebb and flow" as you collect your thoughts and listen to your client's story. Also, it is essential to be sensitive to differences in how eye contact is expressed across cultures. For example, although direct eye contact is usually interpreted as a sign of interest in the middle-class European American culture, some Asian and Native American groups believe direct eye contact is a sign of disrespect (Ivey & Ivey, 2007). Also, for clients who are overly fragile or under much stress and pressure, direct eye contact may increase their level of anxiety.

How do you determine how much eye contact to maintain with your client? There is no universal rule or criteria for what is considered either appropriate or inappropriate eye contact; as already noted, this varies among cultures. A good rule of thumb to follow is to maintain a moderate amount of eye contact while monitoring your client's level of comfort, and to adjust your eye contact accordingly (Young, 2005). Also, it is helpful for you to become aware of your own nonverbal attending behavior, so you can understand how this behavior may affect the counseling relationship. Use Activities 6.1 and 6.2 to gain a deeper understanding of your own attending behaviors.

ACTIVITY 6.1   EYE CONTACT

In dyads, one person is the listener, and the other (i.e., the "speaker") is to speak about anything of interest for about five minutes. During this time, have the listener maintain eye contact as they would normally maintain it in their everyday conversation. After five minutes, take some time to process the experience. What feedback does the "speaker" have regarding the "listener's" level of eye contact? Was it too much? Darting? Too little? Empathic? What was most comfortable? Based on the feedback, do the exercise again, but this time have the listener try to incorporate some of the feedback received about the level of eye contact. Process the activity again, and then switch roles.

ACTIVITY 6.2   NONVERBAL MIRRORING

The purpose of this exercise is to become aware of how your clients might perceive your overall pattern of nonverbal communication (Okun & Kantrowitz, 2007). In this exercise, break up into pairs facing one another. One person will be the "communicator," and the other will serve as the "mirror." For the next five minutes, the communicator can talk about anything he or she wants, and throughout this time the "mirror" is to mirror nonverbally each gesture, facial expression, eye contact, and movement of the communicator. It is important that the mirror does not attempt to "interpret" the message that is being sent by the communicator; he or she is only to mirror the perceived nonverbals. At the end of the five minutes, process this experience with each other. What was it like to see your nonverbals mirrored back to you? Did you learn anything about how you come across to others? Is there anything you would want to change, or do more of?

Body Position

As with eye contact, your **body position** should convey to the client your interest and involvement. Face the client and adopt an open, relaxed, and attentive body posture because this will assist in putting your client at ease. Counselors should not cross arms and legs, and should not sit behind a desk or other barrier. In addition, Egan (2002) recommends that the professional counselor should slightly lean in the upper body toward the client, as this communicates that the counselor is listening to the client and is interested in what the client has to say. Slouching in the chair, or leaning away from the client, may be perceived by the client as a lack of interest or boredom on your part.

Finally, the physical distance between you and your client should be taken into consideration; getting too close can be overwhelming and uncomfortable, whereas too great a distance can make you appear aloof and may be awkward for the client. Although in Western cultures the average physical distance for conversation is typically two to four feet, this "comfort zone" will vary from client to client (Young, 2005). When in doubt, a good idea is to let your client decide the distance by offering to let your client arrange the chairs at an individual comfort level. Counselors should also be aware of their personal space issues and set up personal space boundaries.

Vocal Tone

Have you ever had the experience where you are engaged in conversation with someone and you find yourself becoming increasingly anxious and tense, regardless of the topic? Next time this happens, pay attention to your partner's tone of voice, for you may be unconsciously responding to the emotional tone conveyed in your partner's voice. Emotions are frequently conveyed via **tone of voice**. The pitch, pacing, and volume all can have an effect on how a client responds emotionally to a professional counselor. There is much to be said for a calm and soothing voice in times of distress, especially when the client is in a crisis situation. Do not underestimate the power of this attribute—your control and calmness, which may be one of the greatest benefits to your client.

Your voice can do much to help create a soothing and anxiety-regulating atmosphere for the client. Learn to use your voice as a therapeutic tool. For instance, if your client is overly agitated, it is often helpful to speak more slowly and in a soothing tone because this will help your client to slow things down and begin to focus. Also, to help convey a sense of empathic understanding, it can be helpful to give emphasis to the specific words used by your client. This technique of giving increased vocal emphasis to certain words or short phrases is called **verbal underlining** (Ivey & Ivey, 2007). For example, consider the difference between "You were very hurt by your husband's actions" and "You were *very* hurt by your husband's actions." In the latter sentence, the counselor places the emphasis on the word "very" to help reflect the intensity of the client's experience. Activity 6.3 will help facilitate a greater awareness of the vocal subtleties in the spoken word.

ACTIVITY 6.3   VOCAL TONE

Ivey and Ivey (2007) suggest counselors sensitize themselves to the effects their vocal qualities may have upon their clients. In small groups, assign one person to be the speaker. Instruct the speaker to talk in a normal tone of voice for a few minutes about anything of interest. Have the other group members close their eyes as they listen to the speaker, paying close attention to the tone of voice, pacing, and volume. After two or three minutes, stop and have the members give the speaker feedback on the speaker's voice. What was their reaction to the tone, volume, accent, and rate of speech? After this processing, repeat the exercise, but this time have the speaker make changes in the tone, volume, or pacing of voice. How do the members respond to the changes in vocal qualities? What were the members' emotional responses that corresponded with the various vocal tones? Finally, have the members imagine themselves as clients in counseling. What type of vocal qualities would they prefer to hear?

BASIC LISTENING SEQUENCE

The **basic listening sequence** represents a set of interrelated skills used to achieve three overarching goals: (a) to obtain an overall summary and understanding of the client's presenting issue, (b) to identify the key facts of the client's situation, and (c) to identify the core emotions and feelings the client is experiencing (Ivey & Ivey, 2007). In short, these skills allow you to understand the structure of your client's story. Through the use of these skills, not only will you convey empathy, respect, warmth, and congruence to your client, you will also be setting the foundation for your understanding of the client's issues and the development of subsequent interventions to help achieve a successful resolution to those issues. The skills involved in the basic listening sequence include open and closed questions, paraphrasing, reflection of feelings, and summarizing. An explanation and overview of these skills, examples of each skill in use, and some brief exercises to help you practice these basic listening skills are provided.

Open and Closed Questions

Questioning is a primary skill that allows professional counselors to gather important and specific information about clients. Questions allow us to make an accurate assessment of the client's issues and guide and focus our clients so that we can make the most effective use of the counseling session. However, the use of questioning can be a double-edged sword. Used inappropriately, questioning can impede communication and block client disclosure (Rosenbluh, 1981). Drilling clients with questions can give too much control to the professional counselor. Bombarding clients with questions could confuse and frustrate them and increase their level of anxiety.

Professional counselors definitely do not want counseling sessions to sound like an interrogation. The counselor must be careful to pace the questions appropriately to guard against increasing the client's stress level. Professional counselors need to be aware of how to use questions appropriately and pay close attention to the types of questions used to gather information. The two types of questions examined here are open and closed questions.

OPEN QUESTIONS   **Open questions** usually elicit fuller and more meaningful responses by encouraging the client to talk at greater length. Open questions typically begin with what, how, could, would, or why, and are useful to help begin an interview, to help elaborate the client's story, and to help bring out specific details (Ivey & Ivey, 2007). With open questions, the client can choose the content and direction of the session. Open questions give more control to the client. Following are some examples of the use of open questions:

1. *To begin an interview:* "What would you like to talk about today?" "How can I be of help to you today?" "Tell me why you have come in today"
2. *To elicit details:* "Could you give me an example?" "What do you mean by 'just give up?'" "What do you usually do when you are feeling down?"
3. *To enrich and deepen:* "Tell me more." "What were your feelings when that happened?" "What else is important for me to know?"

As you can see from the above-listed examples, these questions allow room for the client to respond in myriad different ways, which depends on the needs and intentions of the client in the here-and-now of the counseling session. Herein lies the power of open questions: The client, and not the counselor, has the choice to determine the content and the direction of counseling.

Be careful when using *why* questions and questions that are leading in nature. Questions that begin with "Why" often cause the client to intellectualize and can lead to a discussion of reasons. "Why" questions can often cause a client to begin to rationalize or intellectualize their problems, when what we really want them to do is to explore the deeper meaning and feelings behind their issues. In addition, *why* questions can cause the client to become defensive and to feel "put on the spot." When this happens, it is common for the client to become more guarded and to shut down. For example, think back to when you were younger to a time when your parents asked the question, "Why did you do that?" How did you feel, and what was your reaction to them? Take a moment to consider the statements: "Why do you hate yourself?" versus "You say you hate yourself. Help me understand that." Which of these two questions would you prefer your professional counselor to use?

Another roadblock to the use of effective questions involves questions that are leading in nature. Leading questions often contain a hidden agenda because the answer or expectation is already *embedded* within the question. Although well intentioned, these types of questions place too much power into the hands of the professional counselor and tend to push the client into a preconceived direction. Here are a couple of examples of leading questions: "You didn't really want to kill yourself, did you?" "Don't you think if you stop drinking you will feel better?" Notice how the answer is already contained within the question. Try to guard against the use of these types of questions. Professional counselors want to hear a client's story as they understand and experience it. Open questions allow the chance to achieve this end without imposing values and expectations on the client.

CLOSED QUESTIONS   Closed questions can be used when professional counselors need to obtain specific concrete information and get all the facts straight. **Closed questions** typically elicit either a "yes/no" type of response or provide specific factual information, such as the number of drinks a client consumes in a week or the age a client first began experiencing symptoms. In this respect, closed questions are useful and necessary in professional counseling because the counselor must often gather specific information to aid in the assessment of the problem and the development of a treatment focus (James & Gilliland, 2005). Following are examples of closed questions:

- "Are you thinking of killing yourself?"
- "When did these symptoms begin?"
- "Do you have a family member or friend to call on when you are feeling overwhelmed?"
- "How old were you when your parents divorced?"
- "On average, how many days a week do you drink?"

As can be seen from these examples, closed questions are good for obtaining the necessary details to aid in assessment and intervention. However, one must guard against the overuse of closed questions. Use of too many closed questions can cause the client to shut down and become passive because in essence you are training the client to sit back and wait for the next question to answer. A good rule of thumb to follow is to move from the general to the specific in your assessment. In other words, begin with open questions (i.e., general), and as you gather information and hear the client's story, move to more closed questions (i.e., specific) to obtain the specific details important for the assessment and the subsequent intervention plan. Another good rule of thumb is never to ask a question you do not need the answer to.

The following dialogue provides a brief example of how the professional counselor uses a blend of open-ended and closed-ended questions to obtain important information about Janice, who recently discovered the company she works for will be closing operations, and she will need to find another source of income.

JANICE: I've gotten to where I can't even focus at work. My mind just races, and I can't stop thinking about everything.

COUNSELOR (C): You say your mind is racing, and you are having lots of thoughts. Tell me more about some of the thoughts you have been having. (*Open statement/question to facilitate exploration and information gathering.*)

JANICE: That I will never be happy with another job, and that I have wasted my time working for this company. I also wonder how I can ever find another job at my age. This is really painful to consider.

C: You wonder if you will find a satisfying job again and want so much for this pain to go away (*empathic paraphrase*). Tell me more about some of the feelings you have been experiencing. (*Open statement/question*)

JANICE: Mainly down—angry and depressed. I feel this tremendous pain inside my chest, very hurt and sad I guess. I just don't know what my life is going to be like in a few months, and that is scary.

C: You're feeling very hurt and also worried about your future. It is scary. Janice, can you tell me when you began experiencing these symptoms? (*Closed question to identify time line of symptoms.*)

JANICE: I would say about 3 months ago, when I found out my company was going out of business, but really, my symptoms have gotten much worse over the last month.

C: You say they have gotten worse over the last month. What do you make of that? (*Open question to identify client's understanding of her progressing symptoms.*)

JANICE: Well, when I first found out about this, I would talk a lot with my friends and family, but I felt like they were getting sick of hearing me complain all the time. So, lately, I have just been trying to tough it out and deal with it on my own.

C: And is this the first time you have sought counseling for this?

JANICE: Yes.

As this example demonstrates, the professional counselor began with open questions to encourage exploration and to help identify the client's thoughts (e.g., "I will never be happy with another job") and feelings (e.g., anger, grief, fear) associated with the loss of her job. The professional counselor then moved to closed questions to obtain more specific information regarding the duration of her symptoms and her experience in counseling.

OPEN VERSUS CLOSED QUESTIONS   As mentioned earlier, professional counselors often need to use closed questions to identify and bring out specific details to aid in assessment and treatment planning. However, one can often obtain the same information by asking open questions; try to refrain from moving too quickly into a closed questioning approach, unless you are unable to obtain the information otherwise. Consider the following examples of closed questions and their open question counterpart:

Closed: Were you afraid? versus *Open*: What feelings did you experience?

Closed: Are you concerned about what you will do if your husband returns? versus *Open*: How do you think you may react if your husband returns?

Closed: Do you see your drinking as a problem? versus *Open*: What concerns do you have about your drinking?

Notice in these examples that you can probably get all you need to know, and much more, by a subtle change in the wording of your questions to make them more open in nature. Complete Activity 6.4 for some additional practice.

ACTIVITY 6.4   CREATING OPEN QUESTIONS

Change the following leading questions from closed to open questions.
1. Why did you quit your job?
2. Do you think you should stop using drugs?
3. Do you get 8 hours of sleep a night?
4. Did you feel angry with him?
5. Don't you think there are other ways for you to cope with your anger?

Reflecting Skills

The **reflecting skills** represent a set of interventions used to help stimulate clients' exploration of their thoughts and feelings related to the presenting problems. Reflecting skills serve many important purposes. At the most basic level, reflecting skills are a form of active listening that conveys to the client your interest in and understanding of what the client may be struggling with. The reflecting skills allow you to convey empathy, genuineness, and acceptance to the client, and this facilitates the creation of a sense of safety. The reflecting skills also stimulate a deeper exploration and understanding of the problem so that the client can examine the issues more objectively. The reflecting skills covered in this chapter are paraphrasing, reflecting feelings, and summarizing.

PARAPHRASE   A **paraphrase** is how we feed back to the client the essence of what has just been spoken. By paraphrasing, one reflects the *content and thoughts* of the client's message. In other words, a professional counselor is mirroring back to the client, in a nonjudgmental way, an accurate understanding of the client's communication and the implied meaning of that communication. A paraphrase is a reflecting skill used to convey empathic understanding and to facilitate the exploration and clarification of the client's problems (Ivey & Ivey, 2007).

It is important that counselors ensure the paraphrased information is accurate by checking in with the client. For example, after your paraphrase, you might simply say "is that about right?" to assess the accuracy of your paraphrase. This "checking in" also allows for the building of a collaborative relationship with your clients and conveys your interest and care in accurately understanding their message. Inaccurate paraphrasing without affirmation by the client may inaccurately define the primary presenting problem, which may change the direction of the session, or interfere with the development of the most appropriate treatment plan for the client. Young (2005) proposed that reflecting skills provide numerous important functions, which include the following:

1. As a verbal way for communicating empathy.
2. As a form of feedback that enables the client to confirm or reject the impression he or she has been giving.
3. As a way to stimulate further exploration of what the client has been experiencing.
4. As a way to capture important aspects of the client's story that may have been overlooked or covert. (pp. 123–124)

The paraphrase, if used appropriately, is a powerful counseling tool. Appropriate use means professional counselors must develop the ability to take the essence of the client's statement and reflect back the thoughts and facts in *your own words*. When the paraphrase is used accurately, the client will continue to explore and elaborate. Do not "parrot" back to the client word for word what has been said. Parroting back would be a simple restatement, not a paraphrase. An example follows:

> JOAN: I feel so put down and disrespected by my husband. He is just like my father in a lot of ways. He was verbally abusive and full of anger. I never really felt important to him. Why do I let men treat me this way?
>
> C: Your husband is like your father in a lot of ways.

In the above paraphrase, the professional counselor simply parrots back what the client has said, which adds little and keeps the focus superficial. A better response might be the following:

> C: Although you are trying to understand this pattern of hurt and disappointment you have experienced from the important men in your life, it sounds like you are also blaming yourself for this.

To facilitate your skill development in using the paraphrase, you may find it helpful first to identify the key words or content that capture the essence of your client's concern. When you have the key content in mind, try to translate this into your own words. Following are some examples of a client's statements, the possible key themes or words, and the resulting paraphrase.

EXAMPLE 1

Client: I am so fed up with my marriage. I try and try to get through to him, and he just shuts me out.

Possible key themes or words: *fed up, being shut out, failed efforts to connect.*

Paraphrase: You are at your wit's end with this. Despite your efforts to connect, you come up against a closed door. Is that correct?

EXAMPLE 2

Client: Exactly, and that is why I have been thinking about leaving him. I know I deserve much better, but I just keep going back to him. I can't seem to make that first move."

Possible key themes or words: *leaving her husband, being stuck, hesitation, self-worth.*

Paraphrase: "Although a part of you knows this is not the way you want to live your life, it is still difficult to break out of this cycle."

As demonstrated by the examples, identifying the key words or themes can aid in your ability to develop accurate paraphrases that convey the essence of your client's meaning without coming across as superficial. Use Activity 6.5 to practice your paraphrasing skills.

ACTIVITY 6.5   PARAPHRASING

Below are some client statements. Try to identify the key themes or words, and then, based on the key words, develop a paraphrase to your client's statement.
1. I don't know what to do with my life. I hate my job, and everything seems so meaningless. I can barely muster the energy to get out of bed in the morning. Sometimes I just want to sleep for days.
2. I am still in shock that my husband is having an affair. I really can't believe it. I thought we had the perfect marriage. How could I have been so stupid not to see this was happening? I feel like such a fool.
3. I can't tell if I am coming or going. I can't sleep, I have nightmares, and I feel like a zombie throughout the day. I am so tense my body aches. No matter what I do, it just keeps getting worse.

REFLECTING FEELINGS   A wealth of research attests to the usefulness of accessing and working with feelings and emotions in counseling (Greenberg & Pascual-Leone, 2006). Naming and identifying a client's feelings can serve many important functions (Young, 2005). By **reflecting feelings**, a professional counselor can help the client become aware of the emotions experienced in relation to the issue at hand. Reflecting feelings can bring the client to higher levels of self-awareness and can deepen self-disclosure. In addition, reflecting feelings can have a positive impact on the therapeutic relationship, and a convincing amount of research has shown the quality of therapeutic relationship to be one of the strongest predictors of counseling outcomes (Horvath & Bedi, 2002).

It is not the specific theoretical approach of the helper but the strength of the therapeutic relationship that is associated with the successful achievement of the client's counseling goals (Nuttall, 2002). The therapeutic relationship is characterized by an experience of mutual liking, trust, and respect between the client and the helper. In addition, such helper qualities as accurate empathy, unconditional positive regard, and genuineness greatly contribute to the development of the helping relationship (Rogers, 1951). The reflecting skills play an important role in the development of this vital working alliance by conveying these "relationship enhancers" to the client (Young, 2005, p. 55). As with the paraphrase, reflecting feelings can promote the development of accurate empathy and help to create a safe environment for the client.

To reflect feelings, one must be able to recognize and put words to the feeling states observed in the client. What is the best way to practice this? One way is to work on becoming more aware of your own feelings and being able to name the feelings accurately. This awareness will help you to recognize and name accurately the feelings the client may be experiencing. For example, in my counseling skills class, I will walk around the class and ask each student to tell me how he or she is feeling *right now*. The most common responses I receive are "fine," "good," or "ok." Notice, however, that these are not feelings, and do not provide me with any understanding of what my students may be really feeling. Then I explain the importance of being able to identify and name correctly not only the core feelings we all experience as humans (e.g., anger, sadness, fear, surprise, joy, love, disgust), but also to be able to recognize and name accurately moment-to-moment feeling states that represent the finer shadings of the core emotions. For example, some of the finer shadings of anger are irritated, bitter, enraged, frustrated, and sore. By increasing your feeling awareness and feeling word vocabulary, you will be able to identify and respond more easily and correctly to a client's feelings.

How do you identify the feelings your client may be experiencing, especially if the feelings are not explicitly stated? When identifying the emotions of clients, if the feelings are not directly communicated verbally, these feelings may also be found in either the context of the client's communication or inferred from the client's nonverbal behaviors (e.g., facial expression, posture). To identify feelings, it is important to attend not only to what is being said, but also to *how* it is being communicated. Following are practical tips to aid in reflecting a client's feelings (Evans, Hearn, Uhlemann, & Ivey, 2008; Ivey & Ivey, 2007):

1. To aid in identifying a client's feelings:
   a. Pay attention to the affective component of the client's communication.
   b. Pay attention to the clients' behavior (e.g., posture, tone of voice, facial expression).
   c. Use a broad range of words to identify the client's emotions correctly.
   d. Silently name the client's feeling(s) to yourself.
2. When reflecting feelings to your client:
   a. Use an appropriate introductory phrase (e.g., *Sounds like . . . , looks like . . . , you feel . . . , It seems . . .* etc.)
   b. Add a feeling word or emotional label to the stem (e.g., *Sounds like you are angry*).
   c. Add a context or brief paraphrase to help anchor or broaden the reflection. This context should add the link or meaning for the perceived feeling (e.g., *Sounds like you are angry at your father's refusal to put you in his will*).
   d. Pay attention to the tense. Present tense reflections can often be more powerful than past tense reflections (you *feel* angry versus you *felt* angry).

e. Do not repeat the client's exact words (parroting).
f. Reflect mixed emotions (e.g., *You are feeling both angry and hurt about your father's behavior toward you*).
g. Check out the accuracy of the reflection of feeling with the client (e.g., *Am I hearing your correctly; Is that close?; Have I got that right?*).

EXAMPLE 3

Mike: I just sit around the house wondering what to do. We use to spend time with my wife's friends, but now that she is gone, there is no one for me to spend time with. I really miss them, and my own friends seem so busy. I would hate to bore them with my problems.

C: You are feeling both sad and lonely right now, and you are concerned you may be just another burden on your own friends. Is that about right? (*Reflection of feeling with check for accuracy.*)

Mike: Yes, I don't want to bring everyone down with all my problems.

There is one last point to consider when reflecting feelings. If you are presented with a client in a crisis state, you should guard against going too far with uncovering feelings or keeping the primary focus on feelings because this could exacerbate the client's crisis state by overwhelming him or her with emotion. In such cases, strive for a balance of skills to build rapport, and when you do reflect feelings, be sure to keep the focus directly related to the client's presenting concerns (James & Gilliland, 2005). Complete Activity 6.6 to practice identifying feelings so that you can develop accurate reflections of feelings.

ACTIVITY 6.6   REFLECTING FEELINGS

Read each vignette and identify the feelings embedded within this client's communications. When you have identified the feelings, develop your own reflection of the feelings.

1. "I don't know what to do. My husband keeps working late into the night, and I feel like I never get to see him. When we do get some time together, he is moody and reserved. To make matters worse, I saw a charge on our credit card statement to a local hotel. I think he might be having an affair."
2. "Ever since I was mugged I've been having a hard time. Because of the nightmares I can't sleep at night, and am exhausted all during the day. On top of that, I am panicky and nervous all the time. I worry I might be losing my mind."
3. "I can't believe what my father did. He stole all the money from the trust fund grandmother had willed to my brother and me. I have been calling him day and night, and he will not return my calls. I might have to get a lawyer, but I don't know how I am going to afford it. Why would he do this to us?"

SUMMARIZING   The final skill in the basic listening sequence is summarizing. By **summarizing**, a professional counselor can begin to put together the key themes, feelings, and issues the client has presented. By distilling the key issues and themes and reflecting this back to the client, counselors can begin to help clients make sense of what may have originally seemed to be an overwhelming and confusing experience. In addition, when clients are feeling overwhelmed and are flooded with anxiety, they will often go in many directions and tangents, making it difficult for the professional counselor to keep up. When this occurs, brief summaries are often a useful tool to help refocus the client and to reintroduce some structure to the session, which will help to modulate the client's (and counselor's) anxiety. A summary not only should to be used at the end of the session or at the beginning of a new session to recapping the previous session, but also should be used periodically throughout the session, helping to keep a focus and putting together for the client the pertinent issues at hand.

When should a professional counselor summarize? Although much depends on the client and the content being discussed, Evans et al. (2008) offered useful suggestions to help determine when a summary is in order: (a) when your client is rambling, confused, or overly lengthy in comments; (b) when your client presents numerous unrelated ideas; (c) to provide direction to the interview; (d) to help move from one phase of the interview to the next; (e) to end the interview; and (f) to provide an opening to the interview by summing up the prior interview.

When making a summary, you do not have to report back to the client every single detail disclosed. This would require a prodigious memory. The key is to capture the important elements, content, feelings, and issues, and reflect this back to the client in a concise manner. There are three common types of summaries.

1. **Focusing summaries** are often used at the beginning of the session to pull together prior information the client has given and to provide a focus to the session. "Last time we met you were having trouble sleeping, you were having nightmares, and you were feeling panicky throughout the day. We identified some coping skills and relaxation exercises for you to use. Tell me how that has worked out for you so far."
2. **Signal summaries** are used to "signal" to the client that you have captured the essence of their topic, and that the session can move on to the next area of concern. This helps to provide structure and direction to the session. "So before we move on, let me make sure I am understanding things correctly. You discovered your husband is having an affair. . . ."
3. **Planning summaries** help to provide closure and are used to recap the progress, plans, and any recommendations or agreements made. These summaries are good for ending the session on a positive note and to provide a sense of direction for the client. "Let's take a look at what we have covered today. Ever since you were mugged you have been having panic attacks and nightmares. We covered some coping techniques and relaxation exercises for you to practice between now and the next time we meet. . . ." (Young, 2005, pp. 161–163)

To put it all together, here is one more example of a summary statement: "Let me see if I understand you correctly. Yesterday you found out your son has been using cocaine for the last 6 months and has stolen money from you on a number of occasions. You are experiencing a mixture of feelings, especially shock and anger, and you are worried he might turn out to be an addict like your father was. However, you are determined to do all you can to not let that happen to him. How about we discuss some possible directions we can go from here."

This summary captures key issues and feelings without being too wordy, and offers a transition for the counselor and the client to begin identifying some action steps to take. The following example dialogue between Heather and the professional counselor demonstrates the skills of paraphrasing, reflection of feelings, and summarizing.

HEATHER: I really thought things were going well with my husband, so this came as complete shock when I found out about the affair.

C: You were really blindsided by this (*paraphrase*).

HEATHER: Exactly! And I have been trying to push away the pain, but I can't seem to stop thinking about it. I just want to strangle him for putting me through this.

C: Even though you want so much for the pain to go away, it is still there, especially your hurt and anger toward him (*paraphrase with a reflection of feeling*).

HEATHER: Yes, and sometimes I can't tell which is worse, my anger or just the hurt I am going through. I sometimes lay in bed at night and wish something terrible would happen to him. I am not saying I want to kill him or anything, but I just want him to suffer like I am suffering.

C: And this reflects the intensity of your grief right now, wanting to see him suffer too (*reflection of feeling*).

HEATHER: Very true.

C: So in essence, you never expected something like this to happen to you. You were blindsided, and this came as a complete shock. You are feeling very angry and hurt about what has happened, and it has been difficult for you to tough it out and to push away the pain and grief that you have been feeling. Is that about right? (*Summary with check for accuracy.*).

Summary

In this chapter, the basic counseling skills used by professional counselors were reviewed. The use of these skills aids in the development of the counseling relationship with the client and greatly facilitates the creation of a safe therapeutic environment. The nonverbal attending behaviors such as eye contact, body position, and tone of voice communicate interest, warmth, and understanding to the client. In short, be sure to face the client, and adopt an open, relaxed, and attentive body posture while maintaining culturally appropriate eye contact with the client. The tone of voice should be steady and clear, and should be used to convey a sense of safety, warmth, and security for the client.

The skills covered in the basic listening sequence include open and closed questions, paraphrasing, reflection of feelings, and summarizing. The basic listening sequence allows the gathering of important information about the client's issues and facilitates the development of trust and rapport. Finally, the basic listening sequence allows the professional counselor to pull together the key issues to begin the collaborative process of determining a plan of action for the client. Open and closed questions are the skills used to gather information, to aid in assessment, and to provide a focus and direction to the session. Paraphrasing is a reflective skill used to mirror back to the client, in a nonjudgmental way and in one's own words, an accurate understanding of the client's communication and the implied meaning of that communication. Similar to paraphrasing, reflection of feelings is a reflective skill used to convey to the client an understanding of the client's emotional experience. Through this awareness, reflecting feelings can bring the client to higher levels of self-awareness and can deepen self-disclosure.

Finally, summaries allow the pieces to be put together and begin to help clients make sense of what may have originally seemed to be an overwhelming and confusing experience. Summaries can also be used to help keep the session focused, to provide direction to the interview, and to provide closure to the session by reviewing the progress, plans, and any recommendations or agreements made. The basic skills covered in this chapter are fundamental for effective counseling. Using these skills appropriately creates the necessary conditions from which positive change can take place.

Multicultural Counseling

Danica G. Hays and Geneva M. Gray

PREVIEW

As U.S. demographics change to include more diversity, professional counselors are charged with becoming more competent in working with diverse populations. This chapter defines and presents the various dimensions of multicultural counseling, including cultural identity developmental processes and culturally specific information and intervention strategies across the cultural dimensions of socioeconomic status, race, ethnicity, gender, sexual orientation, spirituality, ability level, and age.

"Multicultural counseling," "cross-cultural counseling," and "diversity awareness" are terms used to discuss counseling that occurs with individuals from diverse cultural backgrounds. Multicultural counseling is a method of counseling that takes into consideration the backgrounds and environmental experiences of diverse clients and how special needs might be identified and met through the resources of the helping professions (Axelson, 1999). It involves assessing an individual's needs and values (i.e., individualism) within the context of community value systems (i.e., collectivism). Key terms related to multicultural counseling are presented in Table 7.1; other important concepts are presented throughout the chapter. Activity 7.1 allows you to consider the terms presented in Table 7.1 in concrete and specific ways.

TABLE 7.1 Key Terms in Multicultural Counseling

Key Terms	Definition
Culture	The totality of socially transmitted behavior patterns, arts, beliefs, institutions, and all other products of human work and thought. This could be a particular society at a particular time and place, or a symbolic system of meanings, attitudes, feelings, values, and behaviors that are shared by a group of people, a particular society, or population, and is communicated from one generation to the next via language and observation. Culture regulates and organizes what a group feels, thinks, or does, and may be expressed individually in a variety of ways.

(Continued)

TABLE 7.1 Key Terms in Multicultural Counseling (*Continued*)

Key Terms	Definition
Diversity	Ethnic, gender, racial, and socioeconomic variety in a situation, institution, or group; the coexistence of different ethnic, gender, racial, and socioeconomic groups within one social unit.
Multiculturalism	The preservation of different cultures or cultural identities within a unified society, as a state or nation; a condition in which many cultures coexist within a society and maintain their cultural differences.
Cultural encapsulation	State in which a professional counselor is fused in his or her own culture of origin and is unaware of mutual influences between self and sociocultural context, and holds onto an ethnocentric, monocultural view.
Cultural pluralism	A condition in which minority groups participate fully in the dominant society, yet maintain their cultural differences.
Worldview	The overall perspective from which one sees and interprets the world; a collection of beliefs about life and the universe held by an individual or a group.
Advocacy	The act of pleading or arguing in favor of something, such as a cause, idea, or policy; active support for marginalized individuals or groups.
Discrimination	Treatment or consideration of, or making a distinction in favor of or against, a person or thing based on the group, class, or category to which that person or thing belongs, rather than on individual merit.
Race	An arbitrary classification based on any or a combination of various physical characteristics, such as skin color, facial form, or eye shape. Race is related to **racism**, or the belief or doctrine that inherent differences among the various human races determine cultural or individual achievement, usually involving the idea that one's own race is superior and has the right to rule others. Racism involves hatred or intolerance of another race or other races.
Ethnicity	Characteristic of a people or a group (**ethnic group**) sharing a common and distinctive culture, religion, or language.

ACTIVITY 7.1

Develop examples for each term in the following table and write them inside the empty boxes. Use the definitions provided in Table 7.1.

Key Terms	Examples
Culture	
Diversity	
Multiculturalism	
Cultural encapsulation	
Cultural pluralism	
Worldview	

Key Terms	Examples
Advocacy	
Discrimination	
Race	
Ethnicity	

Over the years, the ideas of multicultural counseling have changed almost as much as U.S. demographics. In 2003, the U.S. Census Bureau reported that foreign-born individuals constituted 11.7% of the population. Of this group, 53.3% were born in Latin America, 25% were born in Asia, 13.7% were born in Europe, and 8% were born in other regions of the world (U.S. Census Bureau, 2003). In addition to changes in the immigrant population, other aspects of the cultural composition of the United States are shifting. For example, "baby boomers" have turned 65 years old by 2007, which marks a shift in the percentage of the elderly population. "Baby boomers" currently make up about 40% of the U.S. population. The U.S. population is also becoming more racially and ethnically diverse with approximately 30% of Americans currently belonging to racial/ethnic minority groups, and projections are that this percentage will increase to 50% within the next 10 years.

Based on these changes, professional counselors must be prepared to provide multicultural counseling services to diverse populations. Since the early 1990s, the counseling profession has expected professional counselors to be multiculturally competent. The American Counseling Association (ACA) adopted the AMCD Multicultural Counseling Competencies and Standards to set forth guidelines for professional counselors to increase their awareness, knowledge, and skills related to multicultural counseling. These 31 standards (Sue, Arredondo, & McDavis, 1992) were designed to ensure professional counselors are self-aware, examine their beliefs and attitudes regarding other cultures, understand how various forms of oppression influence counseling, appreciate other cultural norms and value systems, and intervene in a culturally appropriate manner.

A culturally competent counselor is defined as one who has self-awareness of values and biases, understands client worldviews, and intervenes in a culturally appropriate manner. Increasing one's multicultural competency is a lifelong process and may be increased by continual reflection of one's own assumptions and views about individuals that are culturally similar and different, immersion experiences within others' cultures, and continued training on cultural issues and interventions. In becoming a culturally competent counselor, professional counselors should reflect on the following key issues in multicultural counseling that affect how the profession of counseling considers culture and the appropriate multicultural counseling practice.

KEY ISSUES IN MULTICULTURAL COUNSELING

Etic Versus Emic Debate

A key issue involves the degree to which an individual's culture should be incorporated in counseling. This is often described as the **etic** versus **emic** debate; should multicultural counseling use more general interventions based in Western values that propose to have universal applications to most individuals (etic approach), or should more culturally specific aspects of counseling (emic approaches) be incorporated? Activity 7.2 presents a case example to consider from etic and emic approaches.

Professional counselors who ascribe to the etic perspective suggest that counseling should involve techniques related to the sameness among human beings to create a better understanding of general psychological processes for more systematic and consistent approaches among various professional counselors. Emic approaches allow for the professional counselor to conceptualize the client as an individual and attend to cultural variations and culturally specific interventions. Individuals who promote this approach assert that lack of specialized assessment and treatment in a culturally sensitive manner fails to address how cultural values and environmental stressors affect the presentation of symptoms, or the idioms of distress. Pederson (1996) argued that etic and emic approaches may be combined within the therapeutic relationship. Many professional counselors struggle, however, with the degree to which each should be incorporated in multicultural counseling.

ACTIVITY 7.2

In the following example, discuss how the professional counselor could work with this client from an etic or emic approach, or a combination of both. The client, a Middle Eastern woman, is having difficulty with her role within the family as a woman. She wants to decrease her feelings of discomfort and feel more independent without violating the traditional gender roles within her family.

How Much of Counseling Is Multicultural?

An issue related to the etic versus emic debate is the definition of multicultural counseling itself. Specifically, which cultural identities get included in the definition of multicultural counseling? Should multicultural counseling be defined narrowly to include select cultural groups, such as race and ethnicity, or expanded more broadly to include other identities, such as gender, sexual orientation, socioeconomic status, age, and spirituality? As our understanding of multicultural counseling increases, more and more multicultural theorists are using a broader definition of "multicultural." A general benefit of expanding this definition is that there is an increased understanding of how various cultural identities influence how counseling issues are presented and addressed in counseling. Also, professional counselors may be more willing to acknowledge how individuals' cultural identities intersect in unique ways to create a quite unique construction and presentation of symptoms, available resources, and general value systems.

One major critique of having an expanded view of multicultural counseling is that the more cultural identities that get included in the definition, the less "distinct" the definition of multicultural counseling becomes. In a sense, the question then becomes: "If professional counselors consider most (if not all) of a client's personal and social identities as cultural, then isn't all counseling multicultural?" Also, "What is the difference then between general counseling and multicultural counseling?" Many who prefer a more limited definition of multicultural counseling argue that it allows for more appreciation of major cultural identities (e.g., race, ethnicity) to help generalize to subgroups in more definitive ways and avoid individualizing counseling practice so much that common interventions remain valued. Activity 7.3 presents questions for you to reflect upon in your definition of multicultural counseling.

ACTIVITY 7.3

How do you define multicultural counseling? Which cultural groups are included in that definition? Why? What are the strengths and challenges of applying your definition?

Assessment and Treatment

Another issue involves the dominance of counseling theories based on European/North American cultural values (Katz, 1978). Counseling theories practiced in Western cultures often are constructed based on White cultural values and beliefs that are not always applicable to clients from diverse cultural traditions. Some of the dominant Western values are individualism, action-oriented approaches to problem solving, work ethics, scientific methods, and emphasis on rigid time schedules. These values are present in most counseling theories today and may not be congruent for clients of various racial and ethnic backgrounds.

Neukrug (2006) suggested that because of this emphasis on individualism, expression of feelings, and lack of awareness of how diverse cultures influence and drive behaviors, counseling may not be effective for most clients. Professional counselors may be implementing techniques and interventions that may conflict with client values and worldviews, leading clients to terminate counseling prematurely and creating psychological harm for the client. Activity 7.4 presents some key questions to reflect upon how your values might affect your counseling experience.

Related to the biased nature of counseling theories are the Western views of mental illness. Abnormality according to the U.S. culture may be normal and appropriate in other cultures. Most Western theories that relate to working with couples and families pathologize high interdependency as "enmeshment." Many individuals who do not identify with White cultural values, such as individuals belonging to racial/ethnic minority groups, highly value connections with family and community. Professional counselors may view these individuals as having suboptimal mental health. Another example relates to culturally accepted behaviors and attitudes among various racial/ethnic groups that may be viewed as pathological by Eurocentric counselors. For example, Latino men may demonstrate high masculinity, which is gender appropriate in Latin culture yet may be viewed as pathological on personality tests in the United States (Neukrug, 2003).

Professional counselors with limited knowledge of multicultural issues may lack the understanding of diverse expressions of symptoms, and misdiagnose and mistreat client problems. These key issues should be considered as professional counselors gain an understanding of cultural identity in general.

ACTIVITY 7.4

Consider some values and norms of your own culture. Would you find it offensive or ineffective if a professional counselor did not take these into consideration when helping you with some social or emotional issue? How do you think it would affect the counseling process?

CULTURAL IDENTITY DEVELOPMENT AND MULTICULTURAL COUNSELING

Engaging in multicultural counseling involves understanding cultural makeup of clients and counselors, and how cultural identities change and develop over time. The personal identity model (Figure 7.1) was developed to describe the basic premises that we are all multicultural beings with unique compositions of identities, influenced by sociocultural, environmental, political, and historical events (Arredondo & Glauner, 1992). It serves as a framework for

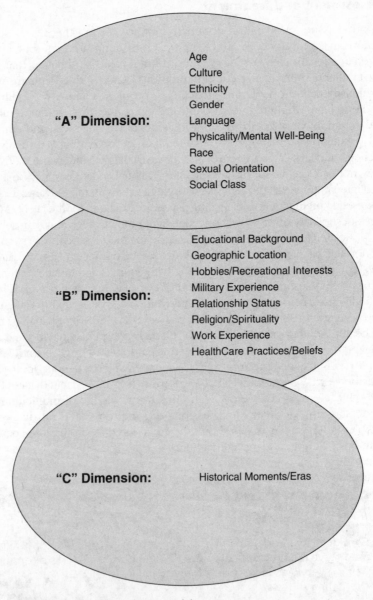

"A" Dimension:

Age
Culture
Ethnicity
Gender
Language
Physicality/Mental Well-Being
Race
Sexual Orientation
Social Class

"B" Dimension:

Educational Background
Geographic Location
Hobbies/Recreational Interests
Military Experience
Relationship Status
Religion/Spirituality
Work Experience
HealthCare Practices/Beliefs

"C" Dimension:

Historical Moments/Eras

FIGURE 7.1 Personal identity model.

understanding the complexities of all individuals, and considers individuals to be unique despite assigned social and cultural categories.

Personal identity is described in the model as involving three dimensions. Dimension A consists of characteristics that are universal for all people. These are characteristics that are predetermined, such as race, gender, ethnicity, language, culture, and sexual orientation. Dimension B consists of characteristics that are not as observable as those in dimension A. These are personal characteristics that may be selected by the individual, such as educational background, geographic location, hobbies, military experience, relationship status, work experience, and health care practices. Dimension C is a composite of positive and negative individual experiences influenced by events in society in which individuals may have little control.

According to the model, the characteristics of dimension B are often dictated by dimensions A and C. An individual's predetermined characteristics and societal experiences are instrumental in shaping his or her experiences of the characteristics in dimension B. Complete Activity 7.5 to identify your personal identity.

ACTIVITY 7.5

Fill out the following tables with your own information.

"A" Dimension:
Age:
Culture:
Ethnicity:
Gender:
Language:
Physical/Mental Well-Being:
Race:

"B" Dimension:
Educational Background:
Geographic Location:
Hobbies/Recreational Interests:
Military Experience:
Relationship Status:
Religion/Spirituality:
Work Experience:
Health Care Practices/Beliefs:

"C" Dimension:
Historical Moments/Eras:

Which of these aspects of your life help to determine who you are? Explain how.

Cultural Identity Development Models

Cultural identity development models refer to descriptions of processes by which individuals make meaning of multiple cultural identities described in the personal identity model, including race, ethnicity, gender, sexual orientation, and spirituality. The degree to which individuals identify with various cultural groups changes with new experiences; cultural identity development is contextual. Professional counselors have different intrapersonal and interpersonal experiences based on how their identity statuses interact with their clients' statuses (see Activity 7.6). Most of these models are based on individuals negotiating their cultural group memberships in the context of oppression experiences.

The purpose of these models is to help explain ways by which individuals come to know themselves culturally and engage in relationships with other individuals from a variety of cultural memberships. Having a strong cultural identity may protect and facilitate mental health and may be helpful in cross-cultural counseling relationships (Poll & Smith, 2003).

Although the models outline developmental issues for cultural identities independently, professional counselors need to consider that cultural identities intersect to create complexities in identity development. In addition, these models are presented linearly, but identity development is a circular process in which individuals move back and forth among statuses while often being characterized by multiple statuses within an identity development model. There are themes common in developing various cultural identities (Table 7.2).

ACTIVITY 7.6

Consider the listed paired identity development statuses within multicultural counseling relationships:
   a. *Contact* counselor and *internalization* client
   b. *Embeddedness-emanation* counselor and *passive acceptance* client
   c. *Encounter* counselor and *disintegration* client;
   d. *Identity synthesis* counselor and *identity acceptance* client
   e. *Achievement* counselor and *moratorium* client

What cognitions, emotions, and behaviors might be associated with each pairing?

Racial and Ethnic Identity Development

Racial identity refers to the psychosocial orientation toward membership in a racial group based partly on attitudes and actions toward other racial groups. **Ethnic identity** refers to individuals' sense of belonging to an ethnic group. It is often influenced by the degree to which an ethnic group conforms to the values of the dominant culture, a process referred to as **acculturation**. Because race and ethnicity are closely related, racial identity development models often describe processes by which individuals retreat, identify, or deny aspects of their ethnicity.

Implicit in racial identity development models is the idea that self-identification with a racial group involves dealing with racism and integrating other aspects of self. Prominent models include models for White (Hardiman, 1982; Helms, 1995), persons of color (Helms, 1995), and biracial identity development (Poston, 1990).

TABLE 7.2 Common Themes of Cultural Identity Development

Themes	Identity Stages/Statuses
Unawareness/denial	Naiveté, contact (WRID)
	Pre-encounter (POCRID)
	Personal identity (BID)
	Passive acceptance (FID)
	Pre-awareness, diffusion (SPID)
Conflict/anxiety	Resistance, disintegration, reintegration, pseudo-independence (WRID)
	Encounter (POCRID)
	Choice of group categorization, enmeshment/denial (BID)
	Revelation (FID)
	Identity confusion, identity tolerance, awareness, initial confusion (SID)
	Awakening, foreclosure (SPID)
Retreat into own group/interact cautiously	Redefinition, immersion/emersion (WRID)
	Immersion, emersion (POCRID)
	Embeddedness-emanation (FID)
	Identity acceptance, identity pride, exploration, deepening commitment, finding and applying the label of bisexuality (SID)
	Moratorium (SPID)
Integrate cultural identity with other identities and other factors	Internalization (WRID)
	Internalization (POCRID)
	Appreciation, integration (BID)
	Synthesis (FID)
	Identity synthesis, identity integration, settling into the identity (SID)
	Recognition, integration, achievement (SPID)
Advocacy	Autonomy (WRID)
	Integrative-awareness (POCRID)
	Active commitment (FID)

Note: BID, biracial identity development (Poston, 1990); FID, feminist identity development (Downing & Roush, 1985); POCRID, people of color racial identity development (Helms, 1995); SID, sexual identity development (Cass, 1979; MaCarn & Fessinger, 1996; Weinberg et al., 1994); SPID, spiritual identity development (Griffith & Griggs, 2001; Poll & Smith, 2003); WRID, White racial identity development (Hardiman, 1982; Helms, 1995).

WHITE RACIAL IDENTITY DEVELOPMENT   Hardiman's (1982) and Helms' (1995) models of White racial identity development (WRID) describe movement from a lack of awareness of one's racial self toward increased awareness and capacity to relinquish privileges associated with Whiteness (e.g., skin tone, values, European descent). The general developmental issues for Whites include the abandonment of entitlement (Helms, 1995) and an integration of their Whiteness with other components of their cultural identities (Hardiman, 1982).

Hardiman constructed a five-stage model: *naiveté, acceptance, resistance, redefinition,* and *internalization.* Whites in the *naiveté* stage early on categorize people by race and receive and transmit messages concerning the amount of power or privilege a particular racial group has. For individuals who move into the *acceptance* stage, there is a belief that there is equal opportunity for all racial groups with Whites serving as the ideal reference group for success. During the *resistance* stage, Whites experience anxiety as they engage in meaningful cross-racial interactions that may challenge earlier meanings assigned to racial groups. With the *redefinition* stage, Whites engage in active self-reflection and attempt to gain self-understanding of ethnic identities independent of attitudes toward other racial/ethnic groups. The final stage, *internalization,* involves Whites defining themselves without the resistance and anxiety characteristics of the other stages.

Helms (1995) portrayed White racial identity development as a six-status model: *contact, disintegration, reintegration, pseudo-independence, immersion-emersion,* and *autonomy.* Individuals in the *contact* status are oblivious to racism and deny that race plays a role in their social interactions. In the *disintegration* status, Whites experience anxiety, guilt, and anger when they encounter events that challenge the idea of racial superiority. To lessen anxiety and other feelings, individuals in the *reintegration* status exhibit intolerance and dislike for individuals of other racial groups. Whites in the *pseudo-independence* status strive to address racism at a superficial level; however, there are discrepancies between attitudes and actual interactions with people of color. For some Whites there are increased efforts to address racism and redefine what it means to be White, known as the *immersion-emersion* status. For the last status, *autonomy,* Whites become social advocates and attempt to relinquish some of the advantages that they have experienced.

PEOPLE OF COLOR RACIAL IDENTITY DEVELOPMENT   Helms (1995) adapted an earlier model of Black identity development to apply broadly to any racial minority, or person of color. There are six statuses associated with this model: *pre-encounter, encounter, immersion, emersion, internalization,* and *integrative-awareness.* During the *pre-encounter* status, there is a strong preference for dominant cultural values either because individuals are unaware of racism or because they minimize the role race plays. People of color in the *encounter* status experience a crisis or conflict that increases their awareness that racism exists. They may begin to see that there are positive aspects of their racial group membership and become distrustful of dominant group members. During the *immersion* and *emersion* statuses, people of color actively reject White culture and have increased racial pride and retreat into their racial community. *Internalization* then occurs for people of color, as they negotiate self-concept and racial group membership. During this status, they may seek out other groups who have experienced oppression. For the final status, *integrative-awareness,* people of color develop a more complex and relative view of all racial groups and actively commit to eliminating all forms of oppression.

BIRACIAL IDENTITY DEVELOPMENT   As the United States becomes increasingly diverse, individuals of multiracial descent will increase in number. Poston (1990) developed a model to examine the identity development processes of biracial individuals, which may be applied to individuals of more than two races. The model contains five stages: *personal identity, choice of group categorization, enmeshment/denial, appreciation,* and *integration.* Individuals typically experience the *personal identity* stage at a young age, when race/ethnicity is not salient. In the *choice of group categorization* stage, biracial individuals experience anxiety and guilt as they select one racial group over another. During the *enmeshment/denial* stage, negative feelings increase because individuals cannot fully express their racial and ethnic backgrounds. In the *appreciation* stage, biracial individuals begin to value their multiple identities. However, some may continue to identify primarily with one reference group. In the final stage, *integration,* biracial individuals increasingly recognize and infuse all aspects of their racial and ethnic heritage.

Feminist Identity Development

Downing and Roush's (1985) model of **feminist identity development** is widely used to understand the process by which women come to know themselves in a gendered world. The model assumes that women experience sexism and enhance their identity as female by addressing sexism. Five stages are proposed in the model: *passive acceptance, revelation, embeddedness-emanation, synthesis,* and *active commitment. Passive acceptance* refers to women adhering to traditional gender roles without awareness of how sexism may perpetuate these roles and create and maintain negative, limiting experiences for them. In the *revelation* stage, women may experience an event that calls into question an earlier notion of men as superior to women and highlights how sexism exists and hinders development. As a result of such experience, women may feel anger and guilt regarding their oppression experiences and engage in dualistic thinking related to gender and sex (i.e., all men are bad and all women are good). Women characterized by the *embeddedness-emanation* stage develop close, supportive relationships with other women to help assist with negative feelings associated with the *revelation* stage. Through this process, they gradually engage with men and consider gender relatively. In the *synthesis* stage, women develop a positive feminist identity by considering that external events may be influenced by sexism as well as other causes. With the final stage, *active commitment,* women seek to advocate for other women and work to eradicate sexism.

Sexual Identity Development

Considering the increasing number of models that seek to describe **sexual identity development** for sexual minorities, we present here models outlining gay (Cass, 1979), lesbian (MaCarn & Fessinger, 1996), and bisexual identity development (Weinberg, Williams, & Pryor, 1994). Cass' (1979) model is widely cited and applied to counseling sexual minorities. It involves the following six stages:

1. *Identity confusion:* Individuals feel "different" and experience inner conflict.
2. *Identity comparison:* Conflict leads to three possible responses of passing as heterosexual while recognizing gay identity, rejecting common portrayal of public gay identity while accepting gay identity, or rejecting identity and seeking to be heterosexual.
3. *Identity tolerance:* There is a desire to connect with other sexual minorities and alienate from heterosexuals.
4. *Identity acceptance:* There is increased contact with the gay community with movement away from simple tolerance of gay identity.
5. *Identity pride:* Gay individuals increase self-disclosure and immersion into gay community with some social activism.
6. *Identity synthesis:* Gay identity is integrated into self-concept.

MaCarn and Fessinger (1996) developed a model for lesbian identity development, adapted from Cass' (1979) model. Their four-stage model examined the simultaneous development of individual and group sexual identity development, as follows:

1. *Awareness:* There is an acknowledgment at individual and group levels that there are other sexual orientations besides heterosexuality.
2. *Exploration:* Individuals begin to experience intimate feelings toward other women and concurrently seek to obtain information about lesbians in the community to assess their degree of belonging.
3. *Deepening commitment:* Individuals solidify their commitment to their sexuality as a lesbian. They are actively committed to a lesbian group identity and culture, and may reject some heterosexual norms.
4. *Identity integration:* Individuals integrate their sexual identity with other aspects of their self-concept and engage fully and securely in their lesbian identity across settings.

Weinberg et al. (1994) outlined three stages of bisexual identity development, a process they saw as occurring for some individuals with an already developed heterosexual identity. In the *initial confusion* stage, individuals experience attraction to both sexes with some discomfort with having to fit into one sexual orientation. When *finding and applying the label of bisexuality,* individuals acknowledge feelings for both sexes and select the label of bisexuality. The final stage, *settling into the identity,* is characterized by self-identification as bisexual with increased self-acceptance.

Spiritual Identity Development

Spiritual identity relates to the degree of connection to individuals' ideas of what their god is. The highlighted models that follow examine spirituality and religiosity; one describes increased awareness of self as a spiritual being (Poll & Smith, 2003), and another highlights the process by which individuals infuse religiosity into their lives (Griffith & Griggs, 2001).

Poll and Smith (2003) outlined a four-stage model whereby individuals become increasingly personally connected to their god. The first phase, *pre-awareness,* involves individuals who do not view themselves as spiritual beings. After a conflict or spiritual learning has occurred, individuals begin to become aware of themselves as spiritual beings in the *awakening* phase. During the *recognition* phase, individuals generalize new spiritual learning across settings until they have integrated their spiritual self into their self-concept and interact authentically with others (i.e., *integration* phase).

The second model (Griffith & Griggs, 2001) is a four-status approach that describes ways individuals experience their faith:

1. *Diffusion:* This status involves a lack of interest in religiosity or participation in religious activities that is largely guided by external motivation.
2. *Foreclosure:* Individuals conform to ideas and practices of religious communities, which creates a crisis because religious identity may be significantly based on personal needs for social approval.
3. *Moratorium:* This status involves active self-reflection and spiritual exploration as individuals confront the anxiety characteristic of the *foreclosure* status.
4. *Achievement:* Core religious values become integrated into all aspects of the individuals' lives, and spiritual inquiry becomes internally motivated.

With an introductory framework for understanding key issues in multicultural counseling and cultural identity development, the remainder of this chapter focuses on counseling culturally diverse individuals and clinical implications. As culturally diverse groups categorized by socioeconomic status, race and ethnicity, gender, sexual orientation, spirituality, disability, and age are introduced, consider how culture is presented in U.S. society (see Activity 7.7).

ACTIVITY 7.7

Peruse several magazines and consider the role of culture in the articles, pictures, and advertisements. Discuss in dyads how race, gender, and sexual orientation are portrayed in various popular magazines. What are the direct and indirect messages in advertisements and articles? How do these messages influence the way we think about ourselves and individuals with other cultural identities?

COUNSELING CULTURALLY DIVERSE INDIVIDUALS

Clients present to counseling with complex cultural identities that involve aspects such as socioeconomic status, race, ethnicity, gender, sexual identity, spiritual affiliation, ability status, and age. These identities intersect to create unique cultural experiences for clients that warrant special considerations in counseling.

Socioeconomic Status and Poverty

Socioeconomic status (SES) relates to individuals' relative position in a cultural group based on social and economic factors. It is typically indicated by household income, education level, occupational status, use of public assistance, and access to health care (World Health Organization, 2003). SES is difficult to define, and household income is often used as a primary indicator of status. Clients belonging to lower SES groups require special attention in counseling because of the inaccessibility of basic resources that affect their physical and psychological well-being. Although there is lack of consensus on what constitutes "low SES," the poverty threshold has been defined as $13,738 for a family of three and $17,603 for a family of four (U.S. Census Bureau, 2001).

More than 31 million Americans live in **poverty**, which involves 11.3% of the U.S. population (U.S. Census Bureau, 1999). When looking closer at statistics, poverty disproportionately affects individuals of racial/ethnic minority statuses: 26.1% of African Americans, 25.6% of Hispanics, 12.5% of Asian Americans, and 31% of Native Americans live below the poverty threshold. In addition, approximately 30% of women who are head of household are poor (U.S. Census Bureau, 1999). Because poverty is often experienced by clients of oppressed statuses (e.g., racial/ethnic minorities, women), its influence in counseling cannot be ignored.

Poverty, closely related to factors such as lower education levels, inadequate housing, malnutrition, and exposure to violence and trauma, prevents access to mental health services and increases clients' sense of vulnerability to mental illness. Research shows that counseling issues such as depression, suicide, post-traumatic stress disorder, behavioral problems, and substance abuse are often associated with poverty and related environmental conditions (Albee, 1999; World Health Organization, 2003). Poor children have an increased risk for lower academic and intellectual achievement, developmental delays, health problems, and dysfunction in social interactions (McLoyd, 1998). Individuals of lower SES groups are two to five times more likely to exhibit criteria for a mental illness compared with individuals in higher SES groups (Bourdon, Rae, Narrow, Manderschild, & Regier, 1994). People of lower SES groups often live in neighborhoods characterized by crime, high unemployment, substandard housing or homelessness, schools with inadequate resources, and substance abuse (Chow, Jaffee, & Snowden, 2003). Individuals with mental illness are overrepresented in these neighborhoods, which often lack available social, psychological, and economic resources.

Poverty becomes a vicious cycle for many clients, as aspects of economic depression, underemployment, and lower educational attainment become self-perpetuating and transcend generations. Within this cycle, individuals' mental health is negatively impacted as they try to cope with related issues. Poverty perpetuates mental illness, and vice versa.

When working with clients of lower SES groups, professional counselors should attend to the connection between SES and environmental factors and evaluate their own biases related to SES. Some areas of exploration may include the following:

- What role does SES play in my client's immediate surroundings (school, neighborhood, community)?
- What types of resources are available to my client in his or her community? Are some of these resources determined by the financial status of that community?
- Do my client's socioeconomic resources affect his or her mental and physical health?
- What have been my experiences with SES? What material, educational, and social resources have been available (or limited) to me?
- How do I view individuals of SES groups different from mine?

In addition, professional counselors are charged with advocating for groups with lower SES. Some ways that professional counselors can work to minimize the impact of poverty in clients' lives include the following:

- Provide psychoeducation to individuals in impoverished neighborhoods about mental health concerns and the role of counseling in addressing these concerns.
- Provide information through community agencies about accessible resources that they may use for a host of issues related to having limited financial resources (e.g., mental health issues, physical health issues, transportation, housing, limited food).
- Because often individuals who lack financial resources and transportation have limited access to counseling services, consider different strategies beyond "counseling in your office for 50 minutes." Some alternatives may include providing in-home counseling to individuals and their families; collaborating with churches or other community organizations to connect to individuals in need of mental health services; and providing counseling to particularly vulnerable groups such as children, elderly individuals, and racial/ethnic minorities.
- Educate others who are not experiencing socioeconomic concerns such as poverty about the role of SES on an individual's mental and physical health. This may include school personnel, other counselors in your mental health agency, or government leaders.

Racial and Ethnic Diversity

In this section, the five major racial and ethnic groups are presented along with a discussion of multiracial individuals.

EUROPEAN AMERICANS   **European Americans** make up most (71%) of the U.S. population and consist of various non-Hispanic backgrounds (U.S. Census Bureau, 2004). During the past decade, the growth rate of this population has slowed, and projections suggest that by 2020 European Americans will compose 64% of the population. However, their numbers are increasing among older age groups, especially the elderly population. There are approximately 50 categories of European Americans, including people from various areas such as England, Italy, Russia, Austria, and France. This group has experienced the most ethnic blending of any other cultural group (Sue & Sue, 2003). European Americans typically include individuals with three or more generations in the United States who vary in immigration experiences.

European American values include individualism, autonomy, status and power, direct communication, linear time orientation, rationality, emphasis on the scientific method, and a nuclear family structure. They may undervalue a group or collectivistic orientation (Katz, 1978). Judeo-Christian beliefs are predominant for the group, and many uphold Protestant values that include individual direction, self-fulfillment through direction, mastery over one's nature, and dedication to moral living (Sue & Sue, 2003). Many counseling theories are based on Western views of individualism and self-determination, and European Americans tend to respond well to counseling theories that stress these common values.

European Americans have a long and dominant history in the United States. They possess the most power in the United States and have had a significant impact on the values and standards of the general U.S. society. Because of these factors, many European Americans are faced with difficulty defining their ethnicities and get placed in a larger category of "Whiteness" (Katz, 1978). Being White affords many special, unearned advantages in U.S. society, known as **White privilege** (McIntosh, 1988). Nugent and Jones (2005) suggest that European Americans are just as much victims of societal forces as other cultural groups because of the indoctrination of racism, privilege, and discrimination passed through generations. As a result, professional counselors should be aware of the role of White privilege and "White guilt" in the lives of many European Americans and work to strengthen their understanding of their ethnicities. Activity 7.8 highlights a reading that allows for deeper reflection on the issue of White privilege.

ACTIVITY 7.8

Review McIntosh's (1988) article on White and male privilege. Identify items that create either a positive or negative reaction for you. Prepare a journal entry describing your reactions to at least five items.

HISPANIC AMERICANS   **Hispanic Americans** constitute approximately 13% of the U.S. population; they are becoming the largest and fastest growing ethnic minority group. Of this group, 60% are Mexican, 10% are Puerto Rican, 3.5% are Cuban, and 28% are from other Latin American countries (U.S. Census Bureau, 2004). It is difficult to estimate accurately the number of Hispanic Americans in the United States because there are numerous undocumented individuals currently living and working in the United States. Several different terms are used to describe Spanish-speaking individuals, such as Latino/Latina, Hispanic, or Chicano/Chicana. The term "Hispanic American" is used here to refer to individuals from Mexico, Puerto Rico, Cuba, El Salvador, Dominican Republic, and other Central and Latin American countries.

Familism is a central theme in the Hispanic culture; this term refers to family unity, loyalty, and respect. Interpersonal relationships within the family and overall community are highly valued and nurtured, and households are often composed of an extended kinship network. The family structure is usually hierarchical with emphasis placed on elderly parents and men, structured gender roles, and child care of younger siblings by older children. In addition, spirituality, particularly Catholicism, has a major influence on this culture with emphasis on prayer, salvation, and charity. Professional counselors should pay close attention to the relationship with the family and spirituality and be willing to include community spiritual leaders as sources of support.

There are several differences among Hispanic American individuals based on immigration status, SES, education level, and acculturation level. Hispanic Americans are currently experiencing difficulty with immigration and establishing citizenship. This struggle has contributed to feelings of distrust and frustration with government and state officials, including social services. Many have fallen victim to disproportionate rates of poverty, unemployment, and substandard living. Because of various oppression experiences, Hispanic Americans also experience problems with alcoholism and substance abuse that further exacerbate their difficulty with functional living. As a result, professional counselors must have some awareness of the roles of racism and discrimination in the lives of many of these clients.

Acculturation conflicts can be a source of stress for many Hispanic American clients. They may struggle with rejection or acceptance of values of the U.S. culture. There may be differences in adolescents and older adults in bicultural values and assimilation. Professional counselors should be prepared to discuss how individuals can negotiate conflict between mainstream values and ethnic group values.

Hispanic Americans may be more likely to seek assistance for mental health issues from community and religious leaders before searching for public assistance because of these barriers. In general, they are more likely to wait longer to seek mental health assistance. Counselors should be aware of potential referral sources for bilingual counseling services.

AFRICAN AMERICANS   **African Americans** make up approximately 12% of the U.S. population; many reside in the southern United States, where they constitute 19% of the population (U.S. Census Bureau, 2004). The African American culture is projected to see a sizable percentage of growth among its teenagers. Much of the research has focused on the lower class and masks a great diversity among African Americans. They are a heterogeneous group in relation to background, heritage, traditions, and skin pigmentation. However, ancestors of many African Americans were brought to the United States as slaves. They have a tumultuous history that has been characterized by racism, poverty, oppression, and discrimination.

African American strength lies in the relationship bonds that extend beyond the biological family. Because about 70% of households are single parent and female led, collaboration among extended family members, neighbors, and community leaders is often the norm in the African American culture. African Americans have elastic family boundaries, and children are readily accepted into the family regardless of the marital status of their parents. Men within the family are more accepting of female work and sharing household responsibilities. Spirituality plays an important role in African American families and is often used as a comfort to oppression and economic struggles. Professional counselors should work with spiritual leaders to support the family and deal with client problems.

Because of oppression experiences and resulting socioeconomic issues, physical and mental health and substance abuse issues, and exposure to and involvement in criminal activity may be factors to consider when working with African American clients. Some issues cited in research include decreased physical health such as cardiovascular problems and HIV/AIDS, problems in academic performance among boys (**disidentification**), disproportionate poverty rates among this population, and unequal numbers of incarcerated African American men.

Professional counselors must be aware of the possible feelings of powerlessness and rage between the environmental factors related to discrimination. Professional counselors should also be aware of the cultural mistrust and lack of trust for social service agencies and medical staff (Phelps, Taylor, & Gerard, 2001). According to Jones (1985), four factors impact how African Americans handle problems: reactions to racial oppression, influence of the majority culture, influence of the African American culture, and personal experiences and endowments. It is important to examine an African American client's response to an adverse situation because these clients may have unique, limited, or reflexive problem-solving skills (Sue & Sue, 2003).

ASIAN AMERICANS   **Asian Americans** compose about 4% of the U.S. population, and most are immigrants from China, India, Vietnam, Korea, Philippines, and Japan. Despite the many misconceptions, Asian Americans are a very diverse group that is experiencing rapid growth in the United States. Estimates suggest that this group will make up 6% of the population by 2020. According to the U.S. Census Bureau (2004), 63% of Asian Americans living in the United States are foreign born. Professional counselors need to gain knowledge of within-group diversity and be careful not to make assumptions about individuals' origins and nationalities.

Asian Americans tend to have a collectivist orientation and place emphasis on family and community. There is also a strong emphasis on older adults as opposed to individualism. The family is usually hierarchical and patriarchal in structure, where men and older adults have higher status. Parenting is authoritarian and directive in nature, and shame may be used to reinforce appropriate behaviors within the family and the community. Children are expected to strive for family goals and not to engage in behaviors that could dishonor the family (i.e., save face).

Other key concepts in understanding Asian Americans may be related to expression of emotions, views on the mind-body connection, and familial conflict related to levels of acculturation (Sue & Sue, 2003). For instance, it may be considered to be immature or out of control to display emotions openly in the Asian American culture. Adhering to more traditional gender roles, fathers provide more of the economic and physical needs of the family, whereas mothers are primarily responsible for meeting the emotional needs of the children. Within the Asian American community, much emphasis is placed on the mind-body connection, and emotional difficulties may be expressed through somatic symptoms. Physical problems cause emotional disturbances; professional counselors should treat somatic complaints as real problems.

Many Asian American children may experience acculturation conflicts with their parents and other family members. This is generally the case when the parents are first-generation and the children are second-generation immigrants. Children are exposed to different cultural standards that often contribute to the conflict with parents who have held to more traditional values. Inability to resolve these differences often leads to identity issues and conflict within the family. Professional counselors should be aware of the possible existence of this struggle and make efforts to inquire about the impact that family may have on the decisions of Asian Americans who are involved in individual counseling.

Similar to many other ethnic minority groups, Asian Americans have experienced racism, discrimination, and stereotypes. They have also struggled with being labeled as the **model**

minority because of examples of individuals from this group being seen as financially successful, intelligent, and nonaggressive. Many Asian Americans experience stress from these stereotypes because of some legitimate struggles that they face on a daily basis. Many issues within the Asian American community, such as discrepancies between education and income, lack of job skills, unemployment, poverty, language barriers, health problems, and juvenile delinquency, may be hidden because of the underuse of community mental health services.

NATIVE AMERICANS   **Native Americans** are the smallest ethnic minority group and include Native American Indians, Alaskan Natives, and Native Hawaiians. There are currently 2.5 million Native Americans living in the United States, and estimates project an increase to 3.1 million by 2020 (U.S. Census Bureau, 2003). About 39% of the Native American population is younger than 29 years old. There are currently 512 Native American tribes in the United States, and about 54% of this group live on reservations.

Native Americans value harmony with nature, cooperation, and holism, and have strong feelings about the loss of their ancestral lands. Other key themes in Native American culture cited in the literature are sharing, noninterference, time orientation, spirituality, nonverbal communication, and extended family network.

Native Americans have experienced a difficult history in the United States since the arrival of European Americans. It is a history of distrust and conflict with local and governmental officials. They have a poverty rate three times higher than that of European Americans and are less likely to have a high school diploma. In addition, Native Americans experience difficulty with survival because of the high rates of unemployment and poverty. Alcoholism and domestic violence are also major concerns in the Native American community.

This tension with the dominant culture may have a negative impact on Native Americans' perceptions of mental health services. Sue and Sue (2003) suggest that this has been due partly to the lack of understanding of Native American traditions, values, and worldviews. Native Americans primarily view mental health and wellness as harmony between mind, body, and spirit. Disharmony among these three dimensions creates illness and is often ameliorated by considering the community. Because of this view, Native Americans may be less likely to seek assistance from professional counselors owing to a lack of inclusion of spiritual beliefs in counseling and lack of outreach to Native American communities, and unwillingness to address contextual factors that may impact the lives of this cultural group.

MULTIRACIAL INDIVIDUALS   In 1967, the United States overturned the law against interracial marriage. Before this formal and "legal" recognition, most **multiracial individuals** in the United States were the product of slaves and slave owners or Native Americans and White Americans. After 1967, the United States experienced a "biracial baby boom," and the U.S. Census began devising methods for counting members of this increasing group.

Currently, 3% of marriages in the United States are interracial (U.S. Census Bureau, 2003). Societal stereotypes regarding interracial marriages still exist and may contribute to the identity problems of multiracial children. Multiracial individuals do not have the same support as their monoracial parents and sometimes experience racial and ethnic ambiguity that may lead to feelings of isolation. It is common for many multiracial individuals to accept the racial/ethnic identity assigned to them by society. Because of the growing numbers of multiracial individuals, professional counselors should be aware of their unique needs and concerns. Also, professional counselors should not assume that a client is a member of a particular race based on the characteristics of one particular group.

RACISM   **Racism** is the classification of groups of individuals based on physical characteristics, such as skin color, eye shape, and hair texture, and inappropriately ascribing intellectual, physical, and psychological traits to them. Subsequently, prejudice and discrimination of groups considered to have "inferior" features have created negative experiences for certain groups (i.e., racial and ethnic minorities). Professional counselors have a responsibility to attend to racism in their clients' lives as well as how they may perpetuate racism themselves:

- Explore your own feelings toward particular racial and ethnic groups with others. How might your views and experiences differ from others'?
- Immerse yourself continually in communities composed of racial and ethnic groups that differ from your own. Reflect on your attitudes and behaviors regarding various experiences. Note any changes in your attitudes and behaviors based on the type of experience, and discuss these changes with others you trust.
- Discuss race and ethnicity with your clients. How has a client's race and ethnicity affected his or her daily experiences? How does your race and ethnicity affect various counseling relationships?
- Educate others in your personal and professional community about concrete instances of racism.

Gender

Messages about gender and gender roles are present in clients' daily lives. Appropriate ways in which men and women should think, behave, and feel are present in media, social interactions, career and education arenas, and family systems. **Gender** is a concept that involves attitudes, behaviors, and relationships associated with being male and female; this concept includes, but is not limited to, biological sex (i.e., chromosomal makeup, hormonal and physical expression of genetic material). Gender roles are roles men and women engage in based on their biological sex (Cook, 1993).

From an early age, females are socialized to be caregivers with traits such as nurturance, dependence, agreeableness, emotionality, and submissiveness. Males are socialized to be rational, autonomous, aggressive, competitive, nonemotional, and powerful. In addition, males receive more negative consequences for embracing feminine characteristics. Bem (1993) coined the term "androcentricism" to describe masculinity as the ideal set of traits for which humans strive that have associated privileges of greater wealth and power in relationships. Additionally, masculinity as an ideal often serves as a basis for most theories of human development. Activity 7.9 provides an opportunity for you to consider how your gender has influenced your opportunities and assumptions.

After the women's movement in the 1960s, greater attention was paid to the role of gender in human development and counseling. In a landmark study exploring gender stereotypes among therapists, Broverman, Broverman, Clarkson, Rosenkrantz, and Vogel (1970) identified that therapists held gender stereotypes and devalued femininity as a healthy characteristic of adults. In this study, healthy adults were described as having predominantly masculine traits. Women were viewed as psychologically less healthy because they were primarily "feminine."

With gender biases present among helping professionals, Chodorow (1978) and Gilligan (1982) proposed that adult development is different for men and women, and that differences should be equally respected. They provided evidence that traditional models of human development favor masculine traits as indicators of mental health. Chodorow discovered that women's sense of self emerges within relationships, as opposed to popular assumptions that healthy development emerges from increased independence. To develop as a healthy man means to reject femininity. Gilligan expanded Chodorow's research to show that gender differences exist in moral development. Specifically, as a result of gender socialization and early developmental experiences, females and males make decisions and find safety in relationships and in autonomy.

Sparse research is available that looks at the intersection of gender and race/ethnicity and the impact of social status (i.e., degree of privilege and power in cross-cultural situations). In general, social status seems to have a negative impact on men. Specifically, men in lower social statuses tend to behave in ways typically stereotyped as feminine. Because traditional gender role socialization is so salient (i.e., men as masculine, and women as feminine), men experience distress as they are often unable to meet the expectations of being fully masculine.

Two groups for which there is some research involve Mexican American and African American families, specifically heterosexual family relationships (Davenport & Yurich, 1991). "Machismo" and "marianismo" are two terms typically identified in Mexican American culture to describe traditional gender role socialization. **Machismo** refers to extreme masculinity, with avoidance of caretaking roles and dominance over other men and women. **Marianismo**, derived from the concept of the Virgin Mary in Catholicism, involves extreme femininity (i.e., passivity, submission to the needs of the family, and belief in male superiority). It is argued that marianismo is an ideal gender role in that women in Latino culture are described as spiritually superior to men and hold special status in the family when they bear children.

Gender roles are less traditional for African American men and women. This may partly be due to the experiences of racism and the restricted power and social status of African American men in society. Although traditional gender roles were present in Africa, slavery diminished men's sense of power within their families because they could no longer protect women, demystifying the myth that men were superior. As a result, women have almost always been in the position of caretaking and working outside the home, while men have been denied social access, leaving them unable to fulfill masculine roles of provider and protector. African American families have been stereotyped as matriarchal, with the female role described as one of strength and resourcefulness (Davenport & Yurich, 1991).

ACTIVITY 7.9 GENDER SELF-EXPLORATION EXERCISE

- Think about your earliest memories when you realized you were a member of your gender. Describe the situation and any feelings and behaviors associated with prescribed roles and expectations.
- In general, what messages did you receive about your gender in your family of origin?
- What opportunities have been available to you because of your gender? What barriers have been present?
- Which gender roles do you still adhere to as an adult?
- How has your gender and related opportunities and barriers affected your physical and psychological well-being?
- How do you think your life would be different if you were another gender?
- How do you think your gender may be helpful as a counselor? Challenging?

SEXISM   Sexism, defined as negative beliefs and behaviors about the ways in which women should be treated based on the notion that femininity is devalued and "less healthy," is closely associated with the concept of androcentrism. The belief in male superiority and the idea that masculinity is considered healthier for adults creates the assumption that women are inferior and deserve negative treatment. Sexism is potentially more harmful for women of color because of the additional experiences of racism and poverty. Some examples of sexism for women include the glass ceiling effect (invisible barrier of occupational and economic success); sexual victimization; physical violence; and promotion of violence, submissiveness, and thinness of women in media.

Women and men may experience negative psychological consequences based on strict conformity to gender roles and failing to meet or rejecting societal standards. Women's problems with gender roles occur when they limit themselves by accepting and conforming to a lower status as designated in society, or when they resist to conform to what is deemed appropriate behaviors for women and experience negative reactions from others. Women are often not allowed to be aggressive and often use indirect and unhealthy coping methods. Even with the women's movement, women may still feel marginalized and disempowered and isolated. These experiences often lead to issues related to development; lack of power and control over their lives; lack of self-confidence; and feelings of anger, guilt, and shame. As a result of the experiences with sexism, there is a higher prevalence of depression, anxiety, and eating disorders for women. Women's symptoms may be a result of unequal power relationships and related social, economic, and political conditions.

Men's problems often result from failing to attain a high status of dominance as prescribed in masculine roles; men may have a lower self-image and cope in destructive ways. Harris (1995) identified key messages men hear about appropriate ways they should express their gender: "Be self-sufficient and don't depend on others." "Don't admit weakness." "Don't show emotions." "Men pursue power and success." "Men are courageous." Masculinity denies mental and physical illness, and men are less likely to seek professional help. In attempts to fulfill these expectations, men experience many physical and psychological issues, including ulcers, heart attacks, completed suicides, hypertension, depression, addiction, problems with intimacy, and stress. Men are more likely to engage in violence (e.g., crimes, domestic violence, assaults) partly because of traditional gender role socialization.

TRANSGENDER INDIVIDUALS   Because most of the focus in counseling has been on men and women corresponding to existing gender categories for their biological sex, there is little known about transgender individuals and their needs in counseling. **Transgender** is a term used to identify individuals who permanently or periodically do not identify with the gender assigned to their biological sex at birth. A related term is "transsexual," which describes individuals who strongly disidentify with their birth sex and seek sex reassignment and hormonal therapy. "Trans individuals," an umbrella term for individuals with evolving gender identities, may possess any sexual orientation (Carroll, Gilroy, & Ryan, 2002).

The increased focus on trans individuals in counseling calls attention to the way gender and sex has been traditionally considered. Professional counselors can play an important advocacy role by accepting trans individuals' experiences and serving as an ally to educate the community and profession on their needs, assisting them to connect to support systems and appropriate occupational opportunities, and identifying strengths that they possess as they deal with societal discrimination. The key to working with this population involves changing the context in which they live, not changing the client.

GENDER-SENSITIVE COUNSELING PRACTICES   Professional associations such as the ACA have attempted to promote gender-sensitive counseling practices with the development of guidelines. Professional counselors are strongly encouraged to review various guidelines for attending to gender in professional practice. Brown and Srebulus (2003) identified some themes of various guidelines:

- Attention to sexist assumptions found in counseling theories, interventions, and assessments
- Focus on counselor biases regarding the influence of gender on mental health and continued evaluation of attitudes toward men and women
- Increased knowledge about the unique needs of men and women
- Increased knowledge of the intersection of sexism and other forms of oppression (e.g., racism, heterosexism)
- Use of nonsexist language and gender-sensitive skills in counseling
- Facilitation of client knowledge of how gender, gender role stereotyping, and sexism affect their physical and psychological health

Sexual Minorities

Although at least 10% of the population identifies with a sexual orientation other than heterosexual (Norton, 1995), there has been little attention to the mental health needs of sexual minorities. Sexual diversity refers to differences in sexual orientation. This section focuses on sexual minorities who identify as gay, lesbian, and bisexual (GLB).

Part of the lack of focus relates to the attitudes and biases of professional counselors. Although homosexuality as a form of mental illness was removed from the *Diagnostic and Statistical Manual of Mental Disorders* in 1973, negative stereotypes and limited understanding of the experiences of individuals who do not identify as heterosexual continue to exist. Chen-Hayes (1997) identified 18 stereotypes that affect GLB clients (Table 7.3). Professional counselors are encouraged to review this seminal article and reflect on which stereotypes they may hold.

GLB individuals experience depression, stress and anxiety, substance abuse, eating disorders, high-risk sexual behaviors, suicide, harassment, and violence. Often, professional counselors identify any mental health concerns in sexually diverse individuals as caused by their sexual orientation, rather than because of the societal discrimination they face. Societal stressors can worsen an existing mental illness for GLB individuals (Dworkin, 2000).

Because sexually diverse clients experience these stereotypes in their daily lives with resulting mental health considerations, the process of self-identifying as GLB (**coming out process**) is complex and difficult. The coming out process is the basis of sexual identity development, discussed earlier in this chapter. Heterosexism, internalized homophobia, and sexual identity management are three concepts that heavily influence an individual's coming out process. Heterosexism refers to the belief that heterosexuality is the normative model for healthy romantic and sexual relationships. Heterosexist individuals often have an irrational fear or hatred of sexual minorities, known as **homophobia**.

Many GLB individuals experience these negative attitudes and increasingly believe that their sexual orientation is morally or socially wrong, resulting in internalized homophobia. As they come to identify their sexual orientation and deal with heterosexism, homophobia, and internalized homophobia, GLB individuals engage in sexual identity management strategies. Some of these strategies include passing as heterosexual or covering or minimizing

TABLE 7.3 Gay, Lesbian, and Bisexual Stereotypes

1. Lesbians, bisexuals, and gays are child molesters.
2. Lesbians and bisexual women really want to be men; gay and bisexual men really want to be women.
3. All gay men secretly desire to wear dresses, and all lesbians secretly desire to wear men's clothes.
4. Bisexuality does not exist; most bisexuals really are either gay or lesbian, or confused.
5. Same-sex relationships never last.
6. You can tell a gay man or lesbian by his or her appearance.
7. Being lesbian, bisexual, gay, or transgendered is due to bad parenting.
8. Lesbians, bisexuals, gays, and transgendered persons do not want children and are unfit parents.
9. Lesbians, bisexuals, gays, and transgendered persons are evil sinners and hate organized religions and spirituality.
10. A really good sexual experience with a heterosexual can turn a lesbian or gay man into a heterosexual.
11. All lesbians, bisexuals, or gays care about is sex. They are all promiscuous and will sleep with anything that moves.
12. If gays and lesbians would blend in more with heterosexuals, they would not be targets of violence and hatred.
13. All gay and bisexual men have HIV/AIDS; lesbians and bisexual women do not have to worry about HIV/AIDS.
14. Lesbians, bisexuals, gay men, and transgendered people are less violent than heterosexuals and traditionally gendered persons.
15. All lesbians, bisexuals, gay men, and transgendered persons are great dancers and have wonderful fashion sense.
16. Same-gender sexual orientations are a White invention.
17. Older lesbians and gays actively recruit younger heterosexuals to be lesbian, gay, or bisexual.
18. Young lesbians, bisexuals, gays, and transgendered persons have plenty of exposure to lesbians, bisexual, gay, and transgendered role models in the media.

Compiled from Chen-Hayes, S. F. (1997). Counseling lesbian, bisexual, and gay persons in couple and family relationships: Overcoming the stereotypes. *Family Journal, 5,* 236–240.

their true orientation to avoid discrimination, and displaying pride for their sexual minority status (Dworkin, 2000). The identity development process for sexual minorities is often complex because of valid safety concerns.

Although the coming out process is an important part of the psychological development of GLB individuals, professional counselors should be careful to not assume that this is the primary reason clients with diverse sexual orientation are seeking therapy. GLB clients may consider counseling for daily issues that are likely affected by others' attitudes regarding their sexual orientation. Some issues that may be unique to sexually diverse individuals include career development, parenting, and relationship status. Examples of these issues include assessing level of safety, job security and sense of belonging with various career options, experiencing legal battles related to custody of children from a previous relationship or barriers to adoption, and not being able to file joint tax returns or receive insurance benefits for their partners.

COUNSELING IMPLICATIONS   To address the specific needs of GLB clients and clients who identify as transgender, the Association for Lesbian, Gay, Bisexual, and Transgender Issues in Counseling (ALGBTIC) developed competencies that correspond to CACREP course areas. Professional counselors should strive to increase their competence for working with this population by examining the ALGBTIC competencies. Some are listed below.

Competent professional counselors will:

- Understand that biological, familial, and psychosocial factors influence the course of development of GLB orientations and transgendered identities. [Human Growth and Development]
- Acknowledge that heterosexism is a worldview and value system that may undermine the health functioning of the sexual orientations, gender identities, and behaviors of gay, lesbian, bisexual, and transgendered (GLBT) persons. [Social and Cultural Foundations]
- Acknowledge the societal prejudice and discrimination experienced by GLBT persons, and assist them in overcoming internalized negative attitudes toward their sexual orientations and gender identities. [Helping Relationships]
- Establish group norms and provide interventions that facilitate the safety and inclusion of GLBT group members. [Group Work]
- Counter the occupational stereotypes that restrict the career development and decision making of GLBT clients. [Career and Lifestyle Development]
- Differentiate between the effects of stigma, reactions to stress, and symptoms of psychopathology when assessing and diagnosing the presenting concerns of GLBT clients. [Appraisal]
- Formulate research questions that acknowledge the inclusion of GLBT participants yet are not biased on stereotypical assumptions regarding these subjects. [Research]
- Know the history of the helping professions including significant factors and events that have compromised service delivery to GLBT populations. [Professional Orientation]

In addition to the ALGBTIC Competencies, following are additional considerations (Sue & Sue, 2003):

- Use gender-neutral language if clients do not specify a gender when referring to their partners.
- Use clients' language when describing their sexual orientation; avoid using the term "homosexual".
- Do not assume that all problems are related to sexual orientation.
- Do not ignore the possible impact of sexual orientation on client problems.
- Focus on sexual orientation to the extent that it is the focus for clients.

Spirituality

The counseling profession is increasingly addressing spirituality in the counseling relationship. **Spirituality** has several dimensions, including search for meaning and purpose; connection to something larger and a sense that one is part of a greater whole; drive for creativity, love, relationships, and personal growth; and value in developing a relationship with a transcendent life force. **Religiosity**, one framework for organizing one's spirituality, refers to construction of and adherence to a belief system of faith, traditions, and community worship (Ceasar & Miranti, 2005). While spirituality and religiosity are related, it is important to assess the degree to which clients identify as spiritual or religious or both.

Because spirituality is such a broad concept that deals with themes of relationships and self-development, many counseling issues may be considered spiritual issues. Clients may present with concerns of isolation, meaninglessness, difficulty connecting with others, and loss of values. Clients' religious beliefs may or may not influence their ways of coping with these issues. Ceasar and Miranti (2005) offer the following reflections for integrating spirituality in counseling:

- How important are spiritual practices in the client's life?
- What is the client's spiritual or religious orientation? To what degree does the client identify with this orientation?
- How does the client view his or her spirituality in relation to the presenting problem (e.g., potential source of strength, cause of current problem, decreasing as a result of current problem)?
- Does the client view the presenting problem as a spiritual issue?
- Is the client willing to explore any spiritual needs?
- From where or whom does the client seek strength and comfort?
- How does the client make meaning in his or her life?

Professional counselors have an ethical responsibility to address diversity issues and promote client growth and development in the counseling process. This responsibility includes addressing spiritual concerns as appropriate. Although addressing spirituality seems to be congruent with the purposes of multicultural counseling, professional counselors may fear imposing their values or may have had negative personal experiences with spirituality and religiosity. Also, professional counselors may lack knowledge of various religious belief systems (Ceasar & Miranti, 2005). Professional counselors are encouraged to review literature describing major religions and their belief systems as they prepare to work with diverse clients.

It is important for professional counselors to be aware of their attitudes, beliefs, knowledge, and experiences related to spirituality and its integration into counseling. The Association for Spiritual, Ethical, and Religious Values in Counseling (ASERVIC) developed the Competencies for Integrating Spirituality into Counseling (see http://aservic.org/CompetenciesforIntegratingSpiritualityintoCounseling.pdf). They include nine competencies, as follows:

1. The professional counselor can explain the distinction between religion and spirituality, including similarities and differences.
2. The professional counselor can describe religious and spiritual beliefs and practices in a cultural context.
3. The professional counselor can engage in self-exploration of religious and spiritual beliefs to increase sensitivity, understanding, and acceptance of diverse belief systems.
4. The professional counselor can describe his or her religious or spiritual belief system and explain the various models of religious or spiritual development across the lifespan.
5. The professional counselor can show sensitivity and acceptance of a variety of religious or spiritual expressions in client communication.
6. The professional counselor can identify limits of his or her understanding of a client's religious or spiritual expression, and demonstrate appropriate referral skills and generate possible referral sources.
7. The professional counselor can assess the relevance of the religious or spiritual domains in the client's therapeutic issues.
8. The professional counselor can be sensitive to and receptive of religious or spiritual themes in the counseling process as befits the expressed preference of each client.

9. The professional counselor can use a client's religious or spiritual beliefs in the pursuit of the client's therapeutic goals as befits the client's expressed preference.

Counseling Individuals With Disabilities

According to the *Americans with Disabilities Act* of 1990 (ADA), Americans with disabilities should be protected against discrimination. According to ADA, **disability** is defined as physical or mental impairment that substantially limits a major life activity. The determination of whether a particular condition is a disability is made on a case-by-case basis. Examples of physical disabilities include vision loss, deafness or hard of hearing, speech impediments, and physical impairment (e.g., arthritis, limited or no use of limbs, wheelchair use). Examples of mental disabilities include major depression, bipolar disorder, and schizophrenia. In addition to protection against discrimination, ADA mandates that businesses make adjustments and accommodations to facilities to make them accessible and appropriate for individuals with disabilities.

Individuals with disabilities have faced several challenges in society related to discrimination that have created social, vocational, educational, and economic segregation. Individuals with disabilities also have been characterized by many myths and stereotypes. For example, many people believe that disabilities are visible, and that physical abilities create the most barriers for this population (American Friends Service Committee, 1998). Similar to the general public, professional counselors often struggle with feelings of guilt and pity toward working with disabled clients.

To assist this population effectively, professional counselors are encouraged to:

- Explore their own personal views of disabilities and challenge any prejudicial assumptions.
- Not make the disability the only focus of counseling. Many individuals with disabilities struggle with other life problems, such as sexuality, divorce, or depression, which may not be directly related to their disability status.
- Identify environmental factors and issues related to negative stereotypes.
- Ask about the disability, but not succumb to the "spread" phenomenon; that is, the belief that the disability impacts unrelated aspects of the individual's life.
- Explore damage related to the individual opportunities for accountability and self-reliance.
- Incorporate family counseling as appropriate.
- Focus on improving the quality of life in rehabilitation. This can be accomplished through community involvement, physical adjustments, and psychosocial adjustments (Vash & Crewe, 2004).
- Gain knowledge about various disabilities and resources available to clients. Activity 7.10 provides a method for increasing your knowledge about disability services at your university.

ACTIVITY 7.10

Visit the office that provides disability services at your university. Interview an employee of that office and gather information on the types of students that typically visit the office, what services are most sought, and any mental health concerns with which these students present. Explore the individual ways by which professional counselors may better meet the needs of individuals with disabilities.

Counseling the Elderly

In 1935, the *Social Security Act* deemed 65 years as the appropriate age for retirement and eligibility for federal retirement funds. According to the U.S. Census Bureau, adults 65 years and older compose 12% of the population. Estimates suggest that the elderly population (adult age 65 years and older) will substantially increase during the years 2010–2030 (U.S. Census Bureau, 2003). The elderly population currently comprises mostly the "baby boomer" generation. "Baby boomers" are individuals born between the years of 1945 and 1965, a period when the United States experienced its largest population growth. The first "baby boomers" will turn 65 years old in 2011, and by 2030, the elderly population will double from that of 2000. With an increase in the number of elderly adults, professional counselors are more likely to be employed in community-based facilities, such as nursing homes, hospices, retirement communities, and day treatment centers.

In general, elderly adults face some major roadblocks to functioning, such as poor economic and physical health, mental health issues, dementia, substance abuse, physical abuse, neglect, and depression (Sue & Sue, 2003). Additionally, many elderly adults are affected by **ageism**, defined as negative attitudes related to the process of aging or elderly people (Doty, 1987). The elderly population has often been viewed as "senile, absent-minded, helpless, and less valuable to society" (McCracken, Hayes, & Dell, 1997, p. 385). Additionally, they have been viewed as having rigid thought processes and little interest in sexual activity (Atkinson & Hackett, 1998). Maples and Abney (2006) suggest there are several challenges related to ageism specific to "baby boomers." "Baby boomers" will be more likely to be affected by declines in social security and by financial insecurity, age discrimination owing to change of demographics in the work environment, and relationship and divorce issues.

In response to the need for appropriate guidelines for working with elderly adults, gerontological competencies were developed in 1973 and provide professional counselors with 16 essential competencies of gerontological counseling. Some of these address end-of-life concerns, social and cultural aspects of aging, importance of family involvement, and roles of professional counselors. The competencies also mandate that all professional counselors be familiar with a variety of service providers in the community who specialize in gerontological counseling. This community care may consist of day treatment, senior centers, residential/long-term care, and wellness programs (Maples & Abney, 2006).

As professional counselors become more competent, it is imperative that they recognize that the elderly are not a homogeneous group and should be treated based on individual needs. According to Maples and Abney (2006), professional counselors are encouraged to assist elderly clients to identify the positive aspects of aging in light of ageism by incorporating creativity, positivism, and wellness into the counseling relationship. It is also important to help promote self-empowerment through helping elderly clients recognize that aging is a natural part of development and helping clients envision a healthy lifestyle until the end of life.

MULTICULTURAL ORGANIZATIONAL DEVELOPMENT: CREATING A CULTURALLY SENSITIVE ENVIRONMENT

Professional counselors may find in their work settings that they may be one of only a few trained in multicultural sensitivity. It is imperative that clients enter the professional counselor's office, whether it be in a school or agency, feeling as though the counselor is sensitive to their cultural identities and privy to salient cultural issues that affect their daily lives.

The good news is that information presented in this chapter can assist professional counselors in a school or agency setting. Having self-awareness, knowledge, and skills for working with culturally diverse individuals is a good foundation for creating a culturally sensitive organization. Following are some additional strategies to employ for increasing multicultural sensitivity within the workplace and creating a positive, therapeutic experience for clients:

- Evaluate collaboratively with other staff in the school or agency the demographics of the setting, what demographics are not being served well, what mental health resources are typically used, and if the purpose of the setting is fulfilling the mental health needs of current and potential clientele.
- Whether clients are waiting in a lobby or sitting in the office in a counseling session, the surrounding environment should be affirming to a variety of cultural identities. Include resources and magazines that represent the experiences of as many cultural groups as possible. Ensure that one cultural group is not overrepresented as to create a sense among particular clients that they do not belong or in general that counseling is not for them.
- Ensure that policies and procedures of the school or agency do not systematically discriminate against certain groups. For example, having a Spanish version of important documents for clients ensures that Latino individuals who speak Spanish as a first language understand their rights and roles as clients.
- Educate staff and other stakeholders in an organization about cultural groups and cultural issues that affect clients. Provide workshops or printed materials to individuals who may not have received training in multicultural sensitivity. Encourage an active, positive dialogue with colleagues about cultural issues.
- Engage in program evaluation to improve the cultural climate of an organization whereby staff and client needs with respect to multicultural sensitivity are assessed as well as their experiences with counseling are explored.
- Collaborate with others in the organization to apply for local and federal grants to expand counseling services to individuals who have limited access to these/such services.

These are just a few activities that can foster a culturally sensitive environment. For each of these strategies, examine through the lens of the various cultural identities presented in this chapter how each can be implemented in concrete ways. Activity 7.11 is helpful in identifying positive and negative cultural stereotypes.

ACTIVITY 7.11

In the table, for each listed cultural identity in the first column, identity positive and negative stereotypes (i.e., what others would say about members of that cultural group) as well as advantages and disadvantages for that group membership (i.e., your personal views on privileges and challenges for your membership). After independently working on the activity, discuss in dyads and small groups, to the extent you are comfortable, your cultural group memberships. Note any surprising findings or challenges with identifying some of the stereotypes, advantages, or disadvantages for particular cultural groups.

Cultural identity	Positive stereotypes	Negative stereotypes	Advantages	Disadvantages
Age				
Gender				
Race				
Ethnicity				
Ability (e.g., physical, cognitive, emotional)				
Spiritual affiliation				
Sexual orientation				
Socioeconomic status				

Summary

Multicultural counseling involves increasing professional counselors' awareness, knowledge, and skills in working with clients who may be diverse with respect to race, ethnicity, SES, gender, sexual orientation, spiritual affiliation, disability, and age. To attend to cultural factors affecting clients, it is imperative that a professional counselor considers personal views on cultural group memberships (see Activity 7.10). In addition, the following are key points to consider as one counsels individuals and families in an increasingly diverse society:

- Attend to the role of culture in counseling by increasing your knowledge of clients' cultural identities. This may be accomplished by discussing with clients how they identify culturally, reviewing the latest research in multicultural counseling, and engaging in self-exploration to identify personal biases and behaviors.
- Increase your knowledge of available resources to help clients develop stronger support networks within communities.
- Pay attention to how SES, especially poverty, plays a role in client mental health.
- Consider new ways to provide counseling services to clients who may not have access or interest in individual counseling.

- Develop a referral resource network as a means to consult on multicultural issues as they arise in counseling.
- Determine ways in which your unique cultural makeup grants you privileges and may oppress you. How can you advocate for others to experience some of the privileges you have? How can you advocate in counseling to end oppression for yourself or other groups?
- Participate in activities that create opportunities to interact with individuals of different races and ethnicities. In these immersion experiences, attend to how your cultural makeup influences the way others respond to you.
- Be cognizant of how differences between and within racial and ethnic groups may be a result of cultural values for a particular group, oppression experiences, or both.
- While there are unique aspects of being of a particular racial/ethnic makeup, consider overarching themes related to being a member of a racial/ethnic minority group compared with that of the dominant racial/ethnic group (e.g., White).
- Increase your understanding of the unique needs of men and women. For both genders, it may be helpful to explore the family

of origin messages received about gender. Reflect upon the benefits and challenges of gender roles as they relate to presenting mental health issues.

- When working with women, assist them to express anger and frustration with sexism and other forms of oppression, empower them by allowing space for their voices, and provide assertiveness and other skills training as needed.
- Consider using holistic counseling approaches, which particularly when used in group counseling, may be suitable for men; these include stress management and relaxation training, nutrition education, exploration of emotions, and assistance with relationship difficulties.
- Assess the degree to which a client's sexual orientation affects his or her mental health status. Consider how sexual identity intersects with spiritual beliefs, gender roles, and race/ethnicity.
- If applicable, reflect upon any privileges in social, educational, and occupational settings you receive based upon your heterosexual identity.

- Some spiritual issues presented in counseling may not be associated with religious beliefs. Keep a broad perspective of spirituality as it applies to a client's presenting situation.
- Consider interventions such as journaling, guided imagery, mindfulness exercises, and meditation and other relaxation techniques when addressing spiritual concerns within a counseling session.
- Acknowledge that many disabilities are not readily apparent by a client's physical presence. Assess any disabilities and clients' experiences without automatically assuming that ability status plays an important role in the presenting problem.
- Familiarize yourself with the ADA of 1990 and other legislation to assist clients with disabilities in dealing with social, academic, and occupational challenges.
- Reflect on your own thoughts about aging and death, and how these thoughts may influence your present attitudes toward counseling elderly populations.

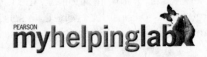

To help further your understanding of some of the topics in this chapter, go to MyHelpingLab at the Pearson.com website and view the following video clip:

- Racial and Ethnic Diversity: *Skills/Processes/Techniques,* Module 11 (Practical Issues: Ethical Dilemmas, "Cultural Considerations in Counseling Sessions").

8

Consultation and Supervision

MARK A. YOUNG AND ALAN BASHAM

PREVIEW

This chapter examines the important counselor activities of consultation and supervision, both of which enable experienced counselors to expand their constructive influence beyond their own clients. Presented are the models, techniques, types of activities, and important skills used to fulfill the role of consultant or supervisor.

USE OF CONSULTATION AND SUPERVISION IN COUNSELING

Not all counseling activity involves working directly with individual clients or groups of clients. This chapter presents two important additional roles for the professional counselor. Experienced counselors often respond to requests from individuals, groups, or organizations to help solve problems when the resources or knowledge at hand are inadequate. This is called consultation. Other accomplished counselors use their expertise and advanced skills to train new and emerging counselors, assuming responsibility for and clinical authority over their work with clients. This is called supervision.

Imagine that you want to backpack into the wilderness to an Alpine lake nestled high in a mountain range. You are determined to go and want to take a few friends along, but you have a serious deficit of knowledge and skill for how to travel and survive in the wilderness. Until this adventurous idea struck, your idea of roughing it was a hotel without room service. What you need is an experienced wilderness guide who will go with you, provide you with gear, help you get to the lake and back, prevent any damage you might inadvertently cause to the environment, perhaps teach you some things about wilderness survival, and make it possible to have a great trip without getting lost, being eaten, or freezing to death. What you need is a wilderness consultant who will help you accomplish this particular trip.

If you want to become highly skilled at exploring the wild places of nature on your own, you will need an expert in wilderness survival who can supervise your training.

This expert supervisor would take you through a course of personal growth and skills development until you were capable of safely exploring the mountains alone. This requires that you learn to trust your wilderness training supervisor and assume the open-minded and open-hearted stance of a learner. The supervisor would undoubtedly ask you to clarify your own motives for seeking such training. He or she would probably praise you for getting it right and correct you when you are headed down the wrong trail. You would be taught to pay attention to yourself, including your strengths and limitations, and to remember the unforgiving demands of the high country. This is necessary, both for your own survival and to ensure that you have a positive, not destructive, effect on the environment. Only when the supervisor believed that you were ready would you be encouraged to explore the wilderness on your own. Activity 8.1 helps you explore your talents, abilities, and skills.

ACTIVITY 8.1

Make a list of your talents, abilities, and skills. For example, are you musically talented? Are you an experienced athlete and team player? Do you know how to obedience train a dog? Be creative in forming your list. Then get together with two or three other students to brainstorm about how your (and their) unique constellation of abilities might be the doorway to effective consultation practice early in your career. For example, if you know how to lead a process group and you understand music, would you be qualified to lead team-building and interpersonal process meetings for an orchestra? Remember, not every counseling consultation is provided for other counselors.

Get the difference? Consider the following definitions of the two terms. **Consultation** is "a voluntary relationship between a professional helper and an individual or *group* that needs help. In such a relationship, the consultant provides assistance by helping to define and resolve a problem or potential problem of the client" (Gladding, 2006, p. 35). Dougherty (2005) described consultation as "a process in which a human service professional assists a consultee with a work-related (or caretaking-related) problem with a client system, with the goal of helping both the consultee and the client system in some specified way" (p. 11).

In contrast, **supervision** is "an intensive, interpersonally focused, individual or group relationship in which a more experienced helping professional is designated to facilitate the development of therapeutic competence in less experienced professionals" (Gladding, 2006, p. 138). Corey, Corey, and Callanan (2003) described supervision as

> . . . a process that involves a supervisor overseeing the professional work of a trainee with three major goals: (1) to enhance the skills and knowledge of the supervisee, (2) to ensure the welfare of the supervisee's clients, and (3) to serve a gatekeeping function for the profession. (p. 320)

Consultation and supervision are similar in some ways and different in others. The first and most obvious similarity is that both activities rely on the competence and expertise of an advanced professional. Supervisors and consultants are able to create constructive change because of what they know or can do better that others know or do less well. Second, consultation and supervision are **tripartite** in nature. Because counseling involves the interaction between counselor and client (or group of clients), it is dyadic in nature; consultation is triadic in nature (Hansen, Himes, & Meier, 1990). Dougherty (2005) described the tripartite relationship of consultation as one involving the three parties of the consultant, a consultee, and the consultee's client system. A consultant interacts with the consultee, who then affects his or her staff, clients, or organization. A counseling supervisor is also engaged in activity that affects both the supervisee and the client. One of the major purposes of supervision is to help the counselor become more effective, which also affects the client. Third, consultation and supervision have some ethical considerations in common. For example, consultants and supervisors (similar to professional counselors) should avoid dual relationships, should refrain from practicing outside the limits of their abilities and training, and should seek positive outcomes for supervisees and their clients or for consultees and their clients or client systems.

How are supervision and consultation different from each other? First, consultation tends to be **collaborative** (Dougherty, 2005), whereas supervision tends to be **authoritative**. While consultant and consultee can work together as equals to solve problems, supervisors carry a higher level of singular responsibility for what their supervisees do in their interactions with clients (Corey et al., 2003). Consultees are free to reject the suggestions of a consultant if they disagree. However, supervisees may not reject the directions given by a professional supervisor and still maintain the supervisory relationship. A second distinction is that supervision is usually imposed by educational, organizational, or credentialing standards, whereas consultation is typically voluntarily sought by the consultee. Third, there is no professional evaluation role implied in consultation because of its collaborative nature (Dougherty, 2005), whereas ongoing performance evaluation is one of the defining attributes of supervision. Fourth, consultation is usually a temporary, task-specific relationship (Dougherty, 2005), whereas supervision is most often an ongoing relationship between professionals that requires time to develop its full potential. Finally, Caplan (1970) suggested that individuals in the consultation relationship are often not of the same professional discipline. It is not unusual for educators or business professionals to call on professional counselors for consultation assistance. However, individuals qualified to supervise counselors and counselors in training are themselves in the counseling field. With this understanding of consultation and supervision as context, the remainder of this chapter describes the important models and techniques of consultation and of supervision.

CONSULTATION

Consultation can be understood by examining the types or models of consultation, the various roles assumed by the consultant, the skills required of an effective consultant, and the variety of professional arenas in which consultation takes place. Although these are described differently by different authors, there are some common themes to the published descriptions of the consultation field. To learn about consultation first-hand from an experienced consultant, complete Activity 8.2.

ACTIVITY 8.2

Interview an experienced professional counselor in your area who provides some form of consultation service. What training and experience were necessary for the consultant to become effective? In what techniques or types of consultation is the counselor most skilled? How did the counselor expand from being a professional counselor into the practice of consultation? What important tips can the counselor provide to help you understand consultation better? Discuss your findings with classmates.

MODELS OF CONSULTATION

Gallesich (1982) identified several models of consultation practice that vary according to the problems faced by the consultee and the intervention techniques used by the consultant. The **education and training model** considers problems that are grounded in a lack of some specific knowledge or skill in the consultee. Intervention is largely a matter of teaching, training, or otherwise providing information either to the consultee or to organizational staff members. The **clinical model** conceptualizes problems in terms of the mental illnesses or dysfunctions of the consultee's clients. This is also known as client-centered **case consultation**. Interventions involve consultant guidance regarding diagnosis and treatment of the consultee's client, which the consultee carries out while the consultant maintains a supportive but nondirective role. The **mental health model** goes beyond a focus on the individual client intentionally to affect the overall competence level of the consultee. Although consideration of a client case may be involved, the consultant's primary objective is to help the consultee become a more effective counselor, leader, or teacher in general. This model is especially important because of its ability to broaden the consultee's impact on community development and on prevention of the adverse social forces that contribute to mental illness, poverty, and suffering.

    Behavioral approaches systematically apply the principles and techniques of learning theory to change client behavior. The consultant guides the consultee in his or her efforts to reduce unwanted client behaviors and to replace them with more facilitative behaviors. **Organizational consultation** uses the knowledge and skill of the consultant to clarify and alter the interpersonal dynamics, organizational structure, or managerial processes of an organization to help maximize its potential. Organizational development interventions include action research, process consultation, team development, and staff training. **Program approaches** focus on development, evaluation, and improvement of the programs through which human service agencies attempt to benefit a particular population or to solve a particular community problem. In an era of increased focus on fiscal accountability and proven program effectiveness, consultation support for human service agencies can help them to maintain their funding, while improving their service to the community.

    The three consultation models presented by Schein (1991) are purchase of expertise, doctor-patient, and process consultation. In the **purchase of expertise model**, the consultee accurately identifies the problem, what sort of help is needed from the consultant, and which consultant would be able to provide appropriate assistance. The consultee pays for and expects to receive expert assistance. Of major importance in this model is the need for the consultee to be correct in his or her assessment of the problem at hand. In the **doctor-patient model**, the client knows that a problem exists, but is unable to identify or solve the problem. The consultee depends more on the judgment and direction of the consultant than in the purchase of expertise model. The consultant is more responsible for the identification and resolution of the problem. The **process consultation model** assumes that some problems require an interactive problem-solving process between the consultant and consultee to produce a workable solution that the consultee can and will adopt. Rather than focus on the content of the problem area, this model attends more to the process by which the consultee's problem is resolved. The expertise provided by the consultant is that of a process observer, guide, and collaborator, while the responsibility for the eventual resolution of the problem remains with the consultee.

A variety of other models exist that conceptualize the field of consultation. Among these is Caplan's (1970) model applicable to the mental health field, which included four types: client-centered case consultation, consultee-centered case consultation, program-centered administrative consultation, and consultee-centered administrative consultation. Blocher (1987) presented seven types of consultation: triadic, technical, collaborative, facilitative, mental health, behavioral, and process. Brown and Srebalus (2003) identified three major models of consultation: mental health, behavioral, and organizational development.

Gladding (2004) provided a helpful synthesis of several of the most comprehensive models of consultation. He described four categories that reflect many of those discussed previously. In the **expert** or **provision model**, the consultant functions as one who has the knowledge and skill to resolve problems that other professionals either cannot or do not have time to deal with. The consultant assumes responsibility for affecting change. A consultant might be hired to provide staff training in conflict resolution because no one else in the organization has the background or ability to do the training.

In the **doctor-patient** or **prescription model**, the consultant functions (as the analogy indicates) by diagnosing the problem and prescribing what the consultee should do about it. This is different from the expert model in that the responsibility for the application of the prescribed action and final "cure" lies with the consultee, not the consultant. The consultant operating from the prescription or doctor-patient model identifies the sources of interpersonal conflict in an organization and presents a list of actions that the management team could carry out to resolve the conflict.

The **mediation model** calls for the consultant to unify the activities and processes of different people who are trying to provide services to the same population. A mediating consultant could bring together the directors of several human service agencies to reduce territoriality and to negotiate a cooperative plan for referral. Finally, in the **process consultation** or **collaboration model**, the consultant facilitates the problem-solving process rather than providing the actual solution. The consultant's efforts are aimed at improving consultees' communication and helping them to work together more effectively to resolve their mutual problems. Activity 8.3 helps you to apply what you have learned about consultation models.

ACTIVITY 8.3   CONSULTATION CASES

Consider the five consultation situations described, and determine which model or models of consultation would best apply for each and explain why.

(Continued)

Case 1

The management team of a family-owned manufacturing business is experiencing difficulty with a transition of leadership. The founder of the company is turning it over to her four adult children, but is having difficulty letting go. She still wants to influence the direction of the company, making sure it does not falter. In addition, the new management team of four siblings wants to establish their leadership by involving all the other managing employees in a team-building process to maximize efficiency and employee satisfaction. Their intention is to empower the broader management team while communicating that they are now in charge of the company. One of the siblings calls you to ask what kind of help they need, if any.

Case 2

A small, rural town has no social service agencies or counseling centers available to help the few hundred people who live there. Some of the citizens called the nearest university to ask if students or faculty could provide community awareness workshops on mental illness, especially to help the families of persons diagnosed with schizophrenia or depression.

Case 3

A professional counselor in a college counseling center is very skilled at helping undergraduate students with typical career, relational, and developmental counseling issues, but has no experience with clinical mental health counseling. She has a new client that she thinks fits the diagnosis of borderline personality disorder, but is unsure. In addition, she feels unable to provide helpful therapy to this client. At the suggestion of her administrative supervisor, she calls a local psychiatrist for assistance.

Case 4

A school principal calls a professional school counselor for problem-solving assistance in dealing with intense interpersonal conflict among the teaching staff. Apparently, there are long-standing grievances among a handful of teachers, along with the gossip, mistrust, hostility, and resistance to change that frequently accompany such problems. Not knowing how to solve the problem himself, the principal calls the professional school counselor for assistance.

Case 5

The director of a community counseling agency wants to know whether or not the programs currently being implemented at her agency are the best or even a reasonable expenditure of the limited funds available. Not knowing how to do program evaluation or action research, she calls on the director of another agency for help with her lack of evaluative expertise.

Consultant Roles

Because consultation is a multifaceted activity, consultants must fulfill many different roles to be effective. Different consultation situations call for different consultation roles, several of which may be synthesized into the professional presence of a single consultant. Following are descriptions of the most common roles assumed by consultants (Dougherty, 2005; Gallesich, 1982; Hansen et al., 1990).

EXPERT   Individuals receiving assistance from a consultant can reasonably and justifiably expect the consultant to know more about the problem or its potential solutions than they do. A consultant often serves as a source of expertise, in knowledge and in skill, which the consultee does not have.

ADVISOR   In part because of their expertise and because it is easier for them to be objective observers of the problem situation, consultants can suggest ideas or courses of action that have yet to be considered by the consultee. Supportive guidance in the right direction often provides the solution needed by the consultee who is seeking assistance.

RESEARCHER   Often consultants function as fact finders, collecting data for use in program evaluation, to aid in decisions about organizational change, or to develop awareness of community and social trends. Sometimes the consultant is asked specifically to conduct research as the major task for an organization; sometimes research is one of the many tasks initiated by the consultant to reach a broader set of objectives.

PROGRAM EVALUATOR   Increasingly, continued funding for human service or educational programs is contingent upon the demonstrated effectiveness of the program. Consultants are often called upon to document program outcomes or to make recommendations for program improvement when the program staff members do not have the time or the ability to conduct such an evaluation themselves.

TEACHER/TRAINER/EDUCATOR   Sometimes the major problem facing a human service professional or organization can be resolved by learning new information or acquiring new skills. In this case, the consultant develops curricula if needed, presents instructional materials, and facilitates learning experiences germane to the subject area.

ADVOCATE   Consultants can advocate for a person or for a position. Advocacy for a person occurs when the consultant champions the rights of an individual or group in the face of injustice or disadvantage. Advocacy for a position occurs when the consultant attempts to persuade others to accept a particular answer or make a certain decision about an issue.

PROCESS SPECIALIST   In this role, the consultant focuses more on the interactive process itself than on the content of the problem. The consultant facilitates constructive interaction among participants to help resolve the problem at hand, while enhancing their understanding of the interpersonal dynamics at work in their setting.

COLLABORATOR   The consultant and consultee share a mutual contribution to problem identification and solution development. They function as equal and interdependent sources of information and judgment, working as partners to create an effective resolution to the issue. Now apply what you have learned about consultant roles by completing Activity 8.4.

ACTIVITY 8.4   CONSULTATION ROLES

Consider again the consultation cases presented in Activity 8.3. Determine which consultant role best fits the needs of each situation and explain why.

Consultation Skills

As evidenced by the types of consultation described earlier, professional counselors who choose to serve as consultants need a variety of skills (Conoley & Conoley, 1991; Dougherty, 2005; Wallace & Hall, 1996). Although some of those skills are likely to be possessed by any effective counselor, others are personal characteristics and areas of expertise that are different from counseling skills per se. An effective consultant must have strong interpersonal skills. There is no substitute for effective communication and a positive, accepting attitude toward others. Communication skills include the willingness and ability to listen. To communicate well with groups and organizations, consultants often need skills in professional writing and in public speaking.

Because most of the problems encountered by professional counselors who serve as consultants emerge from the human nature of consultees and their clients, it is also important to understand people, their motives, needs, shortcomings, and strengths. Consultants should be able to identify problems and have problem-solving skills. It helps to have some background in organizational development, which enables the consultant to understand the environmental setting of some consultations or the nature of an organization that needs help. Because of the heterogeneous nature of society and the importance of treating all individuals with respect, consultants should be aware, inclusive, and considerate of racial and cultural diversity *issues* in the consultation process. Ideally, consultants should have interpersonal experience with and be respectful of the ethnicity of consultees and of their clients.

Consultants must maintain the same level of professional ethics expected of the professional counselor, including appropriate privacy, informed consent, and practicing only within one's level of competence. Consultants must be objective in their efforts to understand and to help resolve consultee problems, especially when contracted by a supervisor to interact with subordinates. Consultants also need skills in group process and team-building. Understanding the typical reasons why working groups are conflicted can enable a consultant to identify quickly and act to resolve the problems of an ineffective team (Basham, Appleton, & Dykeman, 2000). Now use your understanding of the various consultation skills to complete Activity 8.5.

ACTIVITY 8.5   CONSULTATION SKILLS

Consider again the consultation scenarios presented in Activity 8.3. Determine which consultant skills you think would be needed or most effective in each situation and explain why.

Consultation Settings

Consultation performed by professional counselors usually occurs in one of three settings: human service agencies; schools; and a broad category of business, government, and other organizations. Consultant activity among practitioners in mental health and other human service agencies often involves **case consultation** about a specific client, staff training for an agency, or organizational problem solving such as team building and conflict resolution. Much of this activity is **external consultation**; the consultant is often assisting those outside his or her own agency. This situation necessitates that the consultant spend some time getting to know the consultee's practice, professional competencies, and presented problems.

The professional school counselor functions primarily as an **internal consultant**, fulfilling the role of expert resource for a variety of individuals connected to the educational setting (Dougherty, 2005; Erford, 2007a). These include parents, teachers, principals, and sometimes students themselves. The professional school counselor can also have a substantial impact as a systems change agent, using team-building, conflict resolution, and group dynamics skills to help create a more constructive learning and working environment at the school. Because the counselor is contributing to a familiar system, less time is needed to become acquainted with the setting or the consultee than in external consultation. Finally, professional school counselors who are skilled in applied research techniques can assist other educators in program evaluation to improve the quality of educational and counseling services provided (Lusky & Hayes, 2001).

In addition to the expanding role of the professional school counselor as a systems change agent, the past two decades have seen an increase of consultant activity from other professionals in the community (Will, 2003). The role of schools has changed over the years as they have become centers of intervention for such problems as youth violence, teen pregnancy, substance abuse, and child abuse and neglect. Outside consultants to the education system have been instrumental in helping educators provide on-site assistance to children and adolescents.

Many counseling professionals serve as consultants to organizations that are unrelated to the human service or educational fields (Wallace & Hall, 1996). The primary purpose of most organizational consultation is to strengthen the effectiveness of the organization (Dougherty, 2005). Businesses, government agencies, and nonprofit endeavors frequently seek the assistance of professional counselors because the problems faced by the organization are rooted in the interpersonal and group process components of working together. Because professional counselors by nature are supposed to be experts in understanding people, many organizations seek the consultation assistance of a professional counselor to help resolve interpersonal conflicts, train managers to be more effective leaders, create appropriate professional development workshops for employees, help employees manage a changing work environment, and in other ways assist the organization through an applied understanding of human nature. Activity 8.6 helps you to consider your own potential as a consultant.

ACTIVITY 8.6   PERSONAL APPLICATION

Which types of consultation activities would you most like to provide? Which of the consultation skills listed previously do you already possess? Which skills represent lines of growth (not weaknesses) to pursue in your professional development?

SUPERVISION

Supervision is the process by which a helping professional with appropriate training mentors and teaches another individual. It is a process of professional and personal development in which the supervisor challenges, stimulates, and encourages a professional counselor to reach higher levels of competence (Bradley & Kottler, 2001). Bernard and Goodyear (1998) defined **supervision** as

> . . . an intervention provided by a more senior member of a profession to a more junior member or members of that same profession. This relationship is evaluative, extends over time, and has the simultaneous purposes of enhancing the professional functioning of the more junior person(s), monitoring the quality of professional services offered to the client(s) she, he, or they see(s), and serving as a gatekeeper of those who are to enter the particular profession. (p. 6)

Aspects of supervision overlap with consultation in several ways, and for some professionals, supervision often evolves into consultation. Experienced counselors may meet informally with other professionals to discuss ideas about how to work with specific clients or to gain different perspectives, a practice often called **peer supervision**.

Counselor supervision has many purposes, and its focus may change depending on the developmental level of the supervisee. Three main purposes of supervision are (1) facilitation of the counselor's professional and personal development, (2) promotion of counselor competencies, and (3) promotion of accountable counseling services and programs (Bradley & Kottler, 2001). To accomplish the purposes of supervision, the supervisor assumes several different roles, including mentor, advocate, teacher, case consultant, and collaborator, in exploring supervisee counter-transference issues. Through each of these roles, the supervisor engages in specific activities, which may include support, interpersonal and intrapersonal exploration of the supervisee, training, instruction, and evaluation.

Supervisors should also pay attention to diversity issues in supervision (Bernard & Goodyear, 1998). As in the counseling relationship, the potential effect of diversity issues on which supervisor and supervisee differ should be explored openly and honestly as a part of the learning experience for both. In addition, supervisors should assist supervisees to explore the diversity issues of the clients being served and the communities in which they live and work. Appropriate topics for consideration include differences in belief systems; communication and learning styles; and cultural, racial, and gender issues. Reflection 8.1 helps you explore previous experiences with supervision.

REFLECTION 8.1

Before beginning discussion of the models, formats, and interventions of supervision, reflect on previous experiences when you have engaged in supervision, either as the supervisor or supervisee. Can you identify the specific purpose of the supervision? What roles did you (as the supervisee) or the supervisor assume? List the qualities of the supervisor that helped in the process. What qualities did you display that helped the process? Were there any unhelpful qualities displayed?

Models of Supervision

Supervisors employ numerous models including theory-based models, developmental approaches, and models developed specifically for supervision. One group of supervision models is based on counseling theories and can best be described as a direct extension of the particular counseling theory. Supervisors who work from a theory-based supervision model engage with supervisees in a manner that is consistent with their counseling philosophy. At least some of the content, focus, and process of supervision is grounded in the supervisor's counseling model.

Examples of theory-based models include psychodynamic, person-centered, cognitive-behavioral, and systemic supervision. Person-centered supervision believes that the facilitative conditions (e.g., genuineness, empathy, warmth) necessary for counseling apply to the supervisory relationship as well. A successful person-centered supervisor must have a profound trust that the supervisee has the ability and motivation to grow and to explore the therapy situation and the self. A major goal of person-centered supervision is to help the counselor to grow in self-confidence, in self-understanding, and in understanding the therapeutic process (Bernard & Goodyear, 1998).

When the cognitive-behavioral model is used, the purpose of supervision is to teach appropriate counselor behaviors and to extinguish inappropriate behaviors. Additionally, training and supervision should assist the supervisee in developing specific skills, and in applying and refining them. In cognitive-behavioral supervision, counseling skills are behaviorally defined, and supervision employs the principles of learning theory within its procedures (Bernard & Goodyear, 1998).

Developmental supervision approaches focus on how supervisees change as they gain training and supervised experience. Developmental approaches focus on the development of the supervisee and on how the supervisor might work with the supervisee at different developmental levels. Developmental approaches to supervision are based on the assumption that, in the process of moving toward competence, supervisees move through a series of stages that are qualitatively different from one another. Each of these supervisee growth stages requires a qualitatively different supervisory environment for optimal growth to occur (Chagnon & Russell, 1995).

One developmental approach to supervision is the model by Loganbill, Hardy, and Delworth (1982), which focuses on issues supervisees face in their development. Supervisee issues include competence, emotional awareness, autonomy, identity, respect for individual differences, purpose and direction, personal motivation, and professional ethics. The three stages of development are stagnation (e.g., unawareness, dualistic thinking, extreme dependence), confusion (e.g., instability, conflict, fluctuation of feeling regarding ability of self and supervisor), and integration (e.g., calm reorganization, realistic views of self and supervisor). As supervisees deal with each of their issues, they might be at one of the three stages or in transition between stages. In this model, the supervisor's role is to assess each supervisee for each issue and to help the supervisee move to the next stage of development.

Another development approach to supervision, the integrated developmental model by Stoltenberg, McNeill, and Delworth (1988), describes counselor development as progressing through various stages to increasing levels of complexity and sophistication. There are four levels, starting with the beginning level I counselor and ending with the most complex and integrated level III-I counselor. Stoltenberg and Delworth (1987) conceptualized counselor development, and increases in competence and complexity, in terms of eight specific domains of professional functioning and three overriding structures that characterized counselor development. The eight domains of professional functioning addressed by the model are intervention skills, assessment techniques, interpersonal assessment, client conceptualization, individual differences, theoretical orientation, treatment goals and plans, and professional ethics. The three overriding structures are motivation, self-other awareness, and dependency/autonomy (Stoltenberg & Delworth, 1987).

Two strengths of the Stoltenberg and Delworth (1987) integrated developmental model are that it supports a strategic needs-based approach to supervision and indicates specific areas for immediate focus within supervision. The model prescribes a supervision that gives supervisees what they need to further their development by indicating to supervisors a framework from which they can plan their specific supervisory interventions. Apply the supervision models discussed here to the case of Nicole in Case Study 8.1.

CASE STUDY 8.1

Nicole was in her first experience of practicum supervision. During her first session, she was asked to be prepared to show videotaped segments of her counseling sessions during each supervision session. At one of her sessions she told her supervisor that she forgot her tape at home and asked to discuss the client without the videotape. A few sessions later, Nicole again arrived for supervision without a videotape, stating that the video camera failed to record her sessions.

- What developmental issues may Nicole be dealing with?
- What stage or stages of development is she in?
- If you were Nicole, how would you want the supervisor to address your concerns and help you move to the next stage of development?

In addition to theory-based and developmental approaches to supervision, numerous approaches have been developed or modified specifically for supervision. One prominent model is the **discrimination model** (Bernard & Goodyear, 1998), which attends to three separate areas of focus in supervision and assumes three supervisor roles. In the discrimination model, supervisors focus on the following skills of supervisees:

- **Intervention skills**, or what the supervisee is doing in session that is observable by the supervisor
- **Conceptualization skills**, or how the supervisee understands what is occurring in the session, identifies patterns, or chooses interventions
- **Personalization skills**, or the supervisee's personal style

In addition to the three areas of focus, the supervisor chooses one of three roles to accomplish the supervision goals. The roles of the supervisor are as follows:

- *Teacher*—the supervisor teaches specific concepts and techniques and may assign reading to assist the supervisee.
- *Counselor*—the supervisor may help the supervisee focus on personal issues such as discomfort or abilities, and help the supervisee confront personal issues that may affect the counseling sessions.
- *Consultant*—the supervisor may work with the supervisee to identify different interventions, may discuss several models for the supervisee to consider, or may address issues related to specific client populations.

Depending on the chosen role, the supervisor's interactions differ as they work with any of the three focus areas.

The systems approach (Holloway, 1995) is a supervision model that helps supervisors assess supervisee learning needs and teaching interventions. The approach describes seven interrelated factors of the model that contribute to the process and outcome of supervision. The factors include four contextual factors such as the institution, the supervisor, the client and the supervisee along with the supervision functions, the supervision tasks, and the supervision relationship. The supervision relationship is seen as the core factor. These seven factors interact with each other and influence the overall supervisory relationship. As such, supervision is understood as a shared interactional phenomenon (Holloway, 1995).

The Friedlander and Ward model (1984) focuses on six levels, and each level influences the other levels. The model begins with the assumptive world, or the supervisor's past professional and life experience, including trainings, values, cultural background, and worldview. The supervisor's assumptive world influences his or her choice of theoretical orientation, which influences the choice of style or role as supervisor. The supervisor's style or role determines his or her strategy or focus, which influences the choice of format or method. Based on the choice of format or method for supervision, the supervisor chooses the appropriate technique. This model highlights the social influence of the supervisor's assumptive world, and how it affects role, focus, format, and technique.

Supervisors may employ a theory-based model, a developmental model, or an approach that focuses on their social role. Some supervisors may develop an eclectic or integrated approach to supervision (Bernard & Goodyear, 1998). When supervisors develop an integrated approach, they customize their supervision to the needs and differences of the individual or group of supervisees. To explore these differences, see Activity 8.7.

ACTIVITY 8.7

Contact some of the community agencies or schools in your area to learn what supervision they offer to interns and to employees. What models, formats, and interventions do they employ?

Supervision Formats

Counselor supervision is conducted through many different formats, each presenting benefits and drawbacks. Individual supervision is the most widely used form of supervision and is what most people think of when they think of supervision. Group supervision and triadic supervision are also commonly used formats.

Individual supervision is exactly what the term indicates, an individual supervisee meeting with one supervisor. Although there can be great variety in the content of the supervision session, its process and structure are fairly predictable and organized with consistency (Cohen, 2004). Individual sessions usually start with a check-in, which leads to session goals, then the work of the session, and a final check-out. The supervisor begins each session with the check-in to give the supervisee room to discuss what might be most important to cover during that session. The check-in also gives the supervisor information that can be used in setting goals for the supervision session.

Session goals are generally anchored to the respective roles of supervisor and supervisee and to the learning objectives, responsibilities, and criteria for success agreed to in the supervisory contract (Cohen, 2004). Session goals also tie into assessments, evaluations, areas for growth, and interventions or techniques as each of these relate to the current clinical work of the supervisee. Supervision goals may also be set according to the model used by the supervisor, which may focus more on personal insight or growth of the supervisee, better conceptualization of client concerns, or a review of strengths that have been observed to reinforce what is working and what the supervisee is doing well. During individual supervision, the supervisor may employ specific interventions to aid in the process. Some of those interventions will be discussed in a later section.

In many ways, supervision conducted in a group is similar to individual supervision except that it is conducted in a group format. The supervisor uses many of the skills, models, and professional values that characterize individual supervision. Group supervision complements individual supervision and provides another forum in which to implement the roles, learning objectives, and responsibilities agreed to in the supervisory contract. Many university training programs use group supervision at one point or another during practicum and internship, in conjunction with individual supervision. Bernard and Goodyear (1998) defined **group supervision** as

> . . . a regular meeting of a group of supervisees with a designated supervisor, for the purpose of furthering their understanding of themselves as clinicians, of the clients with whom they work, or of services delivery in general, and who are aided in this endeavor by their interaction with each other in the context of group process. (p. 111)

Group supervision can be conducted in several different formats, the choice of which may influence the focus and the goals of the supervision sessions. One sort of group in the clinical setting is organized around basic administrative or organizational issues and is often presumed to focus on the agency's needs. This group is often called a staff meeting, and the structure of the group is typically organized around an agenda that communicates information about policies and procedures, service delivery, productivity, coverage, and record keeping (Cohen, 2004).

A second form of group supervision is a training group, which may include didactic seminars centering on specific clinical matters or issue-oriented sessions and tutorials of interest to the staff. In training groups, members may also review cases or other service delivery issues. These meetings are usually set by the group supervisor.

A third form of group supervision is group clinical supervision, with its major emphasis on facilitating professional growth. Supervisors focus on supervisee development, but they must also understand and manage group process and all the dynamics that can be present in any group format. Group clinical supervision focuses on many of the same issues covered under individual supervision with the added advantages that can be found only in the group format.

Advantages of group supervision include minimized supervisee dependence; opportunities for vicarious learning; exposure to a broader range of clients; and economies of time, money, and expertise. Group supervision also allows for greater quantity and diversity and possibly greater quality of feedback for the supervisee (Bernard & Goodyear, 1998).

Despite the numerous advantages advantages of group supervision, there are some drawbacks to the group format. The group format may not allow individuals to get what they need, and certain group dynamics can impede learning. Confidentiality may be a greater concern for some in group supervision. Some group members may spend too much time on issues not of particular relevance to or interest for the other group members (Bernard & Goodyear, 1998).

Triadic supervision attempts to combine the benefits of individual and group supervision into its session by bringing two supervisees together with one supervisor. This format allows for vicarious learning, exposure to a broader range of clients, and more diverse feedback, while limiting the size and distracting effects that can occur in large group supervision (Bernard & Goodyear, 1998). Now engage in Reflection 8.2.

REFLECTION 8.2

After reviewing the different supervision formats, picture yourself in individual, group, and triadic formats.
- In what format would you feel most comfortable? In what format would you feel most anxious? Discuss your answers, and highlight which elements of each format would affect your comfort level and your anxiety.
- If you were engaged in group supervision, what characteristics do you have that would help the group process? What techniques do you hope your supervisor would employ to help maximize the group supervision process? What characteristics in the participants would impede the group process?

Supervision Interventions

Within the varied supervision formats, supervisors can employ numerous supervision interventions to enhance supervisee experience and learning. These interventions include self-report, process notes, audiotape or videotape, cotherapy, and live supervision. Each intervention can be used in individual, triadic, or group supervision, and some interventions are more commonly used in certain formats. Before proceeding, consider the supervision needs of diverse professional groups by engaging in Reflection 8.3.

REFLECTION 8.3

As we begin to explore supervision interventions, think about other professionals, such as a surgeon, a dentist, or an ophthalmologist. If you were a patient and one of these professionals performed a specific procedure on you, what type of supervision would you hope they had received?

Self-report is seen as an intense tutorial relationship in which the supervisee fine-tunes case conceptualization ability and knowledge of self as each relates to counselor-client relationships. Self-report is commonly used for postgraduate supervision, but is generally viewed as far less appropriate for novice supervisees (Bernard & Goodyear, 1998). In a format similar to self-report, some supervisors find reviewing process notes to be a valuable way of tracking the supervisee's cognitive processes in ways that more active forms of supervision lack (Olsen & Stern, 1990).

Rogers was one of the first to use audiotapes in supervision, which brought about a dramatic shift in the supervision process (Bernard & Goodyear, 1998). The review of audiotape segments can allow the supervision to focus on specific therapy techniques, help the supervisee see the relationship between process and content, focus on how points are made in session, and help the supervisee differentiate between a conversational tone and a therapeutic tone (Goldberg, 1985). Audiotape review also allows supervisees to receive feedback about specific points in a session when they may be struggling personally with their own issues or interpersonally with the client. Many supervisors now use videotape in place of or in addition to audiotape. **Videotape review** allows for the same advantages as audiotape with an additional opportunity to focus on such things as nonverbal communication, incongruence in the client, or lack of synchrony between the client and the supervisee.

With videotape in supervision, professionals' knowledge base and experiential alternatives have increased greatly. Supervisors can better see themselves in the role of the helper, allowing them to be a more complete observer of the work than is possible with just an audiotape (Bernard & Goodyear, 1998). Supervisees can review their tapes privately at their own pace, play selected parts for the supervisor, and come prepared with questions and observations of their own. Supervisors also have the option of picking out particular interactions and keying in on them to share observations about supervisee strengths and areas of growth in assessment and intervention (Cohen, 2004).

Live supervision is used in many training programs and until more recently was considered the hallmark of family therapy training. Live supervision began as an intensive method for working with an individual supervisee, but in more recent years, the team form of live supervision has become more common (Bernard & Goodyear, 1998). When teams are used in live supervision, a group of professional counselors or trainees works together on their cases, with or without a supervisor. Within live supervision, several interventions can be used, such as cotherapy, bug-in-the-ear (BITE), telephone, and the team approach. All these techniques are similar in that they enable the supervisor to monitor the session as it occurs. Each live supervision technique can be modified to fit individual, triadic, and group formats.

During **cotherapy**, or **direct observation**, the supervisor is present in the room with the supervisee, making interventions and comments when appropriate. This intervention permits the supervisor to observe the supervisee while modeling counseling skills in session. When cotherapy is used, most supervisory feedback is given following the session.

Bug-in-the-ear (BITE) and telephone interventions are the two most popular forms of live supervision (Bradley & Ladany, 2001). The BITE method uses a hearing aid type of device to transmit communication from a supervisor watching behind a one-way mirror or closed-circuit television. This intervention has several advantages, including the fact that it allows the supervisor to make minor adjustments or to reinforce the supervisee briefly without interrupting the flow of the counseling session. BITE also protects the therapy relationship more fully than other live supervision interventions because clients are unaware which counselor interventions are the direct suggestions of the supervisor and which originate from the professional counselor (Bernard & Goodyear, 1998). A more recent alternative to BITE is **bug-in-the-eye**, in which supervisors type suggestions from a keyboard in the observation room to be read on a monitor placed behind the client in the therapy room.

Similar to the BITE methods, supervisors may employ telephone interventions to monitor counseling sessions and offer feedback to the supervisee during a counseling session. In contrast to BITE, where the flow of the session is not interrupted, a telephone intervention does disrupt the flow, but can offer the supervisee an opportunity to clarify or discuss the supervisory message. Telephone interventions and BITE methods are the optimal live supervision methods used for communicating brief, uncomplicated, and action-oriented messages, rather than addressing more complicated process issues. When the supervisee needs more clarification than can be provided with a phone directive, the supervisee should leave the session temporarily for a consultation break.

   Supervisory consultation breaks can be used as the sole live supervision intervention or in addition to one of the several types of interventions. This supervisory consultation break should not be confused with the professional counselor's multiple consultation roles described earlier. When supervisory consultation break is used, the supervisee leaves the counseling session to receive more in-depth feedback, to discuss the client process, or to address personal concerns. When a supervisee uses a consultation break, the supervisee must consider how long he or she is out of the room, the impact on the momentum and flow of the session, and the time he or she may need to process the suggestions. Some professional counselors take a break during a therapy session even when there is no one to consult. A temporary break during a session can allow a professional counselor to reflect on an issue, gather his or her thoughts, or regroup before proceeding.

   In addition to or in place of phone-in interventions, some supervisors may choose simply to observe the counseling session, make no interventions during the counseling session, and provide all feedback after the session. When monitoring live sessions, another type of intervention is called **in vivo**, in which the supervisor consults with the supervisee in view of the client. The conversation between the supervisor and the supervisee can be seen as an intervention to heighten the client's awareness of particular dynamics that are present in the session. Another intervention that is similar to in vivo is called a walk-in. The supervisor literally walks into the counseling room to consult directly with the supervisee in view of the client, or to interact with the supervisee and the client. The walk-in does not imply an emergency, and it does not imply the kind of collegiality that is evident with in vivo supervision. A walk-in can be used to redirect the session and to establish certain dynamics between the supervisor and the client or the supervisee and the client. All three interventions involve the supervisor being present behind a one-way mirror and choosing how and when to enter the therapy room. These modes of supervision intrude more on the therapy process than do the methods of phone-in interventions.

   When live supervision is used, presession planning and postsession debriefing are vital parts of the process. The goal of the presession planning is to prepare the supervisee for the upcoming counseling session. The supervisor may help the supervisee to plan for the upcoming session and to focus on the specific learning goals. It is important for the supervisor and the supervisee to complete the presession planning with some clarity about their roles for the counseling session (Bernard & Goodyear, 1998).

   A postsession debriefing allows the supervisor and the supervisee to discuss what transpired in the counseling session. This is a time to share perceptions, review the effectiveness of interventions, offer feedback, address any remaining concerns, and begin planning for the next session. Postsession debriefing is an optimal time for conceptual growth for the supervisee, so the supervisor should allow a proper amount of time for in-depth processing and discussion.

   When conducting live supervision, supervisors may use the various interventions in individual, triadic, and group formats. When using triadic and group formats, supervisors can use the observation rooms as key learning laboratories for the other supervisees. Group members may be asked to watch for specific interventions and work to enhance their conceptualization skills without having the pressure to engage with the client. In the presession and postsession planning, group members can offer additional support, alternative perceptions, and constructive feedback.

When supervisees receive direct observation and coaching through live supervision, there is a greater likelihood that therapy will go well, and that the supervisee will learn more efficiently and profoundly as a result of these successful counseling sessions (Bernard & Goodyear, 1998). Because live supervision provides more safety for client welfare than other forms of supervision, the presence of the supervisor allows supervisees to work with more challenging cases. Another advantage of live supervision is that the supervisee's view of the process of counseling is positively affected because counseling unfolds far more systematically as a result of the input from the supervisor.

The most noted disadvantages of live supervision are the time it demands of supervisors, the cost of facilities, the problem of scheduling cases to accommodate all the individuals involved, and the potential negative reactions from clients (Bernard & Goodyear, 1998). Another disadvantage or potential risk is the danger of the supervisor dominating counseling through live supervision or of supervisee dependence on the supervisor's interventions. To help consolidate your understanding of supervision interventions, complete Activity 8.8 and Reflection 8.4.

ACTIVITY 8.8

Under the direction of the class instructor, divide into small groups and set up role-plays to practice as many of the different kinds of supervision interventions as possible.
- How do the interventions change depending on the specific model of intervention (e.g., phone-in, BITE, walk-in, consultation break)?
- What is the role of the observers? How can your peers best assist your learning?
- When did you feel anxious? How did you respond?
- When using live supervision, make sure you allow time for a presession and postsession meeting.

REFLECTION 8.4

After reviewing each of the supervision interventions, reflect back on the prior question about which type of supervision you would want your surgeon, dentist, or ophthalmologist to have received during his or her training or while he or she was performing your procedure. Rank each of the interventions discussed in this section from most effective to least effective in training the health professional to be competent in performing the particular procedure. Now reflect on your role as a counselor. Does your list of training effectiveness change? How can this experience influence how you approach different supervision interventions?

Supervisory Relationship

Any form of supervision can cause anxiety for the supervisee. Specific efforts should be made to develop a working supervisory relationship that provides a safe learning environment. Supervisors should receive training on supervision models, formats, interventions, and issues specific to supervisee development. Just as a positive and productive relationship is critical to successful counseling, similarly, it is also critical for a successful supervision. (Worthen & McNeill, 1996).

A strong supervisory relationship based on trust and respect is vital to the supervisee's exploration of personal and professional issues while in supervision. Similar to the conditions required to develop a strong relationship between the professional counselor and the client, the supervision literature suggests that several elements are necessary to establish an effective supervisory relationship, including empathic understanding, genuineness, respect, and concreteness. In a positive working relationship, the supervisee's mistakes are not seen as failures; rather, the supervisor works to create an environment of experimentation that allows for supervisee risk taking (Bradley & Ladany, 2001).

Given the nature and purpose of supervision, supervisees often experience anxiety as they are continuously being scrutinized and evaluated by themselves and their supervisors. Within the context of a strong supervisory relationship, however, supervisees can feel that they have a safe space in which to learn to cope with and to tolerate their anxiety. Supervisors should provide supervisees with support, encouragement, and openness (Bradley & Ladany, 2001). Supervisors should also pay attention to differences in belief systems; learning styles; and cultural, racial, and gender issues in supervision (Bernard & Goodyear, 1998). Supervisors should provide a learning environment where the supervisor and the supervisee can readily address potential conflicts and concerns.

Not all professional counselors are capable of being supervisors. First, supervision requires advanced levels of expertise that not all counselors possess. Second, the evaluative scrutiny and honest reflection about another's counseling skills requires a deft balance of support and confrontation that requires special skill to maintain. Third, supervision works only when the relationship between the supervisor and the supervisee consists of trust and mutual respect, especially when the supervisee's own issues are being discussed. Finally, very few professional counselors have received training in supervision skills. Ironically, the same states that require training and certification/licensure to be recognized as a professional counselor do not require specialized training for counselors who supervise counselors in-training seeking to be licensed. Most states do not yet require specific training in supervision before one assumes the role of supervisor. Years of counseling experience and an accumulation of academic credits should not be viewed as sufficient qualifications for supervisors (Bradley & Ladany, 2001). It would be useful to provide novice supervisors with training in specific skills related to supervision before their work with supervisees (Bernard & Goodyear, 1998). Watch for a trend in the availability and requirement of specialized training for counseling supervisors. To further your thoughts on the issues relevant to supervision, complete Activity 8.9.

ACTIVITY 8.9

Develop a list of questions regarding ethical, legal, and client issues regarding supervision. Interview counseling supervisors from community agencies, private practice, or schools to get their answers to the questions. Discuss with the supervisors how they address these issues.

Summary

Consultation and supervision are two important activities through which experienced professional counselors can contribute to the professional development and accomplishments of others, within and outside of the counseling profession. Supervisors are essential to the training of new counselors, guiding neophytes in the development of their counseling skills while ensuring the well-being of the clients of emerging helpers. Consultants are able to use their expertise to modify organizational systems, solve interpersonal problems, and empower others through training. Supervision is required by educational and legal parameters; consultation is voluntarily sought by those seeking assistance. As indicated, many different models, techniques, and skills exist for consultation and supervision. However, successful consultants and supervisors must have advanced professional skills that enable them to accomplish more difficult and varied tasks than are found in individual and group counseling.

CHAPTER

9

Settings and Counseling Career Choices

Nadine E. Garner, James P. Valle,
and Nichole Hinkle

PREVIEW

This chapter describes the unique characteristics of working as a professional counselor in the increasingly multicultural settings of elementary and secondary schools; college and university campuses; the mental health settings of community/agency, hospitals, corrections, and private practice; and the various settings for rehabilitation counselors. The chapter is also an invitation to consider the various counseling career choices in a personal, hands-on way, through the suggested activities and the first-person accounts from practicing counselors entitled, "A Counselor's Reflection." The end of each section contains contact information of related professional organizations, publications, and websites for further research.

COUNSELING CAREER CHOICES

The experiences that a professional counselor will have on the job are shaped by the setting in which the counseling occurs. It is essential, during one's graduate program, to explore carefully the special features of these settings, including the diverse counseling career choices within each setting.

Graduate students who take the initiative to investigate the realities of their intended counseling setting have distinct advantages over students who do not acquire this knowledge. They will be equipped to make an informed decision about their future career plans. They will also appear more attractive to potential employers during the interview process by conveying their understanding of the counselor's role and asking important clarifying questions about the specifics of the position.

Knowledgeable professional counselors are less likely to accept a position and then make the shocking discovery that they are not well matched for the demands of their career choice. They can also avoid the extra expense and time of having to return to school to be trained as a counselor in a different setting, which in some cases could amount to getting an unexpected second master's degree.

Ultimately, well-informed graduates become productive counselors who have an excellent chance of experiencing real job satisfaction in their professional roles. They have chosen to work in a setting that allows them to use their talents in ways that contribute to their clients' progress toward personal growth and wellness.

COUNSELING IN THE SCHOOLS

Background

In the early 1900s, the counselor's role in the schools was to help students find employment (Baker, 2000). As the United States became involved in World War I, counselors emphasized testing young men to place them in the armed forces. By World War II, a counselor was also viewed as someone who could offer counseling services for a student's greater personal development. A series of federal education acts in the ensuing decades provided the resources for counselors to serve students more fully in the areas of academic and career development. By the end of the 20th century, the role of the professional school counselor was propelled into a new era by two major contributions to the field: the comprehensive developmental counseling curriculum, and the creation of national standards for school counseling programs.

Gysbers and Henderson (1988) and Myrick (1987) originally outlined the comprehensive developmental counseling curriculum, which assisted counselors in designing and delivering a curriculum that considered the developmental needs of children at all grade levels. The **ASCA *National Standards for School Counseling Programs*** (Campbell & Dahir, 1997) helped unify the profession on a national level, by providing standards that would be relevant to all school counseling programs. These standards defined three categories in which counselors need to focus (i.e., academic development, career development, personal/social development), regardless of whether the professional school counselor worked at the elementary, middle, or high school level.

Elementary Counseling

Elementary school counselors work with students from kindergarten through grade 5, ordinarily with a primary emphasis on developmental issues and prevention strategies. Counselors assist children in making the adjustment to the school setting by helping them understand basic social and academic skills. Parents and teachers use counselors as consultants regarding student behavior and classroom management. In addition to using traditional counseling methods, elementary counselors use other methods to engage children in counseling. Play therapy techniques can help children participate more fully in the counseling process through the language of play. Puppets, role-plays, drawing, and bibliotherapy are expressive arts methods that counselors can use with younger students, especially children who are less verbal. Text Box 9.1 explains how elementary school students can be positively affected by the work of a sensitive counselor.

Middle School/Junior High Counseling

Middle school counselors work with children in grades 6 through 8, helping them make the transition from elementary school to middle school, and then later from middle school to high school. In these transitions, middle school students have to adapt to different

BOX 9.1

A Counselor's Reflection—Elementary School Counseling

"In reflecting on the time that I have spent as an elementary school counselor, I am humbled by my many opportunities to affect the lives of others and exalted by children's willingness to share their lives with me. In this way, elementary school counseling is similar to the other levels of school counseling. That is, I spent quite a bit of time working either one-on-one or in small groups directly with the students in the schools I served. I also frequently served as an advocate for children on my caseload by attending IEP (Individualized Educational Plan) meetings, community program meetings, or other meetings where I felt like I would be able to advocate for the needs of a child I knew.

"In many other ways, the job of the elementary school counselor is vastly different from that of school counselors at other levels. As an elementary counselor in a rural school setting, I served as the counselor for four different school buildings, which were geographically separated by approximately 20 miles and culturally separated by many different viewpoints and values. This proved to be an additional challenge to the job, as I attempted to address programmatic needs across the various schools in an ecumenical and enthusiastic manner. In comparing my vision of elementary school counseling in graduate school to my actual experience of the job, I think I was most surprised by the fact that there was a fair amount of flexibility in the job. In many ways, this was very good. I enjoyed being able to work with teachers and administrators to determine the programmatic needs of the school. I worked to develop a comprehensive school counseling program, as this idea at the elementary level was fairly novel to this particular district. I really enjoyed creating lessons for different age groups. There is a dramatic difference between addressing bullying with kindergarteners (think puppets!) and sixth-graders (think popular lingo!). This really kept the job interesting and reflective, as it only takes one use of the word "resolution" in a classroom of vacantly staring first-graders to realize that you really have to be adaptive and attentive to the needs of various age groups.

"Reaching out to children by accepting where they are developmentally, and watching them grow over these formative years are very gratifying parts of this job. When I first met Anna, she was an 8-year-old, socially withdrawn, and terrified young girl who moved into the school district from out of state. She drew a picture of herself and shared self-descriptive adjectives with me such as "ugly," "mean," and "stupid." I supported Anna for several years by working one-on-one with her, consulting with teachers, and meeting with her parents. Her teacher came to me one afternoon and shared a new picture that Anna, now 11 years old, had drawn. Her picture showed a smiling girl—with many friends—who felt good about her schoolwork. As an elementary school counselor, I was humbled to realize that, though I was far from the only person who played a role in this young girl's transformation, my unique role in the school allowed me to help her progress. Obviously, not every individual situation has such dramatically positive outcomes; nevertheless, I feel that the job of the counselor offers me the ability to share a few steps in the journey of life with children—and the years from ages 6–12 years provide some uniquely interesting and rewarding times to share these steps."

—Jason Baker, Ph.D.
University Professor and Former
Elementary School Counselor

teachers, complicated schedules, and making and losing friends. Counselors need to be aware of the great degrees of variation in physical and social development between students. Middle school counselors focus on topics such as decision making, conflict resolution, peer pressures, sexuality, career development, and substance abuse. Text Box 9.2 illustrates how important it is for middle school students to have an adult in their lives who cares about their struggles.

BOX 9.2

A Counselor's Reflection—Middle School Counseling

"Being a middle school counselor has brought many rewards and struggles to my life. As a school counselor I have the opportunity to interact with students daily in ways that most people cannot. Everyday I have the opportunity to work with amazing students and be available when they need an attentive listener: from broken hearts to failing grades to the loss of a loved one, to simply popping in to say hello. No two days are the same for a counselor.

"A school counselor is an advocate for children. The most rewarding part of my job is being there for students when they need support. During my first two months as a counselor, I struggled with finding the answer to a student's anxiety issues. I could not get this student to stay in school all day—each day was a challenge for him to just make it to lunchtime. One day the student walked into my office and simply handed me a card and walked out. I opened the card and it said, 'Thanks for everything. It's nice to know that someone cares.' Here I thought I was failing by not being able to help this child with his anxiety, and the whole time all he cared about was feeling cared for.

"One thing that most people do not realize about counselors is that they do not spend the entire day talking with students. There are meetings, phone calls, scheduling, and mandated testing that are also a part of being a counselor. Someone thinking of entering the field needs to remember that it all affects the student one way or another—I would not trade my job for the world!"

—Corissa Fetrow, M.Ed.
Middle School Counselor

High School Counseling

High school counselors emphasize academic advising, educational planning, and career development as they help adolescents graduate to the world of work, higher education, or the armed services. In addition, high school counselors need to be sensitive and responsive to adolescents as they create a sense of identity, which may involve students trying to understand their place in the social context and experimenting with new behaviors. A challenge for high school counselors is to be aware of students who may tend toward violent behaviors well before these students manifest these behaviors and cause a school or personal crisis. Text Box 9.3 provides a picture of how the challenges in the context of high school have changed as a result of technology.

Current Issues Affecting All School Counseling Settings

The *No Child Left Behind Act* **(NCLB) of 2001** (Public Law 107-110) is a federal law that specifies the creation of a national program to raise academic achievement for all students, by closing the achievement gap that exists between socially or economically disadvantaged students and students with more advantages. Although school counselors are not mentioned in this educational reform, the American School Counselor Association (ASCA) responded to this movement by introducing the *ASCA National Model: A Framework for School Counseling Programs* (2005). The model directly involves school counseling programs in school reform by helping counselors design programs that align with the mission of the school and student achievement. Counselors using the model are able to demonstrate to the

BOX 9.3

A Counselor's Reflection—High School Counseling

"When deciding to become a school counselor one has to be prepared to be flexible and have a positive outlook. The challenge every day of a high school counselor is helping those students who just do not care (or say that they do not care). Mental health issues and extremely dysfunctional family lives of students add to the everyday challenges for a high school counselor. Socially, we address current trends such as cyber bullying. This Internet harassment is dangerous and is jeopardizing our personal connection with people as humans. We find many students and teenagers who can't settle their differences with others socially, so they utilize the Internet to attack and say things to someone they would not normally say in person.

"A graduate college professor once told me, 'You have to believe there is a treasure in everyone; in some, you might have to dig deeper to retrieve it.' I believe this is what you have to live by as a school counselor in today's society. One might have to dig very deep to reach the positive attribute in a student, but ultimately there is something there to resurrect. To tap into these teenagers is the ultimate reward, which I call the 'Aha' effect, and it is definitely a unique reward in my job. Students who come back to visit or write 'thank you' notes are other verifications to me that these kids are on their way to becoming productive adults in our society."

—Eric Shellenberger, M.Ed.
High School Counselor

school community how school counseling programs are a vital component in students' personal, academic, and career success.

Traditionally, professional school counselors worked with students through four primary interventions: counseling (individual and group), large group guidance, consultation (with parents, teachers, and administrators), and coordination. More recently, however, the *ASCA National Model* (2005) called for a transformed role for professional school counselors, one that integrated delivery systems (i.e., school guidance curriculum, individual student planning, responsive services, and system support), foundations (i.e., beliefs and philosophy, mission statement, and ASCA content standards for student academic, career, and personal/social development), management system (i.e., agreements, advisory council, use of data, action plans,and time management), and accountability (i.e., results report, school counselor performance standards, and program audit) within the meta-interventions of advocacy, leadership, collaboration, and systemic change.

Career counseling and educational planning continue to be major components of the ASCA model across all grade levels. Complete Activity 9.1 to help you gain insight into career guidance and other activities that take place at a career technical center, as a supplement to understanding the career counseling that occurs in elementary, middle, and high schools. Elementary counselors focus on career awareness, exposing children to the variety of career choices. Middle school counselors assist students in career exploration, by introducing students to software programs that can assist them in taking interest inventories and in researching careers. High school counselors help students with the realities of planning for their upcoming careers.

ACTIVITY 9.1   SCHOOL COUNSELOR'S ROLE IN A CAREER TECHNICAL CENTER

Visit a counselor at a career technical center to gain an understanding of the counselor's role, the overall guidance program, the systemic organization and the responsibilities within it, the referral procedures and resources, and the involvement with special needs students.

The national model also calls for counselors to be accountable and to use data to show how their programs make a difference in students' lives. Although professional school counselors who did not learn about data-driven decision making in their graduate programs may be hesitant to initiate data collection as part of their overall accountability program, it is important for professional school counselors to extend their professional development by including the understanding of data and its relevance to the transformed school counselor's role. It is no longer enough for professional school counselors to list the varied tasks that they perform or to log the time spent on tasks. Professional school counselors make a positive difference in their students' lives every day; however, without the benefit of capturing these data in a form that can be shared with other stakeholders in the school community, these valuable data remain invisible. Collecting and reporting data about the effectiveness of the school counseling program allows counselors to be accountable to their stakeholders, to show the importance of their profession in the lives of the school community, and to assist in program evaluations and modifications.

A challenge for professional school counselors is how to serve all students, as the average counselor has a caseload of about 500 students. When counselors see students individually, they cannot meet with them for weekly, hour-long sessions over an extended time as counselors might in community/agency or private practice settings. The use of a brief, solution-focused counseling approach has received much positive support in the schools (LaFountain & Garner, 1998; Metcalf, 1995; Murphy, 2006). Counselors appreciate its positive, direct, and empowering approach for students and generally see individual students for ten or fewer sessions.

Professional school counselors refer students who have serious, ongoing mental health concerns to outside agencies or private practitioners for longer term psychotherapy. A trend in schools is the appearance of counselors from mental health settings, who are employed by the school district to come directly into the school to facilitate groups and to see individual students who have ongoing issues. While some school counselors welcome the addition of these outside counselors to assist them in their ability to serve students, others are wary that their presence could threaten their jobs.

Professional school counselors and other types of counselors and professionals who work with children are **mandated reporters**, meaning that they are required by law to report suspected child abuse and neglect to the proper authorities. It is not the counselor's role to investigate the suspected maltreatment to substantiate the report; that is the task of the agency that is called upon to conduct an investigation. However, school counselors need to be trained to identify the characteristic behaviors and physical signs that would lead a professional to suspect that child abuse or neglect is occurring. Complete Activity 9.2 to give you a working knowledge of social service agencies and get you thinking about their importance to the functions of a school counselor.

ACTIVITY 9.2   SCHOOL COUNSELORS NEED TO CONNECT WITH SOCIAL SERVICE AGENCIES

Why is it important for school counselors to have a working knowledge of social service agencies? (A version of this question is often asked of applicants in interviews for school counseling positions). Research the functions of a minimum of five social service agencies used by professional school counselors. Be able to describe the services provided and the referral procedures. Give an example of how a school counselor may need to enlist the services of one of these agencies to assist a child in need more effectively.

Counselors need to be aware of the wide range of issues affecting students and be able to respond to them as part of their comprehensive developmental curriculum. Some of these issues include cyber bullying, relational aggression, disabilities, grief and loss, suicide, sexual behaviors, substance abuse, violence, poverty, and child maltreatment. For a comprehensive understanding of the great diversity of issues that professional school counselors address, refer to texts such as *Transforming the School Counseling Profession, 2nd Edition* (Erford, 2007a) and *School Counseling: Foundations and Contemporary Issues* (Sciarra, 2004).

Multicultural Issues in Schools

From the multitude of topics with which school counselors must be familiar, the idea of supporting gay, lesbian, bisexual, transgendered, and questioning (GLBTQ) students and their families is difficult for some counselors and schools to acknowledge. Counselors, teachers, and administrators may have their own personal or religious opinions about homosexuality. However, counselors, regardless of their personal or religious opinions about individuals who are GLBTQ, have an ethical obligation not only to counsel these students, but also to be an active voice in the support of GLBTQ issues (American School Counselor Association, 2004).

Advocacy is defined by the American Counseling Association (2005a) as the "promotion of the well-being of individuals and groups, and the counseling profession within systems and organizations. Advocacy seeks to remove barriers and obstacles that inhibit access, growth, and development." Advocacy is an essential responsibility of school counselors and one of the themes of the *ASCA National Model* (ASCA, 2005). GLBTQ students are a minority population that is in desperate need of counselor advocacy. Activity 9.3 helps you to think about the counselor's role in promoting a climate of support for GLBTQ youth.

ACTIVITY 9.3   PROMOTING A CLIMATE OF SUPPORT FOR ISSUES RELATED TO GLBTQ YOUTH

School counselors need to promote a school climate of support and understanding for issues related to GLBTQ youth. Develop one strategy that you can use to support each of these areas: (1) the student who is GLBTQ, (2) the classroom curricula, and (3) the faculty and staff. What obstacles do you anticipate facing? (Internet resources include: www.outproud.org and www.youthresource.com.)

The data regarding U.S. students who are gay or lesbian are compelling. Approximately 10% of the people in the United States consider themselves to be gay or lesbian, which translates to about three million high school students who are gay or lesbian. It is estimated that one out of every ten middle or high school students is becoming aware of their sexual orientation as gay or lesbian (Sciarra, 2004).

Students who are GLBTQ face adjustment problems, isolation, rejection from unsupportive family and friends, and difficulty seeking help for their concerns. Hershberger and D'Augelli (1995) found that this population of students is also more often the victim of hostility in many forms: verbal harassment, property damage, and sexual and physical assault. A federal task force documented that suicide is the leading cause of death among gay and lesbian adolescents (U.S. Department of Health and Human Services, 1989).

Professional school counselors need to promote a school climate of support and understanding for issues related to GLBTQ youth. Uribe and Harbeck (1992) have pioneered programs to support the whole school community, including counseling support groups for gay students, education and materials, school safety measures, faculty and staff training, human rights advocacy, and dropout prevention strategies. Smith and Chen-Hayes (2004) have created a curriculum for school counselors, complete with activities and lessons for leadership and advocacy.

In addition to working directly with students, professional school counselors work with all of the people who have an impact on children's lives, including parents, teachers, staff, administrators, and the community. School counselors need to view students from a holistic approach, including how all of the environmental characteristics of a child's world and the child's own freedom of choice interact to impact the child. A school counseling position requires having a flexible approach to each school day because it is often unpredictable. A crisis situation or an emergency meeting could change plans for the entire day. It is important for prospective school counselors to spend time with a professional counselor before beginning their career. Activity 9.4 provides valuable information to graduate students considering school counseling.

A professional school counselor's visible presence in the school is enhanced by being seen in hallways, classrooms, meetings, the cafeteria, and the playground. Although school counselors may feel at times that they have so many issues to contend with at once that they cannot adequately address them all, the career choice of a school counselor can be a gratifying one because a school counselor can develop an ongoing relationship with students and their families; observe a student's development over time; and know that he or she is playing an active role in contributing to the student's academic, personal/social, and career success. See Text Box 9.4 for information on professional organizations, publications, and websites for school counseling.

ACTIVITY 9.4   SEEING THE PROFESSION FROM THE INSIDE OUT

Before you enter your practicum or internship semesters, contact local school counselors and inquire whether you can volunteer to help with a special project or event. Getting involved in the activities of school counselors before you undertake your field experiences gives you the advantage of feeling more connected to the profession and more prepared to participate fully in your practicum or internship.

BOX 9.4

Professional Organizations, Publications, and Websites for School Counseling

The **American School Counselor Association** (ASCA) (www.schoolcounselor.org) publishes the journal *Professional School Counseling,* and a wealth of resources for school counselors (e.g., books, videos, manuals, posters) on current topics. The ASCA holds an annual conference at various locations around the United States. Each state also has its own ASCA-affiliated branch, which may publish its own newsletter and journal and hold an annual conference or other professional development activities for school counselors statewide. Counties or regions may also have their own counselor's association, some of which are specifically for school counselors.

COLLEGE/UNIVERSITY COUNSELING AND STUDENT-LIFE SERVICES

While college counseling and student-life services are regarded as separate domains, counselors in both of these career choices have the opportunity to be visible in a college setting, playing an integral role in the life of a campus community. Throughout this chapter, the term **college counseling** is used to describe college and university counseling, unless otherwise noted.

Background

College counseling centers and student-life services have evolved to meet changing cultural needs. Modern college counseling centers were established after World War II to assist returning veterans in the transition to college life and vocational choices. Counseling centers were later affected by the Civil Rights movement and the women's movement of the 1960s and 1970s, as minorities, women, and older students became more prevalent on campus. The field of student-life services also responded to the unique needs of these populations by increasing its offerings.

In the 1980s, college counseling centers began to use a variety of counseling approaches to address students' needs holistically. They took into consideration a client's interpersonal, emotional, physical, and spiritual components. In 1991, the **American College Counseling Association (ACCA)** was created as a division of the American Counseling Association (ACA). The advent of the ACCA, including the publication of the scholarly journal, *Journal of College Counseling,* allowed college counselors to demonstrate their professional identity as distinct from student-life professionals. The field of student-life services is represented by several professional organizations, including the American College Personnel Association (ACPA), the National Association of Student Personnel Administrators (NASPA), the ASCA postsecondary division, and the American Psychological Association (APA) Division 17 (Counseling Psychology). Text Box 9.5 contains further information on professional organizations, publications, and websites related to college counseling and student personnel services.

College counselors and student-life professionals need to be aware of the current demographics of today's college student population. It may be surprising to discover that the "traditional" 18- to 22-year-old full-time undergraduate student constitutes only 16% of the total higher education population. According to the U.S. Department of

BOX 9.5

Professional Organizations, Publications, and Websites for College Counseling

American College Counseling Association (ACCA) publishes the *Journal of College Counseling*; www.collegecounseling.org

American College Personnel Association (ACPA); www.myacpa.org

American Psychological Association (APA) Division 17 (Counseling Psychology); www.apa.org

American School Counselor Association (ASCA) postsecondary division; www.schoolcounselor.org

Journal of American College Health; www.acha.org

Journal of College Student Development; www.jcsdonline.org

Journal of College Student Personnel (currently does not have a website)

Journal of College Student Psychotherapy; www.haworthpressinc.com

National Association of Student Personnel Administrators (NASPA) publishes the *NASPA Journal*; www.naspa.org

New Directions for Student Services; www.josseybass.com

Education (2007), 40% of undergraduate students study part-time, 40% attend a 2-year school, and 58% are 22 years old or older.

It is important for college counselors and student-life professionals to know that undergraduate binge drinking is a more recent dangerous trend that is increasing nationwide, with one in three students drinking intentionally to get drunk. **Binge drinking** is defined for men as having five or more drinks at a time and for women as having four or more drinks at a time (Commission on Substance Abuse at Colleges and Universities, 1994). College counselors and student-life professionals are responding to this phenomenon by initiating programs and services that address awareness, prevention, and intervention.

College and University Counseling

A college counselor's role is multifaceted because college counseling centers typically offer a wide range of services. There is great variation in what a college counselor may actually do. The typical day-to-day roles depend on the type of institution and the size of the counseling staff. Counselors who work at community colleges and small college counseling centers may find that they are expected to take on noncounseling roles, such as new student recruitment or financial aid services (Brown & Srebalus, 2003). College counselors who work in a center with many other counselors are more likely to define a specialty area of counseling for themselves over time (e.g., a specialist in eating disorders, substance abuse, grief and loss, or anxiety and depression).

In addition, college counselors employed by an institution that has separate student-life services to handle noncounseling issues have the opportunity to focus their resources on engaging in a wide range of counseling services. Counselors employed there are able to contribute to the mental health of the campus community in numerous ways, at the center itself and in other locations throughout the campus. They provide academic counseling to students who struggle with time management, motivation, test anxiety, test taking, and public speaking. They see students individually or as couples for personal counseling about difficulties with relationships, family problems, grief, abuse, eating disorders, self-esteem, anxiety, and depression. Activity 9.5 gives you practice in responding to students who refer other students for counseling. Because individual counseling is usually limited to approximately ten sessions per student, professional counselors use a variety of brief counseling approaches. Students whose concerns require longer term therapy are often referred to outside agencies.

ACTIVITY 9.5   HOW WOULD YOU HANDLE THIS CLIENT?

A student brings her roommate in to see you for counseling, saying that her roommate is displaying signs of an eating disorder in the residence hall. The student who is being referred admits that she does need help, but she tells you that she will only work with you in counseling if the roommate attends the counseling session as well, "for moral support." She reasons that because they are roommates, she will tell her what is happening in counseling anyway. What would you do?

College counselors periodically facilitate group experiences that relate to student needs and interests, for instance, building self-esteem or a freshman support group. They also make referrals for psychiatric consultations for students who need care outside the scope of the center. Several times a year, the center may be used as the screening site for national screening programs, such as depression screening and anxiety screening. The center may also maintain a multimedia resource room of mental health information that is available to the entire campus.

College counselors also extend their services into the larger campus community, which increases their visibility and accessibility. They consult with faculty, staff, administrators, and students who express concerns about others who are exhibiting problematic behaviors. Activity 9.6 gives you practice in responding to professors who refer students for counseling.

The counselors present outreach programs to student groups on eating disorders, body image, conflict resolution, sexual safety, and interpersonal relationships; programs to faculty and staff on stress management and communication skills; and contribute to the university's wellness activities. Counselors also become more visible and involved with the life of the campus when they engage in other experiences that expand their professional development. Some of these activities include periodically teaching courses, supervising interns who are in counseling graduate programs on the campus, and conducting research.

ACTIVITY 9.6   HOW WOULD YOU RESPOND TO THIS REFERRAL SOURCE?

A female faculty member refers a male undergraduate student from one of her classes to you, as the college counselor. The student felt comfortable enough with the professor to disclose to her his personal struggles with anxiety and depression. You begin counseling with the student. The professor later sees you on campus and inquires about how the student is doing in counseling. How should you respond?

College counselors are a leading force in the crisis intervention services that are available for emergencies such as suicidal thoughts or attempts, threats, sexual assault, and severe depression. For example, the college counselors at Millersville University in Pennsylvania are members of the Emergency Counseling Team, a group of faculty and staff from all areas of the campus trained in the technique of critical incident stress debriefing (CISD). The Emergency Counseling Team is prepared to be called upon at any time. Members of the team may facilitate groups of students, faculty, and staff who need to process their thoughts and feelings resulting from a crisis such as a student death, a terrorist threat or attack, or a tragic accident.

A casual observer of lively college students walking across campus to class might conclude that college students lead a carefree life; however, college counselors have a different perspective. Counselors who have been working on college campuses for much of their career share similar stories: they have noticed a marked increase in the number of students who present with intense mental health issues. Bishop, Gallagher, and Cohen (2000) identified and classified 46 client problems that are seen in college counseling centers, which are contained in the following categories: relationship difficulties, self-esteem, existential concerns, depression, sexual abuse and harassment, academic concerns, career concerns, stress, anxiety, substance abuse, sexual dysfunction, eating disorders, and unusual behavior such as borderline personality disorder. Text Box 9.6 offers a college counselor's reflection.

BOX 9.6

A Counselor's Reflection—College Counseling

"My friends used to give me a hard time when I would share just how great my job was working in an environment that was so exciting, rewarding, challenging, and flexible. Now I just tell them I have the greatest job in the world. I have been working as a counselor in a college or university counseling center for more than 20 years. My first experience was in 1983—it was the beginning of a journey that I would not trade for anything.

"In the field of counseling there are many settings from which to choose, but there are few that allow you to work with clients who are young, articulate, motivated, and intelligent. Working in a counseling center setting has allowed me to meet and engage in psychotherapy with clients who naturally embody the characteristics that, in my experience, foster the potential for meaningful change. After receiving my Master's degree, I worked for a short period of time with dually diagnosed individuals with moderate to severe emotional disturbances and psychological distress. While the experience was invaluable, working with these clients often yielded results of one step forward and three steps backward. I have great admiration and respect for professionals who have chosen this route for their careers. However, this experience helped me realize how fortunate I had been to work in college counseling centers with clients whose potential for change was more likely.

"My role as a counselor in a university counseling center setting has opened other doors for me at the university and within the community. I greatly enjoy the opportunities I have to provide outreach programming, supervision, and teaching as well as my work with various committees throughout the university. I really appreciate that my experiences every day are diverse. My activities and the people I meet are always changing, and I feel that adds to what makes this job so unique and enjoyable. There is a certain energy and electricity found on a college campus. Counseling with a college population has changed over the last 20-some years. We certainly see much more significant pathology, and our students face more serious issues today. Somehow, though, this has made the reward of witnessing client growth all the more fulfilling for me."

—Joseph F. Lynch, Ph.D.
University Counselor

An ongoing issue on college campuses is the attention given to the topic of student retention, and college counseling centers are being impacted by this growing trend. Administrators are examining retention data to measure the effectiveness of counseling services. Sharkin (2004), in reviewing research that correlated the influence of college counseling on student retention, noted that counseling services can benefit student retention. However, Sharkin cautioned administrators and college counselors against using retention data as the exclusive assessment of a college counselor's impact on student success. The unique, complex part that college counselors play in students' lives cannot be accurately measured by retention data alone. Rather, counselors need to convey proactively to the administration how their comprehensive counseling services are valuable in supporting the institution's overall educational mission.

Student-Life Services

To prepare for a career in student-life services, there are a variety of graduate training programs nationwide, many of which are housed within counselor education programs. The degree programs offered may be called Student Personnel Work in Higher Education, Student Affairs, or a similar title. Depending on how the graduate program is organized, graduate students may take some of the same courses that are part of college counseling degrees, but they will likely do their field work in one or two student-life specialty areas.

On a college or university campus, the career choice of student-life services, also known as student services or student affairs, is generally regarded as a distinct setting from college counseling. The field of **student-life services** is actually a cluster of diverse specialties, which may include admissions, learning services, health and wellness services, food services, financial aid, women's center, residence life, academic advising, international students, global education, registration, and career services.

Because student-life professionals play key roles in important everyday concerns for students, this career choice offers a rich opportunity to develop meaningful relationships with students and to contribute to their academic, personal, and professional development. Student-life professionals are also at the forefront of developing activities to unite the campus community. For example, after the World Trade Center tragedy of September 11, 2001, student-life professionals from the Department of Housing and Residential Programs at Millersville University enlisted the cooperation of the entire campus in designing a visual remembrance of the tragedy. Students, faculty, staff, and administrators took part in an origami project by folding several thousand paper peace cranes, with each crane representing a life lost in the tragedy. The individual cranes were assembled into large mobiles and permanently installed on the campus.

Opinions differ as to whether career counseling should be part of a college counselor's role, or whether it should be handled by a student-life professional in an office outside of the counseling center, as in a career services office. Those who favor keeping career counseling as part of the college counselor's role argue that the history of college counseling is rooted in vocational counseling, and that career development is a fundamental part of a student's personal growth. Those who advocate for the division of roles point to the increased mental health services that college counselors now provide, to adapt to the changing needs of college students.

Regardless of opinion, new college counselors and student-life professionals are likely to find that their role has already been defined for them by the particular setting. Some campuses offer career counseling in the career services office, not at the counseling center. Other campuses have a designated career counselor as a part of the counseling center. Still other campuses expect all counselors at the counseling center to engage in career counseling as part of their caseload. Activity 9.7 provides you with a hands-on experience in the college counseling or student-life services arena.

Student-life professionals who work in career services offices have contact with students at key points in their academic and professional development. They provide career counseling when students need help deciding on a major and when they explore career possibilities. They help students consider graduate school, assisting with the application process and the related graduate entry exams. Career services professionals are a vital resource in preparing students to transition from college life to finding employment. They teach students how to search for jobs, design resumes, and prepare for interviews. They also bring potential employers from various fields to campus for job fairs and on-campus interviews.

ACTIVITY 9.7   VOLUNTEERING AT THE COUNSELING CENTER OR A STUDENT-LIFE SERVICES OFFICE

Contact the director of your college or university's counseling center and inquire whether you can volunteer for an upcoming event. Perhaps, as a master's level student, you can be trained to score screenings (e.g., depression and anxiety awareness day screenings that many campuses offer) or to assist in a campus workshop that the center hosts (e.g., stress management, reducing test anxiety). Or contact the student-life services office on campus. The career services office or the office of residential life will likely have programs for which you can volunteer.

Although student-life services is separate from college counseling, they share a similar niche in that both sets of professionals must be well trained to respond to the myriad developmental needs of college students. In addition, student-life professionals and college counselors can be of most help to students when they know how to interrelate. Sometimes, they simply need to know when to refer students to one another. For example, a counselor who suspects that a student is experiencing academic problems because of an undiagnosed learning disability may refer the student to learning services. A professional in residence life who notices that a new international student is having excessive anxiety making friends may refer the student to the counseling center.

At other times, student-life professionals and college counselors may join forces to amplify their effectiveness. During the **First-Year Experience**, which is a year-long program to help freshmen adjust to the academic, social, and personal aspects of college life, student-life professionals and college counselors can partner to create workshops in areas such as alcohol awareness, sexual safety, and time management. Activity 9.8 provides one way to begin forming impressions about a college or university's student-life services from a distance. Activity 9.9 gives you a glimpse of a counseling center as a potential first-time visitor. Activity 9.10 gives ideas for conducting a research project on your own campus.

ACTIVITY 9.8   CRITIQUING A WEBSITE

Visit the website of your college or university's counseling center or one of its student-life services offices. What services are offered? What special events does it host or coordinate to become a visible presence on campus and to reach out to students? Discuss whether you feel the site's layout and overall presentation would be appealing to students, contains important information, and is easy to navigate.

ACTIVITY 9.9   WOULD A CLIENT FEEL COMFORTABLE THERE?

First impressions are important when helping clients feel comfortable about a new and potentially nerve-wracking situation, such as walking into a counseling center for the first time to seek counseling. Visit the reception area of your college or university's counseling center in person and imagine that you are a student who is considering seeking counseling there. Notice how the environment of the center feels to you, and whether it appears to be an inviting place. Pay attention to things such as the placement of the furniture, artwork, plants, lighting, and brochures and other informational materials. What are some of the positive attributes of this environment? What would you change to make it appear more welcoming?

Multicultural Issues in College Counseling and Student-Life Services

College counselors and student-life professionals must be attuned to the special needs of specific student populations, such as first-generation students, student athletes, and students with disabilities. Two growing populations of students, which will continue to influence how counselors and student-life professionals deliver their services, are international students and reentry women. Students from foreign countries experience the pressure of making a total life adjustment: not only do they have to learn the culture of college life—similar to native-born students—but they also have to manage the added stress of making this transition to college in a country whose culture may be vastly different from their own (Pedersen, 1991). **Reentry women** are women who return to college after an extended time away. They may have spent years raising a family or engaged in other homemaking responsibilities. Although reentry women are often more academically successful than traditional students, they may struggle with issues of self-confidence and role conflict (Padula, 1994).

ACTIVITY 9.10 HOW FAMILIAR IS THE CAMPUS COMMUNITY WITH THE COUNSELING CENTER AND THE STUDENT-LIFE SERVICES?

Conduct a brief investigative study with undergraduate and graduate students and faculty and staff on your campus. Develop a survey or conduct brief interviews with individuals from these groups, asking them about their familiarity with the counseling center and student-life services and the types of services that are provided. Do they know the locations of these various services, and what the confidentiality issues are? Ask faculty and staff members whether they have referred students to any of these services and for what issues. Ask students if they feel that they could turn to these services for help. This study might give you a glimpse of how well informed the campus community might be about the counseling center and the student-life services.

COUNSELING IN MENTAL HEALTH SETTINGS

The field of mental health counseling encompasses a broad spectrum of settings, serving diverse audiences. Community/agency, hospital, corrections, and private practice are four distinct areas where mental health counselors are employed. Complete Activity 9.11 to help you develop your own working definition of mental health counseling.

Background

For most of America's history, the dominant setting for addressing mental health concerns involved state psychiatric hospitals. These institutions primarily served patients with chronic or severe mental illness. By the middle of the 20th century, psychotropic drugs were used to control psychotic behavior, anxiety, and depression with greater effectiveness, enabling otherwise dependent adults to function in the community. Community-based mental health programs began to grow as a consequence of the legislative initiatives of the 1960s, expanding the settings for treatment beyond state-run psychiatric hospitals.

Although legislative changes continue to affect how federal and state funds are allocated, counselors today have more career opportunities than ever. This is an exciting time for trained mental health counselors. In 1986, the National Institute of Mental Health (NIMH) created the category, "mental health counselors." This fifth category of mental health practitioners was added to what existed since its inception in 1940: psychiatry, psychology, social work, and nursing. Mental health counselors serve a cross-section of the population whose clinical problems are considered a normal part of life. Text Box 9.9 provides information regarding professional organizations, publications, and websites related to mental health counseling.

ACTIVITY 9.11 DEVELOPING A WORKING DEFINITION OF MENTAL HEALTH COUNSELING

Visit the website of the Council for the Accreditation of Counseling and Related Educational Programs (CACREP) (www.cacrep.org), which provides an extensive description of mental health counseling. From the information given, develop your own working definition.

Community/Agency Setting

The community/agency setting is a broad setting that offers a host of career opportunities. Community/agency settings provide professional counselors, trained as generalists, a viable starting point for their career. As beginning counselors gain work experience and understanding about their preferences, they may develop a specialty area. Examples of specialty areas, for which mental health counselors in this setting may wish to specialize, include the treatment of juvenile sexual offenders, clients with substance abuse issues, and victims of domestic violence.

The types of **community/agency settings** include government agencies (increasingly funded directly by states or counties as opposed to the federally funded programs of the 1960s) and community-based clinics. These settings currently handle populations with serious and chronic mental illness because these cases are no longer housed solely in hospital settings as they had been in the past decades (Browers, 2005). According to the Substance Abuse and Mental Health Services Administration (2005), mental illness is the leading cause of disability in the United States, with 13% of adults receiving treatment for mental illness in a 1-year period. The increasingly prevalent substance abuse problem, which has gained considerable national attention, can also be addressed in the community/agency setting. Text Box 9.7 offers a counselor's reflection in the area of mental health.

Other examples of community/agency settings include county-funded court diversion programs. **Diversion programs** address the needs of people who have committed certain types of crimes. These programs aim to rehabilitate rather than incarcerate. Diversion programs address offenders who drive under the influence of alcohol, for instance, and counselors are needed to help offenders attend to their behavioral health issues. **Halfway houses**, places where people can learn to function in society with the necessary support after leaving more restrictive settings, and **children and youth services**, organizations that address domestic abuse or neglect, are examples of community/agency settings where mental health counselors may be employed to assist clients in more effectively dealing with their problems. Mental health counselors in this setting may treat substance abuse, intervene in crises, address homelessness, work with clients on probation or parole, or conduct follow-up work for clients released from hospitals after admission for clinical depression or attempted suicide.

Current trends related to counseling in the community include business and industry settings and community career centers (Gladding, 2004; Nugent & Jones, 2005). These settings typically present the counselor with less serious concerns, such as weight management and related wellness issues. Businesses and nonprofit organizations have come to realize that psychologically healthy employees are better equipped to serve the goals of the particular organization. As a result, **Employee Assistance Programs (EAPs)** are now prevalent in businesses, industries, schools, and universities. Services provided by EAPs may address stress management, family issues, or personal issues, including career development. Mental health counselors are equipped with the training needed to facilitate personal growth aims.

Community career centers, which emerged in the 1990s, employ professional counselors who assist clients in the exploration of career options and help with writing resumes, conducting job searches, and learning how to be successful in a job interview. Familiarity with related diagnostic assessments, such as aptitude tests and career assessment instruments, is desirable. The ability to interpret assessment results and to communicate these results effectively to clients is a skill that mental health counselors obtain through training.

BOX 9.7

A Counselor's Reflection—Mental Health Counseling

"I had no idea what I was getting into when I began working as a drug and alcohol counselor for court-committed juveniles. Not only was I counseling adolescent males for drug and alcohol use, I was also dealing with anger, depression, suicidal thoughts, family dysfunction, and about a million other issues that came along with the package. Throughout my first year, there was a persistent underlying question ringing in my head: how can I possibly counsel someone who does not seem to have any intention of changing?

"Believe it or not, that question is also connected to my greatest reward. I am able to see my clients gradually change their behaviors, attitudes, and thoughts. I have the privilege of helping a client move through the process of change, which is definitely a challenge; but that is what I love about it. Every day is something new. Clients progress and regress, laugh, cry, yell, goof off, and work hard. Misbehavior is to be expected. It is my job to learn how to effectively intervene and help my clients find alternative strategies to reach their goals.

"After 8 years at our facility (and several promotions), I feel confident in my skills and abilities, but I am constantly looking to improve them. I also need to keep up-to-date on current trends such as drugs of abuse, drug selling, gangs, current laws and regulations regarding crime, gun use, and fatherhood. This job can be very rewarding and, at times, it can be extremely frustrating. When I entered this field, I had to make a commitment. It's not about me anymore. Parents, the probation system, and the community entrust me to work with adolescents who many would label as being "difficult clients." Drug use is typically just the tip of the iceberg. During 6 to 12 months of treatment, I am ultimately responsible for the life of a child. Does it get any more serious than that?"

—Greg E. Bechtold, M.Ed., CAC
Program Director of a community agency for
court-committed adolescents

Hospitals

Hospitals, previously the most dominant setting for dealing with severe mental illnesses, currently extend their services to address issues that range from dealing with death and dying to maintaining a "wellness lifestyle." **Behavioral health care** is the umbrella term for mental health and substance abuse issues in the hospital setting. The boundary that separates the hospital setting from the community at large has been softened. Counselors working in the hospital setting may go into businesses and schools to provide workshops related to wellness. These might include providing stress management counseling, communication workshops, or conflict resolution strategies. Or they may deal with the kind of crisis, depression, anxiety, or loss that is linked to a medical condition. A professional counselor working in a hospital setting might assist a family dealing with the recent loss of a loved one or a patient dealing with the loss of a limb. Parents whose premature newborn must remain in the hospital for an extended period because of unforeseen complications would likely welcome the assistance of a caring and knowledgeable professional counselor. Situations such as these require counselors who have an aptitude for dealing with grief, pain, and loss, and who are not squeamish in the hospital setting.

The counselor may be assisting "clients" (the term used when treatment is provided outside the hospital) or "patients" (the term used when the treatment is provided inside the hospital) as they deal with lifestyle changes brought on by illness (e.g., heart attack, stroke) (Browers, 2005). The facts that heart disease ranks first as the leading cause of death, and that the largest part of the U.S. population is aging suggest that preventive and remedial efforts in this area would likely integrate the comprehensive skills of the mental health counselor. Professional counselors who are employed by hospitals may provide services that range from educational workshops on stress management techniques in businesses, to bedside counseling of hospice patients dealing with impending and death.

Another area where counselors provide services under the auspices of the hospital involves substance abuse. Hospital care for substance abuse follows a typical sequence. When the condition is acute, as in the case of a college student whose excessive binge drinking requires medical intervention, a hospital stay is warranted. This occurs within the first 3–5 days. Professional counselors who are presented with such a case respond to the crisis by assessing the client's condition. Intermediate care occurs between 7–14 days, followed by a rehabilitation program lasting 1–6 months. Finally, an aftercare component encourages a healthy integration of behavioral change in the client's lifestyle. In each segment of the treatment program, the counselor's role is key.

New mothers pose an entirely different scenario and intervention. In situations where a mother is experiencing clinical postpartum depression, psychiatrists typically prescribe medication, and counselors help the patient do the important work of learning how to function outside the hospital setting. In all these scenarios, mental health counselors are involved to help clients deal with the issues that necessitated hospitalization and to help them develop the skills for independent living. Activity 9.12 encourages you to gain a deeper understanding of the career choice of mental health counseling.

ACTIVITY 9.12   INTERVIEWING A PROFESSIONAL COUNSELOR

Interview a professional counselor working in a community/agency, hospital, corrections setting, or private practice setting. Spend as much time as you are able to at the site. Write a report that includes a description of the counselor's role, the overall counseling program, the mission of the setting, and the referral procedures. Include any other information that the counselor thinks you should know about the setting and your own personal observations and impressions.

Corrections

Corrections is a part of the field of criminal justice. Professional counselors who work in corrections may work in the prison setting, the court, or the community. They may be directly employed by the Department of Corrections or they may work for a private agency that serves the department's needs. The clients served by counselors in this setting undergo a process similar to the following: When an arrest is made for drug possession, the offender is held in jail to await trial. At this point, a mental health professional may be called into the courts to do an assessment, called a court-ordered evaluation. To perform this role, a minimum of a master's degree and licensure or certification is generally required. If the evaluation indicates that a substance abuse treatment program is warranted, the (nonviolent) offender may be sentenced to a diversion program in lieu of incarceration. Diversion programs divert potential inmates from incarceration in overcrowded prisons to treatment facilities within the community and aim to address the issues that caused the problem. The probation department supervises the sentencing to a diversion program, where treatments such as counseling occur.

Stephen K. Valle, president and CEO of AdCare Criminal Justice Services of Worcester, MA, a company that provides comprehensive substance abuse treatment services to correctional facilities nationwide, asserts, "A progressive public safety agency would recognize that a majority of the offenders that appear before them have mental health or substance abuse problems and would try to direct them to a treatment program while they are under their supervision" (personal communication, June 6, 2007). According to Valle, 80% of jail/prison inmates are incarcerated because of addiction, but only about 15% receive treatment.

Progressive judiciary systems recognize the value of comprehensive treatment–based diversion programs that address behavioral change and have established drug courts and mental health courts to deal efficiently with the offender's treatment needs and overcrowded prisons. Professional counselors play an active role throughout the process. They counsel during probation, conduct group and individual counseling to incarcerated inmates, or counsel offenders on parole (Valle & Humphrey, 2003).

The needs of incarcerated inmates often focus on dealing with prison life. Counselors must realize that they are not necessarily perceived as being helpful by their clientele and may be seen as being part of the punitive system. Nevertheless, an advantage to counseling in a corrections setting is that clients must consistently participate in individual and group counseling and complete assigned tasks because their alternative is prison. In contrast to private practice, these clients cannot choose another counselor or neglect paying for the service, so counselors are free to do their best work from beginning to end. Counselors interested in alternative programs need to understand the program, the counselor's role, the political environment, and the funding sources to make informed career decisions.

Private Practice

Beginning counselors commonly make two mistaken assumptions when they consider private practice. The first one is that maintaining a private practice is easier than working in other mental health settings, and the second one is that novice private practitioners can immediately specialize in their favorite treatment area.

Professional counselors and counselors in training often imagine that maintaining a private practice would be an appealing and glamorous career choice; however, both the advantages and the challenges of this setting need to be carefully considered. Some of the benefits of establishing a private practice include the ability to design a creative work schedule, to become a specialist in one or more treatment areas of interest, and to build a potentially profitable business. The challenges of maintaining this independent lifestyle are many. These include meeting or maintaining professional licensure requirements, generating referrals, managing a business, and simultaneously handling a large client caseload. The noncounseling aspects of running one's own business include such tasks as developing marketing strategies, handling finances, retaining employees, and supervising the daily functioning of the office. Text Box 9.8 lists key issues to address when considering private practice as a counseling career choice.

Similar to the broad area of community/agency counseling, the **private practice** setting offers professional counselors the ability to work with a diverse population of clients who present an array of therapeutic concerns. A counselor who contemplates opening a private practice may envision carving out a specialty area such as child and adolescent development, eating disorders, or substance abuse. However, to build a client and referral base in the hopes of becoming financially successful, the private practitioner is likely to find that, at least in the early stages of developing a practice, one must be willing and able to

BOX 9.8

A Counselor's Reflection—Private Practice

"I took the 'big jump' and purchased a 2300-square foot house for my private practice. I rent to five part-time practitioners, all of whom were once my students or colleagues. This is definitely the single most rewarding aspect of my private practice as a counseling psychologist, specifically, the fact that I have been able to facilitate the professional and career development of my truly gifted associates. The key piece of advice here for a master's student is to affiliate yourself with professionals (faculty members or other licensed practitioners) who have private practices such that you will find doors of opportunity opening for you in the world of private practice. In this endeavor, develop networks by joining local provider associations (social work, addictions counseling, psychology, counseling). This provides opportunities for consultation, supervision, and referrals.

"There are a number of important issues to address in considering whether or not you should make part-time or full-time private practice one of your professional goals. They include the following: (a) Should you rent or buy property? (b) How will you purchase professional liability insurance? (c) What will be the source of your referrals? (d) Who will provide supervision and/or consultation for you on difficult clinical issues? (e) What will be your risk-management plan for situations that occur 'after hours' and involve crises such as threats of suicide, homicide, intent to perpetrate abuse? (f) How will you handle the issue of third-party payment (e.g., insurance and publicly funded treatment such as Medicare and Medicaid)? Will you seek to be accepted by them as an approved provider of reimbursable services? (g) How will you manage the federal, state, and local tax issues that confront all small business owners? (h) What licenses or certificates will you need, and what will you need to do in order to earn them? (i) How will you meet the continuing professional education requirements involved in the licensure requirements as well as the ethics codes of our various helping professions? (j) How will you meet the expectation of most professional organizations, which suggests that those in the 'helping professions' should provide some of their services pro bono? These questions may strike the aspiring private practitioner as somewhat daunting, even overwhelming. For me, personally, answering all of them provided a succinct summary of the key challenges of maintaining a private practice.

"The rewards have been many and more than compensate for these challenges. I mentioned the highest reward above, mentoring and supervising my students who have now become accomplished service providers in my practice. The opportunity to serve clients, child protection caseworkers, recovering addicts, children, adolescents, and the family court system has also been very inspiring. One major endeavor that presented itself was to become an expert witness in the Family Court for child protective services cases involving the possible termination of parental rights. This is difficult work, but the openness of judges, attorneys, clients, and caseworkers to the information derived from my psychological evaluations has been very affirming. Many of them have offered unsolicited words of appreciation for my testimony and assistance. In addition, I have learned as much from my clients as they have from me over the years, and for this I am very grateful. I think that the opportunity to work with clients is a gift and an invitation from them to enter their worlds and understand them in ways that others cannot. If in the process, I can facilitate their journeys along life's convoluted pathways, then I feel even more gratified."

—David C. Hill, Ph.D.
Licensed Psychologist and University Professor

address a multitude of issues, rather than specializing in one particular area. Issues that clients may present include family, individual, and career issues; crisis situations; and issues involving diverse lifestyles. As the counseling profession continues to make great strides in reaching out to formerly underrecognized populations, counselors in private practice will increasingly be serving clients who are gay, lesbian, bisexual, and transgendered, and clients with unique ethnic/cultural issues. Developmental concerns related to aging will also increase, as the exceptionally large "baby boomer" population, representing the 76 million children born between 1946 and 1964 (Jones, 2006), reaches retirement age and beyond.

Unique to private practice, relative to much community/agency work, are the funding sources. Private practitioners typically rely on funding from their clients directly or from third-party payments, if their clients have insurance, whereas in many community/agency settings, the funding comes via federal, state, or private-sector grants.

A successful mental health counselor working in the private practice setting must carefully research the considerable demands of this setting before undertaking the role in a full-time capacity. Many professional counselors find that before attempting an independent private practice full-time, success is more readily realized by sharing some of the financial responsibilities through part-time involvement, developing a practice with colleagues, or joining a preexisting practice.

Professional counselors who aspire to work in private practice settings often extend their professional skills and time to other related occupations to build their reputation and supplement their income. These other roles include supervising counselors in training, adjunct teaching at a college or university, and consulting work in educational or community/agency settings (Browers, 2005).

Multicultural Issues in Mental Health Counseling

Not all mental health counselors have received enough training to feel that they can work competently with people who have various disabilities. Current research is focusing on improving counselors' expertise in serving people with disabilities. Strike, Skovholt, and Hummel (2004) studied mental health counselors' self-assessments of their competence in working with people with disabilities, in the areas of self-awareness, perceived knowledge, and perceived skills. Their findings show that the more disability-related counseling experiences that counselors have, the higher their levels of perceived disability competence.

Text Box 9.9, listing professional organizations, publications, and websites for mental health counseling, follows.

BOX 9.9

Professional Organizations, Publications, and Websites for Mental Health Counseling

The American Counseling Association (ACA) publishes the *Journal of Counseling and Development*; www.counseling.org. The ACA offers multimedia resources relevant to each counseling specialty. The ACA has numerous divisions representing specialty areas, which counselors may also join. Each state has a branch of the ACA, and many branches maintain divisions of specialty areas as well.

American Mental Health Counselors Association (AMHCA); www.amhca.org

Council for the Accreditation of Counseling and Related Educational Programs (CACREP); www.cacrep.org

REHABILITATION COUNSELING

While mental health counselors and rehabilitation counselors may share the same settings, the career choices differ. Rehabilitation counseling is a specialty profession that is distinct from mental health counseling in that **rehabilitation counselors** specialize in working with clients who are identified as having a recognized disability. The Americans with Disabilities Act (ADA) describes an **individual with a disability** as a person who "has a physical or mental impairment that substantially limits one or more 'major life activities'" (Zunker, 1994, p. 141). Rehabilitation counselors work in mental health agencies, correctional facilities, university settings, schools, public and private offender and addiction treatment programs for juveniles and adults, hospitals, state rehabilitation agencies, privately supported rehabilitation agencies, and counseling clinics.

The Scope of Practice Statement from the Commission on Rehabilitation Counselor Certification (2003) states that rehabilitation counseling services are provided to people with physical, mental, developmental, cognitive, and emotional disabilities. The intent of rehabilitation counseling is to facilitate the "independence, integration, and inclusion of people with disabilities in employment and the community" (Commission on Rehabilitation Counselor Certification, 2003). It further defines the process of rehabilitation counseling as a systematic process that may use many interventions, such as behavioral, social, psychological, and vocational counseling; collaborating with the client in the formulation of a treatment program; consulting and collaborating with other professionals and services; and supporting the client toward self-advocacy.

Today, people with disabilities who need rehabilitation services are viewed by professional counselors as active consumers of services, who have choices of counselors and services. This perspective represents progress from the more traditional viewpoint of the medical model, which tended to regard people with disabilities as passive recipients who must accept a treatment that is prescribed without their input. Sales (2007) advocates for a collaborative approach to counseling known as the **empowerment model of rehabilitation counseling**: the counselor treats the client as the expert on his or her abilities and disabilities, and the client is encouraged to identify counseling goals.

The shift to considering people with disabilities as active consumers, and as individuals who should be identified as "people" instead of by the disability that they have, is also reflected in the use of **"people first" language**. To project a social model instead of a medical model (which would describe the person as a "patient"), rehabilitation counselors may identify their clients not only as "clients," but also by the descriptions of "a person who needs services," "a consumer," or "a person who has a disability" (as in "a person who has schizophrenia" instead of "a schizophrenic").

While today rehabilitation counselors have multiple roles and serve a diversity of people with disabilities in various settings, the origin of this profession began with vocational rehabilitation. With the passage of the *Vocational Rehabilitation Act* by Congress in 1920, rehabilitation counseling began as a unique profession established by federal legislation to provide rehabilitation services (Fabian & MacDonald-Wilson, 2005). The first rehabilitation counselors were employed within the State-Federal Vocational Rehabilitation (VR) Program. Legislation to reduce the barriers that people with disabilities face continued with the Rehabilitation Amendment of 1992. This amendment helps people with disabilities to transition from school to higher education or employment, by creating ways to connect educational systems and VR systems. The Rehabilitation Amendments of 1998, Title IV of the

Workforce Investment Act (WIA), focuses on increased employment for people with disabilities, by emphasizing collaboration and cooperation across the entire workforce investment system (Wonacott, 2002). The **Americans with Disabilities Act (ADA)** of 1990 further improves the quality of life for people with disabilities by mandating that accommodations are made in public areas, employment environments, and transportation, so that people with disabilities have as much access as possible (Zunker, 1994).

Many national and international professional organizations and journals are dedicated to the advancement of rehabilitation counseling. The National Rehabilitation Counseling Association (NRCA), established in 1958, is a division of the National Rehabilitation Association and publishes the *Journal of Applied Rehabilitation Counseling* (JARC). The American Psychological Association (APA) Division 22 (Rehabilitation Psychology) publishes the journal *Rehabilitation Psychology*. The American Rehabilitation Counseling Association (ARCA) is a division of the ACA and publishes a newsletter. The National Council on Rehabilitation Education (NCRE) publishes the journal, *Rehabilitation Education*.

The International Association of Rehabilitation Professionals (IARP) publishes the journal *RehabPro*. The International Association of Addictions and Offender Counselors (IAAOC) is a division of the ACA and publishes the *Journal of Addictions & Offender Counseling* (JAOC). Text Box 9.10 provides more information on professional organizations, publications, and websites related to rehabilitation counseling.

Rehabilitation counseling has a national certification organization for counselors and a national accrediting body for graduate programs. The Commission on Rehabilitation Counselor Certification is an independent, not-for-profit organization that has certified more than 35,000 Certified Rehabilitation Counselors since 1974 (Commission on Rehabilitation Counselor Certification, n.d.). The Council on Rehabilitation Education accredits graduate programs in Rehabilitation Counselor Education (Council on Rehabilitation Education, n.d.).

The *Revised Strong Interest Inventory* has added another occupational scale—the Rehabilitation Counselor Scale (SII RCS)—to this widely used tool in career guidance (Leierer, Strohmer, Blackwell, Thompson, & Donnay, 2008). The SII RCS is expected to expand the visibility of the field of rehabilitation counseling and play a key role in identifying prospective rehabilitation counselors. The SII RCS will allow students in high schools, colleges, and universities, and other adults to explore how well their personal characteristics match the characteristics of practicing rehabilitation counselors who are satisfied with their chosen profession.

BOX 9.10

Professional Organizations, Publications, and Websites for Rehabilitation Counseling

American Psychological Association (APA) Division 22 (Rehabilitation Psychology) publishes the journal *Rehabilitation Psychology*; www.div22.org/index.php

American Rehabilitation Counseling Association (ARCA) is a division of the ACA and publishes a newsletter; www.arcaweb.org

Commission on Rehabilitation Counselor Certification (CRCC); www.crccertification.com

Council on Rehabilitation Education (CORE); www.core-rehab.org

International Association of Addictions and Offender Counselors (IAAOC) is a member association of the ACA; www.iaaoc.org

People Who Are Served by Rehabilitation Counselors

Although the variety of clients that rehabilitation counselors may serve is too broad to discuss individually in this chapter, several types of people with disabilities who may benefit from the services of a rehabilitation counselor are briefly discussed here: family members of children who have an autism spectrum disorder (ASD), college and university students who have a disability, adolescents and adults who have an addiction, individuals who have survived a traumatic event, individuals who have a chronic mental illness, and individuals who use a vocational rehabilitation counselor. For an in-depth perspective on the great diversity of issues and techniques in rehabilitation counseling, refer to texts such as *Principles and Practices of Case Management in Rehabilitation Counseling, 2nd Edition* (Davis, 2007); *The Psychological and Social Impact of Illness and Disability, 5th Edition* (Dell Orto & Power, 2007); *Rehabilitation Counseling: An Empowerment Perspective* (Sales, 2007); *Rehabilitation Counseling: Basics and Beyond, 4th Edition* (Parker, Szymanski, & Patterson, 2005); and *Counseling Theories and Techniques for Rehabilitation Health Professionals* (Chan, Berven, & Thomas, 2004).

FAMILY MEMBERS OF CHILDREN WHO HAVE AN AUTISM SPECTRUM DISORDER   Rehabilitation counselors work with children, adolescents, and adults who have an ASD to support them in their psychosocial, emotional, and vocational development. Benson and Dewey (2008) suggest that interventions are also needed for the parents of a child with ASD. Parents of children with ASD report experiencing more stress compared with parents of children who do not have ASD. These parents have identified resources to reduce their stress levels: financial assistance, the support of family members, professional supports such as competent helping professionals and parent support groups, and in-home training in managing a child with ASD. Because mothers and fathers tend to place different degrees of importance on the various resources, rehabilitation counselors need to assess the needs from both parents' viewpoints (Benson & Dewey, 2008).

Siblings of children with ASD may benefit from participating in support groups to help them adjust to the challenges they face. Compared with siblings who do not have a child in the family with ASD, siblings of children with ASD are at a higher risk for developing behavioral, social, and emotional problems, including depression and school dropout (Lefkowitz, Crawford, & Dewey, 2007). Support groups may help these siblings gain access to information about ASD and connect with other families who share similar experiences.

COLLEGE AND UNIVERSITY STUDENTS WHO HAVE A DISABILITY   The number of students with disabilities who attend institutions of higher education has increased almost fourfold over the last 30 years (Hennessey & Koch, 2007). Grundy and McGinn (2008) indicated that graduate students who have disabilities face challenges in meeting the demands of graduate school, especially in the areas of defending their thesis, engaging in research, working as a research assistant, and attending professional conferences. Supporting undergraduate and graduate students who have a disability is an important consideration from the standpoints of architectural design and instructional strategies. Universal design for instruction (UDI) is a concept that is intended to provide learners (with and without disabilities) with "an approach to teaching that incorporates proactive design and use of inclusive instructional strategies that benefit an extensive range of learners, including students with disabilities" (McGuire, Scott, & Shaw, 2003). The intent of UDI is for all aspects of a student's experience (i.e., course materials, assignments, and activities) to be accessible. As UDI becomes a more visible component of college campuses, rehabilitation counselors may find themselves becoming more familiar with its principles, which may produce even greater opportunities for rehabilitation counselors to serve the college population.

College and university students who are not only disabled but also from a lower socioeconomic status may tend to use an external locus of control, in which they feel that things happen in their lives because of outside influences such as fate or chance, instead of through their own actions and choices. This external locus of control may be harmful when students use this type of thinking to decide whether or not to use precautions regarding HIV/AIDS protection (Gwandure, 2008). Rehabilitation counselors working with this population need to assess whether their clients believe that their ability to reduce their risk of contracting HIV/AIDS is out of their control and to help them become more assertive in their efforts to keep themselves protected.

ADOLESCENTS AND ADULTS WHO HAVE AN ADDICTION   Rehabilitation counselors working with clients who have addictions are likely to come in contact with the following current techniques as part of their training and may choose to use them with appropriate clients: motivational interviewing and stages of change. **Motivational interviewing** is a counseling style that seeks to increase the client's confidence and hope, while reducing the client's resistance to making a change. It is a positive, empathic alternative to persuasive and confrontational counseling approaches, which may arouse opposition and defensiveness in clients. The motivation to change addictive behaviors in the motivational interviewing approach comes from the counselor's use of strategies such as direct feedback, empathy, and focusing on the client's personal responsibility, and by avoiding arguments, accusations, and labeling (Lewis & Osborn, 2004).

The **stages of change** is only one dimension of the larger transtheoretical model, which is an integrated model for understanding how people make intentional changes in their behavior and how counselors can support their clients during this process. The stages outline the tasks that the client needs to accomplish to dissolve deeply ingrained patterns of a behavior, such as an addiction, and to establish new patterns of healthier functioning. The client begins by being aware that the addiction needs to be changed; articulates that there are more reasons to make a change than there are reasons to keep the addictive behavior; makes a plan; tries it out and revises the plan, while also accepting that relapsing into the old behavior is likely; and, if successful, eventually makes the change part of his or her lifestyle (DiClemente, 2003).

INDIVIDUALS WHO HAVE SURVIVED A TRAUMATIC EVENT   Traumatic events are present in many forms, including natural disasters, terrorist attacks, physical assaults, life-changing illnesses, and physical and psychological injuries in war and accidents. According to Stebnicki (2001, p. 57), "it is estimated that the typical American will spend nearly 12 years of his or her life in a state of limited psychosocial functioning because of chronic illness and disability acquired through disease or injury." This means that most people at some point in their lives may need the assistance of a rehabilitation counselor to support them in their recovery from a traumatic event or the post-traumatic stress disorder that they experience as a result of the event.

INDIVIDUALS WHO HAVE A CHRONIC MENTAL ILLNESS   Individuals who are diagnosed with a chronic mental illness, especially individuals who have one of the disorders of the schizophrenia spectrum, pose significant challenges to themselves, their families, and the mental health care system (Gurovich, Shmukler, Utkin, Stepanova, Sheller, & Turusheva, 2007). These clients often have great difficulty maintaining employment, and they tend to have conflictual or dissolved relationships with family members and other sources of social support. These individuals may require frequent and lengthy hospital stays during periods of relapse. However, once they are discharged, they may fail to comply with outpatient treatment (which likely includes regular medication), reversing the successes that they experienced while hospitalized.

Assertive community treatment teams are being used as an alternative to inpatient and outpatient settings. The treatment team is a fluid arrangement of professionals that can be adapted to fit the needs of the client, both by the types of services provided (e.g., vocational counseling, emergency psychiatric care, group therapy) and the locations that are most convenient for the client, such as in the client's home. The assertive community treatment team has been used effectively to serve clients in their natural settings to maximize the employment, social, and wellness potential of individuals who have a mental illness (Gurovich et al., 2007).

INDIVIDUALS WHO USE A VOCATIONAL REHABILITATION COUNSELOR   All of the people with disabilities described in this section may find that part of their comprehensive rehabilitation plan includes working with a vocational rehabilitation counselor. The primary goal of **vocational rehabilitation** is for people with disabilities to secure competitive employment (Wonacott, 2002), meaning that the individual with the disability is engaging in meaningful career development instead of merely job placement. Vocational rehabilitation counselors are also case managers who design individualized and comprehensive services in collaboration with their client. They advocate for the use of assistive technology, consumer choice, and participation for their clients (Wonacott, 2002).

Person-focused counseling is a key to addressing individual client needs effectively, beginning with understanding the individual's unique circumstances and his or her perspectives on those circumstances. Vocational rehabilitation counselors plan services in partnership with the individual receiving services, so that the individual eventually is empowered to initiate the needed services. Counselors must continuously assess progress, consult with agencies, and coordinate the services needed with an aim toward securing meaningful employment. Text Box 9.11 provides a rehabilitation counselor's reflection on the profession, and Text Box 9.12 is a real-life example of a partnership between a vocational rehabilitation counselor and an individual with a disability. The case shows the importance of focusing on a client's strengths, believing that the client has the ability to transform his or her life, and supporting the client on his or her journey toward independence.

BOX 9.11

A Counselor's Reflection—Rehabilitation Counseling

"Rehabilitation counselors are social activists and address issues of stigma, discrimination, and access for all individuals. We incorporate various strength-based theories, use holistic approaches during our assessments, and examine and attempt to address societal barriers that could deter successful outcomes.

(Continued)

"With financial assistance from the Rehabilitation Services Administration, I was able to pursue and obtain a degree in rehabilitation counseling and work towards my goal of addressing the welfare of the human condition. I found the field to be rich with inspirational practitioners and leaders in research, theory, and policy. I learned that the implementation of rehabilitation services has grown beyond the traditional models of vocational placement. It continues to expand and develop and is one of the fastest growing occupations.

"Since completing my education, I have attained licensure as a clinical professional counselor and have worked as a therapist, vocational evaluator, and rehabilitation director. Through my experiences, I have worked with adults, children, and elderly individuals from a variety of cultures and socioeconomic backgrounds, and with disabilities such as cerebral palsy, traumatic brain injuries, cancer, developmental disorders, mental illnesses, amputations, spinal cord injuries, multiple sclerosis, HIV/AIDS, and post-traumatic stress disorder. I have been touched by the courage and strength of my consumers as they have worked toward their goals of employment and independence. These teachers have expanded upon the foundation that my education provided, and it is with great joy and privilege that I continue in this profession."

—Edward T. Markowski, MA, CRC, LCPC
Rehabilitation Director of a privately
supported, nonprofit rehabilitation agency

BOX 9.12

The Case of Max, the Engineer Who Found His True Passion in Life

This case was related by Thomas Neuville, Ph.D. (personal communication, July 7, 2008), an Associate Professor of Special Education and a former vocational rehabilitation counselor. As a rehabilitation counselor, Thomas met Max (not his real name) after Max became blind in a car accident. Max had been a successful tire engineer by profession, but could not continue in his job after the accident. Thomas also learned that Max's true love was working with wood. Before the accident, Max had a cabinet-making hobby, but he never pursued it professionally because he did not think that he could make a living out of it.

Max's workshop sat dormant after he became blind, but one of the things that Thomas realized was that his client loved cabinet-making so much that he probably would do anything to get back to it, even with his disability. Max had the engineering knowledge that he needed to adapt the tools in his workshop to be able to use them: he designed a way to set up guiding devices on the circular saw so that he could create the cabinets, even though he could no longer see. Thomas' approach to working with Max was to "never think that I had the solution." As Thomas said, "I had no idea how to do these things, but I knew that [Max] knew."

Thomas engaged Max in the solution—in this case, one of business buildup, by forming a business partnership with him. Once Max redesigned all of his tools, they put a business plan together to market the product. After a year, Max was able to continue with the business independently.

Although Max was initially depressed about his blindness, with Thomas' support he was able to transform his life and follow a lifelong dream to have his own cabinet-making business. Max said that he would never have had the opportunity to pursue his true passion in life without the accident. Thomas continued to receive Christmas cards from Max for 10–15 years after their partnership ended. Thomas' ability to form a business partnership with his client is not typical of all vocational rehabilitation counselors in all settings, but in Thomas' situation, he was given a budget and a certain amount of people with whom to work. He had the flexibility and independence in his job to help his clients achieve success in a variety of ways.

Multicultural Issues in Rehabilitation Counseling

In recent years, a multicultural approach to counseling people with disabilities has emerged in the counseling literature and in counseling training programs, when a **minority model of disability** was proposed (Strike, Skovholt, & Hummel, 2004). Considering disability to be a part of the minority model that represents ethnic and racial groups is a change in the social perspective (Gill, 1987). The inclusion of disability in the minority model recognizes that people with disabilities have experienced stigma, prejudice, discrimination, and marginalization (Shapiro, 1993). Pruett and Chan (2006) discuss how essential it is for educators in rehabilitation counseling programs to encourage their students to examine the negative attitudes that they may hold toward people with disabilities or certain specific disability groups, even though students may be able to articulate the profession's egalitarian views of people with disabilities. Activity 9.13 suggests a way to initiate your professional development outside of the classroom setting.

ACTIVITY 9.13   CO-PRESENTING AT A CONFERENCE AS A BEGINNING TO YOUR PROFESSIONAL DEVELOPMENT

Consider the idea of co-presenting a workshop with one of your professors at a local, state, or national professional counseling conference. You may be able to assist your professor by engaging in research or by contributing to the presentation in another capacity. Co-presenting at conferences benefits a graduate student's professional development in many ways. It is an excellent way to (1) develop a scholarly agenda that may carry over into a master's thesis, doctoral dissertation, or into one's career; (2) learn the important skill of sharing information with practicing counselors; (3) gain other perspectives on the various counseling settings and career choices; and (4) network with professionals and other graduate students in the field.

Summary

Professional counselors working in mental health settings can be found in community/agency settings, hospitals, corrections settings, and private practice. It is probable that in all of these settings, counselors will begin their careers as generalists—seeing a variety of clients with wide-ranging concerns—and then perhaps develop a specialty area as they become more experienced and as the work setting allows.

Professional school counselors work with children, parents, teachers, and others within the school community. The setting requires a flexible individual who can adjust quickly to changing demands. School counselors need to be comfortable in highly visible community situations. The job satisfaction rewards are great for counselors who can develop and maintain positive relationships with children, their families, and other school professionals.

College counselors may work in a counseling center or be integrated into student-life services. Historically, they have assisted students with career development and continue to do so depending on the institution. Student-life professionals and college counselors help the diverse, large group of nontraditional students (students older than 22 years) with the reentry issues unique to this population. College counselors must be knowledgeable about the notable problems that undergraduate students typically present, including binge drinking, sexual safety, and eating disorders. Depending on the size of the institution, its vision for counseling and student-life services, and its organizational frame, professional counselors who work in the college setting employ their skills in ways that build relationships with diverse students, faculty, and administrators.

Substance abuse is a significant societal problem, and mental health counselors, regardless of the setting, are likely to work with clients who present issues related to substance abuse. They will also work with clients whose issues range from normal developmental issues to problems that are chronic or severe.

Counselors working in hospitals or prison settings may deal with people whose problems require intensive intervention where they are confined to that particular setting. Or the counselor's work may be primarily preventive, in which the counselor's role is to educate groups of workers at their place of employment on topics such as smoking cessation or the benefits and application of stress management techniques. Rehabilitation counselors work in many of the same settings as mental health counselors; however, their focus is on assisting people who have a recognized disability. Rehabilitation counselors support their clients in functioning as independently as possible and help clients to secure meaningful employment. Professional counselors must carefully consider what constitutes a good match between their own preferences and competencies when choosing the setting in which they will practice their profession.

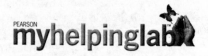

To help further your understanding of some of the topics in this chapter, go to MyHelpingLab at the Pearson.com website and view the following video clips:

- Elementary Counseling: *Child Counseling and Psychotherapy,* Module 4 (Narrative Therapy with Children, "Using Client's Stories to Define the Problem") and Module 9 (Play Therapy, "Using Role Plays and Projection in Play Therapy").
- Middle School/Junior High School Counseling: *Child Counseling and Psychotherapy,* Module 11 (Multimodal Therapy, "Addressing Emotions from a Structural Profile" and "Listing Coping Skills for Dealing with Emotions").
- High School Counseling: *Child Counseling and Psychotherapy,* Module 13 (Reality Therapy, "Exploring a Client's Need for Power" and "Helping Clients Develop 'Their' Goals and Plans").

SECTION THREE

Client Issues and Advocacy

10

Human Development Through the Lifespan

Ann Vernon

PREVIEW

The purpose of this chapter is to describe the developmental characteristics of infancy and toddlerhood (birth to age 3 years); early childhood (ages 4 to 6 years); middle childhood (ages 6 to 11 years); early adolescence, midadolescence, and later adolescence (ages 11 to 24 years); young adulthood (ages 24 to 40 years); middle adulthood (age 40 to 60 years), and later adulthood (ages 60 years and older). The information in these approximate age categories serves as a basis for examples of interventions that helping professionals can use to facilitate development at several of these developmental stages. Because the focus is on the practical application of development theory, readers are encouraged to consult human development books referred to in this chapter for more in-depth information.

LIFESPAN PERSPECTIVE

Life is a journey, with each developmental stage posing a new set of challenges and opportunities, as Robert Munsch (1986) beautifully portrays in his children's book, *Love You Forever*. In this poignant story that describes a mother's unconditional love for her child at each stage of development, Munsch also reminds us that life is a circle; toward the end of our journey, we are once again more dependent as we were in infancy. This process of going full circle, whether as a participant or as an observer, is amazing. As professional counselors, we are in the unique position of not only experiencing our own growth and development, but also facilitating our clients' journey.

According to Baltes (2000), the **lifespan perspective** includes the belief that development is lifelong, but also that it is multidimensional, multidisciplinary and contextual, multidirectional, and plastic. In essence, Baltes maintained that development does not end with early adulthood as the traditional approach emphasized; there are various changes at every stage.

There is some debate about how much capacity for change people have as they get older because some characteristics may become more stable and less plastic. However, there are many different components within the biological, socioemotional, and cognitive dimensions of development that continue to change and develop over time (Santrock, 2004). Complete Activity 10.1 to stimulate your thinking about human development across the lifespan.

ACTIVITY 10.1

What are some things that immediately come to mind when you think about human development throughout the lifespan and the changes that might occur over time? How might these issues and changes have implications for counseling?

Lifespan development is complex, and the field continues to evolve, with greater emphasis on cross-cultural perspectives, including feminism (Gielen & Roopnarine, 2004; Miller & Scholnick, 2000). Broderick and Blewitt (2006) noted that lifespan developmental theory provides an organizational framework for understanding how the different stages of life are linked together, and how the three adaptive processes of growth, maintenance, and regulation of loss are a part of the developmental journey from infancy through old age. As Nugent and Jones (2005, p. 95) stressed, "human development theories focus on helping people of all ages resolve normal conflicts and maintain healthy personal, social, and career development."

Erikson (1950) identified the following stages of psychosocial development, which are reflected throughout the chapter in the specific discussions about lifespan development:

1. **Basic trust versus mistrust** (birth to 1 year). In this stage, infants gain trust from a warm, responsive environment, in contrast to mistrust if they are mistreated or ignored.
2. **Autonomy versus shame and doubt** (1 to 3 years). In this stage, autonomy is nurtured when children can use their skills to make their own decisions.
3. **Initiative versus guilt** (3 to 6 years). Children experiment with who they can become through imaginative play. If parents do not support their ambition and experimentation and expect too much self-control, the child may feel guilty.
4. **Industry versus inferiority** (6 to 11 years). As they become more involved in school, children develop the ability to work with others. If they have negative experiences with peers or in the home or school setting, they may experience feelings of inferiority.
5. **Identity versus role confusion** (adolescence). Developing an identity is a key issue during this stage, but can result in a negative outcome if there is confusion about future adult roles.
6. **Intimacy versus isolation** (young adulthood). Establishing intimate ties with others is a major task at this stage. Individuals who are unable to do this remain isolated.
7. **Generativity versus stagnation** (middle adulthood). Giving to the next generation is the essence of this stage, and individuals who fail to do this feel stagnated without this meaningful sense of accomplishment.
8. **Ego integrity versus despair** (old age). During this time of self-reflection, individuals who have lived satisfying lives develop a feeling of integrity, whereas individuals who perceive they have not lived a satisfying life experience dissatisfaction and fear death.

INFANCY AND TODDLERHOOD

The first 24 months of life constitute **infancy** (Newman & Newman, 2006), when major changes in all areas of development occur at an astonishing pace. During this fascinating, almost magical time, the personality of an infant begins to evolve as the infant begins to establish a presence in this world. Toddlers also make their presence felt by their high energy and their "unpredictable, startling thoughts and actions that keep adults in a state of puzzled amazement" (Newman & Newman, 2006, p. 182). During **toddlerhood** (ages 2 to 3 years), remarkable changes, particularly in locomotion and language development, significantly contribute to the young child's growing autonomy. While there are many developmental accomplishments during this period, the following major ones are described: gross and fine motor development, emotional development, and cognitive/language development.

Motor Development in Infancy and Toddlerhood

Gross and fine motor development are essential during infancy. Santrock (2004) noted that new motor skills are dramatic during the first year of life. By age 3 to 4 months, infants begin to roll over; they can typically sit without support at 6 months; and by 7 to 8 months, they can crawl and stand without support. Infants can generally walk without assistance by 13 months (Feldman, 2003; Santrock, 2004). There can be a 4-month variation as to when these milestones occur, but the sequence of the accomplishments typically does not vary.

Toddlers not only master the above-mentioned skills, but between age 2 and 3 years, locomotion is a key factor; leg muscles are stronger, and children walk, run, and jump several inches from the floor. They seem to be in constant motion and enjoy what their bodies can do.

Fine motor skills, which are almost nonexistent at birth, include reaching and grasping. At about 3 months of age, infants have more control over their head and shoulders, which increases their ability to reach and grasp (Berk, 2003). Fine motor skills follow a gradual progression. Between 6 and 12 months, infants can focus on small objects and reach out to grasp them. Scribbling and turning pages of a book occur between 12 and 18 months.

Fine motor skills continue to develop as toddlers begin to build high block towers and put puzzles together. Their drawings also advance. An 18-month-old can scribble; these scribbles start to become pictures, and toddlers use lines to represent the boundaries of objects by age 3 years (Berk, 2003).

As Feldman (2003) stressed, these norms are based primarily on White Americans, and there are differences in the timing of development relative to cultural, racial, and social groups. African American infants exhibit more accelerated motor development than Whites. Also, variations in the timing of gross or fine motor skills may be affected by malnutrition, which is not only a problem in underdeveloped countries, but also in countries where there is significant poverty.

Emotional Development in Infancy and Toddlerhood

Newman and Newman (2006) identified age-related changes in **emotional differentiation**. In particular, they distinguished between joy and pleasure, weakness and fear, and rage and anger. Infants at 3 months can smile and display rage or anger when they experience physical discomfort. From 6 to 12 months, they are more aware of situations, and their joy, anger, and fear are related to their environment. At 1 year of age, infants not only display elation, but also anxiety, fear, and anger. At age 2 years, they begin to respond to others' emotions and can show love by giving hugs and kisses. A more nonspecific anxiey is also more prevalent during this second year of life, in contrast to the fear of strangers that emerges at about 6 months and the separation anxiety at 9 months (Feldman, 2003).

According to Santrock (2004), toddlers are able to express their feelings verbally. They can say "feel bad" or "dog scare" (p. 218). Toddlerhood is also characterized by the **terrible twos**—if their attempts to achieve greater autonomy are thwarted, anger and its expression through tantrums are common.

Cognitive/Language Development in Infancy and Toddlerhood

What intellectual abilities do infants and toddlers have, and how do these develop over time? **Piaget's cognitive-developmental theory** contributes in part to our knowledge about cognitive development. Because a detailed discussion of Piaget's contributions or those of other theorists is beyond the scope of this chapter, the reader is encouraged to do further research about this important area of development.

Piaget's theory is based on the premise that children discover or construct their knowledge through their own activity, and that they move through four stages of development. The sensorimotor stage, which pertains to the period from birth to 2 years old, is divided into six substages with a progression of development that results in some degree of mental representation (Berk, 2003).

Children move from Piaget's sensorimotor to the **preoperational stage** (ages 2 to 7 years). During this period, mental representation increases dramatically (Berk, 2003), along with make-believe play. Although children younger than 2 years can engage in some make-believe play, such as talking into a toy telephone, after age 2 years, they pretend with less realistic toys. Toddlers are also less self-centered, and their make-believe play is more complex.

With regard to language development, infants cry and coo, then begin to babble (Santrock, 2004). They typically speak their first words at 10 to 15 months, with rapid progression after that. The average 18-month-old has a 50-word vocabulary, which increases to 200 words by age 2 years. Language development continues to increase rapidly during toddlerhood, and by age 3 years, the typical vocabulary is 1000 words, and toddlers' communication is generally understood.

EARLY CHILDHOOD

Curiosity, questioning, and new socialization experiences through exposure to preschool and kindergarten characterize the stage of **early childhood** development. The intriguing changes continue as young children increasingly become more independent and their world broadens. Significant developmental accomplishments in emotional, social, and cognitive development are briefly highlighted.

Social Development in Early Childhood

Play serves an important role for children, in their own skill development and in relation to others. **Associative play**, in which children interact and share, but do not seem to be playing the same game, characterizes 4-year-olds. By age 5 years, children begin to be more cooperative, take turns, and create games (Berk, 1999).

Although children in this age group still engage in make-believe play, they also participate in more structured games that are based more on reality (Newman & Newman, 2006). By the time they are in school and begin spending more time with other children, they learn to share, to deal with conflict, and to be a follower or a leader (Rathus, 2004).

Children at this age prefer same-gender playmates, not only in the United States, but also in other cultures (Newman & Newman, 2006). In addition, they show noticeable gender differences in play behavior: Boys tend to be more involved in rough and tumble play (Rathus, 2004), whereas girls are more inclined to engage in nurturing activities. Also, girls are more cooperative, whereas boys are more aggressive and competitive (Feldman, 2003).

Emotional Development in Early Childhood

Throughout this period, children become increasingly adept at understanding their emotions (Laible & Thompson, 1998). Not only are they able to talk about their feelings, but they can also incorporate them into pretend play, which gives them a better understanding of their feelings and how to express feelings in acceptable ways. Although they gradually develop a better understanding of others' emotions, initially they are quite literal and confuse overt emotional expression with what someone may be feeling (Cobb, 2001). According to Berk (2003), children at this age have difficulty understanding that they can experience different emotions about a situation simultaneously, even though they can understand the idea of experiencing different emotions at different times.

Although they will have made progress managing their emotions, this progress may be very uneven. Their emotional vocabularies are expanding, and they are beginning to understand which emotions are appropriate to specific situations (Izard & Ackerman, 2000). However, because they often lack the ability to verbalize their feelings accurately, young children tend to express them directly through action (Vernon & Clemente, 2005). Complete Activity 10.2 to help you understand more about how children express their emotions.

ACTIVITY 10.2   EMOTIONAL EXPRESSION IN EARLY CHILDHOOD

If you have access to a child between four and 6 years old, ask him or her to speak with you for a few minutes and describe a time recently when he or she got into an argument with a friend or a brother or a sister. Ask the child to tell you about the argument and what feelings he or she had at this time. Then ask the child to draw a picture of these feelings. Afterward, address the following questions:

- How well did the child verbally explain his or her feelings?
- What convergence or discrepancy between the child's drawing and verbal description did you observe?
- What limitations, if any, did you note in the way the child identified his or her feelings?
- Comparing your observations with the literature, how typical or atypical is this child relative to emotional expression?

Cognitive Development in Early Childhood

Preoperational thought patterns characterize the cognitive development of 4-, 5-, and 6-year-olds (Berk, 2003; McDevitt & Ormrod, 2002). Because children are able to represent objects and events mentally, they can think and act more flexibly than during the **sensorimotor stage**. The fact that they can recall past events and envision future ones allows them to connect experiences and thus results in more complex understandings.

Although they become increasingly more adept at relating symbols to each other in meaningful ways, there are some definite limitations. First, they have preoperational **egocentrism**, which is the inability to see things from another perspective. Also characteristic of their cognitive style is what Piaget described as **centration** (Berk, 2003; McDevitt & Ormrod, 2002), which refers to the tendency to focus on one aspect of a situation rather than on a broader view. As a result, they understand things in terms of an either/or framework, and have difficulty grasping cause and effect.

Language progresses rapidly during this period of growth, but children's vocabulary reflects their concrete stage of development. By age 5 years, children can understand almost anything explained to them in context if the examples are specific (Bjorklund, 2000), but they may have difficulty with concepts such as time and space.

Imaginative play and vivid fantasies characterize this period of development, particularly for preschoolers. At age 4 years, they often have imaginary friends and engage in pretend play by themselves and with others, assuming different roles as they act out familiar routines such as going to the store or to the doctor (Cobb, 2001). Activity 10.3 facilitates understanding about imaginative play.

ACTIVITY 10.3   IMAGINARY PLAY

If you have access to several preschool children, ask them to tell you about any imaginary friends they may have. Then observe these children in play to see if they engage in pretend play, and if so, how they assume different roles. Reflect on the similarities and differences with each individual in terms of their imaginary friends and how they engaged in pretend play. Based on what you observed, what did you learn about imaginary play at this stage of development?

Developmental Interventions in Early Childhood

EMOTIONAL DEVELOPMENT IN EARLY CHILDHOOD   Because young children have a limited emotional vocabulary, teaching preschoolers to identify and describe feelings is helpful. A simple strategy is to draw a happy face, a sad face, a mad face, and a worried face on four different paper plates. Secure these to a piece of tag board and put a different colored dot under each face (yellow for happy, blue for sad, red for mad, and green for worried). Then randomly place several of each of the colored dots in a square around the four faces. After explaining what each feeling is, take turns rolling a die and moving a marker along the dots in accordance with the number on the die. Both the child and the professional counselor then share a situation associated with the feeling they "landed" on.

SOCIAL DEVELOPMENT IN EARLY CHILDHOOD   As children begin spending time with other children in preschool, they have increased opportunities to share and cooperate. Facilitating social development is best done in a small group of three to four children. After discussing what sharing means, indicate to the children that they are going to make a snowman (or another object) using the materials in a paper sack (e.g., cotton balls, one pair of scissors, one tube of glue or roll of tape, buttons of different shapes and sizes, pieces of colored construction paper, and five different colored crayons). If possible, videotape children as they work so that after they are finished with the project, you can review the tape and look for examples of cooperation and sharing. If it is not possible to videotape, you can stop at various points throughout the construction of the project and ask for examples of sharing and cooperation.

MIDDLE CHILDHOOD

"Rich years filled with growth and change" is how Cobb (2001, p. 448) characterized **middle childhood**. Although their physical rate of growth has stabilized, 6- to 11-year-olds mature remarkably during these school-age years. Key characteristics relative to social, emotional, and cognitive development are described.

Social Development in Middle Childhood

When they begin formal schooling, children increasingly encounter peers who are different from them with regard to accomplishments, personality, religion, and ethnicity, which enhances their perspective-taking abilities. Consequently, they are better able to communicate with their peers and are more prosocial.

Socialization in the context of a peer group becomes a central issue for children in this age range. Acceptance in a group and a "best friend" contribute significantly to a child's sense of competence (Berger, 2003). Friendships serve important functions; children learn to cooperate and compromise, negotiate, and assume roles as leaders and followers. They also learn how to deal with peer group pressure and rejection.

Throughout this period, friendships become increasingly more intense and intimate, particularly for girls. They generally choose friends who are of the same age, gender, and ethnicity, and who have similar interests (Cobb, 2001; Siegler, DeLoache, & Eisenberg, 2003). As opposed to early childhood, when children are more egocentric and do not need friends as much, children in middle childhood are becoming more dependent on friends for help in academic and social situations, and for companionship and self-validation (Berger, 2003; Siegler et al., 2003). Team play is a new dimension of social development.

Emotional Development in Middle Childhood

A school-aged child's understanding of emotions is more complex than a preschooler's, and in general, the school-aged child is more sensitive, empathic, and better able to recognize and communicate his or her feelings to others (McDevitt & Ormrod, 2002). Berk (2003) pointed out that "children who are sociable, assertive, and good at regulating emotions" (p. 407) are most likely to be empathic and helpful to others.

At this age, children now understand that a person can have two conflicting emotions simultaneously, which extends to self-conscious emotions. In addition, these children have learnt that feelings can change, and that they are not the cause of another person's emotional discomfort (Kaplan, 2000).

During middle childhood, fears and anxieties are related to real life, as opposed to imaginary issues. For example, they are no longer afraid of ghosts, but are worried about tests and grades or being harmed by someone. Happiness is often related to peer acceptance and achieving goals (Siegler et al., 2003).

Cognitive Development in Middle Childhood

During middle childhood, vast differences occur in cognitive development. According to Piaget (1967), a transitional period between preoperational and **concrete operational** thought occurs between the ages of 5 and 7 years, but by age 7 or 8 years, most children are definitely concrete operational thinkers. Berk (2003) noted that this is a major turning point because when children are in this stage, their thinking is more like that of adults. Concrete operational thinkers are able to understand logical operations, such as identity, reversibility, reciprocity, and classification, and can apply them in different contexts, such as friendships, rules in games, or team play. Because play is such an integral part of early and middle childhood, Activity 10.4 is a reflection on this aspect of development.

ACTIVITY 10.4   PLAY IN MIDDLE CHILDHOOD

Think back to when you were a child, or think of a child or children you have seen engage in play activities. First, think of early childhood. What types of games did you play with others? Next, think of games you played as you and friends transitioned through middle childhood. Frequently, children in early childhood participate in make-believe and then structured games based on reality (e.g., playing "house" or "school"). Children in middle childhood frequently participate in more team play and games that have rules (e.g., board games, kickball, other sports that require teams). Based on what you recall about your play, in what ways were you (or children you observed) "typical" according to developmental stereotypes?

School-aged children's thinking is more flexible and rational, and for the most part, they have better problem-solving abilities and organizational skills. They learn best by questioning, exploring, and doing (Gauvain, 2001), and they use language in more sophisticated ways. Despite the growth in cognitive development, there are limitations. Although they can reason more logically, children have difficulty with abstract concepts; they do not readily think about things they cannot see (Cobb, 2001). Because they focus on what they can see, their problem-solving abilities are sometimes limited because they do not consider other possible solutions (Siegler et al., 2003). Children operate from assumptions, mistaking their assumptions for facts and jumping to conclusions. All of these factors affect how children respond to events in their lives.

Developmental Interventions in Middle Childhood

EMOTIONAL DEVELOPMENT   To facilitate emotional development during middle childhood and to help children learn that feelings vary in intensity, professional counselors can engage them in the activity "How Strong" (Vernon, 2006). After discussing how feelings can vary in intensity and sharing several examples, give the child three cans, labeled *strong, mild, weak*. Then give the child a list of situations on individual notecards, such as "someone calls you a name," "someone steals your new bike," and "your best friend moves away." Ask the child to read each situation, write how he would feel in each case, and put each card in one of the cans to signify the degree of intensity of that particular feeling. Discuss why feelings often vary in intensity, and how to decrease the intensity of strong negative emotions.

SOCIAL DEVELOPMENT   Social skills become increasingly important during middle childhood. A classroom guidance intervention to facilitate social development is to play a game similar to musical chairs, in which children move around the circle, and when the music stops, the child left standing draws a "friendship" strip from an envelope and reads it aloud. The child is asked to decide if this is an example of a good or bad friendship behavior and put the strip of paper in the appropriately labeled (good or bad) friendship box after discussing reasons for this classification. Continue the game until there are no chairs left. Examples of behaviors for the friendship behavior strips include "compliments you," "calls you names," "refuses to share," "invites you to play," "spreads rumors about you," and "turns friends against you."

ADOLESCENCE

The relative stability of middle childhood can vanish overnight as children enter puberty, signifying the beginning of early adolescence (ages 11 to 14 years), which is followed by midadolescence (ages 15 to 18 years), and later adolescence (ages 18 to 24 years), often referred to as the beginning of young adulthood. In particular, the first few years of early **adolescence** can be difficult because of the rapid physical changes and the significant cognitive and emotional maturation (Newman & Newman, 2006). Despite some turmoil, however, adolescence can be an exciting time as young people develop more complex social and intimate relationships, gain more autonomy and mastery, and experience many new things.

Early Adolescence

Except during infancy, physical changes occur more rapidly during early adolescence than at any other point in the lifespan (Meece, 2002), affecting the young adolescent in numerous ways. For more specific development that occurs during puberty, the reader is encouraged to consult sources referred to in this chapter.

SOCIAL DEVELOPMENT IN EARLY ADOLESCENCE   As early adolescents become more socially distant from their families, peers play a dominant role and are a vital part of the growing-up process, although in some cultures, this is not as pronounced (McDevitt & Ormrod, 2002; Wolman, 1998). Cobb (2001) aptly described the importance of peers by stating that "in larger numbers, they are socialization agents, guiding adolescents into new, more adult roles. And one on one, they are mirrors into whom adolescents look to glimpse the future within" (p. 591). Jaffe (1998) noted that peers also provide a "safe haven for trying out new beliefs and behaviors" (p. 281), but at the same time, adolescents are very vulnerable to peer ridicule and rejection. Because they have a strong need to belong and to be accepted, and they fear being judged or put down, young adolescents tend to conform to peer norms and expectations (Meece, 2002).

As they get older, friendships become increasingly more intimate (Meece, 2002), and adolescents confide in their peers more than in their parents (Fisher, Munsch, & Greene, 1996). Adolescent friendships are more emotionally bonding and stable than childhood friendships; adolescents want psychological closeness, loyalty, and mutual understanding, and typically choose friends who are like themselves (Berk, 2003).

EMOTIONAL DEVELOPMENT IN EARLY ADOLESCENCE   Heightened emotionality and rapid mood fluctuations characterize this period, with the adolescent shifting from intense sadness to anger to excitement to depression in a brief time. In addition to the unpredictable moodiness that is often accompanied by emotional outbursts, negative and painful emotional states are experienced more frequently (Cobb, 2001; Siegler et al., 2003), along with troublesome emotions, including anxiety, shame, depression, embarrassment, guilt, and loneliness (Vernon, 2004).

Young adolescents are more aware of others' feelings and thoughts. Consequently, they are more sensitive to the ups and downs associated with social interactions, often overreacting to who said what about whom. Although their more advanced cognitive abilities help them interpret unpleasant emotional experiences, this often results in an increase in self-consciousness and self-criticism (Meece, 2002).

There are cultural and gender differences related to the acceptability and expression of feelings. In some cultures, emotional openness is not valued (Saarni, Mumme, & Campos, 1998). Respect for these cultural differences is essential, as well as an understanding of gender differences. For example, girls are often more emotionally expressive and more sensitive to the emotional states of others. Girls frequently also experience more anxiety, shame, guilt, and depression (Garber, Kelley, & Martin, 2002; Meece, 2002). Girls, more so than boys, are depressed by problems in their peer relationships (Nolen-Hoeksema, 2001), and by their appearance and body image (Garber et al., 2002).

The increased intensity of emotions permeates all aspects of early adolescents' lives; they feel confused and anxious about the roller coaster of emotions they may experience (Vernon, 2004). Their negative emotions can be overwhelming, resulting in increased vulnerability. Activity 10.5 invites you to apply developmental theory to a short case study about a young adolescent.

ACTIVITY 10.5   CASE STUDY OF A SEVENTH-GRADE GIRL

The parents of a girl in early adolescence bring her to counseling. She is in seventh grade. According to her parents, she has recently become very quiet and does not spend as much time with them. She stays in her room most of the time and is more withdrawn than usual. She often says she hates school and does not want to go. Her grades have also declined. What types of developmental issues might this adolescent be struggling with, and which aspects would you focus on as her professional counselor?

COGNITIVE DEVELOPMENT IN EARLY ADOLESCENCE   The cognitive changes that gradually occur during adolescence "have far-reaching implications for the young person's psychological development and social relations" (Steinberg, 1996, p. 64) and constitute the most dramatic change in cognition that occurs in anyone's life. Kaplan (2000) noted that **formal operational stage** thinking begins at about age 11 years, but is not consistently attained until at least age 15 to 20 years. As early adolescents move into this realm, they begin to think more abstractly and hypothetically (Cobb, 2001), often engaging in idealization and then comparing themselves and others with these ideal standards.

Steinberg (1996) emphasized that the changes in cognition allow adolescents to think about possibilities, which has a positive impact on their problem-solving abilities. In addition, they become better arguers and do not accept others' viewpoints without questioning them.

With the development of abstract thinking comes an ability to think more logically and hypothesize about the logical sequence of events. Although they are better able to predict consequences of actions, adolescents inconsistently apply these skills to themselves (Cobb, 2001).

Adolescents may see discrepancies between what is and what is supposed to occur conceptually at this period of development. Considerable variability exists in the way early adolescents think. Although thinking continues to improve throughout adolescence, even by the end of middle school, most young adolescents have not attained formal operational thinking (Meece, 2002). Cultural expectations and experiences also influence the development of formal operational thinking, so as Rogoff (1990) stressed, it is important to consider the cultural context with regard to how thinking skills develop.

DEVELOPMENTAL INTERVENTIONS IN EARLY ADOLESCENCE

Emotional Development　The emotional volatility of early adolescence is often confusing and disturbing. The following intervention, intended for small group or classroom guidance, helps adolescents learn to distinguish between helpful and unhelpful ways to manage their moods. Introduce the lesson by discussing how hormonal changes during puberty contribute to mood swings and engage students in a discussion about how adolescents often feel overwhelmed and confused when they experience these. In small groups, have students discuss what they do to manage their moods and record their ideas on newsprint. After each group has shared ideas, give each group a sorting board (a sheet labeled "very helpful," "somewhat helpful," "not at all helpful," "not helpful/negative consequences," and "could be either helpful or unhelpful"). Give them a set of cards per group with a coping strategy listed on each card, such as "listen to music," "write poetry," "attempt suicide," "get drunk," "talk to a parent," "talk to a friend," "punch something or someone," "binge eat," "stop eating," "journal," "talk to a counselor," "leave the scene," and "cut yourself." Have students sort these onto the sorting board. When finished, process the activity by asking students to share which strategies they have used or would like to use to help manage their moods (Vernon, 1998b).

Cognitive Development　Young adolescents' emotions commonly overshadow their ability to think clearly, which affects their problem-solving ability. The following intervention, which can be done with an individual or within a small group or classroom guidance, helps them think more rationally.

Introduce the idea of rational thinking by handing a pair of dark glasses and a pair of glasses with bright lenses to the adolescent. Ask the adolescent to first put on the dark "doom and gloom" glasses and imagine going to a party with these glasses on. What will the party be like? Then have the adolescent put on the brighter glasses; things will look different. What will the party be like? Discuss the idea that the way we look at situations or think about situations affects how we feel about them. Introduce the following concepts, explaining with examples that pertain to adolescence: tunnel vision (i.e., seeing only a small part of the issue), overgeneralizing and "awfulizing" (i.e., blowing the situation out of proportion and assuming the worst), self-downing (i.e., putting oneself down; assuming that you are not good), and mind reading (i.e., assuming you know what someone is thinking without checking it out). Discuss how these negative thinking patterns apply to issues in the adolescent's life, and help identify ways to counteract these by checking out assumptions, not jumping to conclusions, looking at things from multiple perspectives, and looking for other possibilities (Vernon, 1998a).

Midadolescence

Midadolescence is frequently described as a period when teenagers try out adult roles (Dusek, 1996), discover who they are and are not (Cobb, 2001), and establish new beliefs and behaviors (Kaplan, 2000). Depending on when they entered puberty and when formal operational thinking is attained, midadolescence is often a calmer, more predictable stage of development (Vernon & Clemente, 2005).

SOCIAL DEVELOPMENT IN MIDADOLESCENCE   The importance of peer relationships continues into midadolescence, and the increased time spent with peers serves various functions for teenagers to try out various roles, to learn to tolerate individual differences as they come in contact with people who have different values and lifestyles, and to prepare themselves for adult interactions as they begin to form more intimate relationships (Dusek, 1996).

For an adolescent who has attained formal operational thinking, relationships take on a new dimension. Because these adolescents are more self-confident and less egocentric, they are not as dependent on peers for identity and emotional support (Jaffe, 1998). They are also more willing to express their uniqueness and are less likely to conform to peers. Peers continue to be a source of support, however, and play an important role in adolescents' development as friendships become more stable and less exclusive (Broderick & Blewitt, 2006).

Intimate friendships with the same gender and opposite gender increase during midadolescence (Newman & Newman, 2006), with girls seeking these intimate relationships sooner than boys. Teenagers begin to experience casual heterosexual contact through participation in group activities before actual dating begins (Dusek, 1996), typically after age 15 or 16 years (Steinberg, 1996). Sexual experimentation generally increases during this period (Cobb, 2001). Activity 10.6 helps the reader reflect on social development during adolescence.

ACTIVITY 10.6   A HIGH SCHOOL REFLECTION

Think back to when you were in high school. How important were peer relationships to you, and how did these relationships differ from those you were in early adolescence? The literature emphasizes the importance of peer relationships because they serve a variety of functions. How can you apply this statement to your personal experiences? If you could "do it over," what, if anything, would you change about your peer relationships during adolescence?

EMOTIONAL DEVELOPMENT IN MIDADOLESCENCE   In contrast to the emotional upheaval characteristic of early adolescence, more emotional stability comes in midadolescence (Vernon & Clemente, 2005) because adolescents are not as vulnerable and are not as likely to be overwhelmed by their emotions. Kang and Shaver (2004) noted that increased emotional complexity occurs during this period, and that adolescents are able to identify, understand, and express more emotions, and be more empathic.

Although these adolescents are typically more emotionally stable, there is great variability in how they deal with emotionally charged issues depending on their level of cognitive maturation, which accounts for the wide variation in how adolescents manage emotions. More emotionally mature adolescents have better coping skills, and are less likely to behave impulsively or act out behaviorally (Vernon & Al-Mabuk, 1995).

A compounding factor in adolescents' emotional development is depression, which was not well addressed in adolescents until more recently because it was discounted as adolescent turmoil or masked depression (Evans, Van Velsor, & Schumacher, 2002). However, Newman and Newman (2006) reported that about 35% of adolescents experience periods of sadness and depressed feelings regularly.

COGNITIVE DEVELOPMENT IN MIDADOLESCENCE During midadolescence, formal operational thinking continues to develop, although many adolescents and even adults do not reach this level of thinking. Steinberg (1996) stressed that advanced reasoning capabilities develop gradually, that these advanced skills are employed by some adolescents more often than by other adolescents, and that when they apply the advanced skills may depend on the situation. As formal operational thinking develops, adolescents begin to think and behave in qualitatively different ways. According to Newman and Newman (2006), they can also hypothesize, think about the future, be introspective, and detect inconsistency in statements. Their thought processes are more flexible; they are less likely to think in either/or terms, which has a positive effect on how they problem solve (Vernon, 2004).

Although their cognitive abilities have improved considerably since early adolescence, 15- to 18-year-olds are still likely to be inconsistent in their thinking and behavior (Cobb, 2001). As Jaffe (1998) noted, "having an ability doesn't mean that it will be exercised correctly or at all" (p. 112).

DEVELOPMENTAL INTERVENTIONS IN MIDADOLESCENCE

Social Development Although the emotional stability of midadolescence generally affects social relationships in a positive way, adolescents continue to have issues related to rumors, gossip, and unfounded assumptions that can result in interpersonal relationship difficulties. The following intervention (Vernon, 1998b) helps adolescents learn to stop the negative cycle of rumors and assumptions. It is most effective in a classroom or a small group setting.

Introduce the intervention by asking for several volunteers. Whisper a complicated message about a relationship issue to the first volunteer, who passes it on to the second volunteer, who passes it to the third volunteer. The last person states the message out loud, which stimulates discussion about distorted communication. Next, ask the adolescents to identify in writing a time they have been the object of a rumor or gossip, how they felt, and a consequence of the situation. After sharing responses with partners, encourage discussion on how to stop this negative cycle by checking out assumptions; asking themselves if what someone said about them is true, and if not, they do not have to react personally; and not participating in this type of behavior.

Cognitive Development Although many adolescents still live in the "here and now," midadolescence is a period in which they need to begin making decisions about the future.

The following intervention can facilitate that decision-making process. After initiating a discussion with the adolescent about plans after high school, give him or her a set of "what's next" cards (Vernon, 2002) that list examples such as the following, one per card: "full-time job away from the community," "part-time job in the community," "2-year college part time," "2-year college full time," "getting married," "trade or technical school," "4-year college full time," and "joining a branch of the armed services." The adolescent sorts these onto a sheet of paper labeled "very likely," "somewhat likely," "not at all likely." After the sorting is complete, debrief by discussing viable options, obstacles the adolescent may have to overcome, and feelings about these next steps.

Late Adolescence (Emerging Adulthood)

"The new freedoms and responsibilities of emerging adulthood represent major changes in individuals' lives" (Santrock, 2004, p. 441). As young people search for meaning and direction in their lives, a "heightened sensitivity to the process of identity development" ensues (Newman & Newman, 2006, p. 348). Accompanying this search is increasing anxiety and uncertainty about what they want to do with their lives and whether they will be successful.

SOCIAL DEVELOPMENT IN LATE ADOLESCENCE (EMERGING ADULTHOOD)   During this emerging adulthood period, young people are beginning to see themselves as adults and as contributing members of society (Arnett, 2000). They become less dependent on parents, gradually achieving a psychological sense of autonomy in which they are still connected to their parents, but they accept each others' individuality (Broderick & Blewitt, 2006). The degree of autonomy depends on culture.

Feldman (2003) noted that there is a basic need for belongingness, which results in young people's establishment of close relationships with others. Ultimately, a close relationship may become a loving one, although romantic, passionate love is not the norm in every culture. However, for many young adults, choosing a lifelong partner is a major task at this stage of development.

COGNITIVE DEVELOPMENT IN LATE ADOLESCENCE (EMERGING ADULTHOOD)   In contrast to Piaget's theory, which implied that formal operational thinking was the final stage of cognitive development, Labouvie-Vief suggested that there are several cognitive changes that go beyond this stage, including confronting societal paradoxes, using analogies to make comparisons, and reasoning subjectively. Because thinking is more flexible, interpretation and understanding subtleties are more prevalent. Labouvie-Vief labeled this type of thinking as "postformal thought" (Feldman, 2003), which also includes dialectical thinking (arguing, debating, and realizing that issues are not always absolutely right or clear) and the realization that problem resolution involves drawing on past experiences.

Feldman (2003) also discussed Schaie's stages of cognitive development, indicating that in late adolescence and emerging adulthood, "intelligence is applied to specific situations involving the attainment of long-term goals regarding careers, family, and societal contributions" (p. 465). This stage is called the achieving stage, where the decisions they make have lifelong implications, specifically in terms of job and marriage.

Broderick and Blewitt (2006) noted that cognitive functioning during this stage is characterized by acquiring knowledge and becoming more expert in particular areas. A shift to using knowledge to achieve long-term goals also occurs at this time (Feldman, 2003). The reader is encouraged to read about Perry's theory of intellectual and ethical development in the college years, in which he described changes in young adults' knowledge and assumptions of the world. Kitchener's model of reflective judgment also describes the different stages of thinking relative to this period of development (Broderick & Blewitt, 2006). Activity 10.7 encourages reflection about your own intellectual and ethical development.

ACTIVITY 10.7

Research Perry's theory of intellectual and ethical development in the college years. What connections can you make to your own life at this stage? Reflect on any significant changes of worldviews and assumptions, recalling whether or not you became more interested in world news or any world topics. What implications does Perry's theory have for professional counselors seeing adult clients?

SELF-DEVELOPMENT IN LATE ADOLESCENCE (EMERGING ADULTHOOD)   Several important tasks must be assumed by young adults. First, they need to formulate their gender identity. Although role expectations in this culture and some others are more flexible, there are still expectations and choices that young people need to consider (Newman & Newman, 2006). In addition, as they move out into the world, they encounter other adult role models aside from their parents and are faced with the challenge of analyzing beliefs and values they had assumed as children, and re-evaluating them based on their young adult perspectives. Activity 10.8 encourages reflection on changes in beliefs and values during emerging adulthood.

ACTIVITY 10.8

What changes in beliefs and values frequently take place during emerging adulthood? Reflect on your own beliefs and values; how (if at all) were they altered during emerging adulthood? In what ways are your values different from those of your parents or guardians, and how does this affect your relationship with them?

In addition to integrating gender identity and clarifying their personal vision of themselves (Newman & Newman, 2006), later adolescents are more aware of their bodies, and clarify their sexual orientation within the context of intimate relationships.

DEVELOPMENTAL INTERVENTIONS IN LATE ADOLESCENCE (EMERGING ADULTHOOD)

Social Development   Choosing a life partner or becoming involved in a serious romantic relationship often occurs during late adolescence. Sometimes, young adults operate with tunnel vision in that they see only the good aspects of the relationship, so when problems occur, they are often blind-sided and devastated. The following intervention is designed to help them look realistically at romantic relationships.

Give the individual a sheet of paper with a smaller square surrounded by a larger square. In the inside square have the young adult list all the positive traits about the relationship and the individual with whom he is involved. In the outside square, he or she should list all the negative realities represented by the relationship. Process this by discussing the positive and negative aspects of the relationship and the significance and consequences of what he or she has identified. This process helps a young adult clarify the areas of concern and strengths (Vernon, 2002).

Self-development   As young people question their values and continue to define their own roles, an intervention such as the following can provide clarification. First, have the young adult brainstorm a list of strong beliefs and values (i.e., what "matters"). After the list is complete, invite the emerging adult to code these values and beliefs as follows: IM (important to me but not to others close to me), IF (important to me and to my immediate family), IP (important to me and to my partner and/or closest friends), PA (can publicly affirm), A (alienates me from others), E (evident in my behavior, such as work or volunteer activities), TM (takes money), P (proud of), and C (contributes to society, to the "greater good"). After coding, ask the emerging adult to discuss what insights resulted from completing the intervention, and what this tells him or her about "who I am." Encourage dialogue about changes in priorities or actions he or she wishes to make as a result of the insight gained.

EARLY ADULTHOOD

Although **early adulthood** is typically identified as beginning at age 24 years, the tasks associated with this phase may have begun during emerging adulthood, depending on the individual. However, during this stage, three roles evolve: the worker, the committed partner, and the parent (Newman & Newman, 2006). With each of these significant roles come multiple challenges and adjustments.

The Worker in Early Adulthood

Through work, adults "express their personal identity and experience a sense of personal value and social status" (Newman & Newman, 2006, p. 409). In the **early career stage**, the worker questions his or her competence and degree of commitment. How to advance, relate to colleagues and supervisors, and balance work and family are salient issues. Concerns of this nature can create stress as the young worker seeks a fulfilling career and assumes major responsibility for earning a living and navigating the dynamics of the work environment.

As the role of a worker evolves, challenges emerge, including dealing with the demands and expectations of the job and negotiating the hierarchy of authority. As they take on new responsibilities or discover their own limitations, young adults may experience anxiety, coupled with the worry about being financially self-sufficient.

The Partner in Early Adulthood

Developing an intimate relationship may have happened during young adulthood, but with the average age of marriage being delayed, it is likely that committing to an intimate relationship that may involve marriage may not occur until early adulthood, depending on culture. Newman and Newman (2006) identified stages of a committed relationship, beginning with the original attraction and moving to deeper attraction as self-disclosure occurs and partners discover ways in which they are similar. Values and other background characteristics help determine compatibility. The more self-aware young people are, the greater the likelihood that they can select partners with "dimensions of similarity and differences that contribute to intimate relationships" (p. 397).

If the relationship progresses, the next phase occurs as the couple takes new risks in discovering more about each other. At this point, they may experience role compatibility and empathy that strengthens the relationship, or their self-disclosure creates barriers that may lead to a break up if they discover that they are incompatible, or that there are significant undesirable differences. If the relationship endures, intense caring, sexual desire, and euphoria characterize this stage, which may culminate in marriage or an exclusive partnership.

If the couple decides to marry or cohabitate, there are many adjustments. Compromise and flexibility are crucial as couples come to agreement about such issues as spending and saving money, work schedules and habits, relationships with friends and in-laws, alone time versus couple time, eating and sleeping patterns, and other daily living matters. All of these are potential sources of tension, so it is imperative that couples have good communication and conflict management skills to successfully navigate this important task during early adulthood.

The Parent in Early Adulthood

Although not all couples choose to or are able to have children, those who become parents typically do so during this stage of life. According to Newman and Newman (2006), the decision about parenthood is one of the major commitments of early adulthood. These decisions are considered within the context of culture, religious beliefs, family expectations, career aspirations, and personal and family goals.

Feldman (2003) noted that "The birth of a child brings about a dramatic shift in the roles spouses must play . . . and these new positions may overwhelm their ability to respond in their older, although continuing, roles of 'wife' and 'husband'" (p. 507). This shift may be quite stressful given that each parent may adapt to the transition differently. Shapiro, Gottman, and Carrere (2000) noted that although having children is a major responsibility that can be overwhelming as well as rewarding, having children led to greater marital satisfaction for couples who were already satisfied with their relationship. In contrast, couples who had significant conflict before becoming parents had increased difficulty after the birth of the child (Newman & Newman, 2006). Activity 10.9 stimulates thinking about issues relative to significant roles assumed during early adulthood.

ACTIVITY 10.9   ASSUMING ROLES IN EARLY ADULTHOOD

What implications do the roles of worker, partner, and parent have for professional counselors trying to help adult clients? What types of issues related to these three roles may be presented to a professional counselor?

Developmental Interventions in Early Adulthood

Given the many transitions that occur during the early adult stage, an intervention such as the following can help individuals identify changes in roles, responsibilities, routines, and relationships as partners, parents, or workers. Awareness of these changes is the first step in identifying how to deal more effectively with the challenges associated with assuming more responsibility as young adults.

Give the individual a sheet of paper with the words "roles," "relationships," "routines," and "responsibilities" across the top. Under each heading have the individual list three to four changes associated with one or more of the roles partner, parent, or worker. After discussing the changes, work with the individual to minimize the stress associated with the various roles, and identify healthy coping strategies.

Another intervention that addresses the stress and overload that can occur for the young worker, parent, or partner is to give the individual a circle representing a 24-hour day. Ask the individual to divide that circle into sections representing how that time period is currently spent, and then to take another circle and divide it into sections representing how the individual would ideally like the time to be spent. Compare the two circles, and discuss what gets in the way of the ideal circle being the reality. Discuss identifying priorities, establishing realistic and doable goals, and other ways to achieve balance.

MIDDLE ADULTHOOD

According to Broderick and Blewitt (2006), many developmental theorists see the 40s as "a time when reassessment of one's life structure is very likely" (p. 149). Levinson (1992) noted that this questioning of the past, coupled with the reality that life is finite, may result in a midlife crisis. Feldman (2003) stressed that most people make the transition to midlife with little difficulty. Childrearing is typically easier, many adults have been successful in their careers, and for the most part, they are more content with life.

Cognitive and physical changes occur during this period, but because of the increased lifespan and the fact that individuals are healthier at older ages, the "boundaries of middle age are pushed upwards" (Santrock, 2004, p. 514). Aging is different for every individual and varies according to culture, but there are general trends that occur at some point during this developmental stage.

Physical Changes in Middle Adulthood

Although the changes that occur are not as dramatic as during adolescence, by **middle adulthood**, most people experience some change in physical appearance (Santrock, 2004). Skin begins to wrinkle and sag, hair becomes thinner or grayer, and muscle strength decreases while bone loss increases. Vision and hearing can also start to decline, while arthritis and hypertension increase. Typically in the late 40s or early 50s, women go through menopause; men also experience some hormonal changes, including a decrease in testosterone and sperm count (Santrock, 2004).

Cognitive Changes in Middle Adulthood

"Am I losing my memory" is something that middle-aged adults joke about, but at the same time worry about. In reality, sensory and short-term memory do not decline during this period. Although there is some long-term memory loss for some people, Feldman (2003) stressed that "memory declines in middle age are relatively minor" (p. 545). Whether or not intelligence declines with age is controversial. A gradual decline starting at age 25 years is noted in inductive reasoning, spatial orientation, verbal memory, and perceptual speed, but verbal ability increases until about age 40 years and then remains steady throughout the remainder of life (Feldman, 2003).

Key Developmental Tasks in Middle Adulthood

Middle adulthood years can be challenging as adults juggle jobs, children, parents, and partners. Key developmental tasks of midlife include continuation of intimacy and other primary relationships, work productivity, and generativity (Feldman, 2003).

INTIMACY AND RELATIONSHIPS   If there are children and depending on the age during pregnancy, middle-aged adults could be dealing with raising teenagers, launching them into the world, and dealing with the empty nest syndrome (Newman & Newman, 2006). Family roles change as children become adults, and parents need to find other areas of focus. Middle-aged adults may become caretakers for aging parents, which can be a significant challenge (Feldman, 2003). During this period, some parents may also become grandparents, which is another symbol of aging.

WORK   According to Feldman (2003), middle-aged workers are more concerned with pay, working conditions, and policies as opposed to opportunity for advancement or recognition as they were in young adulthood. Many may experience this time as one of high productivity, success, and earning power, but while some older workers experience more job satisfaction than younger workers, burnout also occurs during this period. During the first half of middle adulthood, time and work intensity increase. As adults reach the peak of their career, the energy spent at work may decline, and time with friends and family may increase.

GENERATIVITY   **Generativity**, which refers to the contributions an individual makes to family, community, work, and society, is a concept that was developed by Erikson. According to this perspective, adults in midlife play an important role in mentoring, and focus efforts on continuing their own life by guiding and encouraging future generations (Feldman, 2003). **Stagnation**, which is equivalent to lack of growth, can occur if people feel as if they have not made significant contributions. This may serve as motivation to find more fulfilling, challenging careers or other ways to find meaning in their lives, or it may result in increased rigidity, isolation, and depression if individuals do not have a sense of accomplishment or feel as if they have nothing to contribute to society (Newman & Newman, 2006). Activity 10.10 helps the reader identify issues of middle adulthood.

ACTIVITY 10.10   ROLES IN MIDDLE ADULTHOOD

Place a check mark in all of the following spaces that correctly describe the issues of middle adulthood.

____ 1. reassessment of life structure
____ 2. some long-term memory loss
____ 3. emergence of three roles
____ 4. gradual decline in verbal memory and inductive reasoning
____ 5. decisions about parenthood
____ 6. intelligence is applied to specific situations involving long-term goals
____ 7. hormonal changes

Developmental Interventions in Middle Adulthood

Midlife can be a time when adults experience some dissatisfaction in life and need to find new challenges and opportunities. The following goal-setting intervention is an effective strategy for helping individuals assess their lives and set new goals.

First ask the individual to list 8 to 10 things that are going well in his or her life and to make another list of things he or she would like to change. Next, categorize the things to change into topics such as social, financial, career, family, and spiritual, depending on what was on the list. Then ask the adult to select one item from each category that he or she most wants to change and write these on a separate piece of paper. Next, ask the adult to identify three doable goals for each item that would lead to greater life satisfaction. After discussing the benefits and barriers related to each goal, have the adult identify at least one specific strategy to achieve each of the identified goals, and a timeline.

Another intervention that helps middle-aged adults evaluate how they feel about their life at this stage is to have them complete unfinished sentences such as the following that stimulate discussion about various aspects of life:

"My greatest accomplishment thus far is . . . "

"What I would still like to achieve is . . . "

"As I grow older I feel . . . "

"If I could have done things differently I would have . . . "

"The best thing about being this age is . . . "

"The worst thing about being this age is . . . "

"What I most regret is . . . "

"My family life is . . . "

"My relationships are . . . "

After discussion, invite the middle-aged adult to identify an action plan with goals for the changes he or she wishes to make at this point in life.

LATER ADULTHOOD

In the early 1930s, Carl Jung studied older adult development, concluding that this was a creative period of life as opposed to the prevailing notion that it was characterized by decline and deterioration. For the most part, his theory was ignored, and it was not until more recently that theorists such as Baltes, Cavanaugh, O'Connor and Vallerand, and Schaie revisited this period of life, finding that older adults develop capacities that are noticeably different, involving "reflection, judgment, and knowledge relating to meaningful and cultural experiences" (Nugent & Jones, 2005, p. 107).

During the final 30 years of life, from age 60 on, a period of reinvention occurs. In contrast to the negative stereotypical views about older adulthood, this period of development is characterized by a search for personal meaning as individuals are faced with the opportunity to "invent solutions to their changing conditions . . . they apply the wealth of their life experiences, their perspective on time, and their adaptation to life crises to construct personally satisfying answers to the questions of life's meaning" (Newman & Newman, 2006, p. 470).

This period of reinvention is tempered by the degree to which individuals are able to minimize loss and confront challenges successfully during the later years. However, as Broderick and Blewitt (2006) emphasized, despite loss and physical decline, "for a majority of us, successful development is what we can expect for much of our age" (p. 466). Major developmental tasks during this developmental period involve accepting one's life and achieving satisfaction, redirecting energy to new roles and activities dealing with physical and cognitive changes, and dealing with loss.

Accepting Life in Later Adulthood

Older adults face two tasks related to accepting life and achieving satisfaction. First, they need to reflect on the past and accept the reality of their life, incorporating disappointment, failure, achievement, and successes into an integrated view of self. Second, they need to establish new goals and challenges to maintain optimal functioning (Newman & Newman, 2006). In contrast to the traditional idea that things wind down in later adulthood, older adults fare better if they can achieve a balance between goal achievement and adjustment that may be necessitated by physical limitations or serious stressors.

Redirecting Energy to New Roles and Activities in Later Adulthood

Later adulthood is characterized by many role changes brought about by retirement; death of a spouse, parent, or friends; birth of grandchildren; or assuming new positions as community leaders or volunteers. Each of these changes necessitates adaptation and presents new challenges and opportunities. Older adults cope successfully with these role changes by becoming involved with new activities and developing new interests (Newman & Newman, 2006). Creatively searching for ways to enhance new roles and compensating for one kind of loss by finding another way also contribute to successful aging (Broderick & Blewitt, 2006). Activity 10.11 relates to developmental issues during later adulthood.

ACTIVITY 10.11   DEVELOPMENTAL ISSUES IN LATER ADULTHOOD

Consider the developmental issues that commonly occur in later adulthood and reflect on the following questions:
1. What are some of the negative stereotypes about later adulthood, and how does more recent research differ from these earlier notions?
2. If you were a counselor working with a person in late adulthood, what developmental issues would you expect this client to present?
3. What types of role changes are necessary during this stage of development?

Physical Changes in Later Adulthood

As we age, health concerns increase. Decreased sensory abilities, such as changes in vision and hearing, can have a significant impact on older adults' lives. Arthritis and osteoarthritis constitute another major decline for many older adults and can result in a continuum of physical limitations. The quality of life during this period is affected not only by these two changes, but also by other chronic illnesses. As health declines, dependence on others increases, which can be a difficult role adjustment for the caretaker and the person receiving the care. This is a period when the body begins to break down, and as this occurs, the stress, frustration, and anxiety affect everyone who is affected by an individual's declining health.

Cognitive Changes in Later Adulthood

Cognitive changes do occur in older adulthood. However, because cognition is complex, "it is important to consider that while some dimensions of cognition might decline as we age, others might remain stable or even improve" (Santrock, 2004, p. 598).

Salthouse (2000) indicated that there is a definite decline in the speed of processing information in late adulthood, but stressed that there is a great deal of individual variation in this ability. Changes in attention generally occur at this stage as well, but Rogers and Fisk (2001) noted that while older adults have less selective attention than younger adults, age differences are minimal if older adults have sufficient practice. Santrock (2004) noted non-existent age differences in the area of divided attention when the tasks were simple, but if the tasks were more complex, older adults did not divide their attention as effectively as younger adults. Regarding sustained attention, which is often referred to as vigilance (Santrock, 2004), older adults performed as well as middle-aged and younger adults.

Memory changes also occur during aging, but according to Balota, Dolan, & Duchek (2000), not all aspects of memory decline. Specifically, Santrock (2004) noted that episodic and working memory decline, but not semantic memory, which is knowledge about the world and people's fields of expertise. According to Santrock, good health is associated with less memory decline, and education and socioeconomic status can affect performance on memory tasks.

Although cognitive functioning declines in old age, Santrock (2004) emphasized that the negative effects of memory loss can be mitigated if older adults read, do crossword puzzles, and attend lectures because it is disuse that may cause the atrophy of cognitive skills.

Dealing with Loss in Later Adulthood

It goes without saying that aging adults must adapt to and cope with increasing losses in multiple areas: loss of relationships as people close to them die or suffer from a debilitating illness, loss of abilities (physical, cognitive), and loss of income. According to Piper (1999), another significant loss is meaning: "The old look for their existential place." They ask, "How did my life matter? Was my time well spent? What did I mean to others?" (p. 15).

Newman and Newman (2006) proposed that there are three key processes that help older adults cope with increasing loss. First is selection, which helps individuals narrow goals and limit areas where energy is expended. Second is optimization, finding ways to maximize the achievement of remaining goals. Third is compensation, finding another way to achieve a means to an end when a loss occurs. Broderick and Blewitt (2006) noted that successful coping relates to how well older adults are able to maintain some degree of competence and connectedness to others.

Coming to terms with death is another task for the older adult. Newman and Newman (2006) emphasized that the issue of death becomes more of a reality during this stage of life, not only as it pertains to others, but to themselves as well. With regard to their own death, individuals who accept death as a natural part of the life cycle and appreciate the contributions they have made to society may develop a greater appreciation for life and be more optimistic and enthusiastic about their remaining years.

Developmental Interventions in Later Adulthood

An intervention that helps adults in the later stages of life deal with the concept of "reinventing" themselves is to have them make a list of "Twenty Things I Want To Do." Once the list is complete, ask the adult to rank order these and then code each with one or more of the following symbols: $ (requires money), P (involves physical stamina), M (involves mental challenge, stimulation), I (involves others), V (volunteer activity), S (spiritual), D (doable). This intervention should stimulate thinking and discussion about how the individual wishes to spend time as these later years evolve without as many family and work obligations. Goal setting can be included as a part of this intervention.

A second intervention involves dealing with the multiple losses that can occur during this developmental period. A simple but very cathartic strategy is to have the individual write a letter to the loss, which could be an activity, a person (parent, spouse, child, friend), an ability, a disease, a home or location, work or volunteer activities, or other losses. Encouraging the individual to continue to write these letters facilitates the expression of grief and helps the individual deal more effectively with the loss.

Given the fact that people are living longer than ever before, there is a pressing need for gerontological counseling. Multiple issues arise at this stage of development that differ considerably from those at earlier stages, and counselors need to be well versed in how best to address the needs of this population.

Summary

Knowledge of human development is essential for helping professionals in terms of assessment and intervention. Without this awareness, problems can easily be misdiagnosed, and interventions may be less effective because they are not geared to the appropriate developmental level. Looking through the "lens" of human development also clarifies what is "normal," which helps clients put their problems in perspective and know what to anticipate as they navigate their journey through life.

In working with developmental issues, it is crucial to remember how cultural and diversity factors affect the developmental process. For example, during adolescence, the "need to belong" is very important. Students from families with low socioeconomic status may not be as readily accepted because they cannot live up to the "standards" of the "in" group. This situation accounts, in part, for gang membership—it is a place to belong, even though it may be a negative association. Professional counselors working with clients across the lifespan must be cognizant about how low socioeconomic status, oppression, racism, and prejudice may limit opportunities and result in depression, anxiety, and suicide. It is important to deal with these issues within the context of culture, which means that professionals need to advocate for their clients and address the societal issues that perpetuate problems that occur across the lifespan.

Professional counselors must also remain sensitive to the fact that mastering developmental tasks is more complicated when certain factors come into play. Single mothers living in poverty have more challenges across developmental stages than affluent married women, and teenagers with disabilities may have more obstacles to confront as they deal with typical developmental issues than their nondisabled peers. During emerging adulthood, which is the time to clarify sexual orientation within the context of intimate relationships, gay and lesbian young adults are more likely to experience anxiety, fear, and uncertainty than their heterosexual peers, who do not have societal barriers and biases with which to contend. The developmental journey is significantly affected by these extraneous issues.

There are developmental tasks to master at each stage in the life cycle. Professional counselors can facilitate development in numerous ways, through individual and small group counseling, and classroom guidance, where lessons can facilitate children's and adolescents' understanding of social, emotional, cognitive, and physical development, and self-development. Readers are encouraged to read more in depth about each stage of development covered in this chapter, and to apply the information as they design interventions to facilitate clients' development through the lifespan.

Answer Key

Activity 10.10   Check marks should be placed by items 1, 2, 3, 4, 7.

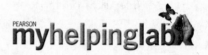

To help further your understanding of some of the topics in this chapter, go to MyHelpingLab at the Pearson.com website and view the following video clips:

- Obtaining an Alcohol/Drug History: *Addictions/Substance Abuse Counseling*, Module 2 (Couples Therapy, "Determining the Extent of Substance Abuse").
- Assessing Motivation for Change: *Addictions/Substance Abuse Counseling*, Module 1 (Integrating Therapy with Twelve-Step Programs, "Increasing Awareness of Obstacles" and "Addressing and Acknowledging Motivation").
- Harm Reduction: *Addictions/Substance Abuse Counseling*, Module 5 (Harm Reduction Therapy, "Assessing Negative Impact of Substance Abuse," "Finding Healthy Alternatives to Substance Use," and "Encouraging Clients to Adhere to Their Goals").
- Engage Support of Family and Significant Others: *Addictions/Substance Abuse Counseling*, Module 2 (Couples Therapy, "Encouraging Teamwork in Recovery Process" and "Challenging Couples to Change Environments").

Assessment, Case Conceptualization, Diagnosis, and Treatment Planning

GAIL MEARS

PREVIEW

This chapter reviews assessment, case conceptualization, diagnosis, and treatment planning in counseling. Assessment is the systematic gathering of information to address a client's presenting concerns effectively. A case conceptualization reflects how the professional counselor understands the nature of the presenting problems and includes a diagnostic formulation. Treatment plans outline counseling outcome expectations and interventions to meet these expectations.

Effective counseling requires many skills. The abilities to gather and interpret information, apply counseling and developmental theories, understand diagnostic frameworks, and engage in collaborative treatment planning are all important parts of the counseling process. This chapter reviews assessment, case conceptualization, diagnosis, and treatment planning.

Assessment is a broad term that includes many structured and unstructured processes for gathering information to understand the issues that bring people to counseling. **Case conceptualization** refers to how professional counselors understand the nature of clients' concerns, how and why the problems have developed, and the types of counseling interventions that might be helpful. **Diagnosis** is the identification of a problem that becomes the target of the counseling intervention. **Treatment planning** provides a road map for the counseling process. Treatment plans identify what the professional counselor and the client are aiming to work on together, and what strategies are to be used to achieve these goals. Each of these is discussed in detail in the following sections.

ASSESSMENT

Assessment is the process of gathering information in a systematic way to evaluate concerns or questions that a client brings to counseling. It is a broad umbrella term that includes intake interviews, tests and inventories, behavioral observations, and relevant information gathered from other sources (Barlow & Durand, 2003; Nystul, 2006). The types of information and gathering methods used depend on many factors, including answers to the following questions:

- What is the presenting question or concern?
- What types of information are commonly used in the field to evaluate this concern?
- Where is counseling taking place (e.g., school, clinic, hospital)?
- What does the client want out of counseling?
- Is the client an accurate reporter regarding the presenting concern? Ordinarily, this depends on the developmental level, motivation, and level of insight and judgment of the client.
- Who is asking for the assessment?
- Why is the question being asked at this time?
- What assessment skills and expertise does the professional counselor have?

The assessment process informs diagnostic formulation and counseling plans, and helps to identify resources that could help the client cope better with the presenting concern. Determining what information to gather is an important assessment skill. Use the cases found in Activity 11.1 to practice identifying important assessment information.

The terms "testing" and "assessment" are often used interchangeably; however, testing is only one type of assessment tool. According to Aiken (2003, p. 474) a **test** is "any device used to evaluate the behavior or performance of a person."

ACTIVITY 11.1

Consider the following cases. In small groups discuss the types of information you think would be useful to gather for each of these cases. Why do you think this information would be useful?

Case 1

Daniel, age 12 years, is brought to the local mental health center because of an escalation in conduct problems. Daniel is referred by the courts and is brought to the center by his mother. Daniel's father left the family and moved out of state 6 months ago. Daniel has had very limited phone contact with his father for the past few months. Recently, Daniel was brought to the police station after breaking several windows in an abandoned house. Daniel reports disinterest in counseling. His mother reports concern about Daniel's behavior and about his emotional state.

Case 2

Susan is a 35-year-old married woman who recently gave birth to her first child. She comes to the center at her husband's request because of feelings of sadness, intrusive thoughts about hurting her baby, irritability, fatigue, and emerging suicidal thoughts. She is fearful of letting the professional counselor know how she feels and is ashamed that she could feel this way about her child.

Case 3

Jason is a 19-year-old second-year college student. He is referred to the college counseling center because of his worry over not being able to decide on a major. He reports guilty feelings that he is wasting his parents' money and increased pressure to choose a major. Jason reports vague ideas about wanting to work in the recreational field, but does not have any clear ideas about what types of jobs there are in this field. He reports no idea about what courses and majors would be consistent with his interests.

Testing and the Counseling Profession

Testing has been an integral part of the counseling profession for a century, with roots in vocational guidance. The counseling field has a long history of using tests and inventories to assist with career planning. However, the field is also rooted in a philosophy of wellness and personal growth. This philosophy has resulted in ambivalence around the use of tests (Nugent & Jones, 2005). Despite concerns about testing, the use of tests by professional counselors has increased over the years. As Prediger (1994, p. 229) noted:

> All one has to do, however, is take a look at the full-page ads in ACA's *Guidepost* and the American Psychological Association's *Monitor,* or stroll past the testing company booths at this ACA National Convention to recognize that testing is bigger business than ever. Fifteen years ago, Tittle and Zytowski (1978) estimated that more than 3,500,000 interest inventories alone are administered each year. My own estimate is that, currently, nearly 10,000,000 clients each year complete "*tests*," "inventories," and other "assessments"—and that estimate does not include school achievement *tests* or college entrance exams.

The history of testing in the United Sates is a tarnished one. Intelligence testing served the political agenda of the eugenics movement in the early 1900s and supported racial and ethnic discrimination. Although these early intelligence tests clearly favored test takers who understood English, were educated, and were familiar with American culture, the results were used to support notions that high numbers of people from minority groups were intellectually inferior, were incapable of self-control, and were "contaminating" the gene pool. Psychologist Henry Goddard used the test results of immigrants at Ellis Island and the testing of school-aged children to support social agendas aimed at identifying and limiting procreation for people deemed to be intellectually inferior (Patrick, 1997).

World War I afforded an opportunity to promote the acceptance of psychology as a science through the use of mass intelligence testing. Robert Yerkes, Henry Goddard, and Lewis Terman, along with others, collaborated to develop the Army Alpha and Beta tests. These were used to determine what types of military functions recruits were intellectually suited for. Despite a clear bias in these tests toward educated and acculturated citizens, not to mention the highly pressured and nonstandardized administration conditions, the results from these mass testing administrations were used to support the belief in racial and ethnic intellectual inferiority (Gould, 1981). In 1925, Hirsch used intelligence testing to correlate intelligence with blood type (meaning ethnic origin) and again supported the prevailing notions of the intellectual inferiority of minority groups (Gregory & Lee, 1986).

The preceding historical discussion highlights counselors' need to be sensitive to the appropriate use of tests and vigilant about discriminatory practices in testing. Professional counselors need to be attentive to cultural biases in tests and use only tests with norms developed on a sample that is representative of the test taker. Professional counselors should also be sensitive to an overinterpretation of test results, understanding that a test provides a limited sample of behavior. Additionally, counselors need to ensure that test results are not used to disadvantage the test taker unfairly.

The use of some tests is regulated by test makers and the purchase of these regulated tests requires advanced levels of education and training. Tests are often categorized by publishers as level A, B, or C. Generally, level A tests are those that require no special training to purchase and administer; level B tests require a master's degree, relevant testing course work, and supervision in the use of the test; level C tests require a doctorate or a license with a scope of practice to interpret these tests and training and supervision in the use of the instrument (Erford, 2006). State licensing boards regulate what types of assessments are within a licensed professional counselor's scope of practice, and ethical standards help counselors determine if they have the requisite education, training, and supervision to administer a given test. Professional counselors should use tests only in counseling practice contexts in which they have specialized training; and for which they understand the testing theory, the concepts of test construction, and statistics; they must select tests that they are trained to administer and interpret, and they must understand the cultural, legal, and ethical issues relevant to testing (American Counseling Association, 2005a).

Despite an earlier history of collaboration between the American Psychological Association, the American Educational Research Association, the National Council on Measurement in Education, the American Speech and Language Hearing Association, and the American Counseling Association, psychologists in some states have tried to limit the use of some standardized tests by counselors. The Fair Access Coalition on Testing was formed to advocate for the testing rights of qualified individuals, including counselors (Clawson, 1997). Activity 11.2 encourages a review of websites to help you to better understand the history, standards, and advocacy efforts related to testing and assessment.

ACTIVITY 11.2

Go to the website for the **Association for Assessment in Counseling and Education** (AACE; a division of the American Counseling Association) at www.theaaceonline.com and review the history and the mission statement of the AACE association. Also, review the testing standards and multicultural assessment competencies posted on this website and the test reviews and other posted information.

Next, go the website for the **Fair Access Coalition on Testing** (FACT) at www.fairaccess.org/ and review the FACT document, *Model Testing Practices,* and other information on the website.

Why Should Professional Counselors Know About Testing?

Most professional counselors have some involvement with tests during their careers. Professional school counselors are often in charge of achievement testing, and in many schools, they are considered the experts in testing. They are called upon to explain test results to parents and use testing evaluations to develop school-based intervention plans. Likewise, mental health and rehabilitation counselors administer tests or interpret testing results to help with diagnosis and treatment planning. Career counselors frequently rely on interest inventories to help guide the career exploration process. The *Strong Interest Inventory* is one of the tests most frequently used by professional counselors. Loesch and Foster's (2005) review of the literature includes the following uses of tests by professional counselors: (1) preliminary problem exploration and diagnosis, (2) selection and screening, (3) placement and planning, (4) facilitation of self-understanding, and (5) licensure or certification.

The Council for Accreditation of Counseling and Related Educational Programs (CACREP) in its 2008 assessment standards requires that CACREP accredited programs provide students with instruction regarding the testing and the relevant statistical concepts; the strategies for the selecting, administering, and interpreting tests; the diversity considerations in testing; and the legal and ethical issues. The following discussion examines the different types of tests and the important concepts associated with testing. First complete Activity 11.3 to demonstrate your understanding of what professional counselors need to know about testing.

ACTIVITY 11.3

Create a two- to three-page letter to a friend that explains (a) why professional counselors need to know about testing, (b) why they should be concerned about practice rights, and (c) what a professional counselor needs to know to become a competent evaluator. Break into small groups and share your letters.

Categories of Tests

Tests are often categorized as standardized or nonstandardized depending on the latitude given to examiners to vary the procedures of administration and scoring. Tests are also categorized as norm-referenced or criterion-referenced depending upon whether the examiner wants to compare a client's results with the results of individuals with similar characteristics, or with some authoritative standard.

STANDARDIZED TESTS **Standardized tests** have defined protocols for administration and scoring. This means that the test is administered in the same way, under similar conditions, whenever it is administered. The methods used for scoring the test are predetermined and are followed consistently. Scores from a standardized test are interpreted in relationship to a norm group (i.e., a group of people who are similar to the test takers in such dimensions as age, gender, and grade) or are measured against some performance criteria. Norms and criteria used for scoring standardized tests are developed through extensive test administrations and statistical analyses. The *Scholastic Assessment Test* (SAT-I) and the *Wechsler Adult Intelligence Scale-III* (WAIS-III) (Wechsler, 1997) are examples of standardized tests.

NONSTANDARDIZED TESTS **Nonstandardized tests** do not have defined administration protocols and have not been extensively studied to create norms or criterion-related scoring protocols. If your instructor gives you a test on the material in this chapter, you may be taking a nonstandardized test.

NORM-REFERENCED TESTS When scores on a test are compared with the scores of a group of people with similar characteristics to the examinee who took the same test, the test is considered a **norm-referenced test**. The *Graduate Record Examination* (GRE) is an example of a norm-referenced, standardized test. The test is administered in the same way whenever it is offered, and an individual's raw scores are compared with the scores of a norm group. This comparison yields a derived score (standardized score or percentile rank) that places individual scores in relationship to the test norms.

CRITERION-REFERENCED TESTS When you take a test and the score is based on performance criteria, you are taking a **criterion-referenced test**. If you are given a test while taking this class, it is likely that the instructor will be looking for some indication that you have mastered the material in this chapter. Your score will likely reflect the number of items answered correctly, and some criterion, such as a grade or percentage score, will be agreed upon. You will be taking a nonstandardized, criterion-related test.

Types of Tests

Tests are frequently categorized as cognitive or affective tests, depending upon whether they measure the thinking and reasoning skills or the personality, interests, and behavioral symptoms.

COGNITIVE TESTS Ordinarily, cognitive tests include intelligence tests, other aptitude tests, and achievement tests.

Intelligence Tests **Intelligence tests** are designed as broad measures of cognitive ability. The *Wechsler Intelligence Scale for Children, -Fourth Edition* (WISC-IV) (Wechsler, 2001) and the *Wechsler Adult Intelligence Scale, -Third Edition* (WAIS-III) (Wechsler, 1997) are the most common tests used to evaluate intellectual functioning in educational and clinical settings (Esters & Ittenbach, 1999). Although there is ongoing controversy regarding the validity of the constructs that underlie intelligence tests (e.g., is general intelligence a useful concept?), it is essential that professional school counselors be familiar with these tests. Use of individual intelligence tests sometimes requires training beyond a master's program, but professional counselors are often called upon to consider the implications of these test results in educational and clinical planning. Group intelligence tests are frequently administered by professional counselors. Examples of group intelligence tests include the *Otis-Lennon School Ability Test* (OLSAT) and the *Cognitive Abilities Test* (CogAT). These tests are correlated to academic achievement and are often used to make educational planning or screening decisions.

Aptitude Tests Intelligence tests are considered to be one type of aptitude test. However, **aptitude tests** also measure a broad range of more specific cognitive abilities or the ability to master particular skill sets. The *O*Net Ability Profiler* (O*Net) developed and used by the U.S. Department of Labor is an example of a multiscale aptitude test and measures verbal abilities, arithmetic reasoning, computation, spatial ability, form perception, clerical perception, motor coordination, finger dexterity, and manual dexterity. Aptitude tests are often used to help students understand personal strengths and challenges, and by employers to help in the hiring process (Aiken, 2003).

Achievement Tests **Achievement tests** are typically used in educational settings and are designed to measure student learning. Examples of achievement tests used by elementary and secondary schools include the *Iowa Tests of Basic Skills,* Form A (ITBS), the *Terra Nova-II,* and the *Stanford Achievement Test, Tenth Edition* (Stanford 10). Professional school counselors are often in charge of or involved in a school's group achievement testing program. Individual achievement tests that measure specific areas of achievement (e.g., reading or math) are used diagnostically by learning disability specialists and school psychologists. Individual diagnostic tests of achievement (e.g., *Woodcock-Johnson Tests of Achievement, Third Edition* [WJ-III] [Woodcock, Mather, & McGrew, 2001], *Wechsler Individual Achievement Test, Second Edition* [WIAT-II] [Wechsler, 2001]) in specific domains are compared against broader measures of intelligence to determine the presence of a learning disability. The diagnosis of a learning disability requires that there be a discrepancy between the measures of general intelligence and achievement in specific areas.

AFFECTIVE TESTS Affective tests include personality inventories, interest inventories, and symptom checklists used for the screening and diagnosis of clinical issues.

Personality Tests and Inventories **Personality tests** and **personality inventories** are designed to measure personality traits, temperament, and levels of pathology. These tests are categorized as objective or projective. **Objective personality tests** are paper and pencil tests that require examinees to answer questions in specific ways (e.g., multiple choice) and can be easily scored. The *Minnesota Multiphasic Personality Inventory-II* (MMPI-2), the *Millon Clinical Multiaxial Inventory-III* (MCMI-III), and the *Myers Briggs Type Indicator* (MBTI) are examples of objective personality tests.

Projective personality tests provide examinees with ambiguous tasks, and examinees' answers can be quite varied. An example of this type of test is the *Rorschach Inkblot Test* (Exner, 1993). Examinees are presented with cards that contain symmetrical inkblots and asked to tell the examiner what they see in the inkblot. Another example of a projective test is the *Thematic Apperception Test* (Rotter, 1946). Examinees are shown pictures and instructed to tell a story about the picture. These tests originated from psychoanalytic ideas and assume that examinees project their psychic conflicts into their answers. The use of these projective tests often involves specialized training.

Interest Inventories **Interest inventories** are an essential tool for career counseling. They are used to help individuals identify their areas of interest and to aid in the process of matching individual preferences to recreational and work contexts. Commonly used interest inventories include the *Strong Interest Inventory* (SII) and Holland's *Self-Directed Search* (SDS) (Aiken, 2003; Watkins, Campbell & McGregor, 1989).

Symptom Checklists **Symptom checklists** measure the presence and intensity of symptoms associated with various problems or disorders. While a diagnosis should not be made solely on endorsed items in a symptom checklist, they are valuable assessment tools. They are also used to monitor the effect of treatment on symptom reduction. Common symptom checklists used in mental health settings to aid in diagnosis and treatment planning include the *Beck Depression Inventory, Second Edition* (BDI-II) (Beck, Steer, & Brown, 1996), *Symptom Checklist-90-Revised* (SCL-90-R) (Derogatis, 1990), *The Child Behavior Checklist* (Achenbach & Rescorla, 2001), and the *Connor's Rating Scales-Revised* (Connors, 1997).

Qualities to Consider When Evaluating Tests

Several qualities help professional counselors decide if a test is a useful tool to administer and how much consideration to give to a test score. Olin and Keatinge (1998, p. 24) cite the following factors as important for test selection: "Is the test accessible? Is the test psychometrically acceptable? Is the test clinically useful? Is the test appropriate for client use?" Another important factor in test selection is whether or not the professional counselor is adequately trained in the administration and interpretation of the test.

If a professional counselor wants to know how depressed a client is, and gives the client the *Beck Depression Inventory-II*, it would be important for the professional counselor to know the reliability and validity of scores derived by this inventory. **Validity** refers to how well a test measures what it is intended to measure, and **reliability** refers to the consistency of scores the test provides.

TYPES OF VALIDITY   In the classic test theory, score validity is frequently described as three types: content validity, criterion-related validity, and construct validity.

Content Validity   **Content validity** refers to how well test questions represent the domain being tested (Aiken, 2003; Olin & Keatinge, 1998). Have you ever taken a test during one of your courses and been surprised that the test focused on only part of the material you were asked to study (perhaps the material you studied less!) and did not represent all of the material you were asked to study? This test probably had low content validity. Suppose you wanted to determine if someone was depressed. As part of your assessment, you administer a depression inventory that asks only about sleep, energy, and appetite. How helpful would this inventory be in evaluating depression? Such an inventory would lack content validity because it did not sample the full range of symptoms associated with depression. Poor sleep, lack of appetite, and fatigue are symptoms associated with depression, but other important symptoms, such as sad mood, hopelessness, and helplessness, have been overlooked. Content validity is frequently determined by experts in the content areas covered by the test. In other words, would these experts agree that the subject matter was sampled in a representative way?

Criterion-related Validity   **Criterion-related validity** refers to the correlation between a test or inventory and another measure (the criterion) that is closely associated with what the test is intended to measure. An intelligence test with an acceptable level of criterion-related validity would be associated with academic achievement, and a test of mechanical aptitude that has an acceptable level of criterion-related validity would be associated with mechanical skill. There are two types of criterion-related validity—concurrent validity and predictive validity. Criterion-related validity is **concurrent** when both measures (i.e., the test and the criterion) exist at the same point in time. It is **predictive** when the closely associated measure (i.e., the criterion) will be available in the future (Aiken, 2003). Do people who are skilled in auto mechanics score well in the mechanical aptitude test (concurrent validity)? What is the correlation between GRE scores taken before beginning graduate school and success later in graduate school (predictive validity)?

Construct Validity   **Construct validity** refers to how effectively a test measures the construct (e.g., intelligence, depression, anxiety) it is intended to measure. Construct validity is determined by multiple methods, including expert judgment, correlation with other measures of this construct, and the internal consistency of the test items (Aiken, 2003). **Convergent validity** refers to the correlation between a test and other measures of a similar construct. **Divergent validity** is the lack of significant correlation between test scores and measures of constructs that are unrelated to the test construct. A test of spatial ability should have a positive correlation with other measures of spatial relations (convergent validity). The same scores should not be related, however, to measures of verbal reasoning (divergent validity). It is important in test construction to evaluate whether there is a relationship between measures of similar constructs. However, for the relationship between similar constructs to be meaningful, there needs to be an absence of correlation between the test and measures of unrelated concepts.

RELIABILITY Reliability refers to the consistency of testing scores. A test cannot be valid unless it is reliable; however, a test could be reliable and not be valid. The purpose of reliability measures is to determine the degree to which a test is free from errors that would cause test scores to vary for random reasons (Aiken, 2003). There are multiple forms of reliability that address the consistency of scores. Reliability can be the correlation between test scores when the test is administered at different times (test-retest reliability), the correlation between scores on two similar versions of a test (alternate forms reliability), and the correlation between items within the test itself (split-half reliability or internal consistency). Table 11.1 provides a brief summary of these various methods for determining score reliability. Finally, Activity 11.4 asks you to apply your understanding of the important concepts in testing by reviewing a test manual of your choice.

TABLE 11.1 Various Types of Reliability

Test-retest (temporal stability)	Correlation between scores on two administrations of the same test within a given time. This reliability measure would be inappropriate when there is a prediction that scores will change over time.
Parallel forms (alternate forms, equivalent forms)	Alternate forms of a test are administered and the scores are correlated with each other.
Split-half reliability	A test is divided into two halves in such a way that there is an assumption that each half is similar. The internal consistency of the test is determined by the correlation between the two sets of scores.
Internal consistency (KR-20, coefficient alpha)	Computer software uses formulas to compute average correlations among items on a scale from a single administration of a test.

ACTIVITY 11.4

In consultation with your course instructor, consider your area of specialization in your test selection, and choose a test that a professional counselor is likely to use. Review the test and the test manual, and answer the following questions.
1. Who is qualified to give this test?
2. What types of clients could be administered this test?
3. Does the test manual detail validity and reliability information? What types of validity and reliability were measured?
4. Under what circumstances would you use this test?

Cultural Fairness

Professional counselors need to consider whether a test is a fair measure to use with a client. Were test norms developed using participants that were representative of the client to be tested? Might language or other barriers affect performance? It is essential for professional counselors to remember that a test may accurately predict differences between majority and minority groups, but that these differences may be a result of environmental disadvantage and not innate qualities. This is an especially important consideration for test interpretation and intervention planning (Skiba, Knesting, & Bush, 2002).

Using Computers in Testing

The use of computers greatly expands professional counselors' testing resources, and computers may provide significant testing benefits. Professional counselors have instant access to testing materials, clients have easy access to test information including test orientation materials and immediate feedback on test results, and tests can be adapted during administration to match the test takers' abilities or knowledge set (Sampson, 2000). Test selection, orientation, administration, and interpretation have the potential to be significantly enhanced by Internet access. Additionally, the Internet provides access to test supervision and consultation that may not be locally available to counselors (Sampson, 2000). However, the use of computers as an assessment vehicle raises interesting legal, ethical, and application considerations. Professional counselors engaged in this practice need to be grounded in necessary technology competencies.

> Although these advancements may improve assessment effectiveness, various unintended negative consequences may occur, such as reduced confidentiality, increased availability of assessments with questionable validity, inadequate or incompetent counselor interventions, and reduced privacy necessary for test administration (Sampson, 2000, p. 78).

Ethical Considerations

The *American Counseling Association Code of Ethics* (2005) is based on the underlying principles of autonomy, beneficence, nonmalifice, justice, and fidelity (Welfel & Patterson, 2005). When selecting, using, and interpreting tests, it is important to consider the following questions: What does the client want (autonomy)? How will a test or test battery be helpful to a client (beneficence)? How could the testing process be harmful to the client (nonmalificence)? Is the test a fair measurement tool for the client (justice)? Are you working in the client's best interest when you use tests in counseling (fidelity)? Goldman (1992) made the case that most professional counselors are not adequately trained to use many standardized intelligence and aptitude tests. He strongly advocated that professional counselors not use testing procedures for which they are not adequately prepared, and instead urged them to consider assessment procedures for which they do have sufficient education and training.

Testing Resources

The *Sixteenth Mental Measurement Yearbook* (Spies & Plake, 2005) and *Tests in Print VII* (Murphy, Spies, & Plake, 2006) are the primary sources of test information (see the website for the Buros Institute in the list for more information on these volumes). Additionally, the

Internet, publication manuals, assessment texts, and information from experts in the testing field are important sources of information (Neukrug, 2007). The following websites are useful resources for professional counselors involved in testing:

- American Counseling Association: *www.counseling.org*
- Association for Assessment in Counseling and Education: *www.theAACEonline.com*
- Fair Access Coalition to Testing: *www.fairaccess.org*
- Buros Institute of Mental Measurements: *www.unl.edu/buros*
- American Educational Research Association: *www.aera.net*
- ERIC Clearinghouse on Assessment and Evaluation: *www.ericae.net*

Intake Interviews

While testing is one form of assessment, the counseling interview is a hallmark of the counseling process. The formality and the content of the intake interview are determined by the context in which the interview occurs. Professional school counselors do not typically do formal intake interviews, and they are typically not developing diagnostic formulations. However, they do use counseling interviews to gather information about student's problems and concerns, and use this information to develop appropriate counseling plans. Mental health counselors often conduct formal intake interviews, write and develop diagnostic formulations based on their clinical assessments, and develop intervention plans that direct treatment. The **intake interview** has three prime objectives:

1. Identifying, evaluating, and exploring the client's chief complaint and the associated counseling goals
2. Obtaining a sense of the client's interpersonal style, interpersonal skills, and personal history
3. Evaluating the client's current life situation and functioning (Sommers-Flannagan & Sommers-Flannagan, 2003, p. 169)

The intake interview, in conjunction with any other types of gathered information, leads to a diagnosis. Erford's (2006) Appendix A included a comprehensive intake assessment for clinical use. In clinical mental health settings, the following types of information are typically gathered during the intake interview:

- Identifying information, such as name, date of birth, relationship status, and ethnicity
- Presenting problem (why is the person seeking counseling) and what symptoms are occurring
- Current functioning, including living arrangements; family, social, academic, vocational, and military status; recreational interests; spiritual practices; and resources
- Past history, including physical/medical, family, social, academic, vocational, legal, substance use, and psychiatric history
- Mental status
- Assessment of suicide and exploration of intent to harm others
- Strengths and resources
- Roadblocks to counseling
- Client's goals for coming to counseling

What Is a Mental Status Examination?

A **mental status examination** "involves the systematic observation of somebody's behavior" (Barlow & Durand, 2003, p. 71). It is a general assessment of primary mental systems, serving in a similar capacity to how a physician's general medical examination covers the major body physical systems. Erford's (2006) Appendix D provided a semistructured mental status exam for clinical use. A mental status exam includes a consideration of the following categories:

- *Appearance and Behavior.* What does the professional counselor observe regarding the client's dress, posture, motor activity, and behavior toward the counselor during the meeting?
- *Speech Patterns.* Is it easy to follow the meaning of the client's sentences? Is speech particularly rapid or slow?
- *Thought Process.* What is the content of the client's thoughts (e.g., obsessions)? Does the client's thinking seem disorganized (as represented by speech that is tangential, hard to follow, or lacks meaning)? Does the client report psychotic symptoms, such as delusions or hallucinations?
- *Mood and Affect.* How does the client report his or her emotional state? What are the counselor's observations of the client's emotional state. A client may report that he or she has felt sad for some time (mood), and the counselor might notice tears and hunched body posture during the interview (affect). In this case, the client's affect would be appropriate to mood.
- *Intellectual Functioning.* What is the professional counselor's estimate of the client's intellectual functioning? This is based on the counselor's observation of the client's level of comprehension and complexity of thinking and speech.
- *Sensorium.* Is the client oriented to his or her surroundings? Is the client aware of where he or she is, what day it is, who he or she is, and who the counselor is?
- *Judgment.* Does the client seem to make decisions that apparently are helpful rather than harmful to himself or herself?
- *Insight.* Does the client have an understanding of his or her problems and the ways in which these problems interfere with his or her life?
- *Reliability.* Is the client a credible reporter?

What Are the Elements of a Suicide Assessment and an Exploration of Intent to Harm Others?

A **suicide assessment** helps to determine if a person is a danger to self or others and includes questions regarding the presence of suicidal or homicidal ideas, plans connected with these ideas, history of suicidal or violent behavior, and history of such behaviors in one's family and social network. Other areas to evaluate when assessing suicidality include the presence of a mood disorder, history of childhood abuse, difficult life events, level of hopelessness, the presence of physical illness, problems with sleeping and eating, agitation, loss, substance use, and the level of available social support (Barlow & Durand, 2003; Sommers-Flanagan & Sommers-Flanagan, 2005).

Intake interviewing is a difficult counseling skill. Counselors need to balance gathering information and developing a supportive relationship. In some clinical settings, the intake interview is a separate process from the counseling itself and is sometimes done by some-one other than the counselor to whom the client will be assigned. However, even in these instances, helping people feel comfortable and listened to is vital. Learning how to do effective intake interviews takes practice. Activity 11.5 gives you and your classmates a chance to practice conducting intake interviews.

ACTIVITY 11.5

Break into groups of three. Rotate roles between professional counselor, client, and observer. Each person will choose one of the following scenarios and develop a character based on this role (feel free to create an alternative role if you prefer).

- A 40-year-old married woman comes to counseling because she found out that her husband had an affair. Although the affair is over, and the couple continues to live together, she continues to feel sad and angry. She has difficulty sleeping and eating, and does not like to go out of the house.
- A 35-year-old man recently was laid off from the brokerage firm he has worked in for the past 8 years. As a result of injuries sustained in a car accident 15 years ago, he has difficulty walking, and relies on a cane to get around. He reports feeling demoralized by the loss of his job. He also finds himself thinking a lot about the accident, and about the activities he can no longer participate in.
- A 17-year-old high school student was recently arrested for shoplifting. The hearing is pending, and the student is very worried about what the consequences will be. This student does not have a history of legal involvement and is beginning the process of applying to colleges.

Practice conducting an intake interview (40 minutes per interview). Use the intake format provided in the previous section to guide your questions. Each person takes a turn being the professional counselor, the client, and the observer. Discuss what this experience was like. Give each other feedback on your interviewing techniques. Were you able to gather information while also developing rapport and demonstrating listening skills? If you struggled with this exercise, remember that you will have a lot of instruction and practice in interviewing throughout your program.

Behavioral Observation

Behavior observations can provide important information not readily available through interviewing or testing. **Behavioral observations** are done in a natural setting in which the client is experiencing the difficulties that precipitated counseling. The purpose of the behavioral observation is to note the frequency of behaviors that are the focus of concern, to notice what precedes these behaviors, and to identify what consequences follow these behaviors (Barlow & Durand, 2003). A professional school counselor might be asked to observe a student with disruptive behavior in the student's classroom. The counselor would want to have a clear understanding of what behaviors are of concern (target behaviors). The counselor would then observe what behaviors of the child, the teacher, and other classmates directly preceded the target behaviors (i.e., antecedent behaviors), and how the student, teacher, and classmates responded to the target behaviors (i.e., consequences).

This type of observation helps the counselor identify the chain of events that leads to the target behaviors, and to understand how these behaviors might be reinforced in the classroom. When the chain of events is understood, the counselor can consult with the teacher and the student to interrupt the chain of events that leads to unwanted behaviors and eliminate reinforcement for these behaviors.

Environmental Assessment

An **environmental assessment** involves a holistic evaluation of the client within his or her environment. "Environmental assessment contributes to the understanding of the dynamics of behavior and is used to determine the impact of environment on the development of the individual, the family, and other groups" (Drummond & Jones, 2006, p. 301). Physical space, organization and supervision of space, materials, peer environment, organization and scheduling, safety, and responsiveness are important environmental factors to consider. Personality; learning, parenting, and teaching styles; school, work, and home environments; and group relationship characteristics are the prospective dimensions of an environmental assessment. The procedures used for these assessments include observation, diagrams, checklists, and rating scales. Environmental dimensions chosen for evaluation and how these dimensions are evaluated depend on the referral or presenting concern. Now apply your understanding of concepts in assessment to the cases presented in Activity 11.6.

ACTIVITY 11.6

Assessment is an important counseling task. The professional counselor, in a planful way, collects and reviews information to address the concerns of the client, while developing a supportive relationship. The types of information the counselor requests depend on the client, the presenting concern, the context in which counseling occurs, and the skills of the counselor. Consider the following case, and list the methods of assessment you would recommend and why. What skills would the professional counselor need to use the identified assessment tools effectively and ethically?

Eric is a 10-year-old boy who is brought to your center by his maternal grandmother. She is currently Eric's legal guardian and is concerned about his recent irritability and increased difficulties in school. Eric came to live with his grandmother last year after his parents divorced, and his father moved out of state. Eric's mother felt unable to care for Eric and asked the grandmother to take over his care. Eric has a younger sister who remains in his mother's care. Eric has always had difficulty in school. He is very active, not particularly interested in classroom work, and often gets into trouble for being inattentive or disrupting the class. He loves skateboarding and is quite good at it. He also makes friends easily, and despite his often impulsive behavior, he is well liked by the other children. More recently, though, he has gotten into several fights, an unusual behavior for Eric, and he is not interested in skateboarding.

CASE CONCEPTUALIZATION

Case conceptualization refers to the way that professional counselors make meaning out of the information they have gathered. The case conceptualization integrates the information gathered during the assessment with counseling and developmental theory, as well as diversity and social justice issues, and leads to a diagnosis and effective treatment planning.

> A case conceptualization is a method and process of summarizing seemingly diverse case information into a brief, coherent statement or "map" that elucidates the client's basic pattern of behavior. The purpose of a well-articulated case conceptualization is to better understand and more effectively treat a client or client-system, that is, a couple or family. In short, a case conceptualization is a clinician's "theory" of a particular case. (Sperry, 2005, p. 190)

Formulating a case conceptualization involves identifying patterns and themes associated with the information gathered during the assessment phases. This might involve patterns in family and social relationships; reaction or adaptation to stress, loss and trauma; impulse control, developmental concerns; clusters of symptoms such as those associated with depression or anxiety; strengths; and resources (Seligman, 2004). Professional counselors should consider information about clients' internal distress (e.g., feelings, thoughts), behavior (i.e., what is the client actually doing), and culture (e.g., what is considered normal or acceptable in the client's family and social network). Biological and developmental issues also need to be considered.

Application of theory is an important aspect of case conceptualization (Murdock, 1991). Counseling theories typically provide a view of human nature: Are people basically good and capable of growth? Are people a product of their environment? Are people basically controlled by biology? Theories also provide views of what promotes emotional well-being, distress, and change, and techniques consistent with the theories. Developmental theories discuss the process of growth and development over the lifespan. They identify stages of development and the developmental issues inherent in each stage, and identify variables that support or challenge development.

Multicultural considerations and attention to social justice are vital to case conceptualization. Professional counselors need to consider how issues such as race, ethnicity, religious beliefs, socioeconomic status, family structure, trauma, and sexual and gender orientation affect a client's presenting concerns and what impact these variables have on the acceptability of, and the access to, counseling.

The themes and patterns identified during the assessment phase are foundational to making a diagnostic formulation. Diagnosis in a broad sense refers to a framework used to identify problems or the focus of intervention. Mental health settings typically use the *Diagnostic and Statistical Manual of Mental Disorders, Fourth Edition-Text Revision* (DSM-IV-TR) (American Psychiatric Association, 2001).

Another aspect of case conceptualization involves the assessment of a client's motivation for counseling. A client may be motivated to come to counseling, yet not ready or interested in making the changes that would likely lead to an improved sense of well-being. Prochaska, DiClemente, and Norcross (1992) reviewed a model of readiness for change that is extremely helpful when trying to develop a case conceptualization and ultimately a treatment plan. According to their model, there are five stages of readiness for change: (1) precontemplation, (2) contemplation, (3) preparation, (4) action, and (5) maintenance.

Sometimes clients come to counseling because other people say they need to make a change, but they are not interested in change or are not ready to do so. This is the **precontemplation stage**. Clients who are thinking about the benefits of change but not ready to make any commitment to change are in the **contemplation stage**. Clients who have made a commitment to change in the very near future and have begun making minor behavioral changes are in the **preparation stage**. Clients who are in the process of practicing the desired changes are in the **action stage**. When change has been initiated, clients need to consider the best ways to ensure that the habits of change continue and to develop strategies to deal effectively with relapses. This is the **maintenance stage**. Professional counselors need to evaluate a client's readiness for change and integrate this information into their case conceptualizations and treatment plans. Successful counseling meets people where they are.

A case conceptualization integrates information into meaningful themes and helps counselors decide on appropriate counseling interventions. Activity 11.7 provides practice in applying concepts in case conceptualization.

ACTIVITY 11.7

Consider the following case and answer the questions that follow the case narrative.

Linda is a first-year college student. She has always been a good student and describes herself as "always trying to do the right thing." She comes from a family reported to be quite conservative in their views. She reports that she and her parents are close, but that when Linda does something that they disapprove of, the consequences are harsh and have ranged from being spanked as a child, to long periods of grounding in adolescence. Linda finds herself attracted to another young woman on campus. She is terrified that she may be a lesbian, and that, if this is true, she will disgrace her family. Linda comes to the counseling center reporting disrupted sleep, constant worry about her sexual orientation, and excessive exercising to distract her attention from her concerns. She reports that she has been crying daily for the past month, is tired most of the time, and has experienced some suicidal thoughts. Linda reports that it is helpful to know that she can come and talk to her professional counselor about anything and not be judged. She is not interested in talking with her parents at this point regarding her current romantic interest or about her distress over past times when she felt judged by them.

A. A case conceptualization should integrate the information that is gathered into categories.
- What do you know about Linda's relationship to her family?
- What do you know about her academic achievement?
- What do you know about her symptoms?
- What do you know about her social relationships?

B. From the above categories of information, the professional counselor can look at patterns and themes.
- Do you see any patterns or themes emerging from the information?
- How does approval of Linda's family (as perceived by Linda) influence her thoughts, feelings, and behavior?
- What are some developmental issues you would expect given her age and life stage?

C. Counseling theories address human nature, what causes emotional distress and well-being, and what promotes change. Bridging theory and case

conceptualization requires professional counselors to apply these theoretical dimensions to the case at hand.
- Consider Linda's case from a client-centered perspective and apply this model's ideas of human nature (self-actualizing), emotional distress and well-being (congruence of self and ideal self, conditions or worth), and what promotes change (unconditional positive regard, genuineness, and empathy) to Linda's case.
- Apply a cognitive or behavioral model of your choice to Linda's case.
- Apply other counseling theories or models of your choice.

D. A diagnosis reflects how the client is functioning at this point in time and what types of distress a client is experiencing.
- In Linda's case, what words would you attach to the symptoms she reports, and how are these symptoms affecting her ability to perform her expected tasks?

E. It is important to consider issues of diversity and social justice.
- What issues need to be considered in this case?

F. Evaluating motivation is an important step.
- Is Linda motivated to engage in counseling?
- What do you think that Linda would like to get out of counseling?
- What is Linda motivated to do at this time?
- What types of strategies would help her attain her goals?
- What model or models of counseling are most consistent with these strategies?

A case conceptualization is your best interpretation based on the information you have. Professional counselors need to be prepared to adjust their case conceptualizations when new information demands a change in perspective.

DIAGNOSIS

Diagnosis is the identification of a disease, disorder, or syndrome based on some form of systematic assessment. Many systems can be used to identify disorders or syndromes. Two common diagnostic systems that professional counselors encounter are the DSM-IV-TR (American Psychiatric Association, 2001) and the *International Classification of Diseases, Ninth Revision, with Clinical Modification* (ICD-9 CM) (NCHS, 2008), currently used in the United States, and the *International Statistical Classification of Diseases, Tenth Edition* (ICD-10) (NCHS, 2008), used internationally.

The DSM-IV-TR is typically used in mental health clinical work and is the manual most professional counselors encounter. The ICD-9 CM and ICD-10 are used in medical settings. The DSM includes a conversion chart so that psychiatric diagnoses can be easily converted to ICD codes. States regulate who can make a clinical diagnosis. Licensed professional counselors are allowed to provide diagnostic assessments in most states. Whether licensed or not, it is necessary for professional counselors to be familiar with DSM diagnostic codes and to consider the implications of a client's diagnosis during the counseling process. Accurate diagnosis is important to treatment planning. The cases presented in Activity 11.8 help you explore the importance of diagnosis to counseling.

ACTIVITY 11.8

In small groups, discuss why considering a diagnosis might be important in the following cases.

Case 1

You are a professional counselor assigned to work with a fourth-grade boy. He has great difficulty completing his work and is falling behind academically. He is unable to complete his written work perfectly and ends up tearing up all of his attempts. He has become more irritable in the past few months and cries easily.

Case 2

You are a career counselor working with a second-year female college student. She was recently hospitalized for an episode during which she did not sleep for many days, had sex with men indiscriminately without using any form of protection, and got in a serious car accident attributed to her reckless driving. She reports that she has a history of severe depression, but that this is the first time she has experienced this type of mania.

The counseling profession has been ambivalent about the use of diagnosis. The humanistic roots of counseling, with its emphasis on development and growth, can seem inconsistent with the use of diagnostic labels (Waldo & Dale, 1993). However, with the advent of licensure for mental health counselors and the workplace requirement for developing DSM diagnostic formulations, diagnosis is now accepted as an important knowledge base for counselors. CACREP (Council for Accreditation of Counseling and Related Educational Programs, 2008, Section 7.h) includes the requirement for all professional counselors to have "an understanding of general principles and methods of case conceptualization, assessment, and/or diagnoses of mental and emotional status."

Professional counselors need to be diligent regarding the use of diagnosis. It is an ethical requirement that counselors providing diagnostic formulations be adequately trained in the use of DSM-IV-TR and that they are accurate in their diagnostic formulations (American Counseling Association, 2005). Professional counselors also need to be sensitive to multicultural and social justice issues, ensuring that the process of diagnosing does not label issues of difference and the normal reactions to social oppression as pathology. The concept of normality is a cultural construction, and what is considered pathological in one culture may be seen as normal in another. In 1851, a southern physician, Dr. Samuel Cartwright, tried to promote a new disease, drapetomania, characterized by a slave's desire to run away (Bynum, 2000). Until 1973, homosexuality was a diagnosable DSM mental illness (Rubinstein, 1995). Counselors often have mixed reactions to the use of diagnosis. Activity 11.9 helps you examine how you and your classmates feel about the use of DSM-IV-TR diagnosis.

ACTIVITY 11.9

In small groups, discuss how you feel about diagnosis as a function of counseling. Consider the potential benefits and disadvantages of diagnosis.

Most cultures have created some classification system to diagnose behaviors that are seen as abnormal. Explanations of abnormal behavior have ranged from possession by demons to the current interest in biochemical explanations. DSM-IV-TR uses a descriptive model, meaning that there is an effort to be atheoretical (earlier versions of the DSM were heavily influenced by psychoanalytic thought), and to consider current symptoms and functional impairments as the basis of a diagnosis (Frances & Egger, 1999). According to the DSM-IV-TR (American Psychiatric Association, 2000, p. xxxi):

> Each of the mental disorders is conceptualized as a clinically significant behavioral or psychological syndrome or pattern that occurs in an individual and that is associated with present distress (e.g., a painful symptom) or disability (i.e., impairment in one or more important areas of functioning) or with a significantly increased risk of suffering death, pain, disability, or an important loss of freedom. In addition, this syndrome or pattern must not be merely an expectable and culturally sanctioned response to a particular event, for example the death of a loved one.

The DSM-IV-TR uses a **multiaxial system**, which provides a richer diagnostic picture than the earlier DSM systems. The DSM-IV-TR also has V codes for conditions that are the focus of treatment, but that do not, in and of themselves, meet the criteria for a mental illness. A client may come into counseling because of conflict with a partner. The client is upset, but not more than would be expected given the reported relational distress. The client is not having difficulty with work, school, self-care, or other expected tasks. This person would be diagnosed on Axis I with a V code: "V61.10 Partner Relational Problems" (p. 737). The DSM-IV-TR also includes an appendix of culture bound syndromes.

Multiaxial System

To understand the way the DSM-IV-TR multiaxial system is used in counseling, consider the following case. Mary comes to counseling because she has been experiencing episodes of intense anxiety that come over her "out of the blue." During these times, she feels like she is "going crazy," and she experiences heart palpitations. The episodes last about 2 hours and have been occurring for the past 2 months. She reports being constantly worried about when the next attack might occur. Mary is a first-year college student, studying biology. She has always been a good student, but is finding it difficult to keep up with her course work. In addition to her classes, she works 20 hours per week in a local restaurant. Mary continues to work and go to classes, but she reports that keeping up with these activities is becoming harder and harder. Mary reports that she has always been a bit "high-strung," but she has never experienced anything like these episodes.

She denies any history of other emotional problems and reports being physically healthy. She denies any substance abuse. Mary's parents recently divorced, and Mary has been worried about both of them and trying to stay in frequent contact with them. She is worried about the financial implications of the divorce and sad over the way her family life has changed. Mary's DSM-IV-TR diagnosis might look like this:

Axis I: 300.01 Panic Disorder without agoraphobia

Axis II: V71.09 No diagnosis

Axis III: None reported

Axis IV: Academic Stress, Parents separation

Avis V: 60

Axis I

Axis I includes **clinical disorders** and **nonclinical disorders** that are the focus of treatment. A diagnosis is not synonymous with a mental disorder. **V codes** on Axis I are used for problems that are the focus of treatment, but not a mental disorder. The following problems and disorders would be noted under Axis I:

- Disorders usually first diagnosed in infancy, childhood, or adolescence (but not mental retardation), including Learning Disorders, Motor Skills Disorders, Communication Disorders, Pervasive Developmental Disorders, Attention Deficit Disorders, Disruptive Behavior Disorders, Feeding and Eating Disorders of Infancy and Early Childhood, Tic Disorders, Elimination Disorders, Separation Anxiety Disorder, Reactive Attachment Disorder of Infancy or Early Childhood, Stereotypic Movement Disorder, and Disorders of Childhood and Infancy Not Otherwise Specified (NOS)
- Cognitive Disorders, including Delirium, Dementia, and Amnestic and other Cognitive Disorders
- Substance Related Disorders, including substance abuse and substance dependence
- Thought disorders including Schizophrenia, Schizophreniform Disorder, Schizoaffective Disorder, Delusional Disorder, Brief Psychotic Disorder, Shared Psychotic Disorder, Psychotic Disorder Due to General Medical Condition, Substance Induced Psychotic Disorder, and Psychotic Disorder Not Otherwise Specified
- Mood Disorders, including Major Depression, Dysthymic Disorder, Depressive Disorder Not Otherwise Specified, Bipolar I and Bipolar II Disorder, Cyclothymic Disorder, Bipolar Disorder Not Otherwise Specified, Mood Disorder Due to General Medical Condition, Substance Induced Mood Disorder, and Mood Disorder Not Otherwise Specified (NOS)
- Anxiety Disorders, including Panic Disorder with and without Agoraphobia, Agoraphobia without a history of Panic Disorder, Specific Phobia, Social Phobia, Obsessive-Compulsive Disorder, Posttraumatic Stress Disorder, Acute Stress Disorder, Generalized Anxiety Disorder, Anxiety Due to a Generalized Medical Condition, Substance-Induced Anxiety Disorder, and Anxiety Disorder Not Otherwise Specified (NOS)
- Somatoform Disorders, including Somatization Disorder, Undifferentiated Somatiform Disorder, Conversion Disorder, Pain Disorder, Hypochondriasis, Body Dysmorphic Disorder, and Somatoform Disorder Not Otherwise Specified
- Factitious Disorders (note: Malingering is not considered a mental disorder)
- Dissociative Disorders, including Dissociative Amnesia, Dissociative Fugue, Dissociative Identity Disorder (previously know as Multiple Personality Disorder), Depersonalization Disorder, and Dissociative Disorder Not Otherwise Specified
- Sexual and Gender Identity Disorders, including Sexual Dysfunctions, Paraphilias, Gender Identity Disorders, and Sexual Disorders Not Otherwise Specified
- Eating Disorders, including Anorexia Nervosa, Bulimia Nervosa, and Eating Disorder Not Otherwise Specified
- Sleep Disorders, including Dyssomnias (primary disturbances in duration and quality and timing of sleep), Parasomnias (primary disturbances in behaviors and actions related to sleep stages, sleep-waking transitions sleep stages, such as sleep walking), Sleep Disturbances Related to Another Mental Disorder, Sleep Disturbance Due to a General Medical Condition, and Substance Induced Sleep Disorder

- Impulse Control Disorders not classified elsewhere, such as Intermittent Explosive Disorder, Kleptomania, Pyromania, Pathological Gambling, Trichotillomania (hair pulling), and Impulse Disorder Not Otherwise Specified
- Adjustment Disorders, including Adjustment Disorder with Depressed Mood, Adjustment Disorder with Anxiety, Adjustment Disorder with Mixed Anxiety and Depressed Mood, Adjustment Disorder with Disturbance of Conduct, Adjustment Disorder with Mixed Disturbance of Emotions and Conduct, and Adjustment Disorder Unspecified
- Other conditions that may be the focus of clinical treatment (V codes)

Axis II

Axis II disorders include Personality Disorders and Mental Retardation. **Personality Disorders** refer to long-standing patterns of relational and functional impairment. Personality Disorders are categorized into three clusters:

- Cluster A includes Paranoid, Schizoid, and Schizotypal Personality Disorders
- Cluster B includes Antisocial, Borderline, Histrionic, and Narcissistic Personality Disorders
- Cluster C includes Avoidant, Dependent, and Obsessive-Compulsive Personality Disorders

Mental Retardation is also coded on Axis II. Mental Retardation must have an age of onset before age 18 years, and is delineated into mild, moderate, and severe categories.

Axis III

Axis III is used to code existing **medical conditions** that are relevant to diagnosis and treatment. Examples of existing medical conditions include diabetes, heart disease, and cancer.

Axis IV

Axis IV is used to record **psychosocial** and **environmental stressors**. The DSM-IV-TR provides a list of common stressors (e.g., academic stress, parent separation, work stress, relationship difficulties), but clinicians should feel free to label items on Axis IV in a concise but descriptive manner. Typically, these are conditions that have been present within the past year. Clinicians can use their discretion to record historical conditions that are relevant to the diagnostic picture.

Axis V

Axis V is used to record the **Global Assessment of Functioning** (GAF). This is a scale from 1-100 (a score or "0" indicates insufficient information for rating). The GAF score considers symptom intensity and functional impairment (the ability to perform expected life tasks). The lower the GAF score, the higher the level of symptom severity or functional impairment or both. Scores of 50 or below indicate serious symptom severity or functional impairment or both; scores between 51 and 60 indicate moderate symptom severity or functional impairment or both; and scores above 61 indicate mild to absent symptom severity and functional impairment. It is often useful to include a GAF score indicating the estimated highest GAF score in the past year. This provides some indication of what level of symptom distress or functional impairment is typical of the client. The cases presented in Activity 11.10 give you practice in thinking diagnostically.

ACTIVITY 11.10

Consider the following cases and answer the questions following the case examples.

Case 1

Mark is a 25-year-old single man who comes to counseling at the request of his mother. Mark is currently unemployed and has no history of successful sustained employment. He periodically picks up short-term jobs for some money to spend. He was an average student in high school and has taken some college courses, although he has not identified an area of major interest. He has no close social relationships and seems to be satisfied spending most of his time alone playing computer games. He is not sure why he was referred for counseling. He reports no distress and says that he is quite comfortable with his current life. He has no current reported medical conditions.

Case 2

Mary is a 16-year-old high school junior, referred by her parents. Mary reports that she has been very sad since her boyfriend of 6 months ended their dating relationship. She notes that she cries every day, is not interested in her usual activities, is not sleeping well, and cannot stop wondering what she "did wrong." She has always been a good student and to date has been able to keep up with her schoolwork, but she reports that it is getting too hard to "keep it together during school." She has stopped spending time with her friends, and spends most of her time after school in her bedroom.

Answer the following questions for each case.
  1. Do you think that there is an Axis I diagnosis? Explain.
  2. Do you think that there is an Axis II diagnosis? Explain.
  3. Is there a reported medical condition that is relevant to the presenting concern? Explain.
  4. What psychosocial/environmental stressors are important in understanding the concerns? Explain.
  5. What level of symptom distress is reported? Explain.
  6. What functional impairments are described? Explain.
  7. Would the client's highest GAF score in the past year be markedly different from the GAF score at intake? Explain.
  8. How helpful do you think counseling would be?

There are benefits and problems associated with diagnosis. The benefits of diagnosis include providing a common language for professionals and clients to describe disorders or problems, a framework that aids in treatment planning and facilitates insurance reimbursement for services, a classification system that facilitates clinical research and helps to determine what treatments are most effective with what types of problems, a framework to help clients understand the problems that they bring to counseling (clients are sometimes relieved to discover a name for the symptoms they have been struggling with), and a classification system that helps clients find support networks with people sharing similar problems (Seligman, 2005).

The problems associated with diagnosis include identifying clients by their diagnosis as opposed to focusing on their unique situations and experiences, limiting counseling to address only pathology, misdiagnosis, biases that tend to pathologize minority clients, and stigmatization that can impede a client's ability to get health and disability insurance and may interfere with the possibilities of some types of employment (Seligman, 2005). Dr. David Satcher, former Surgeon General of the United States, in his groundbreaking *Mental Health Report* (1996), noted that the public sees a stronger correlation between mental illness and violent behavior now than it did in the 1950s. He also noted that most people in need of mental health services did not seek these services because of the stigma attached to mental illness.

According to Welfel and Patterson (2005), professional counselors are likely to make three mistakes in the assessment and diagnostic process. The first mistake occurs when the professional counselor attributes problems to psychological or social issues when there may be an underlining medical condition. The second mistake occurs when the professional counselor considers that there is only one diagnosis that fits a client's condition. Professional counselors need to explore all areas in which a client is experiencing difficulty. The third mistake occurs when a professional counselor relates to a diagnosis as if it is an absolute reality. Counseling is a dynamic process, and areas of concern and focus may shift.

Our knowledge about mental illness is continually evolving, and the DSM-IV-TR has benefits and limitations. Regardless of your counseling specialty area, you need to become familiar with the DSM. If you plan to be a licensed professional counselor, you are required to develop the skills necessary to be a competent and ethical diagnostician. It is vital that professional counselors follow ethical practice in the use of diagnosis. Reviewing the American Counseling Association ethics as instructed in Activity 11.11 can help you better understand what it means to engage in ethical practice when using diagnosis.

ACTIVITY 11.11

Go to the website for the American Counseling Association (www.counseling.org). Find the 2005 *American Counseling Association Code of Ethics*. Read the sections relevant to diagnosis. In small groups, discuss the ethical considerations when making diagnoses in counseling.

TREATMENT PLANNING

What are you and the client agreeing to work on together? What strategies will you use? How will you know if treatment is working? Treatment planning is an essential part of the counseling process and is designed to answer these questions. Without a treatment plan, the professional counselor and the client lack a road map of where they hope to go and how to get there. A good **treatment plan** requires an assessment appropriate to the client's presenting concerns and a case conceptualization that includes an understanding of what the problem is, how it developed, and how to deal with it. Attention should be paid to a client's subjective experience (e.g., feelings, thoughts), behaviors, and the cultural context in which the client lives. The influence of biology on emotional distress needs to be considered and may require consultations with other health care providers. The client's level of motivation needs to be considered. How ready is the client to engage in the change process?

The formality of a treatment plan and the actual form that it takes vary from setting to setting. Professional school counselors help students identify the ways in which the student would like to change, determine with the student the goals of their work together, and identify activities that might help meet these goals. Professional school counselors may not, however, formally detail this in a written treatment plan. A counselor working in a community mental health center frequently needs to develop a written document that is signed by the counselor and the client. This document needs to be periodically reviewed and revised. Regardless of setting, it is important that goals are identified and mutually agreed upon, and the strategies to reach these goals are identified. A counselor should always be able to answer the question, "What are you trying to accomplish?"

Treatment Plans

The format of a treatment plan depends on the setting in which you work. For this discussion, a three-tiered system is outlined including goals, objectives, and interventions or strategies.

Goals are broad statements of desired outcome, as follows:

- James will experience positive mood.
- Mary will be an effective manager of stress.
- Joseph will enjoy high self-esteem.

Objectives are statements of observable or measurable outcome targets, as follows:

- James will report an absence of suicidal ideation.
- Mary will learn time management strategies.
- Joseph will engage in two after-school activities.

Interventions are counseling strategies designed to meet the objectives, as follows:

- James will learn skills to tolerate distress effectively.
- Mary will learn how to use a day planner.
- Joseph will engage in social skills training.

For each counseling goal, objectives are identified to help the client reach the goal. For each objective, strategies are identified to help the client reach the objective. For example:

Goal #1. Susan will be an effective communicator.

Objective 1: Susan will learn anger management strategies.

Intervention 1: Susan will identify situations that trigger anger.

Intervention 2: Susan will learn strategies to de-escalate when angry.

Intervention 3: Susan will participate in assertiveness training.

This system provides a clear road map of the counseling process. Professional counselors need to be prepared for goals to change. Treatment plans should address the major concerns the client brings to counseling; be consistent with the diagnostic formulation; and consider interventions that target thoughts, feelings, behaviors, and social relationships, when appropriate.

When developing treatment plans, it is essential to consider the client's level of motivation. Sometimes clients are motivated to come to counseling and truly want to feel better, but may be less committed to some of the behavior changes that would lead to reduced distress. It is important to evaluate not only your client's desired goals, but also commitment to the change process. The work of Prochaska et al. (1992) helps one to understand a client's readiness to engage in the change process. It is important to match counseling goals, objectives, and strategies to a client's level of readiness for change. Many clients come to counseling not yet ready to engage in actual behavior change. Professional counselors who are able to approach these clients in a supportive, nonjudgmental manner and who have realistic counseling expectations are more successful in developing a therapeutic alliance.

Professional counselors need to evaluate their own areas of competence and what types of services can be effectively delivered in their practice setting. A referral should be made when the client's counseling needs are beyond the professional counselor's scope of competence, or when the required services are unavailable at the facility in which the professional counselor is practicing. The case presented in Activity 11.12 provides an opportunity to practice treatment planning. Activity 11.13 provides an opportunity for personal reflection.

ACTIVITY 11.12   JENNIFER

Consider this case and answer the questions following the case. Share your answers in small groups. Jennifer, a 40-year-old mother of three, comes to counseling because she is feeling "blue," tired, and upset with her appearance. Her friends are encouraging her to take more time for herself and perhaps to join an exercise program. She thinks exercise is a good idea, but does not see how she can fit it into her life because she works 20 hours per week and has many demands with her school-aged children. She reports that she feels responsible for child care and housework when she is not at her job. Jennifer thinks that exercise would reduce her fatigue, probably raise her spirits, and help with her concerns about her appearance. She realizes that there are other issues involved in her mood and self-dissatisfaction, and that finding the time to build in exercise will require that she delegate some of her current responsibilities. She worries that it would be selfish to take this time for herself and is not sure what kind of support she would get from her husband and children.

- How ready is Jennifer to take time for herself or join an exercise program?
- What kinds of interventions would be helpful to help Jennifer decide if she wants to begin taking time for herself or join an exercise program?
- What would Jennifer need to be able to do to take time for activities such as joining an exercise program?

After answering these questions write the following:

1. A goal (*hint*: this is a broad statement about desired change).
2. An objective that would support the goal (*hint*: this is a short-term, measurable, or observable goal).
3. Interventions that would help Jennifer accomplish her objective (*hint*: Jennifer is not yet ready to take time for herself or to join the exercise program. What strategies would be consistent with helping Jennifer move in this direction)?

ACTIVITY 11.13

Identify some change that you are considering making in your life. How committed to change do you think you are? What kinds of interventions would be helpful to you? What kinds of interventions would not be helpful to you?

Comprehensive Models of Assessment and Treatment Planning

Two models of assessment and treatment planning that professional counselors would find helpful to be familiar with are Lazarus's BASIC ID Model (Lazarus & Beutler, 1993) and Seligman's DO A CLIENT MAP model (Seligman, 2004).

BASIC ID   The **BASIC ID** model (Lazarus & Beutler, 1993; Neukrug, 2007) is an assessment model that looks at multiple client domains: **B**ehavior, **A**ffect, **S**ensation, **I**magery, **C**ognition, **I**nterpersonal, and **D**rugs/Biology. The professional counselor evaluates what problems, if any, exist in each of these domains, and treatment objectives are developed from this holistic assessment. Table 11.2 provides an overview of this model.

DO A CLIENT MAP   The **DO A CLIENT MAP** model (Seligman, 2004) includes assessment, case conceptualization, and treatment planning issues. This comprehensive system ensures that counselors consider a broad range of factors in their counseling interventions. Table 11.3 provides a sample of this model. The case presented in Activity 11.14 provides practice in applying the DO A CLIENT MAP and the BASIC ID models of assessment and treatment planning.

TABLE 11.2 Using the BASIC ID Model

Behavior	What does the client do that may be problematic (e.g., isolates self in room; gets into physical fights)?
Affect	What distressing feelings is the client experiencing (e.g., sadness, anger, guilt, shame)?
Sensation	What unwanted physical sensations is the client experiencing (e.g., dizziness, tingling in limbs, headache)?
Imagery	What distressing mental pictures, memories, or dreams is the client experiencing (e.g., images of death, past trauma, failure situations)?
Cognitions	What difficult thoughts is the client having about self, others, or situation (e.g., I am worthless; this is unfair; I deserve better)?
Interpersonal	What problems does the client have in relationship with others (e.g., estranged from family; few friends; abusive relationship)?
Drugs/Biology	What types of substances and what quantity does the client use (e.g., caffeine, medication, illegal drugs, alcohol)? Are there medical/biological issues (e.g., diabetes, thyroid, cancer)?

TABLE 11.3 Sample Client Map

Diagnosis	What is the DSM diagnosis?
Objectives	What are you and the client hoping to accomplish? Objectives are short-term behavior targets for treatment.
Assessment	What do you know about the client and the problem? What information have you gathered that will be helpful to treatment planning?
Clinician-counselor characteristics that would be helpful to the client's progress	What counselor characteristics would facilitate counseling? This might include age, gender, or ethnicity.
Location of treatment	What level of treatment setting will be needed for the client to engage safely and effectively in counseling? Locations could include outpatient settings, inpatient settings, or day treatment programs.
Interventions based on the literature	What treatment models are likely to be most effective? The specific interventions would be drawn from these selected models.
Emphasis	Will the emphasis of counseling be on the past, present, or future? Will counseling be supportive, confrontational, or insight-oriented? Will counseling be client-centered or directive?
Number of people in treatment	Who should be involved in the treatment? Will treatment be individual, family, or group (or some combination of these)? This would be determined by the nature of the problem, the client's resources, and the client's desires.
Timing	How frequently and for how long should this client be seen for counseling? Consideration needs to be given to the level of emergency that exists and the client's ability to work on issues outside of sessions.
Medication	Should the client be referred to a physician or psychiatrist for medication management?
Adjunct services	What services other than counseling will be helpful for the client to achieve the desired change?
Prognosis	What are the reasonable outcome expectations?

ACTIVITY 11.14   BENJAMIN

Review the following case. Using Tables 11.2 and 11.3 for the BASIC ID and the DO A CLIENT MAP models, develop a case conceptualization and treatment plan based on

(Continued)

each model. Discuss the experience of applying each model. In what ways did using these specific models facilitate treatment planning? What was difficult?

Benjamin is a 30-year-old single man referred to counseling because of distress he is experiencing after witnessing a fatal car accident. He reports that he is re-experiencing the distressing images associated with the accident, is feeling very anxious, is unable to sleep, is irritable, and is experiencing an increased sense that life is not worth living.

Benjamin has a history of recurrent depression. He has been treated episodically with a variety of antidepressant medications. At the time of the accident, he was in a period of wellness that had lasted for approximately 6 months.

Benjamin works in a local discount retail store. Because of his history of depression, he has an erratic work history, but has been at this job for 2 years. He is finding it difficult to continue working at this time because of his anxiety, flashbacks, and lack of sleep.

He had been dating a woman for 1 year, but this relationship ended just before the accident at his initiation. He has few friends, but has a supportive immediate family (i.e., parents and an older sister).

Benjamin has a history of substance abuse. He drinks about four nights a week and recently this has escalated to every night. He typically drinks about eight beers per night. He smoked marijuana regularly, but was able to give this up 3 years ago. However, he has begun smoking marijuana again on a daily basis since the accident.

He has a history of multiple hospitalizations because of the suicidal ideation that often accompanies his depressive episodes. Currently, he denies any active suicidal ideation and plan, but the idea that "life is not worth living" intrudes on his thinking.

Summary

This chapter reviewed the major concepts involved in assessment, case conceptualization, diagnosis, and treatment planning. Assessment includes many processes—testing, clinical interviewing, behavioral observation, and collecting information from collateral sources when indicated. This process would need to be done with the client's consent and knowledge, and the counselor needs to consider how this process would benefit or potentially harm the client.

Case conceptualization refers to the meaning counselors make out of the information they gather. A case conceptualization includes looking for themes and patterns, and applying counseling and developmental theory. Issues of diversity and social justice, and an evaluation of clients' motivation for counseling and for change need to be considered.

Diagnosis refers to the framework used for identifying problems that are the target of intervention. The DSM-IV-TR is the diagnostic system with which most counselors need to be familiar. Whether or not a professional counselor provides a DSM diagnosis depends on competency, scope of practice, and practice setting. Understanding the implication of a diagnosis on the client and the counseling relationship is something that all professional counselors need to consider.

The DSM-IV-TR uses a five axial system that includes clinical disorders and other problems that are the focus of treatment, long-standing socioemotional problems, medical conditions, environmental stressors, level of symptom distress, and functional impairment. This five axial system is intended to provide a comprehensive diagnostic picture.

The counseling profession has been ambivalent about the use of diagnosis, and professional counselors need to consider the pros and cons of this process. A diagnosis provides a common language for clinicians, a way of talking about and understanding problems for clients, and a direction for treatment. The problems associated with diagnosis include focusing on the diagnosis rather than the person, limiting the scope of counseling to address only the problems captured in the diagnosis, potential misdiagnosis, and an overfocus on pathology.

Treatment planning is the process of developing mutually agreeable counseling goals, identifying short-term objectives related to each goal that are observable and measurable, and determining treatment strategies that facilitate accomplishing these objectives. Professional counselors need to be careful not to move into problem solving until it is clear what the client wants to address in counseling, and what type of change the client is hoping for. Effective treatment plans are consistent with the client's desires, consider the objectives and interventions that match the client's level of motivation for change, and are within the counselor's scope of competence.

The practice of counseling requires attention to multiple factors. It is an intentional process that demands counseling skills, knowledge of counseling and developmental theory and diagnostic frameworks, attention to the requirements of ethical practice, and the desire to engage collaboratively with clients to develop treatment plans that reflect the counseling goals of the client. Becoming a competent counselor requires dedication, but the journey is exciting!

To help further your understanding of some of the topics in this chapter, go to MyHelpingLab at the Pearson.com website and view the following video clips:

- Intake Interviews: *Skills/Processes/Techniques,* Module 3 (Diagnostic Assessment, "Reviewing Intake Information with Clients").
- Treatment Plans: *Skills/Processes/Techniques,* Module 4 (From Diagnostic Assessment to Formulation, "Proposing a Treatment Plan to a Client").
- Drug and Alcohol Treatment Approaches: *Addictions/Substance Abuse Counseling,* Module 3 (Cognitive Therapy, "Cognitive Therapy Technique of Making Lists"), Module 5 (Harm Reduction Therapy, "Finding Healthy Alternatives to Substance Use"), and Module 7 (Stages of Change, "Arriving at Goals Through Commitment").
- Depression: *Addictions/Substance Abuse Counseling,* Module 4 (Reality Therapy, "Considering Plans for Change").

12 Client Issues

CATHERINE Y. CHANG AND AMY L. MCLEOD

PREVIEW

This chapter provides a broad overview of the general categories of client issues (i.e., drug and alcohol counseling, mental health counseling, career counseling, and rehabilitation counseling). The field of counseling is becoming increasingly specialized with certifications and licensures available for addictions counselors (National Certified Addictions Counselor [NCAC]; Master Addiction Counselor [MAC]), mental health counselors (Licensed Professional Counselor [LPC]—term may vary depending on the state), career counselors, and rehabilitation counselors (Certified Rehabilitation Counselor [CRC]). These areas are not distinct, and clients may enter counseling with a mental health and substance abuse issue, a career and rehabilitation issue, or any combination of the four; it is important for professional counselors to have a basic understanding of each area.

DRUG AND ALCOHOL COUNSELING ISSUES: SUBSTANCE ABUSE AND DEPENDENCE

Consider the following cases. Preston is a 20-year-old, White, male college student. He goes out drinking with friends 4 to 5 nights a week. His friends enjoy laughing at his wild behavior when he is drinking and describe Preston as the life of the party. Preston typically drinks until he passes out. Sometimes when he wakes up in the morning, he cannot remember what happened the night before when he was drinking. Often, he has unprotected sex with young women he meets at bars.

Ty is a 45-year-old, working-class, African American man. He works two jobs to support his family. Ty smokes marijuana daily and occasionally uses crack cocaine. Recently, he tested positive for marijuana on a random drug screen at work. His employer is requiring him to seek substance abuse treatment to keep his job.

Luella is a 55-year-old, Latina, retired schoolteacher. She has never used illegal drugs or alcohol in her life. Two years ago, she was in an automobile accident and was prescribed pain medication by her physician. She still takes the medication daily and has had to increase the dosage. Sometimes she wakes up in the middle of the night sweating, trembling, and feeling nauseous. She has to take the pain medications to make these symptoms subside.

These cases describe examples of typical client issues you may encounter as a professional counselor. Which, if any, of these clients have a problem with substance abuse or dependency? How do you know if a client needs help for these issues? **Substance abuse** is defined as "the habitual misuse of intoxicating and addicting substances, such as alcohol, drugs, and tobacco" (Gladding, 2004, p. 456). Clients with a substance abuse problem may continue to use the substance despite social and interpersonal problems or legal consequences related to the substance. In addition, individuals who meet the criteria for substance abuse may use substances in physically hazardous situations and fail to fulfill major role obligations at work, school, or home (American Psychiatric Association, 2001).

Substance dependence is a more serious problem. Clients with substance dependence frequently use more of a substance than they intended to use and are unable to reduce or control their use of the substance. These individuals spend a great deal of time using the substance and reduce their participation in important social, occupational, or leisure activities (American Psychiatric Association, 2001).

Tolerance is another characteristic of substance abuse. **Tolerance** occurs when the effect of a particular dosage of a substance is lessened because of repeated exposure to the substance (Ray & Ksir, 2004). In other words, one would have to increase the dosage of a substance to achieve the same effect that was once achieved using a smaller dosage.

Withdrawal is also a marker of substance dependence (American Psychiatric Association, 2001). **Withdrawal** indicates physical dependence on a substance. If the substance is not present in the body, an individual with substance dependence may experience symptoms such as increased irritability, sleep disturbance, headaches, fever, nausea, vomiting, diarrhea, tremors, seizures, strokes, or even death (Kottler & Brown, 1996; Ray & Ksir, 2004).

Approximately 35% of adults struggle with some type of substance disorder in their lifetime. Substance disorders are more prevalent among men than women. Approximately 20% of men struggle with alcohol abuse or dependency, and 11.5% of men struggle with drug abuse or dependency in their lifetime, compared with 8% and 5% of women, respectively. Rates of substance abuse and dependency are the highest among adults in early and middle adulthood and generally decrease with age (National Comorbidity Survey Replication, 2005). Activities 12.1 and 12.2 are designed to bring awareness of how the media portrays substance use and the impact of these messages. Activity 12.3 provides an opportunity for self-reflection on personal substance use.

ACTIVITY 12.1

For 2 days, count the number of advertisements or references to alcohol and cigarettes you hear and see in the media. Write a one- to two-page reaction paper discussing your thoughts, feelings, and insights regarding how the media portrays substance use and the impact of these messages.

ACTIVITY 12.2

Watch a movie that focuses on substance abuse (e.g., *The Lost Weekend* [1945], *Clean and Sober* [1988], *The Basketball Diaries* [1995], *Leaving Las Vegas* [1995], *28 Days* [2000], *Traffic* [2000], *Blow* [2001]). Process your thoughts, feelings, and reactions to the portrayal of substance use in the film.

ACTIVITY 12.3

Try this experiential activity to increase your empathy for clients with substance abuse and dependency issues. Identify which mood-altering substances (except for prescribed medications) or activities play a role in your life. These substances and activities may include alcohol, marijuana, cigarettes, caffeine, shopping, gambling, exercise, and sexual activity. Engage in a 2-week period of complete abstinence from all self-identified mood-altering substances and activities, and keep a daily journal of this process. How did you feel physically? What was the most challenging part of remaining abstinent? Were you able to remain abstinent? How will this experience affect your work as a professional counselor with clients who abuse substances?

Drug and Alcohol Treatment Approaches

There are three primary approaches to the treatment of drug and alcohol abuse and dependence: medical model, twelve-step model, and strengths-based approach.

MEDICAL MODEL   Proponents of the **medical model** view addiction as a chronic and progressive disease, similar to diabetes or heart disease. Research provides evidence that a biological basis or genetic predisposition for addiction exists. Treatment based on the medical model may include **detoxification** or medical stabilization, reduction of withdrawal symptoms, the prescription of medications, and intensive therapy designed to increase coping skills and prevent **relapse** or the return to substance use (Kottler & Brown, 1996; van Wormer & Davis, 2003). Total **abstinence** is the goal of treatment based on the medical model. Many hospital and community settings ascribe to the medical model of substance abuse treatment.

TWELVE-STEP MODEL   **Alcoholics Anonymous (AA)** is the original **Twelve-Step Program**. Founded in 1935 by a stockbroker and a surgeon with alcohol problems, AA has grown to be the largest recovery program in the world with approximately two million members in 150 countries (Alcoholics Anonymous, 2006). AA is a self-supported organization for men and women who desire to live a sober life. The twelve-step model of AA includes a spiritual component, but is not affiliated with any religion or religious organization. Members of AA attend meetings, up to several times a day, where they share their stories and offer support for one another. Members of AA believe they are in **recovery** from alcoholism, and that they will always be addicted to alcohol and must take sobriety "one day at a time" for the rest of their lives (Alcoholics Anonymous, 2006). Numerous other twelve-step programs have been developed to help people with addictions to substances other than alcohol and addictions to behaviors, including Narcotics Anonymous (NA), Crystal Meth Anonymous, Gamblers Anonymous, Overeaters Anonymous (OA), Sex and Love Addicts Anonymous, and Al-Anon for family members of alcoholics. The twelve-step model is compatible with the medical model of treatment. Activity 12.4 familiarizes you with twelve-step meetings and helps you gain a better understanding of what clients may experience while attending these meetings. This activity can also help develop empathy for clients.

ACTIVITY 12.4

Identify and attend an open twelve-step meeting or support group in your area. Write a one- to two-page reaction paper to the meeting. Discuss your thoughts, feelings, reactions, comfort level, and any other insights you gained from the experience. The following websites may be helpful in locating a local twelve-step group: Alcoholics Anonymous, www.alcoholics-anonymous.org; Narcotics Anonymous, www.na.org; Gamblers Anonymous, www.gamblersanonymous.org; Al-Anon/Alateen, www.al-anon. alateen.org; Crystal Meth Anonymous, www.crystalmeth.org; Sex and Love Addicts Anonymous, www.slaafws.org; Overeaters Anonymous, www.oa.org.

STRENGTHS-BASED APPROACHES **Strengths-based treatment** approaches are an alternative to the medical model. The goal is **harm reduction**, or minimization of the social, legal, and medical problems associated with unmanaged addiction (van Wormer & Davis, 2003). Total abstinence is considered one among many methods of harm reduction. Learning to control substance use is also considered a valid goal of treatment. Other characteristics of strengths-based treatment approaches include an emphasis on personal choice of the client; viewing the client as a competent person with many positive assets; the cultivation of hope, meaning, and a sense of accomplishment; and the development of a social support system (van Wormer & Davis, 2003).

ACTIVITY 12.5

Learn more about what it is like to work with clients with a drug or alcohol problem by interviewing an addictions counselor. Find out why the professional counselor chose to work in the addictions field, what treatment approach he or she ascribes to, what advice he or she would have for a beginning counselor considering entering the addictions field, what challenges he or she has faced as an addictions counselor, and what aspects of working as an addictions counselor are most rewarding.

Alcohol and Drug Abuse Issues in Special Populations

ADOLESCENTS   Adolescence is a developmental period during which young people attempt to establish independence from their parents, strengthen peer relationships, and develop their own identities. During this period, many adolescents experiment with alcohol and drugs (Burrow-Sanchez, 2006; van Wormer & Davis, 2003). According to the National Council on Alcoholism and Drug Dependence (2000), 80% of high school seniors have used alcohol, 49% have used marijuana, and 9% have used cocaine.

Substance use in adolescence is particularly concerning because early age of first use of alcohol and drugs is a risk factor for the development of substance dependence and other psychological disorders later in life (van Wormer & Davis, 2003). Substance abuse in adolescence is linked with higher rates of unprotected sex, sexual assault and rape, physical violence, and car accidents (van Wormer & Davis, 2003). For these reasons, prevention is critical. **Prevention** efforts include alcohol and drug education programs, and programs designed to increase coping and social resistance skills (Kottler & Brown, 1996). Activity 12.6 introduces professional associations focused on helping clients with substance use difficulties. Activity 12.7 helps you gain awareness and knowledge of the adolescent culture.

ACTIVITY 12.6

Learn more about the division of the American Counseling Association (ACA) for professional counselors interested in addictions, The International Association of Addictions and Offender Counselors (IAAOC). Investigate the IAAOC website, www.iaaoc.org, and read about the history, mission, and current goals of the IAAOC.

ACTIVITY 12.7

Establishing trust and building a therapeutic relationship with adolescent clients can be challenging. Using your client's language is a great way to build rapport. Use the Internet and any other available resources to generate a list of as many slang or street names for drugs as possible. Study the list so that you are familiar with the words adolescent and adult clients may use to talk about drugs.

CULTURALLY DIVERSE CLIENTS   Racial, ethnic, and cultural minority clients are underserved by traditional approaches to substance abuse treatment. Minority groups typically experience greater consequences of substance use, including higher rates of drug-related and alcohol-related deaths and higher rates of incarceration for substance-related activities (van Wormer & Davis, 2003). When working with culturally diverse clients, it is crucial to address issues of oppression and discrimination, and how these experiences relate to substance use. The professional counselor should also discuss the client's level of acculturation, level of education, socioeconomic status, spiritual and religious beliefs, and cultural values and norms (van Wormer & Davis, 2003). The professional counselor should strive to establish a collaborative relationship with the client and explore cultural explanations for the cause of substance abuse and dependency. Treatment should address the client's beliefs about the cause of the problem and may include integrating family and community resources or working with a traditional healer from within the client's culture.

As a professional counselor, one should always be aware of the cultural appropriateness and implications for any intervention. The purpose of Activity 12.8 is to assist in viewing interventions through a cultural lens.

ACTIVITY 12.8

Review the twelve steps of AA and similar organizations. What are your reactions? What cultural groups do you think the twelve steps would be the most and least appropriate for? Why?

MENTAL HEALTH COUNSELING ISSUES

Mental health and school counselors may work with clients on a variety of issues, including depression, anxiety, eating disorders, post-traumatic stress disorder, and suicidal or homicidal thoughts. Substance abuse or dependency issues are also common, as discussed previously in this chapter. In addition to client issues, this section discusses diagnosis in counseling and describes the various levels of mental health treatment. Self awareness is an important component in counselor competence. Activity 12.9 assists you in identifying your emotions and comfort level in working with client's emotions.

ACTIVITY 12.9

Identify which emotions you are most and least comfortable expressing in your personal life. What are the triggers for each of your emotions? What emotions are you most and least comfortable with other people expressing in your presence? How will this affect your work with clients?

Depression

Depression is one of the most common client issues a counselor encounters. Nearly 15 million, or approximately 7%, of adults in the United States experience depression annually. Women are more likely to experience depression than men. The median age of the onset of depression is 32 years; however, clients of any age many present to counseling with symptoms of depression (National Institute for Mental Health, n.d.).

Depression is characterized by persistent feelings of sadness or irritability. Depressed clients may report a loss of interest in hobbies, work, and sexual activity. Sleep disturbance is also a common feature of depression. Some depressed clients may have difficulty falling or staying asleep, whereas others sleep more than usual. Appetite may increase or decrease (American Psychiatric Association, 2000). Isolating from family and friends, crying spells, feelings of hopelessness, and neglecting personal hygiene may also occur during an episode of depression. Culture can dramatically influence the manner in which depressive symptoms are expressed (Activity 12.10 may help you broaden your vocabulary of feeling words to enhance cultural sensitivity and emotional expression). Clients from some cultures may report headaches, problems of the heart, or feelings of guilt or imbalance, which may signal depression (American Psychiatric Association, 2000). Sometimes a client may become so depressed that he or she considers committing suicide. **Suicidal ideation** is a special area of concern discussed later in this section.

ACTIVITY 12.10

Increase your feeling word vocabulary. Generate a list of as many feeling words as possible for each of the following categories of emotions: Mad, Sad, Glad, and Scared. Think about the intensity of each word. How can a vast emotional vocabulary improve your work with clients?

Anxiety

Anxiety is another commonly encountered client issue. In the United States, 3% of the adult population experiences Generalized Anxiety Disorder, 3% experiences Panic Disorder, and 7% experiences Social Phobia (National Comorbidity Survey Replication, 2005) in their lifetime. Similar to depression, women are more likely to experience anxiety than men. **Anxiety**, which typically develops in adolescence or early adulthood, is characterized by excessive or constant worry, restlessness, irritability, and disturbed sleep (American Psychiatric Association, 2001). Clients struggling with anxiety may report a lump in their throat, sweating hands, a racing heart rate, and an upset stomach. Anxiety may be triggered by exposure to specific stimuli, such as being around a large group of people, or may be experienced in a more generalized manner. Some clients experience panic attacks, which may include shortness of breath and chest pains. Sometimes, feelings of anxiety and panic are so intense that people mistake a panic attack for a heart attack and go to the emergency department. Deep breathing can reduce stress and anxiety. Activity 12.11 presents a breathing exercise that you can teach clients who are experiencing anxiety.

ACTIVITY 12.11

Sit up straight and close your eyes. Inhale deeply and slowly. Hold the breath for 3 seconds and exhale slowly. Repeat 10 times. How do you feel?

Eating Disorders

Eating disorders disproportionately affect middle-class to upper-class, White women more than women of color and men (Osvold & Sodowsky, 1993). A primary factor that contributes to the development of eating disorders is the media's emphasis on the idea that to be attractive or of worth one must be thin. The development of an eating disorder may also be influenced by family dynamics, requirements of a sport, or a history of abuse. Two common types of eating disorders are anorexia nervosa and bulimia nervosa. **Anorexia nervosa** is characterized by a client's refusal to maintain minimally normal body weight, a fear of gaining weight, and distorted perceptions of body size and shape (American Psychiatric Association, 2001). Clients with anorexia may drastically restrict their food intake. An estimated 0.5% to 3.7% of girls and women struggle with anorexia nervosa during their lifetime (American Psychiatric Association Work Group on Eating Disorders, 2001). **Bulimia nervosa** involves binge eating and inappropriate compensatory measures to prevent or reduce weight gain (American Psychiatric Association, 2001). Compensatory measures, also referred to as purging behaviors, may include forced or spontaneous vomiting; the use of diuretics, diet pills, and laxatives; and excessive patterns of exercise. An estimated 1.1 % to 4.2% of girls and women experience bulimia nervosa during their lifetime (American Psychiatric Association Work Group on Eating Disorders, 2001).

Trauma

Clients may have experienced a variety of traumatic events, including emotional, physical, and sexual abuse; rape or sexual assault; intimate partner violence; exposure to war or terrorist acts; involvement in an automobile accident; or a natural disaster. Traumatic events result in feelings of fear, helplessness, loss of control, loss of connection with others, and a loss of meaning (Herman, 1997). **Post-traumatic stress disorder (PTSD)** is a DSM-IV-TR (American Psychiatric Association, 2001) classification that includes three main categories of symptoms: (1) hyperarousal, (2) intrusion, and (3) constriction. **Hyperarousal** refers to the persistent expectation of danger and may include a heightened startle response and sleep disturbance (Herman, 1997). **Intrusive symptoms** include vivid nightmares and flashbacks. Children may recreate the traumatic event through play. Emotional numbness, dissociation, and use of drugs and alcohol to dull pain associated with a trauma are examples of **constrictive symptoms**.

Approximately 3.5%, or 7.7 million, U.S. adults experience PTSD each year. Women are more likely to experience PTSD than men. Although clients may experience a traumatic event resulting in PTSD at any age, the median age of onset for PTSD is 23 years (National Institute for Mental Health, n.d.; National Comorbidity Survey Replication, 2005). Empowerment of the client, the re-establishment of safety and structure, mourning losses resulting from the traumatic experience, and reconnecting with systems of social support are goals of trauma work. When working with minority clients, it is important to address the impact of oppression and discrimination in connection with the traumatic event. Activity 12.12 explores the experience of vicarious traumatization, which can affect professional counselors who work with clients with PTSD.

ACTIVITY 12.12

Professional counselors who work with clients who have experienced a traumatic event can experience vicarious traumatization. Self-care is essential for professional counselors who deal with these issues. Generate a list of personal resiliency characteristics and self-care activities you can practice to restore personal wellness.

Clients in Crisis

A crisis is defined as a "brief episode of intense emotional distress in which a person's usual coping efforts are insufficient to handle the challenges confronting the individual" (France, 2002, p. 4). Two types of crises a professional counselor must be prepared to handle are clients expressing **suicidal ideation** (self-harm) and **homicidal ideation** (others' harm). It is essential that professional counselors ask clients directly if they have a plan about how they would harm themselves or someone else, if they have the means to complete the plan, how serious they are about following through with the plan, and if they have ever made a previous attempt at harming themselves or someone else. Minority clients are less likely to disclose suicidal or homicidal thoughts because of distrust of the mental health profession. Professional counselors must take extra measures to establish trust and rapport with these clients.

Professional counselors should be familiar with statistics and risk factors associated with suicide and homicide. Several key risk factors are feelings of hopelessness, uncontrolled anger, reckless behavior, increased substance abuse, increased agitation, isolating from family and friends, feeling trapped, feeling no sense of purpose in life, and dramatic mood changes (American Association of Suicidology, n.d.). The counselor's primary goal is ensuring safety when clients are at risk of harm to themselves or someone else. Professional counselors should evaluate if a client meets the criteria for involuntary commitment to an inpatient setting and if duty to warn applies. **Duty to warn** is related to the 1976 Supreme Court ruling in the *Tarasoff v. Board of Regents of the University of California* case. According to the *Tarasoff* decision:

> When a therapist determines, or pursuant to the standards of his profession should determine, that his patient presents a serious danger of violence to another, he incurs an obligation to use reasonable care to protect the intended victim against such danger.

Case Studies 12.1 through 12.3 help develop your skills in suicide assessment.

CASE STUDY 12.1

Richard is a 55-year-old, middle-class, White man. He began coming to counseling to help cope with work-related stress. Richard has been divorced for 15 years and does not have any family living in his home state. Richard reports drinking alcohol on occasion, approximately two to three liquor drinks every 2 weeks. When Richard arrives for his third session, you notice he is slightly disheveled and appears unusually anxious with rapid and pressured speech. He paces around the room, and you notice the smell of alcohol in his breath. Richard discloses that he was fired from his job today. He feels that he will never find a job that compares to his last job because of his age. When you ask Richard if he has thoughts of hurting himself, he begins to cry and then punches the wall. He says he would not kill himself because he would not give his boss the satisfaction of knowing he drove him to suicide. What questions would you, as the professional counselor, ask Richard? What risk factors can be identified? What ethical issues should be considered? Is it safe to allow Richard to leave your office unaccompanied?

CASE STUDY 12.2

Catalina is a 16-year-old Latina girl who was referred by a teacher at the Catholic high school she attends. Catalina typically scores very good grades and has never been in trouble at school. In the past month, her grades have declined dramatically. She has been sitting by herself in the cafeteria at lunch. She spends most of her time after school in her bedroom by herself and often cries herself to sleep. After two sessions, Catalina tells you that she stole some liquor from a local store and has started drinking to cope with her sadness. She also reveals that she is cutting on her arms and stomach with a razor blade. Five minutes before the counseling session ends, Catalina bursts into tears and tells you that she was raped by a male neighbor. She says that her life is ruined. She begs you not to tell her parents that she is no longer a virgin. Do you think Catalina is at risk for suicide? What risk factors are present? What ethical issues should be considered? How would you handle this situation?

CASE STUDY 12.3

Melton is a 70-year-old African American man. He started coming to counseling after his wife died 2 months ago. Melton and his wife were married for 50 years, and he reports difficulty getting through each day without her. Melton has two adult children who live about 2 hours away; they visit on holidays, but are not particularly present in his life. Melton reports that he has been sleeping about 16 hours per day for the past week. He is tearful during the session. He tells you that he has stopped going to church and has not worked in his garden all week. What's the point, he says, his wife was the one who really liked doing those things. Melton also reveals that he has stopped taking his blood pressure and diabetes medication. He says that he does not want to be on this Earth any longer than he has to be. Do you think Milton is at risk for suicide? What risk factors are present? What ethical issues should be considered? As Melton's counselor, what is your next step?

Diagnosis

The ***Diagnostic and Statistical Manual of Mental Disorders, Fourth Edition-Text Revision* (DSM-IV-TR)** (American Psychiatric Association, 2000) contains descriptions and diagnostic criteria for all mental health and substance abuse disorders recognized by the American Psychiatric Association. The DSM-IV-TR is based on a **multiaxial system of classification**, organized as follows: Axis I, Clinical Disorders and V-Codes; Axis II, Personality Disorders and Developmental Disorders; Axis III, General Medical Conditions; Axis IV, Psychosocial and Environmental Stressors; and Axis V, Global Assessment of Functioning. Criticisms of the *DSM-IV-TR* include overlapping diagnostic categories and biased criteria. Some researchers argue the DSM-IV-TR criteria for depression describe ways in which females are traditionally socialized to express sadness, resulting in the higher rates of diagnosis of depression among women than men (Norman, 2004). In addition, the DSM-IV-TR may fail to account adequately for cultural variation in symptom expression (Atkinson, Bui, & Mori, 2001). Activity 12.13 helps you to become more familiar with the DSM-IV-TR and the culture-bound syndromes.

ACTIVITY 12.13

The DSM-IV-TR includes a section on culture-bound syndromes. Read the descriptions of these syndromes and process your reactions. What similarities and differences do you see compared with the Western expressions of psychological distress? As a professional counselor, how would you respond to a client exhibiting one of the culture-bound syndromes?

Diagnosis is a controversial topic in the counseling profession. Benefits of diagnosis include the establishment of a common language among mental health professionals, a starting point for treatment planning, and the ability to receive reimbursement from insurance companies. Arguments against diagnosis include the belief that labeling a client with a mental disorder can create a self-fulfilling prophecy, and that diagnosis pathologizes and depersonalizes the client (Neukrug, 1999). Activity 12.14 helps you to become more familiar with the role of diagnosis in the daily lives of professional counselors.

ACTIVITY 12.14

Interview a mental health counselor. What types of client issues does the professional counselor encounter most commonly? What is his or her view on diagnosis? What are the most challenging and the most rewarding aspects of being a professional counselor? What are the most important lessons learned from clients?

Mental Health Treatment Settings

INPATIENT TREATMENT FACILITIES Inpatient or hospital-based treatment facilities provide 24-hour care to clients in acute crisis situations. Clients who are suicidal or homicidal may require **inpatient treatment** to ensure their safety and the safety of others. Clients with mental illnesses such as schizophrenia or bipolar disorder may need inpatient treatment to deal with psychosis or manic episodes. Inpatient treatment may also be necessary for clients who have severe eating disorders and are at risk medically. Clients with substance dependence issues may need inpatient detoxification to reduce the medical risk associated with withdrawal symptoms. In inpatient treatment settings, clients receive care from a team of psychiatrists, nurses, professional counselors, and social workers. In the past, 28-day inpatient programs were common. As a result of restrictions imposed by managed care companies, most inpatient programs have been restructured to provide short-term stabilization to clients in crisis.

RESIDENTIAL TREATMENT SETTINGS **Residential treatment** programs provide intensive therapy and a structured living environment for clients struggling with mental health and substance abuse and dependency issues (Neukrug, 1999). Clients who typically enter residential treatment programs may have previously been stabilized in an inpatient setting or may require the structure provided by a residential treatment program because of several episodes of mental health and substance abuse issues. Clients may live at a residential treatment facility, which may also be referred to as a halfway house, three-quarter way house, or recovery residence, for several months while they are developing increased coping skills and focusing on recovery. Some residential programs allow clients to work part-time during treatment.

PARTIAL HOSPITALIZATION **Partial hospitalization** provides intensive therapy for clients for 6–8 hours a day and allows clients to return home in the evenings. Partial hospitalization programs are typically 4–6 weeks in length and include group therapy, family therapy, individual therapy, and support group meetings.

INTENSIVE OUTPATIENT TREATMENT **Intensive outpatient treatment** is appropriate for clients who are functioning at a high level, but need more intensive treatment than outpatient therapy is able to provide. Intensive outpatient treatment typically meets for 2 to 3 hours a day for 4–6 weeks and includes group therapy, family therapy, individual therapy, and support group meetings. Most clients are able to work or attend school full-time while in this type of treatment program.

OUTPATIENT TREATMENT **Outpatient treatment** typically consists of weekly or biweekly sessions of 1 hour in length with a professional counselor. Clients may also attend weekly outpatient groups. Outpatient treatment is appropriate for working with clients on a variety of issues. A referral to a more intensive level of treatment may be necessary when a professional counselor determines that a client is not making progress, is having increased difficulty functioning on a daily basis, or is in danger of harming himself or herself or someone else. It is essential for professional counselors to be aware of the mental health resources available in their community. Activity 12.15 helps you develop your resource list.

ACTIVITY 12.15

Investigate what mental health resources are available in your community. Where could a client go to receive free or low-cost counseling services? Where would you refer a client in crisis? Where could a non–English-speaking client go for counseling? Keep a list of these resources to use in your future work as a professional counselor.

CAREER COUNSELING ISSUES

Which of the following best represents the work of career counselors?

- A 3-year-old loves to play doctor and teacher.
- A preschooler joins her first T-ball league.
- One high school junior considers his college options, while another considers her job opportunities after graduation.
- A college freshman contemplates his major.
- A divorced mother of three considers going back to school.
- A new father quits his full-time job to become a full-time stay-at-home father.
- A 55-year-old begins thinking about retirement.

If you said all of the above, well done! What is career counseling and career development, and why is it an important client issue for professional counselor consideration? When you hear career counseling, you might assume it simply involves helping your client find a job; however, it is more comprehensive than job hunting. Career counseling involves facilitating client development of various life roles. Effective career counseling can assist clients in making smart decisions related to their work and other life roles. Career counseling is especially important because numerous studies indicate that career planning and career counseling are related to job satisfaction and positive mental health (Assouline & Meir, 1987). It is outside the scope of this section to explore the many facets of career counseling and development. In this section, we present a list of important career counseling terms (Table 12.1), a brief introduction to the major theories of career development, some useful resources for career counseling, and, finally, a discussion of diversity issues in career counseling.

Major Theories of Career Development

Career development theories attempt to explain why individuals choose certain careers and how various contexts influence one's career path. Although there are numerous career development theories, most of them can be classified into one of the following four approaches: trait and factor theory, psychodynamic theory, developmental theories, and social cognitive career theory.

TRAIT AND FACTOR THEORY   The **trait and factor theory of career development** (also known as person-environment fit) can be traced back to Frank Parsons who is often referred to as the "father of guidance." It was the major career development theory until the 1950s. The trait and factor approach involves three basic stages, as follows:

"(1) clear understanding of aptitudes, abilities, interests, ambitions, resources, limitations, and their causes; (2) a knowledge of the requirements and conditions of success, advantages and disadvantages, compensations, opportunities, and prospects in different lines of work; and (3) true reasoning on the relations of these two groups of facts" (Parsons, 1909, p. 5).

With its primary focus on assessing one's abilities and interests, the trait and factor approach is didactic and directive.

Although the trait and factor theory has evolved over the years to include more emphasis on the interpersonal nature of careers and lifestyles, the theory has retained its emphasis on the importance of a fit between the individual and the environment. The current trait and factor theory also places more emphasis on the dynamic process between the client and the professional

TABLE 12.1 Important Terms in Career Counseling

Avocation	"a chosen activity, not necessarily pursued for money, that gives satisfaction to the individual and fulfills an important aspect of the person's life" (Neukrug, 1999, p. 264)
Career	"the course of events which constitutes a life; the sequence of occupations and other life roles which combine to express one's commitment to work in his or her total pattern of self-development; the series of remunerated and nonremunerated positions occupied by a person from adolescence through retirement, of which occupation is only one" (Super, 1976, p. 4)
Career counseling	"one-to-one or small group relationship between a client and a counselor with the goal of helping the client(s) integrate and apply an understanding of self and the environment to make the most appropriate career decision and adjustment" (Sears, 1982, p. 139). ". . . A specialty within the profession of counseling, one that fosters vocational development and work adjustment of individuals at each life stage by engaging them in life planning aimed at the psychosocial integration of an individual's abilities, interests, and goals with the work roles structured by the community and occupations organized by companies" (Savickas, 2003, p. 88)
Career development	"a continuous life process through which individuals explore activities, make decisions, and assume a variety of roles. Careers are formulated by the continuous evaluation of personal goals and the perception, assessment, and decisions regarding opportunities to achieve those goals. Career development occurs as educational and vocational pursuits interact with personal goals. It continues over the life span" (National Career Development Association, 2006, p. 6)
Job	"a specific occupation held by an individual at any given time" (Brown & Srebalus, 2003, p. 120)
Leisure	"planned or spontaneous events, usually relatively short term in nature, aimed at enlightening, entertaining, relaxing, or stimulating the individual" (Brown & Srebalus, 2003, p. 120)
Occupation	"a formally classified work activity that involves a group of people working in different situations" (Brown & Srebalus, 2003, p. 120)
Work	"a paid or unpaid systematic activity aimed at producing something of value for one's self, others, or a combination thereof" (Brown & Srebalus, 2003, p. 120)

counselor, and recognizes the importance of affective and cognitive components. It is no longer considered sufficient simply to match a client's traits with job requirements. Rather the match is considered more effective if the client has insight related to his or her unique traits and situational factors that may influence potential career decisions. John Holland is a modern trait and factor theorist. Activity 12.16 helps you bridge theory to practice.

ACTIVITY 12.16

Research Holland's theory of career development and determine how it might be applied to help clients understand their career interests and skills.

PSYCHODYNAMIC THEORY   **Psychodynamic career theory** stresses the importance of unconscious motivation and satisfying emotional needs and is best exemplified by the writings of Anne Roe (1956). According to Roe, one's career choice is influenced by early parenting, and early parent-child interactions form the foundation of one's vocational interests. Through one's career choice, individuals seek to express and satisfy needs that were not met by their parents in childhood.

Roe classified parents as either warm or cold, which resulted in three types of emotional climates: (1) emotional concentration on the child, (2) acceptance of the child, and (3) avoidance of the child. These three emotional climates resulted in six types of parent-child relationships, which influenced the kinds of occupational choices the child would make in the future.

Parenting style eventually results in individuals having one of eight orientations toward the world of work: service, business, organization, technology, outdoor, science, general culture, and arts and entertainment. Although Roe placed great emphasis on the importance of parenting styles on occupational choice, she did not discount the importance of other factors (i.e., genetics, gender, economy, physical appearance, chance factors, family background, and temperament) in career decision making. Psychodynamic career theory has been criticized for being too complex and overemphasizing internal factors such as motivation. Complete Activity 12.17 to become aware of your own career path. Follow this with Reflection 12.1.

ACTIVITY 12.17

Construct a genogram depicting the various career paths of the members of your family. (Visit www.genopro.com for a primer on genograms.)

REFLECTION 12.1

Reflect on your own childhood and your relationship with your parents. Do you believe your parents' parenting styles influenced your career interests and decisions?

DEVELOPMENTAL THEORIES   **Developmental career theories** view one's career choice as a part of a long developmental process beginning with early life events and ending in death. According to developmental career theories, early life experiences, life events and opportunities, and the maturation process all influence one's interests, career exploration, and career outcomes. Ginzberg, Ginsburg, Axelrod, and Herma (1951) are credited with being some of the first theorists to connect developmental theory with occupational choice. Probably the most recognized and extensive career development theory was developed by Super (1957, 1990).

Central to Super's theory is the role of self-concept in career choice and career development. He believed that career development was the process of implementing one's self-concept. How one views oneself is reflected in what one does. According to Super, there are five stages of career development, each with substages and corresponding developmental tasks. The five stages are: growth, exploration, establishment, maintenance, and decline.

The growth stage (birth to 14 years of age) includes the substages of fantasy, interest, and capacity. During the growth stage, individuals begin developing their self-concept as they begin to identify with significant others. The developmental tasks during this stage include gaining self-awareness of interests and abilities, and obtaining an overall understanding of the world of work.

The exploration stage (14 to 24 years of age) includes the tentative substage, the transition substage, and the trial-little commitment substage. During this stage, adolescents and young adults begin testing out their occupational fantasies through school, work, and leisure activities. This stage ends with individuals crystallizing their vocational interests and narrowing their vocational choices.

During the establishment stage (24 to 44 years of age), individuals seek to stabilize their career choice and advance in their chosen career. The substages include trial-commitment and stabilization. Following the establishment stage is the maintenance stage (44 to 64 years of age), which is characterized by maintaining one's current status and enjoying the security of seniority.

The final stage is the decline stage (64 years through death), in which individuals disengage from their careers and begin focusing on retirement, leisure, and avocational activities. The decline stage includes the substages of deceleration and retirement.

In addition to the career development stages, Super believed that individuals engage in various roles, such as child, student, leisurite, citizen, worker, and homemaker. These roles overlap and influence one's vocational development.

SOCIAL COGNITIVE CAREER THEORY   **Social cognitive career theory (SCCT)** (Lent, Brown, & Hackett, 1994, 2002) has its roots in social learning theory and information processing with the key concepts of self-efficacy beliefs ("Can I do it?"), outcome expectations ("If I do it, what will be the outcome?"), and career choice barriers ("What are the consequences of my career choice?"). It is believed that all three concepts influence and are influenced by career interests. One's career interests are influenced by one's values, which motivate the individual to acquire knowledge and develop skills for a specific occupation. Through these experiences, one's behaviors and beliefs are reinforced, which affect one's self-efficacy and outcome expectations.

According to SCCT, contextual and social cognitive factors influence one's career interests, goals, and actions. Because these learning experiences occur within a social context, they are influenced by race/ethnicity, gender, health/disabilities, religious beliefs, and economic factors. These contextual factors include discrimination, socioeconomic status, job availability, educational access, perceived and real barriers, and other environmental factors. All these factors influence one's self-efficacy, which relates to one's career choice. One's career choice can be limited as a result of either faulty self-efficacy or negative outcome expectations. The goal of SCCT is to assist clients in making satisfying career choices by examining self-efficacy, outcome expectations, and perception of career barriers. SCCT is an important contribution to the career development literature because of its integration of social forces (e.g., racism, sexism, classism, homophobia) and contextual/environmental factors (e.g., role models, socialization). Now complete Activity 12.18.

ACTIVITY 12.18

Review the four major career development theories discussed. Which theory best describes your career path? Provide specific examples supporting the theory.

Career Resources

An extensive amount of occupational information is available to assist clients in understanding the nature of work, to gain knowledge about the various careers, and to assist in client self-awareness. Following are some of the most common and useful career resources.

DICTIONARY OF OCCUPATIONAL TITLES   The *Dictionary of Occupational Titles* **(DOT)** (www.occupationalinfo.org) published by the U.S. Department of Labor is a comprehensive classification system of occupations. It details tasks performed, educational requirements, and skills needed for more than 12,000 types of jobs and approximately 30,000 job titles. The DOT provides a nine-digit occupational code for each job. Each set of three digits in the nine-digit code number has a specific purpose and meaning. Together the nine digits provide a unique identification code for a particular occupation, which differentiates it from all other occupations. The first three digits indicate general occupational group. The second series of three digits are the "worker functions ratings," which describe the relationship between the worker and data, people, and things. The last three digits differentiate a particular occupation from other related occupations. For example, professional counselors have the nine digit code of 045.107-010, while marriage and family counselors have the code of 045.107-054. The two codes have the same first six digits, with the last three differentiating the type of counselor.

OCCUPATIONAL OUTLOOK HANDBOOK (OOH)   The *Occupational Outlook Handbook* **(OOH)** is also published by the U.S. Department of Labor (www.bls.gov/oco/). It provides information related to training and education requirements, earnings, expected job prospects, worker tasks, and working conditions for hundreds of jobs. It also provides tips for job searches and information about the job market in each state.

O*NET (OCCUPATIONAL INFORMATION NETWORK)   The O*Net program (www.onetcenter.org), which includes the O*Net database and the O*Net Online, is a free Web-based database and interactive program for exploring and searching occupations. The O*NET database contains information on hundreds of standardized and occupation-specific descriptors. The information from this database forms the heart of O*NET Online, which allows users to explore occupations.

O*Net also provides Career Exploration Tools, a set of assessment instruments for workers and students looking to find or change careers. The Career Exploration Tools include self-assessments that assist users in considering and planning career options by helping users identify work-related interests, what users consider important on the job, and their abilities to explore the occupations that match those attributes. Activity 12.19 gives you the opportunity to complete the self-assessments of the Career Exploration Tools.

ACTIVITY 12.19

Go online to O*Net Online (www.onetcenter.org) and go through the Career Exploration Tools.

Assessment Inventories

Numerous assessment inventories are available to assist clients in their career exploration. The two most widely used career exploration systems in the United States are SIGI-PLUS (System of Interactive Guidance and Information-Plus) and DISCOVER. In addition to career exploration systems, interest inventories that examine client interests in such areas as school subjects, types of people, types of occupation, amusements, and personal characteristics are widely used in career counseling. The *Strong Interest Inventory* categorizes hundreds of careers into a combination of interest theme areas and matches the client's unique interest profile with the careers that are the best fit.

SIGI-PLUS SIGI-PLUS (www.valparint.com/s11.htm) is a career exploration system that offers career guidance based on one's values. The program allows users to perform self-assessments, explore career options, learn about the education and training needed for chosen occupations, obtain practical advice and financial aid information, set career goals, and plan the next steps. The program also provides tips on writing a resume and applying for jobs.

DISCOVER The **DISCOVER** (www.act.org/discover) program offers assessments of career-relevant interests, abilities, and job values that assist the user in exploring occupations. It offers a guidance process that helps users identify their strengths and needs, make good career decisions, and build a plan based on the users' personal profiles. It offers current databases of occupations, college majors, schools and training institutions, financial aid/scholarships, and military options. Users can also learn how to develop good job-seeking skills related to effective resumes, cover letters, job applications, and interviewing skills.

ACTIVITY 12.20

Visit the career center on your campus and see if they have access to SIGI-PLUS and DISCOVER. Explore the use of these programs for your own career decision making so that you can work better with clients with career issues.

In addition to interests and career exploration systems, career counselors can use aptitude inventories, achievement inventories, values scales, and personality inventories to aid in career planning and decision making through increasing self-awareness.

Diversity Issues in Career Counseling

Similar to most traditional counseling theories, most career counseling theories were developed based on the behaviors of White, middle-class, able-bodied heterosexuals; there are numerous unwritten assumptions embedded in these career counseling theories. Although diversity issues such as culture, socioeconomic status, gender, age, and sexual identity are being discussed and analyzed in the career counseling literature, no general theory of multicultural career development has been developed (Osipow & Littlejohn, 1995). It is essential that professional counselors working with diverse populations infuse culturally sensitive practice when extrapolating from these career development theories.

REFLECTION 12.2

Review the career development theories discussed earlier. What aspects of the theories are relevant for diverse groups? What aspects are irrelevant? What additional issues do you think are important to consider when counseling members from a minority group?

REHABILITATION COUNSELING

Is rehabilitation counseling a specialty of counseling, or is it a separate profession requiring separate training? This question has been around as long as rehabilitation counseling and continues to be debated today. The parent organizations of the two professional rehabilitation counseling associations reflect this disparity. The American Rehabilitation Counseling Association (ARCA) is a division of the American Counseling Association, and the National Rehabilitation Counseling Association (NRCA) is a professional division of the National Rehabilitation Association. Give rehabilitation counseling some further thought by completing Reflection 12.3.

REFLECTION 12.3

How do you view rehabilitation counseling? After researching the websites of ARCA and NRCA, and other resources, do you consider rehabilitation counseling a specialty of counseling or a distinct profession? Provide arguments to support your view.

The current definitions of rehabilitation and rehabilitation counseling seem applicable regardless of whether you view rehabilitation counseling as a specialty within the counseling profession or as a distinct profession. **Rehabilitation** refers to "a comprehensive sequence of services, mutually planned by the consumer and rehabilitation counselor to maximize employability, independence, integration, and participation of people with disabilities in the workplace and/or the community" (Jenkins, Patterson, & Szymanski, 1998, p. 2). **Rehabilitation counseling** "is a systematic process which assists persons with physical, mental, developmental, cognitive, and emotional disabilities to achieve their personal, career, and independent living goals in the most integrated setting possible through the application of the counseling process" (Commission on Rehabilitation Counselor Certification, 2007, p. 1). **Rehabilitation counselors** "are committed to facilitating the personal, social, and economic independence of individuals with disabilities. In fulfilling this commitment, rehabilitation counselors work with people, programs, institutions, and service delivery systems" (Commission on Rehabilitation Counselor Certification, 2001, p. 1). **Disability** is defined as "an inability or limitation in performing socially defined tasks, activities, and roles to levels expected within physical and social environments as a result of internal or external factors and their interplay" (Maki & Riggar, 1997a, p. 8).

In addition to a shared definition, rehabilitation as a specialty and rehabilitation as a distinct profession share a common philosophy (Maki & Riggar, 1997a). The rehabilitation philosophy is integrated into the rehabilitation counseling *Scope of Practice,* which outlines the core assumptions of the statement and the underlying values of rehabilitation counseling. The underlying values include the following:

- Value of independence, integration, and inclusion of all people with disabilities in employment and in their communities
- Belief in the dignity and worth of all people
- Commitment to equal justice and advocacy work in the support of individuals with disabilities
- Emphasis on holistic practice
- Recognition of the assets of the person
- Commitment to a comprehensive service plan that includes the consumer and the rehabilitation counselor (see www.crccertification.com/downloads/35scope/scope_ of_practice_%200307I.pdf).

Summary of Rehabilitation Laws

Although the current definition of rehabilitation counseling is comprehensive and includes personal, career, and independent living goals, the early roots of rehabilitation counseling were based in the vocational area and were closely linked with the State-Federal Rehabilitation Program. The relationship between rehabilitation counseling and the State-Federal Rehabilitation Program is intertwined with legislation regarding financial support, education, and civil rights, and the treatment of people with disabilities. Rehabilitation counseling evolved primarily from legislation (Jenkins et al., 1998). Some of the major legislation that impacted the rehabilitation movement includes the following (Maki & Riggar, 1997b; Weed & Field, 2001):

- The *War Risk Insurance Act 1914* provided rehabilitation and vocational training to veterans who were injured during their military service.
- The *Smith-Hughes Act* of 1917 began the vocational rehabilitation movement by providing funding for vocational education.
- The *Smith-Fess Act 1920* provided counseling, training, prosthetic appliance, and job placement for individuals physically disabled from industrial injuries.
- The *Vocational Rehabilitation Program 1935* became a permanent part of the Social Security Act.

- The *Barden-LaFollette Act 1943* broadened the eligibility for disabilities to include individuals with mental illness and retardation, and expanded services for physical restoration.
- The *Vocational Rehabilitation Act* of 1954 (also known as the Hill-Burton Act), and subsequent amendments in 1965, 1967, 1968, and 1973 authorized services for the more severely disabled; extended eligibility status to include individuals who are disadvantaged by reason of age, education, ethnic or other factors; provided funds for graduate training and research; improved facilities at rehabilitation settings; and provided funding for new construction of rehabilitation facilities. It also provided annual evaluations of eligibility.
- The *Rehabilitation Act* of 1973 and 1974 emphasized services to individuals with more severe disabilities and involved the consumer in the rehabilitation process with the establishment of the individual written rehabilitation plan (IWRP).
- The *Education for all Handicapped Children's Act* of 1975 mandated that all states must provide education for all disabled children (ages 3–21) with the rule of least restrictive environment.
- The *Rehabilitation, Comprehensive Services, and Developmental Disabilities Act* of 1978 created the National Institute of Handicapped Research and the National Council on the Handicapped. It also provided for independent living services.
- The *Americans with Disabilities Act* of 1990 prohibited the discrimination against individuals with disabilities in employment, transportation, public accommodations, and activities at state and local governments.
- The *Individuals with Disabilities Education Act* of 1991 and 2004 was an extension of the 1975 *Education for all Handicapped Children's Act.* These acts extended services to include brain injury and autism and transitional services.
- The *Ticket to Work and Work Incentives Improvement Act* of 1999 provided health care and employment preparation and placement services for individuals with disabilities.

Now complete Activity 12.21.

ACTIVITY 12.21

Explore the various acts affecting the practice of rehabilitation counseling.

Disability Eligibility and Demographics

Since the early days of working primarily with the State-Federal Rehabilitation Programs and rehabilitation facilities and rehabilitation hospitals, the settings of rehabilitation counseling practice have expanded drastically to include public and private sectors. Rehabilitation counselors can be found in private rehabilitation and insurance companies, substance abuse agencies, employee assistance programs, schools, and college and university disability service offices. Additionally, disabilities have been expanded to include mental illness, brain injuries, substance abuse, and AIDS (Jenkins et al., 1998). Regardless of the disability (e.g., physical, mental, cognitive) and the setting (e.g., private or public sectors) for services, for individuals to receive services they must have an identifiable and diagnosed disability.

The eligibility for rehabilitation counseling services related to a disability varies depending on the funding source, residence of the client, and other factors. For an individual to be eligible for state-federal rehabilitation services, the individual must have a physical or mental impairment that is stable or slowly progressive, the impairment cannot be acute or of an emergency nature, and the impairment must be documented on file. In addition, the impairment must hinder the individual from employment, and the employability of the individual must benefit from rehabilitation services (Weed & Field, 2001).

The prevalence of disability in the United States is increasing. In 2006, the prevalence of disability ranged from 6.3% (or 2,809,000 individuals) for persons aged 5–15 years old and 52.6% (or 8,922,999 individuals) for persons 75 years old and older with a total prevalence rate of 15% (41,247,000 individuals) for all persons 5 years of age and older. In regard to gender, females 5 years old and older have a slightly higher prevalence rate (15.6%) of disabilities compared with males 5 years old and older (14.4%). There are also differences based on race. The prevalence rate for Whites is 12.7%; for Black/African Americans, 17.5%; for Asians, 6.3%; for Native Americans, 21.7%; and for persons of some other race, 11.9% (www.ilr.cornell.edu/edi/disabilitystatistics/StatusReports/2006-PDF/2006-StatusReport_US.pdf? CFID=3338844&CFTOKEN=25662977, n.d.).

Diversity Issues and Rehabilitation Counseling

As one can see from the previous statistics on the prevalence rate for disabilities, there is a difference based on race. It is expected that the number of disabilities will increase and that the increase will generally come from persons of color based on the prediction that U.S. demographics are shifting, with the current majority race (i.e., White) becoming the minority in the 21st century (Weed & Field, 2001). Given this shift in the demographics and the increasing number of disabilities within ethnic minority groups, rehabilitation counselors must increase their focus on multicultural issues and work toward becoming multiculturally competent. Persons of color who have a disability must be considered from both perspectives: as a person with a disability, and as pertaining to his or her culture. It is also important to acknowledge that people of color with a disability are members of two groups that have historically been marginalized, and that they are at risk for experiencing double discrimination.

Despite the added complexity of considering cultural background and the disability background, it is essential that professional counselors take into consideration both of these identities when providing services. Weed and Field (2001) provided a general outline as a starting point for working with minority clients with disabilities. They recommend self-assessment, which includes awareness of one's own cultural background especially in relation to one's biases regarding disability issues, and client assessment, which includes determination of the client's support system, evaluation of the client's acculturation level, and insight into the client's worldview.

Summary

In this chapter, four main client issues were discussed: drug and alcohol counseling issues, mental health counseling issues, career counseling issues, and rehabilitation counseling. The various treatment models (i.e., medical model, twelve-step model, and strengths-based treatment approaches) related to working with clients with substance abuse and dependency issues were described. The authors also presented special concerns related to substance abuse counseling with adolescents and minority clients.

With regard to mental health counseling, four commonly encountered mental health issues—depressive disorders, anxiety disorders, eating disorders, and post-traumatic stress disorder—were discussed. Additionally, the authors introduced the DSM-IV-TR, which provides descriptions and diagnostic criteria for all formally recognized mental disorders and can be a useful tool for professional counselors when making a diagnosis or forming a clinical impression.

It is also essential that professional counselors are prepared to address crisis situations adequately, including clients with suicidal and homicidal ideations. Professional counselors are advised to consult relevant legal and ethical codes regarding handling a client crisis. Descriptions of various treatment settings and criteria for identifying which type of setting may be most appropriate for clients at various levels of functioning were also presented.

The chapter provided definitions of key terms related to career counseling and an overview of the four major career counseling theories: trait and factor theory, psychodynamic career theory, developmental career theory, and social cognitive career theory. Major career counseling resources were also identified.

Finally, the chapter highlighted key issues in rehabilitation counseling, including the debate over whether rehabilitation counseling is a specialty area under the umbrella of counseling or is a distinct and separate profession. Disability was defined, and the work of rehabilitation counselors was described. Laws related to rehabilitation counseling were also summarized.

Although each of the four areas of counseling discussed in this chapter is distinct, with its own credentialing body, there is great overlap among the issues presented in each area. Clients are likely to enter counseling with any combination of the four issues discussed in this chapter, and professional counselors must be prepared to address the multiple and complex client issues they will encounter.

CHAPTER

13

Advocating for the Counseling Profession

AMY MILSOM

PREVIEW

Little has been written about the concept of professional advocacy in counseling. What does it mean to advocate for the counseling profession? Why is professional advocacy important? In what ways can professional counselors advocate for the profession? The concept of professional advocacy is explored throughout this chapter, and the answers to these questions will become clear.

DEFINING ADVOCACY

According to Gladding (2001), **advocacy** means "actively working for, supporting, or espousing a cause . . . counselors advocate for the welfare of their clients and the profession of counseling" (p. 5). Chi Sigma Iota (1998) suggested that "without advocacy for both counselors and their clients, neither is meaningful" (p. 2). Although both forms of advocacy are important, the focus of this chapter is advocating for professional counselors, or the profession of counseling. Chapter 14 focuses on counselors advocating on behalf of clients.

Synonyms of advocacy include words such as "encouragement," "justification," "promotion," and "recommendation" (*Roget's New Millennium Thesaurus, First Edition [v 1.3.1]*, 2006). By focusing on the synonyms, one can understand better what advocating for the profession might look like. For example, professional counselors might *encourage* someone to seek counseling as opposed to psychotherapy, or they might provide *justification* for various organizations to hire or retain counselors. Additionally, professional counselors could *promote* their services or *recommend* that legislators earmark funding for the training of professional counselors.

A simplistic way of thinking about advocating for the counseling profession is to consider a main emphasis on increasing public awareness. The information that professional counselors want people to be more aware of and the outcomes of their public awareness efforts would be unique. Consider the first two examples presented in the preceding paragraph. By sharing information about the potential benefits of counseling, professional counselors

321

might be able to convince someone to seek counseling services for the first time. Additionally, information shared by a group of professional counselors with their employer regarding the increase in profits generated by clients during the past year might serve as justification for the employer to support each of the staff counselor positions for at least one more year.

BRIEF HISTORY OF COUNSELORS ADVOCATING FOR THE PROFESSION

Professional advocacy can be an individual endeavor or a group effort. Many professional counseling organizations have engaged in formal advocacy efforts at the local, state, and national level. Myers, Sweeney, and White (2002) provided a comprehensive summary of how counselors came to advocate for themselves and their clients, and identified the mid-1900s as the origin of those efforts. That time period marked the emergence of counseling specialty areas and the evolution of professional counseling organizations at the national level. By formally joining together, counselors could promote their specialized skills and knowledge to the public and identify how they differed from other related professionals. Counseling organizations were also able to increase the public's awareness of different types of counselors and to recommend that the government recognize the importance of their efforts. Counselors advocated for the profession by lobbying for federal legislation to provide funding to support the training of school counselors in the 1960s and rehabilitation counselors in the 1970s.

Myers et al. (2002) also identified the establishment of state counselor licensure boards and national accrediting associations (e.g., CACREP, CORE) in the 1970s and 1980s as examples of counselor efforts to advocate for the profession. By creating and maintaining strict standards for training and practice, the counseling profession communicates to the public that entry into the profession is a rigorous process. Counselors continue to advocate for themselves in various ways, as exemplified throughout this chapter.

WHY ADVOCATE?

Understanding what advocacy means is essential. With an awareness of why advocacy is important, however, professional counselors can be purposeful in their efforts. Simply put, Eriksen (1999a) stated that "advocacy efforts are critical to the future of the counseling profession. Only through persistent advocacy have counselors become respected professionals, able to practice without too many constraints what they are trained to do" (p. 33). In essence, professional counselors are encouraged to advocate to retain their unique status among helping professionals and to engage in activities deemed important by the profession.

Although the focus of this chapter is advocating for the counseling profession, clients often indirectly benefit from counselors' professional advocacy efforts. Counselors might advocate for themselves because they know that doing so also benefits the general public. By continually advocating for federal funding to train counselors, rehabilitation counselors have consistently been able to produce graduates. Clients benefit by having access to rehabilitation counseling services. By increasing awareness of their background and the services they can provide, counselors provide information that helps the general public make informed decisions about who might best meet their needs. Finally, by promoting themselves through the development of standards and credentials that encourage self-reflection and regulation, counselors ensure that clients receive services from qualified professionals.

Aside from a general interest in increasing awareness about the counseling profession, professional counselors might have very specific agendas driving their advocacy efforts.

Personal experiences related to things such as job cuts, professional roles, or training standards often spark counselors' desires to take action via advocacy. Activity 13.1 helps you to explore why counselors in your area advocate for themselves and the counseling profession.

ACTIVITY 13.1

What prompts professional counselors in your local area or state to engage in professional advocacy efforts? Interview some professional counselors, counselor educators, or leaders of counseling organizations in your area and ask them to share a time when they felt it necessary to advocate for the counseling profession.
- Ask them to explain what prompted them to engage in advocacy activities, and what advocacy activities they engaged in.
- Inquire about how their advocacy efforts paid off.
- Compare the information you gathered with that of other classmates, and discuss commonalities and differences.
- What main themes arise in their stories?

To examine other reasons professional counselors might engage in professional advocacy efforts, consider the following hypothetical case examples, and respond to the questions that follow. These case studies are intended to help you to understand some of the current issues different types of counselors are facing, and why advocating for themselves and the profession is crucial. The questions that follow in Activity 13.2 encourage you to consider how others view the role of counselors, and to brainstorm specific ways the counselors might respond to their situations.

CASE STUDY 13.1   HIRING PARAPROFESSIONAL COUNSELORS

Since graduating with your master's degree in counseling 10 years ago, you have worked at a mental health counseling agency where your daily responsibilities include providing individual and group counseling, providing case management services, leading community-based workshops, and, recently, supervising junior staff members. You enjoy opportunities to provide direct services to clients the most. Over time, you have seen the staff in your agency increase in size from three to eight based on the growing needs in your community. Your state recently passed legislation permitting the hiring of bachelor's-level counseling paraprofessionals whose responsibilities can include counseling and case management. These individuals cannot provide diagnoses or bill for their services, and their work must be supervised at all times. Because these individuals can be hired at a cheaper rate than master's-level counselors, your agency has decided to downsize the number of full-time professional counselors and replace them with these paraprofessionals. The organization decided they would retain four licensed professional counselors whose main responsibilities would be to provide diagnoses, develop treatment plans, co-lead groups, and supervise the paraprofessionals. Your job is not at stake because you have more experience than most of the other professional counselors; however, you are not sure that you want to continue working at this agency given these changes.

CASE STUDY 13.2   SOCIAL WORKERS REPLACING PROFESSIONAL SCHOOL COUNSELORS

You have worked as an elementary school counselor in a school in your hometown for the past 4 years. You were thrilled to be able to find employment near your family and have enjoyed working with the students, even though your caseload of 400 is way too large. You have a pretty good relationship with your principal. He has allowed you to initiate a rotating schedule of small group interventions and cut back on classroom guidance. Parents and teachers have been very appreciative of your efforts. Nevertheless, the large school district in which you work has decided to eliminate elementary school counselors. They have prioritized a greater emphasis on school-family collaborations, and have decided to hire school social workers because they believe them to be better qualified to coordinate those types of collaborative efforts. You have no interest in, and you do not feel qualified to work in, a middle or high school, and the closest school district that still hires elementary school counselors is an hour drive from your home. Someone suggests that you should pursue the school social work degree.

CASE STUDY 13.3   LICENSED COUNSELOR VERSUS LICENSED PSYCHOLOGIST

Your degree in college counseling has served you well in your position in the office of student support services on a college campus for 20 years. Your main responsibilities have been to provide services to students with disabilities and to students in need of general academic support. You are currently serving in a search committee whose charge is to review applications for a new clinical staff member position at the campus counseling center. This center currently functions as the only option for students needing campus-based counseling services. It historically has been staffed by clinical and counseling psychologists and student interns from those programs. You feel strongly that having a counselor in staff would be important. Additionally, given the existing counselor education program on campus, the addition of a licensed professional counselor could open up possibilities of using that site for counseling student internships. Your efforts are futile, however, and they end up hiring another counseling psychologist.

ACTIVITY 13.2

The three scenarios just described have important implications for clients that are worth exploring (and when you read the next chapter you might want to revisit these scenarios), but for now consider the counseling profession as a whole. For each situation described, ask yourself the following questions:

- Based on their unique experiences, what specific goals might these professional counselors have regarding advocating for the profession?
- What are the potential implications of these hiring decisions on the counseling profession as a whole?

- How are the roles of existing professional counselors in these organizations affected by the hiring decisions?
- What factors do you think led the decision makers in the scenarios (i.e., head of agency or school administrators) to replace or simply not hire professional counselors?
- What, if anything, could the professional counselors have done proactively to prevent the outcomes described in the scenarios?
- What types of information do you think would have been beneficial for the decision makers to know regarding professional counselors that might have led them to different outcomes?
- What, if anything, could the professional counselors in the situations described do *now* to advocate for the counseling profession?

The above-described cases are reflective of situations that occur throughout the United States. Counselors, psychologists, social workers—aren't they all the same? You already have read about the history of the counseling profession, and by now have a basic awareness of issues related to training and licensure. You probably understand more than you did before starting your graduate program that how professional counselors differ from other mental health professionals. To the general public, however, these differences are not so clear. Often, members of the general public are responsible for decisions, such as those in the above-described cases, which affect the counseling profession.

Without knowledge related to differences in training requirements, scope of practice, and credentials among mental health professionals, employers might assume that one professional could be easily replaced with another. Without an appreciation of the unique contributions that professional counselors can offer, employers might underuse them. In talking with professional counselors, you might hear them complain about having to engage in **administrative tasks**, such as coordinating client files, which could easily be completed by office personnel. You might also hear them express frustration related to the agencies that employ them contracting out to other mental health professionals for services that the professional counselors themselves would be qualified to perform. Although numerous factors might cause employers to use professional counselors in those ways, it is likely that an employer's misunderstanding of professional counselors' skills and abilities could be a contributing factor in their decisions regarding counselor roles and responsibilities.

Chi Sigma Iota (1998) suggested that a **proactive** approach to advocacy might serve the counseling profession well:

> Every occupational group must be proactive in the marketplace or they will become extinct over time. Counselors must not only believe in their profession's preparation standards, graduate programs, credentialing requirements, and scope of services, but they must educate, inform, and promote them to legislators, employers, third party payers, and the public at large. (p. 1)

Proactive advocacy may not prevent people or policymakers from questioning various aspects of the counseling profession. Nevertheless, as with the benefits of any type of preventive strategy, proactive advocacy efforts might help to decrease the frequency or delay the onset of concerns from various stakeholders. Consider the suggestion by Crouch and Walz (1992) that advocacy efforts should focus on showing and explaining what professional counselors do, what roles are appropriate for them based on their training, and what the potential benefits are of hiring them.

Gerber and Myers (1997) and Gilchrist and Stringer (1992) discussed the importance of advocates being able to communicate to stakeholders what works, consistent with the current expectation that professional counselors provide data to show their effectiveness. Essentially, questions such as "What do professional counselors do?", "What makes professional counselors different from other mental health professionals?", "Why should I seek counseling?", and "What are the benefits of counseling?" can serve as guides for the type of information that could be shared proactively in their efforts to advocate for the profession. Complete Activity 13.3 to demonstrate your ability to plan, implement, and evaluate a proactive effort to advocate for the counseling profession.

ACTIVITY 13.3

Revisit the questions in Activity 13.2. Generate a list of things you could do to advocate proactively for the counseling profession. After answering the following questions, choose one of your ideas and implement it.
- Who would be your target audience?
- What would you want them to know about counseling?
- How would you assess the effectiveness of your efforts?

CURRENT COUNSELING ADVOCACY AGENDAS

The present goal of the American Counseling Association (ACA) (2006c) regarding professional advocacy is to "increase support for professional counselors and their clients in all appropriate Federal and State laws, regulations, and legislation" (p. 1). Many of their efforts have strong implications for clients, and these issues are discussed in the next chapter. Among the foci of the ACA's efforts to advocate for the counseling profession in general are the recognition of professional counselors being highly qualified to provide mental health services, recognition of the unique training and supervision needs of professional counselors, and recognition of the importance of counseling services. Following is an overview of just a few of the ACA's current advocacy agendas, with an emphasis on implications for the counseling profession.

One of the main agendas of the ACA is to have state and federal governments recognize licensed professional counselors as qualified to provide mental health services. This agenda plays out in relation to the ability of mental health counselors to be included in the list of providers that insurance companies reimburse for services. In 2006, the ACA encouraged members to contact their legislators with the message to "include licensed mental health counselors and marriage and family therapists among the list of providers who can deliver services to Medicare beneficiaries, provided they are legally authorized to perform those services under their state's licensure law" (American Counseling Association, 2006e, p. 1). Recognition that licensed professional counselors are not lesser qualified mental health professionals is an important message inherent in these advocacy efforts. These efforts paid off in 2007 when professional counselors were included as Medicare providers.

Another ACA advocacy agenda addresses a lack of appreciation for the specialized training and supervision needs of professional counselors. In the past, the Department of

Defense's TRICARE Health Services Program forced military personnel to obtain a referral from their physician before they could receive mental health counseling services from a licensed professional counselor (American Counseling Association, 2006a). The program also stipulated that the referring physician must supervise the mental health treatment. Among other concerns, the implied message that a physician is qualified to supervise a professional counselor reflects a lack of information or awareness about counseling as a specialized profession. As a result of this advocacy initiative, professional counselors can now provide services to TRICARE recipients without supervision.

One example of how the ACA (2006d) is advocating to support the growth of the counseling profession is through their focus on the reauthorization of the *Higher Education Act*. Currently, the U.S. House and Senate are in disagreement about whether or not individuals pursuing training in mental health, school, or child and adolescent counseling should be eligible for limited student loan forgiveness. Why is this relevant? Financial concerns might prohibit many individuals from pursuing training in these areas, but the potential for loan forgiveness might make the pursuit of these professions more realistic. By directly influencing the cost of pursuing graduate education, the government can greatly affect the growth and development of the counseling profession.

Finally, the ACA (2006b) consistently has focused on helping to secure funding for school-based professional counselors, based on a concern about potential decreases in funding for the *Elementary and Secondary School Counseling Program Act*. This program provides grant funding for schools to hire professional school counselors and other school-based mental health professionals. In the past, the ACA and other organizations have experienced success in their efforts to prevent elimination of this funding from year to year. Aside from the potential impact of these advocacy efforts on students, acknowledgment of the importance of counseling for school-age students is an important message underlying advocacy efforts in this area.

At any given time, counseling organizations are engaged in a variety of advocacy efforts. The issues discussed previously are only a few of the many agendas being addressed by the ACA when this book was published. In addition, ACA divisions and other counseling organizations engage in various activities to advocate for the profession. Advocacy agendas change as societal issues change, and you are encouraged to explore the types of issues to which the ACA and other counseling organizations currently are dedicating time and resources for advocacy. Activity 13.4 helps you to explore the current advocacy initiatives of various professional counseling organizations.

ACTIVITY 13.4

Search the websites of organizations such as the ACA (www.counseling.org), ACA divisions, Chi Sigma Iota (www.csi-net.org), or the National Board for Certified Counselors (www.nbcc.org).
- What information did you find regarding the advocacy efforts supported or initiated by the counseling organizations?
- What types of long-term advocacy efforts are they engaged in?
- What opportunities and resources do they provide for members who are interested in becoming involved in professional advocacy?
- Who are the individuals recognized for their advocacy efforts?

PREREQUISITES TO EFFECTIVE ADVOCACY

What is required to become an effective advocate for the counseling profession? First, Eriksen (1999a) argued that specific skills are important, and that **advocacy skills** are not that different from counseling skills. She specifically identified basic counseling skills and data-gathering skills as crucial to effective advocacy. Listening and questioning skills are important for understanding concerns expressed by various stakeholders, as are skills in clarifying and summarizing. Oral and written communication skills are valuable for disseminating information accurately, concisely, and clearly. To assess the needs of the counseling profession, data-gathering skills, such as knowing how to conduct needs assessments and how to gather and summarize descriptive information, are crucial.

Eriksen (1999a) also indicated that possessing a clear **professional identity** is necessary before engaging in advocacy efforts for the profession. Similarly, Myers and Sweeney (2004) suggested that professional advocacy efforts require coordinated efforts among counseling organizations. Lack of consistency or coordination within or among various professional counseling organizations can result in unclear messages being sent to the public. In many ways, sharing inconsistent information can potentially be more detrimental to the counseling profession than sharing no information at all. The case in Activity 13.5 helps you to think more clearly about the potential effect of counselors presenting inconsistent identities.

ACTIVITY 13.5

Think back to the case example of social workers replacing the elementary school counselors (Case 2). Suppose lawmakers in your state are trying to determine whether to replace all elementary school counseling positions in the state with social workers, or to redefine the role of elementary school counselors. The state school counseling organization is lobbying to retain elementary school counselors with an emphasis on those individuals mainly providing preventive and responsive services (e.g., direct contact via individual, group, and classroom interventions). A small subset of elementary school counselors whose job responsibilities for the past 5 years have involved teaching classroom guidance lessons, assisting with the design and monitoring of behavioral modification plans, and coordinating testing services are not interested in leading groups or providing individual counseling. They believe the classroom-based services and coordination services not only are important, but also allow them to address the needs of all students. This group of professional school counselors presents a different agenda to legislators.

- If you were these legislators, what would you do with the different information shared by these constituents? How would their perspectives inform your decision?
- Would you favor one group's perspectives over another? If so, which one and why?
- Would your decision be easier if the groups had the same agenda?
- What types of messages would you leave with regarding how elementary school counselors view their roles?

Differing agendas have plagued the counseling profession for years, and because professional counselors are unique individuals, there are bound to be differences in their thoughts and actions. Regarding advocating for the profession, counselors must realize that sometimes it is important to put the needs of the profession as a whole before their own needs. Legislators and other important stakeholders may have a hard time taking a profession seriously if, as a group, they cannot agree on the messages they are sending.

Eriksen (1999a) indicated that conflicts within professional counseling organizations often are major barriers to their professional advocacy efforts. Current threats to a consistent professional identity among counselors include (1) professional counselors identifying first by their specialty areas rather than as professional counselors who work in different settings (e.g., couples and family counselor versus a professional counselor who works with couples and families); (2) professional counselors identifying with other complementary professions before identifying as a counselor (e.g., student affairs counselors overlapping with higher education personnel, or professional school counselors describing themselves as educators); (3) counseling divisions becoming organizations functioning independently from the ACA; (4) inconsistent counselor licensure requirements from state to state; (5) inconsistent training requirements (i.e., counselor education programs do not have to be accredited); and (6) counselor education training programs hiring psychologists or other professionals to teach counseling courses. Complete Activity 13.6 to explore the professional identities of counselors in your local area.

ACTIVITY 13.6

With your classmates, identify professional counselors in your area who represent a variety of specialty areas. Try to interview a few from each area. Consider the issues numbered 1 through 4 in the preceding paragraph as you interview them:
- How do these individuals describe their professional identity?
- What consistencies are there in their descriptions?
- What differences are there in their descriptions?
- If they were to speak as a whole on behalf of the counseling profession, what consistent message could be shared?

A final prerequisite for effective advocacy involves resources. The amount of money and time required varies depending on the types of advocacy activities a professional counselor plans to engage in (Myers & Sweeney, 2004). Even when their desire to advocate is strong, and motivation is high, inadequate financial resources and time constraints might prevent some professional counselors from engaging in advocacy efforts or restrict the scope of their efforts. Professional counselors must be creative in finding inexpensive and efficient ways to advocate for the profession (examples of these are provided later in this chapter), or they must be prepared to exert time and energy securing enough resources in the form of personnel or money to ensure their efforts do not have to be halted partway through. Use Activity 13.7 to discuss other important characteristics that would help someone be an effective advocate.

PROCESS OF ADVOCACY

According to Eriksen (1997), advocating for the profession requires counselors to progress through numerous steps: (1) identify the problem, (2) assess the availability of resources, (3) engage in **strategic planning** activities, (4) train professional counselors to advocate, (5) implement a plan of action, and (6) celebrate accomplishments.

Identify the Problem

A crucial first step in advocacy involves deciding when something is worth advocating for. The last thing counselors want is to be perceived as taking issue with everything that does not exactly work for them or for their clients. The phrase, "choose your battles wisely," comes to mind. Quoting one of the participants in her study, Eriksen (1997) stated "'I think that may be the most challenging part of advocacy is . . . coming to some agreement among ourselves' as to what problems should receive priority attention" (p. 23). Eriksen suggested that problems deemed as having greater threat tend to receive priority, as do problems whose solutions seem feasible. Prioritizing concerns might be simple for individual professional counselors. For groups, however, consensus on which problems are more significant might be more difficult to obtain.

Even when problems are identified, Eriksen (1997) suggested that "problem definition involves using language to frame the problem so that decision-makers and the wider public will be motivated to take action" (p. 23). In other words, professional counselors who are unable to explain their concerns to important **stakeholders** in terms or outcomes that will be meaningful to those individuals are likely to be unsuccessful in securing public or legislative support for their efforts. Activity 13.8 helps you to understand what factors might motivate a counselor to feel strongly about advocating for the counseling profession.

- How much of a concern, on a scale of 1 (low) to 10 (high), are the issues?
- Based on the ratings, which of the concerns does the professional counselor believe warrants action?
- What would happen if the concern is not addressed?
- How motivated is the professional counselor to take action?

Assess the Availability of Resources

As mentioned previously, availability of time and money are important considerations in developing advocacy plans. Factors such as personnel, expertise, motivation, and outside support must also be considered before advocacy plans are finalized. Groups who want to effect change in legislation would need the involvement of someone who possesses knowledge of the legislative system, including timing of advocacy efforts and effective methods and procedures (e.g., letter writing campaigns versus lobbying in person) for contacting legislators. When they are unable to find colleagues who possess that knowledge or hire consultants with that type of expertise, professional counselors might need to consider other ways of advocating for the profession. Additionally, assessing their level of motivation and passion regarding the concerns for which they want to advocate may help professional counselors to determine the time frames for which they are likely to maintain interest and active involvement. Advocacy activities can be designed to fit within reasonable and realistic time frames.

Level of outside support is another key resource area to assess. Outside support might include individuals outside the counseling profession who would support professional counselors' efforts and individuals in key positions who could help professional counselors to access important stakeholders. Professional counselors might enlist support from former clients, from agencies with whom they have partnerships, or from local organizations that benefit from their work. Depending on their advocacy agenda, professional counselors might also target influential community members who might be able to help them communicate their agenda to local government officials or funding agencies or connect them to local media sources. In any event, by determining the amount and type of outside support they have, professional counselors can plan advocacy activities accordingly. Complete Activity 13.9 to explore further the resources that might be available in your community.

ACTIVITY 13.9

Think about possible sources of outside support you may be able to enlist in your community to help your advocacy efforts. Consider the following:
- Which individuals or groups outside the counseling profession might be willing to be involved in this effort?
- How would you decide which outside individuals would be the most influential in advocating for the profession?
- Consider some ways you may contact community support figures or local media sources.

Engage in Strategic Planning Activities

This next step essentially focuses on professional counselors developing ideas for addressing their concerns by designing advocacy plans. Eriksen (1999a) indicated that individual advocacy efforts can be implemented more easily than group efforts. For groups of professional counselors involved in advocating for the profession, Eriksen suggested they use a planning process that involves the creation of a small, representative group of professional counselors. This small planning group would taken on the responsibility for developing long-term plans and short-term goals that reflect the larger group's concerns. The planning group would also develop a list of the activities in which the larger group would engage and allow any materials, documentation, and information to be disseminated to stakeholders. To ensure that all group members are thinking about the issue in the same way, the following questions can be helpful to review during this step:

- What is our main concern?
- Who is our target audience?
- What do we want that audience to know?
- What is a realistic time frame for addressing our concerns?
- How can we best go about addressing our concerns?

Activity 13.10 asks you to consider how decisions might be made concerning the development of a core planning group and the types of decisions for which the group should be responsible.

ACTIVITY 13.10

Think about a group in the Organization to which you belong. Suppose this group decides to generate an advocacy plan designed ultimately to increase membership in the organization. Discuss the following:
- How would your organization determine which individuals should participate in the small, core planning group?
- Would you, as a member, want to have a say in who is chosen for that planning group?
- What types of characteristics do you believe members of the planning group should possess?
- How would you feel if you were not invited to serve as a planning group member?
- What kinds of decisions would this group be responsible for making?

Train Professional Counselors to Advocate

If groups are to advocate effectively, they must have involvement from more than one individual who possesses knowledge and skills to do so. Particularly regarding advocacy efforts that target legislators and other policymakers, the importance of educating your colleagues cannot be dismissed. Eriksen (1999a) believed that training members of an organization for advocacy would help to motivate those members to become involved. Doing so could also result in the group having increased resources in the form of more qualified personnel to carry out advocacy tasks. Eriksen suggested that training should occur in the form of workshops or conferences, and many professional counseling organizations hold sessions related to advocacy. The advocacy knowledge needs of professional counselors before participating in training might include how to approach legislators, kinds of information to share, or what not to do. Skills related to things such as assertiveness, public speaking, and communicating effectively in writing could also be addressed via various training opportunities. Use Activity 13.11 to assess your own readiness to engage in professional advocacy efforts.

ACTIVITY 13.11

Assess your own readiness to engage in professional advocacy activities:
- How confident do you feel in your ability to speak effectively and clearly in public?
- Are you aware of how to express your concerns to legislators?
- Can you identify local counseling organizations that might be willing to partner with you in your efforts?
- Are you able to identify effective formats for sharing information?

Implement a Plan of Action

Implementing an advocacy plan might seem a straightforward step. Nevertheless, many factors are crucial to the success of that implementation. First, a clear, organized strategic plan sets the stage for successful plan implementation. Likewise, ensuring that group members are aware of and competent to perform their assigned tasks is crucial to the success of the group's advocacy efforts. Monitoring the implementation process and assessing any concerns or needs along the way allow professional counselors to make modifications as needed. The core planning team might need to reconvene to revise plans, provide training for other members, or reallocate their resources. In many instances, the time frame for implementing the advocacy plan might limit opportunities to implement modifications.

As all good professional counselors learn, assessing the effectiveness of one's efforts is necessary to inform future actions. Assessment is an important component of this implementation step. Professional counselors engaged in professional advocacy efforts can use short-term goals as ways to engage in ongoing assessment, or, depending on their time frames, they might simply assess final outcomes. Having clear, measurable goals in mind from the start should make assessing those goals manageable. Practice developing potential outcome measures by completing Activity 13.12. Then use Activity 13.13 to discuss further how you might collect outcome data from those measures.

ACTIVITY 13.12

Consider the following **advocacy goals**, and develop outcome measures that could be used to assess whether or not your advocacy efforts were successful:
1. Community members will know how to access counseling services through your agency.

(Continued)

---

2. Administrators will recognize how your efforts affected students academically.
3. Legislators will possess a clear understanding of the unique training that professional counselors receive.

ACTIVITY 13.13

Determine one way to collect outcome data from Activity 13.12 from stakeholders to meet your advocacy goals.

Celebrate Accomplishments

A final step in advocacy is to celebrate. Professional counselors know that it is important to celebrate the little things. It is also important to celebrate the big things. Not only is taking time to reflect on the amount of time and effort shared by the individuals involved important, but also communicating successes to others can be helpful toward future advocacy efforts. Eriksen (1999a) suggested that professional counselors consider documenting and disseminating information about their successes via newsletters or press releases. She also recommended thanking important stakeholders as a way to increase potential support from them over time.

WAYS TO ADVOCATE

By now you should understand why advocacy is important, and you probably have some understanding of how to begin the process of advocating for the profession. Examples of activities that could be used as part of advocacy efforts should help to complete the picture. There are an unlimited number of ways that professional counselors can advocate for the profession. The ACA (2005b) and other counseling organizations have developed resource guides that can be helpful to members during the strategic planning step. The questions mentioned earlier in this chapter regarding who professional counselors are, what professional counselors do, and how professional counselors can make a difference, can be addressed through these advocacy activities. The general goal of advocacy is to share information and increase **public awareness**, with potential outcomes of those efforts ranging from changing public policy, to securing funding to keep a job, to increasing the number of clients who seek counseling services. The following ideas represent only some of the ways that professional counselors can advocate for the profession.

Identifying Yourself as a Professional Counselor

One simple way to advocate for the profession is for professional counselors to identify themselves as professional counselors in any chance they can (American Counseling Association, 2005b; Eriksen, 1999a). This can be as simple as listing **credentials** on letterhead and publications, mentioning involvement in professional counseling organizations, or displaying a counseling license prominently in the office. Some people feel uncomfortable listing numerous professional credentials next to their names, indicating that doing so feels pretentious. Others express a desire to be cautious about alienating clients who might be intimidated by someone whom they perceive to be very well educated. Explore how you and other people react to counselor credentials by completing Activities 13.14 and 13.15.

ACTIVITY 13.14

Test this concern. Obtain some business cards from professional counselors in your area, and ask some of your friends and family members to share their reaction to the information on those cards. Try to find a range of professional counselors—some who list many credentials and others who list only one.
- How often did your friends and family members comment on the credentials?
- Were their reactions more positive or negative?

ACTIVITY 13.15

Think back to a time when you became familiar with a professional's credentials (e.g., a professor, a mental health professional, a physician of any kind). How did you react to this information? Did it change your perception of that professional, or influence your decision to work with or see this professional?

Eriksen (1999a) discussed the importance of taking opportunities to clarify the uniqueness of the counseling profession, particularly when professional counselors are mistakenly referred to as other helping professionals. One might argue that it is simply a matter of semantics to the general public—that by referring to professional counselors as psychologists they mean no harm. It seems likely that most people simply have not differentiated among the professions. This is important to keep in mind, and professional counselors must be careful not to appear defensive about the counseling profession in their efforts to educate the public.

Serve Your Community

Professional counselors can clarify their professional identities not only through displaying their credentials, but also through engaging in activities as a group. The ACA (2005b) suggested that professional counselors consider working as a group to provide services in their local communities. They could host blood drives, gather supplies for local charitable organizations, or find other creative ways to support or raise money for a local cause. An important aspect of these efforts is to publicize the events. Some professional counselors feel uncomfortable doing this because they want their efforts to be viewed as altruistic rather than self-serving. By publicizing their efforts, however, professional counselors can potentially increase awareness about their roles and services. Individuals with whom they interact during the events could be engaged in brief discussion about the counseling services available in the community. However, public knowledge of the event might also increase awareness of the community's needs, and professional counselors can be very intentional about taking opportunities to balance their efforts to advocate for themselves with opportunities to advocate for others, a concept that is addressed in more detail in the next chapter.

Another way that professional counselors can become involved in their communities, securing local support for the services, is to provide professional services outside their typical day-to-day work. Professional counselors might consider the benefits of donating their time to lead an informational workshop through the local library or speak to parents at a PTA meeting (Gilchrist & Stringer, 1992). Topics could include coping with elderly parents, enhancing relationships, and becoming more assertive. Through direct contact with professional counselors, various stakeholders might gain a better understanding of the profession and the importance of the profession.

Similarly, the ACA (2005b) suggested that professional counselors consider participating in the various National Screening Day initiatives related to depression, eating disorders, alcohol, or anxiety disorders. The purpose of these initiatives is to educate the general public about issues, to conduct screenings, and to help people identify places where they can receive help. Through involvement in these events, professional counselors can demonstrate their expertise and explain their services. Complete Activity 13.16 to examine the ways counselors in your local area have been involved in the community. Then complete Activity 13.17 to consider your expertise and ways that you might become involved.

ACTIVITY 13.16

Peruse the local newspaper and bulletin boards throughout this semester.
- With what types of community organizations have local professional counselors been involved?
- How have they, individually or in groups, given back to the community?
- What types of free, public workshops have they offered?
- How effective were their efforts in terms of advocating for the profession?

ACTIVITY 13.17

Identify ways that you can provide a service to your local school or community and also advocate for the counseling profession.
- What types of services do you think are needed?
- How difficult would they be to organize?
- What types of resources would you need?

Choose one of your ideas and implement it.

Use the Media

Disseminating information for advocacy can be done through a variety of media. The ACA (2005b) suggested that professional counselors develop a **media kit** that could be designed specifically to address either a specific issue on which professional counselors are focusing or counseling services specific to one's workplace or area of expertise. They recommended that professional counselors develop and include items such as brochures, flyers, fact sheets, press releases, photographs, summaries of recent events, role statements, frequently asked questions, and biographical information. Professional counselors can be very creative with the formats in which they share information.

The ACA (2005b) suggested that with a media kit in place, professional counselors would be prepared to respond to spur of the moment questions, and they would have comprehensive information available in various formats to accommodate their needs at any given time. Information in a media kit should be updated regularly; for professional counselors working in agencies, perhaps someone could assume the responsibility for compiling information on a regular basis to update the kit. Additionally, professional counselors might consider having information available in formats designed for different target audiences (e.g., information brochures designed for potential clients would look different from ones designed for local policymakers or funding agencies).

Newspapers, radio, and television also serve as useful outlets for professional counseling advocacy efforts. The ACA (2005b) provided examples of press releases and radio spots that professional counselors could use to disseminate information about the profession. Via newspapers, professional counselors can submit letters to the editor in which they attempt to educate the public about important public policy issues affecting professional counselors, advertise their services or special events, or thank the public for their support. Radio spots played during special events could help professional counselors promote awareness of the profession and their services. The ACA suggested that Counseling Awareness Month is a good time to flood the market with messages about the counseling profession. Complete Activity 13.18 and discuss the types of public relations activities that would best fit different situations.

ACTIVITY 13.18

List as many media as you can for disseminating information.
- Discuss the types and amounts of resources (e.g., money, time, personnel) that would be needed for each.
- Which would you recommend for individuals who have small budgets?
- Which would you recommend for individuals who have limited time?

Finally, not much has been written about the use of websites for advocacy, but with more and more people using the Internet, Web-based advocacy efforts seem very timely. In addition to developing and maintaining a website containing information related to services specific to the agencies in which they work, professional counselors should consider the benefits of using their websites to disseminate information about the counseling profession in general. They might provide links to various counseling organizations, display their credentials, and summarize outcome data to show potential benefits. There is no limit to the ways in which professional counselors could use technology to advocate for the profession. Practice your website development skills by completing Activity 13.19.

ACTIVITY 13.19

Design a website either for your counseling program or for a local counseling agency.
- What types of information do you want to share via the website?
- Who is your target audience?
- How will you promote the website?

Target Policymakers

One final way to advocate for the counseling profession is to communicate with **policymakers** at the local, state, and national level. The idea of participating in lobbying efforts was discussed previously, and many counseling organizations offer opportunities for interested members to talk as a group with legislators at state or national levels. Additionally, the ACA provides information on their website regarding current legislation affecting the counseling profession. They also provide sample letters that can be sent by individuals to legislators to express concerns and recommend public policy changes. A more comprehensive perspective on impacting policy is provided by Eriksen (1997) in her book *Making an Impact: A Handbook for Counselor Advocacy*. Eriksen walks professional counselors through various ways to effect change on a systemic level through legislation or the courts. Use Activity 13.20 to plan your own advocacy efforts aimed at policymakers.

ACTIVITY 13.20

Develop an advocacy plan to be implemented during Counseling Awareness Month. Use the steps described previously to identify a goal, target audience, and resources, and to develop and implement your plan.

Summary

Advocating for the counseling profession requires that professional counselors possess knowledge and understanding of what it means to advocate, why advocacy is important, steps involved in advocacy, and ways to advocate. These issues were addressed in this chapter on a very basic level,

and references were made to resources that could be useful in your future advocacy efforts.

Examining the advocacy activities of professional counseling organizations is a good starting point. Professional counselors can seek guidance from professional organizations such as the

American Counseling Association regarding types of issues to focus on and ways to approach advocacy. By examining what types of advocacy efforts have been effective for others, professional counselors can potentially save time and money, and be more effective in their efforts.

To advocate effectively for the profession, professional counselors can expect to engage in many steps. Before developing plans to advocate for the profession, professional counselors must determine what issues are worth advocating for. When they have a specific agenda in mind, if working as a group, they must generate a clear message that they can consistently communicate. Next, after determining the availability of resources, professional counselors can work together to develop and implement their advocacy plan. They should assess the plan's effectiveness along the way if possible, and upon completion at a minimum. Finally, professional counselors are encouraged to share their advocacy successes with others, and particularly with the public.

There are myriad ways to advocate for the profession, and professional counselors are limited only by their own lack of knowledge and the resources available to them. Common methods for advocating include sharing credentials, talking about the counseling profession, and being present in the community. Professional counselors can also use various types of media, including print, broadcast, and Internet. Finally, professional counselors might take political action by interacting with policymakers.

With some knowledge of the advocacy process, a desire to fight for their profession, and minimal resources, professional counselors can potentially make a great impact on the future of the counseling profession. Professional counselors are encouraged to make connections with and gather resources from their local and state counseling organizations. From that point, there are a wide variety of resources available to help guide professional counselors in their individual advocacy efforts.

CHAPTER

14

Advocacy Counseling: Being an Effective Agent of Change for Clients

DONNA M. GIBSON

PREVIEW

Addressing external barriers that interfere with human development is the core purpose of advocacy. Although this purpose can be met by advocating for the profession of counseling, it is often met by advocating at the individual client level. Through an examination of the advocacy competency domains (American Counseling Association, 2006f), specific guidelines are provided on how to increase clients' empowerment and to be a successful advocacy counselor.

ADVOCACY COUNSELING

Advocacy in counseling has traditionally been known as the efforts of professional counselors to support clients based on clients' needs or some social cause (Lee & Walz, 1998). Historically speaking, advocacy has a rich tradition in the fields of social work and education. Over the past decade, there has been a movement within the counseling profession to focus on factors external to clients that adversely affect the emotional and physical well-being of clients (Kiselica & Robinson, 2001). Advocacy in counseling has become known as advocacy counseling with an emphasis on social action and justice.

Advocacy counseling not only includes the actions of professional counselors on behalf of clients, but also includes professional counselors intervening with systems and organizations relevant to clients (Myers, Sweeney, & White, 2002). In considering the "world" (e.g., family, educational, social, political, religious systems) of clients, the context for understanding the problems of clients begins to take shape. However, this conceptualization also includes considering the **barriers** inherent in these systems (e.g., prejudice, socioeconomic issues) that have been encountered by clients. Professional counselors take on the role of advocate when employing social action to confront these issues on behalf of clients, which may result in social justice to confront injustice and inequality in society

(Jackson, 2000; Mays, 2000; Strickland, 2000). Now complete Activity 14.1 on advocacy situations.

ACTIVITY 14.1

Consider some possible advocacy situations for which clients may need your assistance as a professional counselor. Some examples follow:

- A senior citizen who lives at home by himself and is not capable of feeding himself. He does not have family in the area, so there is no one to make sure he is eating.
- A student who recently moved to the area and started school. His teacher has not had time to pay special attention to him, and he is struggling academically and socially. His teacher thinks he is simply a lower achieving student.

Think of other clients or scenarios you may have to advocate for in the future.

Much of the past literature on advocacy counseling focused on strategies employed by professional counselors to address clients' needs through social action or interventions specific to oppressed groups (Myers et al., 2002). This work has spanned across the disciplines of counseling, psychology, social work, sociology, and religion (Kiselica & Robinson, 2001). However, historically, systematic training guidelines and practices of advocacy counseling have not been in place for professional counselors (Eriksen, 1999a). Although advocacy counseling is a professional and ethical responsibility of professional counselors (Field & Baker, 2004), only more recently has attention been given to outlining advocacy competencies for professional counselors.

In this chapter, guidelines for recognizing when advocacy counseling is needed are discussed. In addition, **counseling advocacy competencies** as provided by the American Counseling Association (2006f) are outlined. For each of the competency areas, case examples or applications are provided to illustrate the connection of the case to the competency and the appropriate methods to use as advocacy counselors in working with clients in all types of counseling settings.

When to Advocate

It is essential for professional counselors to integrate the role of advocate into their professional identity. Just as when learning how to apply various theoretical approaches to case conceptualization and treatment planning, professional counselors should identify characteristics within themselves that would make them successful advocates for clients. Values, personalities, and skills taught in counseling programs are necessary to the development of successful professional counselors and are strong contributors to the development of successful advocates (Cigler & Loomis, 1998; Hrebenar, 1997).

In one study, participants reported that an educational approach, relationship building, and good communication are necessary to successful advocacy (Eriksen, 1999a). In addition to these characteristics, a clear sense of professional identity is essential. Professional counselors need knowledge of what and who they represent and what they are promoting in the role of advocate. Finally, other essential elements are required for successful advocacy. Leadership, organizational strength and unity, perseverance, maintaining an advocacy focus at all times, and education and training are components included in successful advocacy counseling. Activity 14.2 helps you to reflect on your own identity as a professional counselor.

ACTIVITY 14.2

How do you identify yourself? Write several sentences about your identity as a professional counselor.

Learning to identify when to advocate has been a focus of educating and training advocates (Eriksen, 1997; Fiedler, 2000; Svec, 1987, 1990). In an effort to provide structure and training standards, the American Counseling Association (2006f) has identified advocacy competencies for professional counselors or counselor educators engaged in these activities. In Figure 14.1, the **advocacy competency domains** are identified as client/student, school/community, and public arena.

In this model, the columns represent the different levels in which advocacy activities can take place. The left-hand column represents the microlevel, which is centered on the client or student. As the advocate progresses to the right, the advocacy activities broaden to include the

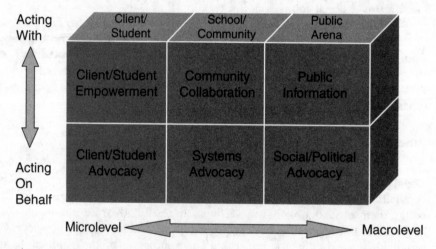

FIGURE 14.1 Advocacy competency domains.
From "Advocacy Competencies [Electronic version]," by J. Lewis, M.S. Arnold, R. House, and R.L. Toporek, 2003. Retrieved December 4, 2006, from http://www.counseling.org/Resources/. Copyright 2003 by the American Counseling Association. Reprinted with permission. No further reproduction authorized without written permission from the American Counseling Association.

systems of the client or student to, finally, the larger systems that affect not only the client or student, but many people. This could include recognition of change needed at a political level.

In Figure 14.1, the rows represent how professional counselors are working as advocates. The top row indicates that professional counselors are working with those groups to make changes. Professional counselors may be working with clients to identify how external barriers have affected their own development and then to identify resources that would help overcome or cope with those barriers. The second row reflects how professional counselors act on behalf of clients to deal with these external barriers. Professional counselors may need to act as allies to clients for clients to gain access to resources. Now complete Activity 14.3.

ACTIVITY 14.3

Activity 14.1 described an elderly man who lives by himself and is having difficulty with everyday functioning.
- Think of a way you, as a professional counselor, can work with the client to overcome these issues.
- What possible community resources could you help him to research?
- Think of a way you can work on behalf of this man to deal with these issues.

Using this model, competencies and advocacy process are outlined throughout this chapter to help professional counselors learn when to empower their clients and when to advocate for them. In addition, methods for empowering and advocating are illustrated in case studies.

Advocacy Competencies for Clients

In the first row of the model in Figure 14.1, client/student empowerment is recognized as the first level for how advocacy counselors work with clients or students. In this chapter, the discussion focuses more on working with clients in counseling versus graduate students in counseling programs, although the process is similar. In working with clients, it is important to remember basic fundamental counseling skills. This includes good communication with clients (Brown, 1988). Having built trusting relationships with the clients, professional counselors understand the importance of empathy and of establishing positive relationships with clients to make advocating effective (Trusty, 1996). Assertive behavior is promoted through empathic understanding and good communication, which is a component of feeling empowered.

CLIENT EMPOWERMENT   In the first level of advocacy counseling, professional counselors incorporate **empowerment** strategies in their direct counseling (American Counseling Association, 2006f). A large component of the empowerment of clients is knowledge. In communicating with clients and developing an empathic understanding of them, the impact of social, political, economic, and cultural factors on their development becomes a part of professional counselors' awareness. Part of the role of advocacy-oriented counselors is to integrate this awareness into the direct counseling relationship with clients to help them understand their own lives in these contexts.

ACTIVITY 14.4

What are some barriers you have encountered in your own development? How have your dealt with these barriers?

In Table 14.1, specific empowerment counselor competencies for the first level of the advocacy competency model are outlined (American Counseling Association, 2006f). In providing direct interventions that help to empower clients, professional counselors can help clients learn to **self-advocate**. A key counseling skill involved in self-advocacy is assessment, as can be seen in the first three competencies in Table 14.1.

Specifically, **problem assessment** is essentially required to discern the need for advocacy. In advocacy models, problem assessment is usually one of the first steps (Eriksen, 1997; Fiedler, 2000; Trusty & Brown, 2005). In problem assessment, professional counselors should identify the etiology of the problem. In other words, where did the problem come from? By systemically examining the problem, professional counselors can assess if problems arise from clients, their families, their work or school environments, the client-family characteristics, the school or work environment characteristics, other environments in which clients interact, or the interactions among the environments. Professional counselors quickly discover that when examining problems systemically, the worldviews of clients are not the only worldviews of importance. The worldviews of the different systems and environments are also important in creating interventions that help to empower clients. In discovering the worldviews of clients and the worldviews from these systemic environments, clients may begin to identify external barriers that affect their development.

A second part of problem assessment is for professional counselors to recognize clients' behaviors and concerns that are responses to systemic or internalized **oppression**, which occurs when another entity imposes an object, label, role, experience, or set of living conditions that is unwanted, is painful, and detracts from the physical and psychological

---

TABLE 14.1 Empowerment Counselor Competencies

In direct interventions, the professional counselor is able to
1. Identify the strengths and resources of clients
2. Identify the social, political, economic, and cultural factors that affect the client
3. Recognize signs indicating that an individual's behaviors and concerns reflect responses to systemic or internalized oppression
4. At an appropriate developmental level, help the individual identify external barriers that affect his or her development
5. Train clients in self-advocacy skills
6. Help clients develop self-advocacy action plans
7. Assist clients in carrying out action plans

From "Advocacy Competencies [Electronic version]," by J. Lewis, M.S. Arnold, R. House, and R.L. Toporek, 2003. Retrieved December 4, 2006, from http://www.counseling.org/Resources/. Copyright 2003 by the American Counseling Association. Reprinted with permission. No further reproduction authorized without written permission from the American Counseling Association.

well-being of the client (Hanna, Talley, & Guindon, 2000). Carefully confronting those behaviors or concerns may help clients gain knowledge about oppression and become more assertive in their efforts to combat these experiences.

In helping clients gain a sense of empowerment, professional counselors need to be reminded that empowerment is an ongoing process. An empowerment-centered philosophy for promoting positive counseling emphasizes that everyone has the ability to shape events in life, rather than being powerless and helpless (Cogan, 1996). Empowered individuals participate in active and meaningful ways in making decisions that affect their life (Fetterman, 1994). In addition, empowerment becomes essential and necessary for clients to self-advocate. Case Study 14.1 presents an application of empowerment counselor competencies.

CASE STUDY 14.1   APPLICATION OF EMPOWERMENT COUNSELOR COMPETENCIES

Mark is a graduate student who has been attending counseling for one semester at the university counseling center. He identifies himself as gay and has been "out" since the start of his graduate studies approximately one and one-half years ago. His family lives in a large city in the southwest. Mark describes his family as religiously and politically conservative. He has not discussed his sexual orientation with them because of their conservative beliefs and values. He reports that they have primarily been concerned that his career choice of student affairs in higher education has influenced him to be more liberal in his values, beliefs, and behaviors.

His reason for coming to counseling was initially to deal with some feelings of anxiety about returning to school at the beginning of the semester. However, the counseling sessions have focused more and more on how his anger is growing toward his family as they continue to make disparaging remarks not only about homosexuals, but also other minority groups. He sometimes avoids their phone calls, and makes only a few visits home. After a recent holiday visit home, he decided to delay coming out to them. He is also committed to his religious beliefs and attends religious study groups. Mark reports that he has found a peace in his relationship with God in regard to his homosexuality. Recently, a friend from the group confronted Mark about his sexual orientation and ended their friendship after learning he is gay.

Questions for consideration follow:

1. What could be some strengths and resources for Mark?
2. What are the social, political, economic, and cultural factors affecting Mark?
3. What are some of the signs that the professional counselor has recognized in Mark that may be a reflection of his response to systemic or internalized oppression?
4. What are some self-advocacy skills you could train Mark to apply to his situation?
5. How would you help Mark carry out his self-advocacy action plan?

In Mark's case, the research indicates that there are several factors to consider in promoting empowerment and self-advocacy. Being a gay man, Mark is considered to be a part of a marginalized population that is frequently overwhelmed by a sense of powerlessness (Savage, Harley, & Nowak, 2005). Powerlessness manifests itself in the form of oppression through language (Kitzinger, 1996), **heterosexism** (Hunter, Shannon, Knox, & Martin, 1998), simultaneous support and curtailment of civil rights (Hartman, 1996), and hate crimes (Cogan,

1996). Mark seems to be experiencing oppression through the language used by his family. His family and religious group member also inflicted oppression through their prejudiced beliefs and values, which they voiced to him. More specific to Mark's family, it seems that he may be experiencing heterosexism, which is the ideology that denies, denigrates, and stigmatizes any nonheterosexual form of behavior, identity, relationship, or community (Herek, 1993). This form of prejudice can make homosexual individuals feel like second-class citizens, promoting feelings of powerlessness and worthlessness.

To increase Mark's self-advocacy, his feelings of empowerment need to be cultivated. To do this, he needs to form coalitions with other marginalized groups in every system that he incorporates into his "world," including his family system. In answering the question about Mark's resources, the answers may help to create an action plan that helps him form these coalitions. A second goal is to help Mark develop an accurate representation of the lives and identities of gay men because he has recently come out to his work and school environments (Savage et al., 2005). How can this be accomplished? Through the identification of Mark's responses and behaviors related to oppression, counseling can offer Mark an outlet to express his emotions about the challenge of being a gay man in a heteropatriarchy society. A third component of Mark's action plan to self-advocate is to focus on Mark learning self-acceptance and acceptance by others. In the midst of oppression, Mark can develop a positive self-identity that can be a source of strength and empowerment. Finally, Mark should be encouraged to put into practice in the "real world" the action steps he has been developing in counseling. Only when he demonstrates these actions himself can empowerment be fully realized.

CLIENT ADVOCACY   As relationships between professional counselors and clients grow, counselors gain awareness of the external factors that act as barriers to clients' development. During this time, professional counselors have a decision to make about how they will act as advocates. The previous section addressed how helping clients gain a sense of empowerment may lead to clients' self-advocacy. However, professional counselors may decide to choose to be the clients' advocates, especially when clients lack access to needed services. Table 14.2 outlines client advocacy counselor competencies.

In advocating for clients, professional counselors are acting for clients and not only with them as in the previous discussion on client empowerment. However, similar to the process of client empowerment and self-advocacy, a problem assessment has to be conducted to determine if client advocacy is warranted, and what needs to be included in the plan of

---

TABLE 14.2 Client Advocacy Counselor Competencies

In environmental interventions on behalf of clients, the counselor is able to
1. Negotiate relevant services on behalf of clients
2. Help clients gain access to needed resources
3. Identify barriers to the well-being of individuals and vulnerable groups
4. Develop an initial plan of action for confronting these barriers
5. Identify potential allies for confronting the barriers
6. Carry out the plan of action

From "Advocacy Competencies [Electronic version]," by J. Lewis, M.S. Arnold, R. House, and R.L. Toporek, 2003. Retrieved December 4, 2006, from http://www.counseling.org/Resources/. Copyright 2003 by the American Counseling Association. Reprinted with permission. No further reproduction authorized without written permission from the American Counseling Association.

action for the advocacy. In the client advocacy counselor competencies, assessing and using available resources is essential to an effective action plan. In a study of counselor advocates, the study participants encouraged advocates to plan advocacy efforts to match their available resources (Eriksen, 1999a). Assessing the systems that are a part of clients' realities helps professional counselors identify any barriers to the well-being of clients, and identify resources for clients. Identification of "human" resources helps in making a plan to include these allies of clients in confronting present and future barriers.

As client advocates, professional counselors have to be able and willing to use the "power" inherent to the role of the counselor position. This means that professional counselors may have certain privileges that accompany their positions, which would facilitate clients' access to information that may have been inaccessible to them (Dinsmore, Chapman, & McCollum, 2000). This "influential power" may be required to negotiate with outside agencies and institutions to provide better services for clients. Additionally, professional counselors may need to act as mediators between clients and institutions, specifically to resolve impasses. Activity 14.5 addresses the "power" of the professional counselor.

ACTIVITY 14.5

What "power" will be inherent in your role as a professional counselor that clients do not possess?

Professional counselors need to be careful not to seem overzealous because it may work against clients. There are several strategies for counselors to remember as they advocate for clients (Ponzo, 1974). First, professional counselors should be flexible and demonstrate the willingness to compromise to persuade others. Second, professional counselors should have some perspective on their own personalities and the impact of their personalities on others. Professional counselors may need to adjust their style to be effective client advocates. Third, professional counselors should understand not only their clients, but also others in various systems, such as agencies and institutions. By employing basic counseling skills (i.e., empathy, warmth, concreteness), professional counselors can gain the trust of the contacts in these various systems. Fourth, professional counselors should learn from the different systems to create advocacy plans that would work in these systems to create change. Finally, professional counselors and clients should set realistic goals. Remembering to work with the resources that are available and delineating short-term versus long-term goals make advocacy plans and interventions successful. Case 14.2 illustrates the application of client advocacy counselor competencies.

CASE STUDY 14.2   APPLICATION OF CLIENT ADVOCACY COUNSELOR COMPETENCIES

Julie is a 25-year-old woman recovering from a crack cocaine addiction. She has been drug-free for 1 year. Julie gave birth to a daughter approximately 5 years ago and relinquished custody to her parents immediately after the birth of her daughter. She has recently experienced more frequent visits with her parents and daughter, but the visits with her daughter continue to be supervised. Currently, Julie continues to live with her boyfriend of 4 years, who chronically abuses alcohol. She reported that he is verbally and emotionally abusive, and she wishes to move out of the house and end the relationship. Julie's current professional counselor has been helping her with her recovery and dealing with the emotional issues that are inherent to her environmental and family systems. The professional counselor referred Julie to a Narcotics Anonymous (NA) group, which Julie attends everyday. Julia's sponsor agreed to have Julia move in with her until Julia is able to arrange for new living arrangements. Julie expressed a desire to continue her sobriety and was inspired about the developing relationship between her and her daughter. However, she is frustrated by the supervised visits and lack of employment she is experiencing.

Questions for consideration follow:

1. What are the relevant services and education systems that may need to be negotiated by the professional counselor on behalf of Julie?
2. How can the professional counselor help Julie gain access to needed resources? What are those resources?
3. What are the barriers to the well-being of Julie?
4. What is an initial plan for confronting those barriers? What are some short-term goals?
5. Who are some of Julie's allies in confronting those barriers?

In the case of Julie, the professional counselor is helping with drug addiction recovery. However, with this client and with many clients, advocacy may be required to address other aspects of the client's experience besides the initial reason for counseling (i.e., recovering from a crack cocaine addiction). In one study of professional counselors who worked with clients dealing with drug addiction, advocacy activities on behalf of clients included obtaining direct services, obtaining practical help for the client, securing support from the client's employer or school, and obtaining information for the client (Graham, Timney, Bois, & Wedgerfield, 1995). For Julie, the professional counselor may want to consider acting as a mediator between Julie and her parents in regard to planning unsupervised visits with her daughter. This may also include obtaining information from the Department of Social Services to consider a plan for future custody and living arrangements. In assessing Julie's resources, it is important for the professional counselor to consider the role of Julie's NA sponsor. A meeting among Julie and her sponsor with the professional counselor may be warranted to create a plan for Julie to move away from her boyfriend and take steps to gain some form of employment. The NA sponsor may be willing to act as an ally of Julie to put her plan into action.

Advocacy Competencies for the Community

In Figure 14.1, the second column of the advocacy competency domains model focuses on **community collaboration** and advocacy. As in the first column that focused on clients, the first row of the second column focuses on how professional counselors can collaborate *with* communities similar to how professional counselors work with clients to help them feel empowered. The second row of the second column focuses on how professional counselors act as advocates for communities or systems.

COMMUNITY COLLABORATION   Professional counselors work in various settings, including public and private K-12 schools, colleges and universities, mental health settings, medical settings, private and public businesses, and rehabilitation settings. Part of the role of the professional counselor is to be attuned to the communities that are being served in those settings. In working with the clients in these communities, professional counselors gain an awareness of recurring themes in the community. Professional counselors may be the first to become aware of specific problems in the community (American Counseling Association, 2006f).

Part of the identity of an advocate is to address problems that are brought into awareness. Professional counselors can choose to share recurring problematic themes with other groups in the community that may also be aware of these issues and are attempting to address these issues. Ethical standards help to guide professional counselors on how this information is shared. Now complete Activity 14.6.

ACTIVITY 14.6

Think of some "themes" or problem situations that you are already aware of within your community. How could these themes affect clients in your future profession?

The main role of professional counselors at this level of advocacy is to act as allies to other organizations in addressing issues of concern in the community. Professional counselors can offer particular skills, such as communication, training, interpersonal relations, assessment, and research, to work in a collaborative effort with other interested groups to address these issues. Table 14.3 outlines community collaboration counselor competencies.

As mentioned in the previous sections, problem assessment is always a key component of advocacy. At this particular level of advocacy, assessment of the problem begins with the recognition of the themes that professional counselors are "hearing" from clients.

TABLE 14.3 Community Collaboration Counselor Competencies

In support of groups working toward systemic change at the community level, the advocacy-oriented counselor is able to
1. Identify environmental factors that impinge upon clients' development
2. Alert community groups with common concerns related to the issue
3. Develop alliances with groups working with change
4. Use effective listening skills to gain understanding of the group's goals
5. Identify strengths and resources that the group members bring to the process of systemic change
6. Communicate recognition of and respect for these strengths and resources
7. Identify and offer skills that the professional counselor can bring to the collaboration
8. Assess the effect of the counselor's interaction with the community

From "Advocacy Competencies [Electronic version]," by J. Lewis, M.S. Arnold, R. House, and R.L. Toporek, 2003. Retrieved December 4, 2006, from http://www.counseling.org/Resources/. Copyright 2003 by the American Counseling Association. Reprinted with permission. No further reproduction authorized without written permission from the American Counseling Association.

However, problem assessment does not begin and end with listening to clients. Professional counselors continue this process as alliances with other community groups are created and expanded. Learning from these other groups about their own perspective on these thematic issues helps to delineate the specific components of the issues. It is essential for professional counselors to know which community groups are aware of or could be affected by these issues. Thus, part of this advocacy process is to identify those groups that could be part of the process of finding solutions to address the issues. Sometimes, the specific community groups that are common to the issue are obvious. For example, in public K-12 schools, common community groups could be mental health, law enforcement, and school board. However, it may not be obvious because of the specificity of the issue, and counselors have to consider potential appropriate groups. Now complete Activity 14.7.

ACTIVITY 14.7

How will you use your skills as a professional counselor to build alliances with community groups? Can you think of specific community groups that will be pertinent to your profession? How might you first contact these groups to begin a collaborative relationship?

Once alliances are formed with community groups, the ability to listen effectively becomes paramount. The professional counselor is at least one member of the alliance trained in effective communication, a skill needed in assessing planning, and implementing interventions to address the issue in the community. Using communication skills, professional counselors can help alliances identify the strengths and resources of community group entities to implement those into the intervention plan. In addition, professional counselors can offer their own specific skills to help in this process. Case study 14.3 illustrates community collaboration for advocacy.

CASE STUDY 14.3   APPLICATION OF COMMUNITY COLLABORATION COUNSELOR ADVOCACIES

At a recent case staffing at a midsize college counseling center, a professional counselor named Joan reported that she has worked with at least five individuals with issues of self-injury in the past month. The other seven professional counselors reported that they had also worked with at least an average of five individuals each on similar issues. After discussing the cases in more depth, the professional counselors concluded that most of the clients reporting these behaviors were freshmen and sophomore young women who lived both on and off campus.

Joan and another professional counselor worked together to determine which other community groups within the college system would be effective in helping to plan interventions. They decided to meet with representatives from student life staff, residence hall staff, and undergraduate academics staff. When meeting with these individuals, it became obvious that self-injury had become an issue for all of these groups. Interventions were designed, and implementation was coordinated through Joan at the counseling center.

Questions for consideration follow:

1. Why do you think those three college community groups were identified with this issue?
2. What do you think became the main goal of this alliance group?
3. What are some of the skills the professional counselors can offer in this situation?
4. How would you assess the effectiveness of the professional counselor's interaction within this community?

One of the great strengths of working with college groups is the ability to use education as a tool in providing effective intervention. In the case of self-injury, three separate groups were identified to assess, plan, and implement strategies for clients in three separate areas of their lives on campus: student life—social environments on campus; residence life—living environments on campus; and undergraduate academics—learning environments on campus. There could be other groups on campus to include in this collaborative effort.

Education of self-injury can act as a method of preventing the stigma associated with it (White, Trepal-Wollenzier, & Nolan, 2002). Self-injury needs to be demystified for not only students on campus, but also for college staff and faculty who are working with students who self-injure. The college counseling center can lead this effort by posting information on the counseling center website and creating and disseminating brochures about self-injury and how to receive help with this issue (Davis & Humphrey, 2000; Prasad & Owns, 2001).

In educating campus groups, an additional group to consider is one that handles judicial affairs. Many campuses have mandatory withdrawal policies for students who engage in disruptive behaviors and suicide attempts (Hodges, 2001). Because self-injury is often erroneously equated with attempted suicide, professional counselors can help these groups understand the differences between suicide and self-injury. Part of the collaboration may help enact new policies that clarify discipline guidelines for students who self-injure.

It is important to consider how effective the professional counselor is in these collaborative efforts. There are a variety of formal and informal methods to use in this process. Asking for feedback from the community groups that are working collaboratively with the professional counselor can be done through a formal written process or informally by gauging the interactions within meetings and other types of communication. If the professional counselor is involved in providing outreach education sessions to students, staff, or faculty, a pre-evaluation and a postevaluation of the education session can be used. Finally, the counseling center may want to employ a confidential method for students who are either engaging in or contemplating self-injury to self-report their concerns. No matter the method, assessing the professional counselor's effectiveness provides information that would be helpful in planning future collaborative activities with community groups. Now complete Activity 14.8.

ACTIVITY 14.8

Create a written evaluation to send to community groups that have collaborated with you in a recent community effort against self-injury. Determine a way citizens considering self-injury could confidentially refer themselves to your agency or school for mental health services.

SYSTEMS ADVOCACY   The second level of advocacy in the community domain of the advocacy competency domains model includes **systems advocacy** (see Fig. 14.1) (American Counseling Association, 2006f). To advocate for small or large systems, it is necessary to understand how systems work (Kiselica & Robinson, 2001). Early in this chapter, clients' systems were discussed to examine how these systems affect clients and how empowerment and advocacy can address systemic issues. In the community domain, systems can include small systems within a community or organization. Smaller systems in schools include teachers, administrators, parents, and students. Larger systems for schools include communities, school districts, and state departments of education. When professional counselors identify systemic factors that are acting as barriers to the development of clients, they may wish to change the environment to prevent some of the problems that are occurring because of these barriers being in place within the system (American Counseling Association, 2006f). In this case, advocacy means changing the system (House & Hayes, 2002).

Regardless of the type of system change, professional counselors engage in processes that help affect change (American Counseling Association, 2006f). These processes require professional counselors to have a vision of change; to be persistent; to provide leadership; to engage in collaboration; to provide systems analysis; and to collect, analyze, and disseminate strong data. In essence, the training professional counselors receive provides the requisite knowledge and skills required in these processes, in effect acting as systems-change leaders. Table 14.4 outlines the competencies for systems advocacy counselors.

Although assessment has been a key component of many of the advocacy competencies discussed in the previous sections of the chapter, research is introduced at this level of the competency model as a requirement. At this level of advocacy, professional counselors and clients are not necessarily the individuals or groups making changes. To make a "case" for change, evidence for the *need* to change has to be provided. Similar to other advocacy competencies, the problem has to be assessed, but the second step is to collect data on how this issue is a problem.

In the previous case scenario on self-injury, the college judicial policy may be to have the student withdraw for any type of injurious behavior. To present this policy as a problem

---

TABLE 14.4 Systems Advocacy Counselor Competencies

In exerting systems-change leadership at the community level, the advocacy-related counselor is able to

1. Identify environmental factors impinging on clients' development
2. Provide and interpret data to show the urgency for change
3. In collaboration with other stakeholders, develop a vision to guide change
4. Analyze the sources of political power and social influence within the system
5. Develop a step-by-step plan for implementing the change process
6. Develop a plan for dealing with probable responses to change
7. Recognize and deal with resistance
8. Assess the effect of counselor's advocacy efforts on the system and constituents

From "Advocacy Competencies [Electronic version]," by J. Lewis, M.S. Arnold, R. House, and R.L. Toporek, 2003. Retrieved December 4, 2006, from http://www.counseling.org/Resources/. Copyright 2003 by the American Counseling Association. Reprinted with permission. No further reproduction authorized without written permission from the American Counseling Association.

in the system, data may need to be collected in determining which students were attempting suicide versus engaging in nonsuicidal self-injury. In addition, outcome data may need to be presented on individuals who received treatment for self-injury and those who did not to determine if intervention plans can be put in place for students who self-injure but are not asked to withdraw from school. Activity 14.9 explores data collection.

ACTIVITY 14.9

What are your strongest data collection skills? What are the areas that need improvement? How will you address both of these areas?

Create a method for collecting data in this case of self-injury.

This level of advocacy continues the collaborative efforts between professional counselors and community groups that are affected by the identified issues. However, the collaboration among the individuals moves to creating a vision for change, analyzing the sources of political power and social influence within the system. Additionally, groups need to create an **action plan** that outlines clear and specific goals in a step-by-step method for implementing change that also shows how to use resources effectively and anticipate difficulties (Trusty & Brown, 2005). This includes methods on how to handle anticipated responses to change, including resistance. Finally, professional counselors need to use their assessment and research skills to evaluate advocacy initiatives (Kiselica & Robinson, 2001). Case Study 14.4 illustrates the application of systems advocacy counselor competencies.

CASE STUDY 14.4   APPLICATION OF SYSTEMS ADVOCACY COUNSELOR COMPETENCIES

In a large public school system, one of the roles of professional school counselors at every high school includes testing. Every counselor at every high school in the school district was required to coordinate and help in the administration of specific tests at the high school level. After some time, the directors of school counseling at these schools identified the theme of testing as being an activity that interfered with the ability of the professional school counselors to perform other roles and duties. At a district-wide school counseling director meeting, one of the school counseling directors brought this issue to the meeting for discussion. They decided that this issue was one that could be changed only at the district level. They created a plan to collect and analyze data about how the activities of the professional school counselors compared with the activities recommended by the American School Counselor Association (ASCA) *National Model for School Counseling Programs* (2005). In addition, they collected data on how much time and effort was devoted to testing responsibilities compared with the recommended activities by the ASCA. After these data were collected and analyzed, all high school counseling directors met with the district superintendent to present this information and ask for the testing duties to be eliminated from the duties required of high school counselors. The superintendent took the issue to his administration team, agreed that the issue had merit, and a testing director position was created for each high school.

Questions for consideration follow:

1. What other data should have been considered by the counseling directors?
2. Who and what do you think were the school counseling directors' political and social power within the system? How could this have been better used?
3. How could the directors handle a refusal from the superintendent?

In public schools, there are many subsystems (e.g., students, teachers, parents, departments, staff, administrators). In this case, it seems that the professional school counselors may have thought they were not fulfilling their counseling duties to many of these subsystems. For these professional school counselors, being in charge of school testing was an ineffective use their time. They also believed it was not consistent with the ASCA (2005) *National Model for School Counseling Programs*. Being able to advocate for systemic change, these school counseling directors were also engaging in leadership activities. This was an example of not only school reform, but also systemic change. To transform school counseling practices, effective leadership by professional school counselors is required (House & Hayes, 2002).

In this example, the school counseling directors were able to present data about the immediate need for change within the smaller systems of the individual high schools and the larger system of the district. There were other components that needed to be considered, however. It is unclear who or what was identified as political resources and social power for this group. Did the professional school counselors consider their constituent groups (e.g., teachers, students, parents, school administrators) as resources for making change? Who at the district level (beyond the superintendent) could have acted as a political resource? This may have been the district-wide assessment coordinator. In addition, this person could have supplied them with additional data to present and act as an ally in the presentation process. Finally, in assessing and evaluating the effectiveness of the advocacy efforts of the professional school counselors, it is easy to note things that could have been conducted differently. However, it is equally important to identify actions and steps that were effective to employ in future systemic advocacy efforts.

Advocacy in the Public Arena

In the final domain of the counselor advocacy competencies model, advocating in the public arena becomes the general focus of professional counselors. Instead of examining oppression and barriers in systems and subsystems, professional counselors advocate at a macrosystemic level for issues regarding human dignity (American Counseling Association, 2006f). Providing **public information** is one method of encouraging the public to become aware of environmental factors that are barriers to all individuals' human development. The second row in the model brings attention to **social advocacy** and **political advocacy**. At this level, professional counselors are employing more direct methods to bring about change in a much larger arena than at the systems level.

PUBLIC INFORMATION   In the first two domains of the model, the focus of the professional counselor was on clients, systems of clients, and systems and communities that involved professional counselors. However, this third domain encourages professional counselors to reach out across disciplines, settings, and theoretical perspectives to share knowledge about human development and expertise in communication. The competencies outlined in Table 14.5 help guide professional counselors in this endeavor.

Chapter 13 addressed advocating for the profession of counseling and outlined several methods that professional counselors can use in actively advocating for the profession. The American Counseling Association (2005b) outlined several techniques for using the media to advocate for the profession. In this third competency domain, these techniques are also applicable to advocating for clients. In essence, when professional counselors advocate for the profession, they are also advocating for clients and against environmental barriers to human development. However, many professional counselors who are beginning advocacy efforts may not feel confident in preparing materials to be used in the media.

In addressing this concern, the American Counseling Association (2005b) provides several guidelines for beginning these efforts. First, professional counselors need to examine ongoing issues that are important concerns to members of counselors' schools, institutions, or communities. In addition, professional counselors need to determine if these same issues are appearing in local newspapers and other media. Second, professional counselors need to determine if their skills and expertise can be used to address these issues. Third, professional counselors need to assess and determine the resources they have to carry out public information activities (e.g., human, monetary, services). Finally, professional counselors need to determine how much time they can devote to these activities. Professional counselors can participate in a variety of activities that can address these

---

TABLE 14.5 Public Information Counselor Competencies

In informing the public about the role of environmental factors in human development, the advocacy-oriented counselor is able to

1. Recognize the impact of oppression and other barriers to healthy development
2. Identify environmental factors that are protective of healthy development
3. Prepare written and multimedia materials that provide clear explanations of the role of specific environmental factors in human development
4. Communicate information in ways that are ethical and appropriate for the target population
5. Disseminate information through various media
6. Identify and collaborate with other professionals who are involved in disseminating public information
7. Assess the influence of public information efforts undertaken by the counselor

---

From "Advocacy Competencies [Electronic version]," by J. Lewis, M.S. Arnold, R. House, and R.L. Toporek, 2003. Retrieved December 4, 2006, from http://www.counseling.org/Resources/. Copyright 2003 by the American Counseling Association. Reprinted with permission. No further reproduction authorized without written permission from the American Counseling Association.

TABLE 14.6 Public Information Activities

1. Sponsor a "thank you" breakfast or other event to honor individuals who contribute to the well-being of your school, agency, or community. Honorees might include individuals who volunteer at your school or in the community, athletic coaches, leaders of youth programs, local politicians, clergy, and law enforcement officials.
2. Provide a presentation before a community or professional group, in workplaces, at public libraries, or other places to increase public awareness for a specific issue.
3. Teach an adult education class at a local college or learning center to boost the visibility and credibility of counseling in the community. Consider the needs and interests of the audience members, such as individuals making important transitions in their lives (e.g., women and men reentering the workforce for various reasons).
4. Send out news releases to area newspapers and periodicals for special events to highlight the issue relevant to the professional counselor's advocacy efforts.
5. Write letters to editors of local newspapers regarding a specific issue. Be specific in the letter, especially if responding to the concerns raised in a previously published letter to the editor.
6. Participate in professional counselor commemoratives to bring public awareness of specific issues (e.g., Black History Month [February], National Alcohol Awareness Month [April], National Child Abuse Prevention Month [April], Older Americans Month [May], National Hispanic Heritage Month [September], Domestic Violence Awareness Month [October]).

From "Advocacy Competencies [Electronic version]," by J. Lewis, M.S. Arnold, R. House, and R.L. Toporek, 2003. Retrieved December 4, 2006, from http://www.counseling.org/Resources/. Copyright 2003 by the American Counseling Association. Reprinted with permission. No further reproduction authorized without written permission from the American Counseling Association.

issues. Examples of public information activities are listed in Table 14.6. Finally, complete Activity 14.10.

ACTIVITY 14.10   APPLICATION OF PUBLIC INFORMATION COMPETENCIES

Using the competencies and public information activities listed in Table 14.6, answer the following questions:
1. What issue at a macrosystemic level are you interested in currently?
2. How could you advocate for this issue using one of the activities listed in Table 14.6?
3. Who are some other professionals that you could involve in disseminating public information on this issue?
4. What resources do you need to do this?
5. How will you assess your efforts in using public information to advocate for this issue?

SOCIAL/POLITICAL ADVOCACY   In the public arena domain of the counselor advocacy competencies model, social/political advocacy is the second level of advocacy to reach a larger and broader arena to address concerns and issues for clients and other individuals who have faced barriers to their human development (American Counseling Association, 2006f). Learning how to use counseling skills and knowledge through public information outlets as a tool to advocate, professional counselors are prepared to carry out social/political advocacy. Table 14.7 lists the social/political advocacy counselor competencies.

TABLE 14.7 Social/Political Advocacy Counselor Competencies

In influencing public policy in a large, public arena, the advocacy-oriented counselor is able to
1. Distinguish problems that can best be resolved through social/political action
2. Identify appropriate mechanisms and avenues for addressing these problems
3. Seek out and join with potential allies
4. Support existing alliances for change
5. With allies, prepare convincing data and rationales for change
6. With allies, lobby legislators and other policymakers
7. Maintain open dialogue with communities and clients to ensure that the social/political advocacy is consistent with the initial goals

---

From "Advocacy Competencies [Electronic version]," by J. Lewis, M.S. Arnold, R. House, and R.L. Toporek, 2003. Retrieved December 4, 2006, from http://www.counseling.org/Resources/. Copyright 2003 by the American Counseling Association. Reprinted with permission. No further reproduction authorized without written permission from the American Counseling Association.

Recently, I attended a national counseling conference in which the director of the National Board of Certified Counselors (NBCC) was describing the NBCC's efforts in expanding licensure internationally. The director reported that he called and was granted an appointment with a high-ranking official with the World Health Organization (WHO) to discuss why licensed professional counseling was essential in different countries. The WHO official is an important decision maker. The NBCC director reported his amazement in gaining this appointment. Hearing this story reminded me of the role of the professional counselor as advocate. Do not be afraid to *ask* for help or simply to present a cause. March (1999) reminds us to meet with people who can make a difference. By educating the individuals who can effect change about harmful conditions to human development, change can be made. These individuals may be local, state, or federal government officials. They may include other officials who work for human health organizations that need to be given data to "make the case" for change for budgetary reasons. Professional counselors may start with local representatives to learn how lobbying and legislatures work in their communities. Professional counselors need to determine what issues need this level of advocacy and the appropriate method of achieving this goal. Finally, professional counselors can use failed attempts to learn how to design and implement social/political advocacy efforts that will succeed. Activity 14.11 presents an application of social/political advocacy counselor competencies.

ACTIVITY 14.11   APPLICATION OF SOCIAL/POLITICAL ADVOCACY COUNSELOR COMPETENCIES

1. Who are the local, state, and national politicians you could approach to present an issue?
2. What is one local issue that you believe could be a national issue to address barriers to human development?
3. Identify two professional counseling organization officials who could act as resources for this issue?
4. What is another discipline that you could approach to be an ally in advocating for this issue?

Summary

Advocacy is a core component of the identity of the professional counselor. Over time, the "look" of advocacy has changed from professional counselors helping clients achieve a sense of empowerment to professional counselors engaging in social action activities on behalf of clients, systems, and communities to bring justice to individuals who are experiencing barriers to their development.

In this chapter, the American Counseling Association (2006f) advocacy competency domains were explained by discussing the various competency levels: client/student (i.e., client/student empowerment, client/student advocacy), community collaboration (i.e., community collaboration, systems advocacy), and public arena (i.e., public information, social/political advocacy). This model illustrates the levels of need for advocacy. In addition, it depicts professional counselors as individuals who can work *with* clients and communities to break down barriers and advocate *for* clients and community systems when required.

To know when to advocate, professional counselors need to engage in problem assessment. By the use of assessment strategies, professional counselors can examine the systems that are interacting with clients and communities to determine if barriers are evident within these systems and preventing the growth of clients or communities. Assessment of these systems also allows professional counselors to determine what resources are available to clients and communities to include in advocacy action plans. These plans can include a range of activities from practicing assertiveness skills in counseling sessions or encouraging a feeling of empowerment by clients, to promoting awareness of domestic violence by providing public information about it through various types of media.

In essence, opportunities to engage in counseling advocacy are abundant and present in most environments in which professional counselors interact on a daily basis. Ethically, professional counselors have an obligation to empower clients/community systems and advocate for those who cannot self-advocate. If professional counselors do not engage in advocacy counseling, in essence, they are part of the barriers to human development and growth.

The Effectiveness of Counseling

15 Accountability in Counseling

BRADLEY T. ERFORD

PREVIEW

Accountability is a central responsibility of all professional counselors. However, accountability is not just tallying the number of clients seen, or how much time has been spent providing various types of services. At its core, accountability demonstrates the effect that a professional counselor has in producing changes in clients and program stakeholders. This chapter presents models and methods for how professional counselors can demonstrate accountability through implementing effective needs assessment, program evaluation, service assessment, and outcome studies. Outcome studies are approached from traditional research methods perspectives, and more contemporary perspectives, including action research and single-subject research designs.

ACCOUNTABILITY

Research has established that counseling is an effective treatment delivery system (see Chapter 16). However, this knowledge alone does not satisfy the public's justified need for continued **accountability** in counseling services, particular on a case-by-case or group-by-group basis. Whiston (1996) stated, "Clients, third-party payers, and school administrators are only a few examples of those who may want data based information concerning a professional counselor's effectiveness" (p. 616). For counseling to remain valued by the public and paid for by third-party payers and clients, professional counselors must provide evidence showing that their work is worthwhile and produces results. Lack of accountability can lead to the elimination of counseling positions, specific counseling practices, and entire delivery systems.

A new era of educational reform and a lack of accountability in the school counseling profession have caused positions to be eliminated from school districts across the United States. Erford, House, and Martin (2007) stated, "School districts, including superintendents and school boards, are primarily focused on increasing student achievement. Professional school counselors must demonstrate that they are central to the success of these efforts" (p. 11). Likewise, third-party insurance payers have made increasing demands for the demonstration of counselor effectiveness with clients. Professional counselors who demonstrate effectiveness may receive more referrals and develop a reputation for skill and efficiency.

Accountability in counseling answers the question, "How are clients different as a result of the services provided by professional counselors?" By the use of assessment techniques to measure outcomes, counselors can provide accountability to clients, funding sources, administrators, and other stakeholders, and demonstrate how their program is affecting member outcomes, development, and achievement. Accountability requires responsibility for professional actions. According to various authors (Erford, 2007a; Issacs, 2003; Loesch & Ritchie, 2004; Myrick, 2003), accountability ordinarily involves the following:

- Identifying and collaborating with stakeholder groups (e.g., advisory committees, clients, parents, teachers, students)
- Collecting data and assessing the needs of clients, staff, and community
- Setting goals and establishing objectives based on data and determined needs
- Implementing effective interventions to address the goals and objectives
- Measuring the outcomes or results of these interventions
- Using these results for program improvement
- Sharing results with major stakeholder groups (e.g., clients, administrators, teachers and staff, parents and guardians, students, school boards, community and business leaders, professional counselors and supervisors)

There are advantages and challenges to conducting accountability studies, although the challenges are often easily overcome by collaborating with colleagues with some accountability expertise. These are outlined in Table 15.1. It is the professional and ethical responsibility of counselors to ensure that the services offered to stakeholders are truly effective. This chapter focuses on the wide-ranging accountability functions of the professional counselor,

---

TABLE 15.1 Advantages and Disadvantages of Accountability Studies

Advantages
1. Data are almost always better than perception when it comes to guiding decision making about programs, practices, and interventions.
2. Accountability studies help show the necessity, efficiency, and effectiveness of counseling services.
3. Accountability studies can help identify professional development and staff development needs.
4. Professional counselors can network to share program results, spreading the word about effective practices.
5. Conducting accountability studies is a professional responsibility and demonstrates commitment to personal and professional improvement.
6. Accountability results can serve a public relations function by informing clients and the public of a counseling program's accomplishments.

Challenges
1. Outcome measures and surveys require some training and skill to develop (sometimes including consultation with experts).
2. It requires time and resources to do quality outcomes research and evaluation, time and resources that could be dedicated to additional service delivery.
3. Many do not understand the nature and purpose of accountability because of misperceptions or previous "bad" experiences.
4. Data are sometimes "overinterpreted" or given undue meaning (e.g., the facts may not support the conclusion). All studies have limitations that must be considered when arriving at conclusions.

including needs assessment, program evaluation, service assessment, and outcome research. This information allows professional counselors to speak the language of decision makers, promoting social and academic advocacy for clients with diverse needs, or overcoming systemic barriers to academic, career, or personal/social success. Toward this end, every professional counselor should be constantly asking and gathering information to answer the question, "Is what I'm doing working with clients?"

Comprehensive evaluations are seldom conducted. More often, bits and pieces of evaluative information are collected, and the "big picture" is often incomplete.

USING A COUNSELING PROGRAM ADVISORY COMMITTEE

A counseling program **advisory committee** serves as a sounding board and steering committee. These committees are commonly used in school, community, or agency counseling environments. The most important factor to consider when composing a counseling program advisory committee is influence. The professional counselor must seek to include individuals who can influence and hold the confidence of program decision makers. In schools, decision makers may include the principal and central office administrators, while in community agencies, decision makers may include program administrators or directors of funding sources. Including influential members on the committee eases the way for necessary programmatic changes and resource attainment.

From a personnel perspective in agencies, it is essential for the program administrator or the representatives from important funding sources to be a member of the advisory committee. In this way, the directors can hear firsthand the ideas and planning that go into recommendations for improvement, and the rationale behind why additional funding may be needed. In addition to the professional counselor, at least several influential stakeholders (e.g., community leaders, activists, politicians, business leaders, parents) should be included. The members can inform the advisory committee of various constituencies' concerns and provide information back to the constituencies regarding actions recommended by the committee.

For school-based committees, it is essential for the principal to be a member of the advisory committee. In this way, the principal can hear firsthand the ideas and planning that go into recommendations for improvement, and the rationale behind why additional funding may be needed. In addition to the professional school counselor(s), at least several influential teachers and parents should be included. Political linkages to parent-teacher organizations often play to the advantage of a professional school counselor because these members can serve as conduits to and from the organizations. The members can inform the advisory committee of various constituencies' concerns and provide information back to the constituencies regarding actions recommended by the committee, or the blockage of the recommended actions.

To round out the committee, an influential school resource person (e.g., school psychologist, special education teacher, reading specialist) and an influential community organization or business leaders should be included. Individuals from the community and businesses are useful for providing an external perspective, and partnerships as well as external funding and resources.

The advisory committee should convene at least twice annually, and more frequently if the program is new or undergoing major changes. The primary role of the advisory committee is to review the results of the needs assessment, make recommendations for program development, review accountability data and outcomes research generated by staff, and locate internal and external funding sources for program development. Locating funding sources often requires the cooperation of directors or principals; this is where it pays off to include directors or principals and other individuals with influence in the committee. The advisory committee can serve a practical and political function, making it a top priority on the professional counselor's agenda. One of the most important roles of the advisory committee is to help professional counselors determine constituent needs and program goals. Now complete Activity 15.1.

ACTIVITY 15.1

Imagine that you are tasked to form a counseling program advisory committee for your school or agency. Who would you invite to participate in the committee and why?

CONDUCTING A NEEDS ASSESSMENT

At least two primary purposes underlie the use of a needs assessment in counseling programs. First, **needs assessment** helps professional counselors understand the needs of various subpopulations of a community. These subpopulations may include clients, congregations, neighborhoods, teachers, parents, students, administrators, community organizations, or local business people. Subpopulations within schools may include subgroups of students experiencing achievement gaps or differential access to rigorous academic programming. Each of these groups holds a stake in the success of the total educational enterprise; they are called **stakeholder** groups. Second, needs assessment helps establish the priorities that guide the construction of a counseling program or group work intervention, and continuous quality improvement of the program. A needs assessment emphasizes what currently exists compared with identified goals and objectives. Assessing the needs of a community or community population provides a trajectory for addressing what the community values and desires to pursue. Needs assessments can be classified as data-driven needs assessments and perceptions-based needs assessments.

Data-Driven Needs Assessment

Data-driven decision making deals with real needs and impact, not perceived needs. Data-driven needs assessment is most frequently used in school systems because standardized assessment is systematically collected primarily due to state and federal initiatives, such as the *No Child Left Behind Act* of 2001. However, this process can also be applied just as easily to community-based mental health practice.

SCHOOL-BASED DATA-DRIVEN NEEDS EXAMPLE **Data-driven needs assessment** begins with an analysis of school-based or community-based performance data. Given the prominence of high-stakes testing and large-scale testing programs required under *No Child Left Behind,* schools are frequently provided with aggregated and disaggregated achievement performance results. **Aggregated** means that all student results are lumped together to show total grade level or school-wide (average) results. Aggregated data are helpful in understanding how the average students perform in a given class, grade, or school, but tell very little about the diversity of learner performance or needs, and nothing about how various subgroups or subpopulations performed. In Table 15.2, the aggregated results are represented by the "Total grade" line at the top for a school with 100 fifth-graders.

TABLE 15.2 Aggregated and Disaggregated Results of a Typical Large-Scale Math Achievement Test for a Total School Fifth-Grade Level

	n	NPR	% in Quartile			
			Q_1	Q_2	Q_3	Q_4
Total grade	**100**	**50**	**19**	**31**	**26**	**24**
Male	48	45	22	34	26	18
Female	52	56	10	31	31	28
Asian	8	72	0	25	38	38
Black	31	37	29	52	13	6
Hispanic	8	43	25	50	25	0
White	52	58	9	30	33	28
Other	1	44	0	100	0	0
Low SES	48	31	36	38	23	3
Non low SES	52	71	5	24	36	35
English (second language)	3	43	0	67	33	0
English (primary language)	97	51	19	30	27	24
Special education	10	25	60	20	20	0
Non special education	90	58	11	31	32	26

Note: n = number of students in sample; NPR = national percentile rank; % in Quartile = percentage of the sample that actually performed in a given quartile.

To understand fully how to use performance data, professional counselors must become proficient in understanding norm-referenced and criterion-referenced score interpretation. While a comprehensive explanation of score interpretation is beyond the scope of this chapter and typically encountered by counselors in an assessment or testing course, what follows can be considered a primer on the interpretation of norm-referenced scores. For a more advanced understanding of interpreting standardized test score data, see two texts by Erford (2007b and 2008a).

In the example in Table 15.2, the mean national percentile rank was 50. A **percentile rank** is most easily understood if one visualizes a lineup of 100 individuals all with certain characteristics in common—in this case they are all fifth-grade math students. When interpreting percentile ranks, the first student on the line is the lowest performing student, whereas the 100th student is the highest performing student. A student's place indicates the relative standing compared with other fifth-grade math students across the United States (thus the term "national percentile rank"). For example, a student scoring at the 79th percentile performed better than 79% of the fifth-graders in the national norm group, or was the 79th student standing in the line. Likewise, a student performing at the 5th percentile would be standing in the fifth place in line and has outperformed 5% of the fifth-graders in the nationwide norm group.

A **quartile** is a commonly used interpretive statistic that divides the percentile rank distribution into four segments. The first quartile includes percentile ranks ranging from less than 1–25, the lowest quarter of a distribution and designated as Q_1. The second quartile (Q_2) includes percentile ranks ranging from 26–50. The third quartile (Q_3) includes percentile ranks ranging from 51–75. The fourth quartile (Q_4) includes percentile ranks ranging from 76 to greater than 99, the highest quarter of the distribution.

Some test publishers also use an interpretive statistic known as stanines. Stanines, short for standard nine, divide a normal distribution into nine segments, albeit in a manner quite different from quartiles. Stanines actually represent one-half standard deviation units. So while each quartile represents 25% of the population, stanines may be composed of varying percentages of the population. The first stanine represents the lowest level of performance, while the ninth stanine represents the highest level of performance, each composing only 4% of the population. In contrast, the fifth stanine represents the middle of the distribution and is composed of 20% of the population.

Parents, teachers, and students understand performance easiest and most accurately when using percentile ranks. Other standardized scores can require some sophistication and may lead to errors in interpretation. Figure 15.1 provides a graphic of the normal curve and commonly used standardized scores the professional counselor may encounter. Each of these standardized scores can be converted into percentile ranks for easy explanation to parents, teachers, and students.

Disaggregated means the data have been broken down by subpopulations so that performance differences between and among groups can be analyzed. Usually, this analysis

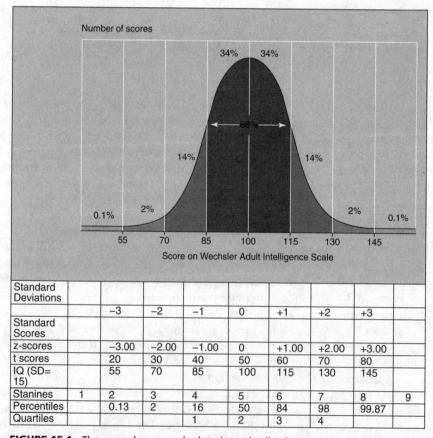

Standard Deviations									
		−3	−2	−1	0	+1	+2	+3	
Standard Scores									
z-scores		−3.00	−2.00	−1.00	0	+1.00	+2.00	+3.00	
t scores		20	30	40	50	60	70	80	
IQ (SD= 15)		55	70	85	100	115	130	145	
Stanines	1	2	3	4	5	6	7	8	9
Percentiles		0.13	2	16	50	84	98	99.87	
Quartiles				1	2	3	4		

FIGURE 15.1   The normal curve and related standardized scores.

involves intergroup differences (e.g., male versus female, race, ethnicity, special education status versus regular education status). Most test publishers can provide this information upon request, broken down by school, by grade level, and even by individual classes. Differences can be determined using statistical methods or by informal comparison. Seeing differences in disaggregated data helps provide hard evidence of gaps in student performance, rather than relying on perceptions. It also provides direction for the types of strategies and interventions needed to close these gaps.

Returning to the data provided in Table 15.2, one can see several noticeable gaps in achievement. First, students from the low socioeconomic status (SES) grouping performed at the 31st percentile rank, on average, whereas students from the non–low SES group (e.g., middle-class and upper-middle-class in this example) performed at the 71st percentile rank, on average. Second, there is a noticeable difference between the average math performance for Black and Hispanic students (37th and 43rd percentile ranks) compared with Asian and White students (72nd and 58th percentile ranks). Third, girls outperformed boys, on average, 56th and 45th percentile rank. From these comparisons of disaggregated data, discussions can ensue, and strategies can be developed to reduce the math performance gap. However, it all starts with the data—hence the name "data-driven." In this way, data provide the impetus and drive behind school improvement plans and responsive school counseling programs. Activity 15.2 encourages you to think further about the disaggregated data in Table 15.2.

ACTIVITY 15.2

How could you use the disaggregated data in Table 15.2 to develop an action plan to enhance the academic performance of these students? What additional data would you need? What areas for improvement would you identify? What strategies and interventions would you recommend or implement?

CLINIC-BASED DATA-DRIVEN NEEDS ASSESSMENT EXAMPLE In an example from clinical practice, Table 15.3 provides treatment change data from the *Beck Anxiety Inventory* (BAI) (Beck & Steer, 1993) for a group of 50 clients seen for a group counseling treatment regimen with no concurrent medication treatment. Analyzing the aggregated data, one would conclude

TABLE 15.3 Aggregated and Disaggregated Data of 50 Clients Treated for Anxiety with a 24-week Group Counseling Regimen on the BAI (Raw Score)

	n	BAI Baseline (A)	BAI (24 sessions) (B)	BAI Change (A-B)
Total sample	**50**	**30**	**20**	**10**
Males	20	26	17.2	8.8
Females	30	32.7	21.9	10.8
White	36	33.3	20.8	12.5
Black	14	21.5	18	3.5
Low SES	20	25.5	22.4	3.1
Non low SES	30	33	18.4	14.6

that the 50 clients began with an average BAI raw score of 30 (moderate-to-severe levels of anxiety symptoms) and finished the group counseling treatment regimen with an average BAI raw score of 20 (mild-to-moderate levels of anxiety)—an average raw score decline of 10 points. On the surface, and on average, these data show that the group treatment was successful in reducing average symptoms of anxiety for the group. However, conscientious professional counselors are interested in determining whether the treatment differentially affected members with various characteristics (e.g., sex, race, SES).

Disaggregating the total sample data in Table 15.3, notice that some differences do appear to exist regarding the effectiveness of the treatment on certain subgroups. For example, low SES participants experienced only a 3-point raw score improvement after treatment, whereas non–low SES participants experienced more than four times that level of symptom relief (i.e., a change of 14.6 raw score points for non–low SES versus a change of only 3 points for low SES participants). Likewise, African American clients reported average BAI raw score declines of only 3.5 points, whereas White participants reported a decline of 12.5 raw score points.

On the surface, one may reach a tentative conclusion that the group counseling treatment was more effective for White and non–low SES participants. Disaggregated data can help professional counselors make decisions about treatment efficacy for prospective clients, and make program improvements to help future clients benefit equitably from an otherwise effective approach or program. Data-driven approaches to needs assessment use existing data, or easy to collect data, to determine client population needs and treatment equity.

These differences can be determined through more advanced statistical procedures or by less sophisticated procedures, such as simply "eyeballing" the data to note gaps in performance. Identified gaps provide objective (not perception-based) evidence of differential results, identifying needs to be addressed. When such needs are identified, professional counselors can begin the process of addressing these needs through well-written objectives, interventions, and programmatic initiatives. (See the later section on converting needs to program goals and objectives.) Now complete Activity 15.3.

ACTIVITY 15.3

How could you use the disaggregated data in Table 15.3 to develop an action plan to enhance the treatment of these clients? What additional data would you need? What areas for improvement would you identify? What strategies and interventions would you recommend or implement?

Perceptions-Based Needs Assessment

In contrast to a data-driven needs assessment, a traditional perceptions-based needs assessment process is more content driven and subjective. Professional counselors are often interested in what clients, community leaders, citizens, teachers, parents, and students perceive as primary needs to be addressed. Before undertaking a **perceptions-based needs assessment**, professional counselors are wise to consider issues of how often to conduct a needs assessment, which stakeholder group to assess, and how to design an efficient needs assessment.

FREQUENCY OF CONDUCTING A NEEDS ASSESSMENT Although it may seem tempting to design and conduct a global needs assessment on an annual basis, such an endeavor would be a massive administrative undertaking. It is probably best to follow a multiyear continuous cycle of assessing programmatic needs. This approach allows ample time for program development and improvements over the course of the cycle. The timing of needs assessments varies for community and school venues. In schools, the American School Counselor Association (ASCA) *National Standards* (Campbell & Dahir, 1997) and *National Model* (American School Counselor Association, 2005) designate the areas of academic, career, and personal-social development as the cornerstones of a comprehensive developmental school counseling program; it makes sense that school community needs be assessed according to these components on a rotating basis.

For a new program or one undergoing tremendous renovations, years 1 and 2 of a 6-year cycle can be spent conducting needs assessment and implementing programmatic changes to address horizontal and vertical articulation issues surrounding student academic development. Years 3 and 4 can be spent on student career development needs, and years 5 and 6 can focus on student personal-social issues. The 6-year cycle could alternate between the three domains addressing half of the domain issues every 3 years (i.e., year 1, academic; year 2, career; year 3, personal/social; year 4, academic; year 5, career; year 6, personal/social). An established school counseling program in good condition requiring only fine-tuning may be put on a 3-year continuous improvement cycle.

Community-based mental health counseling programs may require a comprehensive needs assessment only every 3 to 5 years, or when societal or political changes deem it essential to maintaining quality service levels within the community. The main point here is that assessing needs is part of a much bigger endeavor: that of implementing programmatic changes to improve the counseling program continuously. Implementing changes can be time intensive, and simply a waste of time if not guided by accurate needs assessments and program outcome research. An effective program uses this information to fine-tune its efforts in data-driven decision making.

POPULATIONS TO BE ASSESSED In the broadest sense, any stakeholder group can provide helpful information about the needs of a population or community. However, it is most practical and efficient to seek out individuals who are informed and likely to respond. Community leaders, teachers, administrators, clients, students, and parents are the most likely to be informed of community and school issues and needs, and under most circumstances are the primary stakeholder groups surveyed during a needs assessment. Valuable information can also be garnered from community organizations, local businesses, and the general citizenry. It is just more difficult to obtain a large response sampling from these groups. Information from these stakeholders is probably best obtained through personal contacts and interviews.

Return rate is another factor in the needs assessment process. Return rate is the percent of returned surveys out of those distributed. As in any research sampling procedure, the higher the return rate, the lower the sampling error; this leads to greater confidence in the accuracy of the results. Return rate is generally maximized when the participants are a "captured audience." For example, if a social skills needs assessment of fourth-grade students is conducted in the classroom, the response rate should be nearly 100%. If a needs assessment for parents is sent home, the professional school counselor may be lucky to receive 25% to 50% of the surveys back. The return rate probably would be even lower if mailed to community stakeholders. Whenever possible, surveys should be distributed and collected immediately during client gatherings, community gatherings, faculty meetings, class meetings, and parent gatherings.

Triangulation of needs across populations should be attempted when possible, that is, the highest priority needs should be those agreed to by all or most populations assessed.

This ensures that the community's needs, not an individual's agenda, drive the counseling program. For instance, in a community agency, directors can be powerful influences, and their agendas for the agency may constrict services from being applied where they are most needed. Determining different needs and priorities confirmed by multiple stakeholder groups can provide strong evidence that the director's agenda is off-course. Likewise in a school, if a principal has decided to place a high priority on social skills, but teachers, parents, and students indicate this is a low priority, and far below other issues such as school safety, substance abuse, and study skills, the triangulated responses of the teachers, parents, and students can provide compelling evidence to guide the program's focus.

DESIGNING AN EFFICIENT NEEDS ASSESSMENT Designing an efficient needs assessment is essential to meaningful results. While some experts advocate for a comprehensive needs assessment simultaneously assessing all goals and topics associated with a comprehensive counseling program, others have found it more helpful to focus the assessment on specifically defined topics or issues that are being updated or altered. This chapter focuses on the latter method.

Stone and Bradley (1994) recommended seven methods for determining needs: questionnaires and inventories, analysis of records, personal interviews, counseling statistics, classroom visits, use of outside consultants, and systematic evaluation of the counseling program. Perhaps what is most important is that the needs assessment uses objective methods for data gathering and analysis. It is essential to understand that different questions can be addressed by different methods. Although all of these methods are important and useful, questionnaires (formal or informal surveys) are most commonly used and are the focus here. While open-ended questionnaires are generally easier to design and yield rich and diverse information, such questionnaires are usually more difficult to interpret and translate into goals and objectives.

From a return rate perspective, it is good practice to try to design a needs assessment that is only one page in length (maximum of two pages) and can be completed in only 2 to 3 minutes. The content of the needs assessment should be topical (e.g., social skills, changing families, substance abuse, college application procedures) rather than service related (e.g., individual counseling, group counseling, consultation). Professional counselors should keep in mind that services are simply methods for meeting needs, not needs in themselves. The topics should be related to the program goals (e.g., agency standards or mission statement, the ASCA *National Standards,* local or state standards) so that priority status can be placed on addressing the most pressing needs in comparison to these standards. A good needs assessment directly translates into program development.

In general, the following steps form the basis of an efficient needs assessment:

1. Decide what you need to know.
2. Decide on the best approach to derive what you need to know.
3. Develop the needs assessment instrument or method.
4. Enlist the support of colleagues and a few individuals from the target groups to review and try out items for understanding.
5. Implement the final version on the target groups.
6. Tabulate, analyze, and interpret the results.
7. Translate the results into programmatic goals and objectives.

The design of the scale itself warrants mention. The client survey should ask for the name of the individual completing the form (unless the form is to be completed anonymously). Teacher surveys may ask for the grade level, the number of students in class, or other pertinent information. Parent surveys should ask for the names of the parent's children in case their response to the survey requires contact by the professional counselor. Student surveys should ask for the student's grade and homeroom teacher's name. Questions or response items should be short, to the point, and easily understood. The reading level of the items should also be appropriate for the target audience. Figure 15.2 provides an example of a topic-focused needs assessment for students/clients.

Substantial consideration should also be given to the response format. If the purpose of the survey is to determine the importance or frequency of a potential problem, it is generally best to use a multipoint scale with four to seven choices. For example, Figure 15.2 asks about the frequency of stressors, so the response choices "Almost Never," "Sometimes," "Often," and "Almost always" are appropriate. The response choices "Never" and "Always" do not appear. It is rare that behaviors never or always occur; to include these descriptors may force responses to the center of the distribution and truncate the range of possible results. Also notice how each category has a descriptor. Gone are the days in survey construction when a survey lists the response categories of 0, "Almost never" and 3, "Almost always," and then provides the center points of 1 and 2 with no accompanying descriptor. The reliability problems of such a scale are obvious: Would all respondents agree on what an unlabeled 1 and 2 represent? All choice categories must be accompanied by a verbal descriptor.

Another important response component of a needs assessment is a frequency count. Suppose a professional counselor would want not only to assess the importance of an issue, but to determine how many clients were likely in need of services to address the problems

Name: _____

Place a check mark (✓) in the appropriate space below to indicate how well you handle each issue.

	Almost Never	Sometimes	Often	Almost always	I need help with this	
					Yes	No
1. I am able to focus my thoughts when I need to.						
2. I have a good workout schedule.						
3. I have good time management skills.						
4. I can control my breathing when upset.						
5. I can control my level of stress.						
6. I have good organizational skills.						
7. My muscles are relaxed.						
8. I have good nutritional habits.						
9. I think positive thoughts about myself.						
10. I can readily identify stressors in my life.						

FIGURE 15.2 A focused stress management needs assessment.

stemming from the issue. When possible, the needs assessment should be designed to include an indication of whether the respondent should be targeted for intervention. In Figure 15.2, notice how the far right-hand column asks for a yes or no answer to the statement, "I need help with this." An affirmative response targets the client for future assessment or intervention to address a self-perceived weakness.

Tallying or computing the information from a needs assessment is simple. Tallying simply involves counting the number of clients who may benefit from intervention. Computing the results of a needs assessment is probably best accomplished by assigning a number value to each response category and averaging all responses for a given item. In Figure 15.2, assume that the response categories are assigned the following values: Almost never = 0, Sometimes = 1, Often = 2, and Almost always = 3. For item 1, "I am able to focus my thoughts when I need to," simply add all client response values and divide by the number of responses.

Using the data in Table 15.4, for Item 1, if 50 clients completed the needs assessment, and 10 clients marked "Almost never" ($10 \times 0 = 0$), 12 clients marked "Sometimes" ($12 \times 1 = 12$), 21 clients marked "Often" ($21 \times 2 = 42$), and 7 clients marked "Almost always" ($7 \times 3 = 21$), simply sum the points ($0 + 12 + 42 + 21 = 75$) and divide by the number of client responses (sum of 75 divided by 50 students = 1.50) to compute the average frequency rating (1.50). Although this assumes a ratio scale and is nebulous from a statistical interpretation perspective (i.e., what does a 1.50 really mean?), it does offer a reasonable estimate of the average frequency of a

TABLE 15.4 Data From the Stress Management Needs Assessment ($n = 50$)

	AN (0)	S (1)	O (2)	AA (3)	Yes	No	Average (rank)
1. I am able to focus my thoughts when I need to.	10 (0)	12 (12)	21 (42)	7 (21)	21	29	1.50 (9)
2. I have a good workout schedule.	22 (0)	17 (17)	7 (14)	4 (12)	33	17	0.86 (3)
3. I have good time management skills.	15 (0)	12 (12)	14 (28)	9 (27)	22	28	1.34 (6)
4. I can control my breathing when upset.	29 (0)	12 (12)	7 (14)	2 (6)	42	8	0.64 (1)
5. I can control my level of stress.	24 (0)	9 (9)	10 (20)	7 (21)	33	17	1.00 (4)
6. I have good organizational skills.	14 (0)	9 (9)	17 (34)	10 (30)	19	31	1.46 (8)
7. My muscles are relaxed.	28 (0)	8 (8)	8 (16)	6 (18)	35	15	0.84 (2)
8. I have good nutritional habits.	19 (0)	15 (15)	7 (14)	9 (27)	35	15	1.12 (5)
9. I think positive thoughts about myself.	17 (0)	12 (12)	7 (14)	14 (42)	23	27	1.36 (7)
10. I can readily identify stressors in my life.	6 (0)	9 (9)	10 (20)	25 (75)	4	36	2.08 (10)

Note: Almost Never (AN) = 0; Sometimes (S) = 1; Often (O) = 2; Almost Always (AA) = 3. The tally (no. of clients responding) is entered in each column first followed by the product of the tally and response value; for example, item 1 under the AA (3) column reads 7 (21), meaning that seven clients responded Almost Always and this tally was multiplied by 3, resulting in a product of 21. The rank indicates the order of greatest need, with the lower average scores indicating the greater degrees of need.

behavior, or of the importance of one issue compared with the other issues under study. For example, when viewing the mean computations of the 10 items in Table 14.4, the professional counselor gets a good idea how important Item 1 is compared with the other nine items in the needs assessment. Now complete Activity 15.4.

ACTIVITY 15.4

As a class or as individuals, choose a counseling topic or goal and design a brief perception-based needs assessment to determine the needs of a client group. As a class, complete the needs assessment, tally the responses, conduct descriptive statistics, and prioritize objectives for an intervention program to address group needs.

HELPFUL TIPS FOR DEVELOPING A NEEDS ASSESSMENT A helpful set of common sense guidelines for questionnaire or survey development was provided by Worthen, Sanders, and Fitzpatrick (1997, pp. 355–356):

1. Sequencing questions
   a. Are later responses biased by early questions?
   b. Does the questionnaire begin with easy, unthreatening, but pertinent questions?
   c. Are leading questions avoided (ones that "lead" to a certain response)?
   d. Is there a logical, efficient sequencing of questions (e.g., from general to specific questions; use of filter questions when appropriate)?
   e. Are closed-ended or open-ended questions appropriate? If closed, are the categories exhaustive and mutually exclusive? Do responses result in the desired scale of data for analysis (i.e., nominal, ordinal, interval)?
   f. Are the major issues covered thoroughly while minor issues passed over quickly?
   g. Are questions with similar content grouped logically?
2. Wording questions
   a. Are questions stated precisely (who, what, when, where, why, how)?
   b. Does the questionnaire avoid assuming too much knowledge on the part of the respondent?
   c. Does each item ask only one question?
   d. Is the respondent in a position to answer the question, or must he or she make guesses? If so, are you interested in his or her guesses?
   e. Are definitions clear?
   f. Are emotionally tinged words avoided?
   g. Is the vocabulary at the reading level of the audience? If any technical terminology, jargon, or slang is used, is it the most appropriate way to communicate with this audience?
   h. Are the methods for responding appropriate, clear, and consistent?
   i. Are the questions appropriately brief and uncomplicated?
3. Establishing and keeping rapport and eliciting cooperation
   a. Is the questionnaire easy to answer? (Questions are not overly long or cumbersome.)
   b. Is the time required to respond reasonable?
   c. Does the instrument look attractive (i.e., layout, quality of paper)?
   d. Is there a "respondent orientation?"

   e. Does the cover letter provide an explanation of purpose, sponsorship, method of respondent selection, and anonymity?

   f. Is appropriate incentive provided for the respondent's cooperation?

4. Giving instructions

   a. Is the respondent clearly told how to record responses?

   b. Are instructions for return clear? Is a stamped return envelop provided?

Professional counselors conducting needs assessments must choose an appropriate response format, ordinarily: yes/no (or sometimes), multiscale formats (e.g., almost never, sometimes, frequently, almost always), Likert-type scales (e.g., very dissatisfied, dissatisfied, satisfied, very satisfied), true/false formats, or multiple-choice formats. Note the wording of items, scaling method, and single-page format of the needs assessment presented in Figure 15.2.

CONVERTING NEEDS TO PROGRAM GOALS AND OBJECTIVES If the needs assessment was designed correctly, translating the results into goals and learning objectives is easy. The first step is to prioritize the needs in the order of importance and their relationship to existing components of the program. Prioritization can be accomplished most easily by the use of the tallying, computing, and triangulation strategies mentioned earlier. Next, the needs must be matched with, or translated into, goals aligned with the program mission and standards. Finally, the goals are operationalized through the development of learning objectives. Two texts by Erford (2007a, 2008b) provide an excellent nuts-and-bolts discussion of how to write learning objectives using the **ABCD model**: (A) audience, (B) behavior, (C) conditions, and (D) description of the expected performance criterion.

A reasonable goal stemming from the needs assessment shown in Figure 15.2 would be "To increase clients' abilities to manage stress and anxiety." Notice how the wording of a goal is nebulous and not amenable to measurement as stated. In developing learning objectives related to goals, particular emphasis is given to specific actions that are measurable. For example, a possible objective stemming from this goal could be, "After participating in a group counseling program and learning thought stopping procedures, 80% of the clients will experience a 50% reduction in obsessive thinking over a 1-week period." Another possible objective might be, "After participating in a 6-week program on the importance of exercise with follow-up goal setting monitoring, 80% of members will engage in at least 20 minutes of aerobic exercise at least three times per week." Notice how the objectives designate the audience, the stated behavior, how the behavior will be measured, and the level of expected performance (Erford, 2007a, 2008b). Gain some more familiarity with the ABCD model by completing Activity 15.5.

ACTIVITY 15.5

Write the following statements into measurable behavioral objectives using the ABCD model:

   1. Group members will increase verbal interactions.
   2. Class members will engage in more appropriate social skills with each other during classroom activities.
   3. The client will become less depressed after participating in individual counseling sessions.

EVALUATING PROGRAMS

In this age of accountability, program evaluation is more important than ever. Traditionally, however, professional counselors for many reasons have failed to hold their programs and services accountable or to provide evidence that activities undertaken achieved intended results. Some professional counselors complained that the nature of what counselors do is so abstract and complicated as to render the services and results unmeasurable. Other professional counselors are so busy attempting to meet the needs of clients that they shift time that should be spent in evaluation to responsive interventions. Some lack an understanding of how to implement the methods and procedures of accountability studies. Still others may be unsure of the effectiveness of the services provided, and shy away from accountability unless forced to do so by supervisors.

Whatever the reason, the end result is a lack of accountability that poses dangers for the future of the profession. Each contributes to a shirking of professional and ethical responsibility of ensuring that the services provided to clients are of high quality and are effective in meeting intended needs and goals. Think about it from a business perspective. How long would a business last if it continued to engage in indiscernible or ineffective activities, the value of which were unknown to the business's consumers, managers, or employees? Such businesses are selected out for extinction. Now extend that thought to the counseling profession. Without accountability data to back up service provision, agency and school counseling services are often among the first services to go during budget cutbacks. Evaluation of counseling services must become and remain a top priority.

Stone and Bradley (1994, p. 229) suggested six purposes of evaluation:

> (1) To measure the effectiveness of the . . . program as well as each of the activities included in it. . . . (2) To collect data that, after interpretation, will be meaningful in determining what program modifications are indicated. . . . (3) To determine the level of program acceptance and support from [stakeholders]. . . . (4) To obtain information that can be used to inform the public about the [program]. . . . (5) To collect data that will become an important part of the counselor's evaluation. . . . (6) To analyze the program budget and compare expenditures to future program needs.

In the context of counseling, professional counselors must be concerned with three areas of accountability: (1) process evaluation, (2) service assessment, and (3) results or outcome evaluation. All three are important facets of program evaluation. **Evaluation** is the measurement of worth and indicates that a judgment will be made regarding the effectiveness of a program. In an evaluation process, it is essential to be very specific about what you are measuring and how you are measuring it. This is made clear in the writing of specific learning objectives. Too often, professional counselors are not specific about what they are trying to accomplish, and become frustrated when they fail to measure what they may or may not have achieved. If a person does not know where he or she is heading, the person must either get specific directions (write a specific, measurable objective) or be satisfied with wherever he or she ends up (perhaps an ineffective program).

PROGRAM EVALUATION Program evaluation (also sometimes called **process evaluation** or **program audit**) is akin to the measurement concept of content validity, which is a systematic examination of a test's (in this case, program's) content. Program evaluation asks whether the counseling entity (agency, school system) has a written program, and whether the written program is being fully implemented by the entity (Gysbers & Henderson, 2005). In short, the audit or evaluation of a program involves determining whether there is written program documentation, and whether the program is being implemented appropriately. A program audit frequently provides an analysis of each facet of the comprehensive counseling program (Bowers & Colonna, 2001; Johnson & Johnson, 2003). Auditing the program often points to the areas of programmatic strengths and weaknesses.

For school counselors, the ASCA (2005) *National Model* provided a sample program audit aligning with model components. Sample criteria included "a statement of philosophy has been written for the school counseling program" and "addresses every student's right to a school counseling program" (p. 66). The ASCA suggested that program criteria be evaluated on the following response choices: "None: meaning not in place; In progress: perhaps begun, but not completed; Completed but perhaps not implemented; Implemented: fully implemented; Not Applicable: for situations where the criteria does not apply" (p. 66). In practice, a program audit should be conducted near the end of each academic year. Reports derived from the audit should address program strengths, areas in need of improvement, and long-term and short-term improvement goals. These goals drive program development procedures and activities during subsequent years.

Service Assessment

Service assessments are often requested by agency directors, counselor supervisors, and superintendents and school boards to document how counselors are spending their time. Two types of service assessments are commonly used: event-topic counts and time logs. **Event-topic counts** involve the professional counselor documenting each time an individual is contacted or provided with a counseling service and the nature of the topic addressed. In this way, professional counselors can keep a weekly or monthly tally of the number of clients seen not only for global individual counseling, but specifically for individual counseling for depression, anxiety, behavior, changing family, social skills, anger management, or conflict resolution issues. Such data are quite impressive when aggregated and presented to a supervisor to indicate that, for example, 961 individual counseling sessions were held with clients last year.

A **time log** is sometimes kept by professional counselors to document the amount of time spent in various counseling and non–counseling-related activities. Some school administrators may wish to know the percentage of time counselors actually spend doing group counseling or teacher consultation at the high school level. Time logs require professional counselors to document and categorize their activities for every minute of the workday. In states with mandates for providing direct service activities (e.g., elementary professional counselors must spend at least 50% of their time in the direct service activities of individual counseling, group counseling, and group guidance), time logs may be necessary to document compliance for funding purposes.

While service assessments are helpful for telling what or how much a professional counselor is doing, such assessments give no information about the quality or effectiveness of counselor interventions. The important question becomes, "What good things happen as a result of professional counselors choosing to use their time this way?" After all, what do professional counselors really accomplish if they spend 80% of their time doing group and individual counseling, but have ineffective counseling skills? For this kind of information, we must conduct results or outcome studies. Now complete Activity 15.6.

ACTIVITY 15.6

Keep a time log of all activities you participate in for the next week. Include everything you do from after you wake until you go to sleep. Tabulate and analyze the results. How could you use these data to improve your efficiency as an employee, student, or parent?

RESULTS OR OUTCOMES EVALUATION

Outcome evaluation (also called **results evaluation**) answers the question, how are members different as a result of the intervention? Evaluation is an ongoing, cyclical process represented by the assessment loop shown in Figure 15.3. Many people view accountability or assessment as a discrete component, but it is actually an integrated part of a continuous process for program improvement. All accountability procedures must have the organization's mission in mind because institutional values and needs determine the focus of study. Questions of worth and effectiveness are derived from a confluence of values, needs, goals, and mission, and these questions lead to the determination of what evidence must be collected.

Evidence may exist in many places, but typically is derived using preplanned measures or from the performances or products clients produce during program activities. After information has been gathered, it must be interpreted, and conclusions must be drawn from it regarding the program's or activity's worth, strengths, and weaknesses. Finally, the interpretations and conclusions must be used to change the program or parts of the program to improve it.

Notice how the loop in Figure 15.3 never stops; it represents a continuous process in which assessment results are interpreted and fed back into the improvement process. As assessment information is used to prompt programmatic changes, so are goal setting and the posing of new questions about the revised program recycle. Many professional counselors gather evidence and then stop, believing that the program has been evaluated and the job finished. Why spend valuable time collecting evidence but not use it to improve what you are doing?

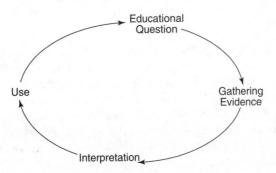

FIGURE 15.3   The assessment cycle.

Important Assessment Terms

Many terms associated with research and evaluation are important to understand. **Evidence** is any data that helps make judgments or decisions, and can be quantitatively or qualitatively derived. **Formative evaluation** is evaluative feedback that occurs during the implementation of a program, and **summative evaluation** is feedback collected at a specified end point in an evaluation process. Although summative evaluation is conducted most frequently, formative evaluation has the advantage of allowing corrective action to occur if an implemented program is shown to be off course. This makes sense when you consider that some programs are expensive to implement in terms of time and money. If you know after one-third of the program has been implemented that desired results are not occurring, midcourse corrections can be made to tailor the program to the audience and the desired outcomes.

A **stakeholder** is anyone involved in or potentially benefiting from the counseling program. Stakeholders may include clients, parents, teachers, professional counselors, administrators, community organizations, and local businesses. A **baseline** is any data gathered to establish a starting point. It is essential to know where clients are so that you can tailor interventions to help facilitate their development. **Inputs** are any resources (e.g., personnel, material) that go into a program; **outcomes** are what stakeholders can do as a result of the program.

A **pretest** is a measure administered before a program is implemented, while a **posttest** is a measure administered after the program or intervention has been completed. If a study calls for a pretest and a post-test, usually there is tremendous overlap in their content because the goal is to determine changes in the individual or group as a result of participating in the program. Any changes that occur in the examinee between administration of the pretest and post-test are usually attributed to the program activities.

Value-added assessment generally uses a pretest-post-test design, but the question posed is, how much value has been added to the client's performance as a result of participating in the program? This is an interesting question to ask because it focuses attention on the timing of interventions and the final yield of an intervention. If 80% of the targeted clients have already met a given criterion, why introduce the concept to the entire group at this time? Would it have been more appropriately introduced earlier in the vertically articulated curriculum? Value-added assessments also focus on the improvements (yield) of the products of a program. For example, elite schools are famous for their desire to produce "creative thinkers and problem solvers," but if students entering the school are selected because of their higher levels of creative thinking and problem-solving capacities, what improvements are these schools really making? Value-added assessment seeks to answer that question by establishing a baseline and evaluating the students' progress over time.

SOURCES OF EVIDENCE Both people and products merit discussion as potential sources of accountability evidence. Almost anyone can serve as a helpful source of evidence: clients, members, students, teachers, staff, administrators, parents, employers, graduates, and community resource people. Numerous products from data collection methods can also be used. A short list includes portfolios, performances, use of ratings from external judges or examiners, observations, local tests, purchased tests, self-assessments, surveys, interviews, focus groups, and client/student work. Each of these sources or products can produce helpful evaluative data, but what is collected results from the specific question to be answered. Some of these sources of evidence are explained in more detail later in this chapter.

Practical Program Evaluation Considerations

To be of practical value, assessment must be connected to real program concerns and the core values of the program. Avoid overwhelming the data collectors, focus on only one or several important questions at a time, and always select measures that yield reliable and valid scores for the purposes under study. Often, ineffective program outcomes stem from poor or inappropriate measurement rather than faulty programming. Be sure to involve the relevant stakeholders and use a variety of approaches. Perhaps most important, do not reinvent the wheel; use what you are already doing to generate useful data about program effectiveness. Also, call upon outside experts to consult on the development and evaluation of a program.

It is good advice to start small and build upon what is found to work; the methods and goals of individual programs are celebrated, and successes can be shared across programs. This often leads to a cross-pollination effect that yields diversity of approach and homogeneity of results. In other words, over time, professional counselors learn from each other what works and implement these strategies with their own populations after necessary refinements based on the needs of a differing client population. Different can still be effective!

Aggregated Outcomes

As mentioned earlier, aggregation is the combining of results to provide a more global or generalized picture of group performance. Although such a practice may de-emphasize subgroup or individual performance, aggregation can be a valuable tool when it comes to evaluating how well counseling programs meet higher level standards or goals. Because of their more abstract or generalized wording, **standards** (sometimes called **goals**) are difficult, if not impossible, to measure directly. This is why curriculum development begins with a statement of standards (goals), which are then described further through a series of **outcomes** (sometimes called **competencies**).

While more specific and well-defined, these outcomes ordinarily are still not amenable to direct measurement in the classic sense. Instead, we rely on specific objectives, such as those discussed in the earlier section on converting needs to program goals and objectives. Objectives are written in such specific, measurable terms that everyone (e.g., clients, professional counselors, teachers, parents, administrators, significant others) can tell when an objective has been met. The use of objectives, outcomes, and goals composes an **aggregated hierarchical model**, and is an important way by which professional counselors can demonstrate the effectiveness of a counseling program. Figure 15.4 provides an example of this aggregated hierarchical model.

In Figure 15.4, note the alignment of objectives to outcomes to goals. Objective 1 measures Competency 1, which is aligned with Standard 1. Likewise, Objective 13 measures Competency 6, which is aligned with Standard 2. Such a hierarchical structure allows the professional counselor to conclude that meeting the lower order objectives provides evidence that higher order outcomes and goals have been successfully met. For example, assume the professional counselor provides evidence that Objectives 1 to 6 have been met. By extension, if Objectives 1 and 2 were met, then Competency 1 was met. If Objectives 3 and 4 were met, then Competency 2 was met. If Objectives 5 and 6 were met, then Competency 3 was met. Because Competencies 1 to 3 were met, the professional counselor has provided evidence that Standard 1 was met. Success! In addition, areas of programmatic strength have been identified.

Again referring to Figure 15.4, now consider a second example in which Objectives 7 to 10 were met, but Objectives 11 to 13 were not met. By extension, if Objectives 7 to 9 were

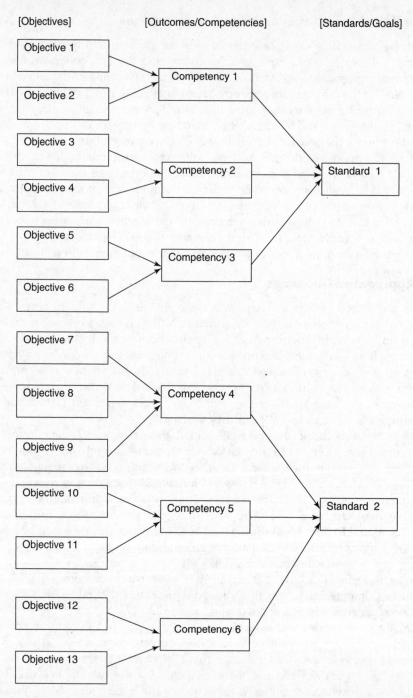

FIGURE 15.4 Aggregated hierarchical model for evaluating the effectiveness of a counseling program.

met, then Competency 4 was met. If Objective 10 was met, but Objective 11 was not met, then Competency 5 either was not met or, more accurately, was only partially met. If Objectives 12 and 13 were not met, then Competency 6 was not met. Now, because of some inconsistent results, interpretation is a bit cloudier. It is most appropriate to conclude that Standard 2 was only partially met because Competency 4 was met, Competency 5 was partially met, and Competency 6 was not met. Given the inconsistency of the outcomes, it would be inappropriate to conclude that Standard 2 had been met; it would be equally inappropriate to conclude that Standard 2 had not been met. A conclusion of "partially met" identifies the hierarchical set of goals, outcomes, and objectives as a programmatic area in need of improvement or providing additional attention to, or revision of, the criteria for successful performance. From these examples, one can see that an aggregated hierarchical model can be a valuable curriculum evaluation method. It also underscores the importance of a measurable objective as the building block of an effective developmental curriculum. Now complete Activity 15.7

ACTIVITY 15.7

Consult Figure 15.4. What would be the conclusion regarding standards attained if each of the odd-numbered objectives were met, but each of the even-numbered objectives were not met? As a professional counselor administering this psychoeducational program, what adjustments would you need to make before implementing the program a second time?

Designing Outcome Studies

While any data collected on counselor effectiveness can be helpful, in most instances, professional counselors should measure outcomes or results by designing a research-type study. A bit of forethought and planning can lead to much more meaningful conclusions. Research studies are typically empirical in nature and involve providing some control over how students are assigned to counseling interventions, and the timing and circumstances under which data are collected. Campbell and Stanley (1963) discussed helpful, easy to implement designs, and several of these designs that may be particularly useful to professional school counselors have been included in Table 15.5.

A comprehensive treatise of this topic is beyond the scope of this book; what follows are some of the relevant points professional counselors should consider when designing outcome studies. Counselors generally receive an entire course in research that can be useful in this context. The interested reader should consult Erford (2008a) for helpful resources on the research methodology and statistical analysis written specifically for professional counselors.

Answering several questions can help the professional counselor determine which research design to use.

1. *Has the treatment already been implemented?* So much for planning ahead! If the intervention has not already occurred, one has many possible options. If the intervention has already occurred, one is relegated to a nonexperimental design, probably a case study or static-group comparison design. It is critical to think about outcomes

assessment in the early stages of planning for an intervention and certainly before the intervention has begun.

2. *Can I randomly assign participants to treatment conditions?* If the answer is yes—outstanding! Control over the random assignment of participants is crucial to implementing true experimental designs. If one does not have control over assignment of participants, the professional counselor must choose a quasiexperimental or non-experimental design.

3. *Can I conduct (one or several) pretests, post-tests, or both?* Usually, measuring the dependent variable before (pretest) and after (post-test) is desirable, although not always essential.

The answers to these questions help the professional counselor choose the most useful and powerful design. For example, if the answers to the three questions are no, yes, and yes, the professional counselor may opt for an experimental design (i.e., designs 7 or 8 in Table 15.5). If the answers are yes, no, and post-test only, one is relegated to a nonexperimental design (designs 2 or 3 in Table 15.5). As one can no doubt surmise, outcome studies require some level of planning early on in program development.

Nearly all true experimental designs involve random assignment of participants, which also randomizes various sources of error allowing for the control of numerous threats to validity. True experimental designs allow causative conclusions to be reached. This is a big advantage when the professional counselor wants to know conclusively if his or her interventions caused significant improvements in clients. For example, if a professional counselor wants to know if a group intervention designed to improve study skills and academic performance was effective, he or she could use the randomized pretest-post-test control group design

---

TABLE 15.5 Common Designs Used for Outcomes Research

Nonexperimental Designs

1. Pretest-post-test single-group design   O I O
2. Case study   I O
3. Static-group comparison   group 1   O
       group 2   I O

Quasi-experimental Designs

4. Two-sample pretest-post-test design   R O
       R I O
5. Nonequivalent control group design   O I O
       O O
6. Time series design   O O O I O O O

True Experimental Designs

7. Randomized pretest-post-test control group design   R O I O
       R O O
8. Randomized post-test only control group design   R I O
       R O

Note: R = participants are randomly assigned to groups; I = intervention (implemented treatment or program); O = observation or other data collection method.

(design 7 in Table 15.5). The counselor would begin by randomly assigning clients into two optimal sized groups, designated control and treatment, and determining a data collection method (e.g., test, survey, observation) to measure an outcome of interest (e.g., depression, stress management skills, anger management skills, social skills). The counselor would begin by administering the "test" (called the pretest) to all participants in the control and treatment conditions. Next, the counselor would implement the intervention (e.g., group counseling experience) to the treatment group, but not to the control group.

The **control group** either would experience nothing (i.e., wait-list control) or may undergo a "placebo" group counseling experience for some issue other than the purpose of the group. Upon conclusion of the treatment program or intervention, the professional counselor would again administer the test (this time called the post-test) to participants in both groups. It would be expected that no change in the control group participants' scores would be observed (i.e., no statistically significant difference between pretest and post-test scores). However, if the counseling intervention was successful, it would be expected that a significant change would be observed in the treatment group (e.g., post-test scores are higher than pretest scores, higher grades at the end of group than at the beginning). The other designs in Table 15.5 could also be used with this or other examples. However, quasiexperimental and nonexperimental designs do not allow the professional counselor to conclude that the treatment was the "cause" of the changes noted in the participants. In many ways, results or outcomes from studies with experimental designs are more valuable and powerful.

A lot of thought must be given to the design of the outcome measure used. Often, non-significant results are not due to the counseling intervention, but are due to the selection of an outcome measure not sensitive enough to show the effect of the treatment. Some outcome measures can be easily obtained because they are a matter of record (e.g., grade point average, percentage grade in math class, number of days absent, number of homework assignments completed), or they already exist in published form (e.g., *Conners Parent Rating Scale-Revised [CPRS-R], Achenbach System of Empirically Based Assessment [ASEBA], Beck Depression Inventory [BDI-II], Children's Depression Inventory [CDI]*). The number of available outcome measures is vast. Still, sometimes professional counselors need to design an outcome measure with sufficient sensitivity and direct applicability to the issue being studied (e.g., adjustment to a divorce, body image, social skills, math self-efficacy). When professional counselors need to develop an outcome measure from scratch, the basics of scale development covered earlier in the discussion of needs assessments can be helpful. In addition, Weiss (1998, pp. 140–142) provided a dozen principles the assessor should consider:

1. Use simple language.
2. Ask only about things that the respondent can be expected to know.
3. Make the question specific.
4. Define terms that are in any way unclear.
5. Avoid yes-no questions.
6. Avoid double negatives.
7. Do not ask double-barreled questions [i.e., two questions in one].
8. Use wording that has been adopted in the field.
9. Include enough information to jog people's memories or to make them aware of features of a phenomenon they might otherwise overlook.
10. Look for secondhand opinions or ratings only when firsthand information is unavailable.
11. Be sensitive to cultural differences.
12. Learn how to deal with difficult respondent groups.

These principles apply to most types of data collection procedures. Professional counselors can use a wide range of procedures, each with advantages and disadvantages. Table 15.6 presents descriptions of several of the most common methods of data collection used by professional school counselors. Finally, complete Activity 15.8.

TABLE 15.6 Common Data Collection Methods

1. *Interviews* of the professional counselors, key personnel, or members of stakeholder groups can provide valuable data. Interviews can be structured, semistructured, or unstructured. **Structured interviews** present a formal sequence of questions to interviewees with no variation in administration, generating clear evidence of strengths and weaknesses. **Unstructured interviews** allow for follow-up and deeper exploration, and are commonly used in qualitative studies. **Semistructured interviews** combine the facets of unstructured and structured approaches. Usually, multiple respondents are required for patterns and conclusions to emerge. Face-to-face interviews are generally better than phone interviews, although they are usually more costly and inconvenient. Careful consideration must be given to question development, and interviewers must guard against introducing bias.

2. *Observations* can be classified as informal or formal. **Informal observations** tend to yield anecdotal data through a "look-and-see" approach. **Formal observations** (or structured observations) usually involve a protocol and predetermined procedures for collecting specific types of data during a specified time period. Structured procedures tend to minimize bias. As an example of observation, professional counselors can be observed implementing a group counseling session by a supervisor or peer.

3. *Written questionnaires, surveys, and rating scales* are usually paper-and-pencil instruments asking a broad range of open-ended or close-ended questions. Questionnaires and rating scales typically ask for factual responses, whereas surveys generally solicit participant perceptions. The greatest weakness of this data collection method is that many surveyed participants do not complete or return the instrument (i.e., low return rate). It also requires a certain level of literacy. Few respondents take the time to write lengthy responses, so usually it is best to keep open-ended questions simple or even close-ended with the opportunity for participants to expand upon a response if needed. Multiscaled response formats (e.g., Likert-type scales) often provide more helpful results than yes-no questions. E-mailed or on-line versions of these instruments are becoming more commonly used.

4. *Program records and schedules* are a naturally occurring and helpful source of evaluation data. If stored on a computer in a database format, this kind of data is particularly accessible, and a professional counselor is well advised to consider this ahead of time when determining how best to maintain electronic records and schedules. Archives should also be kept in good order to facilitate record searches. In particular, professional counselors should keep previous program improvement documents and outcome study reports.

5. *Standardized and counselor-made tests* provide objective sources of measurable client outcomes. Individual, classroom, and school-wide tests can be extremely helpful and powerful measures. Tests exist that measure academic achievement, depression, anxiety, substance use, distraction, career indecision, and myriad other client behaviors. Likewise, professional counselors can design and develop tests to measure client behaviors and characteristics, much like teachers design tests to measure academic achievement.

6. *Academic performance indicators* may include a student's grade point average (GPA) or classroom grade, as well as include daily work behaviors/habits (e.g., attendance, homework completion, disruptions) and attitudes (e.g., academic self-efficacy, attitude toward school). *Products and portfolios* are real-life examples of performance. A **product** is anything created by a client (or the professional counselor) that stemmed from a program standard (e.g., artwork, composition, poster). A **portfolio** is a collection of exemplar products that can be evaluated to determine the quality of an individual's performance.

ACTIVITY 15.8

Using the research designs in Table 15.5 and the data collection methods in Table 15.6, design a simple outcome study using a treatment method, sample, and outcome measure of your choice. Describe how you could implement the study in a clinical setting. What would be the challenges or barriers to conducting the study? What would be the potential benefits? How could you use the results to improve counseling practice?

Single-Subject Research Design

Professional counselors do not always have access to groups of clients that can be randomly assigned to various experimental conditions. Most professional counselors need to document the effectiveness of services one client at a time and for widely varying presenting problems. An interesting form of experimental research design used by practicing professional counselors is the **single-subject research design (SSRD)** (or **single case research design**). SSRD involves an intensive study of a single individual or sometimes of a single group. This type of study examines client changes over a period of time before and after exposure to some treatment or intervention. The pressure for accountability and managed care within all fields of the counseling profession make SSRDs particularly helpful to professional counselors as they strive to document outcomes.

SSRDs start by measuring the state of the individual before the intervention begins. This is called a **baseline** (no treatment) and is designated by *A*. The intervention is designated *B*. Ordinarily, the condition of the client is observed or measured several times during the baseline phase (*A*) and several times during the intervention phase (*B*). A line graph is usually used to display the client's behavioral changes over time. Line graphs are interpreted visually, rather than statistically, and so are popular among mental health professionals and health maintenance organization workers. The behavior being observed or tracked (i.e., the **dependent variable**) is displayed on the vertical axis. Scores on a behavior rating scale, number of times a client gets out of his or her seat without permission, scores on a depression scale, or number of negative self-talk statements are some examples of these observed or tracked behaviors that clients may be trying to change. The horizontal axis usually indicates the observation session (i.e., passage of time). Client observations may occur each hour, day, or session, as determined by the professional counselor. **Data points** indicate the client's score at each time of collection throughout the study, and the slope of the **condition lines** indicates whether a client's condition has changed over time. Figure 15.5 provides a diagram of a commonly used SSRD, the AB design.

There are numerous types of SSRDs, including the AB design, ABA design, ABAB design, BAB design, ABCB design, and multiple-baseline design. The two most commonly used designs by professional counselors (AB and ABAB) are discussed here; the interested reader should see Erford (2008a) for an expanded discussion of SSRDs. The most common, the **AB design**, introduces an intervention to the client after a baseline period during which the client acts as his or her own control. In the AB design, the client is observed or measured for several sessions (i.e., the pretreatment baseline phase, *A*), the intervention is implemented, and the client is observed or measured for several more sessions (the treatment

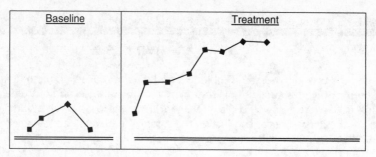

FIGURE 15.5   AB design.

phase, *B*). The general rule of thumb regarding the number of sessions to measure is to keep measuring until a stable pattern emerges, whether the pattern shows the treatment to be effective or ineffective.

A disadvantage of using the AB design is that it does not control for extraneous or con-founding variables. The **ABAB design** may minimize this problem because it includes two baseline periods interspersed with two intervention periods. Initially, the baseline (*A*) is established, and then treatment (*B*) is introduced. When the treatment is shown to have the desired effect, the intervention is withdrawn to collect a second baseline (*A*). If the client's scores on the dependent variable return to a level of diminished effectiveness, the counselor has provided evidence that the intervention was responsible for the changes the client exhibited during the *B* phase. At that point, the treatment is reintroduced (*B*), and more observations are made, the expectation being that a reintroduction of the previously effec-tive treatment will return the client to a more effective condition. The ABAB response pat-tern provides strong evidence that the intervention, not some extraneous or confounding variable, was responsible for changes in the condition of the client. Activity 15.9 asks you to create an outcome study using an SSRD.

ACTIVITY 15.9

Use an SSRD to create an outcome study of a client issue, treatment method, and outcome measure of your choice. Describe how you could implement the study in a clinical setting. What would be the challenges or barriers to conducting the study? What would be the potential benefits? How could you use the results to improve counseling practice?

Action Research

Action research allows professional counselors to focus on changing social, ecological, or client conditions in particular situations or settings by creating a study and intervention to explore and solve a particular problem, usually in the client's environment. Designed and conducted by practitioners or researchers, action research involves the analysis of data to improve practice and solve practical problems. Action research presents the professional

TABLE 15.7 Steps to Develop an Action Research Plan

1. *Identify and clarify the research question.* The main focus of this step should be to make improvements in practice, or troubleshoot and correct existing problems.
2. *Gather data.* In action research, the data are gathered using only a specific or particular group of individuals, and the sample and population are identical. Using more than one method of gathering data (e.g., triangulation) is suggested to provide a more thorough picture of the situation.
3. *Analyze and interpret data.* Any of the aforementioned methods may be used to collect and analyze the data.
4. *Create an action plan.* A main goal of action research is to understand and improve practice in applicable settings. The way to accomplish this goal is to plan and create the steps necessary to alter or improve the situation. The action plan should support and validate the data gathered.
5. *Evaluation and reflection.* When an action plan is created, the next step is to evaluate critically and periodically the plan's effectiveness. Evaluation can be accomplished by validation through testing the claims of improvements in practice (e.g., Does the action plan changes implemented produce the desired outcomes?). Self-evaluation of participants can also be used as a tool for reflection and validity.

From "Research and evaluation in counseling," by B. T. Erford, 2008. Copyright 2008 by Wadsworth, a part of Cengage Learning, Inc. Reproduced by permission. www.cengage.com/permissions.

counselor with many advantages over traditional experimental research procedures because action research requires minimal training; helps develop effective, practice-based solutions for practical problems; and creates a collaborative atmosphere where professionals work together to address and improve conditions affecting clients. Table 15.7 reviews the steps ordinarily considered when developing an action research plan. A more lengthy discussion and some case examples of action research can be found in Erford (2008a). Now complete Activity 15.10.

ACTIVITY 15.10

Design an action research project to address a client issue of your choice. Describe how you could implement the study in a clinical setting. What would be the challenges or barriers to conducting the study? What would be the potential benefits? How could you use the results to improve counseling practice?

REPORTING RESULTS

Although professional counselors, or perhaps an outside consultant, may write most of an accountability report, the counseling program advisory committee should be involved during every step of the process. A comprehensive report may be helpful for analysis purposes by the advisory committee; however, a one- to two-page executive summary should also be prepared for release to administrators, the community, and to other stakeholders and decision makers. Loesch and Ritchie (2004) suggested that dissemination of counseling program results could occur through a written report, verbal presentation, multimedia presentation, journal articles, webpage, television, videotape, posters, e-mail, or newspaper article.

Regardless of the vehicle for dissemination, the results of the program outcomes should be released to relevant stakeholder groups at regular intervals after the results have been reviewed by the advisory committee, professional counselors, and administrators. Results must be circulated for accountability to occur.

As mentioned previously, the results of the outcome studies are used to make substantive program improvements, which then prompt more questions to be studied. And the process cycles again and again. This cycle is essential to the transformation and continuous quality improvement of any counseling program.

Summary

Accountability involves the demonstration of responsibility for professional actions. Professional counselors demonstrate accountability by providing evidence that answers several primary questions. First, what are the needs of the client and stakeholder population? A needs assessment can be implemented using one of two primary methods. A data-driven needs assessment evaluates real needs demonstrated through derived information. Aggregated results are broken down (disaggregated) so that they can be examined at the subgroup level. Such analysis is crucial to demonstrate whether all clients are benefiting from the counseling program and services. A perceptions-based needs assessment assesses what primary stakeholder groups (e.g., clients, directors, teachers, parents) perceive as needs. These perceptions can be gathered through various methods, but some form of quantifiable result is preferred so that various perceived needs can be compared and prioritized.

Second, and particularly relevant to school counselors, is a comprehensive, standards-based program in place? A program evaluation (or audit) should be conducted annually near the end of the year to determine whether a written counseling program is being fully implemented.

Third, what services were implemented to address the identified needs and standards? A service assessment provides an accounting of who did what, how much, and for how long. This type of evidence is helpful in demonstrating that professional counselors are using their time to provide valuable (or even not so valuable) services, and is often requested by administrators. Service assessment is more of a process evaluation (i.e., how one spends one's time) rather than an outcomes evaluation (i.e., what valuable result has occurred by spending one's time that way). In other words, time is a process variable. Results stem from the actions one performs given the precious commodity of time.

Finally, and some would argue most importantly, what was the result of the implemented services? Some argue that results or outcomes studies are the most valuable facet of accountability. The assessment loop shows that the purpose of evaluation is continuous quality improvement. Data are collected to evaluate actions and interventions so that judgments can be made on the worth or value of services and programs. Often, traditional research designs can yield the most helpful and authoritative information about program or event quality, but single subject research designs and action research are making useful and powerful contributions to quality client and program services. Because of the broad ranging nature of goals and outcomes, professional counselors attempting to demonstrate the effectiveness of developmental or psychoeducational interventions may want to use an aggregated hierarchical model in which evidence is collected at the objectives level to demonstrate whether higher order outcomes and goals have been met.

Accountability applies to every facet of a counseling program. Professional counselors must be prepared to engage in accountability activities, continuously collect evidence, and report on program performance. Being responsible for one's actions and the quality of services provided is an important ethical and professional responsibility.

16   Outcome Research in Counseling

Susan H. Eaves and Bradley T. Erford

PREVIEW

Outcome research is intended to answer the question of counseling effectiveness. The outcome of a counseling intervention, occurring in response to the therapeutic process, is measured through outcome research, resulting in knowledge about what is and is not effective. Professional counselors have an ethical responsibility to use counseling methods grounded in theory and empirically validated through research. It is now known that counseling is effective in many forms and for many client conditions. This chapter reviews research on the effectiveness of counseling in several areas: client-counselor characteristics, individual approaches, group approaches, career intervention, and school-based student interventions. This body of information should be used by professional counselors to inform their practice and increase treatment efficacy.

IMPORTANCE OF AND BARRIERS TO OUTCOME RESEARCH

As should have been surmised from the previous chapter, the current practice of counseling is one that is being increasingly dominated by **accountability**. Some researchers (Sexton, Schofield, & Whiston, 1997) suggest that accountability is now a component of professional practice considered more important than theory congruence or philosophical allegiance. Some have viewed this as a negative shift for the field, one that stifles creative independence and instinct, while absorbing time better used in therapy. Instead, it can be viewed as an opportunity to transition from a profession historically based upon theory and intuition to one that would now combine theory, intuition, and science. Because of the inclusion of science, research and its focus on outcome is now a major component of the profession of counseling that has the ability to transform the effectiveness of practice. An understanding of the importance of such outcome research and a closer look at what is known to date are necessary.

The ethical imperative of **nonmaleficence** (i.e., do no harm) is of paramount concern when using counseling interventions. One of the most important means of achieving this end is to use empirically validated research and treatment approaches. To do so, professional counselors must stay abreast of and trained in the most current and empirically supported treatments for the populations they serve. Despite this importance, it is often a neglected aspect of the counseling professional's identity for a variety of reasons. It is not always easy to be a good consumer of outcome research. Outcome research is published in such a wide variety of journals that it is often difficult for counselors to keep abreast of relevant findings (Sexton, 1996). In addition, it is sometimes difficult to decipher results and identify valid and reliable findings that are pertinent to counseling practice. This chapter is designed to assist counselors by summarizing the outcomes research related to professional counseling activities.

Counselors in training are entering the counseling profession at an exciting and dynamic period in history, when the need for counseling services is at an all-time high. According to the National Institute of Mental Health (2007), mental illness is the leading cause of disability in the United States. Approximately one in four individuals (26.2%), ages 15 to 44 years, experience a diagnosable mental disorder in any given year, an increase compared with the 20% reported less than two decades ago (Rice, Kelman, Miller, & Dunmeyer, 1990). In addition, nearly half of the individuals currently diagnosed also meet the criteria for two or more mental health disorders.

While the need for mental health treatment continues to soar, only one in five individuals who need mental health services actually seeks them (Hoagwood, 1999; Kataoka, Zhang & Wells, 2002; U.S. Department of Health and Human Services, 2000). A host of factors contribute to this low rate of help-seeking behaviors, including geographical restrictions, transportation, finances, lack of service knowledge, and stigma. Because of these factors, it is even more important for professional counselors to be adequately prepared to address effectively the innumerable concerns of the individuals who do seek services.

Such effectiveness and preparedness is not only helpful in improving client outcomes, but also is an ethical responsibility. Knowledge and use of empirically validated treatment shown to be effective in counseling outcomes is an obligation of every professional counselor (American Counseling Association, 2005a). Some authors believe that ethical counseling is impossible without a thorough understanding of the current and relevant outcome research (Lambert, 1991; Lambert, Masters & Ogles, 1991). Professional counselors have an obligation to keep abreast of and use empirically validated research and treatment approaches, not only to avoid treatment approaches proven harmful, but also to use the approaches proven most helpful in an effort to maximize effectiveness. Reflection 16.1 invites you to consider the debate concerning empirical data.

REFLECTION 16.1

If a counselor means well, and has a kind and caring disposition, is that enough to prevent doing harm? Is a counselor doing harm by not using empirical data to drive practice and interventions?

Outcome research is vital to the well-being of the client, to the ethical obligations of the counselor, and to the advancement of the field. For the counseling profession itself to continue, it must prove itself effective. To be effective, treatment must be empirically validated by research. If the profession and practice of counseling cannot show improved outcomes for clients, it cannot continue to move forward and receive support. It is crucial for each individual professional counselor to be knowledgeable of the research base, to understand how to use the therapy modalities and treatment approaches validated, and to select and tailor interventions based on best practices.

Despite the existence of overwhelming support for the superiority of systematic, research-based decision-making models (Dawes, 1991, 1994; Johnson, 1988; Tracey, 1991), studies have led researchers to conclude that professional counselors in clinical practice typically refrain from active research (Norcross, Prochaska, & Gallagher, 1989). In addition, most professional counselors do not read current research (Morrow-Bradley & Elliott, 1986), or use research to shape their therapeutic knowledge, skill, or practice (Anderson & Heppner, 1986; Cohen, Sargent & Sechrest, 1986; Falvey, 1989; Howard, 1985). In 1983, Norcross and Prochaska found that selecting a counseling intervention based on outcome research ranked 10th out of 14 reasons for approach selection. In 2000, Norcross stated there was little evidence to believe that trend had improved.

Although the need for outcome research and the subsequent use of it are so necessary, outcome research is blatantly underused. Despite the necessity for empirically supported treatment, outcome research remains underproduced for several reasons. In general, the practitioners who have access to the populations in need of study typically have not been adequately trained in research methods. Additionally, practitioners trained in research methods often have difficulty gaining access to the population in need of study.

Not only is outcome research underproduced, but what is produced is understudied and underused. Often, practitioners prefer to continue using the approaches they are most comfortable with, regardless of their effectiveness. Sexton, Whiston, Bleuer, and Walz (1997) identified seven myths, or misconceived criticisms, used by practitioners in an effort to disregard relevant research findings. Several of these are combined and presented here (pp. 10–15):

1. Research results cannot be trusted and are not useful in practice.
2. Findings are irrelevant to the practitioner because studies examine minute details, not clinical problems.
3. Outcome research looks at groups and evaluates theory, while practitioners are more concerned with individuals and specific techniques.
4. Practitioners are not concerned with statistical significance, but with practical differences.

In addition to these, other reasons professional counselors often resist the idea of assessing their own outcomes include a fear that they are ineffective, reluctance to use time set aside for therapy, and a belief that effectiveness cannot be quantifiably measured. Although some of these criticisms may have held merit in the past, they have largely been discarded by today's professionals. Regardless, they are evidence of the large divide between research and practice that, while narrowing, still seems to exist. Such a research/practice split can also be veiled as a split between individuals advocating the art of counseling versus the science of counseling. Put another way, differences in philosophical ideals and theoretical orientations can become the basis for individuals who believe in clinical intuition and individuals who rely on the scientific method (Sexton et al., 1997). If researchers were to engage in practice, and practitioners were to engage in research, it would be possible to begin bridging the subjective experiences of therapy with the objective evidence of science (Corrie & Callanan, 2001) in such a way as to make research and practice more meaningful and efficacious (Crane & McArthur, 2002).

As stated earlier, the chasm between research and practice has begun to close substantially over the years as practitioners have realized the need for more relevant outcome research, and counseling researchers have made the effort to produce more relevant outcome research. The establishment and rapidly growing control of managed care has also forced the issue. Today, professional counselors must convince third-party payers that they are providing effective services. To practice competitively in this managed care era, counselors must provide proof that interventions used are research-based, empirically sound, and capable of producing desired outcomes (Crane & McArthur, 2002; Hayes, Barlow, & Nelson-Gray, 1999; Kent & Hersen, 2000).

Hayes et al. (1999) advocate for a model that trains practitioners to be researchers by combining clinical and research training, and valuing both equally. This **scientist-practitioner model** teaches professional counselors to view all counseling as a formal research project. By taking a scientific approach to problem identification, using empirical evidence to design treatment interventions, monitor symptoms, and evaluate outcomes, practitioners ideally should become both consumers and producers of research (Crane & McArthur, 2002; Hayes et al, 1999).

Sexton et al. (1997) proposed an integrated process for practitioners and researchers to collaborate to increase the relevance and applicability of outcomes research. Within the proposed model, practitioners and educators devise relevant and critical questions that can be further conceptualized and researched, leading to more relevant graduate training and applicable empirical information. Findings are disseminated to clinicians who can integrate them into clinical practice. For this process to be successful, practitioners must be abreast of the current literature so as to know what information is lacking. They must also digest information produced as a result of their inquiries. Similarly, researchers must understand the difference between clinical efficacy and effectiveness studies for practitioners to view findings as relevant and for them to view making contributions feasible.

The classic and most scientifically sound approach to outcome research involves clinical efficacy studies, which are tightly controlled experiments designed to test a particular intervention. Because of the conditions of random assignment, control groups, standardized measures, and use of practice manuals, these studies are able to show causation. However, these same advantages are often impossible to carry out in naturalistic settings such as community mental health centers, schools, or homes. The second approach, effectiveness research, is most concerned with the use of interventions and techniques with a broad population across multiple settings. These studies test the utility of what works in practical circumstances (James & Mennen, 2001). Reflection 16.2 invites you to consider the gap between research and practice in professional counseling.

REFLECTION 16.2

Of all the many reasons that contribute to the gap between research and practice, what might be some of the most difficult to overcome? What ideas can you think of that could help reduce this problem?

As emphasized earlier, professional counselors have an ethical responsibility to use effective techniques and processes when working with clients and students (American Counseling Association, 2005a; Herlihy & Corey, 2006; Lambert, 1991; Lambert et al., 1991).

Professional counselors must become familiar with the current extant literature on counseling effectiveness, commonly known as **outcome research**, and the procedures for establishing one's own effectiveness, commonly known as accountability (see Chapter 15).

Typically, outcome research involves three separate types of methodology: clinical trials, qualitative reviews, and meta-analytic reviews. Clinical trial studies are common in the existing literature, usually consisting of a single study of a specific type of treatment or approach. Such studies, or **clinical trials**, are important because they use comparison groups (e.g., placebo, wait-list control, alternative treatment), outcome measures, and standardized treatment protocols (Sexton et al., 1997), which when used collectively tremendously enhance the replicability of results. However useful, clinical trials are limited as well because they offer only a single result from a single study, and a subsequent study with a different methodology is likely to yield inconsistent or even contradictory results for reasons that may be impossible to determine.

Problems with clinical trials are frequently seen in the media when a new study is reported that contradicts a previous study, such as is often the case on dietary and health issues. Inconsistencies such as these create confusion in the public and lead to decreased faith in the reliability of research. It is often wiser for professional counselors to use accumulations and summarizations of numerous research results to inform their counseling practice, rather than relying on the potentially unreliable results of a select few.

Instead of relying on individual studies to guide practice, many studies can be identified and collapsed into summaries using quantitative and qualitative methodologies. Advantages and disadvantages accompany each of these approaches. **Qualitative analysis** is a commonly used approach during which researchers examine and summarize robust trends and findings across studies, clients, and contexts. Similar to all experimental methods, qualitative reviews can sometimes result in biased or subjective conclusions, so procedures and criteria must be put into place by researchers to ensure the information is processed systematically, and conclusions are replicable and robust (Cooper, 1982; Ellis, 1991).

Meta-analysis is a specific quantitative technique that amasses and summarizes the results of numerous studies using a meaningful quantitative index, commonly known as an **effect size** (ES). Generally, an ES conveys the magnitude of difference detected as a result of treatment. In other words, when a difference can easily be detected with a relatively small sample, the ES is large. Conversely, a small ES would indicate difficulty in finding even a small difference, requiring a larger sample to detect a difference.

To compute an ES, one simple and commonly used method is to subtract the mean of the control group from the mean of the experimental group, then divide the difference by the standard deviation of the control group $[M_e - M_c]/SD_c$. There are several benefits to using ES. First, the ES from various comparable studies can be combined and averaged to yield a result across several studies. Second, this index can be weighted according to the sample size so that larger, more stable samples are given greater weight than smaller, less stable samples. Several options exist for determining the strength of an ES, including the popular ES range developed by Cohen (1988): ES = 0, no treatment effect; ES = 0.20, small treatment effect; ES = 0.50, medium treatment effect; and ES = 0.80 or more, large effect.

An ES = 0.60 indicates a medium effect, whereas an ES = 0.15 indicates no or little effect.

Another way to interpret ES is in terms of the number of standard deviations above or below the control group mean that a given treatment group score lies. For example, an ES of 0 means that the treatment and control group means were equal, and there was no difference, meaning the average client in the treatment group performed neither better nor worse than the average participant in the control group. In other words, the treatment had no effect, and the average treatment group participant scored at about the 50th percentile of the control group. If ES = 0.50, this indicates that the treatment mean was one-half standard deviation above the mean of the control group. The "medium effect" associated with an ES = 0.50 can also be expressed in terms of percentage outcome; that is, an ES = 0.50 indicates that the average client in the treatment group attained a better outcome than 69% of the control group participants (0.50 standard deviations above the mean is a percentile rank of about 69). Likewise, an ES = 2.00 is not only a large effect (i.e., an ES > 0.80), but also indicates that the average treatment group participant performed better than 98% of control group participants (i.e., 2.0 standard deviations above the mean is the 98th percentile rank).

When an empirical study is correlational (usually involving the computation of a Pearson r), Cohen (1988) suggested interpreting ES according to the following criterion-referenced interpretive range: $r = 0$ (no effect); $r = 0.10$ (small), $r = 0.30$ (medium), $r = 0.50$ (large).

There are many additional formulas for estimating ES, but the reader of group outcome research is likely to encounter these two most frequently in the extant research. While meta-analysis has been commonly used in counseling and psychological research, it is by no means free of criticism (Ioaniddis, Cappelleri, & Lau, 1998; Shadish, 1996; Sharpe, 1997; Sohn, 1997), some of which concludes that combining numerous studies into a single result simply spreads errors from less well-designed studies onto better designed studies. At the very least, readers should view meta-analysis as a potentially helpful procedure for analyzing robust trends across studies, but should view results with some caution, as should be common practice with any research.

HOW EFFECTIVE IS COUNSELING?

Over the past 50 years, the effectiveness of counseling has been explored through numerous studies to reach continually the overwhelming conclusion that counseling is effective. Regardless of the methodology employed to examine the extant literature, counseling is shown to produce more favorable outcomes than placebo treatments and control groups (Table 16.1) (Abramowitz, 1976; Bachar, 1998; Baer & Nietzel, 1991; Bednar & Kaul, 1994; Casey & Berman, 1985; Dagley, Gazda, Eppinger, & Stewart, 1994; Dies & Riester, 1986; Dush, Hirt, & Schroeder, 1983; Fuhriman & Burlingame, 1994a, 1994b; Gazda & Larsen, 1968; Grossman & Hughes, 1992; Hoag & Burlingame, 1997; Kanas, 1986; Kaul & Bednar, 1986; Kraft, 1968; Lambert & Bergin, 1994; Lambert, Weber, & Stykes, 1993; Lubin & Lubin, 1973; Lubin, Lubin, & Sargent, 1972; MacKenzie, 1994, 1995; McRoberts, Burlingame, & Hoag, 1998; Miller & Berman, 1983; Orlinsky & Howard, 1986; Prout & DeMartino, 1986; Roberts & Camasso, 1991; Robinson, Berman, & Neimeyer, 1990; Russell, Greenwald, & Shirk, 1991; Shapiro & Shapiro, 1982; Shirk & Russell, 1992; Smith, Glass, & Miller, 1980; Sternbarger & Budman, 1996; Sugar, 1993; Tillitski, 1990; Toseland & Siporin, 1986; Weisz, Weiss, Alicke, & Klotz, 1987; Zimpfer, 1990a, 1990b). Most studies indicate little or no difference in the effectiveness of counseling regardless of the counseling modality used or the population studied. Individual and group counseling are shown to be effective, although some specific conditions may be more amenable to individual counseling approaches (Hoag & Burlingame, 1997; McRoberts et al., 1998).

Because counseling has superior outcomes compared with **placebo treatments** and **control groups**, there is evidence to support that factors due to counseling are responsible for improvements made. However, it cannot be ignored that there are instances when

TABLE 16.1 Selected Meta-Analytic Studies From the Extant Literature

Source	Outcome Explored	ES
Client/Counselor Characteristics		
Horvath & Symonds (1991)	Working alliance and outcome	Small to medium
Martin, Garske, & Davis (2000)	Therapeutic alliance and outcome	Small to medium
Orlinsky, Grawe, & Parks (1994)	Counselor skill and outcome	Small
Shirk & Karver (2003)	Therapeutic alliance and outcome	Small to medium
Effectiveness of Counseling Adults		
Bachar (1998)	Counseling effectiveness	Large
Baker & Daniels (1989)	Microskills counseling	Large
Cuijpers (1998)	Outreach programs for depression	Medium to large
Dush, Hirt, & Schroeder (1983)	Individual counseling	Large
	Group counseling	Medium
Hoag & Burlingame (1997)	Group counseling	Medium
Lambert, Christensen, & Beutler (1984)	Counseling effectiveness	Large
Lambert, Weber, & Stykes (1993)	Individual counseling	Large
McRoberts, Burlingame, & Hoag (1998)	Individual versus group counseling for depression	Large
Miller & Berman (1983)	Individual counseling	Large
	Group counseling	Large
Mitte (2005)	Cognitive-behavioral therapy for anxiety	Large
	Cognitive-behavioral therapy for depression	Medium to large
Robinson, Berman, & Neimeyer (1990)	Individual counseling for depression	Large
	Group counseling for depression	Large
Shapiro & Shapiro (1982)	Individual counseling	Large
	Group counseling	Large
Smith & Glass (1977)	Counseling effectiveness	Large
Smith, Glass, & Miller (1980)	Individual counseling	Large
	Group counseling	Large
Tillitski (1990)	Individual counseling	Large
	Group counseling	Large
Career and Educational Planning		
Oliver & Spokane (1988)	Career interventions	Large
Whiston, Eder, Rahardja, & Tai (2005)	Educational planning	Small
Whiston, Sexton, & Lasoff (1998)	Career interventions	Small to medium
Youth and School-Based Interventions		
Baker, Swisher, Nadenichek, & Popowicz (1984)	Primary prevention strategies	Medium

TABLE 16.1 Selected Meta-Analytic Studies From the Extant Literature(*Continued*)

Source	Outcome Explored	ES
Bennett & Gibbons (2000)	Cognitive-behavioral therapy for deviant behavior	Small to medium
Bratton, Ray, Rhine, & Jones (2005)	Play therapy	Large
Casey & Berman (1985)	Counseling effectiveness	Medium to large
Kazdin, Bass, Ayers, & Rodgers (1990)	Counseling effectiveness	Large
LeBlanc & Ritchie (2001)	Play therapy	Medium
Prout & DeMartino (1986)	School counseling program	Medium
Prout & Prout (1998)	School counseling program	Large
Stage & Quiroz (1997)	Counseling for disruptive behaviors	Large
Weisz, Weiss, Alicke, & Klotz (1987)	Counseling effectiveness	Large
Weisz, Weiss, Han, Granger, & Morton (1995)	Counseling effectiveness	Medium to large
Whiston et al. (2005)	School counseling program	Small to medium

factors outside of the counseling relationship and independent of the treatment provided may account for improvement in client symptoms. Lambert et al. (1991) reported that factors outside of counseling may account for 43% of client improvement. This is reinforced by studies indicating that 90% of clients seem to improve on their own over time regardless of professional assistance (Lambert, 1976; Mann, Jenkins, & Belsey, 1981). Reflection 16.3 follows.

REFLECTION 16.3

Why do you think spontaneous remission (i.e., un unanticipated reemergence of the symptoms or condition after a period of time when serious displays of the condition were absent) occurs? Have you ever experienced spontaneous remission from a physical or mental health concern?

Even more to the point, only about 6% to 12% of clients experience negative effects from counseling (Bergin & Lambert, 1978; Beutler, Frank, Schieber, Calvert, & Gaines, 1984; Henry, Schacht, & Strupp, 1986; Orlinsky & Howard, 1980; Shapiro & Shapiro, 1982). Sexton (1997) stated that during counseling, "some clients do get worse." It is important to consider, however, that while it is true that some individuals do regress, such instances should not be attributed to counseling alone. Numerous factors may contribute to Sexton's conclusion, including the acknowledgment that there are some counselors who lack the appropriate level of skills. Also, therapeutic relationships or alliances may be of poor quality. Inappropriately prescribed treatments are sometimes to blame as well. Often, issues outside of counseling can contribute to worsening of client symptoms, just as factors outside of counseling can contribute to improvements.

Finally, the process of counseling is often difficult because it brings to surface uncomfortable emotions and awareness (Lambert & Bergin, 1994; Luborsky, McClellan, Woody, O'Brien, & Auerbach, 1985; Orlinsky & Howard, 1980), and if counseling is prematurely terminated before these issues can be resolved, the client condition may be described as worse.

THINK ABOUT IT 16.1

If some clients do get worse after entering counseling, might there ever be times when this is not considered a negative outcome? Explain.

Facets of Counseling That Contribute to Outcomes

With few exceptions, counseling is useful and valuable. Its use and value are consistent across settings and counselors, regardless of theoretical approaches (Garfield & Bergin, 1986; Lambert, 1991; Sexton et al., 1997; Smith et al., 1980; Stiles, Shapiro, & Elliott, 1986). Kazdin (1994) stated that more than 400 variations of therapy currently exist. However, despite differences among them, these therapeutic variations seem to have similarly equivalent effectiveness (Sexton, et al., 1997). For this reason, it is important to focus on the specific facets of counseling that contribute to successful treatment outcomes. In other words, there must be common denominators within the process of counseling, and such commonalities must be considered. While research does support the increased efficacy of certain theoretical approaches with specific mental health conditions, it is generally accepted that counseling is effective regardless of the theory used (Garfield & Bergin, 1986; Lambert, 1991; Sexton et al., 1997; Smith et al., 1980; Stiles et al., 1986).

Putting theoretical orientation aside, many other factors related to counseling effectiveness have been studied, including the length of treatment and the counseling relationship or therapeutic alliance. Treatment length is often connected to therapeutic outcome, with some practitioners concluding that more sessions are more beneficial, whereas other researchers find that most change occurs early on in treatment. Howard, Kopta, Krause, and Orlinsky (1986) concluded that about 50% of improvement occurred by the eighth session, 75% by the 6th month, and 85% by the end of the first year of counseling. These results support the philosophy of brief, solution-focused counselors who indicate that a good deal of change occurs by the eighth session, if it is going to occur (Budman & Gurman, 1988). In general, however, it is accepted that clients who display more severe symptoms and disturbance at the onset of counseling and clients with diagnosable personality disorders (Paris, 2002) have more to gain from a longer course of treatment, and may require longer treatment to show improvements. With a similar rationale, clients who display milder impairment at the onset of counseling seem to make sufficient progress in fewer sessions (Lambert & Bergin, 1994; Shapiro, Barkham, Hardy, & Morrison, 1990).

While research does support the effectiveness of shorter term treatment for clients with milder impairment, terminating treatment after the first several sessions does not produce substantial or long-lasting improvements. Clients who drop out of counseling, known as

premature termination, are problematic in counseling, regardless of the setting, presenting problems, or therapeutic approaches. Some clients never show up for the initial session after referral or setting an appointment. Nearly 49% never arrive for the first session (Phillips & Fagan, 1982). Of those who do follow through with counseling, many terminate counseling by the eighth session (Garfield, 1994). A study conducted by the National Institute for Mental Health (Elkin et al., 1989) found that 69% of children and youth had fewer than six sessions, 19% had between seven and 10 sessions, and only 12% had more than 10 sessions. Howard, Davidson, O'Mahoney, Orlinsky, and Brown (1989) concluded that 44% of private practice clients attended three or fewer sessions, whereas only about 16% made it to the 25th session.

While many factors contribute to premature termination, personal client variables have been found to correlate with these rates. Income, education, and race seem to be related to dropout rates, with clients with lower incomes (Pilkonis, Imber, Lewis, & Rubinsky, 1984), lower educational level (Dubrin & Zastowny, 1988), and African American racial heritage (Sue, McKinney, Allen, & Hall, 1974) more likely to terminate counseling prematurely. Premature dropout rates do not seem to be related to sex (Sledge, Moras, Hartley, & Levine, 1990), age (Garfield & Bergin, 1971), or diagnosis (Garfield, 1986).

While factors related to education, income, and race cannot typically be altered in an effort to improve counseling commitment or engagement, other factors related to the counseling relationship can. Relationship building can reduce dropout rates and can be improved through attention to initial impressions and purposeful counseling activities. The outcome literature indicates that clients are less likely to end counseling prematurely if professional counselors (a) administer complete psychological evaluations (Koran & Costell, 1973; Wirt, 1967); (b) are perceived as trustworthy and competent (Kokotovic & Tracey, 1987; McNeill, May, & Lee, 1987); (c) are perceived as skillful (Baekland & Lundwall, 1975; Sloan, Staples, Cristol, Yorkson, & Whipple, 1975); (d) convey respect, directness, and a strong alliance (Mohl, Martinez, Ticknor, Huang, & Cordell, 1991); and (e) establish mutually agreed upon goals and expectations (Tracey, 1986).

All of the above-mentioned counseling characteristics contribute to the occurrence of a strong match between the client and the professional counselor and are crucial to rapport, therapeutic commitment, and initial outcome. The term **patient-therapist match** is used to refer to the fit experienced by the client and the counselor. This perceived fit determines whether the counselor can resonate with the client, and if the client perceives the counselor as capable of doing so. Match has less to do with matching similarities between client and counselor, and more to do with the client finding the counselor to be agreeable, likable, and possessing characteristics the client wishes to emulate. In general, increased match is found to reduce the likelihood of premature dropout and to increase initial gains made in counseling (Dolinsky, Vaughan, Luber, Mellman, & Roose, 1998). Beutler (1989) estimated that the therapeutic alliance as shown through the client-counselor match may contribute 63% of treatment outcome variance. Likewise, Beutler and Mitchell (1981) estimated that client-therapist compatibility accounted for 60% of treatment outcome, far outweighing the effect of the theoretical approaches used, which accounted for only 10% of the outcome variance.

Therapeutic alliance is similar to match. Several meta-analyses (Horvath & Symonds, 1991; Martin et al., 2000; Shirk & Karver, 2003) have explored the therapeutic alliance as a factor in determining treatment outcome. Considered one of the four primary determinants of treatment outcome (Seligman, 1998), **therapeutic alliance** is defined as a collaborative

TABLE 16.2 Selected Effect Sizes for Specific Facets of Counseling Effectiveness

Study	Characteristic	ES
Hoag & Burlingame (1997)	Group counseling for disruptive behavior	Medium
	Group counseling for anxiety/fear	Medium
	Group counseling for adjustment to divorce	Medium
	Group counseling for social skills	Medium
	Group counseling for depression	Small
Mitte (2005)	Cognitive-behavioral therapy for anxiety	Large
	Cognitive-behavioral therapy for depression	Medium
	Cognitive-behavioral therapy for quality of life	Large
Baker & Daniels (1989)	Microskills counseling	Small

relationship between the client and the professional counselor in which an affective bond has been established (Gaston, 1990; Horvath & Symonds, 1991; Martin et al., 2000; Saunders, Howard, & Orlinsky, 1989). According to Green and Herget (1991, p. 321), "Evidence is mounting that therapist relationship skills and strength of the therapeutic alliance are the most powerful predictors of client outcome." Other authors agree that the therapeutic alliance is important regardless of intervention, discipline, or diagnosis (Krupnick, 1996; Luborsky, Barber, & Crits-Christoph, 1990). Although match is crucial in reducing premature termination and in initial gains made in counseling, therapeutic alliance continues to be influential in determining eventual outcome.

Table 16.2 provides some specific facets of counseling and reported ES. Interested readers are referred to Sexton et al. (1997) for an outstanding comprehensive review of factors that seem to influence counseling effectiveness.

WHICH CLIENT AND PROFESSIONAL COUNSELOR FACTORS CONTRIBUTE TO SUCCESSFUL OUTCOMES?

Although some client and professional counselor factors are important to predicting treatment outcomes, their effects are still small. Sexton et al. (1997, p. 81) concluded, "there is no single counselor or client characteristic, no single theory, or no technique that can account for the success of good counseling." For this reason, researchers have begun to look at the various interactions among the many aspects of counseling.

Counseling is effective in producing positive change despite theoretical application. In response to this, researchers have spent much time identifying client and professional counselor characteristics common across therapeutic approaches that influence or create successful therapeutic outcomes. While such characteristics do show a relationship to outcomes, the ES of these characteristics on treatment outcome appear small (see Table 16.1). As a result, researchers instead have been led to begin exploring the interaction between these factors, including treatment approach, client concern, client characteristics, and professional counselor characteristics (Sexton et al., 1997). In other words, if it is known that cognitive-behavioral therapy is effective for a client with depression (matching client concern with treatment approach), is it possible to match certain client characteristics with specific counselor characteristics to improve treatment effectiveness? This is an important question that warrants much future attention from practitioners, researchers, and counselor educators, as the answer is currently unknown. The remainder of this section explores what is known about the relationship between client and professional counselor factors and treatment outcomes.

The demographic traits of professional counselors have been well studied using correlational procedures. Variables of counselor sex, age, and race have yielded mixed results, however, generally as a result of unsound methodology and the correlational nature of the research (Sexton et al., 1997). Typically, while clients tend to prefer professional counselors they perceive to be similar to them, thereby increasing fit and reducing premature termination, these similarities have little effect on eventual counseling effectiveness (Atkinson, 1985; Atkinson & Schein, 1986; Beck, 1988; Jones, 1982; Terrell & Terrell, 1984; Whiston & Sexton, 1993).

Results of meta-analyses also show little relationship between treatment outcomes and discipline (Prioleau, Murdock, & Brody, 1983), training, or experience (Berman & Norton, 1985; Beutler, Crago, & Arizmendi, 1986; Christenson & Jacobson, 1993; Weisz et al., 1987). These results were not always consistent, however, because experienced therapists (Lyons & Woods, 1991) and professionally trained counselors (Stein & Lambert, 1995) displayed better outcomes compared with individuals with less experience and training. According to Stein and Lambert (1995), experience became an especially salient factor when treating more severely disturbed clients, although it is known that these same individuals make less progress in general compared with less disturbed clients (Burns & Nolen-Hoeksema, 1991; Orlinsky et al., 1994; Stone, Green, Gleser, Whitman, & Roster, 1975). Regarding experience as a factor, however, Svartberg and Stiles (1991) cited evidence to the contrary, concluding through meta-analytic review that counselor effectiveness actually decreases with experience. This observation has led many to consider counseling *skill* as the determining factor in outcomes, rather than training and experience.

The perception of skill as a critical determinant of counseling outcome has resulted in the introduction and validation of **treatment manuals** into professional practice. Such treatment manuals standardize the treatment of certain conditions by providing an empirically validated protocol for professional counselors to follow. Managed care providers encourage the use of such manuals even though early studies on their use have resulted in mixed findings (Luborsky et al., 1985; Robinson et al., 1990; Shaw, 1983). Henry, Strupp, Butler, Schachy, and Binder (1993) indicated that the use of such treatment manuals may result in poorer outcomes, especially affecting counselor-client relationship and perceived supportiveness. More specifically, manuals may increase technical proficiency, while decreasing factors pertinent to the therapeutic alliance.

THINK ABOUT IT 16.2

If you had access to empirically supported treatment protocols for the various conditions and populations you serve, would you use them? What would be the advantages and disadvantages of this?

INDIVIDUAL COUNSELING

According to Nearpass (1990), individual counseling has sometimes been found to be more effective than group counseling. Counselors who primarily used individual counseling were found to be most effective compared with counselors who used other treatment modalities (Wiggins & Wiggins, 1992). Although it was not statistically significant, Weisz et al. (1987) found a larger ES for individual therapy than for group therapy, with ES = 1.04 for individual therapy and ES = 0.62 for group therapy. While this difference was smaller in a subsequent meta-analysis conducted by Weisz et al. (1995), there was still a noticeable difference, with individual counseling (ES = 0.63) producing greater results than group counseling (ES = 0.50).

Several diverse meta-analytic studies have been conducted in mental health clinics, schools, and research laboratories, all of which explore the general effects of individual counseling with children and adolescents. Casey and Berman's (1985) meta-analysis resulted in an ES = 0.71, meaning the average treatment group participant performed better after treatment than 76% of control group participants (i.e., 0.71 standard deviations above the control group mean is the 76th percentile). Similarly, Weisz et al. (1987) reported an ES = 0.79; Kazdin et al. (1990) reported an ES = 0.88; and Weisz et al. (1995) reported an ES = 0.71. Taken together, these meta-analyses indicate the effects of individual counseling to be medium to large.

In another example of the effectiveness of individual counseling interventions, an individual dropout prevention program, comprising tutoring and counseling, significantly improved academic success, confidence, and behavior (Edmondson & White, 1998). In this example, individual counseling was deemed effective without being long in duration. It has been found that brief, individual counseling can be just as effective as long-term counseling. Three approaches to brief counseling designed to address the emotional adjustment of high school students were implemented by Littrell, Malia, and Vanderwood (1995). Participants in each of the three brief interventions reduced anxiety and increased motivation necessary to move them closer to their goals. Similarly, Gingerich and Eisengart (2000) reviewed 15 outcome studies examining the efficacy of solution-focused brief therapy (SFBT) for depression, anxiety, parenting skills, psychosocial adjustment, antisocial behaviors, criminal recidivism, alcohol use, and family conflict. Five of the studies were tightly controlled, and each of these found SFBT to be significantly better than the case of no treatment. However, because these studies were unable to use a control group and did not compare SFBT with another intervention, it was impossible to conclude that outcomes were due to SFBT. Taken collectively, the results of all 15 studies supported the effectiveness of SFBT.

LeBlanc and Ritchie (2001) conducted a meta-analysis of play therapy outcomes designed to add to the findings of Casey and Berman (1985) and Weisz et al. (1987). LeBlanc and Ritchie (2001) reported an ES = 0.66 after conducting a meta-analysis of play therapy outcomes with children. Specifically, they found a strong relationship between treatment effectiveness and the inclusion of parents in counseling with the child, especially when parents were taught therapeutic play behaviors. Parents acting as counselors increased the ES by 0.33 standard deviations. In addition, the length of treatment was shown to be related to outcomes, with the greatest positive effect occurring after 30 treatment sessions. In other words, the ES associated with play therapy continually increased until reaching its maximum ES at about 30 sessions. Finally, play therapy interventions with children were shown to be equally effective as verbal therapies with adults and nonplay therapies with children experiencing emotional difficulties.

Although the effectiveness of specific individual counseling interventions such as play therapy and solution-focused therapy have been stated, even more positive ES have been noted specifically for cognitive-behavioral counseling interventions (Baer & Nietzel, 1991; Bennett & Gibbons, 2000; Durlak, Fuhrman, & Lampman, 1991; Dush et al., 1983) and family therapy (Hazelrigg, Cooper, & Borduin, 1987; Shadish et al., 1993). These studies did not differentiate among youth who were counseled in schools, agencies, or private practice, or by the level of counselor experience, but did find cognitive-behavioral interventions similarly effective across a wide array of populations, settings, and mental health concerns and issues (Kazdin, 1991, 1993, 1994). Similarly, behavioral approaches in individual counseling were found to be most effective when addressing aggressive behavior (Wilson, Lipsey, & Derzon, 2003); Lavoritano and Segal (1992) found that misbehavior decreased as individual counseling progressed.

In addition to examining the specific types of interventions common to individual counseling, several meta-analyses have been conducted examining the effectiveness of individual counseling with specific problems and disorders. Two meta-analyses (Sherman, 1988; Van Etten & Taylor, 1998) of psychotherapeutic treatments for post-traumatic stress disorder found significant ES for individual counseling interventions, both of which reported medium-to-large ES for the use of counseling in reducing symptoms. Solomon and Johnson (2002) found similarities in treatments for post-traumatic stress disorder making them increasingly similar in practice. According to their qualitative review of the literature, most therapies include components to address the meaning of the traumatic events, provide exposure to and reintegration of the trauma, and provide support and coping skills. When these components are included in treatment, experiencing of post-traumatic stress disorder symptoms has been found to shorten from more than 5 years to less than 3 years.

Outcome research has also been conducted to examine the effectiveness of individual counseling for survivors of abuse, with the overall results showing that individual counseling does lead to improvements for this population. When analyzed separately according to the type of abuse (e.g., sexual, physical, emotional, neglect), the strongest and most compelling evidence stems from studies analyzing the effectiveness of individual counseling for sexual abuse. The literature on the other forms of abuse is too limited to draw sound conclusions, although preliminary findings are suggestive of its benefits. Taken together, outcome research in this area is limited by small, nonrandom sampling, inconsistent definitions of abuse, use of unreliable measures, and failure to discern the types of abuse (James & Mennen, 2001). Now complete Reflection 16.4.

REFLECTION 16.4

If you were asked if counseling was effective, if your profession was of use, how would you answer? Could you support your response with scientific evidence from the outcome research literature?

EFFECTIVENESS OF GROUP COUNSELING

The use and effectiveness of individual counseling over group counseling was espoused earlier. However, Prout and DeMartino (1986) found that in some settings, group treatments were more effective than individual interventions, with ES = 0.63 for group counseling and ES = 0.39 for individual counseling. Frequently debated, the question of whether group or individual counseling is more effective continues. McRoberts, Burlingame, and Hoag (1998) found no significant differences between the two interventions when therapist characteristics related to gender, training, and experience were taken into account. In general, group treatment is as effective as individual treatment for most conditions, so long as the group is specific to the focus of treatment (Fuhriman & Burlingame, 1994a). Not only are individual counseling and group counseling equally effective under most circumstances, but also they sometimes can be combined for optimal treatment gains. The simultaneous use of individual and group approaches has been found to be most effective with cases of borderline personality disorder (Slavinsky-Holey, 1983) and eating disorders (Bohanske & Lemberg, 1987).

The effectiveness of group work is a consistent theme in the literature and is found to be useful for children and adults (Abramowitz, 1976; Bednar & Kaul, 1994; Burlingame, Fuhriman, & Mosier, 2003; Dagley et al., 1994; Fuhriman & Burlingame, 1994a, 1994b; Gazda, 1989; Hoag, 1997; Hoag & Burlingame, 1997; Kanas, 1986; Kaul & Bednar, 1986; Lambert & Bergin, 1994; MacKenzie, 1994, 1995; McDermit, Miller, & Brown, 2001; McRoberts et al., 1998; Miller & Berman, 1983; Mitte, 2005; Orlinsky & Howard, 1986; Robinson et al., 1990; Shapiro & Shapiro, 1982; Smith, Glass, & Miller, 1980; Sternbarger & Budman, 1996; Tillitski, 1990; Toseland & Siporin, 1986; Whiston et al., 2005 Zimpfer, 1990a, 1990b). Bachar (1998) reported that the results of meta-analyses of group counseling outcome studies ordinarily yield medium ES.

Group work has specifically been shown as effective with the following issues: depression (Scott & Stradling, 1991; Vandervoot & Fuhriman, 1991), eating disorders (Zimpfer, 1990b), obsessive-compulsive disorder (Krone, Himle, & Nesse, 1991), grief (Zimpfer, 1991), sexual abuse trauma (Alexander, Neimeyer, Follette, Moore, & Harter, 1989; Cahill, Llewelyn, & Pearson, 1991; Winick & Levene, 1992), and other internalizing disorders. There is general agreement that group treatment is outcome-effective and cost-efficient (Scheidlinger, 1993; Yalom & Leszcz, 2005). Group work has also been shown to be effective in addressing externalizing disorders, particularly spousal abuse (Dutton, 1986; Tolman & Bennett, 1990), midlife career changes (Zimpfer, 1989), divorce and separation (Zimpfer, 1990a), bulimia (Zimpfer, 1990b), and bereavement (Zimpfer, 1991). Table 16.3 provides a summary of some available meta-analyses that are referred to throughout the remainder of this section.

TABLE 16.3 Effectiveness of Group Work

Source	Outcome Explored	Effect
Burlingame, Fuhriman, & Mosier (2003)	Group counseling	Medium
Dush, Hirt, & Schroeder (1983)	Group counseling	Medium
Hoag (1997)	Group counseling	Medium
Hoag & Burlingame (1997)	Group counseling	Medium
McDermit, Miller, & Brown (2001)	Group counseling for depression	Large
Miller & Berman (1983)	Group counseling	Large
Robinson, Berman, & Neimeyer (1990)	Group counseling for depression	Large
Shapiro & Shapiro (1982)	Group counseling	Large
Smith, Glass, & Miller (1980)	Group counseling	Large
Tillitski (1990)	Group counseling	Large
Whiston, Eder, Rahardja, & Tai (2005)	Group counseling	Small

Process Issues in Group Outcome Research

The process variables in group work can be difficult to decipher and analyze because of the nature of human interaction. Ordinarily, group process variables include facets such as (1) group planning characteristics, (2) group structure, (3) pregroup training, (4) therapeutic factors, and (4) leader characteristics.

To begin, some of the issues inherent to the **group planning** phase are related to treatment outcomes. McRoberts et al. (1998), in a fascinating, complex, and comprehensive meta-analysis, reported that group work was more effective than individual counseling when 10 or fewer sessions were conducted, confirming the use of group work as a short-term treatment alternative (Budman, Simeone, Reilly, & Demby, 1994; Burlingame & Fuhriman, 1990). However, McRoberts et al. (1998) found no significant differences based on group size (fewer than nine versus nine or more participants), group type (psychoeducational versus process), or group membership (open versus closed).

Regarding **group structure** and its relationship to outcomes, Gazda (1989) identified a trend favoring the use of more structured approaches to group work. Unstructured groups, where the leader is less directive, tend to be related to client difficulties with interpersonal fears, cognitive distortion, subjective distress, and premature termination (Rhode & Stockton, 1994). Structure is especially imperative in the early stages of the group to define boundaries and build trust and cohesion (Keene & Erford, 2007). Lee and Bednar (1977) found that increased structure can lead to lower group cohesion, probably mediated by certain member personality characteristics. Structured group approaches should be used strategically and always matched with member personalities to enhance effectiveness.

Finally, **leader characteristics** are often explored in the group counseling literature to determine their effect on client outcome. Effective leaders have been shown to nurture a sense of hope in group members (Couch & Childers, 1987; Dykeman & Appleton, 1998), and to display encouraging personal characteristics, including a positive attitude and emotionally supportive behaviors (Combs, Avila, & Purky, 1978; Stockton, Morran, & Velboff, 1987). Hadley and Strupp (1976) concluded that group leaders with certain personality traits, including absence of genuineness, coldness, excessive need to make people change, excessive unconscious hostility, greed, lack of interest or warmth, lack of self-awareness, narcissism, pessimism, obsessiveness, sadism, and seductiveness, could be harmful to clients. Lieberman, Yalom, and Miles (1973) reported that nearly 50% of all client casualties are produced by the "aggressive stimulator" leadership style, which involves the leadership characteristics of high stimulus input, intrusiveness, confrontation, challenging but demonstrating, and high positive caring. Group leaders who seek advanced group course work and quality supervision are better able to increase skills and identify ineffective and harmful personal behavior.

Group Counseling With Children

Numerous studies, when taken collectively, indicate that group work with children and adolescents is effective, and as effective as individual counseling (Baer & Nietzel, 1991; Casey & Berman, 1985; Grossman & Hughes, 1992; Prout & DeMartino, 1986; Roberts & Camasso, 1991; Russell, Greenwald & Shirk, 1991; Shirk & Russell, 1992; Weisz et al., 1987). Some studies have pointed to interesting differential effects. For example, Tillitsky (1990) indicated that adolescents reported better outcomes when treated with group counseling rather than with individual counseling, whereas children reported the opposite effect, benefiting more from individual treatment than group work.

Most of the counseling research studies involving children explored the effectiveness of group approaches (Prout & Prout, 1998), although the overall quality and sophistication of these studies was inferior to group outcome studies for adults (Hoag & Burlingame, 1997). Whiston and Sexton (1993) concluded that group approaches with school-aged children were very effective in addressing social skills, discipline, and family adjustment problems. Hoag and Burlingame (1997) reported large ES for depression; medium ES for behavioral disorders, learning disorders, and children of divorce; and small ES for social problems.

Regarding depression in adolescents, Beeferman and Orvaschel (1994) reported that group counseling is a very effective treatment, with the most promising results stemming from a combination of supportive group processes and cognitive-behavioral interventions, combined with behavioral skills training and homework. Although Reynolds and Coats (1986) showed that relaxation training was just as effective as cognitive-behavioral interventions with adolescent group members, other studies (Bauer, Sapp, & Johnson, 2000; Kiselica, Baker, Thomas, & Reddy, 1994) support the use of cognitive-behavioral approaches and relaxation because the combination seems to be particularly effective with high school students.

Group approaches were also shown to produce short-term (Omizo & Omizo, 1988; Pedro-Carroll & Alpert-Gillis, 1997) and long-term (Pedro-Carroll, Sutton, & Wyman, 1999) positive outcomes for children of divorce. Generally, Whiston (2007) suggested that group approaches with children have ample support in the outcome research literature, whereas group work effectiveness with high school students needs further study. This conclusion is of interest because of the general perception that adolescents learn and process best in peer group interactions. Given that group work is effective with children and adults, it is reasonable to conclude that it is also likely to be effective with adolescents; however, group leaders and researchers must collaborate to promote research with this population of students.

EFFECTIVENESS OF GROUP WORK WITH ADULTS   The outcome research on adults is far more compelling and convincing than that available for children and adolescents. Group treatment of depression in adults (Robinson et al., 1990; Vandervoot & Fuhriman, 1991) and of bipolar disorder is quite effective. Group interventions for these mood disorders seem to be helpful in assisting members to access interpersonal support, learn effective coping skills, and understand the nature and course of the conditions. In the treatment of adults with eating disorders, group interventions seem to be very effective as well, and even more effective when coupled with individual counseling. In his review of more than 30 studies of eating disorders, Zimpfer (1990b) concluded that every study resulted in treatment gains, such as reduced binging and purging, improved body image, and lower levels of depression.

Group therapy with adults was highly effective (ES > 0.80) in the treatment of depression, eating disorders, personality disorders, substance abuse, and anxiety disorders, and moderately effective (0.50 < ES < 0.80) for adults with thought disorders, criminal behavior, stress, or neuroticism, or who were sexually abused. No significant relationships were found with the degree of patient diagnosis, group size, pregroup training, membership (open versus closed), therapist experience, or client gender or age (Burlingame et al., 2003).

Differences in outcome can be seen according to different group compositions and warrant mentioning. Members of heterogeneous groups attained an overall ES of only 0.25, whereas members of homogeneous groups attained a significantly higher level of improvement (ES = 0.56) (Burlingame et al., 2003). Group interventions that aimed more directly at underlying, common difficulties that are the focus of the group seem more effective.

Outpatient groups (ES = 0.55) reported more improvement than inpatient groups (ES = 0.20), although this is likely explained by the severity of members' conditions and the current level of crisis prevalent (Burlingame et al., 2003). Mixed-gender adult groups were more efficacious (ES = 0.66) overall than all-male (ES = 0.41) or all-female groups (ES = 0.39). Perhaps the diverse perspectives and interpersonal learning opportunities available in mixed-gender groups accounted for this difference. Reflection 16.5 follows.

REFLECTION 16.5

If you had to choose to use only either individual counseling or group counseling for the remainder of your career, which would you choose, and based on the outcome research, why?

SCHOOL-BASED INTERVENTIONS FOR CHILDREN AND ADOLESCENTS

The National Institute of Child Health and Human Development (2005) reported that approximately 2.7 million children experience severe emotional or behavioral problems, interfering with family relations, peer relationships, and academics. Kazdin and Johnson (1994) found that 17% to 22% of youth younger than 18 years of age have developmental, emotional, or behavioral problems. Doll (1996) indicated that the average school finds 18% to 22% of its students having diagnosable psychiatric disorders requiring intervention; while behavior and attention problems may be most common in primary school settings, depression and suicidal behaviors are more typical of secondary school populations.

As with any area of counseling service, it is critical for professional school counselors to be informed about outcome research and know which interventions are supported. Professional school counselors are employed by schools and provide direct and indirect counseling services at the school sites. In contrast to the traditional individual and group counseling services typically offered by professional counselors in agencies, the services offered by professional school counselors are more diverse and complex, and include increased consultation and collaboration with teachers and administrators, educational planning services, developmental classroom guidance lessons, peer mediation, and comprehensive school counseling programs.

Numerous studies have explored the effectiveness of this broader range of interventions, and Table 16.4 contains results from several meta-analyses, several of which warrant mentioning. In a review of 117 studies published since 1980, Whiston et al. (2005) yielded an overall unweighted ES = 0.46. Other meta-analyses focused more on the specific aspects of school counseling programs. Sink and Stroh (2003) indicated that elementary students who attended schools with a comprehensive school counseling program had slightly higher achievement scores. Sprinthall (1981) and Baker et al. (1984) concluded that primary prevention programs were at least moderately effective. Prout and DeMartino (1986) and Prout and Prout (1998) conducted meta-analyses of school-based individual counseling and concluded that ES for counseling services in schools were medium and large, respectively.

Several qualitative reviews of the literature have been conducted as well. Whiston and Sexton (1993) indicated that positive changes in students generally resulted from the broad range of services offered by professional school counselors. The conclusion of an earlier

TABLE 16.4 Effectiveness of the Specific Facets of Counseling for Youth and School-Based Interventions

Study	Characteristic	ES
Wilson, Gottfredson, & Najaka (2001)	Prevention programs for problem behaviors	None
	For delinquency	None
	For alcohol/drug use	None
	For dropout/attendance	None
Stage & Quiroz (1997)	Decreasing disruptive behavior (all methods)	Large
	With punishment	Medium
	With token economy	Large
	With response cost	Medium
	With reinforcement	Large
	With group behavior modification	Large
	With individual counseling	Small
	With parent training	Medium
	Decreasing disruptive behavior	Large
	Students in regular education	Medium
	With mental retardation	Medium
	With serious emotional disturbances	Large
	With learning disabilities	Large
Bratton, Ray, Rhine, & Jones (2005)	Nondirective play therapy	Large
	Directive play therapy	Medium
	Group play therapy	Medium
	Individual play therapy	Medium
	Parent-led filial trained play therapy	Large
	Play therapy for behavior problems	Large
	Play therapy for social adjustment	Large
	Play therapy for family relationships	Large
Whiston, Eder, Rahardja, & Tai (2005)	School counseling program effectiveness	Small
	Group guidance curricular activities	Small
	Responsive services	Small
	Peer mediation	Small

qualitative review by Borders and Drury (1992) was even more favorable. After examining studies published between 1960 and 1990, they concluded that significant student improvements in academic performance, attitudes, and behaviors resulted from school-based counseling services, leading to a substantial impact on student development. Additional qualitative reviews report similarly positive results. One such review (Gerler, 1985) focused on elementary-aged students and concluded that student affective, interpersonal, and behavioral characteristics are positively affected by school counseling programs. Similarly, St. Claire (1989) suggested that middle school students benefited from school counseling services offered for behavior modification, self-relaxation, and daily progress reports. In a qualitative study of low-performing K-12 students, Wilson (1986) concluded that school counselor strategies and interventions resulted in higher grade point averages across grade levels.

The availability of outcome research in the area of school counseling effectiveness continues to lag compared with the areas of counseling pertaining to career and individual interventions (Whiston, 2007). In addition, the outcomes research in school counseling that is available is replete with methodological limitations. Such limitations are partly due to the complexity of assessing highly variable, multifaceted, and wide-ranging programs. Conclusions about the effectiveness of school counseling interventions should be viewed with caution.

SPECIFIC TYPES OF SCHOOL-BASED INTERVENTIONS   It is important to consider outcomes research within each type of intervention offered because school-based services are multifaceted and may result in different effectiveness rates. Outcomes research that focused on the specific types of school-based interventions is considered. First, Whiston et al. (2005) conducted a meta-analysis to evaluate **developmental classroom guidance** activities. Such activities are used to promote healthy social and emotional development and are typically taught through a variety of methods, including activities, music, drawing, stories, games, worksheets, role playing, puppets, and videos. Whiston et al. concluded that this intervention had primarily small ES across the K-12 curriculum; this may be because many professional school counselors are using materials that have not been studied for their effectiveness (Rowley, Stroh, & Sink, 2005). Although an effect was detected, an even greater effect may result if the materials used were empirically validated.

Regardless, other studies found classroom guidance to be quite effective in addressing personal/affective issues (Rowley et al., 2005), wellness (Omizo, Omizo, & D'Andrea, 1992), academic achievement (Hadley, 1988; Lee, 1993), social competence (Weissburg, Caplan, & Harwood, 1991), school attitude and behavior (Schlossberg, Morris, & Lieberman, 2001), and self-management skills (Brigman & Campbell, 2003; Campbell & Brigman, 2005). In general, the evaluation of materials used for the purposes of classroom developmental guidance is an area of research needing increased attention from empirically oriented practitioners and researchers.

Another type of service specific to school-based counseling is that of **responsive services**. In general, responsive services are services that are aimed at immediate attention and intervention in response to problematic issues that might arise in the school setting, but typically result from personal situations.

While the literature does not always agree on which method is more effective, individual and group counseling responsive services are found to be effective in the remediation of problems displayed by children and adolescents. In a meta-analysis of 58 studies, Whiston et al. (2005) assessed the effectiveness of group counseling interventions and reported an overall ES = 0.35. Group counseling was also determined to be effective for a wide range of school-based behaviors, including discipline problems, social skills training (Whiston & Sexton, 1993), adjustment to divorce (Omizo & Omizo, 1998; Pedro-Carroll & Alpert-Gillis, 1997; Pedro-Carroll et al., 1999), and relaxation (Bauer et al., 2000; Kiselica et al., 1994). Wilson (1986) found group methods to be more effective than individual methods for the purpose of improving the academic performance of low-achieving students. Nearpass (1990) found, however, that individual counseling is more effective. Additional studies conducted by Littrell et al. (1995) concluded that brief, solution-focused approaches to individual counseling were effective with adolescents, indicating lengthier treatment as unnecessary. Thompson and Littrell (1998) reached a similar conclusion when counseling students with learning disabilities.

It is estimated that conflict resolution programs are increasing, with a 40% increase noted in the first half of the 1990s (Shepherd, 1994). However, research on conflict resolution and peer mediation programs in schools continues to be scarce (Burstyn & Stevens, 2001). With the increase in school violence and bullying behaviors on campus, more attention is being focused on the implementation and the effectiveness of such programs. In 2005, Whiston et al. completed a study of peer mediation programs that showed a small effect (ES = 0.39) for improving student knowledge of how to address conflict and potentially problematic situations. While this study did provide evidence of increased knowledge, little is known about the effects of such programs on actual student behaviors and conflict.

One such study that was aimed at examining the effectiveness of peer mediation, conducted by Wilson et al. (2003), found little improvement in aggressive behaviors. However, Lewis and Lewis (1996) noted that findings such as this could be more indicative of the training level of the individuals operating such programs, rather than a result of the program itself. Program implementation was often conducted by noncounselors who lacked the necessary skills. Regardless, Gerber and Terry-Day (1999) concluded that insufficient empirical support exists to say with confidence that the programs are theoretically sound and result in desirable effects. Because of this, there is insufficient cause to warrant the widespread use of peer mediation and conflict resolution programs in schools without more study.

Some outcomes research has focused on specific problem areas, such as disruptive behavior, delinquent behavior, substance use, truancy, moral education, and coping skills. Regarding disruptive classroom behavior, studies show behavior modification techniques to be generally effective. Stage and Quiroz (1997) (see Table 16.4) reported an ES = 0.78, indicating that 78% of treatment group participants receiving behavior modification fared better than the average control group participant. Such effects were noted regardless of the type of behavior modification technique used (i.e., token economies versus response cost procedures versus time-out procedures using contingency delay) (Erford, 1999; Stage & Quiroz, 1997).

Research on **school-based prevention programs for problem behaviors** yielded mixed results. Wilson et al. (2001) concluded that ES were either not significant or extremely small when studying the effectiveness of primary prevention programs. In addition, they found that prevention programs aimed at reducing attendance-related problems were most effective at the high school level (ES = 0.14) compared with elementary (ES = 0.05) or middle schools (ES = 0.09) (see Table 16.4). ES for prevention programs for delinquency (ES = 0.04) or alcohol/drug use (ES = 0.05) were generally not significant. When examined alone, however, a substantial number of these studies were effective for the prevention of drug use (Botvin, Schinke, & Orlandi, 1995; Durlack, 1995; Gottfredson, 1997, 2001; Gottfredson, Wilson, & Najaka, 2001; Tobler & Stratton, 1997) and delinquency (Catalano, Arthur, Hawkins, Bergland, & Olson, 1998; Gottfredson et al., 2001; Hawkins, Farrington, & Catalano, 1998; Lipsey & Derzon, 1998; Samplers & Aber, 1998; Stage & Quiroz, 1997). When analyzed together, differences in studies are lost.

As Tobler and Stratton (1997) noted, how the program is delivered and the student's level of involvement contribute substantially to a program's effectiveness. As is true for many areas of counseling research, the research in this area is "neither vast nor methodologically strong" (Akos, 2004, p. 37). Increased consistency in methodology is required to improve the outcomes research in this area.

CAREER INTERVENTIONS   Career interventions are implemented with students and adults and typically involve interventions aimed at helping individuals define and understand their career interests and abilities, culminating in a plan of action to achieve vocational direction and success. Not only are career interventions helpful in the initial steps of determining aptitude and interests, but also in gaining the skills necessary to seek work, transition to work, cope with work-related stress, and perhaps change areas of work in adulthood. A wealth of outcomes research exists to document the effectiveness of counseling interventions aimed at career development. Oliver and Spokane (1988) reviewed 58 studies (7,311 total participants) conducted between 1950 and 1982 focusing on career counseling interventions. In 1998, Whiston, Sexton, and Lasoff continued Oliver and Spokane's intention through a replication study designed to analyze the results of an additional 47 studies conducted between 1983 and 1995 (4,660 total participants). Such meta-analytic reviews have supported the effectiveness of career counseling with large ES (0.85 and 0.82) (Oliver & Spokane, 1988; Spokane & Oliver, 1983). In general, outcomes research has supported the effectiveness of career interventions, especially individual career counseling and classroom guidance using individual planning services, which coordinates continuous activities designed to assist in the establishment of personal goals and future plans (American School Counselor Association, 2005; Oliver & Spokane, 1988; Whiston et al., 1998).

Evans and Burck (1992) conducted a meta-analysis of 67 studies on the impact of career interventions aimed at providing education in an effort to improve the academic achievement of more than 82,000 primary and secondary school students. Small positive effects (ES = 0.22, unweighted) were found, with the greatest improvements resulting when the program was in its second year with the same students. Overall, providing career education interventions was more beneficial to academic achievement than no education or alternative interventions.

Students benefited from parent consultation about career development and career services, including students considered ethnic minorities, academically gifted, and having disabilities (Sexton et al., 1997). Programs lacking a professional counselor and instead relying on computer-based programs were not as effective (Garis & Niles, 1990; Whiston, Brecheisen, & Stephens, 2003). However, the use of such computerized guidance was helpful when used as a supplemental activity in addition to counselor-directed activities. Student age has also been examined, and is found to be a factor contributing to career counseling success (Sexton et al., 1997). Career focused interventions are least effective for elementary-aged students, who are developmentally unprepared to consider vocational interests and choices. As would be expected, Oliver and Spokane (1988) concluded that career counseling was most effective for junior high and high school students.

Regarding the length of treatment, longer treatment seems more effective and of more benefit than shorter treatment (McAulife & Frederickson, 1990; Pickering & Vacc, 1984; Spokane, 1991). In addition, directive interventions are found to be more efficacious than person-centered interventions in regard to career counseling (Galassi, Crace, Martin, James, & Wallace, 1992). Because length of treatment and therapy modality are considered important variables in determining the effectiveness of career counseling interventions, Sexton et al. (1997) suggested the development and use of standardized and empirically validated treatment manuals to increase the effectiveness and consistency of counseling.

Table 16.5 summarizes ES for the outcomes measured in the meta-analyses conducted by Oliver and Spokane (1988) and Whiston et al. (1998). Overall, 83% of the studies of career intervention reported at least some positive effects (Sexton et al., 1997). Reflection 16.6 follows Table 16.5.

TABLE 16.5 Effectiveness of Career Interventions as Determined by Oliver and Spokane (1988) and Whiston, Sexton, & Lasoff (1998)

Oliver & Spokane ES	Whiston et al. ES	Characteristic
Overall Effect		
0.82	0.45	All studies combined and unweighted
Length of Treatment		
0.31	0.61	Single session intervention
1.01	0.53	2–7 sessions intervention
0.65	0.74	More than 8 sessions intervention
Age of Client		
–0.01	0.04	Elementary school students
1.28	0.42	Middle school students
1.02	0.31	High school students
0.85	0.59	College students
0.82	0.54	Adults
Experience of Counselor		
0.72	0.51	Experienced counselor
0.83	0.81	Counselor in training
0.31	0.29	Counselor-free
0.38	0.60	Other (usually facilitator or group leader)
Treatment Types		
0.74	1.08	Individual counseling
0.62	0.73	Group counseling
0.76	0.36	Group test interpretation
0.75	0.36	Workshop
2.05	0.54	Class
0.59	0.45	Computer intervention
0.10	0.12	Counselor-free
Specific Treatment Outcomes		
2.45	1.40	Accuracy of self-knowledge
0.97	0.73	Securing job or probability of hire
0.40	0.38	Certainty/decidedness
0.88	0.88	Career-related knowledge
1.30	1.03	Skills (interview, writing, and problem-solving)
1.05	0.55	Career maturity

REFLECTION 16.6

After reading through the empirical evidence, what seems to be missing from the outcome research literature?

IMPLICATIONS FOR PROFESSIONAL COUNSELORS

While much helpful outcome research has accumulated over the years, much is still needed to help professional counselors skillfully implement therapeutic interventions. As future professionals in the field, consider ways that you can add to what is known about best practices. Generally, there are three primary ways that professional counselors can help: (1) collaborate with researchers, (2) advocate for outcome research funding, and (3) increase knowledge and use of outcome literature.

Collaborate With Researchers

Students and practitioners alike should make every effort to collaborate with researchers whenever possible. Many forego such opportunities, however, because it is often viewed as costly, complex, time-consuming, and remote. However, for current counseling students, graduating without the ability to evaluate their own effectiveness will provide a distinct disadvantage in their ability to gain employment just as the lack of basic counseling skills and theoretical knowledge would have 10 years ago (Granello & Granello, 1998). Granello and Granello (2001, p. 163) further state, "counselors who cannot demonstrate their successes may find themselves unable to survive professionally."

While in training, counseling students can develop skills necessary to consume, incorporate, and produce outcome research. Counseling students should work alongside professors in an effort to assist with research projects. Although research can be a long and intense process, often taking several years to complete, students can provide valuable aid in conducting portions of studies, contributing to the final product. Not only are students of great help during this process, but they also learn valuable research and evaluation skills that prove useful as future practitioners. Students who become active in research studies begin to understand the research process and are more likely to stay active in research after becoming a professional counselor in the field.

Just as counseling students must assist with research, practitioners too can collaborate with professors, researchers, and other practitioners to conduct site-based action research and program evaluation with clients. Engaging in outcome research does not have to be an impossible task. Simple measures of functioning can be used to measure the effectiveness of treatment and incorporated into routine paperwork obligations. While the results found by one practitioner may seem too small to matter, when combined with the results found by other practitioners, they can lead to meaningful outcomes. Such efforts by practitioners would be invaluable to researchers, as researchers frequently attempt to coordinate such studies, but struggle for lack of access to necessary population samples. Not only can practitioners conduct their own research and collaborate with other counseling professionals, but they should also consider making their worksite available to researchers. Simply making your worksite or willing clients available as a pool of potential participants can lead to a wealth of information when combined with others. The large populations served by professional counselors in schools and community agencies can be particularly useful for outcomes research. Providing access to participants and helping to collect data are the two components of outcome research with which practitioners can be of greatest aid. Most importantly, becoming active in research studies as a student to understand the process and then staying active once you have become a professional counselor in the field is crucial to the future of outcomes research.

Advocate for Outcome Research Funding

In addition to engaging in collaborative research efforts with colleagues and researchers, professional counselors must also advocate for increased funding for outcome research. Ordinarily, funding for research can be obtained from government agencies, private foundations, universities, and professional organizations (Erford, 2008a). Advocating for research funding by these sources is a professional responsibility that generates new practice-improving findings—findings that would help professional counselors understand how better to help their clients meet their goals, help researchers communicate this information to professional counselors, and conduct basic research meant to inform counseling practice. But all this starts with your advocacy efforts.

Increase Knowledge and Use of Outcome Literature

Because research has shown that some practices are more effective than others, and some client problems are helped most by specific counseling models (Sexton, 1999), professional counselors can greatly improve their effectiveness and ethical practice by reading and using knowledge gained from an understanding of the outcomes research. Membership and involvement in national, regional, and state counseling organizations ensures access to the literature through journals and other scholarly publications. Professional counselors should read and use such information to shape their practice. In addition, such information should be passed along to other colleagues, so they too may keep informed on the most recent, relevant, and rigorous information.

Reynolds (2000) introduced a five-step model for practicing professional counselors to use in an effort to increase the use of empirically based treatment.

1. The professional counselor determines the specific clinical question pertinent to the client's progress.
2. The professional counselor seeks out the empirical literature to answer the clinical question.
3. The professional counselor evaluates the evidence found in the literature for its usefulness.
4. The results are used to shape treatment and integrated into counseling interventions.
5. The outcome of the intervention is evaluated.

To move through these steps, the professional counselor must first be aware of what research is available, be able to assess it, have the ability to identify the implications of it, and possess the knowledge and skill to integrate the findings into their practice. Through a systematic process, professional counselors can be encouraged to approach client care more scientifically, not in an effort to dehumanize the experience, but rather in an effort to increase the efficacy of interventions. For counselors to be unconcerned about the outcomes of their interventions is unethical. To maximize effectiveness, professional counselors must combine their professional experience, intuition, and knowledge of theory with the external evidence.

Having stressed the importance of consuming research, it is also important to recall that in reality, most of what works is determined by factors other than the specific counseling technique or intervention chosen. Research shows that this accounts for only 15% of the outcome (Lambert, 1991). The remaining 85% of client outcome is heavily determined by the core conditions of effective helping. Lambert (1991) concluded that 15% of therapeutic outcome is due to client expectations, 40% is due to factors outside of the counseling setting, and 30% is due to core conditions. The point is that although many counselors are oblivious to the current research, others may rush through it to find a solution or the newest technique available for a particular client situation, failing to focus on the importance of establishing a counseling relationship. Instead, it is known that a counselor's level of skillfulness, capacity to conceptualize, and ability to match relationally with the client is equally important to outcomes (Sexton, 1999). Reflection 16.7 follows.

REFLECTION 16.7

What important questions emerge about the effectiveness of counseling that warrant further study? If you were a researcher, how would you gain access to the client population of interest? If you were a practitioner, how would you carry out a research study to examine your own effectiveness, while simultaneously adding to the outcome research?

Putting It All Together—Working for the Future

The current accountability movements in schools and clinics point to the need for practitioners to focus on process and outcome evaluation. It is more essential than ever that students, practitioners, and researchers work together to establish effective practices. In the past, practitioners have often viewed research as artificial, even as a necessary evil. Such a view is counterproductive. Instead, students, practitioners, and researchers must work together—quite literally—to become collaborators in research and consumers of research. Such collaboration would significantly improve our understanding of efficient and effective counseling interventions, to improve personal practice and client outcomes.

The research available on the outcomes of the counseling process has grown substantially and is considered a reliable and valid source of knowledge. Earlier research was in many ways irrelevant to practice; however, that trend has shifted, and a growing body of evidence has evolved that is directly applicable to the specific problems and populations seen daily in practice. Research now shows stable trends supporting the usefulness of some counseling practices over others, the increased value of certain aspects of counseling over others, and the effectiveness of specific models paired with specific problems. The production, proliferation, dissemination, and incorporation of outcome research has the ability to continue moving the profession of counseling increasingly forward, to shape a practice that is not merely one of theory and instinct, but of sound science.

While literally hundreds of studies have explored the effectiveness of the various facets of counseling, much remains unknown. The extant literature on counseling outcomes research to date gives a general idea of what is and is not effective as it relates to work with adults, adolescents, and children, with a multitude of issues, across various counseling settings. As stated previously, no theoretical approach to counseling has shown superiority over another, although some approaches show more promise with specific issues and under certain conditions. This observation has led some researchers to conclude that a great deal of counseling effectiveness is due to core therapeutic conditions common to most counseling approaches. If outcomes research continues to proliferate and flourish, with increasingly more knowledge gained regarding the effectiveness of particular methods, and if this information is used in conjunction with the core conditions of counseling, imagine how much more effective counseling could become. With increased focus on accountability, this is no longer an ideal vision of the future of counseling, but a necessary direction.

Outcomes research is vital to the well-being of the client, the ethical obligations of the counselor, and the advancement of the field. For the counseling profession to remain competitive, it must show effectiveness. To do so, treatment must be empirically validated by research, and improved outcomes must be shown. It is crucial for each individual professional counselor, at a minimum, to be knowledgeable of the research base, to understand how to use the therapy modalities and treatment approaches validated, and to select and tailor interventions based on best practices. Even more so, professional counselors must shift to become producers of outcome research, in addition to consumers, in an effort not only to increase their effectiveness, but also to add substantially to the profession of counseling.

Summary

Simply put, outcome research is intended to answer the question of counseling effectiveness. While the need for counseling services is at an all-time high, so too is the need to prove therapeutic results and effective treatments to practice ethically, reduce harm to the client, gain reimbursement, and advance the field. However, not only do practicing counselors tend to refrain from conducting any outcome research, they also fail to keep informed of the current outcome research and newest empirically validated treatments. Not only is outcome research underproduced, but also what is produced is understudied and underused.

As stated earlier, the chasm between research and practice has begun to close substantially over the years as practitioners have realized the need for more relevant outcome research, and counseling researchers have realized the need for more pertinent and applicable research studies. The scientist-practitioner model has been advocated in training future researchers and practitioners to make everyone effective at research and practice.

Meta-analysis is used to combine statistically results from different studies examining the same variables to analyze across studies the effectiveness of interventions. For each study, an ES is usually calculated, resulting in a numerical index showing if participants receiving the intervention improved beyond participants who did not.

Although Eysenck (1952) initially claimed that psychotherapy was not only ineffective, but also potentially harmful to clients, since that time hundreds of studies have instead supported the effectiveness of such interventions. While a very small percent of individuals do not improve with counseling, and may worsen for a variety of reasons (many of which are unrelated to the counseling itself), outcome research points to the overwhelming conclusion that counseling is helpful for a wide array of populations, presenting with various concerns, in a host of settings. In addition, it is generally accepted today that such positive outcomes are obtained regardless of the theoretical approach. However, it is also known that particular interventions typically are better with certain disorders. Even more important are the interactions of the various facets of the counseling process that are also known to be independently contributory. These interactions are now the focal point of much research.

While still often debated, it is generally accepted that individual counseling and group counseling are about equally effective, although each may be slightly more appropriate or helpful at particular times and in particular conditions. It has also been documented that the combination of the two yields especially promising results.

Likewise, comprehensive school-based programs seem effective in improving student academic performance, social skills, and behavior, although less effective when the focus is on prevention programs related to substance use and delinquency. Nearly all career counseling interventions seem effective when implemented by a professional counselor, whereas interventions using untrained individuals are ineffective if not harmful.

Several implications and suggestions for how professional counselors can help bridge the research-practice gap and tap into a wealth of continuing outcomes research are offered. Professional counselors should also collaborate with researchers and evaluate their own effectiveness, and advocate for increased funding for counseling research. Finally, professional counselors should read, summarize, and disseminate research on effective counseling practice to other practitioners.

The importance of establishing a collaborative relationship with clients cannot be underestimated. While many counselors are unmindful of the current research, others may focus only on current research findings regarding treatment protocols and techniques. Instead, as a professional counselor, strive for a balance that emphasizes the core conditions of counseling, while being knowledgeable of the current outcome literature and examining your own effectiveness.

REFERENCES

Abramowitz, C. V. (1976). The effectiveness of group psychotherapy with children. *Archives of General Psychiatry, 33,* 320–326.

Achenbach, T. M., & Rescorla, L. A. (2001). *Manual for the Achenbach System of Empirically Based Assessment (ASEBA).* Burlington, VT: University of Vermont Department of Psychiatry.

Aiken, L. R. (2003). *Psychological testing and assessment* (11th ed.). Boston: Allyn & Bacon.

Akos, P. (2004). Outcomes research on school counseling. In B. T. Erford (Ed.), *Professional school counseling: A handbook of theories, programs, and practices* (pp. 35–42). Austin, TX: Pro-Ed.

Albee, G. W. (1999). Prevention, not treatment, is the only hope. *Counselling Psychology Quarterly, 12,* 133–146.

Alcoholics Anonymous. (2006). *World Services.* Retrieved December 8, 2006, from http://www.alcoholics-anonymous.org

Alexander, P. C., Neimeyer, R. A., Follette, V. M., Moore, M. K., & Harter, S. (1989). A comparison of group treatments of women sexually abused as children. *Journal of Consulting and Clinical Psychology, 57,* 479–483.

Allen, J. (1992). *Action-oriented research: Promoting school counselor advocacy and accountability.* ERIC Document (ED347477).

American Association of State Counseling Boards. (2007). Retrieved August 28, 2007, from http://www.aascb.org

American Association of Suicidology. (n.d.). *About suicide: Understanding and helping the suicidal person.* Retrieved June 19, 2008, from http://www.suicidology.org/displaycommon.cfm?an=2

American Counseling Association. (1997, May 31). *Know your rights: Mental health, private practice and the law.* ACA national videoconference. Alexandria, VA.

American Counseling Association. (2005a). *American Counseling Association code of ethics* (3rd ed.). Alexandria, VA: Author.

American Counseling Association. (2005b). *Public awareness ideas and strategies for professional counselors.* Alexandria, VA: Author.

American Counseling Association. (2006a). *Access to counseling in Department of Defense's TRICARE Health Services Program.* Retrieved November 20, 2006, from http://www.counseling.org/PublicPolicy/PositionPapers.aspx?AGuid=c667fbb3-b717-40af-9505-99c57267c872

American Counseling Association. (2006b). *Elementary and Secondary School Counseling Program (ESSCP) and FY 2007 federal education funding.* Retrieved November 20, 2006, from http://www.counseling.org/PublicPolicy/PositionPapers.aspx?AGuid=8d08ec97-286e-4b85-ae5c-a053093894d0

American Counseling Association. (2006c). *Public policy and legislative agenda for the second session of the 109th Congress.* Retrieved November 20, 2006, from http://www.counseling.org/Files/FD.ashx?guid=50c41d49-9404-401f-bcfb-262da485204f

American Counseling Association. (2006d). *Reauthorization of the Higher Education Act.* Retrieved November 20, 2006, from http://www.counseling.org/PublicPolicy/PositionPapers.aspx?AGuid=95ff9aea-9d63-446e-8229-54512d172f83

American Counseling Association. (2006e). *Yet another bill introduced including reimbursement of counselors under Medicare.* Retrieved November 20, 2006, from http://www.counseling.org/PublicPolicy/LegislativeUpdate.aspx?AGuid=5fd93ea3-98f4-4fd0-aefa-0767a07e3314

American Counseling Association. (2006f). *Advocacy competencies.* Retrieved December 4, 2006, from http://www.counseling.org/Resources/

American Counseling Association. (2006g). *Licensure requirements for professional counselors.* Alexandria, VA: Author.

American Counseling Association. (2007). *ACA Divisions, Regions and Branches.* Retrieved December 3, 2008, from http://www.counseling.org/AboutUs/DivisionsBranchesAndRegions/TP/Divisions/CT2.aspx

American Friends Service Committee. (1998). *People with disabilities.* Philadelphia: Affirmative Action Office.

American Psychiatric Association. (2001). *Diagnostic and statistical manual of mental disorders* (4th ed., text revised). Washington, DC: Author.

American Psychiatric Association Work Group on Eating Disorders. (2000). Practice guidelines for the treatment of patients with eating disorders. *American Journal of Psychiatry, 157 (1 Supplement),* 1–39.

American School Counselor Association. (2004). *Ethical standards for school counselors.* Alexandria, VA: Author.

American School Counselor Association. (2005). *The ASCA national model: A framework for school counseling programs* (2nd ed.). Alexandria, VA: Author.

Anderson, D. (1992). A case for standards of counseling practice. *Journal of Counseling & Development, 71,* 22–26.

Anderson. T., Ogles, B., & Weis, A. (1999). Creative use of interpersonal skills in building a therapeutic alliance. *Journal of Constructivist Psychology, 12,* 313–330.

Anderson, W. P., & Heppner, P. P. (1986). Counselor applications of research findings to practice: Learning to stay current. *Journal of Counseling and Development, 65,* 152–155.

Arnett, J. J. (2000). Emerging adulthood: A theory of development from the late teens through the twenties. *American Psychologist, 55,* 469–480.

Arredondo, P., & Glauner, T. (1992). *Personal dimensions of identity model.* Tucson, AZ: Empowerment Workshops.

Assouline, M., & Meir, E. I. (1987). Meta-analysis of the relationship between congruence and well-being measures. *Journal of Vocational Behavior, 31,* 319–332.

Atkinson, D. R. (1985). A meta-review of research on cross-cultural counseling and psychotherapy. *Journal of Multicultural Counseling and Development, 13,* 138–153.

Atkinson, D. R., Bui, U., & Mori, S. (2001). Multiculturally sensitive empirically supported treatments—an oxymoron? In J. G. Ponterotto, J. M. Casas, L. A. Suzuki, & C. M. Alexander (Eds.), *Handbook of multicultural counseling* (2nd ed.) (pp. 542–574). Thousand Oaks, CA: Sage Publications.

Atkinson, D. R., & Hackett, G. (1998). *Counseling diverse populations* (2nd ed.). Boston: McGraw-Hill.

Atkinson, D. R., & Schein, S. (1986). Similarity in counseling. *The Counseling Psychologist, 14,* 319–354.

Axelson, J. A. (1999). *Counseling and development in a multicultural society* (3rd ed.). Pacific Grove, CA: Brooks/Cole.

Bachar, E. (1998). Psychotherapy—an active agent: Assessing the effectiveness of psychotherapy and its curative factors. *Israel Journal of Psychiatry and Related Sciences, 35,* 128–135.

Baekland, F., & Lundwall, L. (1975). Dropping out of treatment: A critical review. *Psychological Bulletin, 82,* 738–783.

Baer, R. A., & Nietzel, M. T. (1991). Cognitive and behavioral treatment of impulsivity in children: A meta-analytic review of the outcome literature. *Journal of Clinical Child Psychology, 20,* 400–412.

Baker, S. B. (2000). *School counseling for the 21st century* (3rd ed.). Upper Saddle River, NJ: Merrill/Prentice Hall.

Baker, S. B., & Daniels, T. G. (1989). Integrating research on the Microcounseling Program: A meta-analysis. *Journal of Counseling Psychology, 36,* 213–222.

Baker, S. B., Swisher, J. D., Nadenichek, P. E., & Popowicz, C. L. (1984). Measured effects of primary prevention strategies. *Personnel and Guidance Journal, 62,* 459–464.

Balota, D. A., Dolan, P. O., & Duchek, J. M. (2000). Memory changes in healthy older adults. In E. Tulving & F. I. M. Craik (Eds.), *The Oxford handbook of memory.* New York: Oxford University Press.

Baltes, P. B. (2000). Life-span developmental theory. In A. Kazdin (Ed.), *Encyclopedia of psychology.* Washington, DC: American Psychological Association & Oxford University Press.

Barclay, J. R., Brown, B. M., Gladding, S. T., Goodyear, R. K., Hays, D. G., Hohenshil, T. H., et al. (1981). Counseling and the future: Some views of editorial board members. *The Personnel and Guidance Journal, November,* 131–134.

Barlow, D. H., & Durand, V. M. (2003). *Essentials of abnormal psychology* (3rd ed.). Pacific Grove, CA: Wadsworth-Thomson Learning.

Bartholomew, C. (2003). *Gender-sensitive therapy: Principles and practices.* Prospect Heights, IL: Waveland Press, Inc.

Basham, A., Appleton, V., & Dykeman, C. (2000). *Team-building in education: A how-to guidebook.* Denver, CO: Love Publishing.

Bauer, S. R., Sapp, M., & Johnson, D. (2000). Group counseling strategies for rural at-risk high school students. *The High School Journal, 83,* 41–50.

Beck, A. T. (1988). *Love is never enough.* New York: Harper & Row.

Beck, A. T., & Steer, R. A. (1993). *Manual for the Beck Anxiety Inventory.* San Antonio, TX: The Psychological Corporation.

Beck, A. T., Steer, R. A., & Brown, G. K. (1996). *Beck Depression Inventory* (2nd ed.). San Antonio, TX: The Psychological Corporation.

Bedi, R. P. (2006). Concept mapping the client's perspective on counseling alliance formation. *Journal of Counseling Psychology, 53,* 26–35.

Bednar, R. L., & Kaul, T. J. (1994). Experimental group research: Can the cannon fire? In A. E. Bergin & S. L. Garfield (Eds.), *Handbook of psychotherapy and behavior change* (3rd ed.) (pp. 631–663). New York: Wiley.

Beeferman, D., & Orvaschel, H. (1994). Group psychotherapy for depressed adolescents: A critical review. *International Journal of Group Psychotherapy, 44,* 463–475.

Beers, C. W. (1908). *A mind that found itself.* New York: Longmans, Green, & Co.

Bem, S. L. (1981). *Bem Sex-Role Inventory: Professional manual.* Palo Alto, CA: Consulting Psychologists Press.

Bem, S. L. (1993). *The lenses of gender: Transforming the debate on sexuality inequality.* New Haven, CT: Yale University Press.

Bemak, F., & Espina, M. R. (1999, Winter). Professional counseling licensure: Going from state to state. *ACES Spectrum, 60,* 4–6 & 11.

Bennett, D. S., & Gibbons, T. A. (2000). Efficacy of child cognitive-behavioral interventions for antisocial behavior: A meta-analysis. *Child and Family Behavior Therapy, 22,* 1–15.

Benson, B., & Dewey, D. (2008). Parental stress and needs in families of children with autism spectrum disorder. *International Journal of Disability, Community & Rehabilitation, 7*(1). Retrieved July 5, 2008, from http://www.ijdcr.ca

Berger, K. S. (2003). *The developing person through childhood* (3rd ed.). New York: Worth.

Bergin, A. E., & Lambert, M. J. (1978). The evaluation of therapeutic outcomes. In S. L. Garfield & A. E. Bergin (Eds.), *Handbook of psychotherapy and behavior change: An empirical analysis* (pp. 143–189). New York: Wiley.

Berk, L. E. (1999). *Infants and children.* Boston: Allyn & Bacon.

Berk, L. E. (2003). *Child development* (6th ed.). Boston: Allyn & Bacon.

Berman, J. S., & Norton, N. C. (1985). Does professional training make a therapist more effective? *Psychological Bulletin, 98,* 401–407.

Bernard, J., & Goodyear, R. (1998). *Fundamentals of clinical supervision* (2nd ed.). Boston: Allyn & Bacon.

Beutler, L. E. (1989). Differential treatment selection: The role of diagnosis in psychotherapy. *Psychotherapy, 26,* 271–281.

Beutler, L. E., Crago, M., & Arizmendi, T. G. (1986). Research on therapist variables in psychotherapy. In S. L. Garfield & A. E. Bergin (Eds.), *Handbook of psychotherapy and behavior change* (pp. 257–310). New York: Wiley.

Beutler, L. E., Frank, M., Schieber, S. C., Calvert, S., & Gaines, J. (1984). Comparative effects of group psychotherapies in a short-term inpatient setting: An experience with deterioration effects. *Psychiatry, 47*(1), 66–76.

Beutler, L. E., & Mitchell, R. (1981). Differential psychotherapy outcome among depressed and impulsive patients as a function of analytic and experiential treatment procedures. *Psychiatry, 44,* 297–306.

Bishop, J. B., Gallagher, R. P., & Cohen, D. (2000). College students' problems: Status, trends, and research. In D. C. Davis & K. M. Humphrey (Eds.), *College counseling: Issues for a new millennium* (pp. 109–110). Alexandria, VA: American Counseling Association.

Bjorklund, D. F. (2000). *Children's thinking: Developmental function and individual differences* (3rd ed.). Belmont, CA: Wadsworth.

Blocher, D. (1987). *The professional counselor.* New York: Macmillan.

Bohanske, J., & Lemberg, R. (1987). An intensive group process—retreat model for the treatment of bulimia. *Group, 11,* 228–237.

Borders, L. D., & Bloss, K. K. (1994). Helping students apply the scientist-practitioner model: A teaching approach. *Counselor Education & Supervision, 34,* 172–177.

Borders, L. D., & Drury, S. M. (1992). Comprehensive school counseling programs: A review for policymakers and practitioners. *Journal of Counseling and Development, 70,* 487–498.

Botvin, G. J., Schinke, S., & Orlandi, M. A. (1995). School-based health promotion: Substance abuse and sexual behavior. *Applied Prevention Psychology, 4,* 167–184.

Bourdon, K. H., Rae, D. S., Narrow, W. E., Mandershild, R. W., & Regier, D. A. (1994). National prevalence and treatment of mental and addictive disorders. In R. W. Mandershild & A. Sonnenschein (Eds.), *Mental health: United States* (pp. 22–51). Washington, DC: Center for Mental Health Services.

Bowen, M. (1966). The use of family theory in clinical practice. *Comprehensive Psychiatry, 7,* 345–374.

Bowen, M. (1976). Theory in the practice of psychotherapy. In P. J. Guerin (Ed.), *Family therapy: Theory and practice*. New York: Gardner Press.

Bowers, J. L., & Colonna, H. A. (2001). *Tucson Unified School District guidance and counseling program handbook*. Tucson, AZ: Tucson Unified School District.

Bradley, L., & Kottler, J. (2001a). Overview of counselor supervision. In L. J. Bradley, & N. Ladany (Eds.), *Counselor supervision: Principles, process, and practice* (3rd ed.) (pp. 3–27). Philadelphia: Brunner-Routledge.

Bradley, L., & Ladany, N. (2001b). *Counselor supervision: Principles, process, and practice* (3rd ed.). Philadephia: Brunner-Routledge.

Bradley, L. J., Parr, G., & Gould, L. J. (1999). Counseling and psychotherapy: An integrative perspective. In D. Capuzzi & D. R. Gross (Eds.), *Counseling and psychotherapy: Theories and interventions* (pp. 345–379). Upper Saddle River, NJ: Prentice-Hall.

Bradley, R. W. (1994). Tests and counseling: How did we ever become partners? *Measurement and Evaluation in Counseling and Development, 26,* 224–226.

Bratton, S. C., Ray, D., Rhine, T., & Jones, L. (2005). The efficacy of play therapy with children: A meta-analytic review of treatment outcomes. *Professional Psychology: Research and Practice, 36,* 376–390.

Brigman, G., & Campbell, C. (2003). Helping students improve academic achievement and school success behavior. *Professional School Counseling, 7,* 91–98.

Broderick, P. C., & Blewitt, P. (2006). *The life span: Human development for helping professionals* (2nd ed.). Upper Saddle River, NJ: Pearson Education.

Brooke, B. B. (2001). Professional associations, standards, and credentials in counseling. In D. C. Locke, J. E. Myers, & E. L. Herr (Eds.), *The handbook of counseling* (pp. 55–68). Thousand Oaks, CA: Sage Publications.

Broverman, I., Broverman, D., Clarkson, F., Rosenkrantz, P., & Vogel, S. (1970). Sex role stereotypes and clinical judgments of mental health. *Journal of Consulting and Clinical Psychology, 34,* 1–7.

Browers, R. T. (2005). Counseling in mental health and private practice settings. In D. Capuzzi & D. Gross (Eds.), *Introduction to the counseling profession* (4th ed.) (pp. 357–381). Boston: Allyn & Bacon.

Brown, D. (1988). Empowerment through advocacy. In D. J. Kurpius & D. Brown (Eds.), *Handbook of consultation: An intervention for advocacy and outreach* (pp. 5–17). Alexandria, VA: Association for Counselor Education and Supervision.

Brown, D., & Srebalus, D. J. (2003). *Introduction to the counseling profession* (3rd ed.). Boston: Allyn & Bacon.

Budman, S. H., & Gurman, A. S. (1988). *Theory and practice of brief therapy*. New York: Guilford Press.

Budman, S. H., Simeone, P. G., Reilly, R., & Demby, A. (1994). Progress in short-term and time-limited group psychotherapy: Evidence and implications. In A. Fuhriman & G. M. Burlingame (Eds.), *Handbook of group psychotherapy* (pp. 370–415). New York: Wiley.

Burger, J. M. (2004). *Personality* (6th ed.). Belmont, CA: Wadsworth/Thomson Learning.

Burlingame, G. M., & Fuhriman, A. (1990). Time-limited group therapy. *Counseling Psychologist, 18,* 93–118.

Burlingame, G. M., Fuhriman, A., & Mosier, J. (2003). The differential effectiveness of group psychotherapy: A meta-analytic perspective. *Group Dynamics: Theory, Research, and Practice, 7,* 3–12.

Burns, D. D., & Nolen-Hoeksema, S. (1991). Coping styles, homework compliance, and effectiveness of cognitive-behavioral therapy. *Journal of Consulting and Clinical Psychology, 59,* 305–311.

Burrow-Sanchez, J. J. (2006). Understanding adolescent substance abuse: Prevalence, risk factors, and clinical implications. *Journal of Counseling and Development, 84,* 283–290.

Burstyn, J., & Stevens, R. (2001). Involving the whole school in violence prevention. In J. Burstyn, G. Bender, R. Castella, H. Gordon, D. Guerra, K. Luschen, R. Stevens, & K. Williams (Eds.), *Preventing violence in schools: A challenge to American democracy* (pp. 139–158). Mahwah, NJ: Lawrence Erlbaum.

Bynum, B. (2000). Discarded diagnosis. *Lancet, 356* (9241), 1615.

Cahill, C., Llewelyn, S. P., & Pearson, C. (1991). Treatment of sexual abuse which occurred in childhood: A review. *British Journal of Clinical Psychology, 30,* 1–12.

Campbell, C. A., & Brigman, G. (2005). Closing the achievement gap: A structured approach to group counseling. *Journal for Specialists in Group Work, 30,* 67–82.

Campbell, C. A., & Dahir, C. A. (1997). *Sharing the vision: The national standards for school counseling programs.* Alexandria, VA: American School Counselor Association.

Campbell, D. T., & Stanley, J. C. (1963). *Experimental and quasi-experimental designs for research.* Boston: Houghton Mifflin.

Caplan, G. (1970). *The theory and practice of mental health consultation.* New York: Basic Books.

Capuzzi, D., & Gross, D. (Eds.) (2005). *Introduction to the counseling profession* (4th ed.). Boston: Allyn & Bacon.

Carlson, J., & Ellis, C. M. (2004). Treatment agreement and relapse prevention strategies in couple and family therapy. *The Family Journal, 12,* 352–357.

Carroll, L., Gilroy, P. J., & Ryan, J. (2002). Counseling transgendered, transsexual, and gender-variant clients. *Journal of Counseling and Development, 80,* 131–139.

Carson, J. (1993). *Army Alpha,* Army brass, and the search for Army intelligence. *ISIS: Journal of the History of Science in Society, 84,* 278–309.

Casey, R. J., & Berman, J. S. (1985). The outcome of psychotherapy with children. *Psychological Bulletin, 98,* 388–400.

Cass, V. (1979). Homosexual identity formation: Testing a theoretical model. *Journal of Homosexuality, 4,* 219–235.

Catalano, R. F., Arthur, M. W., Hawkins, J. D., Berglund, L., & Olson, J. J. (1998). Comprehensive community- and school-based interventions to prevent antisocial behavior. In R. Loeber & D. P. Farrington (Eds.), *Serious and violent juvenile offenders: Risk factors and successful interventions* (pp. 248–283). Thousand Oaks, CA: Sage Publications.

Ceasar, P. T., & Miranti, J. G. (2005). Counseling and spirituality. In D. Capuzzi & D. Gross (Eds.), *Introduction to the counseling profession* (4th ed.) (pp. 240–255). Boston: Pearson Allyn & Bacon.

Chagnon, J., & Russell, R. (1995). Assessment of supervisee developmental level and supervision environment across supervisor experience. *Journal of Counseling and Development, 73,* 553–558.

Chan, F., Berven, N. L., & Thomas, K. R. (Eds.). (2004). *Counseling theories and techniques for rehabilitation health professionals.* New York: Springer.

Chen-Hayes, S. F. (1997). Counseling, lesbian, bisexual, and gay persons in couple and family relationships: Overcoming the stereotypes. *Family Journal, 5,* 236–240.

Chester, A., & Bretherton, D. (2001). What makes feminist counseling feminist? *Feminism & Psychology, 11,* 527–545.

Chi Sigma Iota. (1998). *Counselor advocacy leadership conferences I & II.* Retrieved November 15, 2006, from http://www.csinet.org/displaycommon.cfm?an=1&subarticlenbr=70

Choate, L. H. (2005). Editorial comment: Celebrating 7 years of JCC. *Journal of College Counseling, 8,* 3–4.

Chodorow, N. (1978). *The reproduction of mothering.* Berkeley, CA: University of California Press.

Chow, J. C., Jaffee, K., & Snowden, L. (2003). Racial/ethnic disparities in the use of mental health services in poverty areas. *Research and Practice, 93,* 727–797.

Christenson, A., & Jacobson, N. S. (1993). Who (or what) can do psychotherapy: The status and challenge of nonprofessional therapies. *Psychological Science, 5*(1), 8–14.

Cigler, A. J., & Loomis, B. A. (Eds.). (1998). *Interest group politics* (5th ed.). Washington, DC: Congressional Quarterly.

Clawson, T. W. (1997). Control of psychological testing: The threat and a response. *Journal of Counseling & Development, 76,* 90–93.

Clawson, T. W., Eubanks, S., & McCaskill, K. (2007). The school counselor and credentialing: Managing your school counseling program. In J. Wittmer (Ed.), *Managing your school counseling program: K-12 developmental strategies* (3rd ed.). Minneapolis: Educational Media Corporation.

Clawson, T. W., Henderson, D. A., Schweiger, W. K., & Collins, D. R. (2004). *Counselor preparation* (11th ed.). New York: Brunner-Routledge.

Cobb, N. J. (2001). *The child: Infants, children, and adolescents.* Mountain View, CA: Mayfield.

Cochran, J. L., & Cochran, N. H. (2006). *The heart of counseling: A guide to developing therapeutic relationships.* Belmont, CA: Thomson Brooks/Cole.

Cogan, J. C. (1996). The prevention of anti-lesbian/gay hate crimes through social change and empowerment. In E. D. Rothblum & L. A. Bond (Eds.), *Preventing heterosexism and homophobia* (pp. 219–238). Thousand Oaks, CA: Sage Publications.

Cohen, J. (1988). *Statistical power analysis for the behavioral sciences* (2nd ed.). Hillsdale, NJ: Erlbaum.

Cohen, L. H., Sargent, M. M., & Sechrest, L. B. (1986). Use of psychotherapy research by professional psychologists [Special issue: Psychotherapy research]. *American Psychologist, 41*(2), 198–206.

Cohen, R. (2004). *Clinical supervision: What to do and how to do it.* Belmont, CA: Brooks/Cole.

Combs, A. W., Avila, D. L., & Purky, W. W. (1978). *Helping relationships: Basic concepts for the helping process.* Boston: Allyn & Bacon.

Commission on Rehabilitation Counselor Certification. (2001). *Code of professional practice.* Retrieved February 19, 2007, from http://www.crccertification.com/downloads/30code/code_ethics_0506. pdf

Commission on Rehabilitation Counselor Certification. (2003). *Scope of practice for rehabilitation counseling.* Retrieved July 5, 2008, from http://www.crccertification.com/pages/31research. html

Commission on Rehabilitation Counselor Certification. (2007). *Scope of practice for rehabilitation counseling.* Retrieved February 19, 2007, from http://www.crccertification.com/downloads/35scope/Scope_of_Practice. htm

Commission on Rehabilitation Counselor Certification. (n.d.). Retrieved July 5, 2008, from http://www.crccertification.com

Commission on Substance Abuse at Colleges and Universities. (1994). *Rethinking rites of passage: Substance abuse on America's campuses.* New York: Center on Addiction and Substance Abuse at Columbia University.

Connors, C. K. (1997). *Manual for the CRS-R.* North Tonawanda, NY: MHS.

Conoley, J., & Conoley, C. (1991). *School consultation: Practice and training* (2nd ed.). Needham Heights, MA: Allyn & Bacon.

Cook, E. P. (Ed.). (1993). *Women, relationships, and power: Implications for counseling.* Alexandria, VA: American Counseling Association.

Cooper, H. M. (1982). Scientific guidelines for conducting integrative research reviews. *Review of Educational Research, 52,* 291–302.

Corey, G. (2005). *Theory and practice of counseling and psychotherapy* (7th ed.). Belmont, CA: Wadsworth/Thomson Learning.

Corey, G., Corey, M. S., & Callanan, P. (Eds.). (2003). *Issues and ethics in the helping professions* (6th ed.). Pacific Grove, CA: Brooks/Cole.

Corey, M. S., & Corey, G. (2007). *Becoming a helper* (5th ed.). Belmont, CA: Thomson Brooks/Cole.

Corrie, S., & Callanan, M. M. (2001). Therapists' beliefs about research and the scientist-practitioner model in an evidence-based health care climate: A qualitative study. *British Journal of Medical Psychology, 74,* 135–149.

Cottone, R. R. (1992). *Theories and paradigms of counseling and psychotherapy.* Boston: Allyn & Bacon.

Cottone, R. R., & Tarvydas, V. M. (2003). *Ethical and professional issues in counseling.* Upper Saddle River, NJ: Merrill/Prentice Hall.

Couch, R. D., & Childers, J. H. (1987). Leadership strategies for instilling and maintaining hope in group counseling. *Journal for Specialists in Group Work, 12,* 138–143.

Council for Accreditation for Counseling and Related Educational Programs. (2009). *CACREP 2009 standards.* Retrieved January 7, 2009, from http://www.cacrep.org/2009standards. html

Council for Accreditation for Counseling and Related Educational Programs. (2006). *CACREP's core values.* Retrieved February 3, 2006, from http://www.cacrep.org/mission.html

Council for Accreditation of Counseling and Related Educational Programs. (2008). Retrieved March 13, 2007, from http://www.cacrep.org/2008Standards. html

Council on Rehabilitation Counselor Certification. (1994). *Guide to rehabilitation counselor certification.* Arlington Heights, IL: Author.

Council on Rehabilitation Education. (n.d.). Retrieved July 5, 2008, from http://www.core-rehab.org

Cowan, E. W., & Presbury, J. H. (2000). Meeting client resistance and reactance with reverence. *Journal of Counseling & Development, 87,* 411–419.

Crane, D. R., & McArthur, H. (2002). Meeting the needs of evidence-based practice in family therapy: Developing the scientist-practitioner model. *Journal of Family Therapy, 24,* 113–124.

Crane, D. R., Wampler, K. S., Sprenkle, D. H., Sandberg, J. G., & Hovestadt, A. J. (2002). The scientist-practitioner model in marriage and family therapy doctoral programs: Current status. *Journal of Marital and Family Therapy, 1,* 75–83.

Crouch, T., & Walz, G. (1992). *CHDF-partner in professionalism.* ERIC Document (ED347471).

Cuijpers, P. (1998). Psychological outreach programs for the depressed elderly: A meta-analysis of effects and dropout. *International Journal of Geriatric Psychiatry, 13,* 41–48.

Dagley, J .C., Gazda, G. M., Eppinger, S. J., & Stewart, E. A. (1994). Group psychotherapy research with children, preadolescents, and adolescents.

In A. Fuhriman & G. M. Burlingame (Eds.), *Handbook of group psychotherapy* (pp. 340–369). New York: Wiley.

Davenport, D. S., & Yurich, J. M. (1991). Multicultural gender issues. *Journal of Counseling and Development, 70,* 64–71.

Davis, D. C., & Humphrey, K. M. (Eds.) (2000). *College counseling: Issues and strategies for a new millennium.* Alexandria, VA: American Counseling Association.

Davis, M. E. (Ed.). (2007). *Principles and practices of case management in rehabilitation counseling* (2nd ed.). Springfield, IL: Charles C. Thomas.

Dawes, R. M. (1991). Hypothetical studies and civil liberties. *American Psychologist, 46,* 882.

Dawes, R. M. (1994). *House of cards: Psychology and psychotherapy built on myth.* New York: Free Press.

Dell Orto, A. E., & Power, P. W. (Eds.). (2007). *The psychological and social impact of illness and disability* (5th ed.). New York, NY: Springer.

Derogatis, L. R. (1990). *Manual for the SCL-90-R (Symptom Checklist–90–Revised).* Minneapolis: NCS Pearson.

Derogatis, L. R., & Cleary, P. A. (1977). Confirmation of the dimensional structure of the SCL-90: A study in construct validity. *Journal of Clinical Psychology, 33,* 981–989.

DiClemente, C. C. (2003). *Addictions and change: How addictions develop and addicted people recover.* New York: Guilford.

Dies, R. R., & Riester, A. E. (1986). Research on child group psychotherapy: Present status and future directions. In A. E. Riester & I. A. Kraft (Eds.), *Child group psychotherapy: Future tense* (pp. 173–220). Madison, WI: International University Press.

Dinsmore, J. A., Chapman, A., & McCollum, V. J. C. (2000, March). *Client advocacy and social justice: Strategies for developing trainee competence.* Paper presented at the Annual Conference of the American Counseling Association, Washington, DC.

Dolinsky, A., Vaughan, S. C., Luber, B., Mellman, L., & Roose, S. (1998). A match made in heaven?: A pilot study of patient-therapist match. *Journal of Psychotherapy Practice and Research, 7,* 119–125.

Doll, B. (1996). Prevalence of psychiatric disorders in children and youth: An agenda for advocacy by school psychology. *School Psychology Quarterly, 11,* 20–46.

Doty, L. (1987). *Communication and assertion skills for older adults.* New York: Hemisphere.

Dougherty, A. (2005). *Psychological consultation and collaboration in school and community settings* (4th ed.). Belmont, CA: Brooks/Cole.

Downing, N. E., & Roush, K. L. (1985). From passive-acceptance to active commitment: A model of feminist identity development for women. *The Counseling Psychologist, 13,* 695–709.

Drummond, R., & Jones, K. D. (2006). *Assessment procedures for counseling and helping professionals* (6th ed.). Upper Saddle River, NJ: Prentice Hall.

Dubrin, J. R., & Zastowny, T. R. (1988). Predicting early attrition from psychotherapy: An analysis of a large private-practice cohort [Special issue: Psychotherapy and the new health care systems]. *Psychotherapy, 25,* 393–408.

Durlack, J. A. (1995). *School-based prevention programs for children and adolescents.* Thousand Oaks, CA: Sage Publications.

Durlack, J. A., Fuhrman, T., & Lampman, C. (1991). Effectiveness of cognitive-behavior therapy for maladapting children: A meta-analysis. *Psychological Bulletin, 110,* 204–214.

Dusek, J. B. (1996). *Adolescent development and behavior* (3rd ed.). Upper Saddle River, NJ: Prentice Hall.

Dush, D. M., Hirt, M. L., & Schroeder, H. (1983). Self-statement modification with adults: A meta-analysis. *Psychological Bulletin, 94,* 408–422.

Dutton, D. G. (1986). The outcome of court-mandated treatment for wife assault: A quasi-experimental evaluation. *Violence and Victims, 1,* 163–175.

Dworkin, S. H. (2000). Individual therapy with lesbian, gay, and bisexual clients. In R. M. Perez, K. A. DeBord, & K. J. Bieschke (Eds.), *Handbook of counseling and psychotherapy with lesbian, gay, and bisexual clients* (pp. 157–181). Washington, DC: American Psychological Association.

Dykeman, C., & Appleton, V. E. (1998). Group counseling: The efficacy of group work. In D. Capuzzi & D. R. Gross (Eds.), *Introduction to group counseling* (2nd ed.) (pp. 101–129). Denver: Love Publishing Company.

Eaton, J. S. (2006). An overview of U. S. accreditation (revised). Retrieved September 1, 2006, from http://www.chea.org/pdf/OverviewAccred_rev0706. pdf

Edmondson, J. H., & White, J. (1998). A tutorial and counseling program: Helping students at risk of dropping out of school. *Professional School Counseling, 1,* 43–47.

Egan, G. (2002). *The skilled helper: A problem-management and opportunity-development approach to helping* (7th ed.). Pacific Grove, CA: Brooks/Cole.

Eisel v. Board of Education, 597 A.2d 447 (Md. Ct. App. 1991).

Elkin, I., Shea, M. T., Watkins, J. T., Imber, S. D., Sotsky, S., Collins, J. F., et al. (1989). National Institute of Mental Health Treatment of Depression Collaborative Research Program: General effectiveness of treatments. *Archives of General Psychiatry, 46,* 971–982.

Ellis, C. M. (2004). Counselors addressing race: Putting race on the table. *Journal of Counseling and Development, 37,* 1–10.

Ellis, M. V. (1991). Conducting and reporting integrative research reviews: Accumulating scientific knowledge. *Counselor Education and Supervision, 30,* 225–237.

Erford, B. T. (1999). A modified time-out procedure for children with noncompliant or defiant behaviors. *Professional School Counseling, 2,* 205–210.

Erford, B. T. (Ed.). (2006). *Counselor's guide to clinical, personality, and behavioral assessment.* Boston: Houghton Mifflin/Lahaska Press.

Erford, B. T. (Ed.). (2007a). *Transforming the school counseling profession* (2nd ed.). Upper Saddle River, NJ: Pearson Merrill Prentice Hall.

Erford, B. T. (Ed.). (2007b). *Assessment for counselors.* Boston: Houghton Mifflin/Lahaska Press.

Erford, B. T. (Ed.). (2008a). *Research and evaluation in counseling.* Boston: Houghton Mifflin/Lahaska Press.

Erford, B. T. (Ed.). (2008b). *Professional school counseling: A handbook of theories, programs and practices* (2nd ed.). Austin, TX: Pro-Ed.

Erford, B. T., House, R., & Martin, P. (2007). Transforming the school counseling profession. In B. T. Erford (Ed.), *Transforming the school counseling profession* (2nd ed.) (pp. 1–12). Columbus, OH: Pearson Merrill Prentice Hall.

Eriksen, K. P. (1997). *Making an impact: A handbook for counselor advocacy.* Muncie, IN: Accelerated Development.

Eriksen, K. (1999a). Counselor advocacy: A qualitative analysis of leaders' perceptions, organizational activities, and advocacy documents. *Journal of Mental Health Counseling, 21,* 33–49.

Eriksen, K. (1999b). Marriage and family licensing state by state. *The Family Journal: Counseling and Therapy for Couples and Families, 7,* 7–17.

Erikson, E. (1950). *Childhood and society.* New York: Norton.

Esters, I. G., & Ittenbach, R. F. (1999). Contemporary theories and assessments of intelligence: A primer. *Professional School Counseling, 2,* 373–376.

Evans, D. R., Hearn, M. T., Uhlemann, M. R., & Ivey, A. E. (2008). *Essential interviewing: A programmed approach to effective communication.* Belmont, CA: Brooks/Cole.

Evans, J. H., & Burck, H. D. (1992). The effects of career education interventions on academic achievement: A meta-analysis. *Journal of Counseling and Development, 71,* 63–68.

Evans, J. R., Van Velsor, P., & Schumacher, J. E. (2002). Addressing adolescent depression: A role for school counselors. *Professional School Counseling, 5,* 211–218.

Exner, J. E., Jr. (1993). *The Rorschach: A comprehensive system: Vol. 1 Basic foundations* (3rd ed.). New York: Wiley.

Eysenck, H. J. (1952). The effects of psychotherapy: An evaluation. *Journal of Consulting Psychology, 16,* 319–324.

Fabian, E. S., & MacDonald-Wilson, K. L. (2005). Professional practice in rehabilitation service delivery systems and related system resources. In R. M. Parker, E. M. Szymanski, & J. B. Patterson (Eds.), *Rehabilitation counseling: Basics and beyond* (4th ed.) (pp. 55–87). Austin, TX: Pro-Ed.

Falvey, E. (1989). Passion and professionalism: Critical rapprochement for mental health research. *Journal of Mental Health Counseling, 11,* 86–95.

Family Educational Rights and Privacy Act (FERPA). (1974). 20 U.S.C. ∫∫ 1232g.

Feldman, R. S. (2003). *Development across the life span* (3rd ed.). Upper Saddle River, NJ: Pearson Education.

Fetterman, D. M. (1994). In response to Dr. Daniel Stufflebaum's: "Empowerment evaluation, objectivist evaluation, and evaluation standards: Where the future of evaluations should not go and where it needs to go." *Evaluation Practice, 16,* 177–197.

Fiedler, C. R. (2000). *Making a difference: Advocacy competencies for special education professionals.* Boston: Allyn & Bacon.

Field, J. E., & Baker, S. (2004). Defining and examining school counselor advocacy. *Professional School Counseling, 8,* 56–63.

Fischer, L., Schimmel, D., & Kelly, C. (1999). *Teachers and the law* (5th ed.). White Plains, NY: Longman.

Fischer, L., & Sorensen, G. P. (1997). *School law for counselors, psychologists, and social workers* (3rd ed.). White Plains, NY: Longman.

Fisher, J. L., Munsch, J., & Greene, S. M. (1996). Adolescence in intimacy. In G. R. Adams & R. Montejajor (Eds.), *Psychosocial development during adolescence* (Vol. 8) (pp. 95–129). Thousand Oaks, CA: Sage Publications.

Forester-Miller, H., & Davis, T. (1996). *A practitioners guide to ethical decision making*. Retrieved August 4, 2005, from http://www.counseling.org/Content/NavigationMenu/RESOURCES/ETHICS/APRACTITIONERSGUIDETOETHICALDECISIONMAKING/Practitioner_s_Guide. htm

France, K. (2002). Crisis theory and the philosophy of crisis intervention. In *Crisis intervention: A handbook of immediate person-to-person help* (4th ed.) (pp. 3–24). Springfield, IL: Thomas Books.

Frances, A. J., & Egger, H. L. (1999). Whither psychiatric diagnosis. *Australian & New Zealand Journal of Psychiatry, 33*(2), 161–165.

Frankl, V. (1963). *Man's search for meaning*. Boston: Beacon.

Friedlander, J., & Ward, L. (1984). Development and validation of the Supervisory Styles Inventory. *Journal of Counseling Psychology, 31,* 541–557.

Fuhriman, A., & Burlingame, G. M. (1994a). Group psychotherapy: Research and practice. In A. Fuhriman & G. M. Burlingame (Eds.), *Handbook of group psychotherapy* (pp. 3–40). New York: Wiley.

Fuhriman, A., & Burlingame, G. M. (Eds.) (1994b). *Handbook of group psychotherapy* (pp. 3–40). New York: Wiley.

Galassi, J. P., Crace, R. K., Martin, G. A., James, R. M., & Wallace, R. L. (1992). Client preferences and anticipations in career counseling: A preliminary investigation. *Journal of Counseling Psychology, 39,* 46–55.

Gallesich, J. (1982). *The profession and practice of consultation*. San Francisco, CA: Jossey-Bass.

Garber, J., Kelley, M. K., & Martin, N. C. (2002). Developmental trajectories of adolescents' depressive symptoms: Predictors of change. *Journal of Consulting and Clinical Psychology, 70,* 79–95.

Garfield, S. L. (1986). Research on client variables in psychotherapy. In S. L. Garfield & A. E. Bergin (Eds.), *Handbook of psychotherapy and behavior change* (pp. 213–256). New York: Wiley.

Garfield, S. L. (1994). Research on client variables in psychotherapy. In A. E. Bergin & S. L. Garfield (Eds.), *Handbook of psychotherapy and behavior change* (3rd ed.) (pp. 190–228). New York: Wiley.

Garfield, S. L., & Bergin, A. E. (1971). Therapeutic conditions and outcome. *Journal of Abnormal Psychology, 77,* 108–114.

Garfield, S. L., & Bergin, A. E. (1986). Introduction and historical overview. In S. L. Garfield & A. E. Bergin (Eds.), *Handbook of psychotherapy and behavior change* (pp. 3–22). New York: Wiley.

Garis, J. W., & Niles, S. G. (1990). The separate and combined effects of SIGI and DISCOVER and a career planning course on undecided university students. *Career Development Quarterly, 39,* 261–274.

Gaston, L. (1990). The concept of therapeutic alliance and its role in psychotherapy: Theoretical and empirical considerations. *Psychotherapy, 27,* 143–153.

Gaubatz, M. D., & Vera, E. M. (2002). Do formalized gatekeeping procedures increase programs' follow-up with deficient trainees? *Counselor Education & Supervision, 41,* 294–306.

Gauvain, M. (2001). *The social context of cognitive development*. New York: Guilford Press.

Gazda, G. M. (1989). *Group counseling. A developmental approach* (4th ed.). Boston: Allyn & Bacon.

Gazda, G. M., & Larsen, M. J. (1968). A comprehensive appraisal of group and multiple counseling research. *Journal of Research and Development in Education, 1*(2), 57–132.

Gerber, S., & Myers, J. (1997). *Counseling at the crossroads: Let's decide our future*. Papers presented at the annual conference of the Washington Counseling Association. Vancouver, WA. (ERIC Document Reproduction Service No. ED424484).

Gerber, S., & Terry-Day, B. (1999). Does peer mediation really work? *Professional School Counseling, 2,* 169–171.

Gerig, M. (2007). *Foundations for mental health and community counseling: An introduction to the profession*. Upper Saddle River, NJ: Pearson Education, Inc.

Gerler, E. R. (1985). Elementary school counseling research and the classroom learning environment. *Elementary School Guidance and Counseling, 20,* 39–40.

Gielen, U. P., & Roopnarine, J. (2004). *Childhood and adolescence: Cross-cultural perspectives and applications*. London: Praeger.

Gilbert, L. A., & Scher, M. (1999). *Gender and sex in counseling and psychotherapy*. Needham Heights, MA: Allyn & Bacon.

Gilchrist, L. A., & Stringer, M. (1992). Marketing counseling: Guidelines for training and practice. *Counselor Education and Supervision, 31,* 154–162.

Gill, C. J. (1987). A new social perspective on disability and its implications for rehabilitation. In F. S. Cromwell (Ed.), *Sociocultural implications in treatment planning in occupational therapy* (pp. 49–55). New York: Haworth Press.

Gilligan, C. (1982). *In a different voice.* Cambridge, MA: Harvard University Press.

Gingerich, W. J., & Eisengart, S. (2000). Solution focused brief therapy: A review of the outcome research. *Family Process, 39,* 477–498.

Ginzberg, E., Ginsburg, S. W., Axelrod, S., & Herma, J. L. (1951). *Occupational choice: An approach to general theory.* New York: Columbia University Press.

Gladding, S. T. (1996). Bandits: A lesson in identity and direction. *Counselor Education and Supervision, 36,* 99–104.

Gladding, S. T. (2001). *The counseling dictionary.* Upper Saddle River, NJ: Merrill Prentice Hall.

Gladding, S. T. (2002). *Group work: A counseling specialty* (4th ed.). Upper Saddle River, NJ: Prentice Hall.

Gladding, S. T. (2004). *Counseling: A comprehensive profession* (5th ed.). Upper Saddle River, NJ: Pearson Merrill Prentice Hall.

Gladding, S. T. (2005). *Counseling theories: Essential concepts and applications.* Upper Saddle River, NJ: Pearson Merrill Prentice Hall.

Gladding, S. T. (2006). *The counseling dictionary: Concise definitions of frequently used terms* (2nd ed.). Upper Saddle River, NJ: Pearson Education.

Glosoff, H. L. (2005). Early historical perspectives. In D. Capuzzi & D. R. Gross (Eds.), *Introduction to the counseling profession* (4th ed.). Needham Heights, MA: Allyn & Bacon.

Goldberg, D. (1985). Process notes, audio, and videotape: Modes of presentation in psychotherapy training. *Clinical Supervisor, 3,* 3–13.

Goldman, L. (1992). Qualitative assessment: An approach for counselors. *Journal of Counseling and Development, 70,* 616–621.

Gottfredson, D. C. (1997). School-based crime prevention. In L. W. Sherman, D. C. Gottfredson, D. C. (2001). *Schools and delinquency.* New York: Cambridge University Press.

Gottfredson, D. C., Wilson, D. B. & Najaka, S. S. (2001). School-based crime prevention. In L. W. Sherman, D. P. Farrington, B. Welsh, & D. C. MacKenzie (Eds.), *Evidence-based crime prevention.* New York: Harwood Academic.

Gould, J. S. (1981). *The mismeasure of man.* New York: W. W. Norton Company.

Graham, K., Timney, C. B., Bois, C., & Wedgerfield, K. (1995). Continuity of care in addictions treatment: The role of advocacy and coordination in case management. *American Journal of Drug and Alcohol Abuse, 21,* 433–451.

Granello, D. H., & Granello, P. F. (1998). Training counseling students to use outcome research. *Counselor Education and Supervision, 37,* 224–238.

Granello, D. H., & Granello, P. F. (2001). Counseling outcome research: Making practical choices for real-world applications. In G. R. Walz & J. C. Bleuer (Eds.), *Assessment: Issues and challenges for the millennium* (pp. 163–172). Greensboro, NC: ERIC/CASS.

Green, R., & Herget, M. (1991). Outcomes of systemic/strategic team consultation: The importance of therapist warmth and active structuring. *Family Process, 30,* 321–336.

Greenberg, L. S., & Pascual-Leone, A. (2006). Emotion in psychotherapy: A practice friendly review. *Journal of Clinical Psychology: In Session, 62,* 611–630.

Gregory, G. S., & Lee, S. (1986). Psychoeducational assessment of minority groups: Professional implications. *Journal of Counseling and Development, 64,* 635–637.

Griffith, B. A., & Griggs, J. C. (2001). Religious identity status as a model to understand, assess, and interact with client spirituality. *Counseling and Values, 46,* 14–25.

Gross, D. R., & Capuzzi, D. (2005). Counseling the older adult. In D. Capuzzi & D. R. Gross (Eds.), *Introduction to the counseling profession* (4th ed.) (pp. 383–400). Boston: Allyn & Bacon.

Grossman, P. B., & Hughes, J. N. (1992). Self-control interventions with internalizing disorders: A review and analysis. *School Psychology Review, 21,* 229–245.

Grundy, A. L., & McGinn, M. K. (2008). Enabling participation in graduate education: Support for a student researcher who is hard of hearing. *International Journal of Disability, Community & Rehabilitation, 7*(1). Retrieved July 5, 2008, from http://www.ijdcr.ca

Guillot-Miller, L., & Partin, P. W. (2003). Web-based resources for legal and ethical issues in school counseling. *Professional School Counseling, 7,* 52–60.

Gurovich, I. Y., Shmukler, A. B., Utkin, A. A., Stepanova, O. N., Sheller, A. D., & Turusheva, N. B. (2007). The organization of an assertive community treatment unit: The mental health service model and its effectiveness. *International Journal of Disability, Community and Rehabilitation, 6*(2). Retrieved July 5, 2008, from http://www.ijdcr.ca

Guttmacher Institute. (2000). Minors and the right to consent to health care. *The Guttmacher Report on Public Policy, 3*(4), 4–8.

Guttmacher Institute. (2005a). *State policies in brief: Minors' access to contraceptive services.* Washington, DC: Author.

Guttmacher Institute. (2005b). *State policies in brief: Sex and STD/HIV education.* Washington, DC: Author.

Guttmacher Institute. (2007). *An overview of minor consent laws.* Retrieved May 15, 2007, from http://www.guttmacher.org/statecenter/spibs/spibOMCL.pdf

Gwandure, C. (2008). Disability, locus of control and HIV and AIDS prevention and control. *International Journal of Disability, Community and Rehabilitation, 7*(1). Retrieved July 5, 2008, from http://www.ijdcr.ca

Gysbers, N. C., & Henderson, P. (1988). *Developing and managing your school guidance program.* Alexandria, VA: American Association for Counseling and Development.

Gysbers, N. C., & Henderson, P. (2005). *Developing and managing your school counseling program* (4th ed.). Alexandria, VA: American Counseling Association.

Hackney, H. (2001). *Practice issues for the beginning counselor.* Boston: Pearson Education.

Hackney, H., & Cormier, S. (2004). *The professional counselor: A process guide to helping* (4th ed.). Boston: Allyn & Bacon.

Hadley, H. R. (1988). Improving reading scores through a self-esteem intervention program. *Elementary School Guidance and Counseling, 22,* 248–252.

Hadley, S. W., & Strupp, H. H. (1976). Contemporary views of negative effects in psychotherapy. *Archives of General Psychiatry, 33,* 1291–1302.

Halbur, D. A., & Halbur, K. V. (2006). *Developing your theoretical orientation in counseling and psychotherapy.* Boston: Pearson Allyn & Bacon.

Hanna, F. J., Talley, W. B., & Guindon, M. H. (2000). The power of perception: Toward a model of cultural oppression and liberation. *Journal of Counseling and Development, 78,* 430–441.

Hansen, J., Himes, B., & Meier, S. (1990). *Consultation: Concepts and practices.* Englewood Cliffs, NJ: Prentice-Hall.

Hansen, J. C., Stevic, R. R., & Warner, R. W. (1986). *Counseling: Theory and process* (4th ed.). Boston: Allyn & Bacon.

Hansen, J. T. (2006a). Counseling theories within a postmodern epistemology: New roles for theories in counseling practice. *Journal of Counseling and Development, 84,* 291–297.

Hansen, J. T. (2006b). Humanism as moral imperative: Comments on the role of knowing in the helping encounter. *Journal of Humanistic Counseling, Education, and Development, 45,* 115–125.

Hardiman, R. (1982). *White identity development: A process-oriented model for describing the racial consciousness of white Americans.* Doctoral dissertation, University of Massachusetts.

Haring-Hidore, M., & Vacc, N. A. (1988). The scientist-practitioner model in training entry-level counselors. *Journal of Counseling and Development, 6,* 286–288.

Harris, I. M. (1995). *Messages men hear: Constructing masculinities.* Philadelphia: Taylor & Francis.

Hartman, A. (1996). Social policy as a context for lesbian and gay families: The political is personal. In J. Laird & R. J. Green (Eds.), *Lesbians and gays in couples and families: A handbook for therapists* (pp. 69–85). San Francisco: Jossey-Bass.

Hawkins, J. D., Farrington, D. P., & Catalano, R. F. (1998). Reducing violence through the schools. In D. S. Elliott, B. A. Hamburg, & K. R. Williams (Eds.), *Violence in American schools* (pp. 188–216). New York: Cambridge University Press.

Hayes, S. C., Barlow, D. H., & Nelson-Gray, R. O. (1999). *The scientist practitioner: Research and accountability in the age of managed care* (2nd ed.). Boston: Allyn & Bacon.

Hazelrigg, M. D., Cooper, H. M., & Bordvin, C. M. (1987). Evaluating the effectiveness of family therapies: An integrative review and analysis. *Psychological Bulletin, 101,* 428–442.

Helms, J. E. (1995). An update of Helms' white and people of color racial identity. In J. G. Ponterotto, J. M. Casas, & C. M. Alexander (Eds.), *Handbook of multicultural counseling* (pp. 181–198). Thousand Oaks, CA: Sage Publications.

Hennessey, M. L., & Koch, L. (2007). Universal design for instruction in rehabilitation counselor education. *Rehabilitation Education, 21*(3), 187–194.

Henry, W. P., Schacht, T. E., & Strupp, H. H. (1986). Structural analysis of social behavior: Application to a study of interpersonal process in differential psychotherapeutic outcome [Special issue: Psychotherapy research]. *Journal of Consulting and Clinical Psychology, 54,* 27–31.

Henry, W. P., Strupp, H. H., Butler, S. F., Schacht, T. E., & Binder, J. L. (1993). The effects of training in time-limited dynamic psychotherapy: Changes in therapist behavior. *Journal of Consulting and Clinical Psychology, 61,* 434–440.

Heppner, P. P., Kivlighan, Jr., D. M., Wright, G. E., Pledge, D. S., Brossart, D. F., Bellatin, A. M., et al. (1995). Teaching the history of counseling: Training the next generation. *Journal of Counseling and Development, 73,* 337–341.

Herek, G. M. (1993). The context of anti-gay violence: Notes on cultural and psychological heterosexism. In L. D. Garnets & D. C. Kimmel (Eds.), *Psychological perspectives on lesbian and gay male experiences* (pp. 89–107). New York: Columbia University Press.

Herlihy, B., & Corey, G. (2006). *ACA Ethical standards casebook* (6th ed.). Alexandria, VA: American Counseling Association.

Herman, J. (1997). *Trauma and recovery.* New York: Basic Books.

Herr, E. L., & Erford, B. T. (2007). Historical roots and future issues. In B. T. Erford (Ed.), *Transforming the school counseling profession* (2nd ed.) (pp. 13–37). Columbus, OH: Pearson Merrill Prentice Hall.

Hershberger, S., & D'Augelli, A. (1995). The impact of victimization on the mental health and suicidality of lesbian, gay, and bisexual youths. *Developmental Psychology, 31,* 65–74.

Hershenson, D. B., Power, P. W., & Waldo, M. (1996). *Community counseling: Contemporary theory and practice.* Needham Heights, MA: Allyn & Bacon.

Hoag, M. J. (1997). Evaluating the effectiveness of child and adolescent group psychotherapy: A meta-analytic review. *Dissertation Abstracts International: Section B: The Sciences and Engineering, 57*(7-B), 4709.

Hoag, M. J., & Burlingame, G. M. (1997). Evaluating the effectiveness of child and adolescent group treatment: A meta-analytic review. *Journal of Clinical Child Psychology, 26,* 234–246.

Hoagwood, K. (1999). *Summary sheet: Major research findings on child and adolescent mental health.* Washington, DC: National Institute of Mental Health.

Hodges, S. (2001). University counseling centers at the twenty-first century: Looking forward, looking back. *Journal of College Counseling, 4,* 161–174.

Hoffman, R. M. (2001). The measurement of masculinity and femininity: Historical perspectives and implications for counseling. *Journal of Counseling and Development, 79,* 472–485.

Holland, J. L. (1973). *Making vocational choices: A theory of career.* Englewood Cliffs, NJ: Prentice Hall.

Holloway, E. L. (1995). *Clinical supervision: A systems approach.* Thousand Oaks, CA: Sage Publications.

Hopkins, B. R., & Anderson, B. S. (1990). *The counselor and the law* (3rd ed.). Alexandria, VA: American Counseling Association.

Horvath, A. O., & Bedi, R. P. (2002). The alliance. In J. C. Norcross (Ed.), *Psychotherapy relationships that work: Therapist contributions and responsiveness to patients* (pp. 37–69). New York: Oxford University Press.

Horvath, A. O., & Symonds, B. D. (1991). Relation between working alliance and outcome in psychotherapy: A meta-analysis. *Journal of Counseling Psychology, 38*(2), 139–149.

House, R. M., & Hayes, R. L. (2002). School counselors: Becoming key players in school reform. *Professional School Counseling, 5,* 249–256.

Howard, G. S. (1985). Can research in the human sciences become more relevant to practice? *Journal of Counseling and Development, 63,* 539–544.

Howard, K. I., Davidson, C. V., O'Mahoney, M. T., Orlinsky, D. E., & Brown, K. P. (1989). Patterns of psychotherapy utilization. *American Journal of Psychiatry, 146,* 775–778.

Howard, K. I., Kopta, S. M., Krause, M. S., & Orlinsky, D. E. (1986). The dose-effect relationship in psychotherapy [Special issue: Psychotherapy research]. *American Psychologist, 41,* 159–164.

Hrebenar, R. J. (1997). *Interest group politics in America.* Armond, NY: M. E. Sharpe.

Hunter, S., Shannon, C., Knox, J., & Martin, J. I. (1998). *Lesbian, gay, and bisexual youths and adults: Knowledge for human service practice.* Thousand Oaks, CA: Sage Publications.

Individuals with Disabilities Education Improvement Act. (2004). *IDEA 2004 Resources.* Retrieved August 28, 2005, from http://www.ed.gov/policy/speced/guid/idea/idea2004.html

Ioaniddis, J. P. A., Cappelleri, J. C., & Lau, J. (1998). Issues in comparisons between meta-analysis and large trials. *JAMA, 279,* 1089–1093.

Isaacs, M. L. (2003). Data-driven decision making: The engine of accountability. *Professional School Counseling, 6,* 288–295.

Ivey, A. E., & Ivey, M. B. (2007). *Intentional interviewing and counseling: Facilitating client development in a multicultural society* (6th ed.). Belmont, CA: Thomson Brooks/Cole.

Izard, C. E., & Ackerman, B. P. (2000). Motivation, organization, and regulatory functions of discrete emotions. In M. Lewis & J. M. Haviland-Jones (Eds.), *Handbook of emotions* (pp. 253–264). New York: Guilford Press.

Jackson, J. (2000). What ought psychology do? *American Psychologist, 55,* 328–330.

Jaffe, M. L. (1998). *Adolescence.* New York: John Wiley & Sons.

James, R. K., & Gilliland, B. E. (2005). *Crisis intervention strategies* (5th ed.). Belmont, CA: Brooks/Cole.

James, S., & Mennen, F. (2001). Treatment outcome research: How effective are treatments or abused children? *Child and Adolescent Social Work Journal, 18*(2), 73–95.

Jenkins, W. M., Patterson, J. B., & Szymanski, E. M. (1998). Philosophical, historical, and legislative aspects of the rehabilitation counseling profession. In R. M. Parker & E. M. Szymanski (Eds.), *Rehabilitation counseling: Basics and beyond* (3rd ed.) (pp. 1–40). Austin, TX: Pro-Ed.

Johnson, C. D., & Johnson, S. (2003). Results based guidance: A systems approach to student support. *Professional School Counseling, 6,* 180–185.

Johnson, M. (1988, June). *Construct validation of the therapeutic alliance.* Paper presented at the annual meeting of the Society for Psychotherapy Research, Santa Fe, NM.

Jones, A. C. (1985). Psychological functioning in black Americans: A conceptual guide for use in psychotherapy. *Psychotherapy, 22,* 363–369.

Jones, E. E. (1982). Psychotherapists' impressions of treatment outcome as a function of race. *Journal of Clinical Psychology, 38,* 722–732.

Jones, L. Y. (2006, January). Swinging 60's? The first baby boomer looks back-and-forward-on the eve of a milestone. *Smithsonian, 36,* 102–107.

Jourard, S. M. (1971). *The transparent self.* New York: Van Nostrand Reinhold Co.

Kanas, N. (1986). Group psychotherapy with schizophrenics: A review of controlled studies. *International Journal of Group Psychotherapy, 36,* 339–351.

Kang, S. M., & Shaver, P. R. (2004). Individual differences in emotional complexity: Their psychological implications. *Journal of Personality, 72,* 687–726.

Kaplan, P. S. (2000). *A child's odyssey: Child and adolescent development* (3rd ed.). Belmont, CA: Wadsworth.

Kataoka, S. H., Zhang, L., & Wells, K. B. (2002). Unmet need for mental health care among U.S. children: Variation by ethnicity and insurance status. *American Journal of Psychiatry, 159,* 1548–1555.

Katz, J. H. (1978). *White awareness: Handbook for anti-racism training.* Norman, OK: University of Oklahoma Press.

Kaul, T. J., & Bednar, R. L. (1986). Experiential group research: Results, questions, and suggestions. In S. L. Garfield & A. E. Bergin (Eds.), *Handbook of psychotherapy and behavior change* (2nd ed.) (pp. 671–714). New York: Wiley.

Kazdin, A. E. (1991). Effectiveness of psychotherapy with children and adolescents [Special section: Clinical child psychology: Perspectives on child and adolescent therapy]. *Journal of Consulting and Clinical Psychology, 59,* 785–798.

Kazdin, A. E. (1993). Psychotherapy for children and adolescents: Current progress and future research direction. *American Psychologist, 48,* 644–657.

Kazdin, A. E. (1994). Methodology, design and evaluation in psychotherapy research. In A. E. Bergin & S. L. Garfield (Eds.), *Handbook of psychotherapy and behavior change* (3rd ed.) (pp. 19–71). New York: Wiley.

Kazdin, A. E., Bass, D., Ayers, W. A., & Rodgers, A. (1990). Empirical and clinical focus of child and adolescent psychotherapy research. *Journal of Consulting and Clinical Psychology, 58,* 729–740.

Kazdin, A. E., & Johnson, B. (1994). Advances in psychotherapy for children and adolescents: Interrelations of adjustment, development, and intervention. *Journal of School Psychology, 32,* 217–246.

Keene, M., & Erford, B. T. (2007). *Group activities: Firing up for performance.* Columbus, OH: Pearson Merrill Prentice Hall.

Kelly, G. A. (1963). *A theory of personality.* New York: W. W. Norton & Company.

Kent, A. J., & Hersen, M. (2000). An overview of managed mental health care: Past, present and future. In A. Kent & M. Hersen (Eds.), *A psychologist's proactive guide to managed mental health care* (pp. 3–19). Mahwah, MJ: Lawrence Erlbaum Associates.

Kerr, M., & Bowen, M. (1988). *Family evaluation.* New York: Norton.

Kiselica, M. S., Baker, S. B., Thomas, R. N., & Reddy, S. (1994). Effects of stress inoculation training on anxiety, stress, and academic performance among adolescents. *Journal of Counseling Psychology, 41,* 335–342.

Kiselica, M. S., & Robinson, M. (2001). Bringing advocacy counseling to life: The history, issues, and human dramas of social justice work in counseling. *Journal of Counseling and Development, 79,* 387–397.

Kitzinger, C. (1996). Individual action and political strategies: Creating a future free of heterosexism. In E. D. Rothblum & L. A. Bond (Eds.), *Preventing heterosexism and homophobia* (pp. 253–265). Thousand Oaks, CA: Sage Publications.

Kleist, D. M., & White, L. J. (1997). The values of counseling: A disparity between a philosophy of prevention in counseling and counselor practice and training. *Counseling and Values, 41,* 128–141.

Kokotovic, A. M., & Tracey, T. J. (1987). Premature termination at a university counseling center. *Journal of Counseling Psychology, 34,* 80–87.

Koran, L., & Costell, R. (1973). Early termination from group psychotherapy. *International Journal of Group Psychotherapy, 23,* 346–359.

Kottler, J. A. (2003). *On being a therapist.* San Francisco: Jossey Bass.

Kottler, J. A., & Brown, R. W. (1996). *Introduction to therapeutic counseling* (3rd ed.). Pacific Grove, CA: Brooks/Cole.

Kraft, I. A. (1968). An overview of group psychotherapy with adolescents. *International Journal of Group Psychotherapy, 39,* 255–263.

Krone, K. R., Himle, J. A., & Neese, R. M. (1991). A standardized behavioral group treatment program for obsessive-compulsive disorder: Preliminary outcomes. *Behavior Research and Therapy, 29,* 627–631.

Krupnick, J. L. (1996). The role of therapeutic alliance in psychotherapy and pharmacotherapy outcome: Findings in the National Institutes of Mental Health treatment of depression collaborative research program. *Journal of Consulting and Clinical Psychology, 64,* 532–539.

Kunyk, D., & Olson, J. K. (2001). Clarification of conceptualizations of empathy. *Journal of Advanced Nursing, 35,* 317–325.

LaFountain, R. M., & Garner, N. E. (1998). *A school with solutions: Implementing a solution-focused/Adlerian based comprehensive school counseling program.* Alexandria, VA: American School Counselor Association.

Laible, D. J., & Thompson, R. A. (1998). Attachment and emotional understanding in preschool children. *Developmental Psychology, 34,* 1038–1045.

Lambert, M. J. (1976). Spontaneous remission in adult neurotic disorders: A revision and summary. *Psychological Bulletin, 83*(1), 107–119.

Lambert, M. J. (1991). Introduction to psychotherapy research. In L. E. Beutler & M. Crago (Eds.), *Psychotherapy research: An international review of programmatic studies* (pp. 1–23). Washington, DC: American Psychological Association.

Lambert, M. J., & Bergin, A. E. (1994). The effectiveness of psychotherapy. In A. E. Bergin & S. L. Garfield (Eds.), *Handbook of psychotherapy and behavior change* (3rd ed.) (pp. 143–189). New York: Wiley.

Lambert, M. J., Masters, K. S., & Ogles, B. M. (1991). Outcome research in counseling. In C. E. Watkins & L. J. Schneider (Eds.), *Research in counseling* (pp. 51–83). Hillsdale, NJ: Erlbaum.

Lambert, M. J., & Ogles, B. M. (1997). The effectiveness of psychotherapy supervision. In J. C. E. Watkins (Ed.), *Handbook of psychotherapy supervision* (pp. 421–446). New York: Wiley.

Lambert, M. J., Weber, F. D., & Stykes, J. D. (1993, April). *Psychotherapy vs placebo.* Poster presented at the annual meeting of the Western Psychological Association, Phoenix, AZ.

Lambie, G. W. (2005). Child abuse and neglect: A practical guide for professional school counselors. *Professional School Counselors, 8,* 249–259.

Lavoritano, J. E., & Segal, P. B. (1992). Evaluating the efficacy of short-term counseling on adolescents in a school setting. *Adolescence, 27*(107), 535–543.

Lazarus, A. A., & Beutler, L. E. (1993). On technical eclecticism. *Journal of Counseling and Development, 71,* 381–385.

LeBlanc, M., & Ritchie, M. (2001). A meta-analysis of play therapy outcomes. *Counseling Psychology Quarterly, 14,* 149–163.

Lee, C. C., & Walz, G. R. (1998). *Social action: A mandate for counselors.* Alexandria, VA: American Counseling Association.

Lee, F., & Bednar, R. L. (1977). Effects of group structure and risk taking disposition on group behavior, attitudes, and atmosphere. *Journal of Counseling Psychology, 24,* 191–199.

Lee, R. S. (1993). Effects of classroom guidance on student achievement. *Elementary School Guidance and Counseling, 27,* 163–171.

Lefkowitz, E. G., Crawford, S. G., & Dewey, D. (2007). Living with impairment: Behavioral, emotional and social adjustment of siblings of children with autism. *International Journal of Disability, Community and Rehabilitation, 6*(1). Retrieved July 5, 2008, from http://www.ijdcr.ca

Leierer, S. J., Strohmer, D. C., Blackwell, T. L., Thompson, R. C., & Donnay, D. A. C. (2008). The Rehabilitation Counselor Scale: A new scale for the Revised Strong Interest Inventory. *Rehabilitation Counseling Bulletin, 51*(2), 68–75.

Lent, R. W., Brown, S. D., & Hackett, G. (1994). Toward a unifying social cognitive theory of career and academic interest, choice, and performance. *Journal of Vocational Behavior, 45,* 79–122.

Lent, R. W., Brown, S. D., & Hackett, G. (2002). Social cognitive career theory. In D. Brown & Associates (Eds.), *Career choice and development* (4th ed.) (pp. 255–311). San Francisco: Jossey-Bass.

Levinson, D. (1992). *Seasons of a woman's life.* New York: Knopf.

Lewis, M. W., & Lewis, A. C. (1996). Peer helping programs: Helper role, supervisor training, and suicidal behavior. *Journal of Counseling and Development, 74,* 307–313.

Lewis, T. F., & Osborn, C. J. (2004). Solution-focused counseling and motivational interviewing: A consideration of confluence. *Journal of Counseling and Development, 82*(1), 38–48.

Lieberman, M., Yalom, I., & Miles, M. (1973). *Encounter groups: First facts.* New York: Basic Books.

Lipsey, M. W., & Derzon, J. H. (1998). Predictors of violent or serious delinquency in adolescence and early childhood: A synthesis of longitudinal research. In R. Loeber & D. P. Farrington (Eds.), *Serious and violent juvenile offenders: Risk factors and successful interventions* (pp. 86–105). Thousand Oaks, CA: Sage Publications.

Littrell, J. M., Malia, J. A., & Vanderwood, M. (1995). Single-session brief counseling in a high school. *Journal of Counseling and Development, 73,* 451–458.

Loesch, L. C., & Foster, L. H. (2005). Counseling uses of tests. In D. Capuzzi, & D. R. Gross (Eds.), *Welcome to the counseling profession* (4th ed.) (pp. 286–308). Boston: Allyn & Bacon.

Loesch, L. C., & Ritchie, M. H. (2004). *The accountable school counselor.* Austin, TX: Pro-Ed.

Loganbill, C., Hardy, E., & Delworth, U. (1982). Supervision: A conceptual model. *Counseling Psychologist, 10,* 3–42.

Lubin, B., & Lubin, A. W. (1973). The group psychotherapy literature: 1972. *International Journal of Group Psychotherapy, 23,* 474–513.

Lubin, B., Lubin, A. W., & Sargent, C. W. (1972). The group psychotherapy literature: 1972. *International Journal of Group Psychotherapy, 22,* 492–529.

Luborsky, L., Barber, J. P., & Crits-Cristoph, P. (1990). Theory based research for understanding the process of dynamic psychotherapy. *Journal of Consulting and Clinical Psychology, 58,* 281–287.

Luborsky, L., McClellan, A. T., Woody, G. E., O'Brien, C. P., & Auerbach, A. (1985). Therapist success and its determinants. *Archives of General Psychiatry, 42,* 602–611.

Lusky, M., & Hayes, R. (2001). Collaborative consultation and program evaluation. *Journal of Counseling and Development, 79,* 26–38.

Lyons, L. C., & Woods, P. J. (1991). The efficacy of rational-emotive therapy: A quantitative review of the outcome research. *Clinical Psychology Review, 11,* 357–369.

MaCarn, S. R., & Fessinger, R. E. (1996). Revisioning of sexual minority identity formation: A new model of lesbian identity and its implications for counseling and research. *Counseling Psychologist, 24,* 508–534.

MacKenzie, K. R. (1994). Where is here and when is now? The adaptational challenge of mental health reform for group psychotherapy. *International Journal of Group Psychotherapy, 44,* 407–428.

MacKenzie, K. R. (1995). Rationale for group psychotherapy in managed care. In K. R. MacKenzie (Ed.), *Effective use of group psychotherapy in managed care* (pp. 1–26). Washington, DC: American Psychiatric Press.

Maki, D. R., & Riggar, T. F. (1997a). Rehabilitation counseling: Concepts and paradigms. In D. R. Maki & T. F. Riggar (Eds.), *Rehabilitation counseling: Profession and practice* (pp. 3–31). New York: Springer.

Maki, D. R., & Riggar, T. F. (Eds.). (1997b). *Rehabilitation counseling: Profession and practice.* New York: Springer.

Mann, A. H., Jenkins, R., & Belsey, E. (1981). The twelve-month outcome of patients with neurotic illness in general practice. *Psychological Medicine, 11,* 535–550.

Maples, M., & Abney, P. (2006). Baby boomers mature and gerontological counseling comes of age. *Journal of Counseling and Development, 84,* 3–9.

March, P. A. (1999). Ethical responses to media depictions of mental illness: An advocacy approach. *Journal of Humanistic Counseling, Education and Development, 38*(2), 70–79.

Martin, D. J., Garske, J. P., & Davis, M. K. (2000). Relation of the therapeutic alliance with outcome and other variables: A meta-analytic review. *Journal of Consulting and Clinical Psychology, 68,* 438–450.

Maryland Higher Education Commission. (2007). Retrieved August 28, 2007, from http://www.mhec.state.md.us/higherEd/colleges_universities/accreditation.asp

Maryland State Department of Education. (2007). Retrieved August 28, 2007, from http://www.marylandpublicschools.org/MSDE/divisions/certification/

Maslow, A. H. (1968). *Toward a psychology of being* (2nd ed). New York: Van Nostrand.

May, R. (1977). *The meaning of anxiety* (Rev. ed.). New York: Norton.

Mays, V. M. (2000). A social justice agenda. *American Psychologist, 55,* 326–327.

McAuliffe, G., & Frederickson, R. (1990). The effects of program length and participant characteristics on group. *Journal of Employment Counseling, 27*(1), 19–22.

McCracken, J. E., Hayes, J. A., & Dell, D. (1997). Attributions of responsibility for memory problems in older and younger adults. *Journal of Counseling and Development, 75,* 395–391.

McDermit, W., Miller, I. W., & Brown, R. A. (2001). The efficacy of group psychotherapy for depression: A meta-analysis and review of the empirical research. *Clinical Psychology: Science and Practice, 8,* 98–116.

McDevitt, T. M., & Ormrod, J. E. (2002). *Child development and education.* Upper Saddle River, NJ: Pearson Education.

McGuire, J., Scott, S., & Shaw, S. (2003). Universal design for instruction: The paradigm, its principles, and products for enhancing instructional access. *Journal of Postsecondary Education and Disability, 77*(1), 11–21.

McIntosh, P. (1988). *White privilege and male privilege: A personal account of coming to see correspondences through work in women's studies.* Working papers #189, Wellesley College Center for Research on Women, Wellesley, MA.

McLoyd, V. C. (1998). Socioeconomic disadvantage and child development. *American Psychologist, 53,* 185–204.

McNeill, B. W., May, R. J., & Lee, V. E. (1987). Perceptions of counselor source characteristics by premature and successful terminators. *Journal of Counseling Psychology, 34*(1), 86–89.

McRoberts, C., Burlingame, G. M., & Hoag, M. J. (1998). Comparative efficacy of individual and group psychotherapy: A meta-analytic perspective. *Group Dynamics: Theory, Research, and Practice, 2,* 101–117.

McWhirter, B. T., & Ishikawa, M. I. (2005). Individual counseling: Traditional approaches. In D. Capuzzi & D. R. Gross (Eds.), *Introduction to the counseling profession* (4th ed.) (pp. 155–172). Upper Saddle River, NJ: Prentice-Hall.

McWhirter, E. H., (1991). Empowerment in counseling. *Journal of Counseling and Development, 69,* 222–227.

Meece, J. L. (2002). *Child and adolescent development for educators* (2nd ed.). New York: McGraw Hill.

Meichenbaum, D. (1986). Cognitive behavior modification. In F. H. Kanfer & A. P. Goldstein (Eds.), *Helping people change: A textbook of methods* (pp. 346–380). New York: Pergamon.

Meichenbaum, D. (1995). Cognitive-behavioral therapy in historical perspective. In B. M. Bongar & L. E. Beutler (Eds.), *Comprehensive textbook of psychotherapy: Theory and practice* (pp. 140–158). London: Oxford University Press.

Meier, S. T., & Davis, S. R. (2005). *The elements of counseling* (5th ed.). Belmont, CA: Thomson Brooks/Cole.

Metcalf, L. (1995). *Counseling toward solutions: A practical solution-focused program for working with students, teachers, and parents.* West Nyack, NY: The Center for Applied Research in Education.

Miller, P. H., & Scholnick, E. K. (2000). *Toward a feminist developmental psychology.* New York: Routledge.

Miller, R. C., & Berman, J. S. (1983). The efficacy of cognitive behavior therapies: A quantitative review of the research evidence. *Psychological Bulletin, 94,* 39–53.

Mitte, K. (2005). Meta-analysis of cognitive-behavioral treatments for generalized anxiety disorder: A comparison with pharmacotherapy. *Psychological Bulletin, 131,* 785–795.

Mohl, P. C., Martinez, D., Ticknor, C., Huang, M., & Cordell, M. D. (1991). Early dropouts from psychotherapy. *Journal of Nervous and Mental Disease, 179,* 478–481.

Monk, G., Winslade, J., Crocket, K., & Epston, D. (1997). *Narrative therapy in practice.* San Francisco: Jossey-Bass.

Morrow-Bradley, C., & Elliott, R. (1986). Utilization of psychotherapy research by practicing psychotherapists. *American Psychologist, 41,* 188–197.

Munsch, R. (1986). *Love you forever.* Ontario, CA: Firefly.

Murdock, N. L. (1991). Case conceptualization: Applying theory to individuals. *Counselor Education and Supervision, 30,* 355–365.

Murphy, B. C., & Dillon, C. (2008). *Interviewing in action in a multicultural world* (3rd ed.). Belmont, CA: Brooks/Cole, Cengage Learning.

Murphy, J. J. (2006). *Solution-focused counseling in middle and high schools.* Upper Saddle River, NJ: Merrill/Prentice Hall.

Murphy, L. L., Spies, R. A., & Plake, B. S. (2006). *Tests in print (Volume VII).* Lincoln, NE: University of Nebraska Press.

Myers, J., & Sweeney, T. (2004). Advocacy for the counseling profession: Results of a national survey. *Journal of Counseling and Development, 82,* 466.

Myers, J. E., Sweeney, T. J., & White, V. E. (2002). Advocacy for counseling and counselors: A professional imperative. *Journal of Counseling and Development, 80,* 394–402.

Myers, J. E., Sweeney, T. J., & Witmer, J. M. (2000). The wheel of wellness counseling for wellness: A holistic model for treatment planning. *Journal of Counseling and Development, 78,* 251–267.

Myrick, R. D. (1987). *Developmental guidance and counseling: A practical approach.* Minneapolis: Educational Media.

Myrick, R. D. (2003). Accountability: Counselors count. *Professional School Counseling, 6,* 174–179.

National Board of Certified Counselors. (2006a). *2007 Application/NCC: National Certified Counselor Credential* (2007). Retrieved November 15, 2006, from http://www.nbcc.org/extras/pdfs/apps/nccapp.pdf

National Board of Certified Counselors. (2006b). *About NBCC.* Retrieved September 1, 2006, from http://www.nbcc.org/geninfo

National Board of Certified Counselors. (2006c). *Benefits of becoming a National Certified Counselor.* (n.d.). Retrieved November 15, 2006, from http://www.nbcc.org/whyncc

National Career Development Association. (2006). *NCDA policy and procedures 2006–2007.* Retrieved December 10, 2006, from http://www.ncda.org/pdf/policyandprocedures2006_07.pdf

National Center for Health Statistics. (2008). *International classification of diseases, ninth revision, clinical modification* (ICD-9-CM). Hyattsville, MD: Author.

National Center for Health Statistics. (2008). *International classification of diseases, tenth revision* (ICD-10). Hyattsville, MD: Author.

National Commission for Certifying Agencies. (2006). *Accredited certification organizations/programs as of September 30, 2006.* Retrieved November 8, 2006, from http://www.noca.org/ncca/accredorg.htm

National Comorbidity Survey Replication. (2005). *Lifetime prevalence of DSM-IV/WHM-CIDI disorders by sex and cohort.* Retrieved June 19, 2008, from http://www.hcp.med.harvard.edu/ncs

National Council on Alcoholism and Drug Dependence. (2000). *Youth, alcohol, and other drugs.* Retrieved December 10, 2006, from www. ncadd.org/facts/youthalc.html

National Institute of Child Health and Human Development. (2005). *Backgrounder.* Retrieved from http://www.nichd.nih.gov/new/releases/americas_children05_bg_parents.cfm

National Institute of Mental Health. (2007). *Statistics.* Retrieved November 1, 2007, from http://www.nimh.nih.gov/health/statistics/index.shtml

National Institute of Mental Health. (n.d.). *The numbers count: Mental disorders in America.* Retrieved June 19, 2008, from http://www.nimh.nih.gov/health/publications/the-numbers-count-mental-disorders-in-america.shtml

Nearpass, E. L. (1990). Counseling and guidance effectiveness in North American high schools: A meta-analysis of the research findings (Doctoral dissertation, University of Colorado at Boulder, 1989). *Dissertation Abstracts International, 50,* 1984A.

Nelson, K. W., & Southern, S. (2006). Editorial. *The Family Journal: Counseling and Therapy for Couples and Families, 14,* 113.

Neukrug, E. S. (1999). *Theory, practice, and trends in human services: An introduction* (2nd ed.). Boston: Brooks/Cole.

Neukrug, E. S. (2003). *Theory, practice, and trends in human services: An introduction* (4th ed.). Florence, KY: Wadsworth Cengage Learning.

Neukrug, E. S. (2006). *The world of the counselor* (3rd ed.). Florence, KY: Wadsworth Cengage Learning.

Neukrug, E. (2007). *The world of the counselor: An introduction to the counseling profession* (3rd ed.). Belmont, CA: Brooks/Cole-Thomson Learning.

Newman, B. M., & Newman, P. R. (2006). *Development through life: A psychosocial approach* (9th ed.). Belmont, CA: Thompson Wadsworth.

Nichols, M. P., & Schwartz, R. C. (2005). *The essentials of family therapy*. Boston: Allyn & Bacon.

Nolen-Hoeksema, S. (2001). Gender differences in depression. *Current Directions in Psychological Science, 10,* 173–176.

Norcross, J. C. (2000). Toward the delineation of empirically based principles in psychotherapy: Commentary on Beutler (2000). *Prevention and Treatment, 3,* Article 28. Retrieved from http://journals.apa.org/prevention/volume3/pre0030028c.html

Norcross, J. C., & Hill, C. E. (2003). Compendium of empirically supported therapy relationships. In G. P. Koocher, J. C. Norcross, & S. S. Hill, III (Eds.), *Psychologists' desk reference* (2nd ed.) (pp. 202–207). New York: Oxford University Press.

Norcross, J. C., & Prochaska, J. O. (1983). Clinicians' theoretical orientations: Selection, utilization, and efficacy. *Professional Psychology, 14,* 197–208.

Norcross, J. C., Prochaska, J. O., & Gallagher, K. M. (1989). Clinical psychologists in the 1980s: II. Theory, research, and practice. *The Clinical Psychologist, 42*(3), 45–53.

Norman, J. (2004). Gender bias in the diagnosis and treatment of depression. *International Journal of Mental Health, 33*(2), 32–43.

Norton, J. L. (1995). The gay, lesbian, and bisexual populations. In N. A. Vacc, S. B. DeVaney, & J. Wittmer (Eds.), *Experiencing and counseling multicultural and diverse populations* (3rd ed.) (pp. 147–177). Bristol, PA: Accelerated Development.

Nugent, F. A., & Jones, K. D. (2005). *Introduction to the profession of counseling* (4th ed.). Upper Saddle River, NJ: Pearson Merrill Prentice Hall.

Nuttall, J. (2002). Modes of therapeutic relationship in brief dynamic psychotherapy. *Journal of Psychodynamic Process, 89,* 505–523.

Nystul, M. S. (2006). *Introduction to counseling: An art and science perspective* (3rd ed.). Boston: Allyn & Bacon.

Okun, B. F., & Kantrowitz, R. E. (2007). *Effective helping: Interviewing and counseling techniques* (7th ed.). Belmont, CA: Thompson Learning.

Olin, J. T., & Keatinge, C. (1998). *Rapid psychological assessment.* New York: John Wiley & Sons.

Oliver, L. W., & Spokane, A. R. (1988). Career intervention outcome: What contributes to client gain? *Journal of Counseling Psychology, 35,* 447–462.

Olsen, D., & Stern, S. (1990). Issues in the development of a family therapy supervision model. *Clinical Supervisor, 8*(2), 49–65.

Omizo, M. M., & Omizo, S. A. (1988). The effects of participation in group counseling on self-esteem and locus of control among adolescents from divorced families. *The School Counselor, 16,* 54–60.

Omizo, M. M., Omizo, S. A., & D'Andrea, M. J. (1992). Promoting wellness among elementary school children. *Journal of Counseling and Development, 71,* 194–198.

Orlinsky, D. E., Grawe, D., & Parks, B. K. (1994). Process and outcome in psychotherapy. In A. E. Bergin & S. L. Garfield (Eds.), *Handbook of psychotherapy and behavior change* (3rd ed.) (pp. 270–378). New York: Wiley.

Orlinsky, D. E., & Howard, K. I. (1980). Gender and psychotherapeutic outcome. In A. M. Brodsky & R. Hare-Mustin (Eds.), *Women and psychotherapy: An assessment of research and practice* (pp. 3–34). New York: Guilford Press.

Orlinsky, D. E., & Howard, K. I. (1986). Process and outcome in psychotherapy. In S. L. Garfield & A. E. Bergin (Eds.), *Handbook of psychotherapy and behavior change* (2nd ed.) (pp. 361–381). New York: Wiley.

Osipow, S. H., & Littlejohn, E. M. (1995). Toward a multicultural theory of career development: Prospects and dilemmas. In F. T. Leong (Ed.), *Career development and vocational behavior of racial and ethnic minorities* (pp. 251–261). Mahway, NY: Erlbaum.

Osvold, L. L., & Sodowsky, G. R. (1993). Eating disorders of white American, racial and ethnic minority American, and international women. *Journal of Multicultural Counseling and Development, 21,* 143–155.

Oxman, E. B., & Chambliss, C. (2003). Tailoring inpatient group psychotherapy to patients' needs: Size matters! *Research Reports, 143,* 1–9.

Padula, M. A. (1994). Reentry women: A literature review with recommendations for counseling and research. *Journal of Counseling and Development, 73,* 10–16.

Papalia, D. E., Olds, S. W., & Feldman, R. D. (2004). *Human development* (9th ed.). New York: McGraw-Hill.

Paris, J. (2002). Implications of long-term outcome research for the management of patients with borderline personality disorder. *Harvard Review Psychiatry, 10,* 315–323.

Parker, R. M., Szymanski, E. M., & Patterson, J. B. (Eds.). (2005). *Rehabilitation counseling: Basics and beyond* (4th ed.). Austin, TX: Pro-Ed.

Parsons, F. (1909). *Choosing a vocation*. Boston: Houghton Mifflin.

Patrick, J. (1997). Unnatural selection: Intelligence testing, eugenics and American political cultures. *Journal of Social History, 30,* 669–716.

Pedersen, P. (1996). The importance of both similarities and differences in multicultural counseling. *Journal of Counseling and Development, 70,* 6–12.

Pedersen, P. B. (1991). Counseling international students. *Counseling Psychologist, 19,* 10–58.

Pedro-Carroll, J. L., & Alpert-Gillis, L. J. (1997). Preventive interventions for children of divorce: A developmental model for 5 and 6 year old children. *Journal of Primary Prevention, 18,* 5–23.

Pedro-Carroll, J. L., Sutton, S. E., & Wyman, P. A. (1999). A two-year follow-up of a preventive intervention for young children of divorce. *School Psychology Review, 28,* 467–476.

Perls, L. (1970). One Gestalt therapist's approach. In J. Fagan & I. Shepherd (Eds.), *Gestalt therapy now* (pp. 125–129). New York: Harper & Row (Colophon).

Phelps, R. E., Taylor, J. D., & Gerard, P. A. (2001). Cultural mistrust, ethnic identity, racial identity, and self-esteem among ethnically diverse black students. *Journal of Counseling and Development, 79,* 209–216.

Phillips, E. L., & Fagan, P. J. (1982, August). *Attrition: Focus on the intake and first therapy interviews.* Paper presented at the 90th annual convention of the American Psychological Association, Washington, DC.

Piaget, J. (1967). *Six psychological studies*. New York: Random House.

Pickering, J. W., & Vacc, N. A. (1984). Effectiveness of career development interventions for college students: A review of published research. *Vocational Guidance Quarterly, 32*(3), 149–159.

Pilkonis, P. A., Imber, S. D., Lewis, P., & Rubinsky, P. (1984). A comparative outcome study of individual, group and conjoint psychotherapy. *Archives of General Psychiatry, 41,* 431–437.

Piper, M. (1999). *Another country: Navigating the emotional terrain of our elders*. New York: Riverhead Books.

Poll, J. B., & Smith, T. B. (2003). The spiritual self: Toward a conceptualization of spiritual identity development. *Journal of Psychology and Theology, 31,* 129–142.

Ponzo, Z. (1974). A counselor and change: Reminiscences and resolutions. *Personnel and Guidance Journal, 53,* 27–32.

Poston, W. S. C. (1990). The biracial identity development model: A needed addition. *Journal of Counseling and Development, 60,* 152–155.

Prasad, V., & Owens, D. (2001). Using the Internet as a source of self-help for people who self-harm. *Psychiatric Quarterly, 35,* 421–423.

Prediger, D. J. (1994). Tests and counseling: The marriage that prevailed. *Measurement and Evaluation in Counseling and Development, 26,* 227–234.

Prioleau, L., Murdock, M., & Brody, N. (1983). An analysis of psychotherapy versus placebo studies. *Behavioral and Brain Sciences, 6,* 275–310.

Prochaska, J. O., & DiClemente, C. C. (1982). Transtheoretical therapy: Toward a more integrative model of change. *Psychotherapy: Theory, Research and Practice, 20,* 161–173.

Prochaska, J. O., DiClemente, C. C., & Norcross, J. C. (1992). In search of how people change: Applications to addictive behavior. *American Psychologist, 47,* 1102–1114.

Prout, H. T., & DeMartino, R. A. (1986). A meta-analysis of school-based studies of psychotherapy. *Journal of School Psychology, 24,* 285–292.

Prout, S. M., & Prout, H. T. (1998). A meta-analysis of school-based studies of counseling and psychotherapy: An update. *Journal of School Psychology, 36,* 121–136.

Pruett, S. R., & Chan, F. (2006). The development and psychometric validation of the *Disability Attitude Implicit Association Test. Rehabilitation Psychology, 51*(3), 202–213.

Rathus, S. A. (2004). *Voyages in childhood*. Belmont, CA: Wadsworth.

Ray, O., & Ksir, C. (2004). *Drugs, society, and human behavior* (10th ed.). New York: McGraw-Hill.

Rehabilitation Research and Training Center on Disability Demographics and Statistics. (n.d.). *2006 Disability status report: United States*. Retrieved July 1, 2008, from http://www.ilr.cornell.edu/edi/disabilitystatistics/StatusReports/2006-PDF/2006-StatusReport_US.pdf?CFID=3338844&CFTOKEN=25662977

Remley, T. P., Jr. (1992, August). Perspectives from the Executive Director: Are counselors unique? *ACA Guidepost, 4.*

Remley, T. P., Jr., & Herlihy, B. (2007). *Ethical, legal, and professional issues in counseling* (2nd ed. updated). Upper Saddle River, NJ: Pearson Merrill Prentice Hall.

Reynolds, S. (2000). Evidenced based practice and psychotherapy research. *Journal of Mental Health, 9,* 257–266.

Reynolds, W. M., & Coats, K. I. (1986). A comparison of cognitive-behavioral therapy and relaxation training for the treatment of depression in adolescents. *Journal of Counseling and Clinical Psychology, 54,* 653–660.

Rhode, R. I., & Stockton, R. (1994). Group structure: A review. *Journal of Group Psychotherapy, Psychodrama, and Sociometry, 46,* 151–158.

Rice, D. P., Kelman, S., Miller, L. S., & Dunmeyer, S. (1990). *The economic costs of alcohol and drug use and mental illness: 1985* (Report from the Office of Financing and Coverage Policy of the Alcohol, Drug Abuse and Mental Health Administration, U. S. Department of Health and Human Services). San Francisco, CA: Institute for Health and Aging, University of California.

Roberts, A. R., & Camasso, M. J. (1991). The effects of juvenile offender treatment programs on recidivism: A meta-analysis of 46 studies. *Notre Dame Journal of Law, Ethics, & Public Policy, 5,* 421–441.

Robinson, L. A., Berman, J. S., & Neimeyer, R. A. (1990). Psychotherapy for the treatment of depression: A comprehensive review of controlled outcome research. *Psychological Bulletin, 108,* 30–49.

Roe, A. (1956). *The psychology of occupations.* New York: Wiley.

Rogers, C. (1951). *Client-centered therapy.* Boston: Houghton Mifflin.

Rogers, C. (1957). The necessary and sufficient conditions of therapeutic personality change. *Journal of Consulting Psychology, 21,* 95–103.

Rogers, C. R. (1961). *On becoming a person: A therapist's view of psychotherapy.* Boston: Houghton Mifflin.

Rogers, W. A., & Fisk, A. D. (2001). Attention in cognitive aging research. In J. E. Birren & K. W. Schaie (Eds.), *Handbook of the psychology of aging* (5th ed.). San Diego: Academic Press.

Roget's New Millennium Thesaurus, First Edition (v 1.3.1). (2006). Boston: Houghton Mifflin. Retrieved December 2, 2006, from http://thesaurus.reference.com/browse/advocate

Rogoff, B. (1990). *Apprenticeship in thinking: Cognitive development in social context.* New York: Oxford University Press.

Rosenbluh, E. S. (1981). *Emotional first aid.* Louisville, KY: American Academy of Crisis Interveners.

Rotter, J. B. (1946). Thematic Apperception Test: Suggestions for administration and interpretation. *Journal of Personality, 15,* 60–73.

Rowley, W. J., Stroh, H. R., & Sink, C. A. (2005). Comprehensive guidance and counseling programs' use of guidance curricula materials: A survey of national trends. *Professional School Counseling, 8,* 296–304.

Rubinstein, G. (1995). The decision to remove homosexuality from the DSM: Twenty years later. *American Journal of Psychotherapy, 49,* 416–427.

Russell, R. L., Greenwald, S., & Shirk, S. R. (1991). Language change in child psychotherapy: A meta-analytic review. *Journal of Consulting and Clinical Psychology, 59,* 916–919.

Rye, D. R., & Sparks, R. (1999). *Strengthening K-12 school counseling programs: A support system.* Philadelphia: Accelerated Development.

Saarni, C., Mumme, D. L., & Campos, J. J. (1998). Emotional development: Action, communication, and understanding. In W. Dammon (series ed.) & N. Eisenberg (vol. ed.), *Handbook of child psychology (Vol. 3): Social, emotional, and personality development* (5th ed.) (pp. 237–309). New York: John Wiley.

Sales, A. (2007). *Rehabilitation counseling: An empowerment perspective.* Austin, TX: Pro-Ed.

Salthouse, T. A. (2000). Adulthood and aging: Cognitive processes and development. In A. Kazdin (Ed.), *Encyclopedia of psychology.* Washington, D.C.: American Psychological Association & Oxford University Press.

Saltzman, A. (1986). Reporting child abusers and protecting substance abusers. *Social Work, 31,* 474–476.

Samplers, F., & Aber, L. (1998). Evaluations of school-based violence prevention programs. In D. S. Elliott, B. A. Hamburg, & K. R. Williams (Eds.), *Violence in American schools* (pp. 217–252). New York: Cambridge University Press.

Sampson, J. P. (2000). Using the internet to enhance testing in counseling. *Journal of Counseling and Development, 78,* 348–356.

Santrock, J. W. (2004). *Life-span development* (9th ed.). Boston: McGraw Hill.

Satcher, D. (1996). *Mental health: A report of the Surgeon General—Executive summary.* Retrieved March 1, 2007, from http://www.surgeongeneral.gov/library/mentalhealth/home.html

Saunders, S. M., Howard, K. I., & Oklinsky, D. E. (1989). The *Therapeutic Bond Scales*: Psychometric characteristics and relationship to treatment effectiveness. *Psychological Assessment, 1,* 323–330.

Savage, T. A., Harley, D. A., & Nowak, T. M. (2005). Applying social empowerment strategies as tools for self-advocacy in counseling lesbian and gay male clients. *Journal of Counseling and Development, 83,* 131–137.

Savickas, M. L. (2003). Advancing the career counseling profession: Objectives and strategies for the next decade. *The Career Development Quarterly, 52,* 87–96.

Scheidlinger, S. (1993). The small healing group—a historical overview. *Psychotherapy, 32,* 657–668.

Schein, E. (1978). The role of the consultant: Content expert or process facilitator? *Personnel and Guidance Journal, 56,* 339–345.

Schein, E. (1991). Process consultation. *Consulting Psychology Bulletin, 43,* 16–18.

Schlossberg, S. M., Morris, J. D., & Lieberman, M. G. (2001). The effects of a counselor-led guidance intervention on students' behaviors and attitudes. *Professional School Counseling, 4,* 156–174.

Schmidt, J. J. (2002). *Intentional helping: A philosophy for proficient caring relationships.* Upper Saddle River, NJ: Merrill Prentice Hall.

Sciarra, D. T. (2004). *School counseling: Foundations and contemporary issues.* Belmont, CA: Brooks/Cole.

Scott, M. J., & Stradling, S. G. (1991). The cognitive-behavioral approach with depressed clients. *British Journal of Social Work, 21,* 533–544.

Sears, S. (1982). A definition of career guidance terms: A national vocational guidance association perspective. *Vocational Guidance Quarterly, 31,* 137–143.

Seligman, L. (1998). *Selecting effective treatments: A comprehensive, systematic guide to treating mental disorders.* San Francisco, CA: Jossey-Bass, Inc.

Seligman, L. (2004). *Technical and conceptual skills for mental health professionals.* Upper Saddle River, NJ: Pearson Merrill Prentice Hall.

Seligman, L. (2005). Diagnosis in counseling. In D. Capuzzi & D. R. Gross (Eds.), *Welcome to the counseling profession* (4th ed.) (pp. 309–329). Boston: Allyn & Bacon.

Sexton, T., & Whiston, S. (1994). The status of the counseling relationship: An empirical review, theoretical implications, and research directions. *The Counseling Psychologist, 22,* 6–78.

Sexton, T. L. (1996). The relevance of counseling outcome research: Current trends and practical implications. *Journal of Counseling and Development, 24,* 590–600.

Sexton, T. L. (1999). Evidence-based counseling: Implications for counseling practice, preparation, and professionalism. Greensboro, NC: ERIC Clearinghouse on Counseling and Student Services (ERIC Identifier: ED435948).

Sexton, T. L., Schofield, T. L., & Whiston, S. C. (1997). Evidence-based practice: A pragmatic model to unify counseling. *Counseling and Human Development, 30*(3), 1–18.

Sexton, T. L., Whiston, S. C., Bleuer, J. C., & Walz, G. R. (1997). *Integrating outcome research into counseling practice and training.* Alexandria, VA: American Counseling Association.

Shadish, W. R. (1996). Meta-analysis and the exploration of causal mediating processes: A primer of examples, methods, and issues. *Psychological Methods, 1,* 47–65.

Shadish, W. R., Montgomery, L. M., Wilson, P., Wilson, M. R., Bright, L., & Okwumbua, T. (1993). Effects of family and marital psychotherapies: A meta-analysis. *Journal of Consulting and Clinical Psychology, 61,* 992–1002.

Shapiro, A. F., Gottman, J. M., & Carrere, S. (2000). The baby and the marriage: Identifying factors that buffer against decline in marital satisfaction after the first baby arrives. *Journal of Family Psychology, 14,* 124–130.

Shapiro, D. A., Barkham, M., Hardy, G. E., & Morrison, L. A. (1990). The second Sheffield psychotherapy project: Rationale, design and preliminary outcome data. *British Journal of Medical Psychology, 63*(2), 97–108.

Shapiro, D. A., & Shapiro, D. (1982). Meta-analysis of comparative therapy outcome studies: A replication and refinement. *Psychological Bulletin, 92,* 581–604.

Shapiro, J. P. (1993). *No pity: People with disabilities forging a new civil rights movement.* New York: Times Books.

Sharfstein, S. S. (2005). Commentary on "Constituting community: Creating a place for oneself": The healing power of relationships. *Psychiatry, 3,* 212–213.

Sharkin, B. S. (2004). College counseling and student retention: Research findings and implications for counseling centers. *Journal of College Counseling, 7,* 99–108.

Sharpe, D. (1997). Of apples and oranges, file drawers and garbage: Why validity issues in meta-analysis will not go away. *Clinical Psychology Review, 17,* 881–901.

Shaw, B. F. (1983). *Training therapists for the treatment of depression: Collaborative study.* Paper presented at the annual meeting of the Society for Psychotherapy Research, Sheffield, England.

Shearer, R.A., Myers L.B., & Ogan, G.D. (2001). Treatment resistance and ethnicity among female offenders in substance abuse treatment programs. *The Prison Journal, 81*(1), 55–72.

Shepherd, K. K. (1994). Stemming conflict through peer mediation. *School Administrator, 51,* 14–17.

Sherman, J. L. (1988). Effects of psychotherapeutic treatments for PTSD: A meta-analysis of controlled clinical trials. *Journal of Traumatic Stress, 11,* 413–435.

Sherman, L., Gottfredson, W., MacKenzie, D., Eck, J., Reuter, P., & S. Bushway, S. (Eds.) (1997). *Preventing crime: What works, what doesn't, what's promising: A report to the United States Congress* (pp. 5.1–5.71). Washington, DC: U.S. Department of Justice, Office of Justice Programs.

Sheu, H. B., & Sedlacek, W. B. (2002). *Helping seeking-attitudes and coping strategies among college students by race.* Paper presented at the American Psychological Association National Conference, Chicago, IL.

Shirk, S. R., & Karver, M. (2003). Prediction of treatment outcome from relationship variables in child and adolescent therapy: A meta-analytic review. *Journal of Consulting and Clinical Psychology, 71,* 452–464.

Shirk, S. R., & Russell, R. L. (1992). A reevaluation of child therapy effectiveness. *Journal of American Academy of Child and Adolescent Psychiatry, 31,* 703–709.

Siegler, R., DeLoache, J., & Eisenberg, N. (2003). *How children develop.* New York: Worth.

Sink, C. A., & Stroh, H. R. (2003). Raising achievement test scores of early elementary school students through comprehensive school counseling programs. *Professional School Counseling, 6,* 350–364.

Skiba, R. J., Knesting, K., & Bush, L. D. (2002). Culturally competent assessment: More than non-biased tests. *Journal of Child and Family Studies, 11*(1), 61–78.

Slavinsky-Holey, N. (1983). Combining homogeneous group psychotherapies for borderline conditions. *International Journal of Group Psychotherapy, 33,* 297–312.

Sledge, W. H., Moras, K., Hartley, D., & Levine, M. (1990). Effect of time-limited psychotherapy on patient dropout rates. *American Journal of Psychiatry, 147,* 1341–1347.

Sloan, R. B., Staples, F. R., Cristol, A. H., Yorkson, N. J., & Whipple, K. (1975). *Psychotherapy vs behavior change.* Cambridge, MA: Harvard University Press.

Smith, M. L., & Glass, G. V. (1977). Meta-analysis of psychotherapy outcome studies. *American Psychologist, 32,* 752–760.

Smith, M. L., Glass, G. V., & Miller, T. I. (1980). *The benefits of psychotherapy.* Baltimore: Johns Hopkins University Press.

Smith, S. D., & Chen-Hayes, S. F. (2004). Leadership and advocacy for lesbian, bisexual, gay, transgendered, and questioning (LBGTQ) students: Academic, career, and interpersonal success strategies. In R. Perusse & G. E. Goodnough (Eds.), *Leadership, advocacy, and direct service strategies for professional school counselors* (pp. 187–221). Belmont, CA: Brooks/Cole.

Sohn, D. (1997). Questions for meta-analysis. *Psychological Reports, 81,* 3–15.

Solomon, S. D., & Johnson, D. M. (2002). Stress disorder: A practice-friendly review of outcome research. *Journal of Clinical Psychology/In Session: Psychotherapy in Practice, 58,* 947–959.

Sommers-Flannagan, J., & Sommers-Flannagan, R. (2003). *Clinical interviewing* (3rd ed.). Hoboken, NJ: John Wiley & Sons.

Sperry, L. (2005). Case conceptualization: A strategy for incorporating individual, couple, and family dynamics in the treatment process. *American Journal of Family Therapy, 33,* 353–364.

Sperry, L., Carlson, J., & Kjos, D. (2003). *Becoming an effective therapist.* Boston: Allyn & Bacon.

Spies, R. A., & Plake, B. S. (Eds.). (2005). *The sixteenth mental measurements yearbook.* Lincoln, NE: University of Nebraska Press.

Spokane, A. R. (1991). *Career interventions.* Englewood Cliffs, NJ: Prentice Hall.

Spokane, A. R., & Oliver, L. W. (1983). Research integration: Approaches, problems and recommendations for research reporting. *Journal of Counseling Psychology, 30,* 252–257.

Sprinthall, N. A. (1981). A new model for research in the service of guidance and counseling. *Personnel and Guidance Journal, 59,* 487–493.

Stage, S. A., & Quiroz, D. R. (1997). A meta-analysis of interventions to decrease disruptive classroom behavior in public education settings. *School Psychology Review, 26,* 333–369.

St. Claire, K. L. (1989). Middle school counseling research: A resource for school counselors. *Elementary School Guidance and Counseling, 23,* 219–226.

Stebnicki, M. A. (2001). The psychosocial impact on survivors of extraordinary, stressful, and traumatic events: Principles and practices in critical incident response for rehabilitation counselors. *Directions in Rehabilitation Counseling, 12*(6), 57–71.

Stein, D. M., & Lambert, M. J. (1995). Graduate training in psychotherapy: Are therapy outcomes enhanced? *Journal of Consulting and Clinical Psychology, 63,* 182–196.

Steinberg, L. (1996). *Adolescence* (4th ed.). New York: McGraw Hill.

Sternbarger, B. N., & Budman, S. H. (1996). Group psychotherapy and managed behavioral care: Current trends and future challenges. *International Journal of Group Psychotherapy, 46,* 297–309.

Stiles, W. B., Shapiro, D. A., & Elliott, P. (1986). "Are all psychotherapies equivalent?" [Special issue: Psychotherapy research]. *American Psychologist, 41*(2), 165–180.

Stockton, R., Morran, D. K., & Velboff, P. (1987). Leadership of therapeutic small groups. *Journal of Group Psychotherapy, Psychodrama, and Sociometry, 39,* 157–165.

Stoltenberg, C. D., & Delworth, U. (1987). *Supervising counselors and therapists.* San Francisco: Jossey-Bass.

Stoltenberg, C. D., McNeill, B., & Delworth, U. (1998). *IDM supervision.* San Francisco: Jossey-Bass.

Stone, C. B. (2005). *School counseling and principles: Ethics and law.* Alexandria, VA: American School Counselor Association.

Stone, L. A., & Bradley, F. O. (1994). *Foundations of elementary and middle school counseling.* White Plains, NY: Longman.

Stone, W. N., Green, B. L., Gleser, G. C., Whitman, R. M., & Roster, B. B. (1975). Impact of psychosocial factors on the conduct of combined drug and psychotherapy research. *British Journal of Psychiatry, 127,* 432–439.

Strickland, B. R. (2000). Misassumptions, misadventures, and the misuse of psychology. *American Psychologist, 55,* 331–338.

Strike, D. L., Skovholt, T. M., & Hummel, T. J. (2004). Mental health professionals' disability competence: Measuring self-awareness, perceived knowledge, and perceived skills. *Rehabilitation Psychology, 49,* 321–327.

Stuart, S., & Robertson, M. (2003). *Interpersonal psychotherapy: A clinician's guide.* London: Edward Arnold Ltd.

Substance Abuse and Mental Health Services Administration. (2005). *Treatment for mental health problems and unmet treatment needs among all adults.* Retrieved July 7, 2007, from http://oas.samhsa.gov/NSDUH/2k5NSDUH/results.htm#8.1.8

Sue, D. W., Arredondo, P., & McDavis, R. J. (1992). Multicultural counseling competencies and standards: A call to the profession. *Journal of Counseling and Development, 70,* 477–486.

Sue, D. W., & Sue, D. (2003). *Counseling the culturally diverse: Theory and practice* (4th ed.). New York: John Wiley.

Sue, S., McKinney, H., Allen, D., & Hall, J. (1974). Delivery of community mental health services to Black and White clients. *Journal of Consulting and Clinical Psychology, 2,* 794–801.

Sugar, M. (1993). Research in child and adolescent group psychotherapy. *Journal of Child and Adolescent Psychotherapy, 3,* 207–226.

Super, D. (1957). *The psychology of careers.* New York: Harpers.

Super, D. (1976). *Career education and the meaning of work: Monographs on career education.* Washington, DC: The Office of Career Education, U.S. Office of Education.

Super, D. (1990). A life-span, life-space approach to career development. In D. Brown, L. Brooks, & Associates (Eds.), *Career choice and development: Applying contemporary theories to practice* (2nd ed.) (pp. 197–261). San Francisco: Jossey-Bass.

Svartberg, M., & Stiles, T. C. (1991). Comparative effects of short-term psychodynamic psychotherapy: A meta-analysis. *Journal of Consulting and Clinical Psychology, 59,* 704–714.

Svec, H. J. (1987). Youth advocacy and high school dropout. *The High School Journal, 70,* 185–192.

Svec, H. H. (1990). An advocacy model for the school psychologist. *School Psychology International, 11,* 63–70.

Sweeney, T. J. (1995). Accreditation, credentialing, professionalization: The role of specialties. *Journal of Counseling and Development, 74,* 117–126.

Sweeney, T. J. (1998). *Adlerian counseling: A practitioner's approach.* Philadelphia, PA: Accelerated Development.

Tang, M., & Erford, B. T. (2004). The history of school counseling. In B. T. Erford (Ed.), *Professional school counseling: A handbook of theories, programs and practices.* Austin, TX: Pro-Ed.

Terrell, R., & Terrell, S. (1984). Race of counselor, client sex, cultural mistrust level, and premature termination from counseling among black clients. *Journal of Counseling Psychology, 31,* 371–375.

Thompson, R., & Littrell, J. M. (1998). Brief counseling for students with learning disabilities. *Professional School Counseling, 2,* 60–67.

Tillitski, L. (1990). A meta-analysis of estimated effect sizes for group versus individual versus control treatments. *International Journal of Group Psychotherapy, 40,* 215–224.

Tobler, N. S., & Stratton, H. H. (1997). Effectiveness of school-based drug prevention programs: A meta-analysis of the research. *Journal of Primary Prevention, 18,* 71–128.

Tolman, R. A., & Bennett, L. W. (1990). A review of quantitative research on men who batter. *Journal of Interpersonal Violence, 5,* 87–118.

Toseland, R., & Siporin, M. (1986). When to recommend group treatment. *International Journal of Group Psychotherapy, 36,* 171–201.

Tracey, T. J. (1986). The stages of influence in counseling and psychotherapy. In F. Dorn (Ed.), *The social influence process in counseling and psychotherapy* (pp. 107–116). Springfield, IL: Charles C. Thomas.

Tracey, T. J. (1991). Counseling research as an applied science. In C. E. Watkins & L. J. Schneider (Eds.), *Research in counseling* (pp. 3–31). Hillsdale, NJ: Erlbaum.

Trachtman, R. (1999). The money taboo: Its effects in everyday life and in the practice of psychotherapy. *Clinical Social Work Journal, 27,* 275–289.

Trusty, J. (1996). Counseling for dropout prevention: Applications from multicultural counseling. *Journal of Multicultural Counseling and Development, 24,* 105–117.

Trusty, J., & Brown, D. (2005). Advocacy competencies for professional school counselors. *Professional School Counseling, 8,* 259–265.

Tyler, L. E. (1969). *The work of the counselor* (3rd ed.). New York: Appleton-Century-Crofts.

Uribe, V., & Harbeck, K. (1992). Addressing the needs of lesbian, gay, and bisexual youth: The origins of Project 10 and school-based interventions. In K. Harbeck (Ed.), *Coming out of the classroom closet: Gay and lesbian students, teachers, and curricula* (pp. 9–28). New York: Harrington Park Press.

U.S. Bureau of Labor Statistics. (2006–2007). *Occupational outlook handbook.* Retrieved from www.bls.gov/oco/pdf/ocos067.pdf/

U.S. Census Bureau. (1999). *Poverty in the United States: Current population reports: Consumer income.* Washington, DC: Author.

U.S. Census Bureau. (2001). *Poverty in the United States 2000: Current population reports.* Series p60-214. Washington, DC: Author.

U.S. Census Bureau. (2003). *The older population in the United States: March 2002.* Retrieved September 1, 2006, from http://www.census.gov/prod/2003pubs/p20-546.pdf

U.S. Census Bureau. (2004). *The foreign born population in the United States: 2003.* Retrieved September 1, 2006, from http://www.census.gov/prod/2004pubs/p20-551.pdf

U.S. Department of Education, Commission on the Future of Higher Education. (2007). *Growth of the "nontraditional" student.* Retrieved January 11, 2007, from http://www.salliemae.com/about/newsinfo/highereducationstats/

U.S. Department of Health and Human Services. (1989). *Report of the secretary's task force on youth suicide.* Washington, DC: Author.

U.S. Department of Health and Human Services. (2000). *Report of the Surgeon General's Conference on Children's Mental Health: A national action agenda.* Rockville, MD: Author.

Vacha-Haase, T., Davenport, D. S., & Kerewsky, S. D. (2004). Problematic students: Gatekeeping practices of academic professional psychology programs. *Professional Psychology: Research and Practice, 35,* 115–122.

Vaillant, L. M. (1997). *Changing character: Short-term anxiety-regulating psychotherapy for restructuring defenses, affects, and attachment.* New York: Basic Books.

Valle, S. K., & Humphrey, D. (2003). American prisons as alcohol and drug treatment centers: A twenty-year reflection, 1980-2000. In T. F. McGovern & W. L. White (Eds.), *Alcohol problems in the United States: Twenty years of treatment perspective.* Binghamton, NY: Haworth Press.

Vandervoot, D. J., & Fuhriman, A. (1991). The efficacy of group therapy for depression. *Small Group Research, 22,* 320–338.

Van Etten, M. L., & Taylor, S. (1998). Comparative efficacy of treatments for posttraumatic stress disorder: A meta-analysis. *Clinical Psychology and Psychotherapy, 5,* 126–144.

van Wormer, K., & Davis, D. R. (2003). *Addiction treatment: A strengths perspective.* Pacific Grove, CA: Brooks/Cole.

Vash, C. V., & Crewe, N. M. (2004). *Psychology of disability* (2nd ed.). New York: Springer.

Vernon, A. (1998a). *The passport program: A journey through emotional, social, cognitive, and self-development (grades 6–8)*. Champaign, IL: Research Press.

Vernon, A. (1998b). *The passport program: A journey through emotional, social, cognitive, and self-development (grades 9–12)*. Champaign, IL: Research Press.

Vernon, A. (2002). *What works when with children and adolescents: A handbook of individual counseling techniques*. Champaign, IL: Research Press.

Vernon, A. (2004). Counseling children and adolescents: Developmental considerations. In A. Vernon (Ed.), *Counseling children and adolescents* (3rd ed.) (pp. 1–34). Denver, CO: Love Publishing.

Vernon, A. (2006). *Thinking, feeling, behaving: An emotional education curriculum for children*. Champaign, IL: Research Press.

Vernon, A., & Al-Mabuk, R. H. (1995). *What growing up is all about: A parent's guide to child and adolescent development*. Champaign, IL: Research Press.

Vernon, A., & Clemente, R. (2005). *Assessment and intervention with children and adolescents: Developmental and multicultural approaches*. Alexandria, VA: American Counseling Association.

Waldo, M., & Dale, B. W. (1993). Integrating DSM-III-R training into school, marriage and family, and mental health counseling preparation. *Counselor Education and Supervision, 32,* 332–343.

Wallace, H., & Hall, D. (1996). *Psychological consultation: Perspectives and applications*. Pacific Grove, CA: Brooks/Cole.

Wampold, B. E., (2002). An examination of the bases of evidence-based interventions. *School Psychology Quarterly, 17,* 500–507.

Watkins, E. C., Campbell, V. L., & McGregor, P. (1989). The MMPI: Does it have a place in counseling psychology training. *Journal of Personality Assessment, 53,* 413–417.

Wechsler, D. (1997). *Manual for the Wechsler Adult Intelligence Scale, 3rd edition* (WAIS-III). San Antonio, TX: Psychological Corporation.

Wechsler, D. (2001). *Manual for the Wechsler Individual Achievement Test, 2nd edition* (WIAT-II). San Antonio, TX: Psychological Corporation.

Weed, R. O., & Field, T. F. (1994). *Rehabilitation consultant's handbook*. Athens, GA: Elliot & Fitzpatrick, Inc.

Weed, R. O., & Field, T. F. (2001). *Rehabilitation consultant's handbook* (3rd ed.). Athens, GA: Elliott & Fitzpatrick, Inc.

Weinberg, M. S., Williams, C. J., & Pryor, D. W. (1994). *Dual attraction: Understanding bisexuality*. New York: Oxford University Press.

Weiss, C. (1998). *Evaluation* (2nd ed.) Upper Saddle River, NJ: Prentice Hall.

Weissburg, R. P., Caplan, M., & Harwood, R. L. (1991). Promoting competent young people in competence-enhancing environments: A systems-based perspective on primary prevention. *Journal of Consulting and Clinical Psychology, 59,* 830–841.

Weisz, J. R., Weiss, B., Alicke, M. D., & Klotz, M. L. (1987). Effectiveness of psychotherapy with children and adolescents: A meta-analysis for clinicians. *Journal of Consulting and Clinical Psychology, 55,* 542–549.

Weisz, J. R., Weiss, B., Han, S. S., Granger, D. A., & Morton, T. (1995). Effects of psychotherapy with children and adolescents revisited: A meta-analysis of treatment outcome studies. *Psychological Bulletin, 117,* 450–468.

Welfel, E. R., & Patterson, L. E. (2005). *The counseling process: A multitheoretical integrative approach* (6th ed.). Belmont, CA: Thomson Brooks/Cole.

Whiston, S. C. (1996). Accountability through action research: Research methods for practitioners. *Journal of Counseling and Development, 74,* 616–623.

Whiston, S. C. (2007). Outcomes research on school counseling interventions and programs. In B. T. Erford (Ed.), *Transforming the school counseling profession* (2nd ed.). Columbus, OH: Pearson Merrill Prentice Hall.

Whiston, S. C., Brecheisen, B. K., & Stephens, J. (2003). Does treatment modality affect career counseling effectiveness. *Journal of Vocational Behavior, 62,* 390–410.

Whiston, S. C., Eder, K., Rahardja, D., & Tai, W. L. (2005, June). Research supporting school counseling: Comprehensive findings. Paper presented at the annual meeting of the American School Counselor Association, Orlando, FL.

Whiston, S. C., & Sexton, T. L. (1993). An overview of psychotherapy outcome research: Implications for practice. *Professional Psychology: Research and Practice, 24*(1), 43–51.

Whiston, S. C., Sexton, T. L., & Lasoff, D. L. (1998). Career intervention outcome: A replication and extension of Oliver and Spokane (1988). *Journal of Counseling Psychology, 45,* 150–165.

White, M., & Epston, D. (1990). *Narrative means to therapeutic ends.* New York: Norton.

White, V. E., Trepal-Wollenzier, H., & Nolan, J. M. (2002). College student and self-injury: Intervention strategies for counselors. *Journal of College Counseling, 5,* 105–113.

Wiggins, J. D., & Wiggins, A. H. (1992). Elementary students' self-esteem and behavioral ratings related to counselor time-task emphases. *The School Counselor, 39,* 377–381.

Will, C. (2003). Consultation and collaboration: An action research model for the full-service school. *Consulting Psychology Journal: Practice and Research, 55,* 239–248.

Williams, M. E., & Buboltz Jr., W. C. (1999). Content analysis of the *Journal of Counseling and Development. Journal of Counseling and Development, 77,* 344–350.

Wilson, D. B., Gottfredson, D. C., & Najaka, S. S. (2001). School-based prevention of problem behaviors: A meta-analysis. *Journal of Quantitative Criminology, 17,* 247–272.

Wilson, N. S. (1986). Counselor interventions with low-achieving and underachieving elementary, middle, and high school students: A review of literature. *Journal of Counseling and Development, 64,* 628–634.

Wilson, S. J., Lispey, M. W., & Derzon, J. H. (2003). The effects of school-based intervention programs on aggressive behavior: A meta-analysis. *Journal of Consulting and Clinical Psychology, 71,* 136–149.

Winick, C., & Levene, A. (1992). Marathon therapy: Treating rape survivors in a therapeutic community. *Journal of Psychoactive Drugs, 24,* 49–56.

Wirt, W. M. (1967). Psychotherapeutic persistence. *Journal of Consulting Psychology, 31,* 429.

Wolman, B. B. (1998). *Adolescence: Biological and psychosocial perspectives.* Westport, CT: Greenwood Press.

Wonacott, M. E. (2002). *Vocational rehabilitation trends and issues alert.* (Report No. 31). Columbus, OH: Center for Education and Training for Employment. (ERIC Document Reproduction Service No. 462549).

Wood, J. T. (2005). *Gendered lives: Communication, gender, and culture* (6th ed.). Belmont, CA: Wadsworth/Thomson Learning.

Woodcock, R., Mather, N., & McGrew, K. (2001). *Woodcock-Johnson III Tests of Achievement* (WJ III). Itasca, IL: Riverside Publishing.

World Health Organization. (2003). *Investing in mental health.* Retrieved May 14, 2006, from http://www.who.int/mental_health

Worthen, B. B., Sanders, J. R., & Fitzpatrick, J. L. (1997). *Program evaluation: Alternative approaches and practical guidelines* (2nd ed.). New York: Longman.

Worthen, V., & McNeill, B. (1996). A phenomenological investigation of "good" supervision events. *Journal of Counseling Psychology, 31,* 63–75.

Wrenn, C. G. (1962). *The counselor in a changing world.* Washington, DC: American Personnel and Guidance Association.

Yalom, I. D. (2002). *The gift of therapy: An open letter to a new generation of therapists and their patients.* New York: Harper Collins.

Yalom, I. D., & Leszcz, M. (2005). *The theory and practice of group psychotherapy* (5th ed.). New York: Basic Books.

Young, M. E. (2005). *Learning the art of helping: Building blocks and techniques* (3rd ed.). Upper Saddle River, NJ: Pearson Education.

Zhang, H. (1998). Psychological measurement in China. *International Journal of Psychology, 23,* 101–117.

Zimpfer, D. G. (1989). Groups for persons who have cancer. *Journal for Specialists in Group Work, 14,* 98–104.

Zimpfer, D. G. (1990a). Groups for divorce/separation: A review. *Journal for Specialists in Group Work, 15,* 51–60.

Zimpfer, D. G. (1990b). Group work for bulimia: A review of outcomes. *Journal for Specialists in Group Work, 15,* 239–251.

Zimpfer, D. G. (1991). Groups for grief and survivorship after bereavement: A review. *Journal for Specialists in Group Work, 14,* 98–104.

Zunker, V. G. (1994). *Career counseling: Applied concepts of life planning* (4th ed.). Pacific Grove, CA: Brooks/Cole.

Zunker, V. G. (2002). *Career counseling: Applied concepts of life planning* (6th ed.). Pacific Grove, CA: Brooks/Cole.

INDEX